american political behavior

HOWARD D. MEHLINGER
JOHN J. PATRICK

GINN AND COMPANY
(A Xerox Education Company)

GINN AND COMPANY
Home Office: Lexington, Massachusetts 02173
0 — 663 — 23044 — 6

about the authors

HOWARD D. MEHLINGER is Associate Professor of History and Education and Director of the High School Curriculum Center in Government at Indiana University. He holds both M.S. in Ed. and Ph.D. degrees from the University of Kansas. He has eleven years of experience as a world history and American government teacher in Kansas and Pennsylvania high schools. In addition to numerous articles on teaching social studies, he is the co-author of a book on the 1905 Russian Revolution, a bulletin on teaching about totalitarianism, and the co-editor of the 38th yearbook of the National Council for the Social Studies. He is a member of many professional associations, including the National Council for the Social Studies and the American Political Science Association. In 1971 he was a member of the board of Directors of NCSS and a member of the APSA Committee on Pre-Collegiate Education.

JOHN J. PATRICK is Assistant Professor of Social Studies Education and Associate Director of the High School Curriculum Center in Government at Indiana University. He received his Bachelor of Arts from Dartmouth College and the Master and Doctoral degrees from Indiana University. He taught history and civics in two Chicago-area high schools for seven years. In addition to numerous articles in social studies instruction, and curriculum development, he has written *Political Socialization of American Youth*, a research bulletin of the National Council for the Social Studies. He is a member of several professional associations, including the National Council for the Social Studies.

preface to teachers

Knowledge of politics is an essential ingredient of an adequate education. Through the study of politics important lessons can be learned about the management of conflict, the resolution of issues, the distribution of rewards and punishments, the mechanisms of social change, and the maintenance of order.

Knowledge of politics can contribute to the attainment of individual or group goals. Those who understand the political behavior of their society possess a foundation from which to devise fruitful political strategies. For example, understanding the conduct of elections, the activities of political parties, and the factors which influence voter choices can contribute to wiser and more rewarding voter behavior. Comprehension of the ways that public officials make decisions can contribute to the development of effective techniques for influencing the conduct of government.

A major purpose of this book is to increase political knowledge and sophistication. During the past twenty-five years social scientists have greatly expanded our knowledge of political affairs. This book is an attempt to present to high school students up-to-date findings of social scientists about political behavior.

The process of acquiring knowledge of politics ought to be lively and exciting, since the subject is concerned essentially with public controversy, social problems, the articulation of human needs, and the decisions of authorities about who gets what, when, and how. In this book we have tried to capture the vitality and drama of politics through the use of cases which describe the political activities of typical citizens and political leaders. These cases are brief stories about various aspects of political behavior such as voting, demonstrating, bargaining, decision-making, and the like. Simulations, games, political attitude surveys, and data-processing activities are other instructional activities designed to enliven the course.

As a safeguard against biased presentation of information and propaganda, students of political behavior must learn skills of critical thinking and social scientific inquiry. One characteristic of the well-educated person is the ability to make sound judgments about the worth of ideas. Thus, we have tried to design lessons aimed at teaching the skills of using evidence and logic to substantiate factual claims and to consider value claims rationally.

We hope that vastly increased ability to extract meaning from politically relevant experiences and to cope with political demands and challenges is an outcome of studying this book. Certainly this hope is consistent with the traditional American ideal that an informed and politically efficacious citizenry is an essential condition of democracy.

Howard D. Mehlinger
John J. Patrick

table of contents

acknowledgments

The course American Political Behavior is one of the products of the High School Curriculum Center in Government at Indiana University. This Center, sponsored jointly by the School of Education and the Department of Political Science, was established in 1966 through a grant from the U.S. Office of Education, U.S. Department of Health, Education, and Welfare by authority of P.L. 81-152, Title III, Section 302 (c) (15) and P.L. 83-531. The development and evaluation of the preliminary versions of American Political Behavior were supported by this grant.

A great many people have contributed to the development of this program. In the space available it is possible to acknowledge only a small proportion of those who have been helpful throughout the project.

Mr. Shirley Engle, Professor of Education at Indiana University, is the chairman of the High School Curriculum Center in Government. He established the project, set it on its course, and offered continuing advice and encouragement. Members of the Center Advisory Committee at Indiana University, in addition to Mr. Engle, are Mr. Frederick Smith, Professor of Education, Mr. Alfred Diamant, Professor of Political Science, and Mr. William Siffin, Professor of Political Science. Each of these men contributed a number of ideas to the program.

Mr. Fred Coombs, Assistant Professor of Political Science at the University of Illinois, contributed significantly to Unit V, "Unofficial Political Specialists." Mrs. Judy Gillespie, Research Associate at the Center, developed the four simulation-games that accompany the course. Mr. Lee Anderson, Professor of

Political Science at Northwestern University, and Mr. Robert Hanvey, Associate Professor of Education at Indiana University, contributed to chapters 14 and 16, respectively.

Mr. Leroy Rieselbach, Professor of Political Science, Indiana University, was helpful throughout the development of this course. He wrote a paper about political behavior for teachers, taught in a summer institute for the pilot teachers, participated in dissemination institutes, and served as a strict but friendly critic of the materials.

Mr. Gerald Marker, Coordinator for School Social Studies at Indiana University, has been an especially close friend of the project. His counsel and assistance, especially in dissemination activities, have contributed significantly to the project.

Approximately 100 teachers used this course at one time or another during its experimental trials. It is not possible to list each teacher and his school individually, but their role has been invaluable in the development and the evaluation of the course. The authors are deeply indebted to each of them.

We are also grateful to many graduate student assistants who have helped us, especially Mr. Russell Cassity, Mr. Edward Poole, Mr. James Lewellen, Mr. Michael Cabat, and Mr. Eugene Michaels. We also wish to acknowledge the able support of Mrs. Benita Mitten and Miss Connie Carmichael, clerk-typists for the project. A special tribute is due Mrs. Jane Lewis, principal secretary and administrative assistant for the Center. Her cheerful and efficient handling of the many details associated with this project made the entire effort possible.

Finally, the authors wish to thank publishers and copyright holders for permission to reproduce copyrighted material. Specific acknowledgments appear throughout the text.

unit one

introduction to the study of political behavior

chapter 1

What Is Political Behavior?

Political behavior is one kind of human behavior. Human behavior is everything that people do; it includes all human activities. Human behavior is eating, sleeping, breathing, working, loafing, studying, attending church, forming friendships, settling disputes, playing games, voting, driving a car, protesting, and thousands of other things which people do—consciously or unconsciously. In the list above are examples of political behavior.

Political behavior occurs among all groups of people. Political behavior serves human needs; it is a means for solving basic human problems. Human groups cannot do without political behavior.

Increasing your knowledge of political behavior is a main objective of this course. The first step toward attainment of this objective is to consider carefully these two questions:

1. What is political behavior?
2. Why do people behave politically?

A. Four Cases of Political Behavior

The following four examples, or cases, of political behavior can help you begin to answer these two questions. The cases are descriptions of different political behavior. Each case presents some clues about why people behave politically.

Case 1. The Students Open the Gym

Bruce, Mark, Eric, and David were sixth-graders with a problem. They loved to play basketball but had no place to play on weekends and after school. The boys decided to ask their principal at the Faris Elementary School to open the gym for them after school and all day Saturday. They chose Eric to be their spokesman.

Although Mr. Foster, the principal, was sympathetic, he told Eric that it would be against school rules to allow the boys to play in the gym without adult supervision. And there was no money presently available in the school budget to pay teachers to supervise basketball playing in the gym. Furthermore, the principal said that since only four boys wanted to use the gymnasium after school and on Saturdays, he did not believe that the school should use up its small emergency fund simply to satisfy the wishes of four boys in a school with over 600 children.

Eric and his friends were disappointed with the principal's response to their request. They had presented their idea to the main authority of their school, and he had rejected it. What could they do now?

2

Mark was ready to give up. "What can we do?" he said. "Mr. Foster runs this place. Once he says 'no' to something, that finishes it."

David was angry. "Let's start a demonstration," he said. "We'll show Foster that he can't push the sixth-grade students around. I'll bet that I can influence the majority of the fifth- and sixth-grade boys to go along with me. We may feel more strongly about this than the others, but I know most of the guys in the fifth and sixth grade would come to play ball in the gym if it were open."

While David ranted, Eric had an idea. "Dave, I believe you're right when you say that most fifth- and sixth-grade boys want to play basketball after school and on Saturdays."

"Right," said David. "We can prove it by getting them to demonstrate in front of Foster's office tomorrow."

"No," said Eric. "I have a better idea. We can ask them to sign a petition for use of the gym. Then, maybe, Mr. Foster will see that most of the students support us. Then, maybe, he will open the gym."

The boys agreed to Eric's idea for presenting a petition to Mr. Foster. For three days they worked to get signatures. Sixty-five boys signed the petition.

Once again, Eric went to see Mr. Foster and gave him the petition. Mr. Foster said that he was impressed with Eric's leadership ability and with his strong desire to open the gym. He now believed that most fifth- and sixth-grade boys wanted to use the gym. He said that he would request the city school board to give him more money for his budget next year in order that he could hire adult supervisors and open the gym.

Eric replied that this was not enough. He and his friends wanted to play basketball now, not wait until next year. The principal replied that this was impossible. Making an effort to obtain funds to open the gym for next year was the best he could do.

When Eric reported the news to his friends, they became gloomy.

"I knew this wouldn't work," said David. "Foster just doesn't care."

"He does too," said Eric. "But he is not able to do anything now. He can't help it if he doesn't have money to hire teachers to supervise our play in the gym."

"I've got it!" shouted Bruce. "I know how to solve the problem. We'll make phone calls to all of the parents of the students who signed the petition. We'll ask them to volunteer to supervise the gym while we play. They'll do it without pay. Then Mr. Foster will have to let us use the gym."

The boys agreed to Bruce's idea. They asked over 50 parents to help, and they received "yes" answers from 21 people. They presented the names of these parents to Mr. Foster. He called each of the parents to confirm their willingness to help. Then he decided to open the gym three days a week after school and on Saturday afternoon.

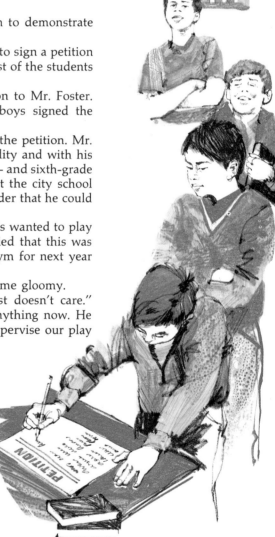

He called Eric to his office to give him the decision. Eric was very happy. The gym would be available for basketball. And so, for the last few weeks, the Faris School gym has been open for both boys and girls. Students play volleyball, basketball, and ping pong. The parent-volunteers supervise. The youngsters and parents clean the gym before they leave. The principal and the children have been happy with this arrangement. The problem has been solved.

Case 2. The Klan Comes to Town

Robert Swanson, mayor of Bloomingdale, paced the floor of his office nervously. He had to make a quick decision, and he did not know what to do. He wiped at his face with a handkerchief and buzzed his secretary. "Bring another cup of coffee, Elaine," he said.

"Yes, sir, Mr. Swanson."

A moment later Elaine appeared with the coffee. "Don't forget your press conference in two hours," said Elaine.

"Thanks for the reminder," said Swanson. "I am trying to prepare for that meeting now." After Elaine left the room, Mayor Swanson reviewed the events leading up to his present problem.

Last week, officers of the Ku Klux Klan in nearby Bedrock had announced that they would come to Bloomingdale to march and distribute leaflets about their organization. Immediately, a public outcry against the Klan march developed in Bloomingdale. Petitions were circulated opposing the Klan appearance. Over 5,000 signatures were attached to one petition that was printed in the *Bloomingdale Evening Star.* It read:

> We, the undersigned, deplore the Ku Klux Klan. It is an organization that spreads hatred among people. It is an organization that would deprive all Negroes and Jews of their rights. Therefore, we believe the Ku Klux Klan members should have no right to publicly parade and speak in Bloomingdale. We demand that Mayor Swanson and the city council prevent the Klan members from holding a demonstration in our city.

The petition started a fierce debate that was carried on in the newspapers, in meetings of organizations in Bloomingdale, and on the streets. An editorial in the *Bloomingdale Evening Star* said:

> We oppose the Ku Klux Klan and everything it stands for. We support the Negro civil rights movement. However, we also support the cause of civil liberties, the cause of free speech. And we oppose any effort to deprive any group, no matter how unworthy, of this basic democratic right. If the right of free speech is denied to the Klan today, it may be denied to a Negro civil rights organization tomorrow. Once we lower the barriers that guard the basic democratic right of free speech, we threaten the very foundations of democratic government.
>
> Thus, even though we are against what the Ku Klux Klan represents, we defend the Klan's right to free speech. We advise Mayor Swanson to permit the Klan to have its public rally.

4

Several letters to the editor of the *Bloomingdale Evening Star* supported the above editorial. Several others opposed it. Two letters, however, were ominous and threatening.

To the editor:

If the Ku Klux Klan is allowed to demonstrate in this city, there will be trouble. You can't expect the black citizens of this community to sit back and watch these hooded hate-mongers march among us. If the city government does not assume its rightful responsibilities to its black citizens, we will have to protect ourselves. We will stand up like men and look the hooded white cowards in the eye. If trouble happens, so be it.

An angry black citizen

To the editor:

If the Ku Klux Klan is not allowed to demonstrate in Bloomingdale, there will be violence. The Klan stands for the salvation of white Anglo-Saxon, Christian America against the threat of Communist conspiracy led by certain so-called civil rights organizations.

Mayor Swanson and the city council have a chance to show whether they support white civilization and Christianity or communism and savagery. If the Mayor decides against America, then the right thinking patriots of this city have the responsibility of setting things straight.

A 100 percent American

Talk of violence and of rioting persisted. The mayor and his advisers became alarmed. Representatives from various organizations advised the mayor. Most of these individuals tried to influence the mayor to stop the Klan from coming to Bloomingdale. They were afraid that trouble would occur that could lead to property damage and human injury. Some of the civic leaders were opposed to free speech for the Klan on principle. They believed that such an undemocratic organization should have no right to freedom of speech.

The mayor tended to agree with these arguments. He wanted to avoid trouble at almost any cost. Yet the arguments of the newspaper editorial kept going through his mind:

Once we lower the barriers that guard the basic democratic right of free speech, we threaten the very foundation of democratic government.

The Bloomingdale Civil Liberties Union supported the newspaper's position. Like the newspaper editors, the Civil Liberties Union members opposed the Klan; but they supported the right of free speech, even for groups like the Klan. They advised the mayor to allow members of the Klan to hold the public rally.

For a week the mayor heard arguments for and against the right of the Klan to demonstrate publicly in Bloomingdale. Civic leaders and ordinary citizens tried to influence him. His decision would have the force of law. What should he do? Only he had the power and the duty to decide.

Case 3. What Is a Park Worth?

Herbert Henson rose slowly from his chair and looked around the council chamber nervously. The room was crowded with angry people. Some in the crowd supported him. But he knew that many were against his ideas. Nevertheless, he felt strongly that he must try once again to influence the Lakeville city council. Henson said:

> Citizens of Lakeville, members of the city council, Mayor Harding, I beg you to follow my advice and build a new park in West Side. The young people of this area have no place to play. The neighborhood is run-down. Our children deserve something more from the city than they have been receiving. Others in this city get what they want. Why are we always left out? We may be black or Mexican and poor, but we're part of this city too.

Henson sat down amid shouts and handclaps. The chairman of the city council gaveled the meeting back to order. He recognized a tall, well-built, distinguished-looking man.

"Mr. Randolph," said the chairman, "you may have the floor."

Robert Randolph spoke:

> I agree that a park is needed in West Side. But this project can wait until another year. What we need immediately is an overpass between the Sunnyside neighborhood and the Kennedy Elementary School. Let me remind you that the children of Sunnyside must cross Highway 62 to get to school. It is a very busy highway. And Amy Wright would be alive today if we had had an overpass on Highway 62. Amy died last month because she had no safe way to walk across this busy street. How many more children must die before we construct an overpass?

The room was quiet as the imposing Mr. Randolph sat down. Others spoke in favor of the proposed overpass and the park.

The chairman of the city council thanked the citizens for their ideas and reminded them that the city government budget would not allow the city to build both an overpass and a park this year. One of the projects would have to be postponed.

Mr. Henson and his friends grumbled as they left Lakeville City Hall.

"I know which project will be postponed," said Henson. "First of all, the city council will take care of those rich, white people in Sunnyside. That's the way the government works. Some big-shot lawyer like Robert Randolph speaks, and the city council listens. When a poor man like me speaks, no one listens or cares."

"Yeah" said Pepe Arroyo, a leader of the Mexican-American group that lives in West Side. "It makes a difference who you are in this town. Those high-class 'gringos' in Sunnyside always get more from the government than we do. The streets in their neighborhood are smooth. Garbage is always picked up on time in Sunnyside. If one of their children is arrested, they get him off quietly and without any serious trouble."

"It's different in old West Side," said Lou Hunter. "Sometimes two weeks go by before they pick up the garbage. The streets are full of holes. And the cops are always around busting our kids' heads."

City Council Votes for Overpass

At the next city council meeting, the councilmen passed a bill to provide funds for the building of an overpass across Highway 62 to connect the Sunnyside neighborhood with the Kennedy Elementary School. The councilmen also passed a resolution declaring that the council recognized the need of West Side for a park. The resolution said that the city council pledged to start a park project as soon as finances would permit.

Herbert Henson, Pepe Arroyo, and their followers were angered. They phoned councilmen, the mayor, and other important public officials to complain. They threatened to withdraw all political support from the mayor if he approved the council's decisions. They reminded the mayor that votes from West Side gave him his victory in the last election.

Mayor Harding was anxious not to offend the West Side voters. But he also believed that the overpass had to be built. He decided to seek a compromise, to reach a settlement that would satisfy both sides in this conflict. He called Herbert Henson and Pepe Arroyo and asked them to come to his office. He also asked the chairman of the city council to be there.

The Mayor's Compromise

At this meeting the mayor suggested that land for the West Side park be purchased immediately. Funds were available for this, although they were not now available to develop the park. However, the mayor pointed out that this development work could begin next year. He pledged that he would see the park project completed before his term in office expired. The chairman of the city council agreed to support this plan. Henson and Arroyo, though not completely satisfied, believed that the mayor really cared about their park project and would complete it. They pledged their continued support of the mayor.

At the next city council meeting, funds were appropriated for the purchase of park land. The mayor publicly pledged to see that this project would be completed within the next two years.

West Side people were pleased because finally they could count upon having a public park in their community. The Sunnyside residents were satisfied that an overpass would be constructed to protect their children. And the mayor was pleased to maintain the political support that he needed to stay in office.

Case 4. The PTA Election

Jerome Marks and his wife gulped down their dinner and rushed to the regular monthly meeting of the Elm Hollow School Parent-Teacher Association. Professor Marks had become a member of the PTA last year, when his son entered the first grade. As a prominent educator at a nearby university, he soon became an important member of the PTA.

The main purpose of this evening's meeting was the election of officers for the next school year. The nominating committee had picked Jerome Marks as its candidate for president. According to the by-laws of the Elm Hollow PTA, the candidates selected by the nominating committee were to be presented to the members at this meeting. Members would be given the opportunity to nominate competing candidates. In the absence of such "nominations from the floor," the professor and other "slated" candidates would become officially the new officers of the Elm Hollow PTA.

Jerome Marks and his wife arrived at the Elm Hollow school at 7:15 P.M. The PTA meeting was scheduled to begin at 7:30. Upon entering the meeting room, he noticed a group of members sitting in a corner of the room. They were talking excitedly. When these people saw the professor and his wife, they immediately stopped talking.

The current president called the meeting to order promptly at 7:30. After discussing some business matters, the president informed the group that the nominating committee had prepared a slate of officers. The slate, with the name of Jerome Marks at the top, was read. The president asked if there were any nominations from the floor. Mr. Samuel Simpson, a prominent lawyer in town, raised his hand. He rose to nominate Laurence Reagan, a medical doctor, for the office of president.

Mr. Simpson's action stirred the group. Never in the history of the Elm Hollow PTA had the members refused to accept candidates presented by the nominating committee. After the president quieted the meeting, Dr. Reagan publicly accepted the nomination. Then, another member suggested that Professor Marks and Dr. Reagan, the two presidential candidates, speak briefly to the group in order that the members of the PTA would be better prepared to choose between the two men. The candidates agreed to do so.

Professor Marks stood up and said:

> I agreed to accept this office as a public service. My desire is to serve this school, the children who attend it, and the parents of these children. I am a Professor of Education and feel that I am highly qualified to do this job.

Dr. Reagan said:

> I accept the nomination. Most of you know my views, so I will simply say that I will be pleased to serve as PTA president.

The president passed out slips of paper to be used as ballots. The PTA members voted. The nominating committee counted the ballots, and announced that Dr. Reagan was the winner by a vote of 43 to 25.

8

Jerome Marks was stunned. Why had he been defeated? Why had his candidacy been challenged? He found the answers to these questions during the coffee hour that followed the meeting.

Betsy Brown, a close friend, told Marks that many members of the PTA had viewed him as a political "leftist," as a radical who favored demonstrations, progressive education, and civil liberties. These people had learned that he belonged to the American Civil Liberties Union. This shocked them. They became determined to save their PTA from leadership by a "civil libertarian."

As they left the meeting, Jerome Marks and his wife overheard some ladies chatting near the door.

"Well, Matilda, we saved our PTA from a take-over by that 'hippie' professor and his intellectual friends."

"Yes," said Matilda, "a little old-fashioned political action saved the day. Fortunately, many of our friends were able to come to the meeting and happily Dr. Reagan agreed to be our candidate."

As he drove home, Professor Marks thought about the PTA election. While he was discouraged by his defeat, he decided that he would continue to work for the PTA. He would begin immediately to build a group of co-workers who shared his educational ideas in order that someone with ideas similar to his might someday be elected president of the Elm Hollow PTA.

B. Aspects of Political Behavior

Political behavior is complex. Several different activities of ordinary citizens and public officials can be called political behavior. Political behavior is mixed with other kinds of behavior. Eating a meal is not ordinarily political behavior. But attending a Jefferson-Jackson Day banquet, or lunching with the mayor to influence city policy, involves political behavior. It is difficult in some cases, therefore, to distinguish exactly political behavior from other kinds of human behavior.

Since political behavior is complex, it is difficult to define precisely. However, main aspects of political behavior can be identified. Consideration of these main aspects can clarify the meaning of political behavior and enable you to use this important term more effectively.

Political Behavior Involves Conflict

A *conflict* is a sharp disagreement or struggle. Conflict means that people clash about what ought to be done in some situation. A conflict results when different individuals want a situation to be settled in opposite ways. For example, there is conflict when two or more individuals seek election to the same public office, like that of mayor, governor, or President. There is conflict when individuals argue about how best to use a limited supply of wealth. Perhaps some individuals want to use funds to clear slums and to build houses for poor people. Perhaps others want to use the same money to build roads.

Identify the political issue in each of the headlines above.

Conflicts arise over issues. An *issue* is a disagreement about what is worth doing and what is not. The following questions could become issues that divide a group of people, that cause conflict among a group. Should the group accept one religious practice rather than another, or should all religions be tolerated? Should the group start a war to conquer another group of people, or should peace be maintained at any cost? What should be the limits of free speech? Should medical care be made available to all members of a society regardless of ability to pay? Should public housing be provided for poor people?

Issues may generate conflicts about values. Values are strong beliefs about what is right or wrong, about what is good or bad. People living together may clash about which goals are best, about which goals to value. For example, different people may wish to use the same resources to achieve different goals. Some may believe that the available resources should be spent to improve the armed forces of the country. These people value security from attack more than other goals. Other people may believe that the available resources should be spent to improve the standard of living of poor people. These people value the achievement of opportunity for poor people more than other goals.

Conflict about methods. In some cases, the conflict is over the best way to reach a goal. For example, two candidates for governor may both want poor people in their state to have better housing; both candidates value the goal of achieving better opportunities for poor people. However, these candidates

What is the issue in conflict here? What are some values held by people (a) who favor strict gun controls and (b) who oppose such controls?

Oliphant © 1968 The Denver Post— The Los Angeles Times Syndicate

IRRESISTIBLE FORCE MEETS . . .   . . . IMMOVABLE OBJECT

may clash over the issue of how best to achieve this goal. One candidate for governor may believe that the government should enter the business of home building in order to provide poor people with low-cost housing. The other candidate may believe that laws should be passed to make it more profitable for private businessmen to build low-cost housing. The two candidates disagree about the method of achieving more low-cost housing.

To show that you understand the meaning of conflict as an aspect of political behavior, refer to the four cases on pages 2–9 and answer these questions.

1. What are the issues in the four cases?
2. What are the value conflicts in the four cases?

Political Behavior Involves the Use of Influence

Influence is the power to control, or direct, the behavior of others. People use many different techniques to try to influence an individual or group. They assemble for public demonstrations, write letters to newspapers, and make phone calls to public officials. They provide financial support, sponsor fund-raising dinners, and go door to door soliciting votes for the political candidate they favor. Americans use such techniques as negotiation, petition, personal contact, election campaign activities, and many other methods to influence the behavior of others.

Political influence requires political resources. An individual's power to influence the behavior of others stems from his ability to use political resources. A *political resource* is the means one person has to influence the behavior of another. Examples of political resources are time, money, votes, control over jobs, control over information, prestige in a group, popularity, intelligence, skill as a negotiator, and the power of public office.

This listing is certainly not complete. In different situations, different assets become political resources. For example, a wealthy businessman who can help to pay for the television appearances of his favorite political candidate may find that one political resource, money, will enable him to exert influence if his candidate is elected to public office. In another situation the ability to make rousing speeches can be an equally valuable resource.

A group of individuals with the same objective usually can wield more power than any single individual. A petition with 10,000 signatures calling for the construction of a new elementary school is likely to be more influential than calls to the local school board from two or three concerned parents. As a member of a group with a common objective, a person with few political resources of his own may be able to combine his assets with others to compete successfully against a person with greater political resources. For example, a group of tenants might organize an effective protest against a landlord to try to influence him to repair an apartment building, while as individuals their complaints were not taken very seriously.

Some individuals with many political resources have little influence on public officials. For example, a wealthy, intelligent individual may not be interested in politics. Instead he may choose to use his wealth and intelligence to support the education of musicians and the promotion of musical activities.

Identify some of the political techniques and resources described in the drawing.

Through the use of influence, an individual or a group may be able to gain an objective. Through the use of influence, an individual may be able to turn values into practice. The successful political candidate who is elected to office may feel obligated to listen to the opinions of individuals who supported his campaign. Their resources—such as time, money, or intelligence—may help them to influence the official to make decisions they favor.

To show that you understand the meaning of influence as an aspect of political behavior, refer to the four cases on pages 2–9 and answer these questions.

1. What techniques are used to try to influence the behavior of others in the four cases?

2. What are the political resources of these individuals or groups?
    a. The four sixth-grade boys
    b. The editor of the *Bloomingdale Evening Star*
    c. Robert Randolph
    d. Herbert Henson
    e. Mayor Harding
    f. Members of the Elm Hollow PTA

3. What is the relationship of political resources to political techniques in Cases 1 and 3?

4. What is the relationship of political resources to the outcomes of Cases 1, 3, and 4?

Policy Decisions May Result from Political Behavior

A policy decision is a choice about what should be done to settle a conflict. Often a policy decision is a choice about how to resolve an issue, a choice about who gets what, when, and how. City councilmen, mayors, governors, congressmen, and the President of the United States are important public officials who make policy decisions daily. They must make decisions about how to settle conflicts. For example, in a recent meeting the city council of Bakerville was faced with the issue of whether or not to allow low-cost, prefabricated homes to be built in the city. Following is an excerpt from the official record of this meeting.

Chairman: This meeting of the city council will now come to order. This evening we will hear testimony on a proposed city ordinance that would revise the housing codes for this city, thereby making possible the construction of low-cost, prefabricated homes. Mr. Wilson will speak for those who wish to change the building codes, and Mr. Ward will present arguments for keeping existing building codes in our community as they are.

Mr. Wilson: I represent the American Fabricated Housing Company. We have built houses in many cities like your own. We provide a chance for low-income families to buy inexpensive, modern homes. A survey of your city reveals that many low-income families cannot afford houses in the city and are forced to find space in substandard apartment dwellings. By the use of prefabrication and assembly-line techniques, we are able to produce good homes at a considerable saving to the buyers. We believe that the city council has an obligation to the poor people of this city to pass the new ordinance, thereby making possible the construction of homes the poor can afford.

Mr. Ward: I represent the home builders, bankers, and realtors of this community. We do not believe that prefabricated homes are needed in this town. There are many houses available for sale. Furthermore, it is not fair to local builders, carpenters, plumbers, and electricians for the American Housing Company to begin building cheap houses in this town and deprive our skilled craftsmen of their income. Moreover, prefabricated homes sell cheaply and look cheap; they will detract from the beauty of the town as they quickly fall apart. For these reasons we oppose the proposed ordinance and urge its defeat.

During the next three weeks many people in Bakerville tried to influence the decision of the city council about the housing ordinance. After much discussion and bargaining, the council passed the ordinance, or law, to allow construction of low-cost homes. This new ordinance is a policy decision; it is a decision that settles a conflict.

Swiss Men Give
Ballot to Women

CLOSURE IS BEATEN
2D TIME IN SENATE

Liechtenstein's Male Electorate
Refuses to Give Women the Vote

Senate, by 8 Votes,
Defeats Campaign
To Curb Filibuster

West Virginia Senate Votes Ban
On Strip Mining in 36 Counties

Senate, 77-3, Votes to Keep
Project to Aid Appalachia

US Lifts
Curbs on
China Travel

Identify the issues and the
policy decisions in the
above headlines.

Policy decisions make winners and losers of people in conflict. The policy decision of the Bakerville City Council benefits some people and hurts others; it is a decision about who gets what, when, and how. The American Housing Company won the opportunity to make profits, and poor families won the opportunity to buy low-cost housing. The people represented by Mr. Ward were the losers in this conflict.

Some policy decisions are compromises. Bargaining that results in compromise is the way many conflicts are settled. A compromise occurs when each party to a conflict agrees to give up *part* of what is wanted in order to gain *some* of what is wanted. Following is an example of the use of bargaining and compromising to settle a conflict.

The garbage collectors in Bakerville said that they would strike unless they received a $20 per week wage increase. The mayor and city council did not want to increase the wages more then $5 per week. But they also wanted to avoid a strike. Thus, they offered the garbage collectors a $12 a week increase. The garbage collectors very much wanted a $20 pay raise. But they also did not want to strike, as they would lose money if they stayed away from work in protest. Thus, the garbage collectors accepted the $12 a week pay raise. The conflict between the city government and the garbage collectors was settled through a compromise. The parties to the conflict reached a bargain that required each party *to give up a little* of what was wanted *in order to get a little*.

Often the alternative to compromise is total victory or total defeat, after a long, costly struggle. To avoid severe struggles or the possibility of total defeat, parties to a conflict often decide to settle their differences through compromise.

To show that you understand the meaning of policy decision as an aspect of political behavior, refer to the four cases on pages 2–9 and answer these questions.

1. What policy decisions were made in these cases?
2. Who made the policy decisions in each case?
3. Can you find an example of compromise in these cases?

Political Behavior Operates within a System of Government and Rules

Journalist Frank Kent some years ago wrote a book called *The Great Game of Politics*, and every student has heard the expression "playing politics." If indeed political activity is something of a game, it cannot be played without a set of rules. *Rules are standards for human behavior.* For example, the rules of baseball are the standards for behavior in a baseball game. These rules control, or direct, the behavior of baseball players. No game would be possible without the rules.

Organized baseball could hardly be played without one or more umpires to interpret and enforce the rules. If a dispute, or conflict, arises, the umpire must make a decision to settle the issue. Umpires are a part of the governmental structure of organized baseball. At the head of this "government" is a Commissioner. He occupies a position created many years ago to save organized baseball from chaotic conditions threatening the game's survival. The "government" of organized baseball includes a group with power to revise the rules of the game from time to time as conditions seem to make changes desirable.

Rules likewise control, or direct, American political behavior. Rules for political behavior are set down in the Constitution of the United States, in the constitutions of the fifty states, and in various laws passed by Congress and the state legislatures. The American government—the national government and the various state and local governments—makes and revises the rules and serves as umpire to enforce the rules and settle disputes.

Carmack in *The Christian Science Monitor.* © The Christian Science Publishing Co.

The umpire speaks.

Rules may be written or unwritten. Very many of the rules which control political behavior in the United States appear in our written law codes. The Constitution names some things which Congress and the President may do, and it also prohibits government officials from engaging in other types of political behavior. Our laws indicate when elections are to be held, how they are to be conducted, which Americans are eligible to vote, who shall pay taxes, and so on.

Americans, however, are also guided in their political behavior by many unwritten rules, or *customs.* It is customary, for example, for the loser of an election to send formal congratulations to the winner and to wish him well. Not every loser will do this, but most of them will observe the custom. Most of the methods used by citizens to influence public officials are simply customary ways of behaving politically.

Most rules are obeyed willingly. Many individuals and groups in the community have some power to enforce rules—parents, teachers, employers, baseball umpires, and the like. But the agency with the most power to enforce rules is the government.

Although a government must be able to enforce rules, it depends upon the willingness of people to follow the rules. For example, it would be very difficult or impossible for policemen to enforce traffic laws if most people were unwilling to obey the laws. However, it is not necessary for a policeman to be present to make most people stop for a red light or to drive on the right side of the highway. Most people in our country readily accept and obey basic traffic rules.

Because most people in our country believe that they should obey the law, the government can maintain order. Since most Americans accept the government's right and duty to make and enforce laws, the government continues to make and enforce laws successfully. Willingness to obey the laws appears to be related to several conditions in a community or nation. Laws

15

are most likely to be obeyed when (a) people feel that the laws are just and necessary, (b) officials who make and enforce the laws are respected by the people, and (c) violations of the law are reasonably certain of being detected and punished.

Rules and government prevent anarchy. *Anarchy is behavior without rules.* For example, if there were no traffic laws to control the behavior of automobile drivers, there would be anarchy on the highways. Every driver would "do his own thing." Wrecks would happen continually. Someone driving a tank, an armored car, or a huge truck could perhaps push his way around; but others would not have the freedom to travel easily or safely.

Anarchy is like trying to play a game of baseball without rules. Without rules, confusion would destroy the baseball game.

Anarchy sometimes is called "the law of the jungle." In a jungle, "might makes right"; conflicts are settled through violence, not by rules. In a jungle no creature is safe and secure from attack.

How does the cartoon illustrate anarchy? What does the cartoonist seem to think about student protest?

"Wait a minute! Who's in charge here?"

Anarchy means that anyone is "free" to do as he pleases so long as he possesses the strength and power to have his way. Anarchy means that there is no security, no order, no peace, and no real freedom to come and go in safety. Anarchy is the opposite of behavior according to rules.

If people are unable to settle conflicts through orderly political behavior, anarchy may destroy the group. Since people fear anarchy, they try to settle conflicts according to rules.

To show that you understand the meaning of rules and government as aspects of political behavior, refer to the four cases on pages 2–9 and answer these questions.

1. Find at least one example of a rule which controlled, or directed, behavior in each of the four cases.

2. Why did individuals behave politically according to rules in the four cases?

16

Political Behavior Is an Important Part of Life

Through political behavior, conflict is managed and rewards and services are distributed.

The stakes of political behavior are very high. Through political behavior, people seek rewards for themselves and for those whom they represent. Policy decisions, the outcomes of political behavior, determine which people gain rewards and which people are denied rewards.

Through political behavior, issues of war or peace, of life or death, and of freedom or oppression are decided. Political behavior produces policy decisions which determine the quantity and quality of many services basic to modern human life, such as water supplies, transportation facilities, postal services, educational opportunities, health care, and so on.

Political behavior is necessary to life within human groups. So long as people disagree and compete, they will need to behave politically to settle conflicts and to maintain order and cooperation.

C. The Pleasant Valley Case

The following case study illustrates several aspects of political behavior discussed on pages 9–17. (1) There is an issue that leads to value conflict. (2) The parties to the conflict use their political resources to try to influence a favorable resolution of the conflict. (3) A public policy decision is made to settle the conflict. (4) The conflict is settled in an orderly way, according to rules accepted by everyone involved in the conflict. (5) Certain people involved in the case felt that they had gained something from the settlement of the conflict. Other people felt that they had lost.

A Letter Starts a Controversy

On April 19 the following letter appeared in the *Pleasant Valley Evening World:*

To the Editor:

Sir, I am a 10th grade student at the local high school. One of my teachers has said things in class that disagree with my religious beliefs, so I was wondering if I am right in not agreeing with my teacher.

This teacher agrees with the university professor who is now in trouble for burning the American flag in his class. My teacher stated that the professor was doing no harm in burning the flag, since it was just a piece of cloth, a symbol. This teacher said, "I don't believe that Professor Smith was doing wrong in burning the flag, after all it wasn't a piece of land he burned."

In my opinion this teacher is totally wrong in saying he was innocent and that he didn't destroy anything but a piece of cloth.

I am 15 years old now and in about two or three years, I will, no doubt, be serving in Vietnam, and be very proud to have a flag that means so much to me. As I have been growing up my parents have taught me to love and respect God and my country. In my Scout work I have learned this also.

17

In the discussion of this professor it was suggested that he had no religion. As an example my teacher said that most of the Bible, as was written by the Apostles and Paul, is only half true. It is my opinion that this teacher is trying to undo all of our beliefs that we have had ever since childhood.

Frankly, I just do not see how this discussion has any connection with English grammar that I am supposed to be learning. It is not my intention to make trouble for this teacher, but I don't agree one bit with all that was said. After thinking, I feel more strongly than ever that this teacher is wrong and that I am right.

I would sign my name to this letter, but I have to face this teacher for the rest of the year. If this teacher wishes to write to the editor as I have done, they may do so.

A Student

The author of the letter remained unknown for several days. But the citizens of Pleasant Valley knew immediately the identity of the teacher. Mrs. Patricia Jackson, a recent college graduate and a first-year teacher of English, had often been the object of community discussion. This letter, therefore, was the last straw for many. Before a week had passed, Mrs. Jackson had lost her teaching job. Why did she lose her job? Why did she become the focus of political conflict? Some background information about Pleasant Valley will help answer these questions.

Pleasant Valley and Mrs. Jackson

Pleasant Valley is a quiet, midwestern town of about 2000 population. It has some light industry but serves primarily as a market town for farmers in the county. One high school serves both the town and nearby rural areas. Children outside the town come to school by bus.

The people of Pleasant Valley are primarily white, Protestant, native Americans. Most are church-going, law-abiding, hard-working loyal citizens. Many are annoyed by people who represent any combination of traits opposed to the community's cherished values.

Mrs. Jackson did not fit easily into the Pleasant Valley way of doing things. She believed that what a person thinks and stands for are more important than how he looks. She was less concerned about her dress and her general appearance than many Pleasant Valley citizens thought appropriate for teachers in the public schools.

Mrs. Jackson believed that she should teach students in her English classes how to speak and write better. She was not interested in requiring them to memorize rules of grammar, nor to diagram sentences. Mrs. Jackson sometimes asked students to watch television programs such as "Batman" to see if they could identify new words and new ways of transmitting ideas. Adults who were critical of Mrs. Jackson's methods of teaching often spoke of that "kooky" new teacher who does not believe in teaching grammar.

Criticism of Mrs. Jackson was common throughout the school year. Parents discussed her teaching among themselves. A few parents protested to the school administration and the board of education. On several occasions Mrs. Jackson was called in by her principal and told she must stop her social comments and spend more time teaching English.

Even during ordinary times Mrs. Jackson would have found teaching in Pleasant Valley difficult. But these were not ordinary times. With a number of Pleasant Valley young men fighting in Vietnam, this was the worst time for a teacher to attack deeply-held values about loyalty and patriotism. Just prior to the time the student's letter appeared in the newspaper, the body of a young Pleasant Valley soldier was returned home—the second fatality of the Vietnam War suffered by the community.

The Flag-Burning Incident

The community was excited also by an incident at one of the state universities about fifty miles from Pleasant Valley and referred to in the student's letter. There, a young English professor, during a lecture on symbolism, responded to a dare by burning a small American flag before his class. Apparently, he did not burn the flag as a sign of protest, nor did he intend to show any disrespect for the United States. He said his purpose was merely to demonstrate that the flag is a piece of cloth. He said the flag acquires meaning only because of the beliefs people have about what it represents. In his view he was merely burning a piece of cloth, not the symbol of the nation. This incident attracted much criticism, and the young professor was soon suspended from his teaching job.

On April 18 one of her sophomore students asked Mrs. Jackson what she thought about the flag-burning incident. She answered that she saw nothing wrong with the actions of the English professor. She said that the professor was merely giving a lecture about flags as political symbols. He did not intend to show disrespect for the flag. Mrs. Jackson's answer prompted the letter sent to the newspaper by one of the students in her class.

More Letters to the Editor

The student's letter stimulated angry community reaction. Around the dinner table in the evening and on the streets during the day, Pleasant Valley citizens discussed Mrs. Jackson, the letter in the newspaper, and what should be done about the entire situation. Some people wrote letters to the *Pleasant Valley Evening World.* Excerpts from four of these letters follow:

> I believe the teacher of the 10th-grade student should be investigated, and if found wrong in his or her beliefs, should be relieved of the job of teaching.

> · And its about time the parents in the school woke up to what is going on in this classroom. I don't think it's right for our school to employ such people to tear down our children's heritage, when their fathers fought long and hard in the World War II, the Korean War, and now their brothers in Vietnam.

Wake up, parents, and as "Column One" [editor's column] said let's THUNDER HARD AND VERY LOUD."

We wish to commend the young student who took the stand against the teacher in the Public Forum letter in Wednesday's paper. That teacher needs to be relieved of duties in our schools.

Our School Board has an urgent responsibility to thoroughly investigate this matter. —To the teacher, whoever he or she may be, I have only one word, written in capital letters, SHAME.

The role played by the newspaper in this incident is not totally clear. Some people charge the newspaper editor with stirring up the community. The newspaper did print the original letter without ever checking to make certain that the charges were accurate. Nor did the newspaper interview Mrs. Jackson and try to present her side of the story. Although the newspaper received letters supporting Mrs. Jackson, none were printed.

The editor said that these letters arrived after the school board had made its decision, and he had no desire to keep the matter burning in the community once a decision had been reached. The editor noted in his column on April 20, "Teachers and instructors are employed to teach various subjects. They are not employed to teach their own values to a captive audience of teen-agers or young adults." Privately and publicly, the newspaper editor indicated that he was against Mrs. Jackson's ideas.

The American Legion Intervenes

On April 24 the *Pleasant Valley Evening World* printed two notices of forthcoming meetings that were destined to be significant in the resolution of the conflict. Members of the local American Legion Post were asked to attend a special meeting at the Legion Home that evening. And it was noted that the regular meeting of the Pleasant Valley School Board was scheduled for the following evening.

At its meeting on the evening of April 24, members of the Pleasant Valley American Legion Post unanimously adopted the following resolution:

TO ALL WHO SEE THESE PRESENTS, GREETINGS:

Whereas, the American Legion is a patriotic organization of men and women who served their country in time of war and national emergency; and

Whereas, the American Legion is constituted by an Act of Congress and charged with the preservation of American principles and respect for the Flag of the United States of America; and

Whereas, it has come to our attention that statements were made by a teacher of Pleasant Valley High School, in the presence of students in the class, upholding a recent act of desecration of the Flag by burning, by an instructor at a nearby state university; and

20

Whereas, we deplore such conduct in Pleasant Valley Schools when there is such great need to instill love of country and respect for the Flag in the minds of our children; and

Whereas these acts are contrary to all that The American Legion stands for and constitute an insult to patriotic citizens;

Therefore, Be It Resolved: that the Pleasant Valley Post, The American Legion, do hereby request that the Board of Trustees of Pleasant Valley School District take conclusive action by terminating the teacher's contract immediately and prohibit said teacher from further teaching in Pleasant Valley schools effective Wednesday, April 26.

Signed: Commander, The American Legion Memorial Post, Pleasant Valley.

The American Legion in Pleasant Valley is not normally a politically active group. Pleasant Valley veterans join the Legion primarily for social rather than political reasons. Nevertheless, in this case, for reasons stated in the proclamation, the Legion believed it had to take a political stand. The Legion was unwilling to stand by and observe passively.

The School Board Meets

As in many communities, the meetings of the school board, while open to the public, do not attract much interest unless the topic for discussion and vote is particularly controversial. More than fifty Pleasant Valley citizens attended the school board meeting on April 25. The meetings are normally conducted in the superintendent's office. As a result of the unusually large attendance for this meeting, business was conducted in the hallway outside the superintendent's office.

The meeting did not last long. Following some opening remarks by the president of the school board, a statement prepared by Mrs. Jackson was read to the audience by the secretary to the board. One week before the meeting on April 25, both Mrs. Jackson and her husband, a Pleasant Valley elementary school teacher, had been offered new contracts for the following school year. According to Mrs. Jackson her contract had included certain conditions that she must agree to. It was understood that if she returned for a second year that she would have to alter her style of teaching in order to lessen the chances of controversy. Mrs. Jackson concluded that she would not be happy teaching under such restrictions and, therefore, together with her husband, elected to return, unsigned, their contracts for the forthcoming year.

Mrs. Jackson's statement that was read to the meeting of the board of education on April 25 contained her beliefs about education and explained why she could not return the following year. It was not technically a letter of resignation, as she had every intention of fulfilling her existing contract but did not intend to sign a new one. In her letter Mrs. Jackson admitted to having made mistakes but re-affirmed her belief "in young minds." She wrote that she would not be shocked by anything students said to her. Furthermore, she stated that teachers must be entirely honest and frank with students.

Following the reading of Mrs. Jackson's letter, the statement adopted on the previous evening and passed unanimously by the American Legion was read. General discussion followed. Some parents reported that their children sided with the student who had written the letter to the newspaper and thereby sparked the controversy. Other parents expressed their fears of what they conceived to be tendencies toward "liberal thinking" in the schools. At one point the meeting was interrupted when some Boy Scouts arrived from their troop meeting. They were greeted with applause.

Witnesses disagree regarding the general tone of the meeting. Some described it as approximating patriotic hysteria. Others believed it to have been a calm discussion of the issues. But all agree that the mood of the meeting was anti-Mrs. Jackson. No one rose to speak in her defense. Nor was Mrs. Jackson present to defend herself.

The Board Makes a Decision

After each person had been given ample opportunity to express his view, the school board retired to executive session. An executive session is one in which members of an organization discuss issues and vote privately without outsiders observing their activities. The board had been absent only a few minutes when they returned to announce their decision to fire Mrs. Jackson immediately and to stop her from teaching further in the Pleasant Valley schools. This order was to take effect the following day, April 26. In effect, the board "fired" Mrs. Jackson but agreed to pay the remainder of her contract. Later, the board's action was interpreted as being one in which Mrs. Jackson's "resignation" was accepted, to become effective immediately. The school board interpreted her letter as a letter of resignation. And the school board agreed to fulfill payment under her existing contract. In this way the school board hoped to forestall any legal action on her part and to avoid unnecessary embarrassment. At the same time, the school board met the demands of some citizens and the American Legion that she not be permitted to teach further in the schools. The school board had thereby settled the crisis in such a way that the citizens of Pleasant Valley were satisfied. And Mrs. Jackson was paid just as if she had continued to work.

The Pleasant Valley incident attracted interest in nearby communities. Other newspapers reported details of the affair. "Letters to the editor" columns contained many notes expressing individual reaction to what had occurred. For the most part the letter-writers condemned the school board and citizens of Pleasant Valley, but they had no visible effect on the final decision. The local chapter of the Civil Liberties Union, a private organization which provides financial and legal support to individuals whose civil liberties are violated, conducted a preliminary inquiry into the case.

The Civil Liberties Union met with several community leaders to try to influence the reinstatement of Mrs. Jackson. As a threat, the Civil Liberties Union said they would take Mrs. Jackson's complaint to a court of law. They claimed that Mrs. Jackson's right of free speech had been taken away unfairly. But the Pleasant Valley school board members believed that their actions had been completely legal. They did not believe that a court of law would rule against them in this case. Thus, they refused to be influenced by the threats of the Civil Liberties Union. They stood firm in their decision to prevent Mrs. Jackson from resuming her teaching duties for the remainder of the school year.

An incident that began by a 15-year-old student expressing a grievance against his English teacher ended by the teacher being forced out of her classroom. Presumably, Pleasant Valley has replaced Mrs. Jackson with a teacher whose teaching methods are more acceptable.

To demonstrate what you have learned about aspects of political behavior, answer these questions about the Pleasant Valley case.

1. What is the main issue in this case?

2. Why did this issue develop?

3. What are the political resources of the parties to the conflict in this case?

4. How did the parties to the conflict in this case try to influence the outcomes of the case?

5. What policy decision was made to settle the conflict in this case?

6. Which groups or individuals were most rewarded by the decision?

7. Why did these groups or individuals have their way?

8. What is the relationship of rules to the political behavior in this case?

9. What does this case indicate about what is political behavior and why people behave politically?

chapter 2

The Social Science Approach to the Study of Political Behavior

Political science is one of the social sciences. Social science is the study of human behavior; and political science is primarily the study of political behavior, one type of human behavior. Increasing your knowledge of the social science approach to the study of political behavior is a main objective of this course.

A. Two Examples of Political Science

Following are two descriptions of the social science approach to the study of political behavior. These examples contain information about how a political scientist does his work and clues about why he does it.

Example 1. Who Voted for Wallace in the 1968 Election?

The 1968 presidential election involved three leading candidates for the office of President. In addition to the candidates of the two major American political parties, Democrat Hubert Humphrey and Republican Richard Nixon, the American Independent party nominated George Wallace. At the time, Wallace was a former governor of Alabama. As governor he had been a symbol of Southern resistance to school desegregation.

In the 1968 election Wallace received about 10 million votes, about 13.5 percent of the total votes cast. Seymour Martin Lipset and Earl Raab wanted to find out what types of people supported George Wallace in this election.*

* Seymour Martin Lipset and Earl Raab, "The Wallace Whitelash," *TRANS-action*, Vol. 7, No. 2 (December, 1969), pp. 22–35. Copyright © December, 1969, by TRANS-action, Inc., New Brunswick, New Jersey.

To answer this question, Lipset and Raab obtained copies of the results of national surveys of voting in the 1968 presidential election. Each national survey was based upon a small sample of voters. Each sample was selected so as to be probably representative of the total national population of voters.

Lipset and Raab studied the results of the national surveys in order to find relationships between certain social characteristics and likelihood of voting for Wallace. These relationships are shown in *Table 1.*

On the basis of the facts shown in *Table 1,* Lipset and Raab concluded that George Wallace received the bulk of his support in the southern states. Lipset and Raab also found that the Wallace voters were more likely to have been (1) manual workers than business and professional workers, (2) low rather than high in educational attainment, (3) low rather than high in income, (4) rural or small-town residents rather than people from larger communities. The figures in *Table 1* also revealed that Wallace had somewhat more support from (5) young voters than older ones and (6) male voters than female voters. Other information in the national surveys permitted Lipset and Raab to reach certain other conclusions about the type of people who supported Wallace. We need not look at these conclusions here. Instead, focus your attention on the information supplied in this example and try to answer these questions:

1. What kind of political behavior were these two political scientists studying?

2. What were the objectives of the political scientists in this study?

3. What techniques did the political scientists use to achieve their objectives?

4. Can you think of any people who would be particularly interested in the conclusions reached by Lipset and Raab? Does your answer to this question provide any clue as to why these political scientists did this work?

Example 2. Public Policy-Making in Levittown

In June, 1958, Levittown, New Jersey, was ready for settlers. The firm of Levitt and Sons, Inc., had carefully planned and built this new suburban community. Herbert Gans was among the first people who moved to Levittown. He came there to conduct a study of human behavior. Some of his questions were about the political behavior of Levittowners, in particular the behavior of public policy-makers and the behavior of those who try to influence public policy.

To answer his questions, Gans became a participant-observer; he lived in Levittown for two years and participated actively in the life of the community. He joined community organizations, attended public meetings, and participated in political activities. As he took part in community affairs, he carefully observed the behavior of people in Levittown. He took notes about the things he saw and heard. He interviewed many people who appeared to be representative of the community. He carefully recorded the information gathered in these interviews. Gans also read newspapers and public documents containing information about life in Levittown.

Table 1. **Voting for Wallace in the 1968 Presidential Election**

SOCIAL CATEGORY	PERCENT WHO VOTED FOR WALLACE	
	South	Non-South
Occupation		
Non-manual	22%	5%
Manual	53	9
Education		
Grade school or less	49	7
High school or less	36	7
Some college	21	5
Income		
Less than $3,000	43	5
$3,000–$6,999	44	10
$7,000–$9,999	42	6
$10,000–$14,999	15	6
$15,000 plus	15	3
Size of Place		
Rural	45	11
2,500–49,999	36	6
50,000–499,999	25	5
500,000–999,999	12	6
1,000,000 plus	—	8
Age		
21–25	—	13
26–29	37	11
30–49	34	8
50 plus	33	3
Sex		
Men	37	9
Women	31	5

25

Willingboro, New Jersey
—formerly Levittown

Herbert J. Gans, *The Levittowners* (New York: Pantheon Books, A Division of Random House, Inc., 1967), pp. 333–367.

From his direct observations, interviews, and reading of documents, Gans gathered and organized many facts. He used these facts to describe and explain human behavior in Levittown, to answer his questions.

Following are some of his findings about influencing policy decisions of the government in Levittown.

1. Government officials tended to make policy decisions that would satisfy large groups of voters who could apply pressure on the decision-makers through their leaders. For example, there is a large Catholic population in Levittown with able leaders in direct contact with government officials. The government officials tended to make policy decisions that pleased this group.

2. Small groups having important political resources were able to influence public policy decisions to a great extent. For example, businessmen who were developing new stores and shopping centers had much influence on policy decisions that concerned their business interests. And representatives of Levitt and Sons, the developer, had considerable influence on the policy decisions of government officials.

3. Government officials tended to ignore the demands of groups with few political resources.

4. Minority groups with few political resources, however, were able to increase their influence on policy decisions by focusing attention on particular issues, generating public conflict about these issues, and organizing group political action, such as circulating petitions and speaking in public meetings.

Use the information presented in this example to answer these questions:

1. What kind of political behavior was Herbert Gans studying?

2. What were his objectives in this study?

3. What techniques did Gans use to achieve his objectives?

4. What are the similarities and differences in the techniques used in Examples 1 and 2?

5. Can you think of any people who would be particularly interested in the conclusions reached by Gans? Does your answer to this question provide any clues as to why Gans did this work?

6. On the basis of information presented in Examples 1 and 2, speculate about what is the social science approach to the study of political behavior?

B. Asking about Political Behavior

Political scientists are curious about political behavior. They want to *describe* political behavior, to *explain* why humans behave politically as they do, and to *predict* the political behavior that is likely to emerge from certain situations. Asking questions is a primary step in the search for knowledge about political behavior.

Four Types of Questions in Political Science

Political science involves the process of asking questions about political behavior. Main types of questions in political science are (a) descriptive, (b) explanatory, (c) predictive, and (d) prescriptive.

A *descriptive* question is about *what* happens: How many people voted for Hubert Humphrey in the 1968 presidential election? What types of people voted for Hubert Humphrey? What is the relationship of racial identity to political party preference? What was President Nixon's policy for ending the Vietnam War?

An *explanatory* question is about *why* something happens: Why did certain types of people vote for Hubert Humphrey in the 1968 presidential election? Why do black people tend to prefer the Democratic party? Why did President Nixon prefer a particular policy for ending the Vietnam War?

A *predictive* question is about *what will happen:* Which candidate will win the next presidential election? Will the present Congress pass legislation that is more liberal than that passed by the previous Congress? Will the United Nations be able to settle the Middle East conflict?

A *prescriptive* question is about *what ought to happen* to reach a certain objective: What policies should Republican party leaders follow in order to attract votes from manual laborers? What changes in public policy should the mayor make in order to attract new industries to his city? What steps should the governor take to make the government function more efficiently?

Characteristics of Good Questions

The political scientist's work can be no better than the questions he asks. Questions direct attention to some things and away from other things. To direct attention fruitfully, questions must be clearly stated, unbiased, and significant.

Good questions are stated clearly. A clearly stated question means the same thing to different people. It focuses the attention of the political scientist directly on what he must do to answer the question. The question "Are men more likely than women to vote in a public election?" is clearly stated. It focuses attention on the relationship between two things, tendency to vote and sex identity. Clearly, to answer this question one must gather facts about the voting tendencies of men and women; one must observe, or question, men and women about their tendencies to vote or not vote in elections.

Here is an example of an unclear question: "How does the President work?" This question is vague. It does not indicate clearly what to do to answer the question, and it is likely to mean different things to different people.

Good questions are unbiased. Unbiased questions help the questioner to make impartial observations and get accurate answers. Here is an example of an unbiased question: "Why are certain types of people likely to participate in nonviolent public

"One more response like that, sir, and I'll be forced to put you down as a hostile respondent."

demonstrations to try to influence public policy decisions?" Now look at an example of a biased question on the same subject: "Why do rabble-rousers foment nonviolent public demonstrations to try to force public officials to change their policies?" The biased question is "loaded" with emotional words that indicate dislike of peaceful public demonstrations. This biased question is not likely to contribute to accurate gathering or reporting of facts about public demonstrations.

Good questions are significant. A significant question is worth asking; it is about something important. In political science a significant question directs attention to important aspects of political behavior, to facts that can help us learn more about how and why people behave politically in certain ways. "What influences the political decisions of congressmen?" is a very significant question in political science. Now look at this question: "What style of overcoats do most congressmen prefer?" This question might be of significance to a clothing designer or salesman, but it is of little or no importance to a political scientist.

To demonstrate what you have learned about the types and uses of questions in political science, answer these questions.

1.   Which of the questions in the following list are descriptive? (b) explanatory? (c) predictive? (d) prescriptive?
   a.   What types of people voted for George Wallace in the 1968 presidential election?
   b.   Why were certain types of people more likely than others to have supported the candidacy of George Wallace in the 1968 presidential election?
   c.   How do residents of Levittown, New Jersey, try to influence public policy decisions?
   d.   Will the voter eligibility laws in my state be changed? *prediction*
   e.   Who are the public policy-makers in Levittown, New Jersey?
   f.   How are political resources related to political influence?
   g.   Since the President wants to attract the votes of white-collar workers, what policies should he support?
   h.   Why are groups with many important political resources likely to be able to influence public policy decisions?

2.   Which of the questions in the following list can be considered acceptable for use by a political scientist? How did you decide which are the acceptable questions?
   a.   What is the relationship of racial identity to party preference?
   b.   What is the effectiveness of government?
   c.   What are the evil consequences of lowering the voting age?
   d.   What is the relationship of hat size to political party preference?
   e.   Are wealthy people more likely than poor people to participate in public elections?

f. Why are all politicians corrupt?

g. Are public policy-makers more likely to prefer cats or dogs as pets?

h. What is the relationship of the President to the people?

i. What are the differences in the ideas of Democratic and Republican members of the United States Senate?

C. Stating Hypotheses and Measuring Variables

Political scientists, like other people, often have hunches, or guesses, about answers to their questions about political behavior. Unlike many other people, political scientists try to test their hunches, to find out whether their beliefs about political behavior are accurate, whether they fit reality.

A preliminary, or tentative, answer to a question about political behavior can be stated as a hypothesis. A hypothesis is a guess about reality, about the way things are, that is stated precisely so that it can be checked against reality.

For example, perhaps you are interested in answering this question; "Do boys who play on varsity athletic teams make better grades than other boys in my school?" You might respond to this question with this hypothesis: *Boys who play on varsity athletic teams achieve lower grade-point averages than do boys who do not play on varsity athletic teams.* As a hypothesis about differences in grade-point averages, this statement is a guess, an untested answer. To decide whether this hypothesis does, or does not, fit the facts, you must gather information about the grade-point averages of athletes and non-athletes in your school.

Alternative Hypotheses

Political scientists are interested in answering questions about participation in politics. One question that they have tried to answer is this: "Are rich people more likely than poor people to take part actively in politics?" A political scientist can respond to this question with these three alternative, or conflicting, hypotheses:

1. Rich people are more likely than poor people to have a high rate of political activity.

2. Rich people are more likely than poor people to have a low rate of political activity.

3. There is little or no difference in the rate of political activity of rich people and poor people.

As alternative hypotheses about political activity, these statements are three conflicting guesses; they are untested answers to a question about differences in political activity. Only one of these conflicting hypotheses can be correct. To find out which hypothesis fits the facts, a political scientist must observe the political behavior of poor people and rich people.

PEANUTS •

By Charles M. Schulz

29

A Hypothesis Shows Relationships between Variables

A statement of an expected relationship between variables is a hypothesis. A variable is something that varies, that can have different values. In mathematics the term variable means a part of an equation that varies, that can have two or more values. For example: 12 = 4x; 12 = 3x; 12 = 6x; 12 = 2x. Since "x" has a different value in each equation, "x" is a variable.

In social science, variables are characteristics of individuals or groups that vary, that have different values. For example, the variables in the preceding alternative hypotheses are *wealth* and *political activity*. Because there are differences in the wealth of individuals, wealth is a variable. In the preceding hypotheses the variable "wealth" has two values, rich and poor. Since there is variation in the political activity of individuals—that is, people are more or less active in politics, political activity is a variable. In the preceding hypotheses, the variable "political activity" has two values, high and low.

Any characteristic of people or groups can be thought of as a variable so long as it has two or more values. For example, sex identity is a variable with two values, male and female. Age is a variable because comparisons among children, teen-agers, young adults, middle-aged people, and elderly people are possible. Political party preference is a variable with the possible values of Democrat, Republican, and Independent. Educational attainment can be considered a variable because a person can be a college graduate (one value), or a non-college graduate (second value). Religious identity can be thought of as a variable because a person can be Protestant (one value), or Catholic (a second value), or Jewish (a third value), or Moslem (a fourth value), etc.

Claims about similarities or differences of human characteristics are hypotheses. Thinking about human characteristics as variables directs attention to degrees of similarity or difference. Thus, thinking about human characteristics as variables increases the precision of a comparison. Comparisons which might have been vague and haphazard can become exact when we identify variables within a hypothesis.

1. In response to each following hypothesis, (a) state two competing or alternative hypotheses, (b) identify the variables in each hypothesis, and (c) specify possible values for each of the variables.

    a. Men are more likely than women to have a high interest in politics.

    b. Protestants are more likely than Catholics to vote in elections.

    c. Young adults are more likely than elderly people to prefer the Democratic party.

    d. There is little or no difference in the political activity of farmers and construction workers.

2. In response to these two questions about political behavior, (a) state a hypothesis in response to the question, (b) identify the variables in your hypothesis, and (c) specify possible values for each of the variables.

    a. Can you compare the political resources of lawyers with the political resources of farmers?

    b. Is violent political activity more likely to occur in democracies or dictatorships?

Measuring Variables

To test a hypothesis, a political scientist must invent a way to measure the variables in the hypothesis. To find out the differences or similarities in human characteristics is to measure variables. For example, in order to find out whether rich people or poor people are more likely to be active in politics, a political scientist must decide what he will do to measure variation in wealth and political activity.

It is easy to invent a technique for measuring some variables. For example, a political scientist who is studying voting differences between rural and urban residents must decide how to measure the variable "place of residence." The researcher might use the Census Bureau's definition of rural (farms and places under 2500 population) and urban (places over 2500 population). In this example the researcher has said clearly what he will do to measure a variable.

It is easy to decide how to measure variables such as sex identity or wealth. A political scientist can decide that people who identify themselves as males will be considered males in his study. Political scientists can decide to measure wealth by observing the income and possessions of individuals. An individual with many expensive possessions and a large income can be called rich, and an individual with few possessions and a small income can be called poor.

It is more difficult to invent a way to measure other variables which a political scientist wants to study. For example, it is difficult to invent ways to measure differences in political attitudes or political opinions. A political scientist cannot observe an attitude or opinion directly in order to measure it. Rather, he must invent a way to observe human behavior that is in some way related to the political attitude or opinion that he wants to study. On the basis of the behavior that he observes directly, the political scientist tries to make accurate judgments about the existence of a political attitude or political opinion.

How does a teacher, for example, make judgments about the attitudes of students on the course he is teaching? One method is to observe student behavior in the classroom: alertness or day-dreaming, asking and answering questions or remaining silent, and so on. On the basis of these observations a teacher could make judgments about the attitudes of students toward his course.

Measuring Sense of Political Efficacy

Sense of *political efficacy* is an attitude that political scientists study. Sense of political efficacy is a feeling that one has the power to influence political decisions and that it is worthwhile to try to do so. A political scientist could observe human behavior directly to try to measure this feeling. During one day he might observe these five examples of human behavior:

> Mrs. Peters, a housewife, is speaking with a neighbor: "I am upset that the state legislature plans to cut its share of money for our local public schools. I am convinced that our schools need that money to hire more teachers and

to update the curriculum. I think I'll write to our State Representative and urge him to fight against the cut."

———————

Mr. Andrews has just left the polling place after casting his ballot: "All the time I was waiting to go into the voting booth I kept thinking, 'Will my vote really make a difference in the election?' I always vote because I know it's my duty, but I figure that it doesn't make much difference what one person decides."

———————

Mrs. James wants to apply for Social Security benefits to which she is entitled: "I think I'll ask my daughter Mary to go with me to the Social Security office tomorrow. I just don't understand the directions and the forms they give you and the complicated language they use. Social Security, to me, is like the rest of the government—it's important, but I just don't understand what it's all about."

———————

Mr. Jonas, a lawyer, is talking to the mayor on the telephone: "Bob, I think something needs to be done about the children's park. Some of the play equipment is broken and could cause an injury. Could you bring this matter to the attention of the Park Department?"

———————

Mr. Arthur is talking with a friend at work: "I get burned up when I read about increases in my taxes. It seems like every couple of months taxes go up—either property taxes, or sales taxes, or income taxes. What's worse is that there isn't anything I can do about it, because people in government don't bother to listen to people like me. They only listen to big shots with lots of money."

On the basis of information in these five examples, a political scientist could decide that Mrs. Peters and Mr. Jonas have a higher sense of political efficacy than Mr. Andrews, Mrs. James, and Mr. Arthur. Both Mrs. Peters and Mr. Jonas appear to believe that they can and should try to influence political decisions. In contrast, the other three individuals *do not* appear to believe that they can or should try to influence political decisions.

This attempt to measure variation in sense of political efficacy is very rough and imprecise. The political scientist has not found very much about the similarities and differences in sense of political efficacy of these five people, and his findings are vague. For example, the political scientist does not know how great or small are the differences in sense of political efficacy among the five individuals. And he cannot compare exactly the sense of political efficacy of the five people.

Political scientists create questionnaires to make more exact measurements of political attitudes. On the basis of responses to their questionnaires, political scientists try to measure similarities or differences in the political attitudes or opinions of different types of people.

A group of political scientists created the following questionnaire to measure variation in sense of political efficacy among different types of people.* People were asked: Do you "agree" or "disagree" with each of the following statements?

1. I don't think public officials care much what people like me think.

2. Voting is the only way that people like me can have any say about how the government runs things.

3. People like me don't have any say about what the government does.

4. Sometimes politics and government seem so complicated that a person like me can't really understand what's going on.

*Adapted from Angus Campbell, Gerald Gurin, and Warren E. Miller, *The Voter Decides* (New York: Harper and Row, Publishers, 1954), pp. 187–194.

Responses to the four statements about sense of political efficacy can be scored by assigning a value of one point for each "disagree" response. For example, a respondent who *disagrees* with each of the four items receives a score of four points; a respondent who disagrees with three items receives a score of three, and so on.

On the basis of this scoring system, a political scientist can define variation in sense of political efficacy as follows:

1. A high sense of political efficacy is a score of four.

2. A medium sense of political efficacy is a score of two or three.

3. A low sense of political efficacy is a score of zero or one.

Asking people to respond to the political-efficacy questionnaire, scoring the responses, and dividing respondents into groups of "high," "medium," and "low" on the basis of their scores is a useful technique for measuring the variable "sense of political efficacy."

One of the questions that political scientists have tried to answer about sense of political efficacy is this: "Do males have a higher sense of political efficacy than females?"

Here are three alternative hypotheses relating the variables of sex identity and sense of political efficacy:

1. Males are more likely than females to have a high sense of political efficacy.

2. Females are more likely than males to have a high sense of political efficacy.

3. There is little or no difference in the sense of political efficacy of males and females.

To measure variation in sense of political efficacy among males and females, Angus Campbell and his associates (above) asked 738 men and 876 women to respond to a questionnaire. These people were selected so as to be probably representative of all adults in the United States. The result of this attempt to measure variation in sense of political efficacy of males and females appears in *Table 2*.

As shown in *Table 2,* males are more likely than females to have a high sense of political efficacy. Thirty-five percent of the males, as compared to 20 percent of the females, expressed a high sense of political efficacy. The questionnaire at the top of page 33 is the instrument used to measure variation in sense of political efficacy, to test hypotheses about this variable.

Table 2. **Relationship of Sex Identity to Sense of Political Efficacy**

	DEGREE OF POLITICAL EFFICACY				
Sex Identity	High	Medium	Low	Unknown	Total
MALE	35%	47%	17%	1%	100%
FEMALE	20%	55%	23%	2%	100%

To demonstrate what you have learned about measuring variables, answer these questions:

1. Here is a definition of political cynicism and a political-cynicism questionnaire. Can you use the definition and questionnaire to write a description of how to measure variation in political cynicism?

    a. Political cynicism means to distrust politicians and government officials and to have a low regard for politicians and government officials.

    b. Do you agree or disagree with each of these five statements?
        (1) In order to get elected, most candidates for political office have to make shady deals.
        (2) Instead of serving the people, politicians spend most of their time getting reelected or reappointed.
        (3) Most of the people running the government are a little crooked.
        (4) A large number of city and county politicians are political hacks.
        (5) People in the government waste a lot of the money we pay in taxes.

2. Can you decide how to measure the variable "age group"?

3. Can you state three alternative hypotheses in which you relate the variables of age group and political cynicism? How would you measure the variables in these hypotheses in order to test the hypotheses?

D. Using Facts to Test Hypotheses

Let us review briefly what has been discussed about the steps a political scientist takes when trying to answer questions about political behavior.

1. He states a belief in the form of a hypothesis.

2. He states alternative or competing hypotheses.

3. He indicates how to measure the variables that are related in the hypotheses.

A political scientist gathers facts, or data, to use as evidence to support or reject hypotheses. A fact, or datum (singular of data), is something that can be accepted as real, as actual or existing. For example, it is a fact that Washington, D.C., is the capital of the United States.

Deciding What Is a Fact

We use our senses—the ability to see, touch, hear, taste, and smell—to decide what is a fact. Something that everyone, or nearly everyone, can agree that he experiences with his senses is considered a fact. For example, it is a fact that Richard Nixon received more votes than Hubert Humphrey in the presidential election of 1968. This fact was established by counting the votes cast for all presidential candidates and observing that Nixon received more votes than other candidates.

A person does not directly experience many of the things that he accepts as facts. For example, most of us have little or no direct experience with experiments in physics. We tend to accept the judgments of experts who conduct scientific experiments in physics about what are the facts of modern physical science.

Making Inferences

Many of the beliefs that we accept as facts are inferences. An *inference* is a judgment about reality—about what is true—that is based on evidence gathered through the senses. Political scientists often make inferences about a large group of people on the basis of facts gathered about a smaller group. For example, political scientists have reported that college graduates tended to vote for Nixon in the presidential election of 1968. To make this observation, a political scientist could have attempted to ask all people in the United States with college backgrounds for whom they voted in the 1968 presidential election. However, this would have been very difficult or impossible to accomplish. Instead political scientists studied a small group, or sample, of college-educated people which was representative of all those in the United States with college backgrounds. When asked for whom they voted, this small sample of college-educated people responded as follows: 54 percent said that they voted for Nixon; 37 percent said that they voted for Humphrey; and 9 percent said that they voted for Wallace. On the basis of the responses of the sample, political scientists made the inference that college graduates throughout the United States tended to vote for Nixon in 1968. This inference about all college graduates is based upon facts about a small representative sample. However, political scientists accept inferences such as this as facts, because they believe that such inferences are very likely to be accurate descriptions of reality.

Facts Confirm or Disconfirm Hypotheses

A hypothesis that *can* be supported with facts is confirmed. A hypothesis that *cannot* be supported with data is rejected, or disconfirmed. For example, one can hypothesize that people with college backgrounds are more likely to vote Republican in a presidential election than are people without college backgrounds. Can this hypothesis be supported with evidence? The graph below presents evidence gathered by the American Institute of Public Opinion about the voting tendencies of individuals of differing educational attainment.

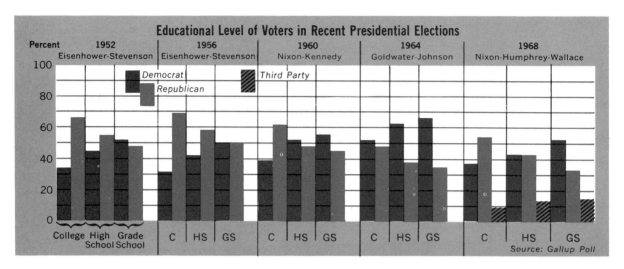

The facts, or data, in the graph support, or confirm, the hypothesis that individuals with a college education are more likely than individuals with non-college backgrounds to support Republican presidential candidates. In four of five elections from 1952–1968, people with college backgrounds tended to vote for the Republican candidate. And in 1964, the year when every group tended to support the Democratic candidate, a smaller proportion of the college-educated people supported the Democratic candidate.

Some facts are more or less general while other facts are specific. The statement that individuals with college backgrounds are more likely to vote Republican in presidential elections than individuals with non-college backgrounds is a very general fact. The statement that individuals with college backgrounds tended to vote for the Republican candidate in the 1968 presidential election is a less general fact than the previous statement. The statement that in 1968, Mr. Smith, a college graduate, voted for Richard Nixon for President is a specific fact.

Obtaining the Facts

How does a political scientist obtain the facts, or data, needed to test a hypothesis? Political scientists use their senses to gather facts about political behavior in three main ways:

1. They ask questions of people about political attitudes or behavior.

2. They observe political behavior directly.

3. They examine products of political behavior.

In the previous examples about voting behavior in presidential elections and about variations in sense of political efficacy, asking questions of people was the technique used to gather data. In the voting-behavior examples, different types of people were asked for whom they voted in presidential elections. In the other example, males and females were asked to respond to a questionnaire designed to measure a person's degree of political efficacy. The responses of individuals to the questions about voting behavior or sense of political efficacy are the data, or the facts, used to confirm or reject hypotheses.

The results of any study based on asking questions of people can be only as good as the questions used to obtain the results. The questions must be as simple, clear, and unbiased as possible, as we saw earlier.

Asking clear questions. A political scientist tries to construct questions that are understandable to the people who will answer the questions. The questions must be worded so that they will mean about the same thing to each person. For example, here are two questions that might be used in a public opinion study.

Question A: Do you approve of the way the President of the United States is doing his job?

Question B: What do you think about the President?

Question A is clearer than Question B. Question B is vague because it does not indicate what the respondents are to evaluate about the President.

In order to write clear questions, a political scientist frequently submits a tentative list of questions to other people for suggestions for improvements. He often tests his questions by trying them out with some people who are like the people he plans to study. For example, if the political scientist is studying the attitudes of college students, he would probably try out the questions on college students. If he finds that these students do not readily understand certain questions, he will try to figure out why the questions are unclear and will change them.

Asking unbiased questions. The wording of questions or statements in a questionnaire must not influence, or bias, the answers. The results of a questionnaire cannot be considered accurate if the wording of the questionnaire distorts the answers. For example, the following biased questions were used by two California congressmen in a political opinion study conducted in their state.* The congressmen wanted to find out the opinions of the people of California about a proposal to raise the salary of members of the House of Representatives. Question A was used by one congressman in his survey.

Question A: A bill is now pending before Congress which would increase the salary of members of Congress from $22,500 to $32,500 per year. Do you favor this 44 percent increase in congressional salaries?

Question B: Do you approve the recommendation of a Presidential Commission to raise congressional salaries to $32,500?

*David Leuthold, *Electioneering in a Democracy* (New York: Wiley, 1968), p. 55.

The biased questions yielded different results. The responses to Question A were mostly negative, and the responses to Question B were mostly positive. Many negative responses to Question A were probably influenced by the stress on "44 percent increase." The emphasis on a "Presidential Commission" in Question B probably influenced many positive responses. This example shows how the wording of questions can bias responses and distort the information gathered through use of the questions.

Observing behavior directly. The study of policy decisions in Levittown, New Jersey, is an example of direct observation as a way to gather facts about the political behavior (pp. 25–26). Herbert Gans lived among the people in Levittown for two years. During this time he observed public policy-makers and those who tried to influence policy decisions. He carefully and systematically recorded his observations. These recorded observations are the facts, or data, that Gans used as evidence to answer his questions about political behavior in Levittown.

Examining behavior products. Examination of products of political behavior is another main approach used to gather facts to support or reject hypotheses. A product of behavior is a record of some type that has resulted from human activity. For example, the artifacts found in Egyptian pyramids or in Indian mounds in North America are products of human behavior in the distant past. Social scientists examine these artifacts as a way to gather facts about the way certain people lived many years ago. Copies of constitutions, newspapers, laws, and speeches are also products of human behavior. Political scientists examine these records to obtain data about past political behavior.

The three main ways of gathering facts—asking questions, observing political behavior directly, and examining behavior products—are often used together by a political scientist trying to answer a question and/or confirm hypotheses. For example, Herbert Gans used each of these techniques for gathering information in his study of political behavior in Levittown, although he depended most on direct observation.

Each of these techniques directs attention to the world of reality as the source of information to confirm or reject beliefs about reality. Each technique depends upon human senses, and aids to those senses, to gather data.

Using information gathered by others. Instead of making personal observations to test hypotheses, a political scientist may use information gathered and organized *by others* who have used one of the three previously mentioned approaches to gathering facts. The study of voter support for Wallace in the 1968 presidential election (pp. 24–25) is an example of using information gathered and organized by others. Lipset and Raab used information gathered and organized by the Gallup Poll, Survey Research Center of the University of Michigan, and other reliable national polling organizations to answer their question about who supported Wallace.

SUGGESTED INTRODUCTION: I'm taking a GALLUP SURVEY. I'd like YOUR opinion on some topics of interest.

Time interview started:
....

The first question I would like to ask you is ...

1. How much thought have you given to the coming November elections -- quite a lot, or only a little?

   1( ) Lot   2( ) Some   3( ) Little   v( ) None

2. On another topic... is your name now recorded in the registration book of the precinct or election district where you now live?

   1( ) Yes 2( ) No 3( ) Don't have to register   v( ) Don't know

Now, I'd like to get your honest opinion on this next question. It doesn't make any difference to me how you vote... I only want to get YOUR views accurately

3. Here is a Gallup Poll ballot. (Tear off attached sheet and hand to respondent. Now suppose the elections for Congress were being held TODAY. Which party would you like to see win in this congressional district. Will you please mark that ballot as you would in a real election if it were being held TODAY --and then drop the folded ballot into the box. (INTERVIEWER: If respondent hands back ballot and says he hasn't made up his mind, or refuses to mark it, say: "Well, would you please mark the ballot for the party toward which you lean, as of today?" (If respondent still can't decide, or refuses to mark ballot, note this on the ballot and be sure to drop it in the box.)

4. Do you, yourself, plan to vote in the election this November, or not?
   I( ) Yes   2( ) No   v( ) Don't Know

   IF YES, ask:
   b. How certain are you that you will vote -- ABSOLUTELY certain, FAIRLY certain, or NOT certain?
   3( ) Absolutely certain   4( ) Fairly   5( ) Not certain

5. Have you heard or read about the ..... Commission?
   I( ) Yes   2( ) No

   IF YES, ask :
   b. Can you tell me what this Commission is or what it does?
   _____
   _____

6. Do you approve or disapprove of the way Nixon is handling his job as president?
   1( ) Approve   2( ) Disapprove   v( ) No Opinion

7a. What do you think is the most important problem facing this country today? _____
   _____

   b. Which political party do you think can do the better job of handling the problem you have just mentioned -- the Republican party or the Democratic party?

   1( ) Republican   2( ) Democratic   3( ) No difference   v( ) D.K.

8. When people around here go to vote on November 3rd for a candidate for Congress, how important will each of the following issues be in their thinking. I'll read you each one and you tell me whether YOU think it is extremely important, fairly important, or not so important?

   a. Inflation -- the high cost of living?
   I( ) Extremely 2( ) Fairly 3( ) Not so   v( ) Don't Know

   b. The racial problem?
   1( ) Extremely 2( ) Fairly 3( ) Not so   v( ) Don't know

   c. Crime and drug addiction?

   d. Vietnam?
   1( ) Extremely 2( ) Fairly 3( ) Not so   v( ) Don't know

   e. Student unrest?
   1( ) Extremely 2( ) Fairly 3( ) Not so   v( ) Don't know

   f. Pollution
   1( ) Extremely 2( ) Fairly 3( ) Not so   v( ) Don't know

9. How often would you say you vote -- always, nearly always, part of the time, or seldom?

   1( )Always   2( )Nearly always   3( ) Part of the time

   4( ) Seldom   5( ) Other _____

13. On the next subject... How would you describe yourself -- as very conservative, fairly conservative, middle-of-the-road, fairly liberal or very liberal?

   1( ) Very conservative   2( ) Fairly Conservative
   3( ) Middle-of-the-road 4( ) Fairly liberal 5( ) Very liberal v( )

13a. Which in your opinion is more to blame for crime and lawlessness in this country -- the individual or society?

   1( ) the individual   2( ) Society   v( ) No opinion

Throughout this book you will be asked to use information collected by other people to develop and test hypotheses about political behavior. However, as you use information gathered by others, take care to investigate the techniques used to measure variables, to gather facts to test hypotheses. Always approach information gathered by others critically to determine the worth of the information.

Exercises on Gathering and Using Facts to Test Hypotheses

To demonstrate what you have learned about gathering and using facts to test hypotheses, complete the following five exercises.

Exercise 1. Use the following information about sense of political efficacy of children to answer these questions: (a) What are the variables in this study? (b) How did the political scientists try to measure the variables in this study? (c) Which of the following alternative hypotheses is confirmed by the data in *Table 3?*

Hypothesis 1. Among eighth-graders, males are much more likely than females to have a high sense of political efficacy.

Hypothesis 2. Among eighth-graders, males are much less likely than females to have a high sense of political efficacy.

Hypothesis 3. Among eighth-graders there is very little or no difference in the sense of political efficacy among males and females.

Two political scientists wanted to measure variation in sense of political efficacy among children. They created the following questionnaire to measure variation in sense of political efficacy.*

*David Easton and Jack Dennis, "The Child's Acquisition of Regime Norms: Political Efficacy," *The American Political Science Review*, Vol. LXI, No. 1 (March, 1967), p. 30.

Questionnaire on Political Efficacy

Do you agree or disagree with each of the following statements?

1. What happens in the government will happen no matter what people do. It is like the weather, there is nothing people can do about it.
2. There are some big, powerful men in the government who are running the whole thing and they do not care about us ordinary people.
3. My family doesn't have any say about what the government does.
4. I don't think people in the government care much about what people like my family think.
5. Citizens don't have a chance to say what they think about running the government.

Responses to these five statements about sense of political efficacy can be scored by assigning a value of one point for each "disagree" response. A score of five or four indicates a high sense of political efficacy.

One of the questions these political scientists tried to answer is this: "Do eighth-grade boys have a higher sense of political efficacy than eighth-grade girls?" To answer this question, they asked 854 eighth-grade boys and 762 eighth-grade girls to respond to their questionnaire. These eighth-graders were selected so as to be probably representative of all eighth-grade children in the United States. The results of this study are shown in *Table 3*.

Table 3. **Relationship of Sex Identity to Sense of Political Efficacy among Eighth-Graders**

| Sex Identity | SENSE OF POLITICAL EFFICACY | | | |
	Low	Medium	High	Total
Boys	18%	30%	52%	100%
Girls	16%	29%	55%	100%

Table 4. **Percentage of Nonwhite Voters Who Voted for the Democratic Presidential Candidate, 1952–1968**

Year	Percent
1952	79%
1956	61
1960	68
1964	94
1968	85

Table 5. **Percentage of Catholic and Protestant Voters Who Voted for the Republican Presidential Candidate, 1952–1968**

Year	Catholic	Protestant
1952	49%	63%
1956	49	63
1960	22	62
1964	24	45
1968	33	49

Source: The American Institute of Public Opinion (The Gallup Poll).

Exercise 2. Following is a hypothesis about the relationship of racial identity to voting choice in presidential elections. Use the evidence in *Table 4* to answer these questions: (a) Is the hypothesis confirmed? (b) Is the hypothesis rejected, or disconfirmed? (c) Is the hypothesis neither confirmed nor disconfirmed by the data?

Hypothesis: Nonwhites have tended to vote for the Democratic candidate in presidential elections during the period 1952–1968.

Exercise 3. Following is a hypothesis about the relationship of religious identity to voting choice in presidential elections. Use the evidence in *Table 5* to answer these questions: (a) Is the hypothesis confirmed? (b) Is the hypothesis rejected, or disconfirmed? (c) Is the hypothesis neither confirmed nor disconfirmed by the data?

Hypothesis: Catholics are more likely than Protestants to vote for the Republican candidate in presidential elections.

41

Exercise 4. Following is a list of factual statements. Which statements are very general facts, which are less general facts, and which are specific facts?

    a. Mr. Jones voted for the Democratic candidate for mayor in the last election.

    b. Mr. Jones is a manual laborer.

    c. In the last mayoral election in our city, manual laborers tended to vote for the Democratic candidate.

    d. On the basis of evidence collected during the past thirty years one can conclude that manual laborers are more likely than other occupational groups to vote Democratic.

    e. In 1964 about 94 percent of the nonwhites voted for the Democratic presidential candidate.

    f. Mr. Jackson is a black man who voted for the Democratic party candidate in the presidential election of 1964.

    g. Black people tend to vote for the Democratic candidate in presidential elections.

Exercise 5. Below is a list of questions taken from different questionnaires used in studies of public opinion. Which of the questions are "good" and which are "bad"? Explain.

    a. Should the United States buy UN bonds to "pick up the tab" for those nations which do not pay?

    b. Should the government help people to get doctors and hospital care at low cost?

    c. Should we act now to correct the tragedy of Cuba?

    d. Should the United States purchase $100 million in United Nations bonds?

    e. The administration has asked $1.6 billion for the war on poverty—an increase of $400 million over the first year. Do you approve?

E. Sampling and Generalization

Political scientists usually want to describe and explain the political attitudes or behavior of very large groups of people. However, to make a study of all people in the United States, or in one of the fifty states, or even in one city would be too costly in time, money, and effort to be worthwhile. Through careful sampling, it is possible to make accurate conclusions about a large group of people on the basis of a study of a very small group of people.

Careful Sampling Involves Random Selection

Sampling involves the selection of a very small number of people from a much larger group of people. To be able to make accurate conclusions about a large group, on the basis of studying a very small sample of the large group, the sample must be selected randomly. Random selection of a sample means that every individual in the larger group has the same chance of getting into the sample as every other individual. For example, assume that you wish to select randomly a sample of 100 students from a population of 500 twelfth-graders in a particular high school. You might put the names of the 500 students in a box, mix the contents thoroughly, and select 100 names in such a way that every individual in the population of 500 students has the same chance of being selected in the sample of 100 students as every other student. Studying the political attitudes of a randomly selected sample of 100 individuals enables generalization about the political attitudes of the total group of 500 individuals from which the sample was drawn.

Suppose you wanted to test hypotheses about the sense of political efficacy of all boys and girls in your school. If you administered the political-efficacy questionnaire on page 40 to a random sample of the students in your school, you could make generalizations about the data from the sample group that also apply to the larger group—all the students in your school. On the basis of data gathered from a small sample, you could confirm or reject hypotheses that apply to a much larger group—all the students from which the sample was selected.

Probability Theory

Studying randomly selected samples to make accurate conclusions about larger groups is based on *probability theory*. For example, pretend that you have a large container in front of you that holds a million marbles of equal size. Half the marbles are red and half are green. You select randomly 100 marbles from the container. According to probability theory, you are very likely, within a 3 percent margin of error, to select 50 green marbles and 50 red marbles. According to probability theory, you are very likely to obtain the same results if you repeat this activity again and again.

It is easy to select a random sample of a relatively small group of people, such as all the students in your school or all the people who live in your neighborhood. It is much more difficult to select a random sample of a much larger population, such as all the people in your state or all the people in the United States. Lists of every individual in a state or in the nation, from which a random sample could be selected, are not available. However, lists of counties, cities, and areas within counties and cities are available. Thus, a random sample of all counties, or of smaller geographic units, in the United States can be selected. Within these smaller areas that have been randomly selected, one can obtain a list of all residents. A random sample of the residents within each geographic unit can be selected. Studying these randomly selected residents of randomly selected geographic areas in the nation provides a random sample of all residents of the United States.

Huffine in *The Wall Street Journal*

"The odds against ever again having four flat tires in a heavy rainstorm are 6,349,833,604,284.6 to 1"

The method of the Gallup Poll for selecting random samples of all Americans is very similar to the method just described. For example, Gallup selects randomly 300 sections of the nation and selects randomly five residents of each section. This random sample of 1500 people is representative of all adults in the United States.

Notice that the size of Gallup's nationally representative sample is relatively small. The size of the sample, beyond a certain minimum size necessary to avoid distortion, is less important than the method of selection. A sample may contain 50 million people, rather than 1500, and yet be unreliable because of faulty selection. According to probability theory, only a randomly selected sample has a very high chance of being an accurate representation of the group from which it was selected.

Random Sampling Is Not Haphazard

Random sampling *does not* mean haphazard sampling. For example, some newspapers and magazines poll their readers about voting preferences or political attitudes. They invite their readers to mail in their responses to a questionnaire. On the basis of whomever chooses to send in answers to the questionnaire, the "pollsters" make conclusions about public opinion. However, this technique for selecting a sample is faulty. The sample is likely to over-represent some kinds of people and underrepresent others. For example, the sample is biased against people who are too poor to buy newspapers or magazines or who do not like to read. And the sample is biased in favor of certain types of people who are likely to respond to a newspaper questionnaire. As the method of selecting a sample in these cases is haphazard, so the results are haphazard and relatively useless.

The Reliability of Random Samples

Many people doubt the reliability of random samples, despite the grounding of this technique in probability theory. Following are two examples that demonstrate the accuracy of studies made with random sampling. The first is a study made of certain political opinions of adult Americans in the 1950's. Two different random samples of all adult Americans were selected. One sample was selected by the AIPO (American Institute of Public Opinion) and the other sample was selected by NORC (National Opinion Research Center). The selection of two different samples provided an opportunity to check the reliability of the random samples. If the responses of each sample to the same questionnaire are similar, then one can assume that both randomly selected samples are accurate. The responses of both samples to one question in this study are shown in *Table 6*.

Table 6 shows the similarity of the percentages of the responses of the two different random samples. This closeness in responses of two independently selected random samples is a powerful demonstration of the reliability of random sampling.

A second example of the reliability of random samples is the comparison of Gallup Poll estimates of presidential election results to the actual election

Polling organizations provide some training for interviewers—often by means of a handbook. On the opposite page are two portions of a handbook of the Survey Research Center of the University of Michigan. One of the circles in the inset diagram shows a polling "segment." The listing sheet identifies the dwellings in such a segment. One or more homes may be chosen for polling.

44

SURVEY
RESEARCH
CENTER

SEGMENT LISTING SHEET

C. PSU _Fall River_

PLACE _Hampton City_

D. SEGMENT NO. _203A_

A. LISTED BY _Susan Metz_ DATE _3/18/'68_

B. UPDATED BY _Susan Metz_ DATE _9/9/'68_

_____ DATE _____

E. TYPE OF SEGMENT:

Take-all ☐

Take-part ☒

Line No.	Description (or address) of Dwelling Unit	Project Number
1.	221 Elm St., upper right	
2.	221 Elm St., upper left	
3.	104 Fieldston Terrace	
4.	127 Fieldston Terrace	
5.	103 Fieldston Terrace	
6.	120 Sherwood St.	
7.	336 Oak St.	
8.	272 Oak St.	
9.	220 Oak St.	
10.	Apartment over large garage behind 272 Oak St., entrance on west side of structure	

Illustration 8-1
SRC Sampling Method

Form S210 (10-67)

SHEET _1_ OF _1_ SHEETS

Table 6. **Responses of Two Samples to This Question:** *If a person wanted to make a speech in your community against churches and religion, should he be allowed to speak or not?*

Sample Group	No	Yes	No Opinion	Total
		RESPONSES		
AIPO	60%	37%	3%	100%
NORC	61%	37%	2%	100%

Source: Samuel A. Stouffer, *Communism, Conformity, and Civil Liberties* (Garden City, N.Y.: Doubleday, 1955), pp. 32–33.

outcome. This comparison, for the presidential elections of 1964 and 1968, is presented in *Table 7.* Furthermore, during the twenty-year period 1948–1968, Gallup Poll estimates of voter behavior in national elections were accurate within a 1.4 percent average margin of error.

Table 7. **Gallup Poll Estimates and Election Results in the Presidential Elections of 1964 and 1968**

	1964		1968		
	Dem.	Rep.	Dem.	Rep.	Third Party
Election Results	61.4%	38.6%	42.9%	43.5%	13.6%
Gallup Estimate	64.0	36.0	42.0	43.0	15.0

Random samples cannot provide absolute certainty of an accurate study. Because the accuracy of studies based on random samples is based on probability theory, one can only claim that random samples are highly likely to yield accurate results. There is always a small margin of error connected with any study based on a random sample. However, random samples are very likely to yield accurate studies. Since there is no good alternative to accurate large-scale studies of political attitudes and political behavior, the random sample is a very valuable tool of the political scientist.

To demonstrate what you have learned about sampling and generalization, complete the following two exercises.

Exercise 1. Evaluate the three examples of sampling which follow. Decide which sampling technique is most likely to produce valid and reliable results in a political-attitude study.

Three teams of researchers were interested in determining attitudes about political efficacy among students in a large midwestern university. The university had 30,000 students. Each team of researchers used the same set of questions to measure political efficacy among the students. But each team of researchers used a different sampling technique.

Sampling Technique of Team I

Team I stopped the first 1000 students whom they met on a street in the middle of the university campus. The team asked the questions about political efficacy to each of these students.

Sampling Technique of Team II

Team II went to the office of the university registrar. This office contained lists of every student enrolled at the university. The researchers assigned a number to the name of each student. All the numbers were placed in a large box and mixed. Then the researchers pulled 300 student numbers out of the box. Each of these 300 students was visited by a researcher and asked to answer the questions about political efficacy.

Sampling Technique of Team III

Team III decided to use a smaller list of students from which to pick a larger sample. These researchers went to the university office where students registered their automobiles. The team obtained a list of 9000 student owners of automobiles. The researchers decided to pick every fifteenth name on this list to include in their sample. Then the researchers visited each of the 600 students in this sample and asked them to answer the questions about political efficacy.

a. Which of these three teams used the best sampling technique? Explain your choice.

b. How widely can the researchers generalize from the data gathered in the above example? Or to say this in another way, how large is the group of students described by factual statements made from these data? Choose one or more of the following groups: (1) all university students in the United States, (2) all university students in the midwestern region of the United States, (3) all university students in the university where this particular attitude survey was made.

c. In order to extend the generalizability of their findings, what must the researchers do?

Exercise 2. In 1936 the *Literary Digest,* a popular magazine, selected a sample of voters in the United States and asked the individuals in this sample for whom they would vote in the upcoming presidential election of 1936, the Republican candidate, Alfred Landon; or the Democratic candidate, Franklin D. Roosevelt. The *Literary Digest* selected a sample of 2,375,000 individuals from lists of automobile and telephone owners in the United States. On the basis of this study the *Literary Digest* predicted that Alfred Landon would win a landslide victory. In fact, Franklin D. Roosevelt won a landslide victory. What was wrong with the *Literary Digest* study?

47

F. Descriptive Beliefs and Explanatory Beliefs

A descriptive belief tells what we can observe about the way things are. The statement, "Water begins to freeze at 32°F," is a descriptive belief. Descriptive beliefs are frequently stated as comparisons: It is cooler in the shade than in the sunlight; alcohol begins to freeze at a lower temperature than does water.

The hypotheses about the sense of political efficacy of eighth-grade students stated on page 40 are *descriptive beliefs.* The statement, "There is little or no difference between the political interest of men and women," is also a descriptive belief, since it tells us about the way something is.

Until this point in the course we have been working with descriptive beliefs. But a political scientist wants to do more than merely *describe* political behavior. He also wants to *explain* why people act as they do. He wants to express explanatory beliefs.

Let us compare a *descriptive* belief with an *explanatory* belief.

Descriptive belief: Men are more likely to be active in political affairs than are women.

Explanatory belief: Men are more likely to be active in political affairs than are women, because men are expected to be more aggressive and competitive than are women.

The *descriptive belief* is limited to reporting *what is* the relationship between variables, in this case between sex identity and political activity. The *explanatory belief* is an attempt to explain *why* the relationship between variables occurs. Both of these beliefs remain hypotheses until reliable evidence can be gathered to show that they present an accurate picture of reality. If these hypotheses can be supported with evidence, then they become factual judgments, or factual statements.

Explanatory beliefs depend upon confirmed *descriptive beliefs.* Unless you are certain of the truth of the statement, "Men are more likely to become political leaders than are women," it is worthless to speculate why that situation exists. Therefore, social scientists must *observe* carefully and *describe* accurately if worthwhile explanations are to become possible.

As you progress through this course you will learn that much evidence has been gathered to support many descriptive hypotheses about political behavior. However, most explanatory hypotheses about political behavior remain unconfirmed. Since human behavior is very complicated, choosing among competing alternative hypotheses about why people act as they do is a very difficult task. While social scientists have developed great skill in accurately describing human behavior through scientific inquiry, they continue to have difficulty confirming explanatory hypotheses. Social scientists are often able to show that some explanatory hypotheses are false. Thus, they can eliminate some competing hypotheses as incorrect. But they are often unable to identify which one, among competing explanatory hypotheses, is the best hypothesis.

Variables May Be Correlated

Social scientists can demonstrate that one or more variables are *correlated.* When variables are correlated, one variable increases or decreases with another variable. For example, political scientists have found that political interest is correlated with income. As income increases, political interest increases. And as income decreases, political interest decreases. The variables, political interest and income, are correlated; they seem to go together.

It is tempting to try to explain an individual's political interest in terms of his income, to say that an increase in income *causes* an increase in political interest. However, to identify a correlation of one variable to another is *not* to identify cause. For example, political scientists have found that several variables in addition to income are correlated with political interest. Some of these variables are occupation, years of schooling, age group, sex identity, and racial identity. Often, it is difficult or impossible to decide which of these several variables, if any, is the cause of high or low political interest. We can say only that these variables "vary" together, or that they are correlated. However, we can hypothesize about the causes of political interest in terms of the variables that are correlated with political interest.

Multi-factor Explanations

Explanations of political behavior are usually *multi-factor explanations.* Several variables (multi-factors) are correlated with a behavior that is the focus of the investigation. Since it is usually impossible to determine which single variable, or factor, is *the* cause of the behavior under investigation, we try to explain the behavior in terms of several variables, or factors.

One way to construct a multi-factor explanation is to combine variables to attempt to explain variation in a human characteristic. *Table 8* shows the relationship of sense of political efficacy to area of residence among a randomly selected sample of students in the tenth, eleventh, and twelfth grades in Toledo, Ohio.*

Table 8.   Relationship of Area of Residence to Sense of Political Efficacy among High School Students

Sense of Political Efficacy	AREA OF RESIDENCE	
	Inner City	Non-Inner City
Low	15%	11%
Medium	42	38
High	43	50
Total	100%	100%
N (number in sample)	331	480

As indicated in *Table 8*, there is a relationship between area of residence and sense of political efficacy. Individuals residing outside the inner-city area are somewhat more likely to have a high sense of political efficacy than individuals residing within the inner-city area. This is a statement that describes the relationship of two variables: area of residence and sense of political efficacy. What happens to this relationship when another factor, racial identity, is added to the analysis? *Table 9* indicates the answer to this question.

Table 9 shows a multi-factor relationship between the variables of racial identity, area of residence, and sense of political efficacy. As shown in *Table 9* blacks are much less likely than whites to have a high sense of political

* Schley R. Lyons, "The Political Socialization of Ghetto Children: Efficacy and Cynicism," *Journal of Politics,* Vol. 32, 1970, pp. 288–304.

49

Table 9. Relationship of Area of Residence and Racial Identity to Sense of Political Efficacy

| Sense of Political Efficacy | AREA OF RESIDENCE | | | |
| | Inner-City | | Non-Inner City | |
	White	Black	White	Black
Low	6%	18%	10%	21%
Medium	38	43	38	43
High	56	39	51	36
Total	100%	100%	99%	100%
N	(81)	(250)	(452)	(28)

efficacy. This relationship holds regardless of area of residence. One can hypothesize that racial identity in combination with area of residence influences variation in sense of political efficacy. Furthermore, since blacks are 75 percent of the inner-city sample, one can hypothesize that racial identity is the main reason for the low sense of political efficacy expressed among the inner-city students.

If we were to carry this example further, our next task would be to add other variables to this analysis. Adding other variables, such as intelligence, father's occupation, and father's educational attainment, would possibly contribute to a fuller explanation of variation in sense of political efficacy among this sample of high school students. A multi-factor explanation can be called a *theory*.

Another way to construct a theory is to combine two or more descriptive beliefs to produce an "if-then" explanatory belief, or theory. An example of combining descriptive hypotheses to form an "if-then" statement of explanation, or theory, follows.

> *Descriptive Hypothesis 1.* Aggressive and competitive people are more likely than nonaggressive and noncompetitive people to be active in political affairs.
>
> *Descriptive Hypothesis 2.* Men are more likely than women to be aggressive and competitive.
>
> *Explanatory Hypothesis, or Theory.* If aggressive and competitive people are more likely than nonaggressive and noncompetitive people to be active in political affairs, and if men are more likely than women to be aggressive and competitive, then one can conclude that men are more likely than women to be active in political affairs.

Two hypotheses, containing the variables of aggressiveness, competitiveness, sex identity, and political activity, are combined to create one explanatory, or theoretical, statement. This theory is an "if-then" statement. If you can believe that hypotheses 1 and 2 are true, then it follows logically that the conclusion is true.

Exercises about Explanatory Statements

To demonstrate what you have learned about explanatory statements, complete the following three exercises.

Exercise 1. Following is a list of statements. Which of these statements are *explanatory beliefs?*

  a. Wealthy people are more likely to be interested in political affairs than are poor people.

  b. Farmers are less likely than lawyers to become political leaders.

  c. Since lawyers tend to have more legal and political training than do farmers, lawyers are more likely than farmers to become political leaders.

  d. People who tend to be interested in politics are more likely to vote in public elections than are people who tend to be uninterested in politics.

  e. Since wealthy people tend to be more interested in politics than poor people do, wealthy people are more likely than poor people to vote in public elections.

  f. Businessmen are likely to have more influence on public policy decisions than construction workers have.

Exercise 2. On the basis of information presented in the following three tables, answer these questions.

  a. What factors seem to be associated with variation in sense of political efficacy among students in this sample?

  b. What generalizations can you make from the data presented in *Tables 10–12?*

  c. What explanatory hypotheses can you make from these data?

  d. What additional questions would you ask to assist in explaining the relationships shown in these tables?

Table 10.   Sense of Political Efficacy of Students in Zenith City

Sense of Political Efficacy	All Students
Low	60%
High	40
Total	100%
N (number in sample)	(400)

Table 11.   School Location and Political Efficacy in Zenith City

Sense of Political Efficacy	Students in Inner-City Schools	Students in Non-Inner City Schools
Low	70%	50%
High	30	50
Total	100%	100%
N	(200)	(200)

Table 12. Political Efficacy, Family Income, and School Location in Zenith City

SENSE OF POLITICAL EFFICACY	FAMILY INCOME			
	Students in Inner-City Schools		Students in Non-Inner-City Schools	
	Low Income	High Income	Low Income	High Income
Low	91%	44%	88%	25%
High	9	56	12	75
Total	100%	100%	100%	100%
N	(110)	(90)	(80)	(120)

Exercise 3. Following are two descriptive beliefs. Combine these descriptive beliefs to construct an "if-then" explanatory belief.

a. Rich people are more likely than poor people to have a high sense of political efficacy.

b. People who express a high sense of political efficacy are more likely than people who express a low sense of political efficacy to participate in public elections.

G. Limitations of Social Scientific Inquiry

Certain kinds of beliefs cannot be confirmed or rejected through scientific inquiry. You have learned that information is gathered from sensory experience to support or to reject hypotheses about political behavior. However, information gained from sensory experience cannot be used to confirm or reject *value judgments* or *beliefs based on faith*. These types of beliefs are not subject to the techniques of social science inquiry.

Value Judgments

A *value judgment* is a claim about what is good or bad, about what people should or should not do, or about what is better or worse. The statement, "Sixty percent of the eligible voters cast their ballots in a recent election," is a *descriptive belief*; the statement, "All eligible American citizens should vote," is a *value judgment*, or *normative belief*. The latter statement expresses what one or more people believe to be "good" political behavior.

As value judgments, normative beliefs cannot be considered right or wrong on the basis of facts. Rather, value judgments are considered right or wrong in terms of personal preferences or the moral or behavior standards of a group.

The statement, "Americans ought to participate actively in politics," is a normative belief. As a value judgment, this statement cannot be confirmed or rejected on the basis of facts. Rather, we may consider this statement to be right or wrong in terms of personal preferences or the moral or behavior standards of Americans. In contrast, the statement, "Most Americans do participate actively in politics," is a descriptive belief. This belief can be judged right or wrong on the basis of facts. One can make observations about the political activity of Americans to reject or confirm this hypothesis.

Normative statements may be changed so that they can be confirmed or rejected on the basis of facts. For example, the statement, "Jim is a *good* high jumper," is a normative statement that may be changed easily into one open to social science inquiry. If we define a "good high jumper" as one who consistently leaps higher than six feet in competition, we need only ask whether Jim meets our standards for deciding who is a "good jumper." This was an easy example because there is little disagreement over the kinds of standards we should use to measure "good jumpers," although other standards are possible.

We could, for instance, have said that a "good jumper" is one who displays good form even when he misses the bar, or one who is a good sport when he loses, or one who trains hard for the sport. The statement, "Jane is a better person than Mary," is much more difficult to confirm or reject on the basis of facts because of the debates that would occur over deciding what is a "good person."

Beliefs Based on Faith

A belief based on faith cannot be tested scientifically, since it cannot be confirmed or rejected in terms of what exists. Following is an example of a belief based on faith: *There is life after death in heaven.* It is not possible to make observations to confirm or to reject this belief. Scientific inquiry cannot be used to test this belief because we cannot make observations about it. We have not said that there is no life after death. We are saying only that this belief is beyond the realm of scientific investigation. The social science approach cannot produce answers to questions that do not lend themselves to making observations to gather facts.

The fact that *normative beliefs* and *beliefs based on faith* cannot be tested scientifically does not make them unimportant. Many of our most significant beliefs are normative or based upon faith. All scientists support some normative beliefs and reject others, and many scientists are religious people who attend church and hold religious beliefs as an "act of faith."

To demonstrate what you have learned about value judgments and beliefs based on faith, complete this exercise. Following is a list of statements. Identify the value judgments, the beliefs based on faith, and the descriptive beliefs in this list.

a. Rich people tend to become political leaders more often than poor people do.

b. Mrs. Jackson was an English teacher.

c. Mrs. Jackson should not have defended the professor who burned the flag.

53

d. Fifty thousand demons can dance on the head of a pin.

e. Rich people tend to participate in political affairs more than poor people do.

f. Invisible demons cause people to have bad luck.

g. Every citizen should vote in public elections.

h. Rich people ought to participate more in political affairs than poor people should.

i. A person can enjoy good fortune by following his horoscope.

j. Black people in the United States tend to participate more in political affairs than do white people.

k. Black people are getting too much involved in politics.

Explain the differences between beliefs based on faith, normative beliefs, and descriptive beliefs.

H. Nonscientific Approaches to the Study of Political Behavior

There are several common, nonscientific approaches that may be used to decide the worth of beliefs. As you read about these nonscientific approaches, decide how useful you think each approach is as a guide to knowledge about reality.

1. The Method of Authority

When trying to settle a dispute about a belief, individuals may appeal to an *authority,* claiming that a "wise man" agrees with them. While the scientific inquiry approach has dominated man's search for truth during the past two hundred years, the method of authority has been a primary approach to justifying beliefs throughout human history. Even today many people prefer to accept the pronouncements of an authority to accepting the findings of science.

The method of authority can be useful. If we need to decide a conflict about the correct spelling of a word, we should consult a dictionary to settle the dispute. We often find it useful to consult books written by authorities to find facts or interpretations of facts. However, the method of authority can also easily lead to the uncritical acceptance of falsehood. For example, in the seventeenth century in Italy the scientist Galileo was forced to renounce some of his scientific findings because they disagreed with the authorities of the Catholic Church. During the rule of dictator Adolf Hitler, in the Nazi-dominated Germany of 1933–1945, Germans had to adjust their beliefs about many things to the pronouncements of Hitler. And in the Soviet Union the authority of political leaders has from time to time overruled the findings of social and biological scientists.

54

2. The Method of Revelation

The method of revelation is sometimes used to decide the worth of conflicting beliefs. A person may claim that he knows the "truth" about some matter, because God has revealed this "truth" to him alone. Such a person may feel compelled to inform others about the "truth" that has been made known to him only.

Most religious truth is based upon divine inspiration. There is no easy way to confirm the claims of those who have experienced revelations. Ultimately, one must accept the word of the prophet on faith or reject his statements of belief.

3. The Method of Appealing to Personal Experience

People frequently appeal to personal experience to justify their beliefs. For example, having known two Germans who lacked a sense of humor, one might conclude that all Germans are humorless. Or having known three brilliant Jews, one might decide that all Jewish people are very intelligent. The chief weakness of the method of appealing to personal experience is that an individual's experiences are always too limited. He is forced to make generalizations on the basis of a very small sample of the total population. In order to verify most beliefs, one must go beyond immediate, direct experiences.

4. The Method of Majority Opinion

The method of majority opinion assumes that if a majority of a group of people accept a belief, it must be correct. Nevertheless, the principle of majority rule has often been shown to be a poor way to confirm beliefs. For example, in medieval Europe most people believed in dragons and demons. As Americans we believe in the majority-rule principle to decide which of alternative public policies should be adopted. We accept the majority-rule principle in government because we believe it is good to trust the many people

Can you think of other ways in which the method of majority opinion is used in advertising? Have you ever used this method to support an argument?

55

who are to be governed to participate in making some political decisions for us. However, the majority-rule principle is not very useful as a method for confirming beliefs about reality.

1. Following are several statements about approaches to confirming beliefs. Distinguish the scientific approaches from the nonscientific approaches. Identify the nonscientific approaches in terms of the following categories: the method of authority, the method of revelation, the method of appealing to personal experience, the method of majority opinion.

    a. I must be right. A majority of Americans agree with me.

    b. My belief seems to be correct. It is supported by statistical evidence about people gathered by the Bureau of the Census.

    c. My belief must be true. It was revealed to me in a dream.

    d. Our leader has said that foreign people are sneaky and deceitful. I believe what he says.

    e. I know ten black men. None is interested in politics. I believe that black people are not interested in politics.

    f. John Smith participates more actively in city council meetings than does Henry Jones. I reached this conclusion after attending every council meeting for one year and keeping careful notes on the discussions that took place there.

2. Tell the difference between scientific and nonscientific approaches to the confirmation of beliefs.

I. Strengths and Weaknesses of Political Science

To answer questions about political behavior, the political scientist observes political behavior to gather facts, organizes these facts, and develops explanations about the facts. Making observations to gather, organize, and explain facts is what scientific inquiry is all about.

Scientific inquiry is the *best* method we have for making decisions about competing alternative hypotheses about reality. It is the best method, because it is the most useful and reliable. The scientific inquiry method produces useful factual judgments, but these factual judgments, these beliefs about reality, are not realities themselves. The beliefs about reality that we hold in our minds and reality itself are two separate things.

It might be helpful to describe the relationship between factual judgments and reality in terms of the relationship between a map of the world and the real world that the map represents. A map is not the real world. It is a picture of the real world. It has been created to serve as a guide to the real world. The more the map corresponds to the real world, the more useful the map is to a traveler. Our factual judgments are like a map. These beliefs are an individual's mental maps of the world in which he lives. But these beliefs are not reality. Some beliefs may correspond more closely to reality than others. We refer to confirmed hypotheses as factual judgments, because such beliefs are our *best judgments* about reality. But these *best judgments* may not correspond exactly to reality. If our factual judgments are useful guides to reality, we retain them, as we would retain a good map. However, when we find that a factual judgment is no longer a useful guide to reality, we revise it, as we purchase a new map when we find the older one is out-of-date.

Beliefs about Reality Must Be Reexamined

Most of our factual judgments are not perfect representations of reality. They are likely to range from very inaccurate to highly accurate. Thus, we face the problem of continuously criticizing our beliefs about reality. In this way we develop new beliefs that may prove more useful than older beliefs. Unlike other approaches to knowledge, the scientific inquiry method demands that we continuously criticize and correct our beliefs.

The scientific inquiry method does not always provide certain and accurate answers. And the scientific method cannot be used to judge beliefs based upon faith or normative beliefs. However, compared to other methods of verifying beliefs, the scientific inquiry method has a major advantage. The scientific inquiry method has built into it the means for correcting mistakes.

The scientific inquiry method is self-corrective, because it demands public discussion and competition between different beliefs. Through public discussion and criticism, inaccurate beliefs are discarded. The scientific inquiry method also demands that disputes between conflicting beliefs be tested by observations of reality, according to unchanging standards.

Democracy Encourages Scientific Inquiry

Because it demands continuous criticism, free exchange of ideas, and open-mindedness, the scientific inquiry method has flourished best in democratic societies. Most dictators, though they have wanted to harness the industrial and military power that modern science produces, fear the full extension of scientific inquiry to all aspects of life. For example, in the Soviet Union, Russian scientists have produced powerful weapons of war, elaborate industrial machinery, and complex space technology. But the Soviet political leaders do not encourage "free" social scientific inquiry. They are unwilling to allow certain beliefs about human behavior, that are based on authority, to be publicly criticized or corrected. In a democratic society free and open discussion of beliefs about human behavior is valued. In a completely democratic society no areas of life are closed to inquiry.

While social science inquiry is a useful way to verify beliefs about reality, several weaknesses surround the statement and use of beliefs that relate variables about political behavior. Two main weaknesses are discussed here.

Many Beliefs Are Tendency Statements

First, most of our beliefs about the relationship of social variables are *tendency statements.* One can always find exceptions to these statements. As *tendency statements,* these beliefs describe trends. They indicate relationships. They show that certain social groups or individuals are likely to do one thing or another.

There are *always* exceptions to tendency statements. By contrast, the propositions of natural science are stated in absolute terms that imply no known exceptions to the propositions. For example, we know of no exceptions to the propositions concerning the laws of earth gravity.

Tendency statements do not allow us to make predictions about human behavior with great confidence. Tendency statements tell us about *past* relationships of social variables, but social conditions are ever-changing. And the relationships of the past, based upon one set of conditions, may be overturned in the future by newly developed and unforeseen social conditions.

Tendency statements indicate trends that may prevail in the immediate future. But only a fool would have complete confidence in predictions based upon tendency statements. While the absolute propositions of natural science can be used to make accurate predictions, tendency statements about human behavior that are guides to past behavior are not necessarily accurate predictors of future behavior.

The Problem of Complex Variables

A *second* main weakness of social science inquiry is that social conditions and human behavior involve so many complex variables that it is difficult to *explain* human behavior. We usually can construct explanatory hypotheses based on multi-factor analysis. However, we cannot with great confidence describe the causes of most types of human behavior.

Other main weaknesses of social science inquiry will be identified and discussed later in this book. While these discussions of limitations and weaknesses should alert you to the dangers of misusing the process of social science inquiry, nevertheless, the process of social science inquiry has been shown to be the most useful device we have for understanding human behavior.

chapter 3

Political Science and Political Behavior

Political science is concerned with attempts to describe and explain political behavior. The successful political scientist makes statements that increase understanding of political behavior. In contrast, political behavior is concerned with attempts to influence decisions that resolve conflicts. The successful politician uses influence successfully to reach his goals.

The study of political behavior is a science. The practice of political behavior is an art. The student of political behavior practices the method of social science inquiry to verify beliefs. The politician practices the arts of political decision-making and persuasion to resolve conflicts. The products of political behavior are value judgments and policy decisions.

The case studies in Chapter 1 presented examples of political actors practicing the arts of political influence and decision-making.

The lessons in Chapter 2 presented the social science inquiry approach to the study of political behavior. The exercises that you completed required you to state and make judgments about beliefs in the manner of the social scientist.

A. Making Value Judgments

It is important for you to learn how to describe and explain political behavior. It is also important for you to evaluate political behavior. In this course you will have an opportunity to make judgments about the way political behavior is. These are factual judgments. You also will have an opportunity to make judgments about the way political behavior ought to be. These are value judgments.

We use standards to help us make judgments about whether a person's behavior is good or bad. For example, teachers expect students to do their own work and to avoid copying the work of others. Thus, schools have rules about classroom cheating. Students who break these rules are considered bad and are punished. Rules are one kind of a standard used to judge a person's behavior. A person who follows the rules is judged as "good." A person who breaks the rules is judged as "bad."

The first step in making a sound value judgment is to distinguish statements of fact and statements of value. The difference between factual and value judgments was discussed on pages 52–53. To test your ability to distinguish statements of fact and value, decide which of the following speakers are stating factual judgments and which are stating value judgments.

SPEAKER 1   SPEAKER 2   SPEAKER 3

The first speaker is making a factual judgment. We do not know whether he prefers, or values, a federal system of government.

The second speaker is making a value judgment. He says that he prefers the government of the United States to all other governments. He does not tell why he prefers the United States government. Perhaps this government satisfies the things he values more than other governments. Someone who holds different values than Speaker 2 might not believe that the American system of government is best. A person who values dictatorship would not consider the government of the United States to be the best in the world.

The third speaker is stating a value judgment. He also tells something about why he holds this value judgment. He reveals that he prefers a weak government to a strong government.

Distinguishing statements of value and fact is important to a careful study of political behavior. Learning to identify the influences on a person's value judgments is another important task that we will pursue throughout this course.

For this lesson, re-read the Pleasant Valley case. You are now required to identify and choose among conflicting value judgments. To assist your reading and investigation, follow these directions.

1. Find at least three direct statements from the Pleasant Valley case that are value judgments of one or more participants.

2. On the basis of their statements or actions decide what values influenced the behavior of:

    a. the student who wrote the initial letter.

    b. Mrs. Patricia Jackson.

    c. the Pleasant Valley American Legion Post.

3. For each of the following participants state in a single sentence whether you believe the political behavior of the participant was right or wrong.

    a. the student who wrote the letter.

    b. the editor of the *Pleasant Valley Evening World.*

    c. the Pleasant Valley American Legion Post.

    d. the school board.

4. Write a paragraph that states the values you hold that led you to make the judgments contained in the answer immediately above.

5. How is making value judgments different from making factual judgments?

B. Making Policy Decisions

The political art of policy decision-making combines factual judgments (judgments about what exists and what does not exist) and value judgments. Before making a policy decision, a politician must be certain that he knows the facts of the case. No useful policy decision can be made without agreement about the facts.

The art of policy decision-making also involves value judgments about the possible consequences of a decision. A politician must consider the consequences that might stem from alternative policy decisions. Then he must decide which of the possible consequences he prefers. This decision is a value judgment. The politician chooses a policy decision that will most likely produce valued outcomes.

In Case 3 on pages 6–7 the mayor of Lakeville and the city council decided to build an overpass across a busy highway. This decision was difficult to make. It was made at the expense of people living in the west end of town. The decision to build the overpass meant that a public park could not be built for the West Side. The consequence of safety for children crossing a busy highway seemed to be valued more than the consequence of more recreational opportunities for West Side.

However, the mayor and the city council also wanted to avoid the consequences of unrest in the West Side people. They valued the continued political support of West Side. Thus, they promised to have a park built as soon as possible. In this way, they were able to achieve another consequence that they valued, the continued political backing of the West Side people.

Policy decision-making is a complex and difficult task. It is the specialty of the politician. Turn back to the case study, "The Klan Comes to Town," on pages 4–5. You will recall that the case ends without a policy decision. The mayor, as a politician, must practice his specialty of policy decision-making. The mayor must decide whether or not to prevent the Ku Klux Klan from holding a rally in his city.

The mayor is faced with a value conflict. He values freedom of speech, but he also values public safety, security, and order. To stop the Klan from holding a rally would be a violation of the American tradition of free speech, but public safety would be protected. To allow the Klan to hold a rally would support the tradition of free speech, but the risks would be great. Public disorder would be a very possible consequence of a Klan rally.

Should this mayor, who values free speech, allow the Klan to hold a rally in his city? Or should the mayor, who also values public safety and order, stop the Klan rally?

1. If you were the mayor, how would you decide this issue?

2. What is the connection between making factual judgments, making value judgments, and making policy decisions?

3. Distinguish the act of policy decision-making from the act of confirming beliefs about political behavior.

61

unit two

similarities and differences in political behavior

chapter 4

Comparing Political Behavior

People of different groups often behave politically in very different ways. Yet, in some very basic ways, the political behavior of all groups of people is very similar.

Increasing your knowledge of similarities and differences in the political behavior of different groups is a main objective of this book. Trying to answer these two questions will help you obtain this objective.

1. What are some basic similarities and differences in the political behavior of different groups of people?

2. Why do these basic similarities and differences exist?

Following are three groups of cases describing political behavior. They can help you begin to answer these two questions.

An Ifugao woman in traditional dress with the decorative tattoos of her tribe.

A. Three Cases about Settling Personal Conflict

The Ifugao, the Dinaric Serbs, and the people of the United States have tended to settle certain types of personal conflicts in different ways. The following three cases reveal similarities and differences in the reactions of these different groups of people to the fundamental human problem of how to resolve conflict.

Case 1. Settling Personal Conflicts through Mediation

The Ifugao (e-few'-gow) people live in rugged mountain country of northern Luzon Island in the Philippines. Disputes in cases where one person has slandered another are settled by a mediator, or go-between, known as a *monkalun*. A *monkalun* is neither an elected nor an appointed official. Rather, any adult man who is a member of a leading family in the Ifugao society can be chosen to serve as a *monkalun*. Any person who complains that he has been slandered chooses a member of one of the leading Ifugao families to serve as a *monkalun*. The *monkalun* tells an accused person of the charges against him and tries to use his influence to bring about a settlement between the conflicting individuals.

The *monkalun* is neither a judge nor a policeman. He has no power to decide which person is right or wrong, to hand down punishments, or to enforce laws. Rather, the *monkalun* tries to settle the conflict by getting the two disputing individuals to make a settlement that is satisfactory to both of them. Since the two parties to the conflict will not speak to one another, the *monkalun* carries messages from one to the other.

64

In a case of slander, the *monkalun* is usually able to settle the conflict by getting the person who did the slandering to pay damages to the person who was harmed. This payment might be farm animals or crops. Typically, the accused will try to bargain with the complainer to lower the cost of the damage payment. Of course, this bargaining by the parties is conducted through the *monkalun*.

If the *monkalun* is unable to arrange a settlement, then the person who was harmed may try to settle the dispute by killing the accused.

Case 2. Settling Personal Conflict through "Blood Vengeance"

In the Dinaric Mountain region of Yugoslavia the Serbian people still talk about the bitter acts of "blood vengeance" that once regularly disrupted this area. Just sixty years or so ago, "blood vengeance" was the only honorable way for a Dinaric Serb to get back at someone who had injured or insulted him. "Blood vengeance" meant that a man who had been personally harmed by slander was expected to kill the man who had harmed him. In this manner he could gain revenge for the harm that had been done.

The "blood vengeance" could take the form of a public fight, but often it was carried out through ambush. The only way to avoid "blood vengeance" was for the person who had caused harm to another to beg for mercy and to pay "blood money" to the avenger. This public humiliation and payment of "blood money" only took place when an individual was afraid to stand up to an avenger. One who paid "blood money" to save his life was despised as a weakling and a coward.

Mediterranean Sea

Personal conflicts were often expanded to long-term "blood feuds" among families in the Dinaric Mountains. One member of a family would try to avenge the harm done to his father, brother, or cousin. This would result in retaliation. Thus, a vicious circle of conflict between individuals or between families would occur.

Although these "blood" conflicts were severe, they were carried out according to rules. Individuals who broke the rules faced the threats of community disapproval and social isolation.

Case 3. Settling Personal Conflict through Judicial Decision

In the United States personal conflicts such as slander are often settled by a judge, or a judge and jury, in a court of law. For example, one person may charge another person with slander and attempt to gain money in return for the damages suffered. The court decides whether payment must be made and, if so, the amount to be paid to the person who has been hurt. Here is an example of a personal conflict involving slander.

Miss Clark was a cashier in a large grocery store owned by Mr. Brown. Miss Clark felt that some of Mr. Brown's employment practices were unfair, and she had complained to officials of her union about his activities. Mr. Brown was annoyed by Miss Clark's action and felt that she should have come to him with her complaints.

One day, several weeks after Miss Clark complained to the union, Mr. Brown accused her of stealing $5 worth of goods from the store. He made his accusations quite loudly in front of several employees and customers.

Miss Clark denied that she had stolen anything from the store and replied that Mr. Brown was only attempting to embarrass her because she had complained to her union about him. She decided to show Mr. Clark that he could not get away with spreading damaging lies about a person. She charged him with slander and sued him for damages.

Mr. Brown protested that Miss Clark had been a dishonest and "upstart" employee. He declared that he would not pay one cent in damages. Miss Clark replied that Mr. Brown should save his protests for the judge, who would decide how to settle this case.

Use your knowledge of issues and rules to help you compare and contrast political behavior in the three preceding cases.

1. What (a) differences and (b) similarities about settling personal conflict are described in these cases?

2. Why did these similarities and differences in settling personal conflict exist?

3. Which of the three techniques for settling personal conflict is best? Explain.

4. What does your answer to question 3 reveal about what are your values and why you have these values?

B. Three Cases about Enforcing Rules

Different people, in different times and places, have created different ways of enforcing rules. The following three cases reveal similarities and differences in the reactions of three groups of people to the fundamental human problem of maintaining rules and social order.

Case 1. Law and Order in a Rocky Mountain Mining Camp

Over a hundred years ago many people went West to "strike it rich." Gold and silver had been discovered in the streams and mountains of the Far West. The Rocky Mountain region was a popular destination for the fortune hunters. They left a heavily populated and highly organized society to seek gold and silver in the sparsely settled wilderness.

The rewards of searching and mining for gold and silver were great, but so were the dangers. Often several people claimed mining rights on the same land. Fist fights, knife fights, and gun battles were usual methods of settling these conflicts over mining claims. Sometimes a miner who had "struck it rich" would be robbed while traveling to the nearest town to spend or to bank his new wealth. Hostile Indians often attacked any white miner they saw.

The daily hardships of the miners were great. They were far removed from the services and conveniences of civilization. Towns were few and far apart. There were few roads, railroads, and stagecoach lines; thus, it was difficult

for the miners to purchase tools, building materials, and food. The power of organized government seldom extended to the barren wilderness where miners prospected for wealth. Each individual had to live by his own wits and courage; each had to care for his own needs.

Zebalin Baxter and his five younger brothers moved to the Rocky Mountain region in 1867. The Baxter brothers had invested their savings in mining equipment. They were determined to make a strike.

After working for many weeks, they finally found gold. Each week their supply increased, and the Baxters became fearful. Would someone discover their "gold strike"? Would someone attack them and take away their mining claim and their newly accumulated wealth? They slept uneasily with loaded guns at their sides.

Rumors of a gold strike brought other miners to the area of the Baxter mine. Soon over a hundred people were living and prospecting for gold in the area. A huge mining camp was established.

One day the Baxter brothers invited everyone in the area to come for a meeting. They proposed that a council be established to make and enforce rules for everyone living in the new mining camp. The people agreed to this idea. By a majority vote, five men were selected to serve on the council. They were given the power to make rules and to settle any conflicts that might arise in the mining camp. Zeke Josephson, the best gunman in the group, was appointed sheriff. Along with two deputies, he was expected to enforce the rules made by the council. The council was given the power to serve as judge and jury for anyone arrested and accused of a crime.

The first conflict to be settled by the council occurred one week later. Zack Brown accused Mike James of stealing food from him. The two men began slugging each other. Sheriff Josephson broke up the fight and brought the men before the council. Zack accused Mike of thievery.

Mike James was brought before the council as an accused thief. After considering the evidence against Mike, the council decided—by a unanimous vote—that he was guilty. The council decided to punish Mike by ruling that he must leave the camp immediately and never return.

Case 2. Law and Order on a Pawnee Buffalo Hunt

Many years ago the Pawnee nation was one of several Indian tribes in the Great Plains region of North America. Among the Pawnee, political decisions were made by a tribal council. All male adults who had proved themselves fit members of the tribe participated.

Buffalo hunt: mural by an Indian artist in the Museum of the Plains Indians, Browning, Montana

During a buffalo hunt, however, political behavior changed greatly. All power was vested in one leader, appointed by the tribal council, for the duration of the hunt. The leader was given command of the ablest warriors, who served as a police force to enforce the hunt-leader's decisions. Individuals who disobeyed the command of the hunt-leader could be killed on the spot.

Why did the political behavior of the Plains Indians change during a buffalo hunt? Buffalo herds provided the Indians with many necessities of life: an abundant source of meat, skins to use in making clothing and in constructing shelters, and bones for making tools and weapons. Without the buffalo as a source of raw materials, the Indians would not have been able to survive easily. Thus, the buffalo hunt was a crucial event in the life of the Indians. The most careful preparations were taken to insure a successful hunt. It made good sense to put the best hunter in charge of these preparations and to give this leader power to control the behavior of the entire tribe during the hunt.

For several years Standing Bear, an able hunter and brave warrior, had been hunt-leader. During the hunting period, which lasted several weeks, Standing Bear directed all movements of the people. He planned strategies for advancing on the buffalo herd and surrounding it for shooting the animals. To disobey Standing Bear could mean instant death. However, at the end of the hunt, Standing Bear became merely another member of the tribe with no more power than any other male adult.

Under Standing Bear's leadership the buffalo hunts had been successful. Members of the tribe believed that his success resulted from ability to enforce the rules of the hunt. He had shown his ability to enforce tribal law fairly and fiercely the first time that he led a buffalo hunt.

68

On the first morning of that hunt, several years before, Standing Bear gave a signal and all the Pawnees began to move up the river. After traveling about twenty miles, the tribe made camp for the night. The next morning three scout groups were sent to look for buffalo. The scouts were forbidden to kill any buffalo, but were told to report to camp immediately if they found a herd.

About noon a scout group reported the presence of a buffalo herd about three miles to the northeast. Immediately the camp became alive. Standing Bear gave orders to prepare for the hunt. Men were sent to a hilltop to make smoke signals calling back the other two scout groups. Standing Bear led his hunters toward the buffalo, dividing the men into two equal groups. He led one group, while the other was led by one of the Soldier Lodge members. Instructions were given not to shoot at the buffalo until Standing Bear gave a signal. Everyone was to be silent and cautious so as not to scare away the herd.

Suddenly Wahan, a young man on his first hunt, shot an arrow into the flank of a buffalo. The animal went down. Other hunters then shot their arrows into the herd. Standing Bear was furious. The shooting had started before he had given the signal. Now it was too late to stop. He ordered the hunt to proceed.

The hunt was successful. Many buffalo were killed, and the Pawnee tribe was happy. But Standing Bear remained furious. He ordered four men to bring Wahan to him. In front of the entire tribe he ordered Wahan to be killed. The death sentence was carried out. Tribal law had been enforced. The rest of the tribe prepared to enjoy a feast in celebration of a successful day of buffalo hunting.

Case 3. The People's Park Protest

The young people enjoyed their park. They had made a park out of a vacant lot owned by a nearby state university. They had transformed a muddy, messy strip of unused land into a playground with grass, flowers, and benches.

The people who used the park were a mixed group. They included "hippies," university students, and so-called "street people"—unemployed university graduates as well as teen-agers who lived in the area but did not work or go to school. The people who had built the park said that "their park" was a place where young mothers could bring their children or students could study or relax, where anyone could "do his thing." In addition, they complained that the city had needed more outdoor recreational facilities for a long time and neither the university nor the city government had taken the problem seriously. They called the lot the "People's Park."

Many people in the neighborhood complained about the activities which took place in the park. There were complaints about noise and messiness. Some people suggested that immoral behavior took place there. They demanded that the university president take steps to stop the "street people" from using the land.

Many members of the university's faculty and administrators also agreed with community residents who wanted the land vacated. They said that the property was owned by the university and that allowing unauthorized individuals to use it would only lead to "lawlessness." Other faculty members said that they liked the idea of a park built by the people who wanted to use it. They argued that since the land was owned by the university, the students who attended the school and the people who lived near the property should have a voice in deciding how the land would be used.

After many meetings with "street people," professors and students, and the university's board of trustees, the university officials decided to settle the problem by making the land into an athletic field to be used by university teams. But the "street people" said they would hold "their park" permanently. They declared that they would never leave "their land" voluntarily. The president of the university ordered a fence built around the property to keep out trespassers. The president believed that the fence would also remind the "street people" that the land belonged to the university.

Despite the fence, and signs which read "University Property—Keep Out," many people continued to come to the park. They climbed over the fence and held parties. The university president called these people trespassers and asked them to stop using the university's land. The "street people" ignored the request.

The day following the president's request 165 policemen moved into the park to expel 50 people who had remained on the university's property. The "street people" decided to fight back. They called for a public rally to protest the action of the university officials and the police. Five hundred young people came to the rally. When the rally ended, they surged into the street and marched toward the park.

70

GO SEE
THE PEOPLES' PARK
Roses · Beautiful · Dignity
THEN YOU WON'T LET THEM
DESTROY THIS LOVELY
CREATIVE THING

One hundred policemen had been called to guard the property. The police and the young protestors faced each other in anger. The protestors called the police "pigs" and threw rocks, bottles, and bricks at them. Several policemen received cuts and bruises. The police shot tear gas into the crowd of protestors and then moved forward with billy clubs swinging. About 130 youths and 20 policemen were injured. Forty-seven youths were arrested.

The arrested youths were charged with trespass and assault. They were tried, found guilty, and fined or sentenced to short jail terms.

In the meantime the university officials ordered the construction of an athletic field for students on the site of the former "people's park." Students now play soccer, rugby, and softball on this field.

Use your knowledge of conflict, government, rules, and anarchy to help you compare and contrast political behavior in these cases.

1. What (a) differences and (b) similarities about enforcing rules are described in these cases?

2. Why did these similarities and differences in enforcing rules exist?

3. What are your value judgments about the outcomes of each of these cases? For example, should Mike James have been banished from the mining camp? Should Wahan have been killed? Should the "park" have been taken away from the "street people" and should the protestors have been punished? Explain.

4. What do your answers to the previous questions reveal about what are your values and why you have these values?

C. Three Cases about Governmental Organization

The Iroquois, the Saudi Arabians, and the people of the United States have created different types of governmental organizations. The following three cases reveal similarities and differences in the reactions of these different groups of people to the fundamental human problem of how to create and maintain government.

Case 1. Government among the Iroquois

Popular opinion had much influence on the government of the Iroquois Indians in the eighteenth century. The Iroquois government was a confederacy of five main tribes: Senecas, Cayugas, Onondagas, Mohawks, and Oneidas. The Confederacy Council, the highest governing group, consisted of 50 chiefs representing the five tribes. The Mohawks and the Oneidas each had 9 representatives; the Onondagas, 14; the Cayugas, 10; and the Senecas, 8. This unequal representation on the Confederacy Council did not mean unequal power, because each tribe could cast only one vote. And no decision could be made unless all five tribes were in favor of it.

Representatives to the Council were chosen by the women of the various villages and could be removed from office if they did not do a good job of representing their people.

Each tribe in the Iroquois confederacy had its own tribal council made up of leading men selected by the women of the tribe. And each village within a tribe had its own governing council of men selected by the women of the village.

All business of the councils—whether Confederacy Council, tribal council, or village council—was conducted publicly and openly. No decision was made without giving all representatives the chance to speak as much as they wanted to about an issue. Council meetings were typically observed by most of the people represented by the council.

The tribal council continues even today to be the typical means of Indian self-government.

Case 2. Government in Saudi Arabia

In Saudi Arabia in the 1960's a king headed the government. He obtained his position through hereditary right and could rule until death.

The king shared power and responsibility with a council of ministers. The king appointed the council of ministers, who in turn appointed lower government officials. There were no political parties and no public elections in Saudi Arabia.

The basic law of Saudi Arabia was the divine law of the religion of Islam. Other laws were made by the king and the council of ministers.

Although the king and the council of ministers ran the government, they depended upon various tribal chieftains and local leaders to help enforce laws and administer services. Thus, the king and the council of ministers had to consider the influence and wishes of these local leaders when making public policy.

Case 3. Government in a Small Midwestern City

Oberlin, Ohio, has a council-manager type of government. The voters of Oberlin elect a city council of seven members. The council appoints a city

King Saud (right) came to the throne of Saudi Arabia upon the death of his father in 1953. He turned over full powers to his brother Faisal in 1964.

74

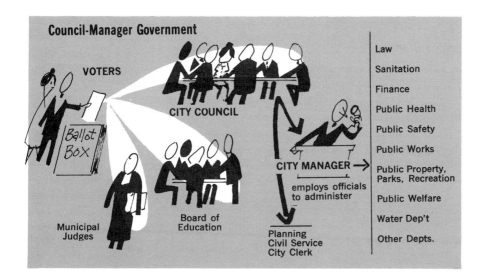

Council-Manager Government

VOTERS

Ballot Box

CITY COUNCIL

Municipal Judges

Board of Education

CITY MANAGER →
employs officials to administer

Planning
Civil Service
City Clerk

Law

Sanitation

Finance

Public Health

Public Safety

Public Works

Public Property, Parks, Recreation

Public Welfare

Water Dep't

Other Depts.

manager. The council has the power and duty to make laws. The city manager has the power and duty to enforce the laws and to administer the business of the city government.

The members of the city council have the power to dismiss the city manager, but only by a five-vote majority or more. The voters of Oberlin have an opportunity periodically to elect new councilmen.

The powers and duties of the city council and the city manager are described in the city charter, a document which describes the plan of government and serves as the basic law in Oberlin.

Use your knowledge of issues, government, rules, influence, policy decision, and anarchy to help you compare and contrast political behavior in these cases.

1. What (a) differences and (b) similarities in governmental organization are described in these cases?

2. Why did these similarities and differences in governmental organization exist?

3. Which of the three types of governmental organization is best? Which is worst? Explain.

4. What does your answer to question 3 reveal about your values and why you have these values?

On the basis of your brief comparative study of the three groups of cases (pp. 64–75), speculate—or guess—about answers to these two basic questions:

5. What are some basic similarities and differences in the political behavior of different groups of people?

6. Why do these basic similarities and differences exist?

What does this cartoon suggest about the use of concepts?

Facts and ideas about similarities and differences in the political behavior of Americans are presented in this unit. As you move through the unit, you will have an opportunity to use these facts and ideas to build a more complete answer to the two questions stated above.

D. Using Concepts to Make Comparisons in Political Science

An important part of the political scientist's work is making comparisons. Hypotheses in political science are statements of similarities and differences, such as: "Rich people are more likely than poor people to have a high rate of political activity." Some hypotheses are statements of comparison between individuals or groups *at a particular time,* for example: "In the 1968 presidential election, rich people were more likely to vote for the Republican party candidate than were poor people." Other hypotheses are statements of comparison about change *over a period of time,* such as: "Poor people were likely to have a higher rate of political activity in 1970 than they did in 1960."

Concepts are tools for making comparisons. A concept is a name for things that go together, that can be grouped, or categorized, on the basis of common characteristics. For example, rich people, poor people, and political activity are concepts that appear in the hypotheses in the preceding paragraph. Rich people are a group or category of individuals with common characteristics, such as much wealth and a high standard of living. We understand the name "poor people" to mean individuals who share certain characteristics, such as little wealth and a low standard of living. Political activity is a group, or category, of human actions with common characteristics, such as attempts to influence public policy.

A concept is a shorthand way of thinking or talking about something. For example, the concept *astronaut* (from two Greek words: *astron,* meaning a star, and *nautes,* meaning a sailor or seaman) was invented to stand for people who are trained to navigate space ships. If someone tells you that he is an astronaut, he has already told you a great deal about himself: about his work, his training program, etc.

Concepts allow us to organize, describe, and communicate facts. Conflict, rules, government, anarchy, policy decision, and political resources are some of the concepts that you have used to organize and interpret facts about political behavior.

Mediation, adjudication, and capitulation are three concepts that can be used to compare the political behavior discussed in the three cases about settling personal conflict on pages 64–66. Mediation means that the parties to a conflict agree to let another individual or group (a mediator) suggest a way to settle the conflict. However, the parties to the conflict are not required to accept the suggestions of the mediator. Adjudication means to settle a personal conflict in a court of law. The parties to the conflict are required to accept the decision of the judge, or adjudicator. Capitulation means that one party to a conflict forces a settlement of the conflict on the other party.

Diagram 1 illustrates the application of these concepts to the three cases. The Ifugao case is an example of mediation. The Dinaric Serbs case is an example of capitulation. The Clark-Brown slander case is an example of adjudication.

Diagram 1. **Techniques for Settling Conflicts**

| | CASE | | |
TECHNIQUES	Ifugao	Dinaric Serbs	Clark-Brown
Capitulation		X	
Mediation	X		
Adjudication			X

The concepts of mediation, adjudication, and capitulation direct our attention to certain details of the cases and away from other details. Using these concepts to compare political behavior is *one* way to interpret the facts in the cases in a meaningful way.

The concepts that we decide to use in a comparison determine the way we see and interpret the facts we are studying. Facts do not "speak for themselves." Facts become meaningful when they are related or organized. Concepts are used to organize and interpret facts, to give them a "voice."

Applying different concepts to the same facts results in different interpretations of the facts. For example, the concepts of formal rules and informal rules can be applied to the interpretation of the three cases about settling personal conflict on pages 64–66. A formal rule is a law that is made and enforced by a government. An informal rule is a custom or tradition that has developed gradually through repeated use. Social pressures, rather than the power of government, are used to enforce informal rules.

Diagram 2. **Type of Rules**

| | CASE | | |
RULES	Ifugao	Dinaric Serbs	Clark-Brown
Informal	X	X	
Formal			X

Diagram 2 illustrates the application of these concepts to the three cases. Case 1—the Ifugao—is an example of informal rules. Case 2—the Dinaric

Serbs—is also an example of informal rules. Case 3—Clark-Brown—is an example of formal rules.

Applying different concepts to the cases about personal conflict leads to different interpretations of the cases. The concepts of mediation, capitulation, and adjudication provide one way to interpret these cases. The concepts of formal rules and informal rules provide another way to interpret these cases.

Concepts are standards for making comparisons. The definition of a particular concept is a standard for deciding whether certain facts are, or are not, examples of the concept. The standard, or definition, that we have used for mediation is this: The parties to a conflict agree to let another individual or group suggest the way to settle the conflict. By applying this standard to the Ifugao case, we see that the facts in the case are an example of mediation.

Variables are concepts. Concepts that are used as variables help us to make comparisons of more or less, higher or lower, or better or worse. For example, one can think of the concept of formal rules as a variable with the values of more and less. One can apply this concept, as a variable, to the cases about enforcing rules on pages 66–72. For example, one can conclude that the rules that are enforced in the "People's Park Protest" case are more formal than the rules that are enforced in the "Rocky Mountain Mining Camp" case.

Concepts can be combined to make general statements of relationships. For example, the concepts of political activity and age groups are combined to make this generalization: Middle-aged people are more likely than either elderly people or young adults to be politically active. *Diagram 3* illustrates this relationship.

Concepts are not to be considered true or false. Rather they are to be viewed as more or less useful in helping to organize and interpret facts. Remember that concepts determine how you see the facts in your surroundings. Some concepts are more helpful than others in showing you the important facts.

To practice the use of concepts to make comparisons, complete these exercises.

1. Use the following two concepts to answer questions about the governmental organization cases on pages 72–75.

Popular control of government means that (a) the people have some way of participating in the selection and removal of important government officials and (b) the people can influence public policy decisions.

Diagram 3. **Political Activity**

DEGREE OF POLITICAL ACTIVITY

AGE GROUP	Low	High
Young	X	
Middle		X
Elderly	X	

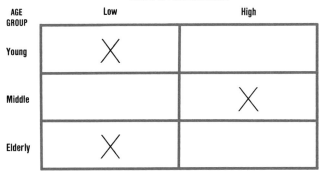

Diagram 4. **Popular Control**

CASE

DEGREE OF CONTROL	Iroquois	Saudi Arabia	Oberlin
Little	A	B	C
Much	D	E	F

78

Separation of governmental power means that independent power to make, enforce, and apply (or interpret) laws is distributed among several individuals or groups. For example, in the United States the Congress makes laws; the President and other officials enforce the laws; courts apply the laws to particular cases.

a. Compare the three cases in terms of *popular control of government.* Use *Diagram 4* to assist your comparison, *but do not mark the diagram.*

b. Compare the three cases in terms of *separation of governmental powers.* Use *Diagram 5* to assist your comparison, but do not mark it.

c. What is the relationship of *popular control of government* to *separation of governmental powers* in the three cases. Use *Diagram 6* to assist your comparison. For example, does Case 1 fit in box A, B, C, or D? In which boxes do Cases 2 and 3 fit.

Diagram 5. **Separation of Powers**

CASE

DEGREE OF SEPARATION	Iroquois	Saudi Arabia	Oberlin
Little	A	B	C
Much	D	E	F

Diagram 6. **Popular Control and Separation of Powers**

DEGREE OF SEPARATION

DEGREE OF POPULAR CONTROL	Little	Much
Little	A	B
Much	C	D

2. What does your use of the two concepts—popular control of government and separation of power—indicate about the relationship of concepts to facts?

3. How are concepts used in comparing political behavior? Discuss concepts as standards and as variables.

79

chapter 5

Culture and Political Behavior

Culture is a main influence on the political behavior of individuals. The concept of *culture* can be used to make comparisons, to identify and interpret similarities and differences in political behavior.

A. What Is Culture?

Culture is the name that social scientists give to the typical beliefs and practices of a group. The groups of people with whom an individual lives form a society. The beliefs and practices that guide the way the people of a society live are their *culture.* For example, in American society we believe in, and therefore practice, compulsory education of the young, monogamy (one husband or wife) in marriage, and freedom of the press to discuss political issues. These are aspects of American culture.

Every human society has a culture. A culture is a human society's way of satisfying group needs and achieving group goals. It includes everything from instructions on how to plant corn or build a fire to the acceptable procedure for obtaining a marriage partner. Humans create culture to solve basic problems, to satisfy basic needs. All people must eat, sleep, and protect themselves from bad weather in order to survive and to live in ways that they enjoy. A culture is a society's fund of wisdom, collected painstakingly throughout its past, that gives the members of the society ready-made solutions to basic problems. It consists of the accumulated thoughts and ideas of many centuries about what is good and bad and about what is true and false. Statements such as "Do unto others as you would have them do unto you," "It is wrong to kill, steal, or lie," and "Education is the key to opportunity" reflect basic values of the American culture. A culture is the value judgments held by most people in a society.

Over a long period of time, a child slowly acquires the culture of his society. In contrast to other animals the behavior of human beings is not controlled largely by instincts. Humans are not born with instincts that control completely how they organize a society, gather food, build shelters, or behave in all the many ways necessary to satisfying their basic needs. Humans must learn how to achieve their goals. Thus, compared to other animals, man's period of childhood helplessness is very long. In the years from infancy through adolescence the child slowly acquires a culture, the skills and knowledge needed for survival.

Language is the key to the creation and continuation of culture. Through language the members of a society communicate their needs and wants to one another. Through a written language the ideas of men who lived long ago can

The Star-Spangled Banner

Francis Scott Key

John Stafford Smith

Every culture has its political aspects.
Show how the items here illustrate
American political culture.

be preserved and passed on to men living today. Thus, some ideas of the ancient Greeks and Romans, along with some ideas of other peoples who lived long ago, are part of our culture today. Without language, culture could not be passed on from group to group or from generation to generation. Without language, every generation would have to start over again to learn solutions to basic human problems, rather than using the solutions handed down from the past and changing or adding to them as the need arises.

The relationship between culture and human behavior is shown by the following story about a trader's wife in Arizona recounted by anthropologist Clyde Kluckhohn in *Mirror for Man.* The trader's wife often enjoyed serving a tasty meal of delicious meat sandwiches to her guests. To some guests the meat in the sandwiches tasted like tuna fish. To others it tasted like chicken. At the end of the meal the hostess would inform her guests that they had eaten rattlesnake meat. Without exception, her guests would become sick and vomit what they had considered earlier a tasty meal.

The guests vomited, because eating rattlesnake meat *was not* part of their culture. They had never learned that rattlesnake meat is edible. While all men must eat, a culture influences what they eat and what they avoid eating.

B. What Is the Relationship of Culture to Political Behavior?

Individuals behave in similar ways when they have similar ideas about what is good or bad or what is true or false. The political beliefs of a group influence the political behavior of group members.

Beliefs about political behavior are part of a culture. For example, in the comparative political behavior lesson on pages 74–75 you identified differences in governmental organization in Saudi Arabia and the United States. These differences in government reflect differences in culture. The Arabians believed that a king should rule and that most people should have little or nothing to say about public policy decisions. These political beliefs were a part of the culture of the people of Saudi Arabia. In contrast, the Americans believe that the people should elect representatives to rule and that the people should have the right to influence public policy decisions. These political beliefs are part of the culture of the American people.

The typical political beliefs of a society can be called a *political culture.* As a culture is typical beliefs about how to behave, a political culture is typical beliefs about how to behave politically. A political culture is one part of a society's culture. For example, in the comparative political behavior lesson on pages 64–66 you noted differences in political behavior of Americans, Ifugao people, and Dinaric Serbian people. Each of these societies has a political culture. These different cultures influence individuals in the three societies to behave differently. The Ifugao believe that a *monkalun* ought to settle conflicts between individuals. This is a value judgment held by most of the Ifugao. In contrast, the Dinaric Serbs believed that conflicts between individuals ought to be settled through "blood vengeance" or the payment of "blood money."

This was a value judgment of the past Dinaric Serbian society. Most people in the United States of America believe that serious disputes between individuals ought to be settled through adjudication in a court of law. This is a value judgment held by most individuals in our society.

Political culture influences political behavior. For example, the belief that decisions ought to be made according to majority vote is part of the American political culture. This political value has influenced Americans to make rules that direct the political behavior of individuals in the American society. For example, Americans elect representatives to government according to majority vote, and elected representatives make laws according to majority vote.

Another illustration of the American political culture is the political value that individuals should have freedom of religion—the freedom to practice any religion or to practice no religion. This political value is supported by the First Amendment of the United States Constitution which provides that all Americans shall have freedom to worship as they please, or not to worship at all if they prefer. Thus, hundreds of different religious practices are found among

At the opening of Parliament a traditional "Speech from the Throne," prepared by the Prime Minister and his Cabinet, is read by Queen Elizabeth. In the United States the President gives a "State of the Union" message when Congress convenes for a new session. What are other similarities and differences in the two political cultures?

the churchgoers in American society. And many Americans belong to no church and follow no organized religious practices. Individuals who value decision-making by majority vote and religious freedom often disapprove of people opposed to these values.

The political value that the American flag is good is yet another example of the American political culture. Thus, it is customary for Americans to express this approval by standing at attention when the flag is raised. Individuals who do not follow this custom are treated as bad citizens. Most Americans are angered or disgusted by such behavior. They may refuse to be friendly with these individuals or even to cooperate with them in any way.

The political culture expresses a society's view of authority. Americans believe that policemen ought to have the authority to arrest lawbreakers. But Americans also believe that policemen should not decide the guilt or innocence of an accused lawbreaker, because an important part of the American political

83

culture is that judges and juries should decide the guilt or innocence of an accused lawbreaker and the punishment to be given. A person who uses power correctly, according to the directions of his political culture, is considered a good citizen. A person who deviates from his political culture when using power is considered a bad citizen, or even a criminal, if his behavior differs greatly from the political culture.

When conflicts within the society are settled in a way that fits the political culture of a society, most individuals will accept these decisions as just and right. Enforcing decisions that most people consider correct is a fairly easy matter. People who believe that a law is just will usually obey it automatically. The power of the government to enforce laws is used to control the behavior of those who would not otherwise obey the law.

To indicate what you have learned about the relationship of culture to political behavior, answer these questions.

1. Each of the following is a statement about political beliefs and behavior. Which of these statements reflect the political culture of the American society?

    a. Individuals should have the right to own property.

    b. Individuals should be equal before the law.

    c. There should be only one political party in a society.

    d. All individuals should be forced to go to church.

    e. Children should follow the directions of the policeman who directs traffic near their school.

    f. No one ought to have the right to criticize the government.

    g. The police have the right to arrest anyone they think might cause trouble.

    h. Americans are expected to vote on election day.

    i. Individuals should have freedom of speech.

    j. Laws should be made and enforced by one man.

    k. The same rights should be granted to all citizens in a society, regardless of race, creed, or national ancestry.

    l. Black people should be allowed to hold positions in government.

    m. The leaders of our government should be elected by majority vote.

2. Study the previous statements again.

    a. Which statements are American political beliefs that are, for the most part, practiced in our society?

    b. Which statements are American political beliefs that are often not lived up to in our society?

3. Explain why there may be a gap between some political beliefs of a society and political behavior in the society.

4. Does the fact that some political beliefs are not widely practiced have any effect on political behavior?

5. What is the relationship of political beliefs to political behavior?

Workers at an auto plant cast their ballots for members of the Supreme Soviet of the Soviet Union in a 1970 election. The ballot lists only one candidate for each office. Those who wish to express disapproval can put their unmarked ballot in the box.

C. Differences in Political Culture

Different countries have different political cultures. And within the same country there are different political cultures among different groups. The concepts of democracy and autocracy provide one way to look at, or interpret, differences in political culture and political behavior.

Democratic Political Beliefs

In the United States most people believe that democracy is good and that children should be taught to accept democratic political beliefs. These are important beliefs in the American political culture. What are democratic beliefs? Below are some political beliefs that most people would call democratic.

Political decisions should be made according to majority vote.

a. Laws should be made by a majority vote of representatives of the people.

b. The leaders of our government should be elected by majority vote.

The rights of individuals should be protected.

a. Individuals should have freedom of speech, religion, and assembly.

b. Individuals should have the right to own property.

c. Individuals should have equality of opportunity.

d. Individuals should be equal before the law.

e. The rights of individuals should be granted to all citizens, regardless of race, creed, or national ancestry.

There should be free competition, regulated by rules, among political groups and ideas.

a. Political conflicts should be decided by free and open exchange of ideas that takes place within a framework of law and order.

b. Political parties should be free to compete with one another for control of the government.

c. Individuals should be free to join different groups that stand for the social and political ideas they favor.

Autocratic Political Beliefs

Autocracy is the opposite of democracy. Democracy means rule by the people with protection of individual (and minority group) rights. Autocracy means rule by one man or by a small elite group. The rights of minorities are not necessarily protected. In some autocratic societies, such as Nazi Germany in 1933–1945, members of minority groups have been jailed or even put to death. Autocratic political systems do not allow competition among political parties. Rather one party, such as the Communist party in the Soviet Union, dominates political life. Ideas are not freely discussed and debated. Instead a "party line," a correct view of the world determined by political leaders, substitutes for the free exchange of ideas. Individuals who dissent from the "party line" may be imprisoned or killed.

Diagramming Political Beliefs

Diagram 7 illustrates the differences between autocratic and democratic political cultures. According to this diagram, two main political beliefs are basic to democratic political culture: (1) a belief in majority rule practices; (2) a belief in protection of the rights of individuals and minorities. The extent to which a group, or nation, believes in and practices majority rule and protection of the rights of minorities is the extent to which the group, or nation, can be called democratic. Majority rule alone does not indicate a democracy, or the enjoyment of real freedom. As the British historian Lord Acton said, "The most certain test by which we judge whether a country is really free is the amount of security enjoyed by minorities."

Diagram 7. **Comparison of Democratic and Autocratic Cultures**

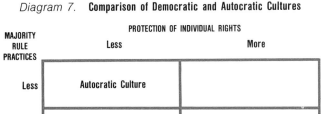

When trying to decide whether a political culture or government is democratic, remember that among the nations of the world there are no perfect democracies. Political cultures or governments are more or less democratic in terms of the standards of majority rule and protection of individual rights. Likewise, no political culture or government is a perfect autocracy. Rather political cultures or governments may be more or less autocratic according to our standards of majority rule and protection of the rights of minorities.

D. Political Beliefs as Indicators of Political Culture

The political beliefs expressed by most people in a society are guides to the political culture of the society. Americans believe that they have a democratic political culture.

To what extent do Americans conform to democratic political beliefs? Data that can provide some clues to this question are presented next.

Political Beliefs of Adults in Two Communities

James Prothro and Charles Grigg, two political scientists, made a study of democratic political beliefs in a northern and in a southern community in the United States.* They selected a random sample of registered voters from each community. The study had two main parts.

First, Prothro and Grigg asked the adults in their samples to agree or disagree with these statements:

*James W. Prothro and Charles M. Grigg, "Fundamental Principles of Democracy: Bases of Agreement and Disagreement," *Journal of Politics,* 1960, Vol. 22, pp. 276–294.

1. Democracy is the best form of government.
2. Public officials should be chosen by majority vote.
3. Every citizen should have an equal chance to influence government policy.
4. The minority should be free to criticize majority decisions.
5. People in the minority should be free to try to win majority support for their opinions.

   Over 90 percent of the adults studied by Prothro and Grigg in the northern and southern communities agreed with statements 1–5.

Next, Prothro and Grigg asked individuals in their samples from both communities to agree or disagree with additional statements. Some of these statements, with responses, are shown below.

6. In a city referendum deciding on tax-supported undertakings, only tax-payers should be allowed to vote.

   Of the individuals responding in both communities, 21 percent disagreed with this statement: 20.8 in the North; 21.2 percent in the South.

7. If a Negro were legally elected mayor of this city, the white people should not allow him to take office.

   Of the individuals responding in both communities, 80.6 percent disagreed with this statement: 88.5 percent in the North; 66.7 percent in the South.

8. If a Communist were legally elected mayor of this city, the people should not allow him to take office.

   Of the individuals responding in both communities, 46.3 percent disagreed with this statement: 49.5 percent in the North; 45.5 percent in the South.

9. If a person wanted to make a speech in this city against churches and religion, he should be allowed to speak.

   Of the individuals responding in both communities, 63 percent agreed with this statement: 67.4 percent in the North; 56.6 percent in the South.

10. A Negro should not be allowed to run for mayor of this city.

    Of the individuals responding in both communities, 75.5 percent disagreed with this statement: 85.6 percent in the North; 56.6 percent in the South.

Answer the following questions about this study of political beliefs in two communities.

1. How do the responses to statements 1–5 compare and contrast with the responses to statements 6–10? What does this comparison reveal about the extent to which some Americans conform to democratic political beliefs as described on page 85.

2. How can you explain the responses to the statements in this study?

Beliefs about Popular Political Participation

Another way to view, or interpret, differences in political culture and political behavior is to examine typical beliefs about political participation. What are the beliefs of the people about how much they ought to participate in politics? What are the beliefs of the people about their chances to influence the government? Do the people trust the government? Compare and contrast the beliefs about popular political participation that are presented in the following two cases.

Case 1. Political participation in Boston's West End. Several years ago a large Italian-American community lived in a downtown section of Boston known as the West End. Most of these Italian-Americans were the children or grandchildren of people who came to this country from Italy. A few of these people were born in Italy and had lived in this country for only a short time.

This primarily low-income area was located at the bottom of the more prosperous Beacon Hill section of Boston. It was bounded by Scollay Square, the Charles River, and the North End section of the city. Today this neighborhood is gone. Under a redevelopment project sponsored by the city, much of the land has been used for the construction of a new complex of government office buildings, high rise apartments, and housing projects.

Sociologist Herbert Gans lived in the West End as a participant observer to study the culture of the Italian-American residents. As part of this study, Gans gathered facts about the political beliefs of these "West Enders." His book, *The Urban Villagers,* presents his findings in detail; but here are his main conclusions about political behavior in the West End.

The West Enders tended to distrust the city government and public officials. They viewed the city government as part of an unfriendly "outside world" which should be avoided as much as possible. They felt that the decisions of city officials usually favored other groups in Boston more than the people of the West End. Furthermore, they believed that most public officials were corrupt and wanted to help themselves rather than the public. Even their own neighborhood leaders were viewed with suspicion. West Enders often believed that if a local leader failed to win a favor for them, it was because he had been "paid off." On the other hand, a politician's success must also mean that he had personally profited from his government transactions.

Most West Enders seldom engaged directly in political affairs. They usually felt that there was little they could do to influence public officials. If

they had a problem or a complaint, they would go to a community leader and ask him to represent them to the government. For example, when the re-development of the West End area was announced by the city government, there were many West Enders who opposed the plan. A few people in the West End attempted to organize public protest activities. But lacking support from the Italian-American community, their efforts failed.

The political activity of most West Enders was restricted to asking neighborhood leaders for favors, expressing political opinions to neighborhood leaders, and voting in public elections. However, many West Enders did not even participate in this limited way. West Enders tended to believe that an individual should have as little to do with government as possible. When efforts by local leaders to stop the redevelopment project by discussion with city officials failed, most West Enders assumed that the problem simply could not be solved. They tended to attribute their lack of success in influencing public officials to the corruption of those in control of government.

When a neighborhood political leader did a favor for a West End resident, the West Ender was expected to express his gratitude by supporting the neighborhood leader's political ambitions. This was usually done by contributing money to the political campaigns of local leaders and by voting for them.

Case 2. Political participation in a small midwestern town. Oberlin College is the largest employer in the small town of Oberlin, Ohio. Many of the town's citizens are employed by the college as teachers, administrators, secretaries, or maintenance workers. About one-fourth of the people in Oberlin are black. Most of the other residents are native-born whites.

In his book *Leadership in a Small Town*, Aaron Wildavsky described political behavior in Oberlin. Here are some of his conclusions about popular political participation in Oberlin in 1961.

There were three types of political participants in Oberlin: active participants, voter-observers, and apathetics. Active participants were very much involved in the political life of the community. These people were leaders with strong feelings of political efficacy and civic responsibility. They believed that they could and should take a part in the making of public policy decisions. They were highly interested in and informed about political affairs. The active participants voted in public elections, took part in political campaigns, and tried directly to influence public opinion and public policy decisions. About 20 percent of the adults in Oberlin were active political participants.

Voter-observers participated in politics much less than the active participants. They tended to vote in public elections and to participate in response to a few issues in which they had a strong personal stake or a special interest. About 45 percent of the Oberlin adults were voter-observers.

Apathetics tended to take no part in political affairs. They usually did not vote in public elections or try to influence public policy decisions. They had little or no feelings of political efficacy or civic responsibility. They tended to be uninterested and uninformed about political affairs. About 35 percent of the adults in Oberlin were politically apathetic.

A majority of Oberlin adults said that they were somewhat interested in political affairs and cared about the performance of the government. They tended to believe that what the government does affects them in important ways. They did not express strong distrust or disrespect of government or public officials.

Although people in Oberlin considered political activity important, very few citizens chose to participate actively. Most of the citizens preferred to spend their time and energy on other activities. However, more than half of these citizens would respond to an issue that affected them directly, such as a rise in taxes, a cutback in services, or a change in the zoning law.

Compare the political cultures of the people in Boston's former West End and Oberlin according to the following directions.

1. Compare the political interest and political activity of the people in Oberlin and the West End. Use *Diagram 8* to assist your comparison.

2. Compare the sense of political efficacy and political trust of the people in Oberlin and the West End. Use *Diagram 9* to assist your comparison.

Diagram 8.   **Comparison of Political Interest and Political Activity**

| | POLITICAL INTEREST | | POLITICAL ACTIVITY | |
CASE	Lower	Higher	Lower	Higher
West End	A	B	C	D
Oberlin	E	F	G	H

Diagram 9.   **Comparison of Political Efficacy and Political Trust**

| | SENSE OF POLITICAL EFFICACY | | SENSE OF POLITICAL TRUST | |
CASE	Lower	Higher	Lower	Higher
West End	A	B	C	D
Oberlin	E	F	G	H

3. What is the relationship of political interest and activity to sense of political efficacy and political trust in the two cases? Use *Diagram 10* to assist your comparison. For example, does the West End case fit in box A, B, C, or D? In which box does the Oberlin case fit?

4. What conclusions can you make about differences in political culture between the people in Oberlin and the West End?

Diagram 10. **A Multi-Factor Comparison**

	Lower efficacy and trust	Higher efficacy and trust
Higher interest and activity	A	B
Lower interest and activity	C	D

E. Conflict as a Result of Cultural Differences

All large societies contain subcultures. A *subculture* is the way of life of a smaller group within the larger society. A subculture includes all the values and attitudes, the standards of right and wrong that guide human behavior in the smaller group. Differences in childrearing practices, religious practices, food preparation and diet, language, and manner of dress also often distinguish a subculture from the larger society.

The United States has many subcultures. Within every large city in America are groups composed of foreign-born people and their descendents. The Mexican-Americans of Los Angeles and southern Texas, the Puerto Rican-Americans of New York and Chicago, the Italian-Americans of New York and Boston, and the Polish-Americans of Chicago and Detroit are merely a few examples of the many groups with distinct subcultures that are part of the American society.

The Amish as a Subculture

None of these groups is as isolated from the larger American culture as the Amish. In his book *Amish Society,* John Hostetler describes the many ways in which culture of the Amish differs from the culture of most Americans. Groups of Amish people live in rural communities in twenty states—notably in Pennsylvania, Ohio, Indiana, Kentucky, and Iowa. The approximately 50,000 Amish people in the United States live chiefly by farming. They are very religious and base their customs and laws upon their interpretation of the Bible. They prefer to live apart from other Americans out of fear that extended contact with the dominant culture would eventually lead to a loss of their unique cultural values.

Two passages from the Bible are often quoted by Amishmen to sum up their view of the world. The first is: "Be not conformed to this world, but be ye transformed by the renewing of your mind that ye may prove what is that good and acceptable and perfect will of God." To the Amish, this means that one should set himself apart from the ways of other people. Consequently the Amish dress in an old-fashioned way and resist strongly any changes in clothing fashion. They refuse to use modern farm machinery, preferring horse-

drawn plows and carts to tractors and trucks. They refuse to buy television sets and to use modern home appliances. They shun electricity, telephones, and automobiles.

The second Biblical quotation that gives a clue to the Amish subculture is: "Be ye not unequally yoked together with unbelievers; for what fellowship hath righteousness with unrighteousness? And what communion hath light with darkness?" To the Amish, this means that they should not marry non-Amish persons, that they should not have business partnerships with "outsiders," and that they should not form friendships with people outside their community.

The Amish have kept their traditions alive by teaching their children to speak a form of German as well as English. The ancestors of the Amish came to America from German-speaking areas of Europe. At home, and within the Amish community generally, German is spoken rather than English. English is used when the Amishman comes into contact with the larger American society.

The Amish attempt to perpetuate their subculture by running their own schools in which the education of Amish children is carefully supervised. Amish children are forbidden to attend public schools for fear that they might reject the Amish way of life in favor of more typical American ways. The traditional Amish culture is preserved by denying Amish children exposure to alternative ways of life during their early childhood years.

The Relationship of the Amish Subculture to Political Behavior

The Amish subculture gives rise to distinct political beliefs. In accordance with his religion, the Amishman is a pacifist. He believes wars, or any kind of fighting, is a sin against God. The Amish are typically law-abiding, hard working, thrifty people. They pride themselves on their orderliness and their readiness to submit to authority. However, they prefer to be left alone, to protect their way of life from domination by outsiders. Thus, when the laws of state or national government conflict with the rules of the Amish society, the Amish are faced with a moral problem. Should they obey the laws of the American government, under which they live, or should they follow the values of their subculture?

The Amish way of life includes political apathy. The Amish readily obey most laws but do not ordinarily organize themselves for political action. Typically they do not participate in election campaigns. The Amish try very hard not to get involved in the political affairs of the larger American society.

Occasionally, however, the Amish way of life brings them into conflict with the government. Such conflict occurs when state or national government laws disagree with Amish religious beliefs. Usually the Amishman chooses to disobey a law rather than to violate a religious belief. For example, in Iowa in the early 1960's, the Amish people became involved in a dispute with government officials over the education of their youngsters. Following is a description of conflict resulting from differences between the Amish subculture and the larger American culture.

Showdown at the Charity Flats School

On November 22, 1965, five public officials representing the state of Iowa forced their way into the Charity Flats school near Hazleton, Iowa. They pushed aside two Amish men who were standing guard before the door of the one-room schoolhouse. Inside the school sixteen Amish children sang "Jesus Loves Me." Several mothers stood around the schoolroom and wept.

Hazleton's Amish children fled when state officials arrived to take them to their new school.

The state government officials had arrived for a "showdown" to end a three-year dispute between the state of Iowa and several Old Order Amish families. For three years the public officials had been trying to force the Amish to improve their schools according to state law or to send their children to public schools. For three years the Amish had resisted the orders of the public officials. The officials had come to take the Amish children to a nearby public school. The children, backed by their parents, were determined to resist. One of the state officials, a truant officer, gently grasped a little girl's shoulder. He told her to move outside and get into a school bus that would take her to a nearby public school. The room was very quiet. Suddenly the girl screamed and pulled away. The other children screamed and wept.

The public officials frowned. They bowed their heads and walked out of the schoolroom. The attempt at a "showdown" to end the Amish school dispute had failed.

Several days later the governor of Iowa, Harold Hughes, called for a halt in the efforts of state officials to force the Amish to obey state educational laws. The state legislature began to consider action to resolve the school dispute. After much debate, the state legislature passed a law in 1967 that protects the right of Old Order Amish children to attend their own schools. The law provides that state laws about compulsory education of children do not apply to children of religious orders whose religious principles conflict with state educational laws. Thus, the "showdown" at the Charity Flats School ended in a temporary victory for the Amish.

History of the Charity Flats dispute. How did the contest between the Amish and the Iowa state government start? Why did the public officials try to force a "showdown" at the Charity Flats School? Why did the Amish win a victory in the state legislature? The following commentary provides answers to these questions.

94

The dispute started on November 8, 1961, when the Oelwein Community School District was formed by consolidating several neighboring school districts. The new Oelwein School Board had to decide how to deal with fifty-three Old Order Amish children who attended two Amish parochial schools in the new consolidated district.

The school board decided to close the Amish schools and require the Amish students to attend a nearby public school. They based their decision on a study by the Iowa State Department of Public Instruction which after investigation reported that the Amish schools did not meet the standards for schools set by Iowa state law. According to the report the Amish schools were run-down and the teachers were not competent. The school board told the Amish to improve their schools or shut them down. They ordered them to hire teachers immediately who could qualify for teachers' licenses from the Iowa State Department of Public Instruction and to add science courses to their curriculum. The Amish teachers had received no schooling beyond the eighth grade.

The Amish refused to obey the school board's orders. They argued that the orders violated their right of religious freedom. The Amish presented the following arguments in support of their position.

> We must send our children to our own schools in order to teach the word of God and to maintain our way of life. If we allow our children to attend the public schools, they will learn sinful ways. They will not be able to live according to the customs of our people.

> The government officials say that they have no objection to the Amish way of life. They say that we are free to live apart according to our ways. Then why don't they let us teach our children, in our own schools, how to live a good Amish life?

> Our people do not harm others. We are good citizens. We work hard and mind our own business. Our children do not become juvenile delinquents and our adults do not become criminals. In our schools we teach our children to have good moral standards. Let us continue to teach them how to be righteous.

> Our educational ideals do not bring harm to other Americans. Our educational system only helps us to make good Amishmen out of our children. Our schools help us to protect our way of life from the perversions of other values.

Public officials state their position. While sympathizing with the Amish, the public officials believed the Amish brand of education to be inferior. They pointed to the aging facilities and outdated textbooks. They criticized the Amish for using teachers having only an eighth-grade education.

The following description of the two Amish schools by Donald Erickson appeared in *Commentary* in January, 1968:

> In keeping with the Plain People's philosophy, their schools are rustic, not to say primitive, and reflect little attention to aesthetics. The two buildings near Hazleton are reasonably clean and cheerful, though finished rather roughly and marred in spots by flaking paint.

Each is furnished with two outdoor privies, a coal shed, and a well with a manual pump. The North school boasts two seesaws, two swings, and some old tires as playground equipment; the South school has none at all.

In each school the only entrance to the single classroom is through a small vestibule, in which there are shelves and nails for lunch buckets and coats. Each classroom has rough board floors; extra-tall windows on two sides for ventilation and light (there is no electricity); short shelves holding a collection of dog-eared books; a kitchen sink with water crock and paper towel dispenser; a large Regulator clock clucking high on the wall; bits of blackboard; five rows of ancient desks; a teacher's desk and chair; two or three sturdy work tables; cardboard boxes full of discarded textbooks; and some roll-up maps that are probably priceless antiques. In the rear of the room, there is a massive stove, which is kept stoked by boys assigned to the task. Pupils' drawings, virtually all of brightly colored rural scenes, are tacked on the walls.

The government officials argued that the primitive Amish schools did not give Amish children a chance to become anything other than Amish farmers. They argued that in these schools the Amish children could not receive an education that could equip them with skills needed to live apart, if they should choose to, from their Amish subculture.

Furthermore, the government officials argued that all groups should receive equal treatment before the law. Thus, the Amish should not be given the right to ignore the school laws. They argued that the laws permit the Amish, or any other group, to have its own schools if these schools meet standards set by state law. But the Amish schools did not meet these standards.

The Amish stubbornly refused to change their schools to meet state requirements. They also stubbornly resisted suggestions to send their children to the public school in Hazleton. The government therefore decided to take action. The county superintendent of schools started the first legal action against the Amish on November 24, 1962. The county attorney prosecuted ten Amishmen for the misdemeanor of sending their children to a school without licensed teachers. All ten were found guilty and fined. Eight refused to pay the fines, on religious principle, and served three days in jail.

School officials attempt a compromise. In January, 1963, the Oelwein School Board tried to reach a compromise settlement with the Amish. They offered to allow the Amish to operate their schools, under the direction of the school board, for two more years. After that time the children would go to public schools. The Amish rejected the offer.

Another compromise was tried in September, 1964. The Oelwein School Board offered to provide special ungraded classrooms for Amish students within the public school on a one-year trial basis. The Amish refused this offer.

A turning point in the Amish school dispute came in September, 1965. Four new members were elected to the Oelwein School Board. During the election campaign, these winning candidates had promised to deal firmly with the Amish if elected. Also the newly elected county attorney had promised to enforce all laws and to give no special treatment to the Amish. Apparently public opinion in Oelwein County was against the Amish in the school dispute.

With the backing of the county attorney, the newly elected Oelwein School Board brought charges against several Amishmen for breaking the state school laws. They were found guilty. The court decided to require the Amishmen to pay a $24 fine at the end of each school day until their children enrolled in the public school in Hazleton.

The Amishmen continued to refuse to send their children to the public school, and daily their fines mounted. By the middle of November, 1965, the Amish owed several thousand dollars in fines to the state for refusing to obey the school laws.

Clearly, the Amish were not to be broken through court action. The county attorney did not want to send the Amishmen to jail or to bankrupt them through the payment of fines. He said that he did not want to punish the Amish. Rather, he wanted to force them to obey the law, just as everyone else had to do.

Plans are made for the showdown. The county attorney worked out a plan that he believed would settle the problem. He decided to use the state truancy laws. He would claim that Amish children who did not attend public schools were truant. Thus, he could legally seize them and force them to attend the Hazleton public school. He even got several important Amish leaders to agree to this plan. They said that their people, who do not believe in violence, would not resist when the public officials came to take their children to the public school.

The truant officer sent a school bus to pick up the Amish children. The children were put on the bus and spent three hours at the public school. Next day, when the school bus came to take the Amish children to the public school, they ran away.

The county officials then decided to take the children out of their one-room schools. The result was the conflict at the Charity Flats School.

The events at the Charity Flats School attracted nationwide attention. Public opinion in Iowa and around the country seemed to favor the Amish cause. Governor Hughes became concerned about the bad publicity for his state. He also believed that the Amish should be able to live a different kind of life if they so desired. He declared publicly, "I am determined to try to find a way, if possible, to make Iowa a place where the Amish people can live and follow their religious beliefs. Why should they be forced to leave Iowa because of a religious issue? Certainly we can find a suitable solution." The governor threw his political weight behind efforts to achieve a solution to the conflict that the Amish could live with.

Eventually a majority of the lawmakers in the Iowa legislature agreed with Governor Hughes on this issue. They sympathized with the plight of the Amish. They also believed that public opinion in Iowa favored the Amish on this issue. Thus, in 1967 the legislature passed a law exempting the Amish, temporarily, from obeying the state educational laws.

1. What is the issue in this case?

2. What is the value conflict in this case?

3. Use the concepts of culture and subculture to interpret the value conflict in this case.

4. What policy decision was made to settle the conflict?

5. Why was this decision made?

Making Value Judgments about the Amish School Dispute

The Amish school dispute attracted nationwide attention. Many editorials were written about the issues involved. Following are conflicting commentaries about the dispute. Read these commentaries carefully and answer the following questions.

1. What conflicting value judgments can you identify in the newspaper editorials?

2. With which value judgment do you agree? How can you justify your position?

In support of the Amish position. Russell Kirk, a news commentator whose articles appear in many newspapers, has written editorials that support the right of the Amish to run their own schools in their own way. Following are excerpts from articles by Kirk which appeared in two Indiana papers, the *Indianapolis Star* and the *Bloomington Tribune.*

Do religious denominations enjoy the right to operate their own schools on their own principles? This question has arisen in several states during recent years, in connection with such religious sects as the Amish and the Mennonites. . . .

If a private school is subversive of public order, or if it leads the young into immorality, political authorities are entitled to intervene. But can they justly meddle with schools which, like those of the Mennonites and Amish, harm no one and are an integral part of a religious community?

The Amish believe that their children do not need schooling beyond the eighth grade. If we can judge schools by their fruits, the Amish seem to succeed. Their children are at least as good in reading, writing, and arithmetic as are typical pupils in an average public school. And Amish people are notably industrious, law-abiding, and well-conducted.

If their children were sent to public schools, they would be denied by the Supreme Court the religious instruction and Bible study essential to the perpetuation of the Amish communities. The typical American public school is scarcely so perfect an institution that a child must be mentally and morally crippled by studying elsewhere.

American society and American schooling need more diversity, not one vast educational monotony. Only a totalitarian state refuses to tolerate the existence of such groups as the Amish.

Destroy the Amish schools, and in time you destroy the Amish sect.

Not wishing to be merged with modern culture, the Amish prefer to educate their own offspring in their own schools, so as to preserve their religious faith. . . .

And now the Iowa legislature has passed an act exempting the Amish, and similar religious groups, from school attendance compulsion. Any religious community established in Iowa for at least ten years may withdraw its children from public schools if the group feels that state instruction is in conflict with their religious doctrines. It is high time, for religious freedom is supposed to be guaranteed by federal and state constitutions. . . .

It is heartening to find freedom of religious and educational choice is approved in at least one state. . . .

In opposition to the Amish position. Several newspaper editorials were written in opposition to the right of the Amish to run their own schools. Following are excerpts from one of these articles in an Iowa newspaper, the *Burlington Hawkeye.*

. . . What the legislature has done is to endorse ignorance by agreeing that the Amish, alone among Iowans, will be permitted to send their children to inferior schools, taught by inferior teachers. . . .

The so-called solution to the Amish problem is filled with ironies and contradictions. First of all, the Amish, nation-wide, are noted for their thrift and business shrewdness and can afford as well as anyone else the cost of adequate education.

Secondly, if a group is to be singled out for exemption from the educational laws, what is to prevent it also from being exempt, on the same grounds, from the sanitation laws, the liquor laws, the tax laws, the usury laws, or any other?

Thirdly, if such an exemption is good for one religious group, why not others? Scores of Catholic parochial schools have been closed for the simple reason that their parishes couldn't afford to meet the state standards for teachers and curriculum. This has been a good thing, I think. But many Catholics may think differently, may prefer to send their children to schools staffed by aged, untrained nuns and part-time housewives, who teach nothing but catechism. Why can't they do it, under the great Iowa "solution"?

chapter 6

Socialization and Political Behavior

Socialization is a main influence on the political behavior of individuals. The concept of *socialization* can be used to make comparisons, to identify and interpret similarities and differences in political behavior.

A. What Is Socialization?

Socialization is the name that social scientists give to the process of becoming an accepted member of a society. Socialization involves the learning of the society's culture. It begins at birth and continues throughout life.

The beliefs that men have a right to own personal property, that public education should be provided for children, that the family should be the basic group in our society, that men should not steal from one another, that government officials should be elected by majority vote are a few examples of the culture of American society. These beliefs, or values, along with many others, are guidelines about how Americans should behave in order to be considered good citizens. When Americans follow these guidelines, their behavior fits the culture of their society. They are considered to be *socialized.*

Because an individual is born in the United States to American parents does not mean that he automatically is socialized, that he instinctively possesses at birth the American culture. An individual is not born with a culture. Rather, the individual is born into a culture that he continues to learn as long as he is part of the society that has created the culture.

As part of the socialization process, a typical American learns to speak English, to accept Judaeo-Christian religious beliefs, and to favor democratic government over dictatorship. Through the socialization process, an infant born in the United States to American parents *learns to become* an American. He is not born with special qualities that make him behave similarly to other Americans and differently from other peoples. Rather, an American becomes socialized through learning the customary ways of behaving in his society at home from his parents, at school from teachers, at church from ministers, and at play and at work from friends.

Because a culture is learned, not inborn, it can also be changed through learning. For example, if an American child is taken to live in a strange country at a young age and grows up in this strange country under the care of people from this country, this child will not learn to behave like other Americans. Rather, he will learn the culture of this other country. He will learn the laws, religion, customs, and language of this other country, because he will have learned these ways of behavior at home, at school, at play, and at work.

100

This relationship between behavior and the social environment is very well described by the anthropologist Clyde Kluckhohn in his book *Mirror for Man:*

From *Mirror for Man* by Clyde Kluckhohn. McGraw-Hill, Inc., 1949. Used with permission.

> Some years ago I met in New York City a young man who did not speak a word of English and was obviously bewildered by American ways. By "blood" he was as American as you or I, for his parents had gone from Indiana to China as missionaries. Orphaned in infancy, he was reared by a Chinese family in a remote village. All who met him found him more *Chinese than American.* The facts of his blue eyes and light hair were less impressive than a Chinese style of gait, Chinese arm and hand movements, Chinese facial expressions and Chinese modes of thought. The biological heritage was American, but the cultural training had been Chinese. He returned to China.

The young man had been socialized into the Chinese society, so he felt more comfortable, more at home, in Chinese society than in American society. The Chinese culture that he had learned from the time he was a child seemed more natural than the strange American culture. Physically this man's heritage was American, but the socialization process that he experienced in China made his cultural heritage Chinese. Thus his behavior was typical of Chinese people.

B. What Is the Relationship of Socialization to Political Behavior?

Through the process of socialization, an individual learns what is considered right and wrong political behavior in his society. *Through socialization, an infant born in the United States of America learns to behave politically in the American way.* Through socialization, the infant learns the political beliefs of his culture. As part of the socialization process, a typical American child learns to obey the commands of a policeman directing traffic, to pledge allegiance to the flag, to select a class president by majority vote, to support freedom of speech, and to express many other typical American political behaviors and beliefs. An American child learns these beliefs and behaviors at home from parents, at school from teachers, at church from ministers, and at play and at work from friends.

What does each part of the drawing show about the method or the content of American political socialization?

The process of learning accepted political beliefs and behavior can be called *political socialization.* As socialization is the learning of a society's culture, so political socialization is the learning of a society's political culture. For example, no child born to American parents instinctively (at birth) possesses the American political culture. Rather, the child is born into a political culture that he continues to learn as long as he is part of the society and the political system that created the political culture. If an American child is taken to live in Russia at a very young age and grows up in Russia with Russian step-parents, he would not behave politically like other Americans. Rather, he would learn the political culture of Russia. He would learn to favor the Russian laws and political beliefs instead of American laws and political beliefs. He would learn to believe that the Russian political system is better than the American political system. He would learn these beliefs and behaviors, through the process of political socialization, at home, at school, at play, and at work.

Socialization Helps to Explain Differences in Behavior

The process of political socialization helps to explain why different people, from the same society, may behave politically in different ways. Although most people within the same society may be exposed to the same political culture, they are not exposed to the political culture in exactly the same way. And they do not learn exactly the same things. For example, Richard and Larry live in the same city. Richard's father is the mayor of the city, and Larry's father is a factory worker. Richard's father and mother are always talking about political affairs at home. Sometimes Richard goes to parties where he meets many of the city's political leaders. By contrast, Larry's father is not interested in politics. He does not even read the newspapers, and he does not vote in elections. It is quite likely that Larry and Richard, although living in the same society with the same political culture, learn different things about the political life of their society from their parents. Because no two individuals have exactly the same experiences, no two individuals are politically socialized in exactly the same way.

To demonstrate what you have learned about the relationship of socialization to political beliefs and behavior, complete the exercise which follows.

Your teacher will show you some pictures of political symbols. You will also receive a "Five-Point Reaction Scale," such as the scale below. Indicate your reaction to each one of the political symbols on this scale.

FIVE-POINT REACTION SCALE

Very Bad Feeling	Bad Feeling	Little or No Feeling	Good Feeling	Very Good Feeling

Your teacher will help you to tabulate and organize the responses of you and your classmates to the pictures of political symbols. On the basis of your tabulation and organization of these responses, answer the following questions.

a. Why do you think you and your classmates responded the way you did to the pictures of political symbols?

b. Do you think most other American teen-agers would have responded to these pictures in the same way that your class responded? Explain your answer.

c. Do you think most Russian teen-agers would have responded to these symbols in the same way that your class responded? Which symbols would most Russian teen-agers have ranked differently from the way your class ranked them? Explain your answer.

d. How are political symbols, political beliefs, and political socialization related?

e. Why do all societies create political symbols?

C. Political Socialization in the Schools

An individual learns the normal, or accepted, political beliefs and behavior of his society from his family, friends, and such official representatives of the society as teachers, policemen, and community leaders.

In our society much political socialization takes place in the schools. On pages 104–105 are several documents about political socialization in American schools. One technique that political scientists use to develop hypotheses is to study documents. *A document is a record of behavior. It is a behavior product.* Diaries, newspaper articles, letters, petitions, and statutes are examples of documents.

Following are several statements about the part that the school is supposed to play in the political socialization process. As you read the documents, decide which of the following statements can be supported with evidence. Be prepared to defend your selections with evidence drawn from the documents.

1. A main purpose of schools is to teach children to love their country.

2. Since freedom of thought is part of the American way of life, American schools do not teach children to believe that they should prefer some political values over others.

3. Since the main purpose of American teachers is to transmit facts to students, teaching about political values has little or no place in the education of American schoolchildren.

4. Political socialization in American schools is conducted only through formal instruction about politics in social studies classes.

5. A main purpose of high school courses in civics and government is to transmit the political culture to children.

6. American schools teach children that democratic political values are superior to other political values.

7. American schools do a very good job of political socialization.

8. Most American school teachers try to promote political stability.

103

Documents about the School as an Agent of Political Socialization

The following statement of philosophy from a midwestern high school expresses one view of the role of the school in political socialization.

We believe that the function of the public school is to preserve the democratic ideal by educating each individual for effective participation in democracy.

Our concept of government rests upon the assumptions that all rights of the government derive from the consent of the governed, that all men are endowed with inalienable rights, that the state exists for the well being of the individual and not the individual for the state, and that the dignity of man may not be violated. Democracy is dependent upon the willing and effective contribution of informed citizens who are capable of responsible self-direction and critical thinking.

This document from an assembly program in a high school auditorium indicates another way in which political socialization takes place.

Fourth Annual "I Am An American Day"

Invocation . . . . A Priest
Pledge of Allegiance . . . . Audience
The Star-Spangled Banner . . . . Audience
Marching On. . . . . High School Choral Club
The Challenge of Citizenship . . . . City Judge
Prayer of Citizenship . . . . A Rabbi
Ode to America . . . . High School Choral Club
Presentation of Citizenship Awards .The Mayor
God Bless America . . . . Audience
Benediction . . . . A Minister

Here is a policy statement on American ideals and values issued by the Kansas State Department of Public Instruction. It is taken from a book by Claude Spencer entitled *Teaching an Understanding of Communism: A Guide for Secondary School Teachers.*

The knowledge of society developed in any culture is an outgrowth of the system of values held by the people who make up that culture.

Our people are committed to a value system which recognizes the unique worth of individual personality and which holds that government is the servant and not the master of man.

It is a primary responsibility of the school to make clear to all youth the nature and the meaning of the democratic values we live by and to develop a deep and abiding loyalty to those values.

All students as a part of basic citizenship education should have a thorough knowledge and understanding of our American heritage of individual liberty and the social, political, and economic benefits derived from it. . . .

104

One of the ways Chinese youth are socialized into their political culture is through participation in youth groups.

In July, 1951, the National Education Association, one of the leading educational organizations for teachers, principals, and administrators in this country, adopted the following resolutions at its national convention.

> The National Education Association strongly asserts that all schools have an obligation to teach the rights, privileges, and the responsibilities of living in a democracy. . . .
>
> The responsibility of the schools is to teach the value of our American way of life, founded as it is on the dignity and worth of the individual; our youth should know it, believe it, and live it continuously. . . .
>
> The Association again reminds the public of the repeated pronouncements of our military leaders and statesmen that education is the basis of our national security and that a well planned, adequately supported system of free public schools is fundamental to the perpetuation of the American way of life.

In addition to the statements on page 103, what other hypotheses can you infer from the evidence provided in the documents? Be prepared to defend your statements with evidence drawn from the documents.

D. Socialization and Roles

As part of the socialization process, an individual learns *roles. Roles are guidelines for behavior.*

Whenever individuals behave in agreement with their culture, they are performing *roles* that their society accepts. An actor in a play is expected to play a role in a certain way in order to be considered a good actor. An individual living in a society is expected to play roles that fit his culture in order to be considered a good citizen.

The performance of roles is a society's culture in action. Roles represent the models for actions of people in a society. As a part of a culture, roles represent guidelines, or directions, for human behavior. Thus, you cannot study the working of a human society apart from its culture.

Roles Are Related to Statuses

An individual's roles in society are related to the positions, or statuses, that he occupies in society. For example, a quarterback on a football team is expected to play a certain role. He is expected to select plays, call signals, and throw passes. His quarterback position, or *status,* on the football team is what determines his role. Because an end has a different position, or status, on the football team, he is expected to follow the orders of the quarterback, not to give them, and to catch passes, not to throw them. The roles of the quarterback and end are different, because they hold different positions, or statuses, on the football team.

Roles Are Interrelated

Every role in a society is related in some way to another role. The role of a parent is related to the role of a child. For example, if American parents are to behave in agreement with American culture, they are expected to provide food and shelter for their child. They are expected to send their child to school. And they are expected to give their child directions about how to behave in many kinds of social situations. The child's role includes living with his parents and obeying their rules.

The role of a teacher is related to the role of pupils. If the behavior of an American teacher is to fit the American culture, the teacher is expected to transmit knowledge to pupils and to keep order in the classroom. The culturally acceptable role of the pupils is to acquire knowledge from the teacher and to respect and obey the teacher's rules.

An Individual Plays Many Roles

What is unexpected about each situation pictured here? How do the drawings illustrate the concept "role"?

Each individual in a society plays many different roles. During the same day, a man may need to play the roles of a father, steelworker, spectator at a football game, and friend to other individuals at a party after the football

game. During the same day, a woman may need to play the roles of a mother, school teacher, and president of the local chapter of the League of Women Voters.

During a lifetime an individual must learn to play the different roles of a child, teen-ager, adult, and elderly adult that are part of his culture. For example, young children are not supposed to play certain roles in American culture, such as driving automobiles or working to earn a living, but adults usually are. Most elderly adults are expected to retire from the task of earning a living once they pass a certain age.

An individual must also learn to play roles related to a sex identity—male or female roles—to earning a living, to recreational activity, and to political activity. For example, it is part of the American culture for girls to wear dresses. Boys are expected to wear trousers. Although many aspects of male and female roles in America are changing, most Americans were socialized with traditional sex roles and express disapproval of individuals who deviate too greatly from them.

In general, individuals who fail to learn the roles that are part of their culture are misfits in their society. They become outcasts. Individuals who learn well the roles that are part of their culture fit in with others in their society.

Political Socialization and Roles

As part of the political socialization process, an individual learns political roles. *Political roles are guidelines for political behavior.* Whenever individuals behave in agreement with their political culture, they are performing political roles that their society accepts.

The performance of political roles is a society's political culture in action. Political roles are the society's blueprints, or models, for political behavior. Political roles represent the expected behavior that flows from the typical political beliefs of the society.

Individuals performing political roles are making the political system of their society function. Political roles are related to the laws and customs of a group of people. For example, the law that the President has the authority to command all military forces is part of the American political culture. This power is given to the President by the Constitution. When the President orders a general to send his troops to an American base in Asia, he is playing the political role of commander-in-chief as indicated by law. However, it is a political custom in the United States that the military should be controlled by civilian leaders. Thus, the President neither wears a military uniform nor identifies too closely with military figures when he plays his commander-in-chief role.

Gen. Charles de Gaulle inspects French Commando troops in London in 1942 as part of his role as head of the French government in exile in World War II.

Status Determines Political Roles

Mrs. Indira Gandhi became Prime Minister of India in 1966.

An individual's political roles are related to the positions, or statuses, that an individual occupies. For example, the President is expected to play certain roles because of his position, or status, as Chief Executive. The President is expected to enforce laws, make treaties with foreign nations, command the nation's military forces, serve as host to visiting leaders of foreign nations, and to play many other roles that go along with his status in our government. A member of the President's White House staff is expected to carry out the orders of the President. His position, or status, on the White House staff determines his role.

On election day, adult citizens in the United States are expected to play the political role of voter. Their status as adults enables them to play this role. By contrast, children, because they occupy a different position, or status, in our society, are not expected to play the role of voter.

An individual's political role is related to his other roles. Individuals who occupy leading positions, or statuses, in the economic system of a society are likely to have more influence on the political decisions than are others who occupy lower positions or statuses. For example, the owner of a business is more likely to have influence on the mayor than is the man who sweeps floors for the businessman. Because the businessman occupies a high position, or status, in the economic system, he is likely to occupy a high position in other parts of a society. Because the floor-sweeper occupies a low position in the economic system, he is likely to occupy a low position in the other parts of a society. Thus, a businessman who has high status is likely to have more power, to play a more influential political role, than is the floor-sweeper.

Political Roles Are Interrelated

Every political role is related in some way to another political role. The role of a political leader, such as the President, a governor, or a mayor, is related to the roles of followers. For example, a mayor is supposed to play the political role of law enforcer in his city, and the people of the city are supposed to play the political roles of law-abiding citizens.

The role of voters is related to the role of an elected public official. Individuals vote for a candidate for public office because they believe that the candidate, if elected, will do certain things to improve the government. They play the political role of voter in order to influence what the government does. The elected public official is supposed to play his political role in a way that satisfies many, if not most, of the people that voted for him. If he fails to play this role, he faces the strong possibility of defeat in the next election.

Each individual assumes many different political roles. During the same day, the mayor may play the political roles of law enforcer, law obeyer, voter, winner of an election, and host to a visiting political leader. During the same day, an ordinary citizen of the same city may play the political roles of law obeyer, voter, participant in a political rally, and discusser of political affairs with a friend.

In a few republics women have risen to the top political leadership positions. Two recent examples are Mrs. Gandhi of India and Prime Minister Golda Meir (left) of Israel.

Socialization Continues throughout Life

During a lifetime an individual must learn to play the different political roles of child, adult, and elderly adult that are part of his political culture. For example, children are not expected to be voters or public political leaders. Most elderly adults are expected to retire from the task of active political leadership. However, there are exceptions to this expectation. Some of our congressmen, Presidents, and judges have been very elderly people.

During a lifetime an individual must learn to play political roles related to a sex identity—male and female roles. In the American political culture, men are expected to be more interested and active in politics than are women. The United States has never had a woman President, and very few women become lawmakers or judges. However, in recent years American women have shown more political interest and activity than ever before. Perhaps this increased female political activity indicates that a part of our political culture is changing.

Individuals who fail to learn or to play the roles that are part of their political culture are misfits in their society. At least, they are considered bad citizens. They may become criminals or outcasts. Individuals who learn well the roles that are part of their political culture fit in with others in their political system. They are considered good citizens.

Two Ways of Playing Politics

The relationship between political roles, political socialization, and political behavior is shown by this fictional account of a high school student government election.

Jim and Nick had campaigned hard against each other. Both boys wanted to be student government president. Both boys were school leaders and believed that becoming student government president was one of the highest honors anyone could achieve in the school.

During the campaign Jim tried to influence students to vote for him by pointing out that he had much experience as a leader in school clubs during the past three years. Nick tried to influence students to vote for him by telling

109

everyone that he was much smarter and much nicer than Jim. Nick publicly said that Jim was dull and lazy. He often called Jim names when he talked about the election.

Jim and Nick competed to fill the school's hallways with political signs. Jim's campaign workers had been able to finish making their signs before Nick's followers had completed their signs. So they were able to place Jim's signs in the most prominent places. Nick became angry and publicly ripped down some of Jim's signs. He said that it was not fair for one candidate to "hog" all the best places.

On election day Jim stood in front of the school. As the students passed by, he shook hands with as many as possible and asked them to please vote for him. Nick also stood out in front of the school and shook hands with as many students as possible and asked for their votes. However, several times he yelled at students who wore signs on their coats that favored Jim. He called these students stupid and said that they would be sorry if he lost the election. When all the votes were counted, Jim had won a landslide victory.

Use the concepts of socialization and role to hypothesize about why Nick probably lost the election by a landslide vote.

E. Personality and Political Behavior

Since no two individuals have exactly the same personality, no two individuals behave politically in exactly the same way. These personality and political-behavior differences result from the differences in political socialization that exist in every society. The political culture of any society is not learned in exactly the same way by each individual.

Personality is all the characteristics of behavior that distinguish one individual from another. It is an individual's way of reacting to his environment. No two individuals have exactly the same personality because no two individuals have exactly the same physical and cultural heritage or exactly the same personal experiences.

The relationship between personality, socialization, and culture is shown by the following example. James and Robert are identical twins. This means that they have the same physical inheritance, the same inborn capabilities. They look almost exactly alike. A short time after birth their parents died. James was adopted by a doctor and went to live in a big city. Robert was adopted by a poor farmer who lived in an isolated mountainous region. James completed college and became a high school teacher. Robert dropped out of school after completing the eighth grade. He became a farm laborer. James likes to read books, attend plays, and to play classical music on the piano. Robert seldom reads books and likes to play folk music on the guitar. On radio he listens to popular and country music.

Jim and Robert behave differently because they have had different experiences. Even though Jim and Robert were identical twins, they learned to behave differently because they grew up in different cultural environments and were socialized in different ways.

110

Personality Affects Political Behavior

Personality and individual political behavior differ because almost all people have a different physical, or biological, heritage. (Only identical twins possess the same physical inheritance.) Because of limited mental ability inherited from parents, some individuals are not able to learn certain political roles. No amount of teaching can fit a mentally slow person for the role of Supreme Court judge. Also, some individuals are able to acquire political skills more easily than others because they are born with more mental ability. People with high mental ability are more likely to become political leaders, if they so choose, than are individuals who are born with low mental ability.

Personality and individual political behavior differ because no two people have exactly the same cultural heritage. Since no two individuals have exactly the same experiences, no two individuals are socialized politically in exactly the same way. Because of personality differences that result from differences in political socialization, no two individuals play the same political role in exactly the same way. For example, no two Supreme Court justices play the judicial role in exactly the same way.

Because of the influence of political socialization upon personality development, the political behavior of most individuals in American society fits the American political culture most of the time. With a knowledge of American political culture, you can predict much of the political behavior of Americans in certain typical situations. For example, you know that a group of American lawmakers, whether congressmen, state assemblymen, or city councilmen, will not make laws without a majority vote. The idea of majority rule is a basic part of the American political culture.

Predicting Political Behavior Is Risky

However, you cannot predict many kinds of political behavior solely on the basis of knowledge of a political culture. While a political role represents what people might do in typical situations, people do not always act in expected ways. Because of differences in personality, different individuals may have different views of how they should behave politically. Thus, without knowledge of an individual's personality, it may be difficult or impossible to predict his political behavior in certain situations. Because of personality differences, there may be a variation between role and role behavior, between what a person ought to do and what he does.

For example, citizens in the American society are taught that playing their roles properly requires them to vote in elections of public officials. Yet, many American citizens do not vote in elections. Many citizens believe that they have little personal or political power. Therefore, they do not vote, nor do they participate in politics in other ways. The role behavior of these non-voting citizens departs from the American citizen role, from what American citizens are expected to do. Personality characteristics, feelings of personal inferiority and powerlessness, account for the gap between role and role behavior in this case, that is, between the expected behavior and the actual behavior.

F. The Meanings of Black Power: An Example of Differences in Political Socialization

"Black power" has become a rallying cry and symbol of many black political leaders and their followers. Stokely Carmichael was prominent among the leaders who used this slogan. During a protest march through Mississippi in 1966, Carmichael spoke to a crowd at Greenwood. He said:

> We've been saying freedom for six years. . . . from now on when they ask what you want, you know what to tell them. Black power! Black power! Black power!

As a slogan and political symbol, "black power" means different things to different people. To many people the slogan means that blacks must acquire more political and economic power to gain more control over their lives. They believe that blacks should own the stores and control the schools in black neighborhoods. They believe that black people should be very active in politics to gain more influence in government. They support black candidates for public office. However, to some people "black power" means the use of threats and violence to gain political and economic objectives. To these people "black power" means black supremacy, black domination of whites. To other people "black power" means that blacks should avoid social contact with whites, that blacks should have control of the government, the economic resources, and all other aspects of social life within their separate communities.

Stokely Carmichael is shown during an address given in the Watts district of Los Angeles in 1966.

112

Some black leaders have believed that the "black power" slogan could harm their crusades for civil rights and equal opportunities. For example, according to *The New York Times* in July, 1966, Roy Wilkins, leader of the NAACP (National Association for the Advancement of Colored People) said:

> No matter how endlessly they try to explain it, the term black power means anti-white power.
>
> . . . It has to mean going it alone. It has to mean separatism. Now separatism . . . offers a disadvantaged minority little except a chance to shrivel and die. . . It is a reverse Mississippi, a reverse Hitler, a reverse Ku Klux Klan. . . We of the NAACP will have none of this. We have fought it too long.

The New York Times also quoted the late Martin Luther King, Jr., former leader of the SCLC (Southern Christian Leadership Conference) as saying:

> It is absolutely necessary for the Negro to gain power, but the term "black power" is unfortunate because it tends to give the impression of black nationalism. . . We must never seek power exclusively for the Negro, but the sharing of power with the white people. Any other course is exchanging one form of tyranny for another. Black supremacy would be equally evil as white supremacy.

Two University of Michigan political scientists, Joel Aberbach and Jack Walker, decided to make a study of the reactions of both blacks and whites to the slogan "black power." They chose to conduct a random-sample survey in Detroit, Michigan.

J. D. Aberbach and J. L. Walker, "The Meanings of Black Power: A Comparison of White and Black Interpretations of a Political Slogan," *The American Political Science Review* (June, 1970), pp. 367–388.

In the summer of 1967, Detroit experienced severe riots in the city's black ghettos. Detroit has a large black population. Many of its black residents are migrants from the rural South who came north seeking employment in the automobile factories and steel mills of that city.

The following tables show some of the conclusions drawn from this survey. *Table 1* shows the general reactions of whites and blacks to the slogan "black power."

Table 1. **Black Power Interpretations, by Race**

Question: What do the words "black power" mean to you?

Reaction	Blacks	Whites
Unfavorable response	49.6%	80.7%
Favorable response	42.2	10.7
Don't know	8.2	8.6
	100%	100%
Number of respondents	461	394

What is the relationship of racial identity to reactions to the "black power" slogan?

The survey also showed that blacks who had favorable reactions to the slogan "black power" tended to interpret black power as an attempt by blacks working together to gain equal rights, to achieve greater political power, or to improve their living conditions. Here are some of the definitions which those who favored black power gave:

"Negroes getting the same opportunities as whites when qualified."

"To me it means an open door into integration."

"We people getting together, agreeing on issues and attempting to reach a common goal.

"Togetherness among Negroes; but it means you can get along with others."

"It means being true to yourself and recognize yourself as a black American who can accomplish good things in life."

Notice that nearly one-half of the blacks gave what Aberbach and Walker considered to be "unfavorable" interpretations of the "black power" slogan. A response was counted as unfavorable if the respondent (a) showed contempt for the term, (b) gave some other sign of disapproval, (c) said that "black power" meant racism or "blacks ruling over whites," or (d) associated the term with trouble, rioting, and disorder.

Tables 2–4 focus attention on the blacks in the Detroit survey who gave *favorable* reactions to the term "black power." Aberbach and Walker called a reaction "favorable" if the respondent interpreted "black power" to mean either (a) black unity or (b) a fair share for black people.

Table 2. **Percentages of Blacks Who Gave Favorable* Reactions to the Term "Black Power"—Classified according to Their Ages and Regions of Birth**

| | REGION OF BIRTH | | |
Present Age	South–Came to Michigan after age 21	South–Came to Michigan before age 21	Born in Michigan
10–19	—	33%	67%
20–29	39%	46	59
30–39	21	44	58
40–49	52	64	55
50–59	35	63	—
60–69	17	33	—

*Interpretating "black power" to mean either black unity or a fair share for blacks.

Table 2 shows how the reactions of blacks to the term "black power" varied according to age and region of birth. The table shows only the percentage in each category who gave a *favorable* reaction to the term "black power." For example, of blacks in their twenties 39 percent of those who were born in the

114

South and arrived in Michigan after age 21 gave a favorable reaction to the term; thus 61 percent of this group presumably gave either an unfavorable or "Don't know" reaction to the term. Of the Southern-born blacks (age 20–29) who came before age 21 to Michigan, 46 percent gave a favorable reaction to the term "black power" while 54 percent presumably reacted unfavorably or "Don't know." Among the Michigan-born blacks (age 20–29), 59 percent gave a favorable reaction to the term—with 41 percent giving an unfavorable or "Don't know" reaction.

What is the relationship of region of birth to favorable reactions to the "black power" slogan?

Table 3 shows differences by church membership among those who reacted favorably to the "black power" slogan. For example, 33 percent of Southern-born black church members gave a favorable reaction to the term "black power," with presumably 67 percent of this group giving an unfavorable or "Don't know" reaction.

Table 3. **Percentages of Black Church Members and Non-Members Favorable to "Black Power" Slogan**

AFFILIATION	PLACE OF BIRTH	
	South	Michigan
Church member	33%	39%
Non-member	48	67

What is the relationship between church membership and favorable reaction to the "black power" slogan?

Aberbach and Walker were interested in adding another variable to their study: level of trust in government. They wanted to see what relationship might exist between trust in government, church membership, place of birth, and reaction to the "black power" slogan. To measure level of trust in government, the investigators asked the blacks in their survey the following questions:

1. How much do you think we can trust the government in Detroit to do what is right: (a) just about always (b) most of the time (c) some of the time (d) almost never?

2. How much do you feel that having elections makes the government in Detroit pay attention to what the people think: (a) a good deal (b) some (c) not very much?

3. How much do you think you can trust the government in Washington to do what is right: (a) just about always (b) most of the time (c) some of the time (d) almost never?

4. Would you say that the government in Washington is pretty much run for the benefit of a few big interests or that it is run for the benefit of all the people?

5. How much do you feel that having elections makes the government in Washington pay attention to what the people think: (a) a good deal (b) some (c) not very much?

Aberbach and Walker could then compare differences in favorable responses to the "black power" slogan between blacks who are high or low in trust in government, between blacks who are church members or non-members, and between blacks who were born in the South or in Michigan. *Table 4* shows their results.

Level of Trust in Government	PLACE OF BIRTH: CHURCH MEMBER:	South		Michigan	
		Yes	No	Yes	No
High		20%	29%	38%	58%
Low		55	66	44	77

Table 4. Percentages of Blacks Giving a Favorable Reaction to the Slogan "Black Power" according to Three Variables

What is the relationship between trust in government, church membership, place of birth, and favorable reaction to the "black power" slogan?

Tables 1–4 suggest differences in socialization among respondents in this study. Using the data presented in these tables, answer the following questions.

1. What are the variables in this study?

2. How are these variables combined? Why are they combined in this way?

3. What explanation, from data in *Tables 2–4*, can be presented for the differences in the responses of blacks shown in *Table 1?*

4. What hypotheses can you make about the relationship of political socialization to differences in responses to the "black power" slogan?

In 1966 in Canton, Mississippi, the leaders of three major civil rights organizations marched arm-in-arm. At left is Martin Luther King, Jr. In the center is Floyd McKissick of CORE, and at the right Stokely Carmichael.

chapter 7

Socioeconomic Status and Political Behavior

Similarities and differences in political behavior can be viewed in terms of status. Status means the position that an individual holds within a group. Status is connected to role (p. 105). A person is expected to behave in certain ways, to play a certain role, because of the position he holds in a group.

We can relate similarities and differences in political behavior to status differences in numerous ways. For example, similarities and differences in the political behavior of females and males, of lawyers and farmers, of leaders and followers can be studied as status differences. This chapter compares political behavior in terms of socioeconomic status differences.

A. What Is Socioeconomic Status?

In all societies some individuals have higher status than other individuals. In all societies individuals who possess more of the things the society values are considered to have a better position, or a higher rank, in the society than those who possess fewer such things.

Socioeconomic status is the label that social scientists apply to a person's rank in our society. Individuals with a high rank are said to have high socioeconomic status. Individuals with a low rank are said to have a low socioeconomic status. The "economic" in this label signifies that an individual's income and material possessions are among the most important standards used to judge a person's social rank. However, wealth alone does not determine rank.

Characteristics Associated with Socioeconomic Status

What are standards, or criteria, used by individuals in our society to rank themselves and others socially? The social characteristics typically identified with social position appear in the chart on the next page.

In American society well-to-do people usually have more prestige, or a higher rank, than poor people. An individual or family with a large income can afford a nice home in a high-prestige neighborhood. High income or wealth also permits the individual to acquire other "badges of success"—one or more expensive cars, the best in household furnishings, perhaps a summer home, and so on. High income also opens the doors to membership in high-prestige social organizations—the Country Club, for example. High educational attainment as represented by a college degree is in itself a "badge of success" and tends to give a person high social rank. But the college education is even more important as a means of entering a high-prestige occupation, such as business executive, physician, lawyer, and the like. And high-prestige occupations *tend*

Social Characteristics Associated with Upper and Lower Status Individuals in the American Society	
UPPER STATUS	LOWER STATUS
High income	Low income
Many material possessions	Few material possessions
High-prestige occupation	Low-prestige occupation
High educational attainment	Low educational attainment
Membership in high-prestige social organizations	Membership in low-prestige social organizations or no organizational affiliation
Residence in high-prestige neighborhood	Residence in low-prestige neighborhood
Many outstanding accomplishments	Few or no outstanding accomplishments

to pay high incomes. In short, many of the socioeconomic status characteristics are interrelated.

Mr. Smith has a higher socioeconomic status than Mr. Brown when judged by the social characteristics listed on the chart. Mr. Smith is a graduate of an outstanding university. He is an important executive in a textile factory. He earns about $45,000 a year, lives in an expensive home, and is a leader in many important civic and social organizations. In contrast, Mr. Brown is a high school graduate. He is a machine operator in the textile factory. He earns $9000 a year, lives in a five-room apartment, and belongs to no high prestige social or civic organizations.

Occasionally a person with little wealth enjoys a high social rank. A few occupations enjoy high prestige but do not provide high incomes—the ministry, for example. Or a person's high social rank may rest chiefly on some outstanding accomplishment which brings him high honors but not very much money. And a wealthy person may fail to obtain high social rank if it is generally known that he got his money through illegal activities.

Open and Closed Societies

Opportunities to earn a higher socioeconomic status vary from society to society. In an *open society* there is much opportunity for individuals with low socioeconomic status to move to a higher socioeconomic position. In a *closed society* there is little or no opportunity for individuals with a low position in the society to rise to a higher position. *Diagram 11* shows the differences between open and closed societies.

118

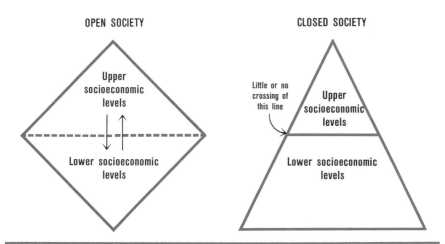

Diagram 11. **Differences between Open and Closed Societies**

OPEN SOCIETY

Upper socioeconomic levels

Lower socioeconomic levels

CLOSED SOCIETY

Little or no crossing of this line

Upper socioeconomic levels

Lower socioeconomic levels

There are no completely open societies and no completely closed societies. Rather different societies can be thought of as more or less open or more or less closed according to the amount of opportunity that lower status people have to improve their positions in the society. The American society and several societies in Europe have tended to be open. Through educational opportunities and job opportunities many individuals have been able to move from lower to higher positions.

Notice the difference in the shapes of the open and closed societies in *Diagram 11*. A diamond shape is used to distinguish the open society and a pyramid shape to distinguish the closed society. The diamond shape shows that in an open society most people occupy positions in the middle of the society. There are fewer people in positions at the very top or very bottom. By contrast, the pyramid shape shows that in a closed society most people occupy positions at the bottom. Very few people occupy positions at the higher levels.

Measuring Socioeconomic Status

To demonstrate what you have learned about socioeconomic status, read these descriptions and complete the exercises that follow.

Mr. Green is president of the First National Bank in Lynnville. He is a graduate of Harvard University. He earns over $100,000 a year. He recently moved into a new home in the city's finest residential area. His $90,000 house has four bathrooms, six bedrooms, and a big yard with a swimming pool. Mr. Green belongs to many organizations in this city. He is a member of the Chamber of Commerce, the school board, and the exclusive Town Club. His four children attend an expensive private boarding school.

Mr. Jackson works as janitor in the First National Bank in Lynnville. He completed the eighth grade before dropping out of school. He earns less than $5000 a year. He pays $60 monthly rent for a three-room apartment in a run-down section of town. He has never been invited to join any of the community's service clubs. He sees the inside of the Town Club only when Mr. Green pays him extra money to do some cleaning there. His three children attend the local public schools.

Mr. Jones is a bookkeeper in the First National Bank in Lynnville. He graduated from high school and completed a two-year correspondence course in accounting. He earns $8500 a year. He owns a small frame home in a neat residential section. His two children attend the public school. He has never been to the Town Club. His only social contacts with Mr. Green are at social affairs related to the First National Bank.

Mr. Thomas is a lawyer. One of his chief clients is the First National Bank in Lynnville. He graduated from the law school at the state university. He has a successful law practice and earns over $20,000 per year. His three children attend the local public schools. Mr. Thomas belongs to several civic and social organizations, but has not yet been invited to join the Town Club.

1. Rank the individuals in the preceding descriptions according to the following position ranking scale.

— ? —	— ? —	— ? —	— ? —
Highest	**Upper Middle**	**Lower Middle**	**Lowest**

2. Which of the following variables did you use to make your rankings of the four individuals?

sex identity	family size
educational attainment	organization membership
occupation	place of residence
income	age group
political trust	sense of political efficacy

3. Explain how you used the variables to rank the four individuals.

B. The Relationship of Socioeconomic Status to Political Behavior

Data from four studies about socioeconomic status and political behavior appear below.

A study of voters in four Wisconsin cities indicated that about one-fourth of the voters were very active in political affairs.* *Table 5* presents data about these very active political participants.

What are the variables in *Table 5*?

What generalizations can you make from the data in *Table 5*?

*Robert R. Alford and Harry M. Scoble, "Sources of Local Political Involvement," *American Political Science Review,* Vol. LXII, No. 4 (December, 1968), pp. 1192–1206.

Table 5.   Socioeconomic Status and Political Involvement

SOCIOECONOMIC CHARACTERISTIC	Percent High in Local Political Involvement
EDUCATION	
Non-graduate of high school	13%
High school graduate	23
Some college	43
OCCUPATION	
Manual	16
Non-manual	37
INCOME	
Lower	16
Higher	32

Table 6.   Socioeconomic Status and Political Activity

SOCIOECONOMIC CHARACTERISTIC	LEVEL OF POLITICAL ACTIVITY			Percent of total sample
	Very Active	Slightly Active	Apathetic	
EDUCATION				
Did not complete high school	9%	16%	29%	**18%**
High school graduate	17	32	50	**33**
College graduate	74	52	22	**48**
INCOME LEVEL				
Lower	40	81	79*	**67**
Higher	60	19	18*	**33**

*Those not answering were excluded from the table.

A study of adults in Oberlin, Ohio, showed that a little more than 20 percent were very active in political affairs. *Table 6* presents data about these very active political participants.*

What are the variables in *Table 6?*

What generalizations can you make from the data in *Table 6?*

*Aaron Wildavsky, *Leadership in a Small Town* (Towata, N.J.: The Bedminster Press, 1964), pp. 16–21.

121

A nationwide survey of adult Americans showed that about 10 percent of the adult population can be called very active political participants. This study revealed the relationships of political activity to socioeconomic status shown in *Table 7*.*

*Julian L. Woodward and Elmo Roper, "Political Activity of American Citizens," *American Political Science Review*, Vol. 44 (December, 1950), p. 135.

Table 7. **Socioeconomic Status and Level of Political Activity**

SOCIOECONOMIC STATUS	Very Active	Fairly Active	Fairly Inactive	Very Inactive
High	36%	33%	23%	8%
Upper middle	24	26	34	16
Lower middle	11	19	38	32
Low	3	9	31	57

What are the variables in *Table 7?*

What generalization can you make from these data?

Answer these questions about *Tables 5–7*.

1. From the data in these tables, what generalizations can you make about the relationship of socioeconomic status to political behavior?

2. What hypotheses can you make to explain the relationship of socio-economic status to political behavior?

C. Portraits of Four Types of Citizens

The following four descriptions illustrate the relationships of socioeconomic status, socialization, personality, and political behavior. As you read these descriptions compare and contrast the political behavior styles of the four men.

A Man with "Clout"

Fred Miller grew up in a comfortable home. His father was a successful lawyer with a high income. His parents belonged to several leading social and civic organizations.

In school Fred was a capable student and a respected athlete. He never doubted that he was an important member of his school and community. He learned that every citizen has both a right and a duty to participate in politics through reading, listening, discussing, forming and expressing opinions, and voting. Seeing his parents participate in political activities helped to convince him of the importance of these duties.

In college Fred was further encouraged by his studies, his teachers, and his friends to succeed in being an important, responsible citizen. He also learned how to deal with people effectively. Fred became confident that goals could be achieved and changes could be made through political participation.

After graduating from college, Fred went into business for himself. Through a combination of wise business deals and a few years of hard work, Fred became owner of a large and profitable restaurant chain. With this business doing well, Fred bought a row of apartment houses in a dilapidated section of his city.

Differences in socio-economic status are reflected in housing—and also in clothing, furniture, recreational interests, and general life style.

Fred's political activity. Fred became a leader in the local organization of the Republican party. Although he has never run for public office, Fred supports certain candidates in every election. He gives money and time, and uses his considerable influence in the community in support of "his" candidates. They are often elected.

In return for substantial support in an election campaign, Fred Miller expects "his" candidates to do favors for him. Because Fred has been successful in getting candidates elected and in getting policies adopted that he favors, he has become known as a man with "clout," or much influence, in the local government.

Fred Miller uses his "clout" to further his business interests and to help his friends. For example, when a bill that would have hurt Fred's restaurant business was proposed in the city council, Fred and several other restaurant owners joined to oppose the bill. They spoke against the bill at meetings of business executives and clubs and in other public speeches. Most importantly, Fred Miller contacted the mayor and three city councilmen and told them that he and his friends would oppose them in the next election if they allowed the bill to pass. The bill was defeated, and Fred Miller's reputation as a "man with clout" was confirmed.

Fred Miller uses customary channels of political influence. He has not participated in protest marches, sit-ins, pickets, or other types of protest demonstrations. Rather, he makes political bargains through direct contact with public officials and community leaders.

123

A new problem arises. Fred had never had any major difficulties until the summer when the people living in his apartment houses began complaining particularly loudly about the condition of the buildings. Fred knew they were in poor condition, but he rarely went to that neighborhood to notice that his apartments had become rat-infested, filthy, and run-down. The plumbing needed fixing, and the walls were cracked and shabby. Many of the dwellings were severe fire hazards. Fred either ignored the complaints or made only minimal efforts to correct extreme problems. As long as Fred could keep the apartments rented, he thought conditions must be generally satisfactory. Besides, Fred believed that his tenants did not take proper care of their apartments and would only damage them again if he made repairs. Moreover, Fred reasoned that he would have to raise the rents if he made improvements. Most of his tenants could not afford a rent increase. Therefore, Fred consoled himself by thinking that the present situation was best for everyone.

In response to many complaints from tenement residents, the city government devised a plan to set stricter construction, sanitation, and maintenance standards for housing in the city. This housing plan was designed to please the tenants in the slum section of the city, where Fred Miller's apartments were located. The mayor seemed anxious to please the voters in the slum section, because they were becoming increasingly militant and critical of the city government. Some slum-area residents had recently formed a large and tightly organized political action group.

Fred mobilizes his political resources. Fred Miller believed the proposed housing plan would cost him much money. So he quickly arranged a meeting of people who owned other apartment houses in the slum neighborhood. Fred opened the meeting with the following remarks: "It seems to me that we should send someone to meet with the mayor and the directors of the sanitation and housing departments. Our representative could explain our position and present all the arguments against this proposed plan. We can probably convince them not to put the plan into operation. But even if the mayor decides to carry it out, perhaps we can get him to water it down, make it less harmful to us."

Mr. Larson spoke up next: "This might work, Fred, but maybe we should also get a petition signed by the landlords and present it to the mayor at the same time. The more people we have on our side, the more convincing we'll be."

"Good idea, Larson," replied Fred, and the others nodded in agreement. "I'll appoint a committee to get the petition ready. We'd better select someone tonight to represent us at a meeting with the mayor, that is, if you all think arranging the meeting is a good idea."

"I think it would help our cause to get some of the people in town on our side," remarked Frank Hays. "Suppose I write a letter supporting our position to the editor of the paper."

"No, I don't think that's a good idea, Frank," Fred replied. "If we do that, we'll arouse more opposition than support. But why not send such a letter to other businessmen who would be likely to agree with us anyway?"

124

"I suppose that makes sense," Frank responded.

The landlords decided that Fred should ask for a meeting with the mayor and represent all of the property owners at this meeting. Fred was less confident than usual. He knew that he faced a difficult challenge. While he could apply pressure to the mayor, his opposition was stronger this time than ever before. He was not sure that he had enough "clout" to win this political battle.

An Apolitical Man

Frank Hays has been a close friend and neighbor to Fred Miller since childhood. Frank and Fred attended elementary school, high school, and college together. During his youth Frank, along with Fred, enjoyed the privileges and opportunities of wealth.

After completing college, Frank Hays went to work in his father's bank. He became president of the bank when his father retired. He also owns much property, including apartment buildings in the slum section of the city.

Unlike his friend Fred Miller, Frank Hays is not very interested in politics. He pays attention to political news in the newspapers and on television, and he usually votes in public elections. However, he does not belong to any political organizations and does not take part actively in election campaigns.

Frank Hays is an *apolitical* man, a person who is not involved in political affairs. Frank Hays prefers to use his time, money, energy, and skills to pursue his business interests and hobbies. Whenever he has a problem involving the city government, he asks Fred to use his "clout" to settle the problem. In the conflict about new housing standards, Frank looks to Fred Miller for leadership.

An Apathetic Citizen

Joe Johnson was born in the hills of eastern Kentucky, where he lived in an overcrowded shack until the age of eight. Then his family moved to the slum section of Fred Miller's city. Since his father made very little money, Joe's family could not afford luxuries and had to do without some necessities. For example, the food was mostly inexpensive starches and not as nourishing as meals which include lean meat, fresh fruits, and vegetables. Sometimes their clothing had patches, or did not fit well, or was not warm enough. There was no money to provide the children with adequate medical or dental care.

Joe received an inferior education. Because of the poverty of the area and the toughness of the neighborhood, it was very hard to get good teachers. The slum-area schools were poorly equipped. Most students did not think education was important, but everyone had to attend school until the age of sixteen. Joe's parents had almost no education, and they gave their children little encouragement to succeed in school.

Joe's parents lacked knowledge and interest in politics, so they never participated. If they mentioned politics at all, their only comment was that it should be left to people who knew more than they did. Joe's parents tended to take things as they came and resisted involvement in any activity which required much effort. For example, a social worker once tried to organize the people in Joe's neighborhood against merchants who appeared to be overcharging their customers. A well-organized and determined group could have forced these businessmen to abandon unfair practices, but it would have taken much time and work. The social worker was unable to find enough people willing to carry out the project.

Seeing no prospects for an exciting career by remaining in school, Joe decided he might as well quit at sixteen and begin working. He soon married and started a family, still earning low wages at whatever job was available. The only place he could afford to live was in a slum area, where the houses were in bad condition. Joe lived in one of Fred Miller's houses.

Joe knew little about politics and cared less. He never voted, skipped news stories in papers and magazines, and almost never discussed public issues. His worries about money made him feel that he had no control over his life. He felt he would always be dependent on outside sources—a boss, a loan company, or an unemployment check to keep his family going. He felt especially inferior when trying to deal with people of higher status than himself. Joe Johnson was an *apathetic* citizen.

Joe's political inadequacies were also typical of many other people in his neighborhood. This became evident one summer when political action was needed. The condition of the buildings in the neighborhood were intolerable, but the tenants could not afford to make repairs. Fred Miller, the landlord, refused to help. Several times during the spring and summer Joe and some of the other tenants had called Fred's office and complained about bad plumbing, crumbling walls, broken windows, and rats. Each time Fred promised to do something but then failed to carry out his promises. The tenants grew more and more discouraged and resentful. Although many of the tenants felt the same as Joe, they had no formal organization and no contacts with influential people. Effective action against the landlords seemed impossible.

A Political Activist

While Joe Johnson and his friends complained among themselves about their housing problem, Larry Mason was busy trying to solve the problem through political action. During the past year Larry Mason, with several other young men, had formed the Community Organization for Underprivileged People (COUP) to help poor people deal more effectively with public officials and businessmen in the community.

Larry Mason, the founder and director of COUP, is an extraordinary young man. He was born and raised in Joe Johnson's neighborhood. His family was poor and large, and Larry had to quit school at age sixteen to help support his younger brothers and sisters.

After two years of working at frustrating, low-paying jobs, Larry became a "runner" for a local gambling syndicate. As a "runner" Larry collected bets for "numbers," "policy," and "bolito" gambling operations.

Through these activities Larry earned a sizable income and became known in the neighborhood as a man with "good connections." Larry sometimes used his new wealth and influence with the gambling syndicate to do favors for his friends. Larry was becoming a neighborhood leader when the police cracked down on the local gambling operation and arrested Larry. He was sentenced to three years in prison.

Larry decides to use his political skills. During his term in prison, Larry passed the time by reading. He read articles about the problems of poor people in America, and biographies of courageous leaders who had worked hard to improve the lives of their followers. Much of what he read caused him to reexamine his old ideas. He decided he had wasted his time trying to get rich by helping the syndicate take money from poor people. "I'm tired," he said, "of living in a town where poor people are always being shoved around by everyone else." He felt that it was time for poor people to start speaking up for themselves, because, as he said, "there isn't anybody else looking out for us anyway."

When Larry left prison, he returned to his former neighborhood. He persuaded five friends to help him form an organization to aid underprivileged people. At first these men continued in their regular jobs as manual laborers and only helped to organize COUP in their spare time. However, Larry's ability to talk to the people of his neighborhood, as well as favorable publicity for some of COUP's initial projects, enabled COUP to grow in size and effectiveness. Larry and his friends eventually left their old jobs to become full-time administrators of the political action organization.

People in the neighborhood depended on COUP to help them apply pressure on public officials to get such services for the neighborhood as better garbage collection, street repair, recreation facilities, and better police protection. COUP encouraged the unemployed to enter work-training programs and sometimes helped them to find jobs. COUP helped poor people to work with welfare department officials and to obtain the assistance of lawyers. Through his leadership of COUP, Larry Mason hopes to convince the people of his

In Somerville, Massachusetts, tenants used a variety of political techniques to persuade the city government to pass a rent-control law.

neighborhood that there is strength in unity and that "clout" can be generated from a tightly-knit and well-led organization.

COUP puts pressure on City Hall. During the past month Larry Mason has been pressuring the city government to do something about the condition of the tenements in his neighborhood. He told the mayor and the councilman from his area that he could guarantee a sizable bloc of votes for them in the next election if they helped now to improve the neighborhood. He threatened to cause trouble for the city government if the housing problems were not solved.

While the city government officials hesitated, trying to decide how to react to the issue about housing standards, Larry Mason and COUP increased their pressure. Picketers parading around City Hall carried signs insisting that the city government accept COUP's demands.

At an open meeting of COUP, Larry Mason urged the people of his neighborhood to remain united. Mason declared:

> We must stand up like men and refuse to cooperate with those who would oppress us. Let the mayor and his cronies see that together we have more power than the landlords. We must convince the mayor that he will lose the next election if he doesn't help us now.

128

Larry's audience cheered as he finished his speech. Joe Johnson was among those attending the meeting. A friend had asked him to come. After listening to Mason's speech, Joe Johnson decided to join COUP. Joe had never heard anyone so much like himself speak so forcefully. "Maybe Mason is right," he said to his friends. "Maybe we can do something about our problems if we stick together and stand up like men against the big-shots in this city."

1. Compare the political behavior of the four men in terms of these concepts: (a) sense of political efficacy, (b) degree of political interest, (c) degree of political activity, (d) amount of political resources, (e) amount of political influence, (f) political techniques, or style of political behavior, (g) main political objectives.

2. Try to explain the similarities and differences in political behavior, identified in answer to the first question, in terms of the following concepts: (a) political socialization, (b) personality, (c) socioeconomic status.

D. Two Cases about Socioeconomic Status and Political Behavior

The following cases describe some of the relationships between socio-economic status and political behavior. Following your reading of these cases, you will have a chance to apply many of the concepts used in this unit to an analysis of these two studies.

The Campout in Charleston

Failure to extend the 1964 Economic Opportunity Act forced the West Virginia Welfare Department to decrease the state's Aid to Families with Dependent Children of the Unemployed (AFDCU). AFDCU provided a minimum income to unemployed men with dependents in return for their labor on public projects at the rate of a dollar an hour. By attending special education classes, it was possible for men to increase the $165 per month allowance to as much as $250 per month. Now with cuts in aid, this total was in jeopardy.

William Mitchell, Billy Ray Flemings, and Clifford Atcheley were all included under the AFDCU program. They agreed that unless special action by the West Virginia legislature was taken, a great hardship would be placed on them and their families. They had been barely able to get along on their income under the previous program. A cut in aid would deprive their families of even the basic necessities. Somehow, they thought, our plight must be brought to the attention of the responsible state officials and the general public.

The three men decided that they could best dramatize their needs and enlist the sympathy of the public by camping out on the lawn in front of the Capitol. They chose a site directly across the street from the governor's mansion. They pitched a tent and set up housekeeping there, declaring that they would remain, fasting and praying, until the legislature took steps to restore their welfare payments. This would require a special legislative session.

This event, unusual in West Virginia, was given wide coverage in the press and on radio and TV. The initial public reaction seemed to be one of bewilderment. A public demonstration such as this by poor people was a new experience for "tradition-bound" West Virginia. As the demonstration continued, commentary in the mass media and public opinion throughout the state appeared to be against both the methods and the goals of the demonstrators.

A counter demonstration begins. Vernon Lyons, a factory worker and taxpayer, was quite upset over the actions of the three AFDCU workers. He declared that he disliked the idea of paying increased taxes to support "those people who could find jobs if they weren't too lazy to work." Lyons decided that he could best counteract the pressure of the welfare recipients on the legislature and the governor by using the same tactics. Therefore, Lyons and his two sons, on "behalf of the taxpayers," also set up a tent on the Capitol grounds with a sign "Taxpayer's Campgrounds, Welcome." Lyons said he would remain at his "workingmen's" camp until the governor assured him that no new taxes would be levied and that the statehouse lawn would not again be desecrated in such a manner.

Over the last fifteen years the effects of unemployment, depression of the coal-mining industry, and other economic problems of Appalachia had increased the number of welfare recipients in West Virginia to record proportions. The state's middle-class taxpayers had developed an increasingly hostile attitude toward those receiving financial aid from the state. The intensity of this hostility became apparent when the activities on the statehouse lawn were publicized. A storm of protest was hurled at all concerned, in the form of letters-to-the-editor of various newspapers and protests to the governor and legislators. But instead of grappling with the question of whether or not cuts in welfare payments should be restored, the public controversy centered primarily on whether citizens have the right to protest decisions of government by camping on the statehouse lawn.

On the third day of the camp-in, the governor released a statement expressing confidence that a special session of the legislature would be convened late in the following month to deal with the problems of public welfare as well as a number of other matters requiring attention. This announcement was encouraging to the welfare campers. William Mitchell said, "I'm willing to go home now. That's what we wanted the governor to do, call a special session. We just wanted him to make an effort for us, and it looks like he's doing it."

Mitchell's colleagues, however, were less optimistic. They noted that the governor had failed to specify a date for calling the special session; they thought his statement was vague. An outdoor worship service and rally at the campsite that evening by supporters of their cause convinced the three welfare campers to remain on the Capitol grounds until the governor's position was clarified. Three days later the campers met with the governor in his office. However, he was unable to give them a firm date for calling a special session of the legislature, and the protestors remained.

The protestors go home. Finally, after eleven days on the Capitol grounds, the poor people broke camp and went home, declaring, "If no action is taken to call a special session, we will be back. We didn't do all we set out to do. But if we hadn't come, the AFDCU program would not be saved." Apparently the men had become discouraged and had decided that their tactics were not proving successful, since the governor had not agreed to their demands.

The "workingmen's" camp remained. Vernon Lyons told a reporter, "I figure on staying until the governor assures me that working people's taxes won't be raised to pay for more welfare, and until he assures me there'll be a law passed against any more camping on the grass like this." Pointing to bare patches in the grass left after the removal of the "poor people's" camp, he said, "Just look what we've done. It's a disgrace—people ruining the Capitol lawn. I hate what I've done, but it's for a good cause."

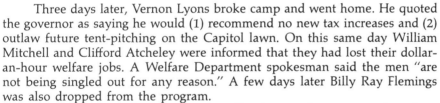

Three days later, Vernon Lyons broke camp and went home. He quoted the governor as saying he would (1) recommend no new tax increases and (2) outlaw future tent-pitching on the Capitol lawn. On this same day William Mitchell and Clifford Atcheley were informed that they had lost their dollar-an-hour welfare jobs. A Welfare Department spokesman said the men "are not being singled out for any reason." A few days later Billy Ray Flemings was also dropped from the program.

On the eighteenth day after the affair began, the governor issued an executive order designed to "protect the beauty and value of the area known as the Capitol Complex." Among other rules and regulations was the following: "No person, persons, groups of persons, nor any organization shall erect tents or any other temporary or permanent shelter or shelters on the Capitol grounds. . . ." A special session of the legislature was not called.

1. What was the issue in this case?

2. What public policy decisions were made in this case?

3. Why were the unemployed "campers" unsuccessful in achieving their objective in this case? Use the concepts of socioeconomic status, socialization, culture, and personality to help you organize answers to this question.

4. Do you approve of the outcome of this case? Explain.

The Montgomery Boycott

On December 1, 1955, Mrs. Rosa Parks, a frail, soft-spoken Negro lady, made a fateful decision in Montgomery, Alabama. She refused to give up her seat on a bus to a white man. Her behavior violated the law in Alabama. For refusing to yield her seat, she was arrested and charged with breaking the law. The arrest of Rosa Parks aroused the anger of Negroes in Montgomery. They vowed to strike at segregation laws, at laws that forced them to take a "back seat" to whites, at laws that made them "second-class citizens." The response of Montgomery Negroes to this arrest had far-reaching effects on Montgomery, on Alabama, and on the United States.

Why did Rosa Parks take a stand against segregation of the races on a Montgomery bus? Mrs. Parks "tells it as it was" on that eventful December 1, 1955.

> I spontaneously made that decision—without any leadership. You can't be told what to do. You have to be motivated—you have to feel that you will not be pushed around.
>
> • • •
>
> For a white person to take the seat I would have had to stand. It was not at all pre-arranged. It just happened that the driver made a demand and I just didn't feel like obeying his demand. . . .
> . . . I had been working all day on the job. I was quite tired after spending a full day working. I handle and work on clothing that white people wear. That didn't come in my mind but this is what I wanted to know; when and how would we ever determine our rights as human beings? The section of the bus where I was sitting was what we called the colored section. . . . And just as soon as enough white passengers got on the bus to take what we consider their seats and then a few over, that meant that we would have to move back for them even though there was no room to move back. It was an imposition as far as I was concerned. . . .
> Just having paid for a seat and riding for only a couple of blocks and then having to stand was too much. These other persons had got on the bus after I did—it meant that I didn't have a right to do anything but get on the bus, give them my fare, and then be pushed wherever they wanted me.*

When Mrs. Parks refused to give up her bus seat to the white man, the bus driver called a policeman who arrested Mrs. Parks. She was first put into jail, then released after she posted $100 bond. Her trial was set for December 5.

The message of Mrs. Parks's arrest spread quickly throughout the Negro community in Montgomery. About forty Negro leaders decided to meet on the evening of December 2 to discuss the Rosa Parks incident. Nearly every Negro organization in Montgomery was represented at this meeting. Every leader reported that Montgomery Negroes were seething with anger over the

Mrs. Rosa Parks

*Joanne Grant, *Black Protest*. (Greenwich, Connecticut: Fawcett Publications, Inc., 1968), pp. 277–278. Reprinted by permission of Highlander Center, Knoxville, Tennessee.

132

affair. After years of suffering indignities, abuse, and injustice on the buses of Montgomery, the blacks had had enough. Their leaders voted to organize a bus boycott at the December 2 meeting. Leaflets were printed to spread word of the boycott. They declared:

> Don't ride the bus to work, to town, to school, or any place Monday, December 5.
>
> ———————
>
> Another Negro woman has been arrested and put in jail because she refused to give up her bus seat.
>
> ———————
>
> Don't ride the buses to work, to town, to school, or anywhere on Monday. If you work, take a cab, or share a ride, or walk.
>
> ———————
>
> Come to a mass meeting, Monday at 7:00 P.M. at the Holt Street Baptist Church for further instruction.*

*Stride Toward Freedom by Martin Luther King, Jr., p. 48 (hardbound edition). Copyright 1958 by Martin Luther King, Jr. Reprinted by permission of Harper & Row, Publishers.

The call for a bus boycott received an overwhelmingly positive response from the black people of Montgomery.

Why did the Montgomery Negroes respond favorably to the bus boycott idea? Any attempt to answer this question must begin with a description of race relations and the living conditions of Negroes in Montgomery, Alabama, in the 1950's.

Background of Negro unrest. The segregation system dominated relations between blacks and whites in Montgomery. It was against the law for a white man and a black man to ride in a taxi together. They could not sit together in the buses. Rather, the front portions of the bus were reserved for whites and the back of the bus was set aside for Negroes. Blacks were to give up their seats to incoming white passengers if necessary. Blacks and whites attended separate schools and separate churches. They used separate recreational facilities; there were "white" cemeteries and "black" cemetaries, "white" parks and "black" parks. This was the law.

Politically Montgomery's blacks were nearly powerless. In 1954 there were only about 2000 Negroes registered to vote, out of about 30,000 Negroes of voting age in Montgomery County. Not one Negro held public office in the city or county of Montgomery, although blacks comprised over one-third of the population of this area. Less than 10 percent of Negroes of voting age were registered to vote in the state of Alabama at this time. Legal barriers and social and economic pressures had been erected by the white leaders of Alabama to keep Negro voting limited.

Most blacks in Montgomery were deprived economically. For example, in 1950 the medium income for whites in this city was $1730 per year, as compared with $970 per year for blacks. Only 31 percent of the black families in Montgomery had flush toilets in their homes in contrast to 94 percent of the white families.

In addition to their low economic and political status, Negroes were subject to verbal and physical abuse. On the streets and in buses, black men and women frequently were called "niggers," "black apes," and "black cows." Negroes who talked back to whites were physically assaulted to "put them in their place."

Following her arrest, Mrs. Parks was fingerprinted at police headquarters.

Black anger turns into action. Such were the conditions of life for Negroes in Montgomery prior to December 1, 1955. When the Rosa Parks incident occurred, the anger of Montgomery's black people boiled over. They were ready and willing to strike out in some way against the white-dominated social system under which they had suffered for so long. The organization of the bus boycott gave them a long-awaited opportunity to do something to lash out against the segregation system. Denied political influence through the usual channels—mass voting and political office holding—they had no ready or easy access to those who held political power. Blacks had only one avenue open to make effective demands on the political system —orderly public protest.

On December 5, Mrs. Parks was tried for breaking the city segregation laws. The judge found her guilty and fined her $10 and court costs. Mrs. Parks appealed the decision to the Alabama Court of Appeals.

While Rosa Parks stood trial, the black people of Montgomery were conducting a nearly total boycott of the buses. Their objective was to show the white people of Montgomery, and the white-owned and -managed bus company, that they were tired of being treated unfairly.

At 7:00 P.M. on December 5, people gathered at the Holt Street Baptist Church for the mass meeting that had been advertised in the boycott leaflets distributed earlier. They realized that if the boycott were to succeed, organization and cooperation were necessary. They voted to organize the Montgomery Improvement Association (MIA) and elected a young minister, the Reverend Martin Luther King, Jr., to be its chairman.

King expressed his feelings about the MIA in his speech at the mass meeting:

We are here this evening to say to those who have mistreated us so long that we are tired—tired of being segregated and humiliated; tired of being kicked about by the brutal feet of oppression. We have no alternative but to protest. For many years we have shown amazing patience. We have sometimes given our white brothers the feeling that we liked the way we were being treated. But we come here tonight to be saved from that patience that makes us patient with anything less than freedom and justice. . . .

One of the great glories of democracy is the right to protest for right. . . .
We will be guided by the highest principles of law and order. . . .
Our method will be that of persuasion, not coercion.

134

MIA defines its goals. At the conclusion of King's speech, the newly created MIA adopted three resolutions that became the objectives of the bus boycott. The resolutions declared that Negroes would not ride the buses again until:

1. Courteous treatment by the bus operators was guaranteed.
2. Passengers were seated on a first-come, first-served basis—Negroes seating from the back of the bus toward the front while whites seated from the front toward the back.
3. Negro bus operators were employed on predominantly Negro routes.

Martin Luther King realized quickly that the key to the success of the MIA and its bus boycott was efficient organization. Thus King organized several committees to deal with such problems as finance, transportation, and strategy. He persuaded the most able black leaders in Montgomery to work on these committees.

Finding temporary transportation. King's most pressing problem was transportation to and from work for the thousands of blacks who formerly rode the buses to work. At first, Negro-owned taxi companies had volunteered to transport boycotters for the same ten-cent fare that they paid on the buses. But the Montgomery Police Commissioner said that this was against the law and stopped the taxis from offering cut-rate service.

The MIA reacted by organizing volunteer car pools. Over three hundred people offered their cars and their services to transport bus boycotters to and from work free. Transportation schedules were organized, printed, and distributed. "Dispatch" and "pick-up" stations were set up around the city. After a short time the car-pool system was running efficiently. Even so, many people by choice or necessity walked to work or to town in order to show publicly their defiance of the segregated bus system.

At first the bus company and the white political leaders of Montgomery refused to take the bus boycott or the MIA seriously. They believed that after a few days the boycotters would be tired of doing without bus service and the boycott would collapse. They did not believe that the Negroes were capable of organizing a successful voluntary transport system or of maintaining the spirit of cooperation and sacrifice needed to make the boycott work.

However, the white political leaders quickly gave up these ideas as the boycott continued day after day. And, day after day, the bus company lost money. Since 75 percent of its patrons had been Negroes, the boycott was hitting the bus company owners where it hurt most—in the pocketbook.

Negotiations requested. Finally the bus company officials asked city political leaders to help negotiate a settlement with the MIA. Through orderly, well-organized public protest, the Negroes of Montgomery—formerly without political power—were brought into direct contact with the leading political figures of the city.

As spokesman for the MIA, Martin Luther King presented the three demands (p. 135) of the boycotters. After lengthy discussion only one of the demands, courteous treatment of Negro bus passengers, was accepted by the bus company. But they declared that an end to traditional seating arrangements was against the law. The city political leaders had no intention of changing that law. Furthermore, the bus company officials said that they would not hire any Negro bus drivers. The MIA leaders were not satisfied with the reaction of the bus company officials to their demands. The meeting broke up without settling the conflict. The boycott continued.

Another meeting between white city leaders, MIA leaders, and bus company officials was called for December 17 in the mayor's office. Again the meeting ended without a settlement. It appeared that there was no easy way to negotiate the conflict. Montgomery's political leaders and bus company officials realized that an end to segregation on the buses could lead eventually to an end to segregation of other activities and services. They had been socialized to accept segregation as natural and just. This long-standing tradition of the South would not be given up easily. However, Montgomery's blacks were equally determined to undermine the system of segregation which had handicapped them for so long. Without access to the usual channels of political action, they continued to use orderly public protest, the only legal political technique open to them. They continued their bus boycott, and they learned that group solidarity brought political power. As isolated individuals they had been weak; but through union, they found strength. Through efficient organization they were able to wield political power.

Whites adopt a "get tough" policy. With the breakdown of negotiations, the opponents of the MIA turned to other tactics to end the boycott. The city political leaders launched a "get tough" policy against the boycotters. The mayor delivered a speech on television denouncing the MIA and its leaders. City policemen began to harass the Negro drivers in the voluntary car pool. Blacks waiting to be picked up by vehicles in the car pool were arrested as

Martin Luther King was charged with violating the state's anti-boycott law. He is seen at the right greeting some friends as he arrived at Montgomery County Court House for the second day of his trial.

"hitchhikers." Police stopped and questioned black drivers about their driver's licenses and automobile registrations. Drivers in the car pool were accused of traffic violations and arrested. Finally, Martin Luther King was arrested while participating in a car pool. He was accused of driving 30 miles an hour in a 25-mile-per-hour zone. Throughout these difficulties the MIA leaders kept emphasizing: "stick together," "cooperate," "don't let them scare us or divide us."

The Montgomery blacks did "stick together." The "get tough" policy failed. The boycott continued into its fortieth day. Many white people, staunch believers in the segregated way of life, became desperately angry about the continued success of the boycott. By the end of January, 1956, obscene phone calls and threatening unsigned letters began to pile up in the offices of the MIA. On January 30, King's home was bombed. Two nights later a stick of dynamite was thrown onto the lawn of another MIA leader. But the violence and threats did not shake the determination of the Negro people. The boycott continued.

Legal maneuvering was directed against the MIA to stop the boycott. A Montgomery lawyer called the attention of the city political leaders to an old state law against boycotts. The law stated that when two or more persons cooperate to prevent the operation of a business, without just cause, they shall be guilty of a crime. On February 13, the Montgomery County Grand Jury was called into session to decide whether the boycotters were breaking this law. The jury, composed of seventeen whites and one Negro, decided that the boycott was illegal and that boycott leaders could be arrested. After this decision, over one hundred Negro leaders, including Martin Luther King, were arrested and thrown into jail. The white political leaders were certain that these arrests would end the boycott. But the Negroes only became more determined. They remained united, and the boycott continued.

Martin Luther King was fined $500 and court costs, or 386 days at hard labor in the county jail. Rather than sentencing the other defendants, the judge entered a continuance until the case of King, who had appealed this decision, would be decided.

Negroes file a civil rights suit. Negro leaders fought back, also, by filing a suit in the United States district court. This suit asked the court to prevent the city commissioners of Montgomery from violating the civil rights of Negro motorists and pedestrians. On June 4, 1956, the Federal court declared that the bus segregation laws of Alabama were unconstitutional. The Negroes were jubilant, but victory was not yet complete. The city commissioners appealed the Federal court decision to the United States Supreme Court. On November 13, 1956, the victory of the MIA was complete; the United States Supreme Court upheld the decision of the Federal district court. The Supreme Court agreed that the bus segregation laws contradicted the Constitution of the United States and were, henceforth, null and void.

The bus boycott, which had continued for over one year, ended on December 20 when the bus integration order reached Montgomery. The objectives of the boycott had been achieved. Certainly the nationwide attention drawn to the anti-segregation cause of the MIA by its boycott had been instrumental in achieving the goal of ending segregation on buses in Montgomery. The activities of the MIA had become front-page news around the nation. Much sympathy had been generated for the cause of the bus boycotters.

But problems over bus transportation were not yet ended for the Negro community of Montgomery. In January the homes of several Montgomery Negroes were bombed. Four Negro churches were bombed, causing over $70,000 worth of damage. White "toughs" beat a few black men and women who rode the desegregated buses. However, influential white leaders in Montgomery denounced the violence against blacks. After a short time these violent efforts to prevent the integration of bus transportation ended.

Recently, Rosa Parks, then living in Detroit, received another in a long series of awards honoring her part in the ending of bus segregation laws. Her behavior on December 1, 1955, which appears so extraordinary to many people, does not seem startling to Rosa Parks. "It's always amazing to me that people thought it was. It seems to me it's natural to want to be treated as a human being," she said.

1. What was the main issue in this case?

2. What public policy decisions were made in this case?

3. Why did the following groups react as they did to the conflict in this case? Use the concepts of socioeconomic status, socialization, culture, and personality to help you organize answers to this question.

    a. the city commissioners of Montgomery
    b. the bus company officials
    c. white people who were hostile to the MIA
    d. the leaders of the MIA
    e. black people who supported the MIA
    f. the judges of the Federal district court and the United States Supreme Court

4. Why was the MIA successful in achieving its objectives in this case?

5. What is your evaluation of the political behavior of the opposing groups in this case? Explain.

chapter 8

Political Alienation and Loyalty

Individuals can be compared and contrasted in terms of political alienation and loyalty. What are political alienation and loyalty? How do individuals become committed to or alienated from their country and government? What are some consequences of political alienation and loyalty?

A. What Is Political Loyalty?

Loyalty is faithfulness or allegiance to a person, group, or set of ideas. Main objects of political loyalty among most people are their nation, its fundamental ideals, and its system of government. Lesser objects of political loyalty are political parties and political pressure groups.

Each of the following statements provides some clues about the speaker's political loyalty to the nation. Decide which speaker of each pair (1a or 1b, etc.) is the "more loyal" and which is the "less loyal." Be prepared to defend your choices.

Speaker 1a: Perhaps the greatest privilege ever offered an American is the opportunity to give his life for his country. The quiet courage that enables a man to make this noble sacrifice entitles him to join the ranks of those heroes who have made America great.

Speaker 1b. I love my country, but I will not kill for it. God's commandment is clear: "Thou shalt not kill." I can kill no man, whatever the risks, however noble the cause, for my first obligation is to obey God. By living a moral life, in agreement with God's will, I can best serve my country.

Speaker 2a: A good American supports his President. Once a President is elected, he is the leader and should be followed. To oppose him is wrong.

Speaker 2b: The President's policies are bad for our country. They violate our national ideals. If his policies are not changed, our nation will be ruined. All good Americans should join to resist the President's policies.

Speaker 3a: Every American should support the law. To those who criticize our nation, I say: "Love it or leave it."

Speaker 3b: Every good citizen must be willing to protest unjust laws or acts of public officials. If a law is unfair or immoral, then the citizen who truly loves his country must strive to change that law. Public demonstrations and passive resistance may be necessary to overthrow evil policies or laws and to achieve justice.

Types of Loyalty

From the preceding lesson it should be clear that it is very difficult to decide who is loyal, who is disloyal, and who is most loyal. It would be difficult to find a person who lacks loyalty. When a person is accused of *disloyalty*, it generally does not mean that he has no loyalty but rather that his loyalties are different from those of the accuser. Let us look first at some different types of loyalties.

Loyalty to other people. One type of loyalty is the feeling of attachment people have for their family and friends. For example, in American society, families and relatives are expected to come to one another's aid in times of trouble. We expect people to defend their families and friends against unfair accusations. A young person who told lies about a friend would in a sense be considered "disloyal" to his friendship.

Loyalty to groups. Many of the groups to which we belong command our loyalty. Students loyal to their school cheer for their own team, not for the opponents. School clubs, church groups, civic organizations, perhaps the company we work for, and political parties are other groups which share our loyalty. A person maintains his loyalty to these groups either because their goals and beliefs are similar to his own or because of his attachment and interest in others who belong to these organizations.

Loyalty to beliefs and ideas. Another type of loyalty is the strong belief in certain attitudes or ideas. During periods of religious persecution, Christians and Jews have been willing to die for their beliefs rather than to renounce, or be "disloyal" to, them. Some people are fiercely loyal to the idea of private enterprise. Others are similarly attached to the idea of socialism.

National loyalty. Most people in the world have a sense of national loyalty. This feeling of attachment to the nation is acquired early in the socialization process. Reciting the pledge of allegiance and singing the national anthem are ways that children learn national loyalty. Observing national holidays and reading stories about national heroes are two other ways in which national loyalty is fostered. Participation in youth organizations (Scouts, 4-H Clubs, and the like) and school club activities helps young people acquire the political culture. Such participation helps to produce allegiance to the nation.

As a result of political socialization, Americans tend to identify with their nation. They say "we" defeated the Germans in World War II, although they may have been too young to fight; and they say "we" are in Vietnam. Either "we" must win there or "we" must leave, depending upon the individual's point of view. This sense of identification can provide enormous satisfaction for the individual citizen. It allows us to feel that we have participated in the acts of American heroes, such as "our" landing on the moon. (Would you have been as excited if the Russians had landed first?) Feelings of patriotism can also blind us to improper actions committed by our own countrymen, actions we would condemn if committed by other nations.

Even though most Americans have a sense of national loyalty, we can be sure that it does not mean the same thing to everyone. In fact, "national loyalty" seems to be a general term for all of an individual's group loyalties. Therefore, when a man joins the army to defend his nation, he is defending people and associations that are most important to him. These friends and associations may not be identical to those being defended by the man who is fighting by his side. Thus, one man may fight because he believes that the United States is a nation where one is free to be Jewish, another to be Roman Catholic, another to be Protestant, and still another not to attend church at all. In each case the "nation" stands for their beliefs; thus the nation's survival is important to the survival of the groups with which they identify.

People are loyal to the nation as a result of the satisfactions they get from many group identifications and because people believe that the nation supports these groups. For example, a Democrat and a Republican will disagree on certain domestic policies. Nevertheless, Democrats and Republicans can be equally loyal to the nation so long as it continues to be a place in which the beliefs of each are protected or seem to be protected.

Conflicting loyalties. Any individual is able at the same time to be loyal to a variety of groups, including family, friends, club, employer, church, and government. Often these loyalties overlap and support each other. Sally Thompson is a member of a Girl Scout troop sponsored by her church. These two groups lend support to one another. Moreover, both teach national loyalty, as do Sally's family and her school.

In other cases a person's loyalties may conflict. Jane Atwood lives on the same block as Sally and attends the same school. As youngsters they played together a great deal, but are now just casual friends. Jane and her family are members of a religious sect which believes that the flag-salute ceremony is contrary to the teaching of the Bible. Jane's family and church provide her with one view of the meaning of national loyalty, while her school and community give her a different meaning of the concept.

Some societies try to suppress any expression of loyalty which differs from that of the leaders of the government. The family, church, school, labor organizations, communications media, and other groups and organizations are expected to support the goals and policies of the governmental leaders. Dissent and criticism are branded as disloyalty. A free society, on the other hand, can put up with quite a large number of different points of view. It makes some provision for people who, for example, have conscientious objections to fighting in a war or saluting the flag.

Occasionally, conflicting loyalties force a person to make fundamental choices between groups and beliefs. A young man, for example, may have been taught that it is honorable to serve one's country in the armed services; but he has come to believe that his country today is engaged in an immoral war. He feels that service in the army would be an act of disloyalty to his new beliefs. If he chooses to be loyal to his new beliefs, he may cut himself off from his family and former associates. He experiences a sense of *alienation*.

B. What Is Political Alienation?

A person's loyalty to one group may exclude him from another group. For example, a person who joins a hippie clan may be expressing his feeling of isolation from other groups with whom he once associated. He probably has feelings of *alienation.*

An *alien* is a foreigner living outside his own country. We say that a person is alienated when he feels like a stranger even in familiar surroundings. An alienated person rejects, or feels rejected by, social groups with which he once had close attachments—family, friends, school, church, and the like.

A politically alienated person is one who rejects, or feels rejected by, his society and its political system. He has serious gripes about his government and does not think that his complaints can be corrected through the traditional machinery of government. The politically alienated person has lost faith in his government and the laws, customs, and beliefs which support it.

Some politically alienated individuals become *political activists* who seek to overthrow the existing political system. These radical political activists tend to have a high sense of power and personal efficacy. An alienated political activist may be willing to engage in conspiracy or violence to bring about the changes he seeks.

Other politically alienated individuals are *political apathetics* who seek to withdraw from the political system. These political dropouts tend to have a low sense of power and personal efficacy. They avoid activities that would show support for the established political system. However, they are not interested in revolutionary political activity.

(1) Decide which of the following speakers are alienated from the political system or culture of the United States. (2) Then group the alienated speakers into two categories: (a) the alienated activist and (b) the alienated apathetic. Be prepared to defend your choices.

Speaker 1: Someone told me that the city government wants to add fluoride to our water. I think it has something to do with teeth. I don't know much about it. They will probably do what is best, and I will accept their decision.

A commune is a small social unit of families and individuals who share possessions and work duties.

Speaker 2: My friends and I are tired of this phoney society and the phoney politicians who run it. We're organizing our own commune on some wilderness land that my uncle left to me in his will. Living in this commune will give us a chance to be free from the corruption and insincerity of the straight world. Why don't you join us?

Speaker 3: I don't really care who gets elected to public office. I'm satisfied with my life. Whatever happens, it's not likely to affect me very much. I'll still have my job, my family, and my home.

Speaker 4: The whole society is sick. It has to be torn apart and rebuilt. Burn, baby, burn—that's the only political slogan that's worth anything.

Speaker 5:   Some of my friends have tried to get me involved in politics, but I have resisted. I enjoy the Boy Scout group I work with. I like to work with the boys and think I am making a contribution to our society in that way. Boy Scouts and my family take up just about all my free time.

Speaker 6:   The government and the political big-shots in this country have always cheated people like me. But what can we do about it? We have to sit back and take their abuse. There's no sense in trying to overthrow the government, but don't expect me to cooperate with the public officials or obey the law if I can get away with it.

Speaker 7:   Most public officials in this country are socialist traitors who have forgotten the true American heritage. No peaceful efforts can make these public officials change their ways. Therefore, I have started an underground organization of true patriots who will save this country from socialism. If necessary, we will violently overthrow the government in order to preserve the true American way of life.

Speaker 8:   My friends and I have been working hard to elect Jones as governor of our state. We believe that he is a very able man who will begin to solve the serious problems of air pollution, traffic congestion, and unemployment that afflict our state. It appears that he has a good chance to win this election.

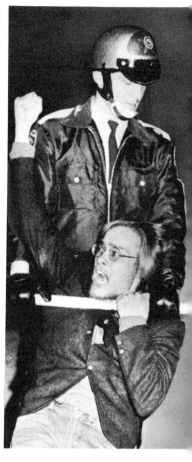

C. Profiles of Politically Alienated Americans

Some political alienation presumably exists in every society. Societies with a high degree of political alienation may be verging on revolution or disintegration. Societies with a low degree of political alienation tend to be stable and to accomplish changes in an orderly and gradual fashion.

A Profile of Alienated Youth

Recently many Americans have been concerned about a seeming increase in public protest and alienation among young people. In 1969, the polling organization of Daniel Yankelovich, Inc., was hired by CBS News to make a study of political alienation and activism among American youth.* A questionnaire designed to reveal political attitudes and beliefs was administered to a national sample of young Americans, ages 17–23. This study indicated that no more than 1 percent of American youth could be classified as "revolutionaries." To be labeled a revolutionary, a respondent had to support these beliefs:

1. The American system is not flexible enough and radical change is needed.
2. The social system is too rotten for repair.

*Daniel Yankelovich, *Generations Apart* (Columbia Broadcasting System, 1967).

143

3. A mass revolutionary political party should be created.

4. Destruction or mutilation of property is acceptable in order to achieve worthwhile goals.

5. Assaulting police is acceptable in order to achieve worthwhile goals.

6. Holding an important public official or national leader captive is acceptable in order to achieve worthwhile goals.

According to the Yankelovich study, an additional 10 percent of American youth could be classified as "radical dissidents." These individuals wanted sweeping changes in American life and sympathized with revolutionary activities and techniques. However, they had less extreme beliefs than the "revolutionaries."

While the "revolutionaries" were obviously politically alienated, many of the "radical dissidents" merely verged on political alienation. The remaining 89 percent of the respondents in the Yankelovich study were classified as "moderate reformers" (23 percent), "middle of the road" (48 percent), and "conservative" (19 percent). These respondents were obviously not politically alienated.

Table 8 reveals the characteristics of the "revolutionary" and the "radical dissident" that emerged from the Yankelovich study. In studying the table, notice that the column 1 figures refer to all the youth in the national sample. The figures in column 2 apply to the 1 percent of the sample classified as "revolutionary." The figures in column 3 apply to the 10 percent of the sample classified as "radical dissident."

On the basis of information in *Table 8*, what inferences can you make about the main characteristics of the "revolutionary"?

On the basis of information in *Table 8*, what inferences can you make about the main characteristics of the "radical dissident" youth in America?

Table 8. **Characteristics of the "Revolutionary" and the "Radical Dissident"**

CHARACTERISTICS	Total Youth	Total Revolutionary Youth	Total Radical Dissident Youth
Sex			
Male	45%	71%	44%
Female	55	29	56
Age			
17 years old	18	2	18
18–19 years old	35	29	33
20–21 years old	25	49	34
22–23 years old	23	20	15
Race			
White	91	81	74
Nonwhite	9	19	26
Parents' Income			
Under $10,000	49	36	55
$10,000–$14,999	29	20	24
$15,000 or more	22	44	21
Father's Occupation			
White Collar	41	58	46
Blue Collar	46	31	27
Other	13	11	27
Religion			
Protestant	58	7	50
Catholic	27	7	25
Jewish	5	12	8
Other	2	14	5
None	8	61	12
Education			
College	20	81	20
Non-College	80	19	80

A Profile of the Black Rioter

During the 1960's numerous civil disorders occurred in the black neighborhoods of major American cities. These riots were expressions of severe alienation. However, only a minority of urban blacks participated in or supported these riots. A study of the political attitudes of black Americans indicates that "most Negroes . . . though they speak in terms that would seem to justify the riots, reject violence both as a general strategy and as an approach they would be willing to take part in themselves."* Only 8 percent of a sample of blacks from fifteen major cities said that they would join in a riot, and only an additional 15 percent of this sample said that they would "be ready to use violence" to try to gain their rights.

What are the characteristics of the black people who are so alienated that they are ready to resort to violence? The National Advisory Commission on Civil Disorders drew the following profile of the black rioter, based on information gathered from eyewitness accounts, sample surveys in Detroit and Newark, and arrest records of rioters in twenty-two cities.

*Supplemental Studies for the National Advisory Commission (Washington: Government Printing Office, 1968), p. 51.

The typical rioter in the summer of 1967 was a Negro, unmarried male between the ages of 15 and 23. . . . He was . . . a lifelong resident of the city in which the riot took place. Economically his position was about the same as his Negro neighbors who did not actively participate in the riot.

Although he had not, usually, graduated from high school, he was somewhat better educated than the average inner-city Negro, having at least attended high school for a time.

Nevertheless, he was more likely to be working in a menial or low status job as an unskilled laborer. If he was employed, he was not working full time and his employment was frequently interrupted by periods of unemployment.

He feels strongly that he deserves a better job and that he is barred from achieving it, not because of lack of training, ability, or ambition, but because of discrimination by employers.

. . . He takes great pride in his race and believes that in some respects Negroes are superior to whites. He is extremely hostile to whites, but his hostility is more apt to be a product of social and economic class than of race; he is almost equally hostile toward middle-class Negroes.

He is substantially better informed about politics than Negroes who were not involved in the riots. He is more likely to be actively engaged in civil rights efforts, but is extremely distrustful of the political system and of political leaders.

Report of the National Advisory Commission on Civil Disorders (Washington: Government Printing Office, 1968), pp. 73–77.

1. What are similarities and differences in the characteristics of the black rioter and the "revolutionary" or "radical dissident" youth?

2. What speculations can you offer about why some Americans become politically alienated?

D. Sources of Political Alienation

Why are most people loyal to a nation or political system? Why does political alienation develop among others? These questions are difficult to answer precisely, since different people may have many different reasons for expressing political loyalty or alienation. However, in every case the social groups such as family, friends, and work groups to which an individual belongs play a large part in shaping his attitudes towards his country.

Through the groups to which they belong, most Americans learn to be loyal to their nation, government, and political culture. They are socialized to believe that commitment to national goals and to the national welfare is good, as we saw on page 101.

The political socialization process produces many Americans who remain loyal and committed to the political system. Yet some Americans become alienated. Other Americans shift back and forth between expressions of political loyalty and alienation. The following four cases provide some clues about sources of political alienation in the United States.

Case 1. The Bomb Makers

Mary B. was raised in a white, Protestant, middle-class home in a small midwestern town. Her father, an insurance salesman, earns about $25,000 per year. Mary is an only child.

Mary was popular in high school, earned academic honors, and attended a small eastern women's college. After graduation Mary and one of her friends traveled throughout Europe for nearly six months, listening and talking to many different kinds of people.

Uncertain of what career she might begin, Mary decided to attend graduate school at a nearby state university. There Mary made new friends who took part in community action programs designed to help poor people. These students tutored disadvantaged children to help them improve their reading and writing skills. They helped unemployed adults find jobs. They tried to instruct poor people in political protest tactics, to help them organize rent strikes in slum housing, and to provide legal assistance to poor people who could not afford lawyers.

As Mary became involved in these activities, her political attitudes began to change. She realized that she had led a sheltered life and had been unaware of the suffering and problems of poor people. She became increasingly disgusted with people who seemed to be ignoring the problems of the disadvantaged.

At a graduate student party she met Jim, a student much different from other men she had known in her home town. Jim had been involved in many political protest activities and was currently a leader of a radical political organization. Soon they were dating regularly. Mary wrote to her parents about Jim and his ideas and was hurt when they disapproved. Mary also began to see less and less of her former friends, and she found excuses to avoid going home to visit her parents because she disliked arguing with them about her new friends and her new ideas.

146

Gradually, as a result of her new friendships and new attitudes, Mary began to feel like an outsider. Because she and Jim dressed differently than many of the students on campus, they were often treated rudely by people who disapproved of their appearance. Since many of Jim's and Mary's friends were active in radical student groups, soon Mary began joining them in protest marches to dramatize their opposition to American foreign policy and to the treatment of poor people in American society.

After participating in many protest marches, sit-in demonstrations, and political rallies, Mary and her friends became very disillusioned with their seemingly ineffective efforts to change the political system through peaceful protest. They started to discuss the use of violence as a means to influence political change. These discussions led to the conversion of a basement apartment into an underground bomb factory, where Mary and her friends began to make homemade firebombs to use in future acts of political violence.

Today Mary is an angry, frustrated young woman. She is happiest when she is with Jim, but she sees the United States as a hostile, unfriendly place for herself and her friends.

Case 2. The Underground Soldier

John M. is a dentist in a West Coast city and a veteran of the Korean War. Until recently he was a law-abiding citizen.

A few months ago John was discussing politics with one of his patients. They agreed that something should be done to stop the peace marchers. In John's view the peace marchers were merely prolonging the war in Vietnam and giving aid and comfort to the enemy. His patient suggested that John attend a meeting with him where a few others who had the same point of view would discuss what could be done to save the country from the "peaceniks."

John attended the meeting and made some new friends. He also learned some new ways of thinking about the United States. The speakers and the organization's pamphlets said that peace activities were part of a Communist conspiracy. The pamphlets asserted that the colleges and universities were run by Communists. He was told that even the Federal government was controlled by Communists. The effort to pass firearms legislation in Congress was nothing more than a plot to disarm patriots like himself, thereby letting the Communists take over easily. He was told that civil rights legislation was designed by Communists to weaken the United States.

At first John doubted much of what he was told. But gradually it all began to make sense. He now distrusts most government officials, believing they are either working for the Communists or are subtly influenced by Communist ideas. As a result he has joined an organization of "underground soldiers" who are committed to saving the "true" American heritage. They take part in a number of illegal activities in order to fight for their version of "truth and justice." John and his friends managed to smuggle some guns from Mexico so that the weapons would not be registered and traced to them. They are stockpiling the weapons to be ready to defend their homes against any attempted Communist takeover. These "underground soldiers" participate in secret military training activities. They send threatening letters and make threatening phone calls to public officials who favor policies that John and his friends believe are sponsored by the Communists.

John has become alienated from the "mainstream" of American life, which he believes is drifting toward communism. He has become alienated from his government, which he believes is led by Communists and Communist sympathizers. He is fearful that the nation may collapse; he is also frightened that his illegal activities will be discovered and he will be arrested. Nevertheless, he believes that if he and his friends stand firm, they can root out the traitors and save the nation.

Case 3. The Betrayed

This case is based on an account found in Morton Grodzins, *The Loyal and the Disloyal* (New York: World Publishing Company, 1956), pp. 106–131.

During World War II more than six thousand Americans formally declared that they were disloyal to the United States. These were Americans of Japanese ancestry. Why did they renounce their loyalty to the United States?

For nearly a century Japanese had migrated to the United States, where they settled primarily on the West Coast, especially in California. The Japanese were not always welcome. Particularly in California they met discrimination in obtaining housing, purchasing land, and finding employment. Nevertheless, by 1941, second-generation Japanese-Americans were beginning to be accepted. They had good reason to think that in the future Japanese-Americans would have the same opportunities as other Americans.

December 7, 1941, dramatically changed the lives of American citizens of Japanese ancestry. On that day Japanese airplanes bombed Pearl Harbor, and the old hostilities against people of Japanese ancestry reappeared. Many Americans feared that the Japanese-Americans were a dangerous threat to the nation's security, more loyal to Japan than to the United States. Therefore, it became official national policy in 1942 to evacuate to detention camps all Japanese aliens and American citizens of Japanese ancestry living in Washington, Oregon, California, and Arizona. Even those with as little as one-sixteenth Japanese ancestry and who were even unaware of their Japanese background were forced to relocate. These people had to give up jobs, homes, and possessions to move to one of ten evacuation centers. Most of the camps were in the arid regions of the western states.

Scenes at the relocation camps in 1942 are shown below and on the next page —along with a notice of the evacuation orders.

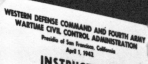

The suddenness of the move caused the evacuees severe financial hardship. They were given little chance to sell their belongings; and when they could sell their possessions, it was at a price far below real value. The relocation camps were equipped with barracks, barbed wire, guards, and searchlights. Originally the Japanese-Americans were to be locked up in these camps for the duration of the war.

In less than a year some government officials had decided that the evacuation policy had been a mistake and were trying to change it. Some officials believed the entire scheme was unjust. Others argued that the plan treated recent Japanese immigrants who might be loyal to Japan the same as Japanese-American citizens who had been born in the United States and who had spent their entire lives here. Others were shocked at the living conditions within the camps. Still others believed that the policy was too costly in money and human resources.

A Nisei is a native-born citizen of the United States having Japanese immigrant parents.

In January, 1943, the government announced that it would accept volunteers for an all-Nisei (pronounced nee-say) combat unit. To find these volunteers, a general registration of all the adults seventeen years of age and older was ordered for all ten camps.

Each adult in the camp was asked to fill out a questionnaire. The most crucial question was: "Will you swear unqualified allegiance to the United States of America . . . and forswear any form of allegiance or obedience to the Japanese emperor?" When the registration was completed, nearly 31,000 people had answered "yes" to the loyalty question; more than 6000 "no," and 3000 others either answered "no" or qualified their answers.

What kind of people answered "no" and why? Here are some typical answers:

"I am loyal to this country, it's the only one I know, but my husband is an alien and I want to be where he is. The only place we know is Sacramento and if we can't go there we might as well go to Japan."

"My loyalty is now more to Japan than to the United States. That's what my conscience tells me to say. Before evacuation it was different. We were making a pretty good living. Then this thing came and took our property. A country that wants you or wants your loyalty doesn't treat you this way."

"You people say a Jap's a Jap. You've ruined our future. We had something to look forward to, now it is all ruined."

"My dad is fifty-eight years old now. He has been here thirty years at least. He came to this country with nothing but a bed roll. He worked on the railroads and in the beet fields. If I told you the hardships he had, you wouldn't believe me. I owe a lot to my father. All through his life he was working for me. During these last years he was happy because he thought he was coming to the place where his son would have a good life. I am the only son. I have to carry on the family name. My mind is made up. I know my father is planning

150

to return to Japan. I know he expects me to say "no" so that there will be no possibility that the family will be separated. There isn't much I can do for my father anymore; I can't work for him the way I used to. But I can at least quiet his mind on this.

Case 4. The Rioters

On the evening of April 4, 1968, a large, tense crowd gathered at 14th and U Streets in Washington, D.C. These people had just heard a news report that civil rights leader Dr. Martin Luther King had been shot by a white man while standing on his motel balcony in Memphis. At 8:19 P.M. newscasters reported that Dr. King had died. At first there was a quiet anxiety throughout the area. Later that evening President Johnson spoke over television and radio to express sorrow for Dr. King's death. The President urged people not to respond to this tragedy with violent behavior, and he reminded them that Dr. King had stood for nonviolence.

Black people in Washington reacted in various ways to the assassination. Many felt quiet, prayerful sorrow at the loss of a great man whose leadership had meant so much to them. Some reacted with uncontrolled fury, wanting to destroy aimlessly to avenge the death of this great black leader. Others wanted to use the death of Dr. King to start revolutionary activity among black people, activity aimed at crippling or overturning the government. Numerous black people in Washington decided to take part in a destructive riot that lasted two days and resulted in enormous and costly damage.

This case is based on information in Ben W. Gilbert, *Ten Blocks From the White House: Anatomy of the Washington Riots of 1968* (New York: Frederick A. Praeger, Publishers, 1968).

Who participated and why? What social and economic factors made an estimated 20,000 persons riot—one out of every eight residents of the affected areas? Did rioters come from certain limited groups in the community? What motivated the typical rioter? These and related questions are hard to answer because of limited information. But newsmen at the riot scene talked to many people. Also much information was recorded about the 7600 rioters actually arrested. Along with personal observations and recollections, this information gives a fairly accurate, although complex, picture of conditions in Washington and of the rioters.

(1) Housing in the riot areas was in bad condition and extremely crowded. Inhabited almost completely by blacks, the areas had been expected to explode when racial riots occurred in other big cities during previous years.

(2) In the area where the riot started, black militants had support.

(3) While a great many blacks had government jobs or decent jobs in private industry, there were complaints that promotion was infrequent and pay inadequate. Unemployment and underemployment were big problems, and the majority of blacks still held menial jobs at low pay.

(4) In some areas blacks and whites lived side by side. But large areas of the city were completely poor and black. Many whites had left Washington to live in the suburbs, leaving a black majority within the city.

(5) At least 90 percent of the public school pupils in the District were black. Many whites sent their children to private schools. There were charges that the public schools offered students an inferior education.

A lone soldier guards a deserted Washington street shortly before a curfew went into effect as an aftermath of the riot.

(6) In 1967 the old three-member board of commissioners which governed Washington under the watchful eye of Congress was replaced by a single commissioner (popularly called "mayor"), an assistant commissioner, and a nine-member council—all appointed by the President. The President appointed a black man, Walter Washington, to be the first "mayor." The city council was given limited power to enact ordinances and to review the budget. But this was not really the "home rule" which many black citizens in Washington demanded.

(7) Blacks believed that too many ghetto stores were white-owned and operated. Too few Negroes had responsible positions in these stores. There were complaints against merchants for unfair pricing, high credit rates, shoddy merchandise, and other discriminatory actions against slum residents. Citizens were beginning to demand more black ownership and management in business.

Some observers believe that these conditions provided all the ingredients for a major outbreak. Only a spark like Dr. King's murder was needed to set off the explosion. Others contend that the murder was not a motivating factor. For some, rioting was an outlet for anger against the white man who shot Dr. King or against the whole white race for past and present injustices. Others claimed it was not a "race thing" or a product of hatred, but simply a release of tension. Adventure or greed motivated still others.

Some extreme black militants, later questioned in an anonymous interview, said they used King's assassination to justify the riot to the masses of basically nonviolent people. Their motives were frankly racial and revolutionary; their fire bombings were designed to give incentive to the masses. Once things got started, the hysteria became infectious. People began to participate "because everyone else did."

The majority of rioters were not burning buildings but were looting. Those breaking windows and starting fires tended to be teen-agers and men in their early twenties, but everybody joined in the looting.

Of those arrested 98 percent were black and 91 percent male, although a much greater percentage of women rioters was seen. The arrested rioters tended to be (a) young (average age 24.6 years), (b) residents of the District, (c) blue-collar workers but not at the lowest poverty levels, (d) high school dropouts, and (e) persons without previous police records.

Some looters needed what they took and some did not. Some intended to hurt particular merchants; others considered it just a game. Some were sorry later, but many were anxious to do it again.

Use information provided in this chapter, in particular from the four preceding cases, to assist your discussion of these questions.

1. What is the relationship of group identification to the development of political alienation?

2. How are public policies related to the development of political alienation among certain groups?

3. What is the relationship of socioeconomic status to the development of political alienation?

4. How are (a) sense of political efficacy and (b) sense of personal power related to the development of political alienation?

5. What general statements can you make about the sources of political alienation and national loyalty in our society?

E. National Loyalty and the Right to Dissent

Most Americans share some fundamental beliefs about their country. One is a belief in rule by law. Law establishes order, prevents chaos and anarchy, and provides protection and freedom. American law is supposed to be applied equally to all, without discrimination. Furthermore, no man is supposed to be above the law.

Nearly all Americans also believe in the principle of majority rule and the protection of the rights of minorities. According to this principle, differences of opinion should be settled by debate and by vote. The losers in a political debate agree to abide by the decisions of the majority; the majority meanwhile is prohibited by law from infringing upon the rights of the minority. These rights include allowing the minority to continue to argue for its views in the hope that today's minority might become the majority in a future election.

Right to Dissent Is Fundamental to Democracy

The First Amendment to the Constitution guarantees American citizens protection of their rights of free speech and assembly. The rights of the minority would be meaningless without this protection. The right to say what one thinks, to petition the government, and to assemble peaceably with others to discuss public issues is essential for a healthy democratic system. How can public leaders know whether their policies are sound if they do not have the chance to hear what citizens honestly believe about government policies? Thus, *dissent,* the right to disagree openly with policies one believes are bad, is also fundamental to democracy.

Political dissent is a long and honorable American tradition. Indeed, many who came as original settlers to the colonies were dissenters, men and women who disliked the official Church of England and came seeking to practice their own religious beliefs. Throughout our history there have been many great dissenters, including Abraham Lincoln. As a United States Congressman he spoke out against American foreign policy during the Mexican War in the belief that President Polk's reasons for fighting the Mexicans were wrong.

Dissent and National Security

Almost everyone agrees that freedom of speech and dissent are basic to the American way of life. But many disagree about how much dissent should be allowed. Many Americans agree with the naval hero of the 1790's, Stephen Decatur, who said, "Our country, may she always be right, but our country right or wrong." They say that during a national crisis, such as a war, all Americans must line up solidly behind the government even if they do not agree with government policy.

Other Americans agree with Carl Schurz's modification of Decatur's famous words, "When right, to be kept right; when wrong to be put right." They say that it is the duty of loyal Americans to protest government actions which they think are wrong. They believe that freedom of speech or the right to dissent should not be limited even during a national crisis. These Americans feel that patriotism involves constructive criticism as well as conformity to established traditions.

Both of these viewpoints raise difficult questions. For example, can a society remain democratic if the people blindly follow their leaders, "right or wrong"? But can a society remain stable, can it be kept in order, if everyone is "free" to decide how to "put right" the affairs of the nation?

In a democratic society questions about national loyalty and the right to dissent are often difficult to decide because of the democratic traditions of freedom of speech and protection of minority rights. The right to criticize and disagree with the policies of the government are a basic part of every democratic political culture. However, such criticism and dissent can possibly result in social disorder or even anarchy. Every democratic society faces the difficult problem of balancing the right of freedom to dissent with the need for conformity to existing rules, of balancing the right of individuals to be different with the need for conformity. Every democratic society must find answers to the questions of what should be the relationship between liberty and loyalty, and when does dissent become disloyalty?

Questions about national loyalty and the right to dissent are also complicated by the fact that people disagree about the meaning of loyalty. For example, one group of people may participate in a peace march to dramatize their belief that the government's foreign policies are harmful to the United States. Other Americans march to show their support for the President's policies. Both groups consider themselves loyal Americans—and both groups are likely to remain loyal Americans so long as the nation is sufficiently free and open to accommodate the broad range of beliefs they represent.

Comparing Loyalty in Dictatorships and Democracies

There are basic differences between the way democratic and totalitarian leaders treat questions of loyalty. In a totalitarian state any means available is used to make citizens conform totally to the goals and policies of the leaders. A totalitarian state does not allow individuals to participate in groups which do not give full support to the national leaders and their policies. If the churches oppose the political leaders, church officials will be arrested and the churches will be forced to conform. The state tries to destroy or weaken existing groups and to replace them with new groups which will promote acceptance of the leader's policies.

In Nazi Germany the "ideal" family was one in which the father was a Nazi, the mother a member of the Association of Nazi Women, the daughter a member of the Association of German Girls, the son a member of Hitler Youth, and they all met once a year at the Nazi Congress in Nuremberg. In this way a totalitarian regime tried to ensure that there were no competing loyalties in the state. All loyalties in Nazi Germany were directed toward the nation and its leader.

While no totalitarian state has ever been completely successful in rooting out all group loyalties and affiliations which it does not control, that is the goal. The end result—so totalitarian leaders believe—is a population that is completely loyal to the national leaders and their policies.

Democracy has an entirely different set of beliefs. In the United States a person is supposed to be free to believe what he wishes, to do what he wants, and to associate with whomever he chooses. The only major exception to these practices is to limit the activities of those whose policies would prevent others from exercising their freedom. Thus, atheists are not free to burn churches because they think churches are unimportant. Nevertheless, if one believes that churches are given unfair privileges, he may say so and try to convince others to support his views.

The question of when one man's freedom harms others is sometimes difficult to decide. It has led to much legislation and is often argued in the courts. Nevertheless, the principle is clear. In a democracy one is free to organize a group and to advocate policies that are exactly opposite to those promoted by the national leaders. Indeed, a good citizen is often viewed as one who actively seeks to convince others that a current policy should be changed.

Following are two cases which raise important questions about the right to dissent, the meaning of national loyalty, and the need to balance conformity to tradition with criticism of tradition.

Case 1. Protest at the Pentagon

On October 21, 1967, over 30,000 Americans marched in Washington from the Lincoln Memorial to the Pentagon, headquarters of the Joint Chiefs of Staff and the Defense Department. Their purpose was to protest the government's use of military force in Vietnam.

155

The day before the protest many people were worried that the demonstration would lead to disorder and violence. An editorial in the *Washington Post* of October 20, 1967, expressed the fears of many Americans on the eve of the protest at the Pentagon.

> The Americans who plan to march tomorrow from the Lincoln Memorial to the Pentagon in protest against the war in Vietnam have an indubitable right to do so. This form of expressing dissent from a policy of their government is honored by tradition and protected by the Constitution. It bears witness to a freedom which is at once a source of strength to America and an essential element of American life. When all this has been said, however, it is vital for the marchers to remember that the constitutional right which they exercise is a right to assemble *peaceably* and that it must be exercised in good order and in conformity with valid laws.

The protestors gathered slowly and peacefully in front of the Lincoln Memorial during the morning and early afternoon. They were a very mixed group: middle-aged housewives standing next to long-haired hippies, veterans of earlier American wars along with self-proclaimed opponents of all war. There were clean-shaven men in neat business suits and shabbily dressed, bearded, shaggy-haired nonconformists. But mostly there were high school and college students, both clean-cut and shaggy haired, representing schools from all parts of the country.

Many demonstrators carried signs with slogans such as "We Don't Want Violence," "Stop the War Now," "Impeach Lyndon B. Johnson," and "Make Love, Not War." A few demonstrators carried the flags of the nation's enemies in Vietnam, the Viet Cong and the North Vietnamese, and signs that proclaimed support for the Viet Cong.

From the steps of the Lincoln Memorial, speakers told of their opposition to the war in Vietnam. Several speakers denounced the war. Some called for peaceful protest according to the law. Others called for active resistance to the government and the war effort, even to the point of breaking the law.

At about 2:30 in the afternoon the demonstrators began leaving the Lincoln Memorial to march to the Pentagon. Carrying banners and signs, shouting slogans, and talking among themselves, the marchers slowly moved toward the Pentagon.

At the Pentagon the demonstrators were faced by several hundred Federal marshals and army troops who were on hand to maintain order. There had been reports that some demonstrators would try to enter the Pentagon and disrupt the work going on inside the building. The soldiers had orders to keep all protestors out of the building.

At about 5:30 the first serious disorder took place. About 3000 protestors attempted to charge through the ranks of soldiers to enter the Pentagon. About thirty of the protestors forced their way into the building.

"Push 'em out," a captain shouted.

"A Company, move up and push 'em out," he ordered. The soldiers moved forward, swinging their rifle butts and pushing the demonstrators back.

Not since 1932, when President Hoover called out a thousand men to put down the "Bonus March," had soldiers been called for riot-control duty in Washington, D.C.

156

The demonstrators retreated, holding their heads and arms in pain. Blood had been spilled on the Pentagon steps. As a result of this action, several demonstrators were arrested.

Throughout the evening the crowd of demonstrators continued to face the soldiers and marshals. Occasionally a group of demonstrators would shout something at the troops or at another group of demonstrators.

Mostly the demonstrators gathered together in small groups and talked. Some talked in disgust about the behavior of those who had tried to force their way into the Pentagon. They said that the demonstrators should not break laws. Others in the crowd talked proudly of violent protest. They said that the American government was corrupt and that the laws should be broken. They vowed to express their contempt for the law and to change society, by revolution if necessary.

Groups of protestors argued about what to do next. Some wanted to "protest with their bodies." They wanted to rush into the Pentagon and to cause as much disorder and destruction as possible. They believed that through civil disobedience they might best influence public opinion. Others disagreed. They believed that the best way to influence public opinion would be to express their dissent in an orderly way, according to the rules. The ideas of these two groups are represented by these fictional speeches.

Robert, a young leader of the anti-war demonstration, proclaimed:

> Let's protest until we tear this corrupt government apart. This government is immoral. It orders the destruction of people and property in a faraway land. It oppresses poor people in this country. Against a brutal government such as ours, orderly dissent makes no sense. Let us begin the task of wholesale and widespread resistance to the laws. Let's turn this society upside down. Let's disrupt the Pentagon, this awful headquarters of our national war machine.

George, another young leader, disagreed with Robert. George replied:

> I'm against the war in Vietnam. I believe that it is a mistake for our country to waste human lives and money there. These resources should be used at home to solve the problems of poverty that exist here. But I stand for orderly protest. I don't want to destroy my government; I want to improve it. I'm not against America; I am for its betterment. I believe that to be a loyal American today one must disagree with the government's Vietnam policy. But I don't want to tear our society apart. And I don't want us to cause disruption and destruction here at the Pentagon today.

Later that evening, at about 11:45, some of the protestors became unruly and pressed against the soldiers. The soldiers using rifle butts, and marshals swinging clubs, beat back the crowd. Several more of the demonstrators were arrested.

After this outburst most of the demonstrators settled down to spend the night in a vigil of protest outside the Pentagon. At about 6 o'clock in the morning most of them picked up their belongings and headed for home. Only a few stayed outside the Pentagon for a second day of protest.

A peace demonstrator taunts military police during the confrontation in front of the Pentagon.

By nightfall of this second day of demonstrating, only about 400 protestors remained. By midnight quiet reigned; all the protestors had left.

During the two-day protest 684 people had been arrested for disorderly conduct. Their cases were heard in the days following the demonstration. Most of those arrested were convicted and given suspended sentences. A few received small fines and short jail sentences of thirty days or less.

Among the other results of the protest march were forty-seven people injured, with the most serious casualty being a broken arm. The two-day cost to the Federal government was $1,078,500. Most of this money was spent to transport, maintain, and pay soldiers, marshals, and police.

Case 2. The Civil Rights Protestors

In the 1960's civil disobedience was a tactic used by some black people to overturn laws that supported segregation. For example, in some cities black people were prohibited by state and local law from being served at lunch counters in department stores. Black youth would sometimes occupy all the counter stools and refuse to leave when requested to do so. They insisted on staying until they were served, thereby violating the local law. These youth were trained to be nonviolent, to avoid striking back when hit or insulted, and to go peaceably when arrested.

Martin Luther King, Jr., was a major leader of peaceful protest activities that involved civil disobedience. Dr. King believed that civil disobedience was a proper reaction to "unjust laws," which he defined as laws that a minority is forced to obey but which are not applied to the majority. According to King, segregation laws, which discriminated against black people, were "unjust laws."

One of the most dramatic applications of Dr. King's ideas about civil disobedience as a tool of black protestors came in Birmingham, Alabama, in the spring of 1963. King expressed the bitterness of black people toward

158

segregation laws in an attempt to explain the basis for the protest activities in Birmingham:

> We have waited for more than 340 years for our constitutional and God-given rights. The nations of Asia and Africa are moving with jet-like speed toward gaining political independence, but we still creep at horse-and-buggy pace toward gaining a cup of coffee at a lunch counter. Perhaps it is easy for those who have never felt the stinging darts of segregation to say, "Wait." But when you have seen vicious mobs lynch your mothers and fathers at will and drown your sisters and brothers at whim; when you have seen hate-filled policemen curse, kick, and even kill your black brothers and sisters; when you see the vast majority of your twenty million Negro brothers smothering in an airtight cage of poverty in the midst of an affluent society; when you suddenly find your tongue twisted and your speech stammering as you seek to explain to your six-year-old daughter why she can't go to the public amusement park that has just been advertised on television, and see tears welling up in her eyes when she is told that Funtown is closed to colored children, and see ominous clouds of inferiority beginning to form in her little mental sky, and see her beginning to distort her personality by developing an unconscious bitterness toward white people; when you have to concoct an answer for a five-year-old son who is asking: "Daddy, why do white people treat colored people so mean?"; when you take a cross-country drive and find it necessary to sleep night after night in the uncomfortable corners of your automobile because no motel will accept you; when you are humiliated day in and day out by nagging signs reading "white" and "colored"; when your first name becomes "nigger," your middle name becomes "boy" (however old you are), and your last name becomes "John," and your wife and mother are never given the respected title "Mrs."; when you are harried by day and haunted by night by the fact that you are a Negro, living constantly at tiptoe stance, never quite knowing what to expect next, and are plagued with inner fears and outer resentments; when you are forever fighting a degenerating sense of "nobodiness"—then you will understand why we find it difficult to wait. There comes a time when the cup of endurance runs over, and men are no longer willing to be plunged into the abyss of despair. I hope, sirs, you can understand our legitimate and unavoidable impatience.*

* Martin Luther King, Jr. *Why We Can't Wait* (New York: Harper and Row, 1964), pp. 83–84.

At the head of the Southern Christian Leadership Conference (SCLC), a civil rights organization, Dr. King marched into Birmingham in April, 1963. He called Birmingham the most "segregated city in America."

During the next two months Dr. King and his followers daily protested on the streets of Birmingham. King said that his purpose was to draw the attention of the nation to the problems of black people, to show that black people in America had neither the freedom of other people guaranteed by the Constitution nor equal opportunities to make a decent living.

King and his followers believed that segregation laws and customs were wrong. They intended to change these laws. They decided to break the segregation laws and go to jail, if necessary, to draw nationwide attention to their cause.

The Rev. Ralph Abernathy (left) and Dr. Martin Luther King lead a long line of chanting black demonstrators in their attempt to march on city hall in Birmingham. Police intercepted them short of their goal.

By contrast, the law-enforcement officials of Birmingham, led by the police commissioner, believed it was their duty to stand behind their state and city laws and to arrest law violators. When Negroes, led by King, marched through the streets of Birmingham without legal march permits, the police believed that it was their duty to break up the march. The police commissioner said that King and his followers had no legal right to march in the streets, that the marchers were a threat to public order and safety, and that if they did not disperse peaceably they would be arrested.

Dr. King and his followers refused to obey the police chief's orders to stop their public demonstrations. Instead they demonstrated peacefully, if illegally. They sang songs such as "We Shall Overcome," and they carried signs saying "freedom now" and "end segregation." The Birmingham police reacted to the peaceful, but illegal, protest with force. They used police dogs and powerful streams of water from fire hoses to stop the demonstrators. Many black protestors were arrested, including Dr. King, until the jails were overflowing. But the protest marches continued.

The protest marches in Birmingham finally ended when the city officials made some concessions to the demands of the protestors. They announced an agreement to provide for the desegregation of lunch counters, public restrooms, and other public facilities; the release from jail of arrested demonstrators; the hiring of more Negro workers for city jobs; and the establishment of a biracial committee to discuss problems of race relations in Birmingham.

Use information from this chapter, particularly from the preceding two cases, to assist your discussion of these questions.

1. Were all of the dissenters in the preceding cases politically alienated? Explain. What is the difference between a dissenter who is politically alienated and a dissenter who is not politically alienated?

2. Some people have claimed that it is permissable to break the law for a "just cause." Do you agree? Explain.

3. What limitations should be placed upon dissent in our society? Explain.

4. When discussing national loyalty or patriotism, some people stress the duty to conform to authority. Others stress the responsibility to dissent constructively, when necessary, from authority.

  a. Would you stress either conformity or dissent in a discussion of the meaning of national loyalty and patriotism?

  b. Are there different views of national loyalty and patriotism among your classmates?

5. What are the relationships of culture, socialization, socioeconomic status, role, and group identifications to the political behavior of the "protestors" and the "law enforcers" in the preceding cases?

6. What are your value judgments about the political behavior of the "protestors" and the "law enforcers" in the preceding cases?

The violence in Birmingham aroused nationwide sympathy for the civil rights movement. Marchers in Boston call for Federal action.

unit three

elections and the behavior of voters

chapter 9

Selecting Leaders of Government

Every society selects certain individuals to be leaders of government and gives these leaders the power to settle conflicts and to distribute rewards within the society. Every society faces the problems of deciding how to select its rulers and how to transfer ruling power from one group to another.

A society's method of choosing governmental leaders has crucial consequences. The extent to which a society enjoys political stability, peace, order, and justice is related to its methods of selecting its rulers. The surest way to determine the extent to which a society is democratic or antidemocratic is to examine its method of selecting rulers. A democratic society selects its governmental leaders through majority vote of the people and protects the rights of those in the minority. A democratic society offers regular opportunity to vote new individuals to ruling positions.

A. Different Ways of Selecting Governmental Leaders

How should rulers be selected? How long should they stay in power? How should they be replaced when their period of rule comes to an end? Answers to these questions have varied greatly from society to society throughout history. Following are five examples of reactions to the common human problem of how to select rulers and to transfer power.

Example 1. Long Live the King *hereditary*

The young man stood proudly before the Assembly of Nobles that crowded the church to witness his coronation. He was outwardly solemn, but inwardly very happy. A few days before, he had been very sad. His father, the king for thirty years, had died. He had loved his father; it had been difficult to hide his emotions on that terrible day. But today, as his father's oldest son and heir, he would be crowned king. Could he match his father's accomplishments in war and peace? Could he successfully defend his nation and rule his people? Would he make wise and just laws? Thoughts of happiness and pride, mingled with sadness and worry, ran through his mind as he waited for the crown to be placed on his head by the bishop.

After the coronation ceremony, the new king rode through the main street of his city. The people cheered for their new ruler. Happy shouts of "Long live the king" filled the air.

Example 2. The People's Choice *popular vote*

The *Daily Times*, the largest newspaper in the capital city, carried a bold headline proclaiming the election of a new President of the nation. The election had been very close. Fifty-five percent of those who had voted had chosen him to be the new President. His most important opponent had received 42 percent of the vote.

The newspaper carried a victory message from the new President. He congratulated his opponents for conducting a fair and vigorous, if losing, campaign. He thanked the people of the nation for giving him majority support. He pledged that during his four-year term of office he would try to live up to the great record of his predecessor, who was now retiring from public life.

Example 3. Power Struggle *unlimited conflict*

The radio commentator interrupted the scheduled programs to broadcast this startling news to his nation.

"Citizens, our beloved leader has died. He suffered a heart attack and died before a doctor could reach him. His body will be displayed publicly tomorrow. All loyal citizens are requested to pay tribute to our fallen leader. Please remain calm."

Despite the broadcaster's plea to remain calm, the nation was thrown into turmoil. The leader had ruled for twenty years with an iron hand. He had appeared to be vigorous and healthy. No thought had been given to the selection of a new leader to take his place. He had completely dominated the political life of the nation. Suddenly he was gone. The power that he had controlled for so long was now available. Who would claim it?

Two leaders who had worked under the fallen leader claimed the right to succeed him. Each man began to line up support for his claims. People openly talked of the possibility of civil war. The people of this great nation waited nervously for the power struggle from which would emerge their new leader.

Example 4. The Elders Choose a Leader   *vote of an Elite*

The council of elders had been secluded for three days and nights. During this time they faced the problem of choosing a new ruler from among the eligible men of the tribe. They were allowed to choose only from among a select group of warriors, men who had won special honor in battle. Thus, at the start of the discussion, the council considered carefully the merits of only twenty-four eligible candidates. By the end of the third day, the list was narrowed to two preferred leaders. A vote was taken among the council. Each elder then voted for one of the two final candidates. When the new leader's name was announced to the tribe, the people gave a roar of approval.

Example 5. The Party's Choice   *leaders of an Party leaders*

The voters stood in long lines and waited patiently and quietly to cast their votes. For several weeks by radio, television, and newspaper advertisements the leaders of the country's only political party had reminded all citizens of their obligation to vote. Now the time had come for the people to approve the candidates whom the leaders of the party had selected.

Each voter received a ballot which listed the names of the candidates. There was one candidate for each office. The voters had the right to approve or reject the candidates. However, the leaders of the party expected the voters to approve the official list of candidates. They were not disappointed.

1. What is the method for selecting governmental leaders in each example?

2. Why are different societies likely to have different selection methods?

3. Why do all societies develop an established way of selecting leaders of government?

4. Which of the methods of selecting rulers are likely to contribute greatly to political stability and orderly behavior? Explain.

5. Which of the selection methods are likely to contribute to the practice of democracy? Explain.

6. Which of the methods of selecting leaders do you prefer? Why?

7. Which of the preceding questions (a) can be answered with facts? (b) Which must be answered with hypotheses? (c) Which one requires a value judgment? (d) What are the differences between questions that are answered with facts, hypotheses, and value judgments?

B. Selecting Leaders of Government through Public Elections

A public election is a method of selecting or approving rulers by popular vote. Public elections are conducted according to rules. Thus, power to govern is transferred from individual to individual and from group to group in an orderly way.

166

The main consequence of selecting leaders of government according to established rules is political and social stability. A leader who has been selected according to the rules of his society is accepted as *legitimate.* In other words, the people accept his right to govern because he has been chosen according to the rules of the society. Individuals in the society have been socialized to accept these rules.

Public elections provide an opportunity for most citizens to participate in politics. Only a few citizens become political leaders or activists, but through public elections masses of citizens have the chance to influence the selection and direction of political leadership. Public elections give masses of citizens the chance to feel a fundamental involvement in the political life of their country.

On the opposite page an Italian citizen studies some election posters. Below are election scenes in India (left) and Algeria (right).

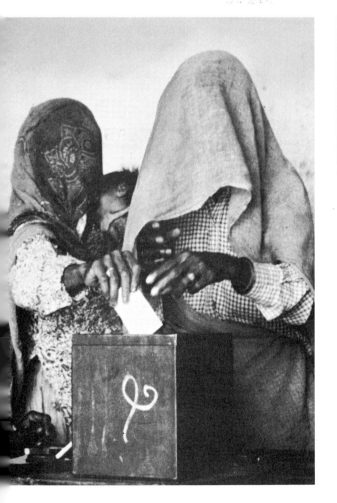

J. Mirachi. Copyright
Saturday Review, Inc. 1967

"Well, that's democracy
for you. My vote nullifies
your vote."

What does this cartoon suggest about the implications of extending the right to vote to all adults regardless of social class?

A society's method of selecting its rulers is an important clue to whether or not the society honors democratic values. In a democratically oriented society, different leaders have the opportunity to compete for the support of the people. Rulers are chosen through popular vote in open, competitive elections. Losers have the chance to criticize the victors and to try again to win power in a future election.

In a nondemocratic society, open competition between two or more political parties is not allowed. People with unapproved political ideas are not allowed to work openly to achieve control of the government.

Competitive and Noncompetitive Public Elections

Modern societies use two types of public elections, competitive and noncompetitive. Some countries conduct noncompetitive, one-party public elections. For example, in the Soviet Union the rulers allow only the Communist party to function. Prior to an election in the Soviet Union, the Communist party selects one candidate for each public office. The people can vote either for or against the official list of candidates. The official candidates typically receive almost 100 percent approval.

Since there is only one political party and one candidate for each office, there is no open competition or conflict in Soviet elections. An election campaign serves chiefly as a demonstration of popular unity and support for the leaders and ideas of the Communist party. Competition for positions of leadership in the Communist party and Soviet government takes place within party circles. The masses of Soviet people are not able to influence the selection of leaders through voting.

Many countries conduct competitive public elections in which voters have the right to choose governmental leaders from among candidates of two or more political parties. For example, in most West European countries there are several political parties which compete for control of the government. Election campaigns feature conflicts among different personalities and ideas representing political parties with diverse points of view. Voters have the opportunity to judge a variety of competing viewpoints and candidates in these countries.

In a two-party or multi-party system, representatives from different parties will almost certainly be elected to the legislature (Congress or Parliament). And sometimes members of different parties have positions in the executive branch. Losing parties are willing to accept temporarily the right of the winners to rule so long as the winners have achieved victory according to the accepted rules. The winners are obligated to allow the losing parties to criticize the winners and to attempt to win control of the government in future elections.

In the United States adult citizens choose public officials through periodic public elections. The two major political parties, the Democratic and Republican, select the competing candidates and manage the election campaign according to state and Federal laws. These political parties are organizations which strive to gain and maintain the power to make and carry out public policy. The main goal of the Democratic and Republican parties is to win elections to public office so that the party can reap the rewards of controlling the government.

Nominating Candidates by the Direct Primary

The Democratic and Republican parties select potential leaders of government through formal nomination procedures. The direct primary is a preliminary election in which the public votes to select candidates to represent each party in a general election to public office.

Most states use the *closed primary*, in which a voter (a) indicates in some manner his party choice and then (b) receives only the ballot of that party. Generally a voter must be registered in advance as a Republican or Democrat in order to vote in the primary, and he gets only the ballot of the party for which he is registered. A few states allow voters registered as "Independent" to ask for the ballot of either party. In some states any voter can ask for the ballot of *either* party; but if he is switching from his choice in the last primary, an election official may issue a "challenge." Then the voter must take an oath that he supported his new party in the previous general election or intends to do so in the coming election. Of course, there is no way of proving the matter.

An *open primary*, used in a few states, is a nominating election open to any eligible voter. In most of these states the voter gets one Democratic and one Republican ballot, both the same size and color. In the privacy of the voting booth, the voter marks one ballot and discards the other. Where voting machines are used, the voter moves the levers of only one party—and the other ballot is automatically locked.

People favoring the closed primary argue that the direct primary is a *party* election and that people unwilling to be identified with a particular party have no business participating. The closed primary, they say, cuts down "outside interference" in the party's choice of its candidates.

In most states using primary elections the candidate who wins the most votes (a plurality) for a particular office wins the nomination. However, in a few states, all located in the South, a candidate must win a majority of the votes cast in his party's primary in order to win the nomination. If no candidate receives a majority of the votes, then the two candidates with the highest number of votes must compete in a "run-off" election to determine the party's nominee.

In some areas one political party tends to dominate or control political affairs. For example, in some rural areas of Kansas the Republican candidates typically prevail. The Democratic party offers little real competition. Likewise, in some urban areas, such as Brooklyn or Gary, the Democratic nominee usually wins the general election. In these areas of one-party domination, the primary election usually determines the winner for public office, since the opposing party tends to offer little or no challenge to the dominant party in the subsequent general election.

The photos suggest the tumult at the 1968 Democratic convention (top) and the relative calm at the 1964 convention (bottom) where Lyndon Johnson was nominated by acclamation. Straw hats reminiscent of GOP dominance early in the century often reappear at Republican national conventions.

Nominating Candidates by Party Conventions

A party convention is used to nominate candidates for Congress or for state government offices in a very few states. A political party nominating convention is a meeting of party members who have been selected as delegates to nominate party candidates. The delegates act as representatives for party members throughout the state. In some direct-primary states the party convention is used to endorse a list of candidates. The endorsed candidate presumably has an advantage in the ensuing primary election, since the ballot will show that he is the convention's choice.

Other Election Activities of Political Parties

Political parties organize and manage the election campaigns of candidates who have been nominated to represent the party. Through election campaigns a political party tries to advertise its candidates and their ideas in order to attract support for the party. Thus, election campaigns are likely to feature severe and boisterous clashes of personalities and ideas.

Officials of the local government organize and manage the general election. However, representatives of the competing political parties are present at the polls, or voting places, on election day. "Watchers" from each party are present to guard their party's interests and to see that the votes are counted fairly. Party members are available to pass out campaign literature as "last minute" appeals to the voters.

Political parties function to limit and channel the conflict between individuals and their ideas which must be part of any free and open public election. By organizing and conducting periodic public elections, according to rules, the political parties regulate conflict between rivals for governmental leadership. The winning party is a temporary holder of power, it must continue to seek public support to remain in control of the government. The losing party is a temporary "loyal opposition" which continues to examine and criticize the public officials of the winning party with the objective of gaining control of the government. During and after election campaigns, rival candidates and parties are free to criticize and compete for the power to make and carry out public policy.

Kuekes in the *Cleveland Plain Dealer*

THE MORNING AFTER

What does this cartoon show about basic values shared by Democrats and Republicans?

Political parties often help voters to see more clearly what the issues are in the election. At the national and state levels the issues are set forth in party platforms.

In the United States the leading governmental officials—the President, state governors, mayors, and local, state, and national lawmakers—are chosen through the votes of citizens. How does this election process work? What are the "rules of the game" for this very important political activity? Following is an example of how the election process works in the United States. This example is about the election of a mayor in a northern industrial city.

C. Gary Elects a Mayor

The "rules of the game" for an American election are clearly illustrated in the following example. Essentially, these rules are very similar for any election of a public official in the United States. The selection of American mayors, governors, and lawmakers in large and small cities, and in different parts of the country, is done in various ways. However, certain basic rules pervade any American public election, since all Americans are influenced by a common political culture and a common legal structure, or system of laws.

Although the following case reveals main characteristics of public elections in the United States, realize that some features of the election in this case are associated with local conditions that do not apply to other places in our country. Also, most local elections are not contested as bitterly and dramatically, or with as much nationwide publicity, as this one.

Population Characteristics of Gary

Gary, a city of over 180,000 people, is located in Lake County in the extreme northwestern corner of Indiana. Large numbers of Gary's working population have employment in the city's steel mills and related industries.

Gary's population consists of people of many different national backgrounds. The first groups to come to Gary, seeking work in the newly built steel mills, were immigrants from southern and eastern Europe: Poles, Yugoslavs, Czechs, Slovaks, Greeks, Hungarians, Romanians, Italians, Lithuanians, Ukrainians, and Russians. Most of these eastern and southern European immigrants arrived during the years 1905–1920.

During recent years, 1940 until the present, four new groups of people have come to Gary seeking work in the steel mills: Negroes from the Southern states, white Americans from the Southern states, Puerto Ricans, and Mexicans. Negroes have been by far the largest of these four new groups of migrants to Gary. Prior to 1940, Negroes were less than 15 percent of the city's total population. The proportion of blacks in the city grew to almost 60 percent by 1970.

The relationships among the different ethnic (nationality) groups of Gary have been reasonably friendly for the most part. If the various ethnic ingredients thrown into Gary's "melting pot" did not always "melt," the pot did not boil over. Some friction existed between the city's earlier inhabitants and the Negro and Latin-American newcomers. But this friction did not seriously disrupt the political and social stability of Gary. Unlike many racially mixed Northern cities, no rioting had occurred in Gary prior to 1967.

The descendants of eastern European immigrants ran the city of Gary for many years. Their representatives regularly held most of the public offices, including the very important mayor's office. The Negro, Mexican, and Puerto Rican people in Gary have not been as well represented in government. Most important, before 1967 no Negro or Latin American had ever been elected mayor of Gary. In 1967 Richard G. Hatcher, a 33-year-old Negro lawyer, set out to change the balance of political power in Gary.

172

Hatcher Seeks the Democratic Nomination for Mayor

After much careful planning, Hatcher announced, early in 1967, that he would be a Democratic party candidate for mayor. At that time he was president of the Gary City Council. Many whites expressed shock and annoyance that a black would run for mayor. Gary's blacks, however, were inspired to try to gain greater political power in a city where, despite the fact that they were the majority of the population, they had not influenced governmental decision-making to any great extent.

Could Richard Hatcher become Gary's first Negro mayor. No city in the northern United States had ever before elected a Negro mayor. Hatcher's first hurdle was to win the nomination of his party, the Democratic party, as a candidate for mayor. In the Indiana election system candidates for public offices must be nominated in a *primary election* that takes place in May. This primary election is the means by which the members of each political party decide upon candidates to represent their party in the general election in November.

Competing against Hatcher for the Democratic nomination were the incumbent, Mayor A. Martin Katz, and businessman Bernard Konrady. Businessman Joseph B. Radigan was the only contender for the Republican nomination for mayor. Radigan, a furniture store owner, was a member of an old Gary family and a civic leader who had served on many civic committees.

During March and April of 1967, Hatcher, Katz, and Konrady campaigned vigorously among the Democratic voters of Gary. Both Hatcher and Katz had support among black and white Democrats. However, Hatcher had more backing from blacks than did Katz. Konrady appealed only to white voters. On May 7, the primary election day, the Democratic voters of Gary chose Richard Hatcher to be their candidate for mayor. Since no Republican opposed Joseph Radigan, he automatically became the Republican candidate.

Hatcher's Advantages and Disadvantages

Hatcher should have been able to look forward to an easy campaign and victory in his political battle with Republican candidate Radigan. After all, Gary had not elected a Republican mayor since 1942. And in Lake County, Indiana, most political offices had been controlled by Democrats for over thirty-five years. In recent years most Democratic candidates for public office in Gary had won overwhelming victories. Consequently, the Republican organization in Gary had become weak and ineffective. But the candidacy of Richard G. Hatcher shot new life into the decaying Gary Republican party forces.

As the campaign battle between Radigan and Hatcher progressed, it was obvious that many white Democrats were supporting the Republican Radigan against the Democrat Hatcher. Why? The answer is complicated, but to a considerable extent racial prejudice against Negroes was involved.

Many of Gary's whites preferred to keep apart from Gary's Negroes as much as possible. In the past whites had often refused to sell their homes or to rent apartments to Negroes. Whenever black families moved into a previously all-white neighborhood, most of the white people would eventually move away. Thus Negro and white housing was largely segregated.

Further complicating Hatcher's drive to win the mayor's office was his record as a supporter of civil rights for black people. To his supporters, Hatcher's efforts to protect the rights of free speech and equality of opportunity for black people made him appear as a champion of democracy. However, to many people in Gary, Hatcher's efforts in support of civil rights was a mark against him. To these people Hatcher appeared to be a dangerous political radical.

The Democratic Party Chairman Opposes Hatcher

A great blow to the Hatcher campaign came when the Lake County Democratic party chairman decided to throw his political power against Hatcher. Many members of the county Democratic organization followed the chairman's leadership and worked to defeat their fellow Democrat, Richard Hatcher.

The Democratic party chairman was asked to explain his highly unusual stand. After all, it is customary for a party chairman to work for the election of *all* of his party's candidates. He claimed that he was putting patriotism, loyalty to his country, before loyalty to his political party. He said that Hatcher was a dangerous political radical who might undermine good government in Gary. Here is a sample of the party chairman's comments about Hatcher during the campaign as reported in the *Washington Post* of October 29, 1967.

> I am not against Richard Hatcher because he is a Negro. I am against him because of the kind of man he is . . .
>
> He's made treasonous statements about Vietnam. He's supported the ACLU. He was for an open-occupancy law. He's refused to denounce Stokely Carmichael and Rap Brown by name. He's got people around him who defend draft dodgers, flag desecrators, draft-card burners. I'm not against him because he's a Negro, but because I think he's dangerous.

The ACLU, American Civil Liberties Union, is an organization that defends the right of all individuals to enjoy the benefits of the Bill of Rights of the United States Constitution.

The party chairman called upon Hatcher to denounce two radical Negro leaders, Stokely Carmichael and Rap Brown, and to denounce violence and civil disorder. Only then, the party chairman said, would he consider supporting Hatcher's bid for the mayor's office.

Hatcher denounced violence and civil disorder publicly. But he refused to denounce Carmichael and Brown by name. He said that these men did not live in Gary and had nothing to do with Gary politics. Therefore, he saw no reason to mention their names.

Hatcher claimed that the party chairman's real reasons for not lending support were that the Democratic nominee was a Negro and that he would not take orders from the party chairman. Here is a sample from the *Gary Post-Tribune* of Hatcher's comments about the party chairman during the campaign:

> The party chairman is against me because I'm a Negro. He is also against me because he can see control of Gary slipping out of his grasp.

Richard Hatcher walks past his election headquarters, which is decorated with his election slogan.

Many important Democratic party leaders rushed to defend Hatcher against charges that Hatcher was a dangerous political radical. Indiana Senators Birch Bayh and Vance Hartke, Indiana Governor Roger Branigan, Vice-President Hubert Humphrey, and New York Senator Robert Kennedy, along with many other leading Democrats, vouched for Hatcher's patriotism and for his political ability. These leaders denounced the party chairman for not supporting Hatcher. On September 14 Vice-President Humphrey embraced Hatcher publicly and called him "a man of merit, experience, character, education, willingness, and capacity to serve."

The party chairman replied to his critics: "I will carry this fight through to the very end, no matter how it may endanger my political future. I shall fight for the principle that loyalty to my country comes first and my loyalty to my party comes second."

The party chairman, although criticized sharply by state and national Democratic leaders, was strongly supported by many white local Democrats who hailed him for having "the guts to stand up and say what everybody is thinking."

Attitudes of People in Gary

The attitudes of many people in Gary revealed the severity of this political campaign. Many white people who had always voted Democratic were declaring that this year they would vote for Radigan, although they would support other Democratic candidates for public office. Some of the reasons that these white Democrats gave for supporting a Republican candidate for mayor are representative of comments that were made throughout Gary in the autumn of 1967.

> *Steelworker*—The decent people of Gary don't want a black mayor. Gary used to be a nice place to live in before the blacks came here. If they win the mayor's office, Gary won't be a fit place for a white man to live in. I never voted for a Republican before, but this year, Radigan's my man.

175

Housewife—I haven't got anything against the Negroes. Some of my best friends are Negroes. But Hatcher is a dangerous radical. He has big-shot friends in the civil rights movement who will control his decisions if he gets elected. We Gary people don't want outsiders running our city.

Neighborhood grocery store owner—The black people are trying to take over this city, and the whites have to stop them.

Lawyer—I disagree strongly with some of Hatcher's plans for the development of Gary. I usually vote Democratic, but Joseph Radigan appears to be better qualified than Richard Hatcher to lead Gary.

Not all white Democrats agreed with the above ideas:

Businessman—I've always supported the Democratic Party. I see no reason to stop now. Hatcher is well qualified to run this city.

Housewife—Richard Hatcher pledges to clean up this city. I believe him. Therefore, I'm with him all the way.

Black citizens were nearly unanimous in their support of Hatcher:

Steelworker—Hatcher's my man. He's going to turn this city around. I've never before worked in a political campaign, but I'm behind Hatcher one hundred percent.

Housewife—Dick Hatcher is a fine man. He'll lead Gary real good.

Unemployed young man—If Hatcher don't get elected, there is going to be trouble in this town. We've got the votes, baby, and the whites better not steal them away from us.

Secretary—I don't care much for Richard Hatcher, but I prefer him, or any Democrat, to Radigan.

For the first time in over twenty years Republicans could anticipate victory. They were making every effort to take advantage of this unexpected chance to gain political power.

October, 1967, was filled with hectic campaign activity. Political interest was higher in Gary than ever before. Speeches, parades, rallies, and newspaper advertising were all used to influence voters. Hatcher and Radigan spoke many times to large and small groups hoping to win support. Both candidates knew the election would be close, and they overlooked no possibilities to gain votes. Many observers predicted that the election would be decided by less than 2000 votes, a close decision indeed.

Voter Registration Becomes an Issue

An important part of the campaign strategy revolved around the competition to register voters. Both Hatcher's supporters and his opponents worked vigorously to register as many favorable voters as possible. In Gary, as elsewhere in the United States, a person may not vote on election day unless he has been registered previously as an eligible voter. This is the law. Voter registration requirements vary in this country from state to state. But in Gary, as elsewhere in Indiana in 1967, a person had to be at least 21 years of age, an American citizen, a resident of the state for at least six months, and a resident of his county for at least 60 days to be eligible to register as a voter.

The anti-Hatcher forces had a slight advantage in this race to register voters. The Democratic party chairman also held the post of county clerk. This gave him membership on the Lake County Election Board, which supervises elections within the county.

Furthermore, the Hatcher forces faced the handicap of overcoming low Negro voter registration totals. Although Negroes comprised almost 60 percent of Gary's population, they made up slightly less than half of the total number of registered voters. Thus, even if all Negro voters would vote for Hatcher (highly unlikely), he would still need about 10 percent of the "white" vote to win.

Workers for the Lake County Election Board made themselves available daily to Gary residents who wished to register to vote. Workers who supported Hatcher tended to stress the registration of Negroes, while Radigan supporters tended to stress registration of people likely to vote against Hatcher.

The voter-registration competition resulted in a charge that a few of Hatcher's opponents were using illegal voter registration tactics in their drive to defeat Hatcher. During the week before the November 7th election, Hatcher filed suit in the Federal district court. He charged Lake County Election Board workers with breaking Federal law in their registration activities. Hatcher claimed that his opponents were adding "ghost voters" to their list of eligible voters. Presumably, people who would vote against Hatcher would be paid to vote under the names of the "ghost voters." Furthermore, Hatcher charged that many names of registered Negro voters were being unfairly taken off the registered voter lists.

Hatcher sent a telegram to United States Attorney General Ramsey Clark stating, according to the *Chicago Sun-Times,* that he had "absolute and undeniable proof that certain prominent election officials are engaged in massive fraudulent registrations in white areas in order to steal the election. Without immediate Federal intervention a fair election cannot be held and the people of Gary will be robbed of their inherent and constitutional rights." On November 3 the United States Justice Department filed suit against five Lake County election officials charging that "they have padded white voter rolls and illegally purged Negro voters. . . ." Attorney General Clark said that he took this action to protect the rights of Gary's Negro voters under the Fifteenth Amendment to the Constitution, the "equal rights" clause of the Fourteenth Amendment, and the Voting Rights Act of 1965.

On November 6, election eve, an FBI agent testified before a three-judge Federal panel that he found evidence of "massive registration of nonexistent white voters who presumably would vote against Hatcher." Then a Gary precinct committeewoman testified that she had "signed voter-registration applications for approximately 48 persons who didn't exist."

After hearing testimony, the three-judge panel ordered that 4845 Negroes who had been removed from the voter registration list be put back on the eligible voter rolls. The court also set guidelines for a fair election.

According to the *Gary Post-Tribune,* when the party chairman was asked about the Federal court action, he said:

> The election board has taken every precaution to prevent ghost voting, and those persons we know to be illegally registered will be identified as such on the official registration records in the hands of election board officials at each polling place.
>
> We expect these persons to be challenged at the polls. This is the right that can be exercised by any election board official right down to the precinct level or by any eligible voter. . . .

Both Hatcher and Radigan made public statements about the voting registration controversy. According to the *Gary Post-Tribune,* Hatcher said:

> Two weeks ago I made a charge and a challenge: I charged that an attempt was being made to take many thousands of living and legitimate midtown voters off the rolls, and that at the same time there was a plot to register and vote many thousand phantom voters against me. I challenged my opponent to meet with me and any impartial person he might suggest and review my evidence, and the evidence that he was aware that this plan was in the making.
>
> Since then, the Federal Bureau of Investigation has investigated the situation in Gary; and now upon evidence of vote fraud supplied by them, the Justice Department has brought suit against those who were conniving to steal this election.
>
> Now that my charges have been verified, will Mr. Radigan accept my challenge and meet with me, and face the facts of his implication in this scheme?
>
> If he will not, the choice for the people of Gary will be clear. They can vote for elections as usual, and machine politics, or they can vote for honest elections and independent leadership.

Radigan's statement in the Gary newspaper follows:

My position on the conduct of the election has not changed, and I continue to stand by my statements made last week at a press conference and given wide circulation by the press.

I again repeat my principles and beliefs concerning this election:

1. I have continually urged an honest election. At public meetings and in official statements from my headquarters I have asked for a complete investigation to clear the air and guarantee our citizens an honest election.

2. No one who meets all residence and registration requirements should be deprived of his right to vote.

3. Persons who do not meet these qualifications should not be permitted to vote.

4. Fraud is fraud, wherever found, and I have not, nor will I now, apply double standards to this type of activity.

Outcome of the Gary Election

As election day neared, tensions rose in Gary. Many feared that civil disorders, even large-scale rioting, might occur. As a result of these fears, Governor Roger Branigan ordered an Indiana National Guard unit to duty in the Gary area as a precaution against massive civil disorder. Radigan, Hatcher, and prominent public officials appealed to the people of Gary to behave in an orderly way on election day and to accept whatever decision would be yielded by the election process.

Outside his Gary law office, candidate Hatcher chats with a prospective voter.

On November 7, election day, the several polling places located in various Gary neighborhoods were unusually busy. Over 70 percent of those who could qualify to vote did vote this election day. This was quite a contrast to the less than 60 percent of the electorate which usually votes in an American election.

Voters stood in long lines and waited patiently to cast their votes. All the fears of massive disorder were unfounded. Outgoing Mayor Katz called this election day one of the most orderly, peaceful, and quiet in Gary history. The appeals of Radigan, Hatcher, and a host of other civic leaders were heeded by Gary's citizens. Despite severe tensions and conflicts, people obeyed the rules, and a political decision was reached in terms of the rules. Later that evening Hatcher was named the victor. The official tally of votes gave Hatcher 39,330 votes to 37,941 votes for Radigan.

A crisis in the life of Gary, Indiana, had passed. The streets were quiet and tension-free for the first time in weeks. Political power had been peacefully turned over to a Negro mayor-elect, Richard G. Hatcher.

Hatcher's victory had been based almost entirely upon Negro votes. He received about 95 percent of the Negro votes. The city's white people gave Hatcher no more than about 15 percent of their votes, most of them from Latin Americans and Jews. Yet, as Hatcher took office, the bitterness that had marked the campaign began to recede.

In victory, according to a long-standing American political custom, Hatcher was publicly magnanimous. He publicly described Radigan as "a worthy adversary who truly fought a hard battle. Gary certainly needs his talents and the talents of others like him. There is much they can do."

In defeat, according to a long-standing American political custom, Radigan was gracious and accommodating. In a public statement he said, "I now offer my congratulations and every hope for a successful administration."

Aftermath of the Gary Election

Later Joseph Radigan, along with former Mayor Katz, began to be prominent supporters of the Hatcher administration. Following the lead of Radigan and Katz, other prominent white leaders began to actively support the new Hatcher administration. The growing mood of much of the white community became one of guarded and hesitant toleration. "The guy wanted the job; let's see what he can do with it." Hatcher's former opponents, in line with the American political culture, became his supporters or his "loyal opposition." If many Garyites still resented the fact that Hatcher was mayor, they would still respect the mayoral role, the mayoral institution. And they would work to unseat Hatcher at the next election, according to the "rules of the game."

In May, 1971, Hatcher won renomination in the Democratic primary by a big margin over a black candidate endorsed by the Democratic committee.

A further consequence of the Gary election was renewed hope for many of Gary's Negroes. Often in the past they had lapsed into passive political apathy or angry political alienation. They had felt that they could not successfully make demands upon the political system. There had been speculation that many Gary blacks were growing tired of obeying the political rules. Conforming to the rules had not appeared to pay off. There had been talk of possible Negro riots in Gary.

180

Bob Laster in the (Gary) *Post-Tribune*

Let's Get the Gifts in Deserving Stockings

Anachronism

But Hatcher's victory appears to have changed this massive Negro political alienation, at least temporarily. His brand of "black power," according to the "rules of the game," is evidence that the American political system can adjust effectively to meet demands upon it from masses of Negroes.

Discussing the campaign a few days before the election, Hatcher said:

I hear a great deal these days about how lucky we are in Gary not to have had any riots or serious civil disturbances. It is not luck alone that has prevented serious difficulty in Gary—it is something much more tangible and identifiable than that.

Gary has something many of these other cities did not have and that is an element called hope. There is an honest and genuine hope in the hearts of most people here that things are going to be better in Gary and that Gary has a chance to lead the way in this nation. I think my election in November is a part of that total feeling of hope. It is a feeling that must neither be frustrated nor betrayed.*

1. How did the political parties select candidates to represent them in this election?

2. How did rules (laws and customs) influence the political behavior of (a) the candidates for mayor, (b) the voters, (c) the voter registrars?

3. What are the political roles of a winning and losing candidate in an American election: (a) How is the winner expected to behave? (b) the loser? (c) What good result does society expect when winner and loser act in these customary ways?

4. What were the short-run consequences of this election?

What does the cartoon on the left tell about the political role of the newly elected mayor? The Mauldin cartoon on the right appeared two days after Hatcher's election. White voter reaction against the Negro struggle for equality is sometimes called "the backlash vote." What point is Mauldin making?

* *The Washington Post,* November 12, 1967.

181

Above is a scene at the 1936 Democratic convention, where Franklin Roosevelt was nominated for his second term. Lyndon Johnson faced no opposition in the 1964 Democratic convention, but there was disunity in the Republican camp over the nomination of Senator Barry Goldwater.

5. What are five or six basic characteristics of public elections in the United States?

6. What were some unusual, or irregular, characteristics of this mayoral election?

7. To what extent do American public elections reflect the characteristics of democracy?

D. Electing a President

The Presidency is the leading position in the government of the United States. As the chief executive, the President is responsible for carrying out the nation's laws. As head of the government, the President has the power to make decisions that affect the lives of all American citizens. As chief representative of the people, the President is a symbol of the United States to the peoples of the world.

Since the Presidency is the foremost position in the American government, it is vitally important to the life of the country to select capable Presidents. How is the American President selected? Does this method of selection contribute to, or detract from, the possibility of selecting a capable President?

National Party Conventions Nominate Candidates

The first part of the presidential election process is the nomination of candidates to compete for the Presidency. Every four years the political parties hold nominating conventions. The convention is a meeting of select party members from throughout the country. The nominating conventions are the creations and responsibilities of the political parties. Neither the Constitution nor Federal laws prescribe how candidates for President of the United States must be nominated.

Prior to the national party conventions, individuals seeking the nomination of their party announce their intentions and begin to campaign. For example, in the early part of 1968, Robert Kennedy, Eugene McCarthy, and Hubert Humphrey actively sought the nomination of the Democratic party. Richard Nixon, Nelson Rockefeller, and Ronald Reagan were prominent pursuers of the Republican nomination in 1968. Each candidate for nomination tried to gain the support of delegates to his party's convention, since the delegates would select the party's presidential candidate.

The convention delegates are chosen by popular vote in primary elections in fifteen states and the District of Columbia. In the other states, delegates are chosen by state party conventions or by committees of party leaders.

The size of the delegations from each state varies according to the population of the state and the support that the state has given to party candidates in recent elections. For example, states with large populations and states where the voters supported Republican candidates for national office in 1968 would have more delegates, and more votes, at the 1972 Republican National Convention than would small states and states where voters supported Democratic candidates in 1968.

All the persons seeking to be the party's "standard bearer" in the coming presidential election will have their names presented to the convention. A majority of delegate votes is needed to nominate a candidate. In 1968 a majority of the 2989 delegates to the Democratic National Convention voted for Hubert Humphrey as their presidential candidate. A majority of the 1333 delegates to the 1968 Republican National Convention voted for Richard Nixon to represent their party in the presidential election. The delegates usually endorse the presidential candidate's choice as the party's candidate for Vice-President of the United States.

Other Convention Activities

In addition to selecting the party candidates for President and Vice-President, delegates to a national convention approve a party platform. A platform is a statement of political ideals and policy positions. A platform is really a "bundle of compromises" between different groups within the party who have conflicting ideas. As such, it is a very general statement that is aimed at holding together diverse groups in the party so that they can cooperate to elect the party's presidential candidate.

The competition of candidates to win the party's nomination is likely to create divisions and bitterness among party members. A fundamental purpose of the party convention is to "bind the wounds" of recent conflict so that the party can present a united front of cooperation in the upcoming election. Thus the winner of the nomination usually makes complimentary remarks about the losers and asks for party unity in support of his candidacy.

Following the conventions, which are held in July or August of the election year, the rival candidates campaign to present their ideas and to attract voter support. On the Tuesday following the first Monday in November, the voters across the country indicate their preferences among the rival candidates.

The Electoral College System

Unlike the nomination process, the election system is defined by state and Federal laws. The Constitution of the United States requires that an Electoral College, or group of electors, select the President and Vice-President. (See Article II and Amendment XII of the Constitution.) However, the Electoral College functions much differently than its designers intended.

Some delegates at the Constitutional Convention in 1787 favored direct election of the President by the people. Others believed that the President should be elected by the national legislature (Congress). The idea of election by an Electoral College was really a compromise. The states would choose electors, who in turn would elect the President.

Under this plan, as altered by the Twelfth Amendment, (1) each state would choose as many presidential electors as its total of Senators and Representatives in Congress; (2) the state legislature would decide how the electors were to be chosen; (3) each elector would cast a separate ballot for President and for Vice-President; (4) the ballots would be opened and counted before a meeting of the Congress; (5) the person receiving a majority of the votes

184

cast for President would become the President, and the person receiving a majority of the votes cast for Vice-President would become the Vice-President; (6) if no candidate obtained a majority of the votes cast for President or Vice-President, the House of Representatives would choose the President and the Senate would choose the Vice-President.

The writers of the Constitution expected that the presidential electors in each state would study, discuss, and carefully vote for a highly capable President from among the country's prominent leaders. The system worked as the "Founding Fathers" intended only during the first and second presidential elections, when George Washington was chosen, without opposition, as the Chief Executive.

With the retirement of George Washington from public life, competition for the Presidency developed between newly organized political parties. The growth and development of competing political parties led to changes in the election system. The Electoral College of the Founding Fathers remained in the Constitution, but it was made to function in ways that the writers of the Constitution had not intended or foreseen. The major change was the emergence of a popular vote to control the selection and behavior of the presidential electors.

Today, the members of the Electoral College go through the formalities required by the Constitution. However, the voters across the country have the real power to select the President. The members of the Electoral College from each state are expected to vote for the candidate who receives a majority of the popular votes in their state.

The Electoral College System in the 1968 Election

The 1968 presidential election illustrates the Electoral College system as it developed over the years. On November 5, 1968, over 73 million Americans voted in a public election to choose a President and Vice-President. The Republican candidate, Richard M. Nixon, received 31,770,237 votes, or 43.4 percent of the total popular vote. The Democratic candidate, Hubert H. Humphrey, received 31,270,533 votes, or 42.7 percent of the total popular vote. George C. Wallace, the American Independent party candidate, received 9,906,141 votes, or 13.5 percent of the total popular vote. A variety of other minority party candidates received a total of 239,908 votes—less than 1 percent of the total popular vote.

Although Richard Nixon was the winner of the popular vote, the masses of people could not formally elect him to the Presidency. Rather, in each state people were technically choosing between competing lists of Republican, Democratic, and American Independent party electors. For example, the state of Wisconsin had the right to select twelve electors, since it had two Senators and ten members of the House of Representatives. Richard Nixon, the Republican candidate, won a majority of the popular votes in Wisconsin. According to the "winner-take-all" system practiced in every state, the twelve electors selected to represent Wisconsin in the Electoral College were those of the Republican party. These presidential electors met in Madison, the state capital,

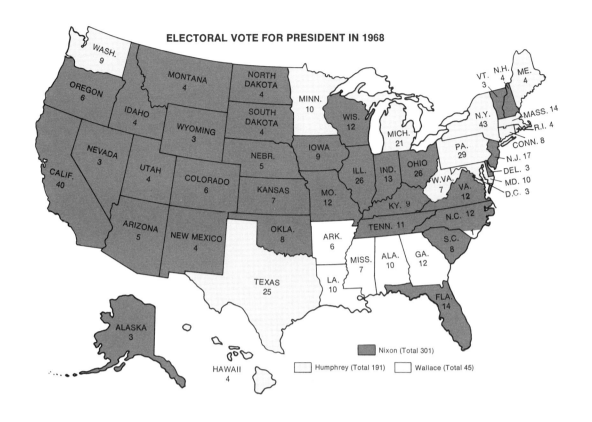

ELECTORAL VOTE FOR PRESIDENT IN 1968

Nixon (Total 301)
Humphrey (Total 191)
Wallace (Total 45)

THE POPULAR VOTE FOR PRESIDENT IN 1968

(State vote in thousands)

N = Nixon 31,770,237
H = Humphrey . . . 31,270,533
W = Wallace 9,906,141

	N	H	W
Alabama	147	197	691
Alaska	38	35	10
Arizona	267	171	47
Arkansas	189	185	236
California	3,468	3,244	487
Colorado	409	335	61
Connecticut	557	622	68
Delaware	97	89	28
Dist. of Columbia	31	140	
Florida	887	677	624
Georgia	380	334	536
Hawaii	91	141	3
Idaho	165	89	37
Illinois	2,175	2,040	390
Indiana	1,068	807	243

	N	H	W
Iowa	619	477	66
Kansas	479	303	89
Kentucky	462	398	193
Louisiana	258	310	530
Maine	169	217	6
Maryland	518	538	179
Massachusetts	767	1,469	87
Michigan	1,371	1,593	332
Minnesota	659	855	69
Mississippi	89	151	415
Missouri	812	791	206
Montana	139	114	20
Nebraska	321	171	45
Nevada	73	61	20
New Hampshire	155	131	11
New Jersey	1,325	1,264	262
New Mexico	170	130	26
New York	3,008	3,378	359

	N	H	W
North Carolina	627	464	496
North Dakota	139	95	14
Ohio	1,791	1,701	467
Oklahoma	450	302	192
Oregon	408	359	50
Pennsylvania	2,090	2,259	379
Rhode Island	122	247	158
South Carolina	254	197	215
South Dakota	150	118	13
Tennessee	473	351	425
Texas	1,228	1,267	581
Utah	239	157	27
Vermont	85	70	5
Virginia	590	442	320
Washington	589	616	97
West Virginia	308	374	73
Wisconsin	810	749	128
Wyoming	71	45	11

186

in December to cast their ballots for the Republican candidates, Richard Nixon and Spiro Agnew. These ballots were sealed and sent to Washington, D.C.

On January 6, 1969, the President of the Senate opened the sealed ballots from each of the fifty states and the District of Columbia. The votes were counted before the members of both houses of Congress. Richard Nixon received 302 electoral votes and was officially declared the President. He needed at least 270 of the 538 electoral votes to gain a majority. His running-mate, Spiro Agnew, also received 302 electoral votes and was officially declared the Vice-President. Democrat Hubert Humphrey and his running-mate, Edmund Muskie, received 191 electoral votes, and the "third party" team of George Wallace and Curtis LeMay received 45 electoral votes. Although everyone had known since November 6 that Nixon and Agnew had won the election, their victory did not become official until the electoral votes were counted on January 6.

The members of the Electoral College are expected to vote for the candidate that receives a majority of the popular vote in their state, but the Constitution allows them to vote as they please. Thus, it is legally possible for the electors to vote for candidates other than those selected in their states by the popular vote. For example, in 1960 an elector from Oklahoma voted for Senator Harry Byrd of Virginia even though a majority of Oklahoma's popular vote had gone to Richard Nixon. However, electors rarely have broken their pledges to follow the popular vote.

In the event that no candidate receives a majority of the electoral votes, the Constitution requires that the House of Representatives choose the President. In this special election, each of the fifty state delegations in the House would have one vote; and it would require a majority of twenty-six votes to elect a President. The House would select a President from among the three candidates with the most electoral votes. In 1800 and in 1824 the House of Representatives chose the President in this manner.

E. Should We Change Our Method of Nominating Presidential Candidates?

Although our system for nominating presidential candidates has worked satisfactorily, critics have urged reform. Following are arguments for and against the current method of nominating presidential candidates.

Arguments against the Convention Method of Nomination

The main argument against the nominating convention is that it limits popular participation. In most of the states, party leaders, rather than popular votes, select delegates to the party conventions. Thus, the critics argue, most of the convention delegates are under the influence of their political party leaders rather than the masses of people. According to the critics, the convention system is open to selection of a presidential candidate through political deals rather than by the will of the people.

Many advocates of change in the nomination procedure have suggested some type of nationwide popular primary election as the best means for selecting presidential candidates. Estes Kefauver, the late Democratic senator from Tennessee, was a strong supporter of nomination through primary elections. Following is an excerpt from a statement by Kefauver, before the Senate Judiciary Committee in 1961, in favor of electoral reform:

> The primary method of nomination works well in selecting Governors and Members of Congress in many states. It should be extended to the choice of candidates for President and Vice-President and thus continue the evolution toward more democratic methods of choosing our presidential and vice-presidential candidates. The more the people have a chance to speak their minds, the closer we get to grassroots opinions and desires, the better our democracy works.

> Presidential primary elections in all the states would require candidates to discuss the issues publicly. Such public debate will help to inform and enlighten public opinion via press, radio, and television, and it would pave the way for broadening and strengthening the democratic process.

> It will also result, I believe, in better government and government more responsible to the people. A candidate for President who has been nominated by the people instead of the conventions will be, if elected, more responsive to the will of the people and more obligated to the people than to politicians.

> Experience shows that presidential primaries arouse public interest and stimulate discussions of public issues, as well as of the character, convictions, and abilities of those who aspire to the highest offices in the land. They also increase the participation of eligible voters in presidential elections and overcome the apathy induced by the feeling that the people have little real choice in the selection of their candidates for President and Vice-President.

What is Mauldin's view on the national nominating conventions?

©1968 Chicago Sun-Times   MAULDIN (Miami Beach)

"THERE'S GOT TO BE A BETTER WAY FOR US TO TRAVEL."

In this period of struggle between the democracies and the dictatorships, the method of choosing the men who lead our nation should leave no room for doubt, at home or abroad, that our leaders have been elected after the fullest possible freedom of choice by our people. The archaic convention system does not necessarily register the preferences of the people.

Arguments for the Convention Method of Nomination

The main arguments in support of national nominating conventions are (1) that they serve to maintain political party unity, (2) that they involve less expense than the alternative proposal of nationwide primary elections, and (3) that they have worked adequately to produce competent presidential candidates. Furthermore, supporters of the convention system believe that the conventions do reflect the popular will in selecting candidates.

Many of the supporters of the convention system believe that some minor changes should be made to improve the conduct of the conventions. However, these supporters of conventions are united in the belief that this method of nominating presidential candidates is superior to any alternative.

One of the many staunch supporters of the convention system was the late Clinton Rossiter, a well-known professor of political science. Following is an excerpt from Rossiter's argument in support of conventions.*

* Clinton Rossiter, *The American Presidency* (New York: Harcourt Brace Jovanovich, Inc., A Harvest Book, 1960), pp. 192–194.

Quite to the contrary of accepted legend, the convention has done a remarkable job over the years in giving the voters of each party the man whom they, too, would have selected had they been faced with the necessity of making a responsible choice. The convention is anxious to satisfy, not frustrate, the hopes of the members of the party; if the [people] give an unmistakable sound, the [convention] will echo it gladly and faithfully. If they . . . cannot agree on a clear choice, the convention will choose their man for them . . . and the choice, moreover, will be made finally with near or complete unanimity. One of the undeniable merits of the convention, as opposed to the primary, is that it heals most of the wounds that are inevitably laid open in the rough process of making so momentous a political decision. . . .

The convention . . . is a clear if not brilliant success. It meets the one test to which we like to put all our institutions: it does the job it is asked to do, and does it remarkably well. . . .

The nominating convention fills a constitutional void; it unites and inspires each of the parties; it arouses interest in [public election] through which we choose our President. We will have to hear more convincing charges than have hitherto been pressed before we tamper with this venerable instrument of American democracy.

1. What are the main arguments in opposition to the convention system for nominating presidential candidates?

2. What are the main arguments in favor of the convention system?

3. What is your evaluation of the arguments of Estes Kefauver and Clinton Rossiter concerning reform of the nominating process?

About a third of the states choose delegates to the national conventions in a statewide primary election. The dates for the primaries range from March to June of the election year. About ten of the states give the voters a chance to express a preference among the contenders for their party's nomination. A contender who makes a poor showing in an early primary may decide to withdraw from the race. Four days after Senator Eugene McCarthy (campaigning at left) made a strong showing against an organized write-in vote for President Lyndon Johnson in the 1968 primary in New Hampshire, Senator Robert F. Kennedy announced his candidacy for the Democratic nomination. Two weeks later Lyndon Johnson announced that he would not run for reelection. Then Hubert Humphrey promptly entered the race.

The Boston Globe
MORNING EDITION
MONDAY, APRIL 1, 1968

LBJ STUNS THE NATION: *"I shall not seek and I will not accept the nomination of my party for another term as your President."*
(Complete text on Page 14)

Johnson Won't Run in '68

The assassination of Robert Kennedy (campaigning opposite) at a victory celebration following the California primary left the race to Humphrey (right) and McCarthy. Richard Nixon (below) had relatively clear sailing after Governor George Romney (above) withdrew early in the Republican race for President.

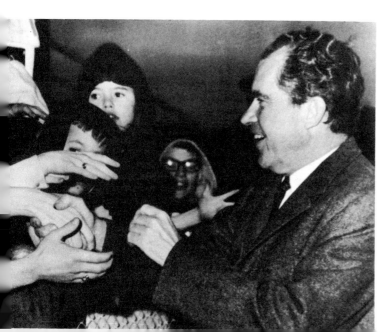

F. Should We Alter or Abolish the Electoral College?

The Electoral College system has been under attack. Critics have said that the system suffers from several weaknesses, and have urged its alteration or abolishment.

The Case against the Electoral College

The most serious criticism is that under the Electoral College system a candidate with more popular votes than any of his opponents may fail to win the Presidency. Twice in our history, in 1876 and 1888, candidates with the most popular votes failed to get a majority of the electoral votes. See *Table 1* below.

Table 1. **Popular Votes and Electoral Votes in 1876 and 1888**

Year	Candidates	Popular Vote	Electoral Vote
1876	Hayes	4,033,950	185
	Tilden	4,284,757	184
1888	Cleveland	5,540,050	168
	Harrison	5,444,337	233

The "winner-take-all" method of choosing electors in each state is the major reason for the possibility of electing a President with minority popular support. For example, a candidate needs only to win the popular vote in a state by one vote in order to gain all the electoral votes of the state. Thus, a candidate could win 270 electoral votes, enough to be elected, by winning the popular vote in several states by a very small margin of victory. At the same time this candidate could lose the popular vote in several states by a very large margin and lose the nationwide popular vote to his rival while winning the Presidency.

A second major criticism of the Electoral College system is that the law does not require the presidential electors to vote for the candidate who has received a majority of the popular votes in their state. Although electors pledge to vote for the winning candidates in their states, and most electors have honored their pledges, there is the possibility in some future election for presidential electors to violate the public trust and disregard the popular vote in selecting a President.

A third criticism is that the states with less population are favored over the states with more population in the distribution of electoral votes. For example, the population of New York State is roughly 58 times more than the population of Alaska. Yet New York's total of electoral votes is only 13 times that of Alaska.

A fourth criticism is that the present system encourages candidates to focus attention on a few heavily populated states and to neglect the voters

Engelhardt in the *St. Louis Post-Dispatch*

"Without me, where'd be all the excitement?"

in other states. Under the "winner-take-all" system of gaining electoral votes, it was possible to win the Presidency in 1968 by winning the popular vote in the twelve largest states, which had a total of 281 electoral votes.

A Proposal for Abolishing the Electoral College

Many political leaders have urged the abolition of the Electoral College in favor of direct popular election of the President and Vice-President. Senator Birch Bayh of Indiana was the major spokesman in 1970 for an amendment to the Constitution to abolish the Electoral College and allow the people to elect the President directly. In the event that no candidate obtained at least 40 percent of the popular votes, a "run-off" election between the top two vote-getters would determine the winner.

Following is an excerpt from one of Senator Bayh's arguments in favor of direct popular election of the President:

Unless we accept the argument that the people should not be trusted to choose their President and Vice-President, there is absolutely no valid argument against the direct popular election amendment now being debated. . . .

Any system that retains the electoral vote, no matter what scheme is devised to divide the vote, can elect a President who is not the first choice of the people.

If our political system is ever to be truly democratic and truly responsive to the will of the people, it must let the people elect their President.*

Explain the cartoonist's signs on the voting booth. At the right is a facsimile of a certificate of electoral votes cast in one state in the 1968 election.

* Birch Bayh, "U.S. Hasn't Corrected Election Inadequacies." Bloomington, Indiana: *Daily Herald-Telephone.* September 12, 1970. (From syndicated column of John P. Roche.)

193

Proposals for Altering the Electoral College

Many political leaders have suggested the reform, rather than the abolishment, of the Electoral College system. One widely discussed plan for reforming the system would divide the electoral vote of each state in proportion to the popular vote cast in the state. For example, Vermont has three electoral votes. If a candidate wins two-thirds of the popular vote in Vermont, he would receive two of the three electoral votes. The loser, who received one-third of the popular votes in the state, would receive one of the state's three electoral votes. This proportional system of dividing electoral votes would do away with the electors to insure that the electoral votes would reflect the popular votes. The supporters of the proportional system say that their plan retains the strengths of the Electoral College system while doing away with its main weaknesses.

Many leaders wish to retain the essential features of the present electoral system. Abolishing the electors is the only change they would make. They would have the electoral vote tied directly to the popular vote without the use of presidential electors to cast their ballots ceremoniously.

1. What are the main arguments against the Electoral College system?

2. What are the main arguments in favor of retaining the essential features of the Electoral College system?

3. What is your evaluation of the arguments presented here for altering or abolishing the Electoral College?

chapter 10

Popular Participation in Election Campaigns and Voting

The citizen's right to vote is basic to American politics. Through voting in public elections, ordinary people have a chance to select public officials and to influence the direction of public policy. From childhood through adulthood, Americans are told that they should show interest in politics and vote in public elections. To what extent do American citizens exercise their right to vote? Are some groups in our society more likely than others to participate in the public election process? If there are differences between groups in degree of participation in the public election process, why do these differences exist?

A. Who Votes in American Elections?

Following are three tables about popular participation in public elections in the United States. On the basis of data presented in these tables, what generalizations can you make about (1) the extent of popular participation in the public election process and (2) the relationship of tendency to vote to each of the following variables:

    a. age group

    b. racial identity

    c. sex identity

    d. educational attainment

    e. occupation

    f. income

    g. socioeconomic status

    h. area of residence

Table 2. **Percentage of the Electorate Voting in National Elections, 1940–1970**

Year	CIVILIANS OF VOTING AGE	
	Percent Voting for President	Percent Voting for Congressman
1940	59.2%	55.7%
1942		33.9
1944	52.9	49.8
1946		37.4
1948	51.3	48.4
1950		41.6
1952	62.6	58.6
1954		42.4
1956	60.1	56.6
1958		43.4
1960	64.0	59.6
1962		46.7
1964	62.9	58.7
1966		46.3
1968	61.8	55.8
1970		43.8

Source: *Statistical Abstract*

195

Table 3. Percentage of Different Types of Nonvoters in Four Presidential Elections

| | PERCENT OF GROUP NOT VOTING | | | |
	1948	1952	1956	1960
Sex				
Male	31%	21%	20%	21%
Female	41	31	32	31
Age				
21–34	44	32	36	32
35–44	34	24	26	25
45–54	25	21	22	21
55 and over	37	23	21	25
Race				
White	34	21	24	24
Negro	64	67	65	51
Type of Community				
Metropolitan areas	17	21	25	23
Towns and cities	37	27	23	27
Rural areas	59	32	30	26
Education				
Grade School	45	38	39	36
High School	33	20	26	25
College	21	10	10	15
Occupation of Head of Family				
Professional and managerial	25	12	21	27
Other white collar	19	19	30	36
Skilled and semi-skilled	29	26	32	39
Unskilled	50	40	48	49
Income				
Very low	54	47	47	40
Medium	26	24	31	28
Higher	18	12	18	18

Adapted from Robert E. Lane, *Political Life* (New York: The Free Press, 1959), pp. 48–49.

196

Table 4. Comparative Voting Turnout of Different Groups in 1964	
Group	Percent in Each Group Who Voted in the 1964 Presidential Election
Employment	
Employed men	67%
Unemployed men	50
Occupation	
White-collar workers	77
Service workers	67
Farm workers	60
White-collar men at age 45	82
Income	
Very low	45
High	77
Very high	85
Age Group	
Less than 25	45
Ages 25–44	66
Ages 45–64	75
Over 75	60
Sex	
Men	65
Women	60
Racial Identity	
Whites	65
Blacks	52
Area of Residence	
Metropolitan area	64
Non-metropolitan area	60
Educational Level	
A year or more of college	73
Less than eighth-grade	44

Source of data: J. W. Friedheim, *Where Are the Voters?* (Washington: The National Press, 1968), pp. 41–44.

Social scientists will be watching for the impact of 18-year-old voters on future elections.

B. The Influence of Laws upon Voter Turnout in Public Elections

Most Americans have the right to vote in public elections, but a large number of eligible Americans do not vote. *Table 2* indicates that more than one-third of the electorate does not vote in presidential elections. Less than half of the electorate participate in off-year congressional elections.

Elections that occur in the years between presidential elections are called off-year elections.

Why are some individuals more likely than others to vote in a public election? Several factors, or variables, can help us to account for differences in degree of political participation of different individuals. Election laws, or the legal factor, can account for some of the nonparticipation.

Legal Qualifications for Voting

Every society that provides opportunities for citizens to vote for political leaders also establishes legal qualifications for voting. The main purpose of these legal qualifications is to prevent unfit individuals from voting. Individuals are judged unfit as voters in terms of the political culture, the predominant political values and attitudes in the society. In times past in American history, black people, women, men without property, and men who did not believe in God were judged undesirable as voters. However, changes in our political culture are reflected by changes in voting laws. Today women, black people, propertyless men, and nonbelievers in religion have the legal right to vote in all states.

In line with the political culture of current American society, aliens, nonresidents, convicts, and children are the main groups that are considered unfit voters. Laws exist that prevent them from voting.

The Constitution of the United States gives the state governments chief responsibility over voting and elections, but it puts some restrictions on the power of the states to determine the right to vote. The Fifteenth Amendment declares that no state may prevent an individual from voting "on account of race, color, or previous condition of servitude." The Nineteenth Amendment provides that no state may prevent women from voting. The Twenty-fourth Amendment says that the states may not require the payment of a poll tax as a qualification for voting.

In order to vote in each of the fifty states an individual must be an American citizen, have reached a certain minimum age, and be a resident of the state for a certain period of time. We shall look at each of these requirements, and then look at other barriers which have existed in recent years.

Citizenship as a Barrier to Voting

A person who is neither a "natural-born" nor a "naturalized" citizen of the United States can neither vote nor be a candidate for public office. These restrictions upon aliens, or non-citizens, are law in all fifty states.

An individual is a natural-born citizen if (a) he was born within the boundaries of the United States, or (b) he was born anywhere in the world to parents who are United States citizens.

198

A citizen of another country may become a naturalized citizen of the United States by satisfying certain legal requirements: (1) Petition for naturalization: Any alien who has lived in the United States for five years or more, who is at least 18 years old, who has been permitted to establish his home in the United States, and who can speak, read, and write English may make a petition to become an American citizen. (2) Examination: The applicant for citizenship must prove that he can meet the English language requirement, has good moral character, and has established legal residence in the United States. (3) Final court hearing: The person seeking citizenship appears in court and takes the oath of allegiance to the United States of America. He then becomes a naturalized citizen and is entitled to the same rights and duties as any other American citizen.

An eighteen-year-old registers to vote in Decatur, Georgia.

Age as a Barrier to Voting

Until Georgia reduced the voting age to 18 in 1943, the minimum age had always been 21—the age of adulthood under the English common law which the colonists brought with them to America. Kentucky reduced the voting age to 18 in 1955. When Alaska and Hawaii entered the Union in 1959, Alaska's constitution set the voting age at 19 and Hawaii's constitution at age 20. Efforts in a number of other states during the 1950's and 1960's to lower the voting age failed.

Measures to lower the voting age appeared on the ballots of fifteen states in 1970. One third of the proposals passed. Alaska went to age 18; Montana and Massachusetts to age 19; and Maine and Nebraska to age 20.

Earlier in 1970, during deliberations on extending the Voting Rights Act of 1965 for another five years, Congress inserted a provision for a nationwide 18-year-old voting age. The bill provided machinery for a swift court test of the measure so that 18-year-olds would become eligible in 1971. Some critics of the measure argued that this kind of policy decision should be made by constitutional amendment. Those favoring direct action by Congress said that a lowering of the voting age was long overdue and that amending the Constitution would take "too long." Some contended that today's young people are better informed and more mature and responsible than young people of an earlier time.

In December, 1970, the Supreme Court handed down a decision on the amendments to the Voting Rights Act. The Court held that Congress acted properly in giving the vote to 18-year-olds *in Federal elections*. But, said the Court, Congress exceeded its authority in lowering the voting age for state and local elections. To resolve the problem of having separate Federal and state ballots in future elections, Congress in 1971 proposed an amendment lowering the voting age to 18. It was ratified within four months.

Mobility as a Barrier to Voting

All states require that a voter must have resided in the state for a certain period of time, generally six months to two years. Most states also have a local residence requirement (ranging from one month to six months) in the county

199

and/or voting district. Residency restrictions on the right to vote presume that a newcomer to a state or county would be unfit to vote for lack of time to become acquainted with candidates and issues in the state or local election.

Mobile people, those who change their place of residence, are the victims of these residency requirements. It is estimated that from six to eight million people lost their vote in the 1968 presidential election because they had not lived long enough in their new homes to satisfy the residency requirements. These people had moved from one state to another or from one part of a state to another part.

Many of America's better educated people—doctors, lawyers, educators, engineers, and businessmen—are among the more mobile elements of the population. The residency laws work against them when they are compelled, for business or professional reasons, to change their place of residence.

While some few months of residence may increase the fitness of a person to vote in a state or local election, this argument does not apply to presidential elections. A person moving from Ohio to Colorado two months before a presidential election has not thereby become less fit to choose between the candidates for President.

To remedy this unfairness, Congress in 1970 added a second provision to the law extending the Voting Rights Act (p. 199). It establishes a uniform residence requirement of 30 days in the state or political subdivision for voting in presidential elections. This means that states will have to provide newcomers to a state or county with a separate ballot to vote for President and Vice-President if the state chooses to retain its other residency requirements.

The Decline of Other Legal Requirements for Voting

Throughout American history, legal barriers to voting have gradually broken down. During America's colonial period, only white males were allowed to vote. Seven of the thirteen colonies required an individual to own land in order to vote. The other six colonies required evidence of personal property or a tax payment of all voters. A few colonies required a person to profess some kind of orthodox religious belief in order to vote.

Property and tax-paying qualifications continued in force after the thirteen colonies gained independence. Several states retained property ownership qualifications for voting until the 1840's and 1850's. New Western states that came into the Union during the nineteenth century usually did not establish property qualifications for voting.

The Nineteenth Amendment provided for woman's suffrage (the right to vote). And much earlier the Fifteenth Amendment ended *legal* restrictions on the right of Negroes to vote. As we shall see, however, blacks in some states were kept from the polls by a variety of other devices. One of these was the poll tax, which was finally removed as a requirement for voting in 1964 by the Twenty-fourth Amendment.

Literacy tests have also been a barrier to voting until very recently. It is estimated that such tests prevented around one million people from voting in the early 1960's. Such tests had been used for many years to hinder the registration of black voters in certain Southern states. The Voting Rights Act of 1965, mentioned earlier, suspended the use of literacy tests in states where there was clear evidence of racial discrimination in voting. Then when that law was extended in 1970, Congress added a third major provision: a permanent ban against any literacy test as a qualification for voting in any public elections throughout the country.

Literacy tests were based on the belief that a person cannot vote intelligently without at least a low level of reading ability. (Today, of course, even nonreaders can get considerable "voter education" by means of radio and television.) The state literacy test in New York was typical of several. It consisted of reading a paragraph and answering eight simple questions about it.

Other states, especially in the South, required a prospective voter to read a section of the state constitution and to interpret its meaning to the satisfaction of the voting registrar. Time after time Negroes, even those with college degrees, "failed" such tests. On the other hand, the Civil Rights Commission found in one state where few Negroes were registered that thousands of white voters who were unable even to write their name on the election register had "passed" the literacy test.

The Voting Rights of Black People: Using the Law to Change the Law

In spite of the fact that large groups of people have been denied the ballot in the past, a belief in "government by the people" has been an important element of the American political culture. Compared with most other countries, the United States was a leader in granting the ballot to more and more people.

A major exception to this general trend was the erection of barriers to black voters in the South at the end of the Reconstruction period in the 1870's. The Fifteenth Amendment had barred the states from making race or color a condition for voting. Nevertheless, Southern states devised other means of keeping blacks from registering and voting:

Literacy tests, as we have seen, could be "scored" to pass illiterate whites and to reject even educated blacks.

Poll taxes required that individuals pay a fee, usually one or two dollars, to be eligible to vote. In a few states the prospective voter had to pay any unpaid back poll tax as well as the current tax. Moreover, the individual could escape the tax by not voting. The poll tax, of course, stopped many poor blacks, as well as whites, from voting.

Economic and social pressures besides the poll tax included dismissal from a job if a black man asked for the ballot. Threats and actual beatings, house burnings, and even murders were used to terrorize the black community.

White-primary laws provided that only enrolled party members could vote in a primary election. The Democratic party would then refuse to enroll any black members, claiming that the party was sort of a private club and not an arm of the government. In states with white-primary laws the winners in the

Copyright © 1962 St. Louis Post-Dispatch, reproduced by courtesy of Bill Mauldin

"By th' way, what's that big word?"

This 1962 cartoon leveled criticism at the uneven standards used in the administration of literacy tests in some states.

"THE SUGAR SHACK"

Taking advantage of rights gained under the Voting Rights Act of 1965, blacks in rural Alabama flocked to the polls in 1966. This is a polling place near Peachtree, Alabama.

Democratic party election almost always won in the general election. Thus blacks had little or no chance to influence the elections.

The *Grandfather Clause* was first used in Louisiana in 1898. It gave permanent voter registration to anyone whose father or grandfather was qualified to vote as of January 1, 1867. All other people had to pass a literacy test to qualify to vote. Since the only fathers and grandfathers who were registered voters in 1867 were white, the only voters who were allowed permanent voter registration were white. Most blacks had to pass the unfair literacy test described earlier. The Grandfather Clause worked so well in restricting black voting that it spread to several other Southern states.

Most of the devices to keep blacks from voting took the form of state laws which were passed to get around the Fifteenth Amendment. How could blacks knock down these legal barriers? Some black leaders decided to use the law courts to win political rights.

A citizen who believes that a law harms him in some special way or deprives him of his constitutional rights may start a case in court. Eventually the case may reach the United States Supreme Court. The Court may decide that the citizen's claim is valid—that the law is unconstitutional and therefore may not be enforced.

202

The National Association for the Advancement of Colored People (NAACP) led the fight. The first breakthrough came in 1915, when NAACP lawyers presented their case against the Grandfather Clause in the Oklahoma state constitution. The Supreme Court declared the clause unconstitutional, or null and void. Other victories by means of law suits came slowly. Then in 1944 the white-primary laws were declared unconstitutional by the United States Supreme Court in the case of *Smith* v. *Allbright.*

In addition to seeking changes in the law by means of court action, the NAACP and other black organizations in alliance with white sympathizers worked for new Federal laws to broaden voting rights. The Civil Rights Acts of 1957 and 1960 gave the United States Attorney General the right to bring suits against election officials practicing racial discrimination. The Civil Rights Act of 1964 required that literacy tests must be given in writing and that anyone with at least a sixth-grade education must be considered literate.

We have seen that the Voting Rights Act of 1965 suspended the use of literacy tests in certain areas. That law also permitted Federal officials to register Negro voters in areas where local officials were thwarting Negro voter registration. The Voting Rights Act was extended in 1970 with an outright ban on literacy tests (p. 200).

Federal intervention in voter registration has led to a dramatic increase in election participation by blacks. In 1900 Louisiana had only 5320 blacks registered to vote, and Alabama only about 3000. As late as 1940 in eleven Southern states only 250,000 Negroes, or 5 percent of the black population, were registered to vote. By 1970 over three million Southern blacks were registered, and further gains were expected.

The chart on this page shows the dramatic impact of legal change upon the right to vote. Federal law has forced state and local governments in several states to relax their restrictions on the voter registration of black people.

Social pressures and traditional apathy still limit the participation of black people in public elections. Some white leaders still try to influence black people to stay out of political affairs. Some older black people have grown accustomed to nonparticipation in politics. However, many younger blacks have accepted the challenge of improving their opportunities through political activity. They aim to use political action to improve their lot in life.

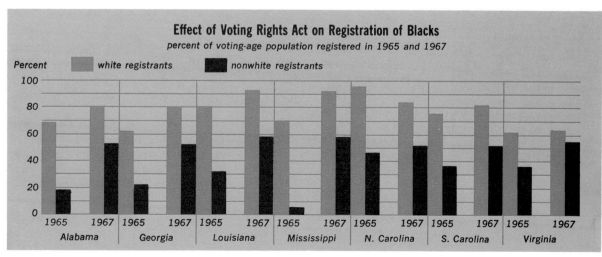

Effect of Voting Rights Act on Registration of Blacks
percent of voting-age population registered in 1965 and 1967

Answer these questions to demonstrate what you have learned about the influence of laws upon voting in public elections.

1. How do voting laws influence popular participation in public elections?

2. What reasons are used to defend the various legal restrictions on voting?

3. How have black people used the law to change their role in public elections?

4. What is the relationship of culture and socialization to legal requirements for voting?

5. Which of the following statements can be supported with evidence?

    a. There is little difference in the percentage of the nation's population that votes in a presidential election today and the percentage that voted in 1850.

    b. In every state in the United States, an individual must be a citizen, 21 years old, and a resident of the state for one year to qualify to vote.

    c. In the United States the fifty state governments, rather than the national government, have the main duty and power to establish voting qualifications.

    d. It is easier to qualify to vote in some states than in others.

    e. The national government has almost no influence on voting qualifications in the various states.

    f. Many individuals lose the right to vote in state and local elections simply by moving their place of residence.

    g. Part of the American political culture is the belief that some persons are more fit than others to participate in government by voting. Legal qualifications for voting reflect this part of the American political culture.

C. Non-Legal Factors That Influence Voter Turnout in Public Elections

Failure to satisfy legal requirements explains why some people do not vote in public elections. However, the legal factor does not explain why several million American citizens choose not to register or often fail to vote if registered.

Personal Factors and Voter Turnout

Political scientists have speculated that personal factors can contribute to an explanation of nonvoting in public elections. Personal factors are such variables as sense of political efficacy, political interest, sense of civic duty, and concern with election outcome.

Political scientists who have studied the relationship of these personal factors to nonvoting have defined these variables as follows: *Sense of political efficacy* is a person's beliefs about how much power people like him have over what public officials do. For example, people with a high sense of political efficacy believe that they can and should influence governmental decisions. People with a low sense of political efficacy believe that they can do little or nothing about what government does. (See pages 31–34 for a discussion of sense of political efficacy.)

Political interest refers to the amount of interest a person has in the election campaign. People with a high degree of political interest are very concerned about campaign issues and the characteristics of the candidates.

Concern about the election outcome means caring about who wins an election and about the results that might stem from the election outcome. A person with a low degree of concern about the election outcome cares little or nothing about which candidates win or what these candidates might do once they assume public office.

Sense of civic duty is the responsibility a person feels to participate in a public election. A person with a high sense of civic duty believes that he should take part in a public election and that those who fail to participate are not very good citizens.

Political scientists have constructed questionnaires to measure these personal factors, or variables, and administered these questionnaires to randomly selected samples that are representative of the population of the United States. Some of their findings are revealed in *Diagrams 1–4*.

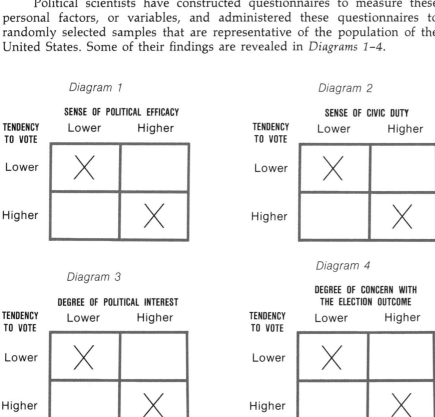

Diagram 1

TENDENCY TO VOTE	SENSE OF POLITICAL EFFICACY	
	Lower	Higher
Lower	X	
Higher		X

Diagram 2

TENDENCY TO VOTE	SENSE OF CIVIC DUTY	
	Lower	Higher
Lower	X	
Higher		X

Diagram 3

TENDENCY TO VOTE	DEGREE OF POLITICAL INTEREST	
	Lower	Higher
Lower	X	
Higher		X

Diagram 4

TENDENCY TO VOTE	DEGREE OF CONCERN WITH THE ELECTION OUTCOME	
	Lower	Higher
Lower	X	
Higher		X

205

What is the relationship of each of the four personal factors to tendency to vote as indicated in these diagrams?

Political scientists sometimes combine the four personal factors just studied under the concept *personal involvement in politics*. Hence, a *high sense of personal involvement in politics* is indicated by a high sense of political efficacy, a high degree of political interest, a high sense of civic duty, and a high degree of concern about the election outcome. A *low sense of personal involvement in politics* is indicated by a low ranking in each of the four personal factors. On the basis of *Diagrams 1–4*, and the discussion in the preceding paragraphs, indicate the correct relationships between personal involvement in politics and tendency to vote in *Diagram 5*. For example, should a mark be placed in box A, B, C, or D to indicate this relationship?

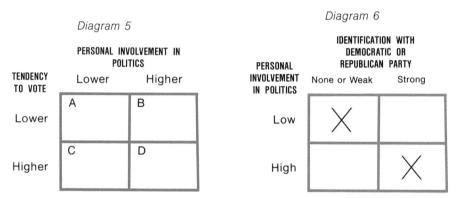

Findings about the relationship of personal involvement in politics to several other variables are indicated in *Diagrams 6–8*. Use evidence provided in the diagrams to answer the questions that follow the diagrams.

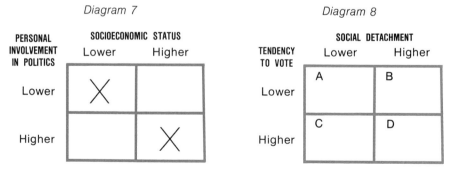

What is the relationship of political party identification to sense of personal involvement in politics?

From evidence presented in *Diagrams 1–6*, what inferences can you make about the relationship of political party identification to tendency to vote?

From the evidence presented in *Diagrams 1-6*, how would you attempt to explain the relationship that you inferred between political party identification and tendency to vote.

What is the relationship of socioeconomic status to personal involvement in politics?

From evidence presented in *Diagrams 1-7*, what inferences can you make about the relationship of socioeconomic status to tendency to vote?

From the evidence presented in *Diagrams 1-7*, how would you attempt to explain the relationship that you inferred between socioeconomic status and tendency to vote?

Social detachment is another variable which political scientists have applied to studies of political participation. A *high degree of social detachment* means that an individual is a marginal member of society, a fringe person who is not involved in activities that are basic to the functioning of a society. A person with a high degree of social detachment has little or no stake in the success of the society and shows little interest in trying to support the groups that comprise the society. A low degree of social detachment means that an individual is involved extensively in the affairs of his society. A person with a low degree of social detachment has a great concern for the success of his society and works hard to support the groups that comprise the society.

Based on this definitional discussion of social detachment, what is your hypothesis about the relationship of social detachment to tendency to vote? State your hypothesis in terms of *Diagram 8*. For example, would you place a mark in Box A, B, C, or D to indicate your hypothesis?

How would you attempt to explain your hypothesis about social detachment and tendency to vote?

The Impact of Situations on Participation in Public Elections

The statement that low socioeconomic status is related to a low rate of political participation is a *tendency statement*. Some poor people are quite active in politics. How can one account for such exceptions to this and other generalizations about political behavior?

Differences in situation, from one time or place to another, can account for some of the exceptions to our generalization about socioeconomic status and political participation. For example, black people throughout our country have tended to have less socioeconomic advantages than whites. And, reflecting our generalization, blacks have tended to participate in public elections to a lesser degree than whites. However, in New Haven, Connecticut, the situation was different.

In a case study of political behavior in New Haven in the late 1950's, Robert A. Dahl reported that black people in that community were active in political affairs, even though they tended to be of lower socioeconomic status. Dahl rated a sample of whites and blacks on their degree of political participation. Among those rated "high" in election campaign participation, and participation in local political affairs generally, Dahl found a larger percentage of blacks than of whites.

Political activity held rewards for black people in New Haven. The political parties provided blacks with chances to get good jobs in the city government and to play important roles in the community. Thus many black people, though of lower socioeconomic status, were motivated to participate actively in political affairs as a means to personal advancement.

This New Haven example reminds us that explanations and descriptions of political behavior that apply to a particular group at a particular time and place may not apply to different groups at different times and places. Keep in mind that one can usually find exceptions to generalizations about political behavior.

Complete these exercises about factors related to popular participation in public elections.

1. On the basis of the evidence on pages 195–208, identify factors, or variables, associated with nonvoting in public elections.

2. What explanatory hypotheses can be constructed from the variables associated with nonvoting in public elections?

3. Apply the explanatory hypotheses, constructed in response to question 2, to the question of whether a person with much political information and political skill is more or less likely to participate in a public election campaign.

4. Apply your explanation of nonvoting to the question of whether a person with a high degree of political alienation is more or less likely to vote than a person with little or no political alienation.

5. Apply your explanation of nonvoting to the question of why black people are less likely than white people to vote in public elections.

6. Which of the following variables could be used to construct explanatory hypotheses about the political participation of black people in New Haven? Justify your choice of variables.

   a. sense of political efficacy
   b. sense of civic duty
   c. political interest
   d. concern with election outcome
   e. socioeconomic status

7. *Table 2* on page 195 shows that people are more likely to vote in a presidential election than in an off-year congressional election. Speculate about differences in participation in these elections in terms of the factors that you identified in answer to question 1 above.

8. Evaluate the following statement, about motivating people to vote, in terms of the factors that you identified in answer to question 1.

   The best way to motivate people to vote is to advertise, through all the communications media, that to be considered a good citizen a person must vote on election day.

9. Does your attempt to explain nonvoting clearly indicate what causes nonvoting?

208

10. Why are several variables, rather than a single factor, or variable, used in your attempted explanation of nonvoting?

11. What are some weaknesses, and limitations, of our attempts to explain political behavior?

D. Who Ought to Participate in Public Elections?

This chapter has thus far made many *descriptive* and *explanatory* statements about the participation of American citizens in public elections. It has not made *prescriptive* statements—value judgments—about popular participation. Nevertheless, "ought questions" about popular participation in public elections do concern us and must be considered.

A main theme of democracy is the belief that people ought to participate in elections. Yet many Americans participate little or not at all. In many elections less than half of the citizens eligible to vote actually bother to cast their ballots. Many, perhaps most, of the voters seem to know little about important public issues and are unfamiliar with most of the candidates on the ballot.

The gap between the "ideal" and the "real" political participation of Americans has led some people to be disappointed about American politics. However, one could respond by saying: "Well, I think our ideals are too unrealistic. When one considers how complex public issues have become and how much pressure Americans have on them to do other things, I believe American citizens are quite active in politics." Or another could respond: "It is true that we fall short of our ideals. We should look for new and more efficient ways to bring Americans into the public election process." While people might agree about the facts of political participation in the United States, they might react to the evidence quite differently. These different reactions are differences in evaluation.

In this lesson you are asked to evaluate conflicting statements about popular participation in public elections and to justify your evaluations.

As you evaluate the following statements, try to avoid inconsistency, or contradiction, in your value judgments. For example, your value judgments are inconsistent, or contradictory, if you agree (a) with one speaker who opposes a law which would permit more people to vote and (b) with another speaker who believes that every adult citizen should have the opportunity to vote in every public election. Strive for consistency as you react to the statements of each of the following speakers.

Speaker 1: Every citizen should vote in public elections, because one vote can make a difference. In 1839 Marcus Morton was elected governor of Massachusetts by a margin of one vote out of 102,066. In the 1916 presidential election Charles Evans Hughes defeated Woodrow Wilson in California by a margin of 4000 votes out of the nearly one million cast. Less than one additional vote per precinct for Hughes would have won California for him, and with the addition of California's electoral votes he would have won the election. John F. Kennedy defeated Richard Nixon in 1960 by 112,803 popular votes out of 68.8 million total votes. This was a margin of less than one vote per precinct. In the 1968 election, Nixon's margin was very thin in Illinois and California. If Humphrey had won those two states, he would have become the new President rather than Nixon. One vote can make a difference!

Speaker 2: Some people do not vote because they are against all of the candidates. People who do not like any of the candidates have a perfect right to sit out the election.

Speaker 3: Even if one were to conclude that all the choices are unsatisfactory, it would be necessary to choose among them. Those who do not vote because they dislike all the candidates probably dislike some candidates less than others. The nonvoter helps the worst candidate's cause as much as the others. Edmund Burke said it best: "The only thing necessary for the triumph of evil is for good men to do nothing."

"I'd like to have voted, but the line was too long."

Speaker 4: Perhaps we should not be overly concerned that less than two-thirds of the electorate participates in public elections. Maybe nonparticipation is a sign of general satisfaction with the political situation. We would have more reason to be concerned if suddenly all Americans were to become eager to participate and were making all sorts of demands on the government. Intense political activity by large numbers of people could result in severe conflict and disorder.

Speaker 5:   Most of the people who fail to vote should not vote. They do not know the candidates. They are ignorant of the issues. We might be better off if we did not encourage people who lack education to vote. Maybe our democracy is better off because many lower status citizens are apathetic about politics.

Speaker 6:   You do not have to have a lot of money or a lot of education to know whether the government is doing a good job. If you're living in a ghetto, you know very well if the services you receive from the city are adequate. Someone once compared democracy to buying shoes. Making a shoe, like running the government, requires special knowledge and skill. But when you go to buy a pair of shoes, you know better than the shoemaker whether the shoes fit you or not. Every citizen is competent to judge whether the government is pinching him or whether the policies of the government "fit," or satisfy, him. I think many Americans, especially poor Americans and members of oppressed minority groups, are sick of having decisions made for them by upper-class and middle-class elites. We have a right to participate in making the rules that affect us. That's what "Black Power" is all about. Black people want to gain control over the institutions that affect them. They want black policemen, black businesses, black-controlled schools, and so on. But to gain power and influence in the government, people have to participate in public elections.

Speaker 7:   People should have some say in the decisions that affect their lives. People who don't participate in public elections, or other forms of political activity, give up their most basic human rights. Since political participation is the essence of a democracy, no country where 40 percent of the people regularly fail to vote can call itself a democracy.

Speaker 8:   Many people don't participate in public elections because they are too busy with their own affairs. The typical working man is too busy caring for his family and making a living to be too excited about politics. There appears to be little that a typical working man can get out of giving his precious time and energy to working in an election campaign. Furthermore, it seems to make little difference whether one man or another gets elected. The typical working man gets little or no benefit from taking the time to vote.

Speaker 9:   I believe that every citizen has the duty to vote in a public election. Therefore, I would propose that the government make a law that requires every citizen to vote or be subject to payment of a fine. This is the only way to make certain that our public officials will be elected according to the democratic principle of majority rule.

Speaker 10:   Restrictive registration procedures are a major reason for low participation in public elections. In many states people must re-register if they neglect to vote in a four-year period. As registration procedures are often bothersome, I suggest that every citizen in every state be permanently registered to vote.

Election laws in other democratic nations seem to encourage higher rates of voting. In these nations, such as Italy, West Germany, Norway, Sweden, and Denmark, voter registration is the responsibility of the government rather than of the individual. For example, in Italy local government officials compile lists of eligible voters. This results in the automatic registration of all citizens. Once a voter gets on the registration rolls, he stays there until he dies.

Partly as a consequence of their voter-registration procedures and election-day administration, European democracies can boast of much higher rates of voter turnout than the United States. For example, in Italy over 90 percent of eligible voters usually turn out to vote. In West Germany, from 1950 to 1970, around 78 to 88 percent of the electorate voted.

Speaker 11: Procedures for administering elections also discourage some people from voting. For example, polling places in many areas close too early. Potential voters must stand in long lines at overcrowded polling places after working all day. Many decide that voting is not worth this extra time and effort. Why can't we make Sunday, a typical day off from work, the election day? Then individuals can have a greater opportunity to vote. In Italy elections are held over a two-day period, on Sunday and Monday, in order to encourage voter participation.

Speaker 12: Residency laws also serve to discourage too many people from voting. No one should have to live in a state or local community longer than six months to qualify to vote. Many people who must move from place to place because of their jobs are prevented from voting by unfair residency laws.

Speaker 13: Congressmen who voted in 1970 to ban the use of literacy tests as a qualification for voting made a good policy decision. These tests are devices for denying underprivileged people the right to vote. All Americans have the right to vote if they are to be first-class citizens. Some states have used the literacy test as a device for stopping black people from voting. Many working-class people who have been deprived of a chance for an education have also been discriminated against by the literacy tests. The vote enables people to influence the government to serve their interests. Uneducated people ought to have this right as well as educated people.

Speaker 14: Certainly, the literacy test should be employed as a barrier preventing ignorant or uneducated people from voting. Our form of government depends upon intelligent, educated citizens. Those who cannot read at least at a sixth-grade level should not have the right to vote. Their votes can be too easily influenced by propaganda. They are too likely to vote mindlessly for a political party label without studying the issues and without considering the merits of the candidates. We need to encourage intelligent voting, if democracy is to survive.

Speaker 15: Our present residency and registration laws should not be changed. They were made to protect all of us from the influence of irresponsible or ignorant voters. To eliminate these laws would permit undesirable people to vote.

1. Identify the speakers with whom you agree or disagree.

2. Are there any contradictory, or conflicting, beliefs among the speakers with whom you agree? If so, what are they? And if so, which beliefs must you reject in order to resolve the inconsistency?

3. Explain why you agree or disagree with each of the speakers in the preceding discussion. Do you find any statement with which you agree in part? Explain.

4. Is there disagreement among your classmates in their evaluation of the different speakers? Explain.

chapter 11

Influences on Voting in Public Elections

In the privacy of the voting booth, American citizens influence their country's destiny through their choice of governmental leaders. What influences a voter to prefer one candidate to another? Do American voters choose the candidate who they believe will best serve the community or the candidate who will best serve their own interests? Do American voters carefully study the candidates and the issues? Do American voters think for themselves, or do they mindlessly follow the advice of relatives, friends, or prominent leaders? How can one explain the choices of American voters? In this chapter you will study information that pertains to these questions.

A. Voting Tendencies of Various Groups in Recent Presidential Elections

Which candidates do different kinds of American voters tend to choose in presidential elections? Relationships between several variables and candidate preferences of voters in presidential elections are indicated in *Table 5*. This table reveals that in five consecutive presidential elections certain social groups tended to prefer either the Democratic or Republican candidates.

On the basis of information presented in *Table 5*, what generalizations can you make about the relationship of the following variables to voter choices in presidential elections:

a. educational attainment

b. occupation

c. racial identity

d. age group

e. sex identity

f. religious identity

g. political party preference

Following are descriptions of typical Americans. Use evidence from previous discussions and tables to support your answers to the following questions about these descriptions.

1. In a presidential election which of the three individuals described below is most likely to vote (a) for the Democratic candidates? (b) for the Republican candidates?

2. In a presidential election which of the three individuals is (a) most likely to vote? (b) least likely to vote?

3. What are some weaknesses of attempting to predict political party preference, candidate choice, and likelihood of voting solely on the basis of social characteristics?

214

AYC AYC Table 5. **Percentage of Vote by Groups in Presidential Elections, 1952–1968** AYC

	1952		1956		1960		1964		1968		
	Dem. %	Rep. %	D %	R %	D %	R %	D %	R %	D %	R %	Wallace %
NATIONAL	44.6	55.4	42.2	57.8	50.1	49.9	61.3	38.7	43.0	43.4	13.6
Men	47	53	45	55	52	48	60	40	41	43	16
Women	42	58	39	61	49	51	62	38	45	43	12
White	43	57	41	59	49	51	59	41	38	47	15
Nonwhite	79	21	61	39	68	32	94	6	85	12	3
College	34	66	31	69	39	61	52	48	37	54	9
High school	45	55	42	58	52	48	62	38	42	43	15
Grade school	52	48	50	50	55	45	66	34	52	33	15
Prof. & bus.	36	64	32	68	42	58	54	46	34	56	10
White collar	40	60	37	63	48	52	57	43	41	47	12
Manual	55	45	50	50	60	40	71	29	50	35	15
Farmers	33	67	46	54	48	52	53	47	29	51	20
Under 30	51	49	43	57	54	46	64	36	47	38	15
30–49	47	53	45	55	54	46	63	37	44	41	15
50 & older	39	61	39	61	46	54	59	41	41	47	12
Protestant	37	63	37	63	38	62	55	45	35	49	16
Catholic	56	44	51	49	78	22	76	24	59	33	8
Republicans	8	92	4	96	5	95	20	80	9	86	5
Democrats	77	23	85	15	84	16	87	13	74	12	14
Independents	35	65	30	70	43	57	56	44	31	44	25

Source: Estimates from a national survey by The American Institute of Public Opinion (The Gallup Poll).

H.L. Cabrera

Descriptions of Individuals

Mr. Pietrowski is a steelworker. He is a semi-skilled worker who earns about $8000 a year. He is an officer of his local labor union. He attends the Catholic Church, is a member of the Elks Club, and regularly participates in social activities. He is a high school graduate. He is forty-six years old and has lived in this large eastern seaboard city all of his life. His father migrated to this country from Poland in 1920.

Mr. Young is the owner of a large department store on the main street of a small midwestern city, population about 45,000. He is the president of the local Chamber of Commerce and is a leader in the city's civic and social activities. He earns over $50,000 a year and lives in a plush home on the edge of the city. He attends the Presbyterian Church. He graduated from his state university with a degree in business administration. He is forty-five years old.

Mr. Jameson is a migrant laborer. He works at odd jobs on farms or in small rural towns. Every summer and fall he works as a fruit picker. He travels from town to town looking for work. Often he is unemployed. He earns about $4000 a year. He was baptized into the Baptist Church, but rarely attends church services. He does not belong to a labor union or to any social clubs. He dropped out of school at the end of the eighth grade. *Republican*

B. Four Types of Voters

Why does a voter cast his ballot for one candidate rather than another? Each of the following descriptions, of four types of voters, is a different answer to this question. Each description accounts for the behavior of some American voters. Decide which of the descriptions accounts for the behavior of most American voters. In other words, decide which of the four types of voters is the more accurate picture of reality.

The Public-Minded Independent

The "public-minded independent" is very informed about political affairs. Prior to casting his ballot, he carefully examines the issues of the election campaign and the strengths and weaknesses of the candidates. After much thoughtful consideration, the "public-minded independent" casts a ballot for the candidate who he believes will best serve the community.

The "public-minded independent" resists the attempts of relatives, friends, work associates, or politicians to influence his choice of candidates. Rather, the "public-minded independent" thinks for himself and considers the needs of the community before his own interests when deciding for whom to vote. For example, in deciding whether or not to support a candidate who wants to raise taxes to build more schools, the "public-minded independent's" first consideration is whether new schools are needed. If so, he supports the candidate even though it will cost him more money.

The Thoughtless Participant

Another view of American voter behavior is that the voter thoughtlessly goes along with his family, friends, or work associates when deciding for whom to vote. The "thoughtless participant" is uninformed about the issues of the campaign and the characteristics of the competing candidates. The "thoughtless participant" knows very little about politics or government and does not take the time or effort to consider carefully for whom he will vote. He prefers the political party that his family, friends, or work associates support and usually votes for all the candidates of this political party, even though he may not know the names of many of these candidates.

The Manipulated Subject

The "manipulated subject" is most susceptible to the persuasion techniques of modern advertising and propaganda. The messages of the mass media have more influence on him than do the opinions and recommendations of family, friends, and organization leaders. He votes for the candidate who has conducted the flashiest and most clever campaign. Persuasive slogans or political advertisements presented on television, radio, or in newspapers usually impress and influence the "manipulated subject."

The "manipulated subject" does not think for himself. Rather, he accepts without questioning the thinking of political leaders as projected via the mass media. To win the allegiance of the "manipulated subject" a candidate is "packaged and sold" like a carton of soft drinks or a box of cereal.

The Self-Interested Partisan

A "partisan" is a person who tends to express a strong preference for a particular political party and to vote for its candidates. A "self-interested partisan" is loyal to a particular political party because it supports policies that help him, and the people whom he identifies with, in some important ways. However, the "self-interested partisan" is ready and willing to shift his political allegiances whenever it appears that candidates of the other party are more likely to help him than are the candidates of his own party.

The groups to which the "self-interested partisan" belongs—his family, his occupational group, his racial or ethnic group, and so on—influence his political party preference and his choice of candidates, since he tends to have interests and goals that are similar to others like himself. Thus, with others like himself the "self-interested partisan" is not a "thoughtless" voter; he carefully considers his election choices.

However, unlike the "public-minded independent," the "self-interested partisan" is not well-informed about a wide range of political issues. Rather, he tends to be somewhat informed only about the few issues which might directly affect him. And the "self-interested partisan" tends to give his vote to the party and candidates that hold beliefs about those issues that seem to serve his needs. For example, on an issue such as aid to education, the partisan who thinks the government takes too much money from him is likely to support the party which guarantees not to raise taxes to finance school improvements.

It is difficult to manipulate the political thinking of the "self-interested partisan" through the mass media. His first loyalty is to his political party. Television, newspaper, or radio messages that contradict his party loyalty, as long as this loyalty seems to serve him, are disregarded, or filtered out.

The "self-interested partisan's" identification with a particular political party makes it easy for him to choose between rival political candidates. The positions of his party and its candidates concerning issues of direct importance to him provide him with a ready-made point of view, which he accepts so long as it appears to serve his needs and interests. However, his acceptance of the party point of view, indeed his loyalty to the party, depends upon his belief that his party identification helps him, and those like him, in important ways.

Each model, or type, of voter—the public-minded independent, the thoughtless participant, the manipulated subject, and the self-interested partisan—represents the voting behavior tendencies of many citizens. A particular voter may tend to be a public-minded independent, yet he may show some of the characteristics of a self-interested partisan. Another voter may tend to be a thoughtless participant who also exhibits some of the qualities of a manipulated subject. Remember that most voters tend to behave more or less like one of the four descriptions, or models. Which model do you think is the better description of American voters? In the next section you are provided with evidence to use in deciding which of the four models best describes the voting behavior of most Americans.

C. Factors Influencing the Candidate Choices of American Voters

Several factors appear to be related to the candidate choices of American voters. Evidence classified in terms of these factors is presented on pages 218–232. On the basis of this evidence, decide which of the four types of voters described above is the best model, or picture, of voter behavior in the United States.

The Political Knowledge of Voters

Many American voters tend to be ignorant of fundamental facts of politics and government. Numerous surveys have revealed the following evidence:

(1) Many voters do not know who represents them in Congress. For example, less than half the people can name their Congressman and only slightly more than half the people can name one of their two Senators.

(2) Less than half of the public knows which party controls Congress at any particular time.

(3) A majority of the public is unable to identify fundamental characteristics of such governmental institutions as the Congress, the Supreme Court, and the Electoral College.

MASSACHUSETTS CHAPTER

Americans for **D**emocratic **A**ction

27 School Street (Room 401)   Boston Mass 02108

BAY STATE ► CITIZEN

LEGISLATIVE SUPPLEMENT

Roll-Call Record of 1970 General Court

A number of organizations including Americans for Democratic Action (ADA), the League of Women Voters, the Ripon Society, and the AFL-CIO engage in programs to educate voters. Two reports on Massachusetts legislators are shown here. Similar reports on Congress are prepared by the national offices of ADA and the AFL-CIO.

House of Representatives

1. REDUCING SIZE OF HOUSE. ADA opposed this Initiative Amendment to the Constitution. Failed in Joint Session 69-191(1/4 of elected members required)(Nay=ADA+) 2/25/70.

2. SHEA-WELLS BILL. ADA favored this test of the legality of sending Massachusetts citizens to fight in a war not declared by Congress. Engrossed 136-89(Yea=ADA+) 3/16/70.

3. BIRTH CONTROL. ADA supported Rep. Newman's attempt to save her bill to repeal the law restricting birth control information and devices to married women. Motion failed 81-142 (Yea=ADA+) 3/24/70.

4. WITNESS IMMUNITY. ADA opposed this bill to compel witnesses to give up their 5th amendment rights in exchange for immunity from prosecution. Rep. Backman's motion to kill the bill failed 28-189(Yea=ADA+) 4/13/70.

5. PRAYERS IN SCHOOL. ADA opposed permitting public

* * * * * * * * * * * * * *
* Massachusetts ADA has chosen *
* key roll calls taken in each *
* House during the 1970 sess- *
* ion of the General Court. *
* These roll calls do not pre- *
* sent a complete picture of a *
* legislator's performance, *
* but they do provide an ob- *
* jective measure of each mem- *
* bers position on issues wh- *
* ich ADA considered to be of *
* significance during the *
* past session. *
* *
* We hope that this record *
* will be used, not just as a *
* basis for judgement on the *
* past, but as a guide for *
* citizens in expressing their *
* * * * * * * * * * * * * *

13. WELFARE AFFIDAVITS. ADA opposed this measure to require affidavits from welfare applicants giving the name and address of fathers of dependent children. Motion to kill the bill failed 104-107(Yea=ADA+) 7/27/70.

14. CIVIL SERVICE. ADA favored a program to recruit career executives in the Commonwealth. A motion to reconsider a vote killing the bill failed 98-115(Yes= ADA+) 7/28/70.

15. RENT CONTROL. ADA favored S1551, a state-wide local option rent control bill.

Massachusetts House of Representatives Voting Record on Selected Roll-Calls

		1	2	3	4	5	6	7	8	9	10	11	12
Natick	Keane, Francis M.(D)	+	–	A	+	–	+	+	+	–	A	–	
Hyde Park	Kearney, Joseph M.(D)	+	–	+	–	A	+	–	+	–	A	–	
Uxbridge	Kenney, Frederick Leo (D)	+	–	+	+	–	+	–	+	–	+	+	
Feeding Hills	Kerr, Walter T.(D)	+	–	–	+	–	+	–	+	–	+	+	
Everett	Keverian, George (D)	+	+	+	+	+	+	+	+	–	+	+	
Lowell	Kiernan, Cornelius F.(D)	+	A	–	+	+	+	A	+	–	+	+	
Pittsfield	Kitterman, William I.(D)	+	–	+	–	+	+	–	+	–	+	+	
Chicopee	Kulig, Mitsie T.(D)	+	–	+	–	–	+	–	+	–	+	+	
Fall River	Kuss, Matthew J.(D)	–	–	–	–	–	–	–	–	–	+	+	
Gardner	LaFontaine, Raymond M.(D)	+	–	+	+	–	+	+	+	–	+	+	
Waltham	Landry, Richard E.(D)	–	+	A	+	–	+	+	+	+	+	+	
Boston	Langone, Joseph A., 3rd(D)	+	–	–	A	–	+	–	+	A	–	+	

KEY TO SYMBOLS

+ = a vote favored by ADA

– = a vote opposed by ADA

A = the member was absent or abstained from voting

p+ or p– = the member paired and was absent

P+ or P– = the member paired and was present

P = the member was present and abstained from voting

Official Labor Record

of the

MASSACHUSETTS HOUSE OF REPRESENTATIVES

and the

MASSACHUSETTS SENATE

1969-1970 Session

Published by Americans for Democratic Action, Washington, D.C.

Vol. 25, No. 1   ◆   January 1970

ADA WORLD

ADA VOTE ANALYSIS HITS NIXON RECORD

Massachusetts State Labor Council AFL-CIO

6 BEACON STREET, BOSTON, MASS.

ROLL CALL NO. 1
This roll call was on the veto by Governor Sargent of the pay raise bill for state employees and was taken on July 22, 1969. The House voted to override the veto by 195 to 32 with 13 representatives not voting. A Yea vote to override is a right vote. A Nay vote not to override is a wrong vote. N-V indicated not voting.

ROLL CALL NO. 2
Senate No. 262, the Council bill to make eligible for unemployment benefits, employees locked out due to a labor dispute was before the House for a third reading.
A resolve to kill Senate 262, which was to send this bill to a study was moved and the vote was on the resolve.

ROLL CALL NO. 3
Senate No. 262 the Council bill to provide unemployment benefits to employees locked out because of a labor dispute was before the House for engrossment.
A motion to kill S. 262 by referring it to the next annual session was made and the vote was on this motion.

ROLL CALL NO. 4
The House had passed Senate No. 262 to be engrossed. S. 262 was the State Council bill to provide that employees locked out during a labor dispute would be eligible to receive unemployment compensation. The vote to reconsider engrossment of S. 262 would again subject the bill to an engrossment vote if successful. Therefore, a vote against reconsideration was a right vote. A Nay vote a wrong vote.

ROLL CALL NO. 5
This was the roll call vote on an amendment to the State Constitution to cut the size of the House from the present 240 to 160.
Labor was definitely opposed to this change. 191 Senators and Representatives voted against the amendment with 69 for it and 16 absent or not voting.

R is a right vote
W is a wrong vote
NV is not voting

HOUSE ROLL CALL

DEMOCRATS	1	2	3	4	5
Bartley	R	R	NV	R	R
McGee	R	R	R	R	R
Murphy, P.	R	R	R	R	R
Aguiar	R	W	W	W	R
Ahearn	R	R	R	R	W

(4) Most adults know very little about current political issues.

(5) Most voters know little or nothing about the content of the political party platforms in presidential elections.

(6) Less than two-thirds of the voters report that they have heard or read anything about either candidate in a particular congressional election in their district. Less than one-third of the voters report that they have heard or read anything about the candidates of both parties in a particular congressional election.

(7) Typically, less than one-third of American voters are able to identify correctly the differences between Republican and Democratic policies concerning certain important issues related to foreign-aid programs, international involvement, influence of big business in government, influence of unions in government, segregation of schools, aid to education, and the like. For example, less than one-third of Americans can identify differences between Republicans and Democrats concerning the advisability of Federal aid to education. Only about one-third can identify Republican and Democratic differences concerning the influence of big business and labor unions in government.

The results of a national "current events test," conducted and documented in 1967 by a major television network, further reveals the level of political knowledge of the general public. The test consisted of simple questions about current political leaders and current issues. A score of 60 percent was interpreted as equivalent to a tenth-grade standard of education. However, the average score of a national sample was 48 percent.

It has been estimated that less than 10 percent of the adult population are careful and regular readers of political news. Paying close attention to the facts of politics is not tremendously important to most people; they prefer to spend their leisure time in other ways.

What does the previous evidence suggest about the relationship of political knowledge to the candidate choices of American voters?

The Influence of Election Campaigns on Voting

Election campaigns are activities designed to influence the behavior of voters. Victory on election day is the main purpose of a political campaign. Through various campaign strategies and activities, political party organizations attempt to influence the voter to support their candidates for election to public office. Other purposes of a political campaign are to publicize the ideas and the name of a political party, to raise money for the political party, and to recruit workers and supporters for the party.

Through an election campaign, a candidate for public office tries to (1) keep the votes of party supporters, (2) encourage as many party supporters as possible to turn out to vote on election day, (3) win the support of political independents, and (4) win the support, even if temporary, of people not closely identified with the opposition party.

One way to view the impact of election campaigns on voter choices is to find out what percentage of the voters decide for whom to vote before and during election campaigns. What does *Table 6*, and the facts about the 1968

220

Table 6. Time of Decision on Voter Choice for President

TIME DECIDED	1948	1952	1956	1960	1964
Before Conventions	37%	31%	57%	30%	40%
During Conventions	28	34	18	30	25
During Campaign	26	31	21	36	33
Don't Remember	9	4	4	4	3

Source: © Copyright by Institute for Social Research, University of Michigan. Reprinted with permission of Institute for Social Research.

presidential election in the following paragraph, suggest about the influence of election campaigns on voting?

In the 1968 election, 78 percent of a national sample of voters reported that they never intended to vote for a presidential candidate other than the one they voted for. Only 22 percent of the voters reported that during the election campaign they switched their support from one to another of the three main presidential candidates.

In fairly close elections the events of the political campaign can be decisive. As many as one-third of the voters may decide for whom to vote during the political campaign. This group consists of weak party identifiers and political independents. Presumably, political issues and the appeal of candidates determine their voting choices rather than political party identification. In a close election these "undecided" voters hold the balance of power. And the candidate waging the best campaign is most likely to capture the election by gaining the support of the minority of the voters who make their decision during the campaign.

Relationship of Group Identification to Voting

Table 5 on page 215 reveals relationships between candidate preference and social-group membership. How are these relationships developed? To what extent do social-group memberships influence voting? Three concepts that

Table 7. Relationship of Primary-Group Membership to Voting

RESPONDENT VOTED	FRIENDS VOTED		SPOUSE VOTED		FAMILY VOTED		WORK ASSOCIATES VOTED	
	Dem.	Rep.	Dem.	Rep.	Dem.	Rep.	Dem.	Rep.
Democrat	89%	7%	80%	8%	83%	15%	79%	24%
Republican	11	93	20	92	17	85	21	76

Source: Angus Campbell and others, *The American Voter.*

can help us to answer these questions are (a) primary-group identification, (b) secondary-group identification, and (c) cross-pressure.

Primary groups and voting. Primary groups have a direct and far-reaching influence on an individual's beliefs and behavior. Usually primary groups are those in which individuals have a close, "face-to-face" relationship. The family, friendship groups, and small groups of fellow workers are examples of primary groups. What does *Table 7* reveal about the relationship of primary-group membership to voting?

Secondary groups and voting. Secondary groups have an indirect, and usually less extensive, influence on an individual's beliefs and behavior. Religious organizations, political parties, social classes, and occupational groupings are examples of secondary groups. An individual may identify with several secondary groups, but his contact with them is usually impersonal.

Several million Americans are members of a labor union. This is one kind of secondary group. Political commentators often speak about the influence of union membership on voting behavior. National union leaders often endorse particular candidates for President and Congress. Some candidates of both major parties win union endorsement, but the record shows that far more Democrats than Republicans get the union "seal of approval." Just how much influence does a labor union—and its leaders—have on the voting behavior of union members?

Studies of how members of the United Auto Workers (UAW) voted in the 1952 and 1956 presidential elections provides some evidence in answer to the above question. As you read the evidence, however, keep in mind that it relates to only *one* labor union in *two* elections. Certain unions—and particular union leaders—work harder than do others in trying to influence the votes of union members. The UAW has a long record of strong political activity.

In his book *When Labor Votes,* Arthur Kornhauser reports that in the 1952 presidential election two-thirds of the members of the UAW voted for the Democratic candidate, Adlai Stevenson. However, nearly 75 percent of UAW members strongly attached to the UAW and its leaders voted for Stevenson. Slightly more than 50 percent of UAW members who had a weak identification with the UAW and its leaders voted for Stevenson.

Two political scientists studied the voting behavior of UAW members in Detroit in the 1956 election. In Detroit—and elsewhere—the UAW leaders have been strong supporters of the Democratic party. Also it has been UAW policy to try to interest their members in political participation and to put political pressure on government officials to undertake policies favored by UAW leaders. Over 75 percent of UAW members in Detroit in 1956 considered themselves Democrats. Only 10 percent identified with the Republican party. Almost 15 percent identified themselves as political independents. Of those auto workers who voted in the 1956 election, 72 percent cast their ballots for Democratic candidate Adlai Stevenson. Thus, strong auto-worker support came for Stevenson in a year when he received only 42.2 percent of the vote throughout the nation.

The 1956 study of UAW members also revealed that 65 percent favored more influence for labor unions on governmental decisions. More than 65 percent said that "it was all right" for unions to campaign actively in behalf of Democratic candidate Adlai Stevenson. The 1956 Detroit study also showed that individuals who strongly identified with the UAW were more likely to follow the political advice of the union leaders than were individuals who did not identify with the union.

Cross-pressures and voting. Social cross-pressures tend to limit or undercut the influence of primary and secondary groups on voting behavior. Individuals belong to several primary and secondary groups and identify with several of these groups. When different groups with which an individual identifies reveal contradictory political preferences, then a cross-pressure situation is established. For example, Sally Smith grew up in a family with fairly strong Republican leanings. She now lives a few miles from her parents' home and sees them often. Her husband, a machinist and shop steward for his labor union, is a Democrat. Sally is caught between two opposing influences; she is in a cross-pressure situation. Sally may resolve the contradictory influences (1) by not voting, or (2) by splitting her vote between Republican and Democratic candidates, or (3) by favoring the stronger of the conflicting influences. In our open society such opposing influences are commonplace. Note in the following examples how a person can be subject to social cross-pressures or to consistent social pressures on voter behavior.

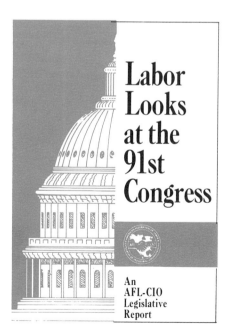

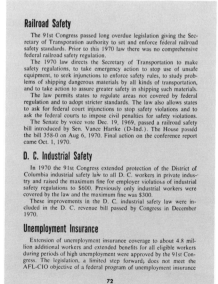

Railroad Safety

The 91st Congress passed long overdue legislation giving the Secretary of Transportation authority to set and enforce federal railroad safety standards. Prior to this 1970 law there was no comprehensive federal railroad safety regulation.

The 1970 law directs the Secretary of Transportation to make safety regulations, to take emergency action to stop use of unsafe equipment, to seek injunctions to enforce safety rules, to study problems of shipping dangerous materials by all kinds of transportation, and to take action to assure greater safety in shipping such materials.

The law permits states to regulate areas not covered by federal regulation and to adopt stricter standards. The law also allows states to ask for federal court injunctions to stop safety violations and to ask the federal courts to impose civil penalties for safety violations.

The Senate by voice vote Dec. 19, 1969, passed a railroad safety bill introduced by Sen. Vance Hartke (D-Ind.). The House passed the bill 358-0 on Aug 6, 1970. Final action on the conference report came Oct. 1, 1970.

D. C. Industrial Safety

In 1970 the 91st Congress extended protection of the District of Columbia industrial safety law to all D. C. workers in private industry and raised the maximum fine for employer violations of industrial safety regulations to $600. Previously only industrial workers were covered by the law and the maximum fine was $300.

These improvements in the D. C. industrial safety law were included in the D. C. revenue bill passed by Congress in December 1970.

Unemployment Insurance

Extension of unemployment insurance coverage to about 4.8 million additional workers and extended benefits for all eligible workers during periods of high unemployment were approved by the 91st Congress. The legislation, a limited step forward, does not meet the AFL-CIO objective of a federal program of unemployment insurance

72

As part of its political-education program, the AFL-CIO regularly publishes a legislative report on what Congress has done, or failed to do, about a wide range of policy issues.

Mr. Jankowski is a corporation executive. He is a Roman Catholic and a Polish-American. His parents are pro-Democratic. Some of his personal friends are supporters of the Democratic party. Most of his business associates are pro-Republican. His wife and her parents support the Republican party candidates. Clearly, Mr. Jankowski is torn between contradictory political influences and is caught in a social cross-pressure situation concerning voting choice and political party preference.

Mr. Brown is a business associate of Mr. Jankowski. Mr. Brown is a Protestant. His parents, wife, and close friends are pro-Republican. Mr. Brown is *not* caught in a cross-pressure situation. Rather, the social forces that surround him influence him consistently in the direction of preference for Republican party candidates.

Individuals faced by nonconflicting social pressures, such as Mr. Brown, tend to have consistent political attitudes, to vote for candidates of one party, to decide for whom to vote early in an election campaign, or before the campaign begins, and to have strong views about politics.

By contrast, individuals faced with social cross-pressures, such as Mr. Jankowski, tend to have conflicting political attitudes, to vote a split ticket (voting for candidates of different parties in the same election), to decide for whom to vote late in a campaign, and to have weak and shifting views about politics. Often a cross-pressure can only be settled by not voting or by showing little political interest. People influenced by social cross-pressures are usually political independents.

Large numbers of Americans are affected by social cross-pressures. Political scientists hypothesize that this has a stabilizing and moderating influence in politics. They speculate that if all Americans were strongly partisan, political conflicts might become too heated and too severe. This could lead to violence and social upheaval. Furthermore, individuals influenced by social cross-pressures often become political independents shifting voting preference from party to party. Opposing candidates must regularly compete for their support at every election. Often these independent voters hold the balance of power between the Republicans and Democrats. Thus, both Republicans and Democrats are forced to modify and moderate their views in order to appeal to the political independents and the weak party identifiers.

Political Party Policies, Group Identification, and Voting

Table 5 on page 215 reveals voting tendencies of certain social groups in recent presidential elections. *Table 8* reveals the political party preferences of certain groups in American society. Notice the similarities in the two tables. For example, both tables reveal that professionals and businessmen, upper-income people, and college-educated people are more likely to prefer Republicans than are manual workers, lower-income people, and high school graduates. Both tables reveal that black people are likely to prefer Democrats.

Caution. Before looking at further information about political party preferences, it is useful to emphasize the limitations of such information as provided in Tables 5 and 8. Conclusions about the relationships between social groups and political party preference describe what people *tend* to do. They show that certain individuals are highly likely to identify with one political party and highly unlikely to identify with the opposing party. Since these conclusions are tendency statements, there are always exceptions. For example, although manual workers *tend to* vote for Democratic candidates, 60 percent of manual workers voted for Republican Dwight Eisenhower in the presidential election of 1956. Although college-educated individuals *tend to* support Republican candidates, 52 percent of college-educated individuals voted for Democratic candidate Lyndon Johnson in the presidential election of 1964.

Another limitation of conclusions about social groups and political party preference is that they describe tendencies of the past. While they also indicate trends that may prevail in the future, they do not predict the future with complete accuracy. For example, while there is much statistical information to show that workingmen of Irish, Polish, and Italian ancestry have tended to vote for Democratic candidates in the presidential elections of 1960, 1964, and 1968, some political analysts foresee a majority of this group switching to the Republican party in future elections. These political analysts would say that relying entirely on statistical data of past political preference would not necessarily help us to detect new trends in American voter behavior.

Table 8. **Political Party Preferences by Group Membership, 1968**

	REPUBLICAN	DEMOCRAT	INDEPENDENT
NATIONAL	27%	46%	27%
Sex			
Men	28	44	28
Women	26	48	26
Race			
White	29	43	28
Nonwhite	7	75	18
Education			
College	35	31	34
High school	25	47	28
Grade school	23	56	21
Occupation			
Prof. & business	33	35	32
Clerical & sales	28	43	29
Farmers	35	44	21
Manual workers	19	52	29
Labor union members	9	59	32
Nonunion workers	29	44	27
Age			
21–29 years	22	38	40
30–49 years	24	48	28
50 or over	31	48	21
Religion			
Protestant	31	42	27
Catholic	18	55	27
Jewish	7	69	24
Income			
$10,000 & over	33	37	30
$7,000–$9,999	23	46	31
$5,000–$6,999	22	49	29
$3,000–$4,999	24	51	25
Under $3,000	27	53	20

Source: The American Institute of Public Opinion (The Gallup Poll).

A third limitation of conclusions showing the relationship of social groups and political attitudes and behavior is that they disregard the personality factor. Every individual has a unique personality due to unique social experiences and inborn potentialities. Thus, individuals are not likely to respond in the exact same way to the same influences. For example, some unskilled, Roman Catholic workers regularly vote Republican, even though most unskilled, Roman Catholic workers regularly vote Democratic. And some upper socio-economic status corporation executives vote Democratic consistently, even though most upper status corporation executives consistently vote Republican.

Social groupings in the American society are composed of various types of individuals. Although strong pressures are exerted for conformity within any social group, other forces tend to undercut these conformist pressures. Social cross-pressures are examples of these undercutting forces. Personality differences also work against conformity. A complex society, such as the American society, contains many possibilities for social cross-pressures and wide variation in personality and behavior.

Examining Political Party Differences

A study of the party platforms of the Democratic and Republican parties over the past twenty to thirty years indicates that both major political parties try to appeal to as many citizens as possible. Many planks in the opposing platforms say almost the same thing: continued opposition to Communist aggression, support of the United Nations, national-defense strength "second to none," higher Social Security benefits, stabilization of farm income (but not full agreement on how to do this), and so on. The party in power "points with pride" to its accomplishments. The party out of power uses its platform to recite what is wrong in national affairs, blames the ruling party for the sad conditions, and promises to set things straight.

However, the party platforms do reveal differences in policies supported by the Democrats and Republicans. These differences in ideas and programs help to account for the different appeals that each party has for different groups in our society. Gerald M. Pomper has reported, in *Elections in America,* his study of Democratic and Republican party platforms from 1944–1964. He concluded that Republicans have placed more emphasis than Democrats on improving national-defense capability and on such governmental issues as the relationship of the Federal government to the state governments and governmental budgetary reform. By contrast Democrats have placed more emphasis than Republicans on social-welfare programs and policies to aid labor unions. Pomper concluded that "Republicans have tended to be regarded as better managers of the government and to be more trusted on issues of war and peace. Democrats have been regarded more highly in terms of domestic policy and group benefits."

One way to view differences in the policy positions of the two major parties is to study the results of a survey of political beliefs Democratic and Republican party leaders have. The party leaders in this study were delegates to the Republican and Democratic national conventions of 1956. *Table 9* shows

226

differences in the response of Democrats and Republicans to several issues. On the basis of evidence in this table, what inferences can you make about differences in policy positions of the Democratic and Republican parties?

Realize that differences between the two political parties, revealed in party platforms and the survey of party leaders, represent tendencies and points of emphasis. For example, both parties have supported programs to assist black people, poor people, and labor unions. Both parties have encouraged the development and prosperity of private business. Furthermore, both parties share many important goals. Their differences most often are in means to achieve objectives, rather than in the objectives.

Table 9. **Responses of Political Party Leaders to Selected Issues**

ISSUES	DEMOCRATS	REPUBLICANS	ISSUES	DEMOCRATS	REPUBLICANS
Public ownership of natural resources should be:			Regulation of trade unions should be:		
			a. increased	59.3%	86.4%
a. increased	57.5%	12.9%	b. decreased	12.4	4.5
b. decreased	18.6	51.9	c. kept the same	28.3	9.2
c. kept the same	23.8	35.2	Corporate income tax should be:		
Federal aid to education should be:			a. increased	32.3	4.0
a. increased	66.2	22.3	b. decreased	23.3	61.5
b. decreased	13.4	43.2	c. kept the same	44.4	34.5
c. kept the same	20.4	34.5	Tax on large incomes should be:		
Federal programs of slum clearance and public housing should be:			a. increased	27.0	5.4
			b. decreased	23.1	56.9
			c. kept the same	49.9	37.7
a. increased	78.4	40.1	Tax on business should be:		
b. decreased	5.6	21.6			
c. kept the same	16.0	38.3	a. increased	12.6	1.0
Social Security benefits should be:			b. decreased	38.3	71.1
			c. kept the same	49.1	27.8
a. increased	60.0	22.5	Tax on middle incomes should be:		
b. decreased	3.9	13.1			
c. kept the same	36.1	64.4	a. increased	2.7	0.8
Minimum wages should be:			b. decreased	50.2	63.9
			c. kept the same	47.1	35.3
a. increased	50.0	15.5	Tax on small incomes should be:		
b. decreased	4.7	12.5			
c. kept the same	45.2	72.0	a. increased	1.4	2.9
Government regulation of business should be:			b. decreased	79.2	65.0
			c. kept the same	19.4	32.1
a. increased	20.2	0.6			
b. decreased	38.5	84.1			
c. kept the same	41.3	15.3			

Adapted from H. McCloskey, P. J. Hoffman, and R. O'Hara, "Issue Conflict and Consensus among Party Leaders and Followers," *American Political Science Review*, Vol. 54 (1960), pp. 405–427.

INCREASES IN U.S. MILITARY STRENGTH
JAN. 1961 TO DATE

150% INCREASE IN THE NUMBER OF NUCLEAR WARHEADS AND A

200% INCREASE IN TOTAL MEGATONNAGE OUR STRATEG ALERT FORCE

PLATFORM COMMITTEE
1964 DEMOCRATIC
NATIONAL CONVENTION

Platforms of the major parties are usually lengthy documents. In the photo Secretary of Defense Robert McNamara appears before the platform committee at the 1964 Democratic convention.

What does the evidence on pages 225–227 suggest about the relationship of political party policies, group identification, personal interest, and voting?

The Relationship of Political Party Identification to Voting

Political party identification refers to an individual's preference for the leaders, the policies, and the image of a particular party. What do the following tables, and the list of factual statements, indicate about (1) the development and extent of political party identifications of American voters and (2) the relationship of political party identification to voting?

Table 10. **Party Identifications of Americans, 1940–1968**

	1940	1947	1952	1956	1960	1964	1966	1968
Democrats	41%	45%	47%	44%	46%	51%	42%	47%
Independents	20	21	22	24	23	22	31	26
Republicans	38	27	27	29	27	24	27	27

Source: The American Institute of Public Opinion (The Gallup Poll).

Table 11. **Relation of Parents' Political Party Preference to That of Children**

Party Preference of Respondent	Both Dem.	Both Rep.	One Rep. One Dem.	One Dem. or Rep.; Other Uncertain	Both Shifted	Don't Know about Either	Neither Voted
Strong Democrat	36%	7%	12%	14%	11%	15%	15%
Weak Democrat	36	9	32	23	23	21	22
Independent	16	20	10	33	39	30	36
Weak Republican	6	30	22	12	14	9	9
Strong Republican	6	33	22	15	11	3	3
None, minor party, or unknown	—	1	2	3	2	22	15

Table 12. **Relationship of Political Party Identification to Time of Voter's Decision in the 1964 Presidential Election**

Time of Vote Choice Decision	Strong Democrat	Democrat	Independent	Republican	Strong Republican
Before Convention	59%	38%	30%	29%	36%
During Convention	24	26	23	25	30
During Campaign	17	36	47	46	34

Source: W. H. Flanigan, *Political Behavior of the American Electorate.*

Table 13. **Relationship of Political Party Identification to Voting in Presidential Elections**

Political Party Identification	1952 D %	1952 R %	1956 D %	1956 R %	1960 D %	1960 R %	1964 D %	1964 R %	1968 D %	1968 R %	1968 3rd Party %
NATIONAL	44.6	55.4	42.2	57.8	50.1	49.9	61.3	38.7	43.0	43.4	13.6
Republicans	8	92	4	96	5	95	20	80	9	86	5
Democrats	77	23	85	15	84	16	87	13	74	12	14
Neither Rep. nor Dem.	35	65	30	70	43	57	56	44	31	44	25

Source: The American Institute of Public Opinion (The Gallup Poll).

Additional facts about political party identification that have been revealed in nationwide studies are:

(1) Roughly 75 percent of American adults express identification with either the Democratic or Republican parties.

(2) Roughly 20 percent of American adults have switched political party identification, although many more have occasionally voted for candidates of the other party.

(3) About 50 percent of the voters have supported the presidential candidate of the "other" party at least once.

(4) Almost 50 percent of the voters view the two major political parties in terms of benefits to themselves and the primary and secondary groups with which they identify. For example, these voters choose to identify with either the Democratic or Republican party because of their beliefs about party policies that affect them. They choose to support the party that they believe will help them, or those with whom they identify, in some important way.

(5) Individuals who express a strong preference for a political party tend to view the political world through the lenses of their political party identification. An individual's beliefs about how his party reacts to an issue colors and influences his reactions to the same issue. In this way a political party identity serves as a filter for political attitudes and beliefs about issues. Rather than carefully studying issues prior to making decisions about policies, the partisan uses his understanding of his political party's position as a guide to his own position about an issue.

(6) Currently, about one-fourth of American voters do not identify with either the Republican or Democratic party. Another one-third of voters *weakly identify* with either the Republicans or Democrats. These *weak* party identifiers and independents are most open to the appeals of provocative issues or attractive candidates as main influencers of their voting choices.

Political analysts say that Eisenhower's personality led many weak identifiers with the Democratic party to switch away from their own party's candidate, Adlai Stevenson (left), in 1952 and again in 1956.

The Influence of Situation on Voting

Provocative issues, appealing candidates, or social upheavals are situational factors that can influence voting behavior to a great extent. Several presidential elections provide examples of the influence of situation on voting.

The "Great Depression" of the 1930's was a severe social upheaval that influenced political party identification and voting. Prior to the "Great Depression" the Republican party dominated the American political scene. More people identified with the Republican party than with the Democratic party. Since the depression, associated in the minds of many people with Republican policies, the Democrats have been the majority party. Since the 1930's in one election after another, a majority of black voters have supported Democrats, most manual workers have supported Democrats, and most businessmen and college-educated people have supported Republicans. From time to time deviations in these voting patterns have occurred, because of the appeal of issues and candidates; but the persistence of these voting tendencies, related to political party identity, has been impressive.

Some political scientists believe that severe social conflicts of the 1960's— related to race relations, the Vietnam War, and radical student protest—are creating extensive changes in political party identification and voting. These political scientists point to the number of voters who supported George Wallace in the presidential election of 1968 in traditional areas of Democratic party strength, such as manual workers and young adults. In addition, Republican candidates appear to be gaining increased support among all groups, except black people, that have supported the Democrats strongly during the past two generations. The presidential and congressional elections of the 1970's will indicate whether or not a major realignment of party preferences and candidate choices is taking place among American voters.

In 1964 Barry Goldwater (right) failed to hold the support of many Republicans and to win the support of Independents, thus giving President Lyndon Johnson a landslide victory.

The presidential elections of 1952, 1956, and 1960 provide examples of the influence of issues and candidates upon the voting choices of independents, weak party identifiers, and a few strong party identifiers. In the presidential elections of 1952 and 1956 many typical Democratic voters supported Democrats for Congress, showing that their switch to the Republican presidential candidate was based on the personal appeal of Eisenhower rather than upon the overall appeal of the Republican party. Also, independent voters were mostly for Eisenhower, which is another indication of his great personal appeal. However, in 1964 a majority of independent voters and 20 percent of typical Republican voters switched to the support of Democrat Lyndon Johnson. This switch was partially a response to the *negative* appeal of Republican candidate Barry Goldwater, who supported some policies that many voters viewed as too extreme to be acceptable.

The presidential campaign of 1960 featured the major issue of Democrat John Kennedy's Roman Catholic religious identification. Many usual Democratic voters switched to Republican Richard Nixon because they preferred not to have a Catholic as President. Some Roman Catholics who usually voted Republican supported Kennedy in this election.

What does *Table 14* reveal about the relationship of situation to voting?

Table 14. **Democratic Vote in 1952 and 1960 by Religion and Occupational Class**

| | 1952 | | | 1960 | | |
	Catholic	Protestant	Total	Catholic	Protestant	Total
Manual Workers	64%	52%	56%	85%	47%	60%
Non-manual Occupations	38	28	34	75	29	45
Total	55	42		81	38	

Source: Robert R. Alford, *Party and Society* (Chicago: Rand McNally, 1963), pp. 242–243.

To demonstrate your knowledge of factors influencing the candidate choices of American voters, complete these exercises.

1. Below are five descriptions of typical individuals. Answer the questions that follow each description. Apply these concepts—primary group, secondary group, and cross-pressure—to the discussion of each question.

Mr. Sam Jones has lived in Centerville all of his life. His mother, father, five brothers, and six uncles and aunts all live in Centerville. Next month the citizens of Centerville will be selecting a mayor. Two strong candidates are running for the mayor's office. Mr. Brown, the Democratic candidate, has been a long-time friend of the Jones family. Sam's mother, father, brothers, uncles, and aunts are all campaigning for Mr. Brown against his Republican opponent, Mr. Green. For whom do you think Sam Jones is likely to vote? Why?

In 1968 Steve Smith worked in a steel mill. He rode to work daily with a group of fellow workers. These men were close friends who hunt and fish together, play cards together, and in general have a good time with one another during off-work hours. Steve's friends supported Republican Richard Nixon in the presidential campaign of 1968. However, Steve was a strong supporter of the steelworker's union. He believed that the union leaders watched out for the best interests of the union members. He had always followed the political advice of the union leaders in the past. The union leaders were campaigning for Democrat Hubert Humphrey. Furthermore, Steve's wife and parents were life-long Democrats who were supporting Humphrey. Steve was also very religious. He went to church every Sunday. He looked up to the minister of the church and often followed his advice. The minister had told Steve that he was supporting George Wallace for President. How was Steve likely to vote? Why?

The year is 1970. George Johnson is a black man who lives in Chicago. He is a manual worker. His wife and two brothers prefer the Democratic party. He belongs to a labor union. The union leader has urged all members to support Democratic party candidates in the upcoming election. Mr. Johnson also admires several black civil rights leaders. In the newspapers he read that these civil rights leaders were urging all blacks to support the Democratic party candidates. Mr. Johnson also believes that members of civil rights organizations around the country are supporting Democratic party candidates. He identifies strongly with these organizations. Mr. Johnson is deciding for whom to vote. Which candidate is he likely to support? Why?

Mr. Murphy has just moved to Centerville. He is not familiar with local political issues. His wife is not very interested in politics and seldom bothers to vote. Mr. Murphy belongs to no social organizations. He spends most of his off-work time watching television or drinking beer at the corner tavern. He is a bus driver. His three close friends care little or nothing about politics. Which political party is Mr. Murphy likely to support? Why?

Mr. Goldman is an upper-income, college-educated businessman. He is white, a Protestant, and a member of the Chamber of Commerce, the American Association of Manufacturers, and the Rotary Club. He is very much against labor unions. He lives in a wealthy suburb. He strongly identifies with big business interests in the United States. Which political party is Mr. Goldman most likely to support? Why?

2. What are some weaknesses of social group analysis of political party preference, and candidate choice, as required in exercise number one above?

3. Why have black people tended to favor Democratic party candidates?

4. Why are businessmen more likely than manual workers to favor Republican party candidates?

5. Which of these models, or types, accounts for the behavior of most American voters: (a) the Public-Minded Independent, (b) the Thoughtless

Participant, (c) the Manipulated Subject, (d) the Self-Interested Partisan? Explain. (See pages 216–218 for a description of each type.

6. Which of these models of voter behavior would be most difficult for many people to practice? Explain.

7. Which of these models of voter behavior is most desirable? Explain.

D. The Impact of Voting on Government

Congresswoman Shirley Chisholm of Brooklyn gives an impassioned speech to members of the New York Democratic State Committee.

Upon signing the Voting Rights Act of 1965, President Lyndon Johnson said, "The vote is the most powerful instrument ever devised by man for breaking down injustice and destroying the terrible walls that imprison men because they are different from other men." President Johnson suggested, in this statement, that voting is an important political resource, that through the ballot common people can influence the government.

People who believe in democracy stress that voting in public elections is a means to influence public officials. Through the vote citizens can defeat unsatisfactory public officials and support those who are suitable. Abraham Lincoln's famous phrase, "government of the people, by the people, and for the people" only has meaning in our country if the vote is an important political resource.

Some people believe that voting has little or no impact on the making of public policy. These people view voting as merely a political ritual (ceremony) which gives citizens the feeling that they can influence policies.

Does voting in public elections really pay off? How useful is the vote as a political resource? What is the impact of voting on public policy decisions? Are individuals and groups really better off because of using the right to vote?

Evidence on the following pages suggests answers to these questions. However, realize that this evidence, though useful and highly suggestive, is limited in scope.

Black Votes and Black Power

Prior to the 1960's a majority of black adults were not registered to vote and did not participate in public elections. During the 1960's increased political awareness among blacks in combination with the enactment of laws to protect and extend voting rights led to vastly increased participation of black people in public elections (p. 203).

Kenneth A. Gibson flashes the victory sign after being sworn in as Newark's first Negro mayor in July, 1970.

One way to study the effectiveness of the vote as a political resource is to compare and contrast the privileges and opportunities of black Americans before and after their widespread use of the ballot. If, indeed, voting has an impact upon public policy, then there must be a connection between black votes and the capability of black people to influence public policy.

During the 1960's the Federal government enacted major civil rights laws that increased the opportunities of black people in education, employment, housing, and the use of public facilities. Certainly increased voting by black people did not account entirely for the passage of these laws. The 1960's were years of unusual concern for the rights of disadvantaged people. During this decade black people showed considerable political skill and determination in seeking their rights through activities such as picketing, boycotts, sit-ins, strikes, and protest marches. Black voting in combination with other political activities contributed to passage of laws favorable to black people.

Black voters are often in a good position to influence the outcome of presidential elections. Many black voters live in the large cities of the heavily populated states with the most electoral votes. When these black people choose to cast their votes as a bloc, to unite in support of a candidate, they sometimes have the power to "swing" a close election to the presidential candidate who appears ready to help them the most. Thus, the hopes and desires of the black voters of large cities in states such as California, Pennsylvania, New Jersey, Illinois, Ohio, Michigan, Texas, and New York were not ignored in the party platforms and campaign promises of presidential candidates in the 1960's. In addition, congressional and senatorial candidates in states with large black populations paid more and more attention to the views of black voters.

Julian Bond, a member of the Georgia State Legislature, responds to a question at a press conference in 1970.

Another indicator of increased black voting power is the vast increase in black public officials that occurred during the 1960's. During that decade President Johnson appointed the first black Cabinet member, Robert Weaver, and the first black Supreme Court justice, Thurgood Marshall. By the end of the 1960's there were 168 black state legislators, 48 black mayors, 575 other elected city officials, 362 black school board members, and 99 black sheriffs, police chiefs, and constables. In 1969 there were nine black members of the House of Representatives and one black member of the Senate. Although these totals are small, they represented a vast increase in the number of black public officials in 1969 as compared to 1960. Certainly, increased use of the ballot led to an increase in the number of black public officials.

In local elections in various parts of the United States black voters helped bring such gains as (1) better educational opportunities through access to better schools and through improvements in school facilities, (2) improved legal protection and police services, and (3) improved public services, such as garbage collection, street maintenance, and recreational facilities.

These kinds of gains have not been won by all blacks in every part of the United States. And black people have more of these kinds of opportunities in some communities than in others. However, there does appear to be a relationship between political activity among blacks, particularly voting, and the achieving and keeping of educational opportunities, public services, and

235

legal protection. In addition, it must be noted that the ballot has not been a very powerful political resource in helping blacks to achieve greater social equality or vastly improve their living standards.

The following case, about the impact of black voting in Tuskegee, Alabama, describes both the power and the limitations of the vote as a political resource.

Black Power in Tuskegee

Tuskegee is a small town in Macon County in Alabama. It is the home of Tuskegee Institute, the famous school for Negroes founded by Booker T. Washington. Tuskegee is in the heart of the deep South's "black belt." A majority of Tuskegee's inhabitants are Negro. However, until 1962 a majority of the registered voters in Tuskegee were whites, as the graph on the opposite page shows.

Until recently, Negro voter registration and voter turnout had been low in Tuskegee, as elsewhere in the South. This was primarily a result of the southern tradition of segregation and legal discrimination against blacks. Both legal and social barriers had been erected to prevent large numbers of blacks from voting, as we have seen.

Although they were a minority of the population of Tuskegee, white people ran the city government. The white public officials of Tuskegee made policy that favored whites. The government provided many services for whites that were not provided for Negroes. For example, the streets in the white neighborhoods were paved while streets in the black neighborhoods remained unpaved. Garbage was picked up three times a week in the white neighborhoods. The city provided garbage collection service only once a week for the black neighborhoods. City housing laws prevented blacks from moving to certain sections of the city. Recreation facilities were segregated.

The Macon County Democratic Club (MCDC) tried to organize blacks in Tuskegee for the purpose of influencing the local government. The MCDC worked hard to register black voters. Before every election, the MCDC met to choose the candidates most likely to favor Negro interests. Then the MCDC would urge all blacks in Tuskegee to vote for the MCDC-selected candidates. In this way the MCDC hoped to gain influence over public officials that they helped elect.

For the most part the attempts of the MCDC to influence public officials failed. Prior to the election of 1964, black voters were a minority. It was impossible for this minority group to elect a Negro to public office. Even when they helped to elect a white man, the white official felt compelled to follow the traditions of the white community. This meant that blacks continued to be discriminated against in the distribution of public services.

Finally in 1964 tradition was shattered. Tuskegee blacks achieved a majority of the registered voters. The MCDC encouraged several Negroes to run for public office. Several white candidates for office promised to support black interests if elected. The MCDC agreed to back those white candidates who would support policies favorable to black people.

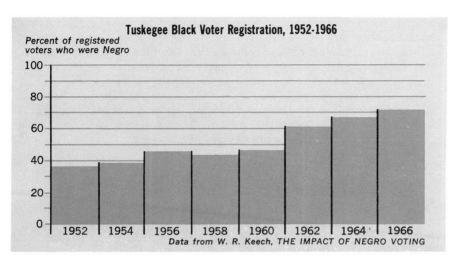

Tuskegee Black Voter Registration, 1952-1966

Percent of registered
voters who were Negro

Data from W. R. Keech, THE IMPACT OF NEGRO VOTING

In the local election of 1964 the MCDC delivered the black vote in support of its slate of candidates. Every candidate on the MCDC slate was elected. Thus, a white man who had promised to support Negro interests was elected mayor. Four white men who had promised to support Negro interests were elected to the city council. For the first time since Reconstruction days, two blacks were elected to the city council. Two were elected to the school board, two as justices of the peace, and the new county sheriff was a Negro. Black power had been demonstrated in this election.

The MCDC had been in a position to influence the selection of an all-Negro slate of candidates. It chose not to do this, because it wanted to demonstrate that it was willing and able to cooperate with whites. Although it is a majority political force in Tuskegee, it realized that blacks would remain a minority political force in the state of Alabama. The MCDC hoped that its willingness to cooperate with white people would encourage whites in other parts of Alabama to cooperate with Negroes. The MCDC desired to use black power to help Negroes, not to hurt whites.

Black voting power in Tuskegee helped to change some public policies in Tuskegee. But the vote alone did not account for the changes. Rather, the MCDC continued to remind public officials that they had been elected to office with black votes. Therefore, Tuskegee blacks expected some favors from the government. This constant pressure that the MCDC applied to public officials, along with the black voting power that the MCDC commanded, influenced public officials to take action.

One of the first actions of the government in behalf of Negroes was to pave the streets in the black neighborhoods. Garbage collection service was changed. Both black and white neighborhoods received equal garbage collection service. The new city council, elected with the support of black voting power, abolished housing laws that discriminated against Negroes. Public parks and swimming pools were integrated.

237

An obvious benefit to the black community came in the distribution of appointments to city jobs. Before 1964 no Negroes had been appointed to serve on local government boards and commissions. After the election of 1964, many blacks received such appointments. Two were appointed to the city library board. Three blacks were appointed to the housing commission. Three were placed on the city planning board. One was put on the medical board, and four were appointed to the board of directors of the city-county hospital. Five blacks were placed on the recreation board. Black voting power had won black representation on every appointive board in Tuskegee.

The Dean of the College of Arts and Sciences at Tuskegee Institute talks with a student group.

Voting power did not win social and economic advancement for blacks as a group in Tuskegee. Many whites, true to their traditions, continued to treat Negroes with disdain. Poor Negroes with low living standards tended to remain poor and with low living standards.

However, black voting power won impressive legal and political gains for blacks in Tuskegee. But it is important to remember that these changes did not come about until Negroes became a majority of the voters in Tuskegee. It is important to remember that bloc voting by Negroes helped to achieve these results. Further it is important to note that the vote alone did not win more rights and services for Tuskegee's blacks. Rather, a strong organization, the MCDC, was needed to organize voters to influence public policy. And the MCDC was needed to pressure public officials to carry out their election promises.

1. How effective was voting as a political resource in Tuskegee? Discuss the limitations as well as the power of the vote as an influencer of public policy decisions.

2. What is your evaluation of the political tactics and strategies of the MCDC? Do you approve or disapprove of their kind of "black power"?

Three Views of the Impact of Voting on Public Policy

Following are three descriptions of the impact of voting on public policy. On the basis of evidence presented in Unit Three, pages 164–238, decide which of the descriptions is the more accurate view of the relationship of voting to the making of public policy. As in several other exercises in this course, you are required to think in terms of more-or-less rather than either-or. Each of the three descriptions tells us something about the election process in the United States. You are required to decide which of the descriptions is the more accurate picture of reality as indicated in evidence presented previously.

Elections as mandates. Some people view public elections as providing mandates for public policy. A "mandate" authorizes a representative to act in behalf of his constituents. The "mandate" view of public elections holds that elections are great debates over issues between rival candidates. The voters indicate their public policy preferences by voting for the candidate who represents their ideas about the issues debated in the election campaign. Thus, the winning candidate is given a "mandate" by the voters to attempt to enact certain public policies.

The "mandate" view of public elections suggests that voters hold the power to control the policy decisions of public officials. Government is a direct reflection of the wishes of the people. Public officials who violate their "mandates" are turned out of office by dissatisfied and angry voters.

Elections as indirect influencers of public policy. Some people view elections as indirectly influencing, not directly controlling, the policy decisions of public officials. The "indirect influence" view of elections holds that voters control directly the jobs of elected public officials. Thus, these public officials must pay attention to the moods and desires of the voters. However, the masses of voters do not, indeed cannot, indicate specific policy directions to the winning candidates. There are many issues raised in most election campaigns, and different groups of voters usually support the winning candidate for different reasons. Thus, the winning candidate receives a popular endorsement from the voters, in terms of which to make policy, rather than a mandate.

The "indirect influence" view of elections suggests that the elected official is not committed to follow exactly a program of policies indicated specifically by the voters. The voters are not able to dictate exactly what the public official must do. Yet the elected official must always consider the reactions of the voters when making policy decisions, since the voters control the public official's job and can end his political career through the power of the ballot. The need to win public approval in an election serves to restrain, and thereby to influence, the actions of the elected public official.

Elections as rituals. Another view of public elections is that they are basically ritualistic, or ceremonial. The main function of elections and voting is to legitimize the right of public officials to make policy, that is, to make people feel they have helped choose their public officials and to give the people a feeling of political participation so that they will readily accept the authority of public officials. The "ritual" view of elections holds that the voters do not have the opportunity to make meaningful choices between candidates with conflicting ideas about policies. Rather, the rival candidates strive to blur, or disguise, any real differences in beliefs. Thus, the voter must choose candidates on the basis of personality, campaign advertising, or traditional, but thoughtless, political party loyalty.

The "ritual" view of elections suggests that the voter has little or no influence over the making of public policy, since candidates are elected in the absence of meaningful debates about policy questions. The public official is seen as relatively free from the influence of the voters so long as he avoids blunders that could result in a loss of public confidence in his ability.

1. On the basis of evidence presented in this unit, which of these views of elections is the more accurate account of the impact of voting on public policy: (a) the "mandate" view, (b) the "indirect influence" view, or (c) the "ritual" view. Explain.

2. Which view of elections is most desirable? Explain.

"Well, there's the choice—which one would you prefer to have hitting you over the head, Alvin?"

Mahood, © *The Times* (London)

240

I SAY GIVE EIGHTEEN-YEAR-OLDS THE VOTE.

GET THEIR PROTESTS OFF THE STREETS —

AND INTO THE VOTING BOOTHS.

WHY SHOULDN'T THEY BE AS INEFFECTIVE AS THE REST OF US?

©1970 Jules Feiffer 5-3

241

Congressional Record

PROCEEDINGS AND DEBATES OF THE 92ᵈ CONGRESS, FIRST SESSIO...

United States of America

WASHINGTON, THURSDAY, FEBRUARY 11, 1971

Vol. 117

No...

House of Representatives

The House was not in session today. Its next meeting will be held on Wednesday, February 17, 1971, at 12 o'clock no...

Senate

THURSDAY, FEBRUARY 11, 1971

(Legislative day of Tuesday, January 26, 1971)

THE JOURNAL

Mr. MANSFIELD. Mr. President, I ask unanimous consent that the Journal of the proceedings of Wednesday, February 10, 1971, be approved.

The PRESIDENT pro tempore. Without objection, it is so ordered.

COMMITTEE MEETINGS DURING SENATE SESSION

Mr. MANSFIELD. Mr. President, I ask unanimous consent that all committees be authorized to meet during the session of the Senate today.

The PRESIDENT pro tempore. Without objection, it is so ordered.

POSTAL SERVICE PASSPORT APPLICATION FEES

Mr. MANSFIELD. Mr. President, I ask unanimous consent that the Senate proceed to the consideration of Calendar No. 6, S. 531.

The PRESIDENT pro tempore. Is there objection?

There being no objection, the bill (S. 531) to authorize the U.S. Postal Service to receive the fee of $2 for execution of an application for a passport for a... was ordered to be engrossed for a third reading, read the third time, and passed, as follows:

S. 531

Be it enacted by the Senate and House of Representatives of the United States of America in Congress assembled, That the period begin... June...

ment and shall continue in eff... 30, 1973.

EXECUTIVE SES...

Mr. MANSFIELD. Mr. P... unanimous consent that into executive session, t... tain nominations on the... endar.

The PRESIDENT p... there objection?

There being no obje... proceeded to consider...

NATIONAL CREDI...

The legislative cler... sundry nomination... Credit Union Board...

Mr. MANSFIELD... unanimous consent... be considered en bl...

The PRESIDEN... out objection, the... consider... en blo...

tion, the are no ob... —Mr. MANSFIE...

...unanimous cons...

MESSAGE FROM THE PRESIDENT

A message in writing from the President of the United States was communicated to the Senate by Mr. Geisler, one of his secretaries.

EXECUTIVE MESSAGE REFERRED

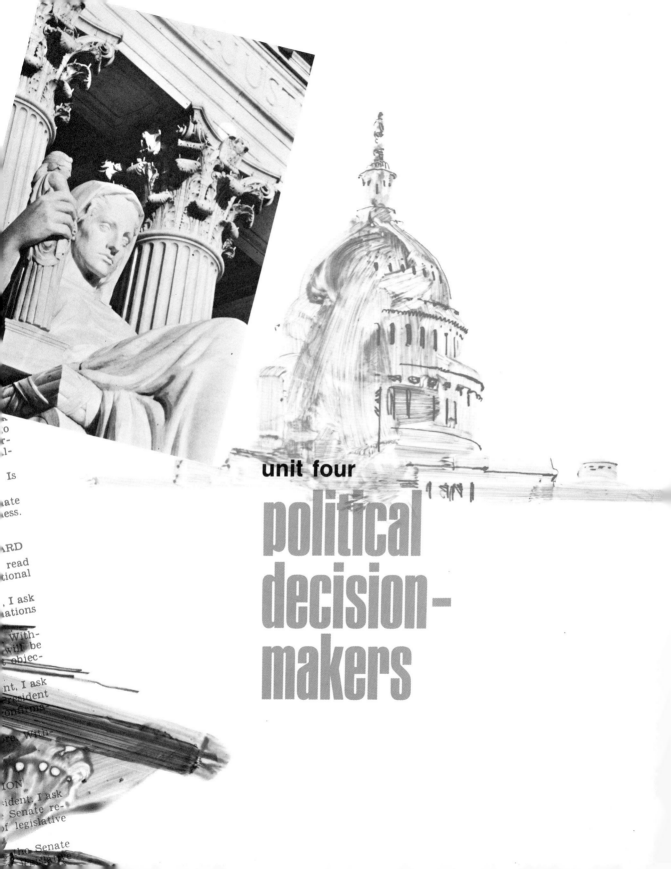

unit four

political decision-makers

chapter 12

Introduction to the Study of Political Decision-Makers

Units Four and Five are about government in the United States, about some of the people in government who make important political decisions, and about some people who do not work for government but who influence government policies. These units provide some answers to questions like these: What types of people become government leaders? How do they become leaders? Why do the leaders behave as they do? What kinds of decisions do political leaders make and what are the factors that influence their decisions?

Nancy Jefferson's assignment in American Government for today is related to one of the above questions: "What kinds of decisions do political leaders make?" Her specific assignment is to list twenty ways in which government has an impact on her personal life. Before leaving her classroom yesterday, Nancy had jotted down half a dozen items. "The others won't come easy," she thought to herself. Let's follow Nancy through the morning to see how easy or difficult the assignment really is.

A. In the Presence of Government

Nancy Jefferson, an attractive, friendly high school student in Chicago, was awakened at 7:00 A.M. Daylight Saving Time by her electric alarm clock. Federal law prescribes when clocks are to be moved forward an hour in the spring—and back an hour in the fall. Nancy lives in the Central Time Zone, an area designated by the Federal government. The electricity for Nancy's alarm clock is provided by a private company whose service is regulated by the state of Illinois. In some cities the electricity would have been provided by a government-owned utility.

Stretching and yawning, Nancy heads for the bathroom, where she brushes her teeth with water that is stored, purified, tested, and transported by the city of Chicago and with toothpaste containing fluoride, a substance found helpful in fighting tooth decay. Research in dental health is supported by the government. Another government agency, the Food and Drug Administration, approved the use of fluoride in Nancy's toothpaste.

Nancy returns to her bedroom where she begins to dress. She chooses a cotton blouse that was manufactured in the United States. The cotton in the blouse was part of a crop subsidized by the Federal government. The blouse manufacturer also received a kind of subsidy, since the Federal government has put a tax on blouses produced in other countries and sold in the United States in order to give some protection to the American blouse manufacturer from foreign competition. (Laws that provide subsidies to cotton farmers and

manufacturers mean that Nancy had to pay a bit more for the blouse than if the subsidies did not exist.) She also slips on a pair of imitation alligator shoes. Nancy had wanted real alligator shoes but could not find any at a price she could afford. The shoe clerk told her that the government has decided to protect alligators from hunters; therefore, very few alligator hides are now available, driving up the price on the few alligator shoes that are manufactured.

Neither the imitation alligator shoes nor the cotton blouse were manufactured in Chicago. The blouse was part of a shipment transported from a New England textile mill to Chicago by truck; the shoes arrived by railroad. Both railroad companies and trucking companies are regulated by the Interstate Commerce Commission, a government agency. (If the shoes and blouse had arrived by airplane, they would have landed at O'Hare Field, a government supported and operated airport, under conditions approved by the Federal Aviation Administration.)

Nancy goes into the kitchen, greets her father, and kisses her mother, leaving a slight smudge of a lipstick which is judged to be suitable for sale by public health authorities. She sits down at the table to drink a glass of milk (inspected and approved by government inspectors), shakes cereal out of a box clearly labeled as required by the government, and starts to munch on government-inspected bacon.

As she eats her breakfast, she watches the weather report on television. The weather report was based upon data provided by the government weather bureau, and the television program was broadcast at a frequency assigned by

The illustrations above suggest some important activities of government: collecting taxes, insuring bank deposits, printing money, and carrying mail.

245

the Federal Communications Commission. Although the television set itself was manufactured and sold by a private company, some of its components were invented or perfected in laboratories supported by government funds.

Finishing her breakfast, Nancy picks up her schoolbooks (selected by a state textbook adoption committee and paid for by the state of Illinois), walks down the stairs of her apartment house (financed with a low-interest mortgage guaranteed by the Federal Housing Administration), and runs out to the sidewalk built with tax money.

Soon she is at school, a publicly owned and managed agency, where she meets her friends, including those who arrived on buses operated by the city of Chicago. She goes to class where she meets her teacher, a government employee, whose education was supported in part by public funds. At noon she hurries to the cafeteria where she buys her lunch. She uses money that was printed and minted by the government. The cost of lunch is a bit less than would otherwise be the case because some of the food is provided at reduced cost by the government. Lunch is interrupted by a fire drill. (The state requires at least one fire drill each month.)

Before going to her next class, Nancy has a chance to visit briefly with her friend John (Social Security number 514-24-6215 and draft card number 14-41-31-117). She asks him to mail a letter, which for the small price of an airmail stamp she assumes the government will deliver to her brother at a military base overseas. Her parting words are "I must run now and finish my Government assignment. I'll never think of twenty ways that government has an effect on my personal life."

1. List four examples of government *regulation* in the story about Nancy Jefferson.

2. List four examples in which government provides *goods* or *services* to citizens.

3. Describe briefly one instance from the story in which a different policy decision by a government leader would make a difference in Nancy's life.

4. Make a list of activities in which you engage each day that are not affected by government in any way.

B. Some Important Rules That Influence Government in the United States

Suppose you were asked to describe professional football for a person who knew nothing about the game. It probably would not help him very much to begin by describing the key plays from the last championship game or by listing your favorite players. He cannot be expected to appreciate the players' skills until he knows something about the rules that influence their play.

You would need to explain how many players there are on each side and the purpose of the game. He should know how many tries a team has to advance the football ten yards, the number of points allowed for a touchdown, a safety, a field goal, and an "extra point." It might be important for him to know the penalties for violations of the rules. And you may have to define such terms as punt, forward pass, huddle, lateral, block, and tackle. In short, full appreciation of a coach's defensive strategy or a quarterback's passing skill begins with knowledge of the fundamental rules of the game.

This is also true of government. A full appreciation of the strategy used to change an important government policy or of the way a President performs his job depends upon a knowledge of the fundamental rules of American politics and government. But while the rules and procedures for playing football are relatively simple and easy to understand, the rules and procedures for the conduct of government are very complex. In a single course we can study only the most basic rules and procedures for American politics and government. Nevertheless, an understanding of even a few basic rules will help one better to understand the American political system.

Basic Features of American Government

Throughout your study of Units Four and Five you will learn about specific rules and procedures that influence the political behavior of the President, members of Congress, and other political leaders. However, there are some general features of the American political system you should understand before examining any of its parts.

The United States has a constitutional government. A constitutional government is one in which officials derive their authority to make, implement, and enforce their decisions from a written constitution. They may not legally assume responsibilities beyond the authority either stated or implied by the constitution.

Since 1789 the Constitution of the United States has been a major influence on the behavior of American political leaders. Whenever an important official enters office, he is asked to pledge his loyalty to the Constitution and swear that he will abide by its terms.

While the Constitution has been changed by amendments and some clauses may be interpreted differently today than they were in the past, the existence of the Constitution assures that governmental affairs will be conducted in similar ways by all public officials.

The Constitution is the foundation of the American legal system. The Constitution is a written plan for government. It tells how the government is to be set up and how it is to work. It describes how laws are to be made and enforced. It tells what the government can and cannot do. It describes the powers of government officials.

As *Diagram 1* shows, all laws made by governments in the United States must agree with the Constitution.

A democratic-republican form of government. The American government is *democratic* in that ultimate decision-making power lies with the people. By their votes Americans can change policies by changing political leaders. It is a *republican* form of government because most policy decisions are made

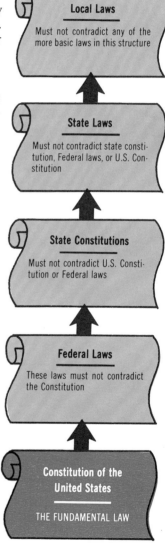

Diagram 1.

The Constitution Is the Foundation of the American Government

Local Laws

Must not contradict any of the more basic laws in this structure

State Laws

Must not contradict state constitution, Federal laws, or U.S. Constitution

State Constitutions

Must not contradict U.S. Constitution or Federal laws

Federal Laws

These laws must not contradict the Constitution

Constitution of the United States

THE FUNDAMENTAL LAW

by representatives, not by the citizens themselves. As compared to direct democracy in which all citizens gather to discuss and to decide policy, Americans elect officials to represent their views and to choose policies that are in their best interests.

The fact that we have a "democratic-republican" form of government has been a major influence on political activity in the United States. It has led, for example, to the emergence of strong political parties to choose candidates, to suggest policy alternatives, and to conduct campaigns. Study *Diagram 2.*

Diagram 2.   **Elements of Democratic-Republican Government**

People choose decision-makers in regular competitive elections

Political parties offer candidates and policy alternatives

Elected leaders must be responsive to the voters or risk defeat at the polls

A federal system of government. A federal system is characterized by a *division of powers* between the central government and its chief subdivisions—in our country, the fifty states. The United States is a federation of states with a strong central government. Both the states and the national government derive their authority from the people by means of the same document, the Constitution.

A *federal* system may be contrasted with a *unitary* system in which all political subdivisions draw their authority from the central government. In the United States neither the state governments nor the national government are dependent upon the other for their power. And local governments derive their authority from the respective state governments, rather than from the national government. The Constitution clearly assigns some responsibilities to the national government only (for example, coining money); other powers are reserved to the states (for example, establishing local governments); while still other powers are shared by the national and state governments (for example, ability to tax).

The federal system has been a major influence on political activity in the United States. For example, each state has considerable freedom to establish its own laws governing elections. This means that each state decides what residency requirements must be met in order for its citizens to be eligible to vote. The federal system provides that in some matters, such as recruiting men and women for the armed services or delivering mail, the national government may reach people directly. In other matters, such as education, health, and safety, when the national government wishes to provide services for all Americans, it may have to rely upon the state governments to administer its programs. *Diagram 3* illustrates the division of powers.

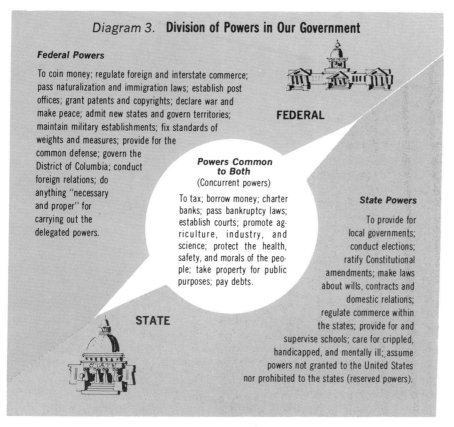

Diagram 3. Division of Powers in Our Government

Federal Powers

To coin money; regulate foreign and interstate commerce; pass naturalization and immigration laws; establish post offices; grant patents and copyrights; declare war and make peace; admit new states and govern territories; maintain military establishments; fix standards of weights and measures; provide for the common defense; govern the District of Columbia; conduct foreign relations; do anything "necessary and proper" for carrying out the delegated powers.

FEDERAL

Powers Common to Both
(Concurrent powers)

To tax; borrow money; charter banks; pass bankruptcy laws; establish courts; promote agriculture, industry, and science; protect the health, safety, and morals of the people; take property for public purposes; pay debts.

State Powers

To provide for local governments; conduct elections; ratify Constitutional amendments; make laws about wills, contracts and domestic relations; regulate commerce within the states; provide for and supervise schools; care for crippled, handicapped, and mentally ill; assume powers not granted to the United States nor prohibited to the states (reserved powers).

STATE

Power is separated among various branches of government. The Constitution provides for a separation of powers at the national level among three major branches of government: the executive branch, the legislative branch, and the judicial branch. These branches are said to be separated partly because each has a different function. The Congress primarily passes laws; the President primarily administers laws; and the Supreme Court primarily decides disputes growing out of law. This separation of responsibility is not so neat and clear-cut as generally believed and as described above. Nevertheless, the Constitution assigns different functions to different branches of the national government.

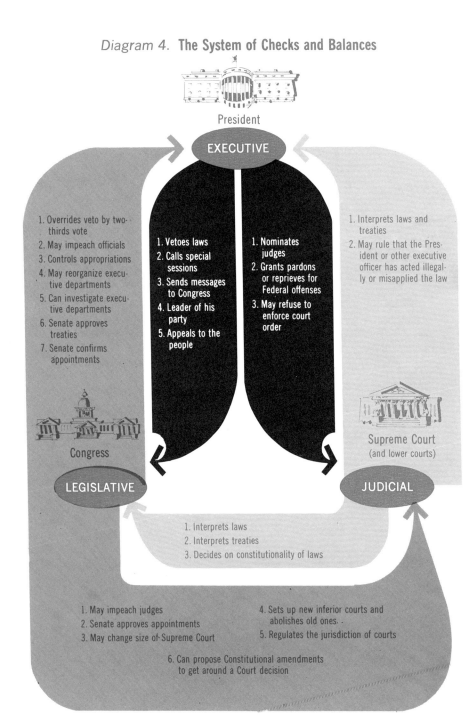

Diagram 4. **The System of Checks and Balances**

President

EXECUTIVE

1. Overrides veto by two-
   thirds vote
2. May impeach officials
3. Controls appropriations
4. May reorganize execu-
   tive departments
5. Can investigate execu-
   tive departments
6. Senate approves
   treaties
7. Senate confirms
   appointments

1. Vetoes laws
2. Calls special
   sessions
3. Sends messages
   to Congress
4. Leader of his
   party
5. Appeals to the
   people

1. Nominates
   judges
2. Grants pardons
   or reprieves for
   Federal offenses
3. May refuse to
   enforce court
   order

1. Interprets laws and
   treaties
2. May rule that the President or other executive
   officer has acted illegally or misapplied the law

Congress

LEGISLATIVE

Supreme Court
(and lower courts)

JUDICIAL

1. Interprets laws
2. Interprets treaties
3. Decides on constitutionality of laws

1. May impeach judges
2. Senate approves appointments
3. May change size of Supreme Court

4. Sets up new inferior courts and
   abolishes old ones.
5. Regulates the jurisdiction of courts

6. Can propose Constitutional amendments
   to get around a Court decision

250

The three branches check and balance one another. The Constitution does not provide for *absolute* separation of the lawmaking, executive, and judicial powers. Each branch has some power to check the other two. And in practice there is some mutual sharing of responsibility, especially by Congress and the President. This tends to create something of a balance of political power among the three branches of the central government, and none can easily gain control over the others.

The most important checks are shown in *Diagram 4*. Notice that the Senate must give consent to treaties and approve many appointments made by the President. The President may veto bills passed by Congress, but Congress can override his veto by a two-thirds vote in each house. The Supreme Court may set aside (declare unconstitutional) a law passed by Congress and signed by the President. Thus, while we have the principle of separation of powers, we also have close connections between the three departments through the check-and-balance system.

Most of the checks and balances are specifically listed in the Constitution. But some have developed over the years with custom and usage. For example, the President as leader of his party exerts strong influence over its members in Congress.

Constitutionalism, the democratic-republican form of government, federalism, and the *separation of powers* among the three branches of the national government have the combined effect of preventing the total, uncontrolled use of political power by a single individual or group of people. Since political power is spread throughout the political system and since public officials are subject to restraints by citizens, it is necessary for public officials to bargain and to negotiate with others in order to govern. The American form of government makes politics a necessary fact of life.

C. Two Ways of Viewing Politics and Government

Anyone who has used binoculars knows that you will view a scene differently depending upon which end of the binoculars you peer through. If you are sitting in the back of a theater and want a close-up view of the leading actor, you will use the binoculars to magnify the scene. You will then see the actor's face more clearly, but other people on the stage may no longer be in view. On the other hand, if you were primarily interested in seeing the total scene and less interested in focusing upon one person, you might turn the glasses around and look through the opposite end.

Certain social science concepts can serve us as if they were binoculars. Some concepts lead us to concentrate on the total social process. Such a concept is *system*. Other concepts, such as *role*, lead us to focus on smaller units within the whole rather than upon the big picture. Thus, what we see depends a great deal upon which concepts we use.

Depending upon your purpose it may be useful to study the system as a whole, or it might be useful to focus upon parts within the system. For example, think of your body as a system. It is composed of many parts working together to make you function as a whole. For many purposes it is useful to think of yourself as a system—the total you. In other cases, such as when you are being examined for glasses, it is more useful to concentrate on only one of your parts. For an eye examination, it is not necessary for the optometrist to remember that your eyes are in a skull attached to your trunk that moves about on legs. He will satisfy you if he helps you see better.

Previous units have focused *primarily* upon elements of the whole, bringing these parts into sharp focus. The lessons provided insights into the behavior of typical American citizens. In Units Four and Five we study the behavior of American political leaders.

In Unit Four, three chief concepts—role, recruitment, and decision-making—are used to organize our inquiry. For example, in the chapter on congressional role, we identify the role or roles congressmen play and the customs, rules, and procedures that influence the congressional role. We ask what kind of people become members of Congress and what factors influence a congressman's decisions. We shall be less concerned with how Congress as an institution relates to other government institutions and how Congress compares to other legislative assemblies; these questions would be appropriate for analyzing the total system.

Of course, just as the optometrist should never forget that your eyes are a part of your total body, so should we never forget that each of the roles we are examining is a part of a total political system. The roles do not and cannot exist in isolation. An analysis that concentrates upon the elements within a system can serve us by drawing our attention to the ways individual parts of the total political system function.

Social scientists can study any social institution (family, church, labor unions, government, and so on) by using either of the two approaches described above. Let us see how the two analytical approaches might be used to study the American high school.

Studying the High School by a "Systems" Approach

A "systems" approach to a study of American high schools would focus on such questions as these: What kind of relationship exists between the high school and the local community? How does supervision by the school board affect activities within the high school? In what ways do parents influence curriculum decisions made in the high school? How do American high schools today compare with those a generation or a century ago? How do American high schools compare with high schools in other countries? What are the relationships between high schools and elementary schools, between high schools and vocational schools, between high schools and colleges or universities, and between high schools and other educational organizations in the United States? What is the relationship between the city and county school systems in the same county?

Diagrams 5, 6, and 7 suggest some of the ways a person might think about high schools if he were interested primarily in analyzing high schools as part of an educational system.

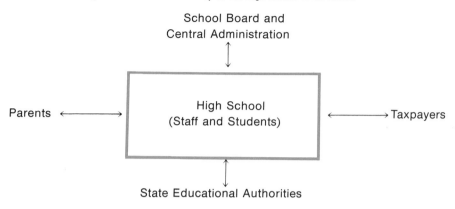

Diagram 5. **The Relationship of the High School to Its Clients**

School Board and
Central Administration

Parents ←——————→ High School
(Staff and Students) ←——————→ Taxpayers

State Educational Authorities

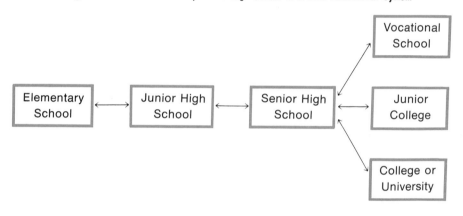

Diagram 6. **The Relationship of the High School to a Total Educational System**

Elementary
School ←——→ Junior High
School ←——→ Senior High
School

Vocational
School

Junior
College

College or
University

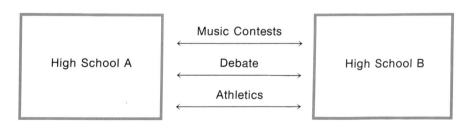

Diagram 7. **The Relationship of a High School to Other High Schools**

High School A

Music Contests

Debate

Athletics

High School B

The diagrams above do not exhaust all that might be learned through a systems analysis of American high schools, but the diagrams do show the kind of topics such an analysis focuses on.

A Second Approach to the Study of the High School

Suppose we were to concentrate upon one school rather than upon the interactions among schools. We might see that in any particular high school a number of *roles* can be identified. The interaction among these roles produces a social action referred to generally as a "high school education." *Diagram 8* reveals some of the major roles that exist in every school and some of the simple transactions that occur among these roles.

What aspects of the role of principal do these pictures suggest?

Diagram 8. **Some Roles That Are Important within a High School**

HIGH SCHOOL

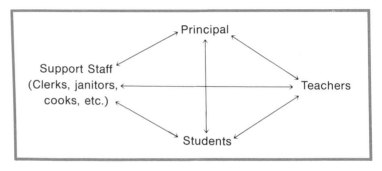

Principal

Support Staff
(Clerks, janitors,
cooks, etc.)

Teachers

Students

Let's select one of these roles, the high school principal, and apply the three major concepts to be used in each of the chapters in Unit Four: *role,* *recruitment,* and *decision-making.*

254

Role. In analyzing the principal's role it would be important first to remember that in any situation the *role* a person plays depends upon the position, or status, he occupies. In other words, the man who is a principal is able to act in certain ways because of the position he holds, rather than because of who he is, his personality, and so on. Any person who occupies the position of principal has the authority to behave as a principal. The expectations people have about the way principals should behave—the rules and customs that accompany the status of principal—comprise what is called the principal's *role.*

At one time the principal was the "principal" teacher (first or most important teacher). Today, principals in large high schools rarely teach at all. Most of their time is devoted to the management of the school. They plan school schedules, interview prospective faculty members, hold meetings with parents, represent the school at official functions, administer the school budget, establish and administer many school rules, punish or supervise those who punish students for violation of school rules, distribute rewards for student and faculty achievement, and together with faculty and student committees plan new programs, including instructional programs, for their schools.

The principal's role is shaped by many customs, rules, and procedures. For example, he is not free usually to alter the curriculum drastically because some courses may be required by state regulations for high school graduation, because his curriculum must correspond to a general plan approved by the school board, and because the courses must satisfy the teachers, students, and parents. He is not free to abolish by himself extracurricular activities that he considers unnecessary. He has only the amount of money to spend that is allocated to him by the school board. Tenure rules and the teachers' association may prevent him from replacing mediocre teachers with "above average" instructors.

He is expected to be a "good" man. His moral behavior should conform to the standards of the community he serves. He is expected to be fair and honest. When he is angry, he is not expected to use profanity in front of his students. He is expected to dress and behave in a manner that will set an example for the faculty and student body.

Recruitment. What kinds of people become senior high school principals? A study published in 1965 of approximately 16,000 high school principals produced the following generalizations:

(1) Almost nine out of ten high school principals are men.

(2) Most have small-town and working-class origins. Therefore, becoming a high school principal is for many of these men a move upward in socio-economic status.

(3) They tend to be appointed to their first principalship at a relatively early age (early to mid-thirties).

(4) About 90 percent of the principals have earned a master's degree. Only 10 percent had a bachelor's degree or less; only three percent had a doctorate.

(5) Nearly all principals have had some teaching experience prior to becoming principals. About 60 percent of the principals had between 4 and 14 years of teaching experience prior to becoming principals.

(6) Over one-third of the principals moved to their first principalship directly from the high school classroom. About one-fifth became principals after serving as assistant principals or vice principals. About 14 percent became principals directly from the position of fulltime coach or athletic director.

(7) About three-fifths of the principals expressed satisfaction with educational administration as a career, but only one-fourth indicated they had no desire to move to another position. Many wanted to become superintendents; others wished to move to larger high schools.

What consequences might follow from having these kinds of people become principals as compared to other kinds of people? Do the principals appear to be trained for their roles?

Decision-making. High school principals are called upon daily to make important policy decisions for their schools. Therefore, in each high school, the principal is an important decision-maker. Policy issues can usually be decided in a number of ways. Nevertheless, a principal is not entirely free to choose from among the possible choices. He is limited in part by his role. The customs, rules, and procedures which shape the role and his relationships with other people—faculty, students, school officials, parents—all have a part in determining his decision. His personal beliefs, formed by his prior experiences and by his personality, are also important. His decision leads to new actions that ultimately lead to new decisions. By studying decision-making we learn not only about how an individual role is played but also how the role is linked to other parts of the system.

The following case study provides an opportunity to study the principal's role. It also provides some examples of the basic elements of decision-making.

Crisis at Webster Senior High

The buzzer on the telephone brought Principal George Baxter of Webster Senior High School to attention. He picked up the receiver and heard his secretary say, "Willie Smith and Julia Lincoln are here for their appointment. Shall I send them in?"

"Give me two or three more minutes," Mr. Baxter replied. "I'll call you when I am ready."

He returned the phone to its cradle and swung around in his chair to face the window in his office. "Two or three minutes!" he thought. "I won't be ready in two or three years to solve this problem!"

Two weeks ago, when the new school year began, it had not occurred to him that he would face this kind of problem. Most students seemed happy to be back. He had assembled what he believed to be the best faculty ever at Webster Senior High.

And the coaches were predicting an outstanding football season. Then, last Monday, his troubles began.

Webster Senior High is the only high school in a small midwestern town. The school has 1540 students in grades nine to twelve. Approximately 20 percent of the students are black. Mr. Baxter's trouble arose from a growing tension between white and black students and the forthcoming elections for cheerleaders.

Cheerleader selection at Webster High. Traditionally, cheerleader elections are held each fall at Webster Senior High on the Friday prior to the first football game. On that day each high school student who wishes to be considered as a cheerleader leads one cheer at a school-wide pep assembly to demonstrate her skill. Following the assembly all the students vote for the five students they consider to be the best cheerleaders. The five who receive the greatest number of votes are elected.

Traditionally, only white girls have been elected. While one or two black girls have entered the competition each year, none has ever been elected.

On Monday, a group of black students charged that no black cheerleaders had ever been elected because of prejudice on the part of white students. They announced that this year at least one black girl would have to be elected cheerleader or there would be trouble. Willie Smith, a halfback on the varsity football team, said that neither he nor any of the other fifteen black football players would compete this year unless there was at least one black cheerleader.

Since the announcement by the black students on Monday, Mr. Baxter had been able to think of little else. First of all, he did not doubt that if the election were permitted to run as usual, no black girl would be chosen cheerleader. This was not because there were no capable black candidates. But a series of small fights between black and white students had created ill-feeling, and many angry white students seemed certain to vote only for white candidates. Secondly, cheerleader try-outs and elections were conducted by the student council. Whenever possible, Mr. Baxter tried to avoid interfering in matters that were directly the student council's responsibility. In the past whenever he tried to influence a student council decision, it had caused a student uproar. The student council had met on Tuesday following the announcement by the black students and decided that the present system of electing cheerleaders was the most democratic process imaginable and that the elections should proceed as planned.

Consultation with the faculty. Mr. Baxter discussed the entire issue in a faculty meeting on Wednesday. The faculty was badly divided. (1) Some were angry that the blacks had threatened trouble and were against giving in to their demands. (2) Others were sympathetic to the black demands and argued that if the elections could not be held without discrimination against blacks, there should be no elections at all. The school could simply do without cheerleaders. (3) The coaches, fearful of what a black walkout would do to chances for a successful season, urged that one of the five cheerleader positions be saved for a black cheerleader. The black girls could compete for that slot while the white candidates competed for the other four positions.

In the meantime Mr. Baxter was receiving advice from other sources. The newspaper ran a story on the problem at Webster High and noted that racial harmony in Webster City depended upon how the problem was resolved. A delegation of black parents called upon Mr. Baxter and pleaded for a fair election in which black girls would have the same chance to be elected as white girls. Many white parents also visited Mr. Baxter and urged him not to interfere in a student council matter but to be prepared to maintain order in the school if trouble broke out.

Mr. Baxter called the superintendent of schools to ask his advice. Superintendent Henderson's secretary said that he was out of town but that the whole affair and Mr. Baxter's handling of the incident would be reviewed by the school board at its next regular meeting.

Mr. Baxter's dilemma. To summarize, here is Mr. Baxter's problem: More than anything else he wants a happy, peaceful school. He knows that cheerleader elections in the past have been unfair to black candidates. But since no one had complained, he had not interfered. This time, if he stands by and does nothing, there will surely be trouble. If he orders the student council to change its procedures, he will be under fire by many white students—and many parents and perhaps the school board as well. And what is a fair decision after all? Would it be best to have no cheerleaders this year, as some faculty members believe? Would it be better to recognize race and apply a quota system? Or would it be better to let the majority of Webster High students decide the issue for themselves in the election? The responsibility to decide was his.

Mr. Baxter picked up his telephone and rang his secretary. "Send Willie and Julia in. I'm ready to give them my decision."

1. What decision do you think would be best? What decision do you think Mr. Baxter made?

2. What are some of the factors that Mr. Baxter must consider in making his decision?

3. Can Mr. Baxter predict the consequences that will follow from any of the decisions available to him?

4. Would all principals make the same decision that Mr. Baxter will make? What factors might lead other people to make the same decision or different decisions if they were the principal?

D. Political Decision-Makers and Political Specialists

Unlike typical American citizens who devote only a small part of their time to political affairs, some Americans are engaged in politics daily. Politics and government are their primary interests. Some of these people are employed by government. They include the President of the United States, members of Congress, Supreme Court justices, Federal bureaucrats, governors, state legislators, and mayors. We shall call these people *political decision-makers.* Other individuals do not hold official positions in the government, but they try to influence the policy decisions of government officials. We shall call these people *unofficial political specialists.*

Political Decision-Makers

In Unit Four you will study about political decision-makers. A decision-maker is one who holds a position which enables him to make policy decisions that are binding on other people. There are decision-makers in families, churches, schools, clubs, and corporations. But we shall be concerned with government decision-makers only. Sometimes public policy decisions are made by one person, or in the name of one person, as when the President decides. Other decisions are made by a group. For example, while each Supreme Court justice first decides each case for himself, he contributes to a final group decision that is binding. Each senator must decide whether he will support a bill or not, but his decision by itself is not as significant as the decision made by the Senate as a whole.

When studying political decision-makers, we shall depend primarily upon three major concepts: *role, recruitment,* and *decision-making.* We are less concerned with how specific individuals have behaved in a role as we are concerned with the norms, values, rules, customs, and procedures that make up the role. *Recruitment* will help us to determine what kinds of people become political decision-makers, how they are selected, and how they are trained for their positions.

While the norms, customs, and procedures for arriving at decisions vary in different roles, all of the decision-makers do make *political decisions.* A central purpose of government is to produce such decisions. Political decisions may be distinguished from other decisions by one important characteristic. Political decisions tend to be *accommodational* decisions. Political decisions seek to find a point at which all contending parties can be satisfied.

Political decisions do not have to "make sense" or be fully consistent with other political decisions. Political decisions, rather, are decisions which tend to make the greatest number of most interested people satisfied with the outcome. For example, scientific evidence suggests that smoking cigarettes can be damaging to one's health. In light of this finding the Federal government has taken a number of steps to discourage the use of cigarettes. Cigarette packages now contain a health warning to users, and television and radio may not broadcast commercials by cigarette manufacturers. These actions represent policy decisions to discourage smoking. On the other hand, the government did not ban cigarettes. (This would make cigarette smokers unhappy.) And the government continues to provide various forms of support to tobacco growers, thereby keeping tobacco farmers partially happy in spite of the war on cigarette smoking.

Unofficial Political Specialists

Unit Five is about *unofficial political specialists.* They are "unofficial" because they do not hold official positions in the government. Thus, the mayor of a city might be called an "official" political leader. The local Republican party

259

Which of the persons shown on these two pages are political decision-makers? Which are unofficial political specialists? At the right is United States Senator Edward Brooke of Massachusetts. From left to right at the bottom are the following: the head of the Patrolmen's Benevolent Association in New York City; a mayor; a newspaper editor; and United States Secretary of State William P. Rogers.

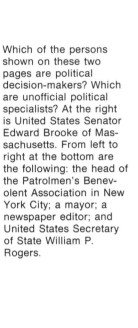

chairman who advises the mayor and who helps gather support for the mayor is an "unofficial" political specialist, because he does not hold public office. Examples of unofficial political specialists are newspaper editors, lobbyists, and political party leaders. While each of these specialists undoubtedly makes decisions, their decisions do not have the same authority and are not binding on the public, as governmental decisions are. For this reason we shall use the term "political specialist" rather than "political decision-maker" to describe them.

The most important characteristic of unofficial political specialists is that they devote far more time to political affairs than do typical citizens. In addition, most have access to political resources not available to typical citizens. Among these resources are the leadership of a large organization, access to the communications media, and possession of important knowledge that government leaders need.

The head of the AFL-CIO is an unofficial political specialist. While much of his activity is related to advancing the economic goals of union members, the AFL-CIO president is a significant political force in this country. He tries to help elect public officials who favor the labor point of view, and he tries to influence public policies that favor labor.

Dr. Martin Luther King was an important unofficial political specialist. He was a recognized leader of many black people who were demand-

ing civil rights reform. He was able to bring pressure to bear upon the political system and to gain many of the reforms he desired. Yet, Dr. King held no official position in the government.

The publisher of *The New York Times* is an important unofficial political specialist. *The New York Times* can influence the opinion of many citizens and government leaders by the articles it publishes or chooses not to publish and by its editorial columns.

While each of the unofficial political specialist roles is different and attracts different kinds of people, each can influence public policy decisions. Each is important to understanding how government is managed in the United States.

To show your understanding of the material in this chapter, complete the following exercises.

1. Decide which of the persons pictured on pages 260–261 would fit our definition of (a) *political decision-makers*, and (b) *unofficial political specialists*.

2. The President wants to keep taxes at the current rate. Some Congressmen want to lower taxes immediately, especially for low-income individuals. Finally, a law is passed that keeps taxes the same for the current year and lowers taxes on low-income people for the following year. Why is this an example of a *political decision*?

3. Following are five statements about government in the United States:

   a. The United States has a constitutional government.

   b. The United States has a democratic-republican form of government.

   c. The United States has a federal system of government.

   d. In the American system of government power is separated among various branches of the government.

   e. The three branches check and balance one another.

Below are a series of statements which illustrate the statements above. Match each statement below with one of the statements in the list above.

(1) The Congress passes laws; the President administers laws; and the Supreme Court interprets the law.

(2) While the Congress passes laws, the President can veto legislation preventing bills from becoming law.

(3) Each of the fifty states has its own regulations regarding health, safety, and education. Nevertheless, the Congress has appropriated money to help states increase the quality of health, safety, and education in their states.

(4) The government has limits to what it is legally able to do. Moreover, Congress is not free to pass any kind of law it wishes.

(5) Voters in the United States make very few policy decisions directly, but voters have regular opportunities to elect government policy-makers.

chapter 13

The Presidential Role

A Gallup Poll of 1501 adults in the United States in December, 1968, posed the following question: "What man that you have heard or read about, living today in any part of the world, do you admire the most?" The ten most frequently mentioned in the order of their frequency were as follows:

1. Former President Dwight D. Eisenhower
2. President Lyndon B. Johnson
3. Senator Edward M. Kennedy
4. Reverend Billy Graham
5. President-elect Richard M. Nixon
6. Vice President and presidential candidate Hubert Humphrey
7. Presidential candidate George C. Wallace
8. Pope Paul VI
9. Former President Harry S. Truman
10. Presidential candidate and Senator Eugene J. McCarthy

Eight of the ten "most admired" men were either Presidents, former Presidents, presidential candidates, or prominently mentioned as candidates.

A March, 1969, survey of 1504 Americans contains clues to the amount of trust we ascribe to four important roles in the government. The survey team asked the respondents to react to this statement: "The President [then Governor, United States Senators, and Supreme Court] can be trusted to do what is good for the people." Just over half of the respondents agreed that the Supreme Court "can be trusted to do what is good for the people." For Senators the agreement vote was 54 percent; for governor, 58 percent; and for President, 64 percent.

Americans know the President, seem to admire him as a person, and trust him to do what is good for them. How do we select our Presidents? What is a President expected to do once elected? And how does he make decisions on public policy issues? These three questions relating to *recruitment, role,* and *decision-making* are the focus of this chapter.

A. What Kind of Person Should Be President?

Imagine that the picture of the person above represents a future President of the United States. What kind of person would you want him to be? Should he be old or young, rich or poor, handsome or plain, black or white? Or should "he" be a "she"? Probably you would agree that his or her physical appearance is less important than other qualities. Suppose you could design the ideal President, what qualities are absolutely necessary for him to have?

List ten or more character and personality traits that you believe to be most desirable for a President to have. Since honesty is a trait that nearly all Americans expect of the President, you might begin your list with "honesty."

Probably most of the qualities you have listed would be found in many people. Certainly most Americans would like to think they possess these traits. For example, honesty heads your list. Who would want a *dishonest* President? Yet not only our President should be honest; ideally we want all people to be honest.

This leads to some important questions: If the qualities we desire in a President are in many cases those we expect to find in other people, how can we choose a President on the basis of these personal traits? If all Americans possess these qualities at least to some degree, how then do we choose for President the man who demonstrates them to an extraordinary degree? And how can we be certain that a presidential candidate has the qualities we consider important?

Very few Americans have an opportunity to meet presidential candidates and to know them well. Voters, therefore, draw conclusions about the qualities of presidential candidates chiefly from newspapers, radio, television, and other media. On the basis of what they read and hear, Americans draw conclusions about the character and personality traits of presidential candidates.

Americans are not entirely open-minded when drawing conclusions about candidates. Political party loyalty, nationality or racial identity, region of country, and the like influence our impressions. That is, we tend to see and hear what we want to see and hear. For example, if we are strong Republicans and always vote for Republican candidates, we are more eager to find the qualities we prefer in the Republican candidate than in the Democratic candidate. And we shall probably conclude that the Republican candidate is better. If we are strong Democrats, the reverse process takes place.

Nevertheless, presidential candidates know that Americans expect to find certain qualities in their Presidents. Candidates, therefore, try to conduct campaigns which hopefully will convince the public that they possess the desired traits. For example, most Americans want their President to be a "strong but humble leader." Therefore, candidates for President do their best to give the impression that they are strong but humble men. No presidential candidate in memory has ever announced publicly that he would do anything or pay any price to become President, although many behave in this way. Such an announcement would raise questions about the candidate's humility. Rather, the candidate seeks to give the impression that he is "willing to serve if called upon by the American people," and then he works feverishly to make certain that the "call" is made.

Perhaps you are beginning to appreciate one of the complex tasks of a campaign manager for a presidential candidate. Americans expect to find certain qualities in their political leaders. While these qualities are often difficult to define, a potential presidential candidate and his political manager must decide upon the traits they believe Americans desire in a President and then plan a campaign that proves that their man possesses these qualities.

Off to the Races

In the months preceding the national party conventions it is not unusual for men interested in the presidential nomination to deny that they are seeking the office. The cartoon shows four potential Republican nominees in 1963 denying an interest in the nomination.

Bill Crawford. Reprinted by permission of Newspaper Enterprise Association

Your task is to imagine yourself as the campaign manager for a presidential candidate. What would you ask the candidate to do during the campaign to demonstrate that he has at least *one* of the qualities that you listed? (Incidentally, what quality do you think is being exhibited when candidates kiss babies?)

B. Formal and Informal Rules on Presidential Recruitment

Look again at the list of qualities you believe a President should have. Would it be easy to choose a President on the basis of these traits alone? Of course not. There are several reasons for this: (1) The qualities are too widely shared among many Americans. (2) There is much disagreement about the criteria for measuring each trait. (3) There is no easy way to determine whether a specific candidate has the desired qualities to the right degree.

To make the recruitment of presidential candidates easier, a number of *formal* and *informal rules* have appeared which guide the recruitment process. *Formal rules* are rules that exist in a formal or legal manner for all to see, as in the Constitution. *Informal rules*, on the other hand, are a result of custom and tradition. They may not appear in writing, but most people are familiar with them and are guided by them.

Formal Rules

Certain formal rules specify who can and who cannot be President of the United States. These rules are found in Article II, Section 1, and Amendment XXII of the Constitution in the Appendix.

According to Article II, a person is not eligible for the Presidency unless he is (1) a natural-born citizen of the United States, (2) at least thirty-five years old, and (3) a resident of the United States for at least fourteen years.

The Twenty-second Amendment adds another formal rule. It limits the President to two terms of his own or to only one additional term in office if he has served more than two years of his predecessor's term. In other words, no President may serve more than ten years in office.

These two rules exclude certain portions of the American population. More than one-half of Americans are less than 35 years old; therefore, of the more than 200 million Americans in 1970, only about 83 million could meet the age requirement to become President. In addition, any naturalized American citizen is ineligible by definition to become President, and any natural-born citizen must have lived at least fourteen years of his life within the borders of the United States. The Twenty-second Amendment makes certain that Presidents cannot continue in office as long as they wish and are able to be elected.

In addition, no one can be President of the United States who has not been elected to that office. Article II and Amendment XII of the Constitution specify the formal rules governing presidential elections.

Article II of the Constitution stipulates that each state select as many electors as there are members in Congress from that state. The method of choosing electors is left up to the states, but a common set of practices has developed. In each state each political party nominates a set of electors who are expected to vote for the party's nominee for President. The set of party electors receiving the most popular votes receives all the electoral votes of that state. The electors of all the states comprise the Electoral College. Article II also states that no Federal official, such as a member of Congress or a Federal judge, may serve as an elector. It also stipulates that Congress determines when the electors will be chosen.

The Twelfth Amendment describes the manner in which the Electoral College functions. The electors meet in their state capitals on the first Monday after the second Wednesday in December to cast their ballots. The candidate receiving the majority of electoral votes of the entire Electoral College is chosen President. If no candidate receives a majority of the electoral votes, the selection goes to the House of Representatives. This body chooses among the three candidates who have received the highest number of electoral votes. If no candidate for Vice-President receives a majority of electoral votes, the Senate chooses between the two highest candidates for the office. A set of ballots from each state is sent by the electors by registered mail to the President of the Senate. He opens all of the electoral ballots on January 6 in the presence of both houses of Congress.

Therefore, we start with a set of formal rules that determine who can be President. A man cannot legally buy or force his way into the White House; he must be elected, and he must be elected according to a set of formal procedures. He is not eligible for election unless he is at least thirty-five years of age, is a natural-born citizen, and has lived fourteen years of his life in the

United States. When he is elected President of the United States, he can be reelected only once.

Informal Rules

While the Constitution provides the legal framework within which we choose our Presidents, knowing the formal rules for presidential recruitment is not enough. Informal rules and procedures that have developed over the years play an equally important part. For example, political parties are not provided for in the Constitution, but they are quite important to the process of electing a President. While one could legally be elected President without the support of a political party, in practice it is impossible to do so. No candidate can expect to be elected President without being nominated by one or the other of the two major political parties. This means that the recruitment of Presidents is in the hands of political parties.

For a man to be elected President, he must first win the support of a political party, preferably one of the two major political parties, since they have the greater opportunity to select a President. From the point of view of the political party, the name of the game is winning. It costs a great deal of money to mount a presidential election campaign. In the 1968 campaign, twenty-one Republican campaign committees reported spending more than $20 million to elect Richard M. Nixon. The unsuccessful Democratic campaign of Hubert H. Humphrey cost a similar amount.

These enormous expenditures are worth the prize to be won. The prize consists of jobs, power, prestige, strength, and the opportunity to carry through programs. One person has written: "Win the election; never mind the expense; defeat is the most expensive of all contests."

When President Nixon was elected in 1968, he had the opportunity to appoint approximately 6500 people to important Federal positions. If a popular presidential candidate can also sweep other members of his party into office at national, state, and local levels, additional jobs for members of his party result. For those who have supported the successful candidate, winning the election provides the opportunity to carry out programs they favor. Consequently, the prize for winning is very high in any presidential election, and both major parties are careful to select candidates who are most likely to win.

Candidate Factors Considered by the Major Parties

What are the factors which leaders of the two major political parties have in mind when they choose a candidate?

Personality. One factor is the personality of the candidate himself. To be President, one must be ambitious. A President must welcome public exposure and be physically and emotionally strong. He must have the ability to convince people to work together for the fulfillment of a program. If he shuns crowds, prefers to work by himself rather than to meet people, or dislikes bargaining with people in order to meet goals, he is unlikely to be very happy in the job of President.

267

Nearly all the Presidents have been professional politicians. They have had experience in the Congress, as governors, as judges, or in some other political role. Most have spent many years in politics and through this experience have acquired skills in mobilizing resources and in getting groups with different interests to work together. The candidate's political experience can easily be examined, and party leaders can judge whether he has proved to be an effective politician.

Geography. Ordinarily a person has a better chance of being selected as a candidate for President by a major party if he comes from a pivotal state—one that could go either to the Republicans or to the Democrats—and which controls a large number of electoral votes. California, for example, is a major pivotal state today.

By choosing a candidate from such a pivotal state, it may be possible to swing that state's vote to the party, thereby winning all the electoral votes of that state. Of thirty-eight presidential candidates from 1868 to 1968, twenty-two were from New York, Ohio, and Illinois. These three states control a large number of electoral votes. In 1968 New York had 43 electoral votes; Ohio, 26; and Illinois, 26. These are truly pivotal states. Sometimes they have voted Republican; in other cases Democratic. Therefore, the party leaders of these states have much to say about the selection of presidential candidates for the two major parties.

Sex, race, and ethnic background. There are no legal barriers to the selection of Presidents based upon sex, race, or ethnic background. Yet party

President Lyndon Johnson on the campaign trail projects a warm personality as he greets voters in New York State.

leaders know that many Americans hold a number of prejudices and that these must be considered in choosing a candidate for President. No woman has ever been selected as a major party's candidate for President or Vice President, nor is one likely to be nominated in the near future. Senator Margaret Chase Smith once campaigned unsuccessfully for the Republican nomination, but she was easily defeated.

Moreover, all the major-party candidates for President have been white. Some minor parties have chosen Negroes as candidates for President, as in 1968 when Dick Gregory was chosen as a candidate for President by the Peace and Freedom party. However, since blacks comprise only around 12 percent of the population, no major political party has been willing to risk losing an election by choosing a candidate who would automatically be rejected by prejudiced white voters. In addition, presidential candidates have been chosen primarily from families that have northern European backgrounds, especially English backgrounds. No President has been elected whose family immigrated from southern Europe, eastern Europe, the Middle East, Asia, Latin America, or Africa.

Religion and morality. Americans expect their Presidents to be religious men. More specifically, they are expected to be Christian. Until very recently they were expected to be Protestant. The election of President John F. Kennedy marked the first time that a Roman Catholic was elected President. Jews, Moslems, Hindus, and Buddhists stand little chance of being elected President, nor would a professed atheist be accepted by a political party as a candidate. Even if a man has weak religious commitments, he is expected at least to act interested in religion when he becomes a presidential candidate.

Americans also expect their leaders to be moral men. Therefore, violations of widely accepted standards of morality by a man interested in becoming President would cost him the candidacy of his party. While divorce is widely practiced in the United States, it is opposed by so many people that a man who is divorced or who has in some other way had an unhappy married life is not likely to be selected by a political party. Exceptions to this unwritten rule have occurred, but they have occurred only when the candidate's other qualities were considered impressive enough to outweigh this factor.

Socioeconomic status. There are many stories about poor boys who struggle and ultimately succeed in becoming President. The fact is that less than a half dozen Presidents have risen from the ranks of the very poor. Most of our Presidents have grown up in the upper-middle class. Several, such as George Washington, Franklin D. Roosevelt, and John F. Kennedy, were very wealthy. Most Presidents have come from families in which the parents could provide their children with a good education.

Presidential candidates are not supposed to represent a particular interest or organization. Therefore, while many candidates have come from an upper-middle-class background, they are not ordinarily selected from corporate offices. The president of United States Steel Corporation, for example, would

269

In the 1872 election the Republicans publicized the humble, workingman backgrounds of U. S. Grant, the Galena (Illinois) tanner, and his running-mate Henry Wilson, the Natick (Mass.) shoemaker.

not likely be chosen as a presidential candidate because he would be seen as favoring "big business" against the interests of labor. On the other hand, no political party is likely to choose the head of the AFL-CIO or the United Auto Workers for President because he would be seen as likely to represent the interests of labor against business. Perhaps this helps to explain why presidential candidates tend to be chosen from a background of politics rather than either business or labor experience.

Miscellaneous. Much more might be said about the factors that political parties keep in mind when choosing a presidential candidate. In an age of television the parties obviously want someone who will appear attractive on television and who is a good speaker. It is important that while a candidate has had an active political life that he has avoided becoming entangled in controversial affairs that might alienate large numbers of voters. He should have few enemies either in the party or in the public at large. All things being equal, he should have a record of party loyalty. And he should have had some direct experience with foreign as well as domestic affairs.

If all of these factors are considered, who stands a chance of becoming President of the United States from the approximately 80 million people who are legally eligible? It is likely that few more than a hundred men are "available" at the time of any given election. From these one hundred who are able to meet each of the criteria stated above, the party chooses the one it thinks will have the best chance of being elected. In short, the question for American voters is not who among all the men in the United States is most qualified to be President and has the most desirable qualities expected in a President. Rather, the question is who in the estimate of a group of political leaders stands the best chance on a given day every four years to capture a majority of the electoral votes.

Applying What You Have Learned about Presidential Recruitment

The chart on page 271 provides information about eight characteristics of American Presidents who have served during this century. Study it carefully; then answer each of these questions:

1. Which of the *formal rules* and which of the *informal rules* seem to have been followed in the selection of each President?

2. Which of the rules were violated in specific cases?

3. Explain, if possible, any exceptions to the rules that you find.

270

BACKGROUND CHARACTERISTICS OF TWENTIETH-CENTURY PRESIDENTS

PRESIDENT	HOME STATE WHEN ELECTED	AGE ON TAKING OFFICE	ANCESTRY	RELIGION	FAMILY BACKGROUND	EDUCATION	OCCUPATION	POLITICAL EXPERIENCE
Theodore Roosevelt	New York	42	Dutch	Dutch Reform	Wealthy, urban	Harvard	Rancher, soldier, politician	Vice-President, Governor
William H. Taft	Ohio	51	English	Unitarian	Wealthy, professional	Yale	Lawyer	Cabinet officer
Woodrow Wilson	New Jersey	56	Scotch-Irish	Presbyterian	Ministry	Princeton	University professor	Governor
Warren G. Harding	Ohio	55	English	Baptist	Farm	Ohio Central College	Newspaper publisher	Senator
Calvin Coolidge	Massachusetts	51	English	Congregational	Small merchant	Amherst	Lawyer	Governor
Herbert Hoover	California	54	Swiss-German	Quaker	Farmer, small merchant	Stanford	Engineer	Cabinet officer
Franklin D. Roosevelt	New York	51	Dutch	Episcopalian	Country squires, wealthy, small town	Harvard	Politics	Governor
Harry Truman	Missouri	60	Scotch-Irish, English	Baptist	Small town, poor	Kansas City School of Law	Politics	Vice-President, Senator
Dwight D. Eisenhower	New York	62	Swiss-German	Presbyterian	Small town, poor	West Point	Soldier	None
John F. Kennedy	Massachusetts	43	Irish	Roman Catholic	Wealthy, business	Harvard	Politics	Senator
Lyndon B. Johnson	Texas	55	English, French, German	Christian Church	Small town, modest means	Southwest Texas State Teachers College	Politics	Vice-President, Senator
Richard M. Nixon	New York	56	Irish	Quaker	Small town, merchant	Whittier College, Duke	Politics	Vice-President, Senator

Source: Adapted from Francis Heller, *The Presidency: A Modern Perspective* (Random House, 1960), p. 46.

C. An Overview of Presidential Role

KENNEDY SQUEAKS BY NIXON

LBJ WINS IN LANDSLIDE

NIXON DEFEATS HUMPHREY

What an exhilarating but sobering moment it must be for a candidate to know that he has won the Presidency of the United States. It is exhilarating because to be chosen President is the highest honor this nation can bestow upon any of its citizens. A President has been chosen for membership in an exclusive club that in 1970 registered only thirty-seven members, tracing back to George Washington. From the Tuesday in November when he is elected, to the twentieth of January when he leaves office, the eyes of the world will

George Washington is shown taking the oath of office on a balcony of Federal Hall in New York City, where the new government was first located. This is a reproduction of an original drawing made at the time of the inauguration.

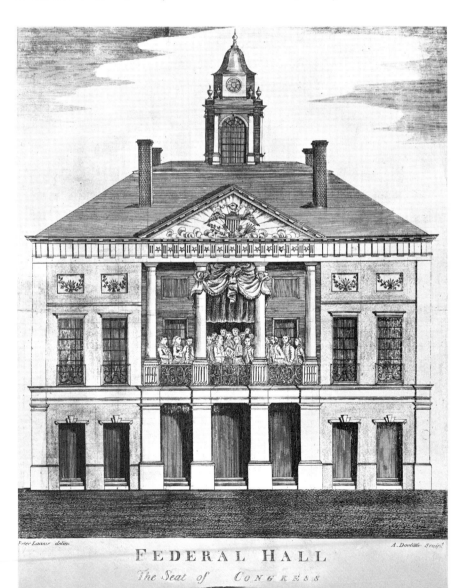

Peter Lacour delin.

A. Doolittle Sculp.

FEDERAL HALL

The Seat of CONGRESS

be upon the new President. What he says and does will be recorded and broadcast to the world. His face will be recognized by millions of people. Regardless of how successful he is as President, his place in history is assured.

It must also be a sobering moment for the newly elected President, because with the Presidency comes the greatest burden of responsibility that any man can have. The United States Presidency is one of the most powerful offices in the world. This is true because the United States is one of the most powerful nations in the world. Decisions made by the President affect not only the millions of citizens of the United States but inevitably touch additional millions of other people scattered around the world. Presidential decisions affect the welfare, even the lives, of Americans and many other people. Very few men could fail to be sobered by this thought.

The President's power stems from the authority granted the office in the Constitution. The President may officially act in ways permitted no other American because the Constitution says he can, and Americans accept the Constitution as the supreme law of the land. It is the chief rule book which determines how the "game" will be played in the United States. Moreover, while the framers of the Constitution divided Federal power among three branches of government—the President, Congress, and the courts—no single individual dominates a branch of the government so exclusively as the President dominates the presidential branch. And no branch of the government is so free to act so swiftly and decisively as the President can in areas of defense policy, foreign affairs, and, in many cases, domestic affairs.

The power of the Presidency also stems from the fact that Americans expect the President to act. Numerous studies of American citizens have demonstrated that while few Americans understand fully many of the issues facing their country, most will support the President in whatever action he takes. Most Americans seem to assume that the President will know best; and, therefore, whatever action he takes will be supported by them.

How do we train our Presidents? How do we prepare men to fill the most powerful and decisive office in the world? Imagine for a moment that you had just been elected President of the United States. Where would you turn for advice? How would you find out how one should act as President of the United States? How would you learn what the presidential role is?

The Constitution Provides Guidelines

One place you might look is in the Constitution, for it lays down the general guidelines for the office. The Constitution establishes the rules by which the President must act. According to Article II, Section 2: (1) The President is Commander-in-Chief of the armed forces: Army, Navy and Air Force and the National Guard when it is called into Federal service.

(2) To assist him in carrying out his duties, the President may call upon the heads of the various executive departments to provide him with advice and information. In practice the heads of executive departments, such as the Department of Health, Education, and Welfare or the Department of Labor, serve the President as members of his Cabinet.

(3) The President has the power to make treaties with the consent of two-thirds of the Senate.

(4) The President has the power to appoint ambassadors and consuls, judges of the Supreme Court, and many other officials also with the approval of the Senate.

(5) The President also has the power to appoint public officials to fill vacancies temporarily without senatorial consent if the vacancies occur during a senatorial recess. These appointments, however, are strictly limited to a single session of Congress.

Article II, Section 3, gives the President the following additional powers and duties: (6) He is expected to deliver a "State of the Union" message to Congress at the opening of each congressional session. He also sends special messages to Congress from time to time. (7) The President has the power to convene the Congress when they are not in session, if necessary. (8) The President meets with heads of state, ambassadors, and other public officials from foreign countries and commissions officers of the United States.

Other Ways of Learning the Presidential Role

The President may also learn about his role from his predecessors. Recent Presidents have written books about their activities in the Presidency, about the kinds of decisions they faced, and about how they met these decisions. In addition, Presidents often contact former Presidents to discuss problems. President Johnson frequently contacted Presidents Eisenhower and Truman. In addition, President Johnson met several times with President-elect Nixon before his inauguration. Furthermore, President Nixon established an elaborate task force that eased the transition between the Johnson Administration and the Nixon Administration. It was the job of this task force to contact key members of the Johnson Administration and learn what projects were under way within each agency. Members of the Nixon Cabinet worked closely with members of the Johnson Cabinet in preparation for their new roles.

A new President also draws upon his own prior experience in politics to prepare himself for the presidential role. Most Presidents have had widespread political experience, either as members of Congress or as governors of large states. In these roles they have had to cope with governmental problems

Prior to his inauguration, Richard Nixon met several times with President Johnson.

and have had to organize staff members to help manage political problems. Of course, the Presidency is enormously more complex than the governorship of a state or a senatorial office. Nevertheless, most men who have been elected President have had some experience that helps them in their new position.

Recruiting Personnel

Much of the time of the new President, both before he assumes office and immediately after he takes up the presidential role, is spent recruiting personnel to work with him. This is especially true if the new President is of a different political party than his predecessor. President Nixon, for example, faced the task of filling about 70 Cabinet and sub-Cabinet posts, about 300 other major government jobs, and a total of nearly 3000 senior Federal positions. Nearly 6500 patronage jobs were available to him to fill by appointment. While most positions in the Federal government are obtained by civil service examinations and are filled by career people who cannot be replaced for political reasons, many of the most important Federal offices are filled by direct appointment.

Nevertheless, while many new people appear in Washington following the election of a new President, hundreds of thousands of other people continue to work for the new President as they did for his predecessor. In every agency of the government skilled, experienced, professional staff workers are available to train their new bosses. This is true even in the White House itself where the vast majority of workers in the Executive Office—secretaries, clerks, chauffeurs, cooks, maids, and other employees in the White House— remain to serve the new President. A few White House employees can trace their service back through several Presidents. Undoubtedly, the career employees remaining in their jobs from one administration to the next help make the task of the new President easier.

The President Has a Large Staff

What do we provide the President to enable him to fulfill his role? First of all, we provide the President with help. As the size of our nation has grown and the scope of its activities has increased, so has the number of employees needed to provide the desired services. George Washington was responsible for supervising a total of about 1000 employees scattered through the few agencies and departments that were his responsibility. Today's President, on the other hand, must keep track of approximately 2000 departments, agencies, bureaus, commissions, and committees that employ approximately two million people.

Earlier in our history Presidents had only a clerk or two to help them. Often these had to be borrowed from other departments of the government, such as the army. Not until 1857 did Congress appropriate funds to hire a private secretary, a White House steward, and a messenger for the President. Grover Cleveland answered most of his mail in long hand. Woodrow Wilson wrote out many of the state documents himself. Herbert Hoover was the first President for whom Congress provided three secretaries.

The Executive Office of the President was created in 1939 when Franklin Roosevelt was President. At that time President Roosevelt designated the administrative offices in the White House, the Bureau of the Budget, and several other agencies the Executive Office. The office of the President has changed much from the early days, when the President read and answered most of his own mail and wrote his own speeches, to the Presidency of today when the President supervises and coordinates the activities of many assistants who do most of these jobs for him.

Salary and Fringe Benefits

We also provide the President with a salary of $200,000 per year, plus a $50,000 tax-free expense allowance, the use of the White House, and use of many other facilities. The President is free from most of the bothersome details that take up much of the typical American's life. The President has his own physician who checks him regularly, even daily; and the President does not have to wait in the doctor's office for an appointment. His personal barber can give him a haircut at the President's own convenience. The President has his own movie theater and, until recently, his own private swimming pool. When he needs new clothing, someone buys it for him. He can eat whenever and whatever he wants. He merely notifies his cook that he is ready to eat and what he would like to have.

Sailing was one of President Franklin Roosevelt's hobbies.

When the President prepares to travel, all his travel arrangements will be made for him by others. If he chooses to go by automobile, he can travel rapidly in a chauffeured limousine with a police escort. He will not be caught in traffic jams; he will not wait for stop lights. All traffic stops while the President moves by. If he chooses to fly, Air Force pilots are waiting to take him in the most modern jet aircraft to any place that he desires. And if he wishes to leave the pressures of the White House and have a brief vacation, he may travel quickly to Camp David in Maryland.

He has instant access to the best communications system in the world. Not only does he have the same sources of communication that many citizens have—newspapers, television and radio—but he has outlets for each of the major wire services in the White House. He can talk by telephone or by wireless radio to points all around the globe. By special telephone hookup he can talk almost instantly to the political leaders in the Soviet Union. Whenever he travels, this vast communications network travels with him. In short, no other man in the world has as many conveniences placed at his disposal to make it possible for him to focus all his energies upon his job. What the nature of that job is and why such enormous resources are necessary we look at next.

D. The Multiple Roles of the President

In the previous lesson you learned about the scope and importance of the presidential role, about some of the ways a President learns to play his role, and about a few of the resources we provide the President to enable him to perform his role successfully. In this lesson we shall examine more closely what a President actually does. You will learn that there are many aspects of the presidential role. This one presidential role can be divided into at least eight parts. These eight roles are: *head of state, chief diplomat, commander-in-chief, chief executive, chief legislator, chief economic planner, party chief,* and *representative of all the people.* In addition to these official roles, Presidents also fulfill roles as fathers, husbands, grandfathers, and citizens as do many other Americans.

As head of state, President Eisenhower welcomes Queen Elizabeth on a state visit, and President Nixon presents the Young American Medal for Volunteer Service to one of the winners.

Head of State

The President of the United States is our nation's official host to visiting royalty and heads of governments. When foreign ambassadors present their credentials to our government, they do so to the President of the United States. The President is expected to bestow medals on American heroes, unveil monuments, light the annual Christmas tree, hunt Easter eggs on the White

277

House lawn with Washington children, throw out the first baseball to start the baseball season, give the first dime to the polio drive, and buy the first Christmas seals. As *head of state,* the President receives important civic and business leaders of our country and has his picture taken with them to symbolize their visits. He meets with visiting Girl Scouts, movie stars, and sports champions. When astronauts return from outer space, he is the first one to call and offer his congratulations.

The President proclaims the Fourth of July, Labor Day, and Thanksgiving. He announces American Education Week and other special "weeks" throughout the year. When the nation has lost a hero, the President leads the nation in mourning by attendance at the funeral or at the commemorative religious ceremonies.

To millions of people in other nations, the President of the United States *is* the United States. When he speaks, he speaks for all Americans; when he travels abroad, he represents the United States. His actions, his words, his every behavior communicate America to the millions of people around the world.

Some Americans believe that the ceremonial activities of the President of the United States interfere with his more important responsibilities. Nevertheless, these ceremonial functions are one part of the President's job. The President fulfills duties performed by kings in other countries. He is as much a symbol of the United States as are the flag and the Statue of Liberty.

Chief Diplomat

While there is much that remains the same in foreign policy from one administration to another, each administration confronts new issues that require new policies. And while most foreign policy decisions need not demand the President's attention and can be resolved by others, the President must approve the general direction of American foreign policy. He will frequently make the most important decisions himself after listening to the advice of others. The Constitution gives him the sole power to initiate and to negotiate treaties with foreign countries, although the Senate must finally approve such treaties. The President receives foreign ambassadors. He can, if he wishes, indicate that a particular ambassador is no longer acceptable to this country and ask the ambassador's nation to recall him. He appoints ambassadors and ministers to other countries with the advice and consent of the Senate.

The Constitution provides some checks on the President's diplomatic powers. Treaties must be approved by the Senate before they can be put into effect. The Senate must also confirm the appointment of ambassadors and ministers to foreign countries. Many treaties cannot be carried out until the House of Representatives agrees to authorize the funds needed to make the treaty effective. Nevertheless, the initiative in foreign policy and control over foreign policy are in the President's hands if he chooses to take them.

The President may make Executive Agreements without submitting them to the Senate. Under these arrangements President Franklin Roosevelt recognized the USSR in 1933, swapped some American destroyers for naval bases with England in 1940, and concluded arrangements with England and the Soviet

Union in 1945 for the conclusion of the war with Germany and Japan. Only the President can "recognize" a country. Since 1949 Presidents Truman, Eisenhower, Kennedy, Johnson, and Nixon have refused to extend recognition to the government of Red China.

The President, more than any other official in the country, has access to information upon which diplomatic decisions can be made. The Central Intelligence Agency, the National Security Council, as well as the intelligence divisions of the various armed services and the State Department report directly to the President. He is not obligated to share this privileged, highly secret information with others. Therefore, Congress and the courts may be in the dark regarding the specific policies we are following and why we are following them. By his actions the President can influence for many years the relationship of our nation to other nations of the world.

Commander-in-Chief

Closely related to his role as chief diplomat is the President's role as Commander-in-Chief of the armed services. The President is "super-general" and "super-admiral" for the United States. He, more than any other person, can decide whether we shall have war or peace.

The Constitution assigns some war-making powers to Congress. The Congress has authority to declare war, to tax for common defense, to raise and support armies, to provide and maintain a navy, to make rules governing the army and navy, and so on. Nevertheless, Congress has never declared war except at the request of the President, and the President can and often has sent troops wherever he wished without asking the permission of Congress.

By his actions, the President may start a war and thereafter wage it. The last time that Congress declared war, in 1941, Japan had already attacked the United States. Since that time, the United States has fought bloody engagements in Korea and Vietnam. In neither case did the President ask for, nor did Congress grant, a declaration of war. Moreover, Presidents have intervened in a number of circumstances that might have led to violent conflict. For example, President Eisenhower sent troops to Lebanon in 1957; President Johnson intervened in the Dominican Republic in 1965; and President Kennedy authorized an unsuccessful invasion of Cuba in 1961.

In the hands of the President of the United States, we have placed the greatest military power the world has ever known. The President is the only American citizen who has the power to decide whether to launch atomic warfare. If the President decides to attack another nation with atomic weapons, whether he initiates the attack himself or whether he is responding to attacks by another country, he has the capacity to obliterate all life on this planet. The enormity of this power should be the most sobering aspect of choosing a President. According to their own accounts, it is the most sobering responsibility that a President assumes.

The President can also, if he chooses, use the military to put down revolt within our own nation. The President is not only "super-general" and "super-admiral," he is also "super-sheriff." When local police and state militia are unable to control rioting and civil disorder within an American city, the President can use, and on occasion has used, Federal troops to bring an end to violence. During such national disasters as a flood or earthquake, the President can use his authority as Commander-in-Chief to send airlifts of supplies or dispatch troops to prevent looting.

Probably the framers of the Constitution assumed that General Washington would act directly as Commander-in-Chief of the armed forces. It is true that Washington himself led troops for a time during the Whiskey Rebellion of 1792. But even when the President has not been at the front leading his troops into battle, the President sometimes makes the final decisions regarding military tactics. Lincoln chose the generals who were to lead the Union armies during the Civil War. President Truman made the decision to drop the atomic bomb on Hiroshima and Nagasaki. President Truman decided to replace General MacArthur, when MacArthur's statements contradicted the policies of the Truman Administration. And President Johnson chose the targets and decided whether to bomb or not bomb target sites in North Vietnam. It is clear that one of the major roles of the President of the United States continues to be leader of the American armed forces.

President Roosevelt discusses Pacific war strategy in 1944 with two of his naval commanders.

Chief Executive

Perhaps one of the most far-reaching and difficult roles of the Presidency is that of *chief executive*. The Constitution specifies that the executive branch will execute (carry out) the laws passed by the Congress. The government engages in many services authorized by Congress. The mail must be delivered, meat inspected, the stock market supervised, airline traffic regulated, crime investigated, new dams built, and so on. These and thousands of other activities require Federal employees. Most of these employees are civil servants. They are employees who spend their lives working for the government, just as other people work for private business. The President may appoint leaders of each of these activities.

While the President has many employees to help him, it is ultimately his responsibility to make certain that the business of government is conducted efficiently. It is not unusual to hear the President blamed for an increase in crime in Washington, D.C., for inefficient postal service, for not choosing more honest men. In short, most of the business of the Federal government is ultimately the responsibility of the President. It is apparent that he cannot begin to know all the people who are working for the government; he cannot supervise all of its activities. He can only hope that the men and women he appoints to supervise those activities do so honestly and efficiently and that the government meets its obligations to its citizens. It is easy to understand why his role as chief executive is perhaps his most frustrating one.

Chief Legislator

The Constitution clearly specifies that the function of Congress is to pass legislation. Nevertheless, certain legislative responsibilities were reserved for the President. He can, for example, veto legislation that has been passed by Congress and thereby prevent it from becoming law. Moreover, the Constitution provides that the President may recommend to Congress measures that he thinks the legislators should consider. In effect, the President has the power to initiate legislation if he wishes.

The power to initiate legislation, to make suggestions to Congress, has taken the form of messages and reports to Congress on many topics. Each President normally gives a State of the Union address at the start of each new session of Congress. Thereafter, he is likely to send special messages about legislation he would like to have considered.

However, the President's legislative power goes beyond merely making recommendations to Congress. In actual fact, most of the major legislative measures considered by Congress each year have originated in the executive branch. The ideas for such legislation often begin within executive departments of the government. In many cases the legislation is drafted almost entirely by executive officials. It is then introduced into Congress, both in the House and Senate, by members of the President's political party.

Once the legislation is introduced, it is taken up by committees. At committee hearings members of the administration defend the legislation which they drafted. The President holds "breakfasts" and other meetings for House and Senate leaders to encourage them toward the passage of desired legislation. He conducts press conferences to explain the purpose of the legislation to representatives of the news media. He sometimes speaks directly to American citizens to encourage them to pressure their congressmen to vote for legislation that he wants. In many cases, therefore, the legislation which comes from Congress is legislation that was planned and engineered by the President.

Many early Presidents felt that the President's legislative role should be quite small. They believed that the President should not interfere with the right of Congress to make law. Some Presidents would not even speak up in defense of legislation that they wanted passed. Recent Presidents have not been that timid. Most of them have considered one of their principal roles to be making certain that legislation they believe vital to the American public makes its way through Congress. Therefore, the President spends much time meeting with congressional leaders and with his own presidential aides in devising strategies for influencing Congress.

The hands of President Johnson rest on the Civil Rights Act of 1964 after he signed the historic measure into law.

Chief Economic Planner

Americans have always taken much pride in their system of "free enterprise." The role of government in the American economy traditionally has been to insure stable conditions within which business could operate freely. Increasingly in modern times, the role of government in the economy has grown. Particularly since the administration of Franklin Roosevelt, the President's job has included developing programs to help the economy run smoothly.

Prior to 1921 the business of deciding how much money the government would need each year was left to Congress. But by the end of World War I it was clear that this was an inefficient way to do business. Therefore, in 1921 the Bureau of the Budget was established within the executive branch. The Bureau's job was to create a national budget to be presented to Congress each year. This shifted the responsibility for planning the national budget from Congress to the Presidency. At first the Bureau of the Budget was housed in the Department of the Treasury; later, it was moved to the Executive Office of the President.

Today all programs of the Federal government must be cleared by the Office of Management and Budget before they can be submitted to Congress. The director of the Office of Management and Budget is one of the most important presidential assistants. It is his responsibility to coordinate all the requests of the various agencies of the government into a single budget to be presented to the Congress for approval. To prepare the budget, the President must decide his programs and his policies for the coming fiscal year. The opinions of Congress about the President's policies and programs are largely expressed through their treatment of his budget. By budget additions or deletions Congress decides which of the President's programs will be put into operation.

The passage of the Employment Act of 1946 gave new duties to the President. This act requires the President to send to Congress an annual economic report describing the state of the nation's economy. This report covers not only the activities of the government itself but also the economic status of the nation as a whole. To assist the President in this task the Council of Economic Advisers was established. The Council examines various aspects of the national economy and makes recommendations to the President about such problems as increasing employment for American citizens, finding ways of curbing inflation, and so on. The Employment Act of 1946 established the principle that the government—specifically the executive branch—could undertake policies that would affect the business and economic life of the nation. Since that time, the national government's policies on taxing, Federal spending, and many other issues have greatly influenced the economic life of the nation. Employment, prices, and the rate of growth of the economy are all affected by decisions made by the President and his economic advisers.

Party Chief

The Constitution does not require the President to be the leader of a political party. Nevertheless, with the exception of George Washington, every President has been recognized as the leader of a political party.

In his role as *party chief* the President must sometimes engage in activities that seem contrary to other roles that he performs. For example, while he is *head of state,* representing all American citizens, he is at the same time the head of the Democratic or Republican party. Therefore, when he chooses people to hold key positions in the government, he is likely to choose members of his own political party. He chooses these people not only because he may

President Johnson was playing his role of party chief when he campaigned in California with the Democratic candidate for United States Senator, Pierre Salinger, who had formerly been Press Secretary for Presidents Kennedy and Johnson.

believe that they are more committed to his policies than would be members of the other party, but he must also reward members of his party for their faithful activity during the election campaign.

In his role as party chief the President will try to strengthen his political party while he is in office to improve his own chances for reelection, or, if he chooses not to run for reelection, to make it more likely that a member of his own party will be chosen to succeed him. As head of his party, the President often assists members of his own party who are running for office, lending his support where he can to make certain that they will be elected.

On the other hand, as *chief legislator* he must have the support of congressmen of both parties. Therefore, he must be careful that he does not express so much favoritism for one political party that he is always opposed by members of the other party when he needs them to support legislation he wishes to have passed. One way Presidents have sometimes resolved the conflict between the *head of state* role and *party chief* role is to assign much of the strictly party political activity to the Vice-President.

The President frequently finds himself walking a very narrow path, trying to appear to represent all Americans at the same time that he is providing vigorous leadership for his own party. In his capacity as *party chief* he selects the national chairman of his party and helps plan strategies for future elections. He gives speeches that help the party pay for the election campaign. And he may establish a President's Club with a membership fee of $1000 entitling the member to attend a White House dinner. The membership fee for the President's Club will go into the party treasury.

Representative of All the People

President Truman once referred to the President as "lobbyist for all the people." The President is the only person who is elected by all Americans. According to this view he has, in effect, a national constituency as compared to a Senator or Representative, whose constituency is limited to the congressional district or state from which he is elected. Therefore, the President more than any other person has an opportunity and an obligation to consider the needs of the entire nation.

Occasionally a Senator or Representative may face contradictions between what he believes to be best for the nation as a whole and what his constituency wants. For example, it may be very costly to continue to build ships in an old, inefficient shipyard. The President may believe that we could spend our money better in other ways. Nevertheless, it is very difficult for the congressman from the district that contains the shipyard to vote in favor of its closing, for it means the loss of jobs to many people in that district. The President, on the other hand, may see a way of using the money saved by abolishing the shipyard to create many more jobs in another part of the country. It is, therefore, one of the principal roles of the President to try to identify what is sometimes referred to as "the national interest" and try to promote it whenever he can.

While only one individual can be President of the United States at any single moment, the office of the President requires the time, energy, and loyalty of thousands of men and women. While the President has responsibility for treaty-making in his role as *chief diplomat*, the actual work in drafting and negotiating a treaty is done by many other people. In some cases the President may be familiar with only the general purposes of the treaty, knowing little about the specific details.

The vast majority of the President's legislative program does not originate with him but begins in the various departments and agencies of the Federal bureaucracy. Unless he is on record as being opposed to a program desired by an agency and unless the cost of the program exceeds the agency's budget, the President is likely to recommend the program to Congress, although he may have only a vague conception of how the program would actually operate.

In short, the President is the most well-known and final decision-maker in the United States. Yet his decisions depend upon the work and prior decisions of many other people.

E. A Typical Day in the Life of a President

In the previous lesson you learned that the President has at least eight roles to fulfill. During any typical day the President may engage in each of these eight roles. In the following exercise you will have an opportunity to apply what you have learned about presidential role. Below is a schedule that might be "typical" for a President of the United States. This schedule is based upon actual schedules of recent Presidents. Nevertheless, any actual day's schedule can rarely be typical, because on some days the President may be engaged in a single crisis or activity that may call for all his time and energy. This means that his other roles are likely to be neglected. However, this hypothetical schedule allows one to observe all the things a President might do in a day that would relate to all his roles. The following schedule is typical of the varied kinds of activities that occupy the President's time and shows us the length of work day the President normally faces.

Your task is to take each of the roles described in the preceding lesson and listed below and decide which of the President's activities during the day represents one of the eight roles in action. Note that an additional role—father and husband—has been added, since during any particular day the President also acts in that role. Some of the items on the schedule may be of more than one role type.

Head of State (HS)   Chief Economic Planner (CEP)
Chief Diplomat (CD)   Party Chief (PC)
Commander-in-Chief (CC)   Representative of All the
Chief Executive (CE)   People (RP)
Chief Legislator (CL)   Father and Husband (FH)

Presidential Calendar—February 12, 19—

6:30—President is awakened by guard; he shaves and dresses.

7:00—President watches television news in his bedroom and glances through three morning newspapers.

7:30—Two assistants enter his bedroom. One hands the President the *Congressional Record* for the preceding day. A few pages have been clipped to indicate specific references he should read. The second assistant, the appointments secretary, briefs the President on his schedule for the day and hands him a folder containing brief notes which explain why each person with an appointment wishes to see him.

7:50—Meeting completed, assistants leave; and President joins his wife for breakfast. They talk about personal matters, especially the forthcoming marriage of their daughter.

8:15—President arrives at his office and finds atop his desk a notebook of clippings containing current news items and commentary. This notebook, approximately thirty pages long, is put together daily by three assistants drawing upon newspapers and journals from across the nation. President scans through the articles rapidly, making some marginal notes by articles that capture his interest.

8:25—President telephones the Secretary of Defense, expressing concern about the increase in civilian casualties in Vietnam as reported in the press. He believes that the Air Force is too careless in its bombing raids and sometimes causes needless damage to civilian life and property.

8:35—Personal secretary enters room, bringing with her a number of documents for the President to sign and a few selected letters from the early morning mail she believes the President would like to read personally. He reads the letters, dictates directions for answering them, and signs documents.

8:53—Meets with four congressional leaders of his party to discuss strategy for passing a bill that is of great interest to the President. President reminds congressional leaders how important this legislation is to the nation and to their own party.

9:20—President steps from his office to an adjoining room where he is presented an award by the National Audubon Society in appreciation of his efforts to preserve nesting grounds for wild birds. President thanks members of the Society for the honor. Photographers snap pictures.

9:35—President returns to office and places three telephone calls:
—(1) to Senator Smith, a long-time friend who is recovering from an illness. President urges him to get well soon.
—(2) to Murphy, a labor leader whose union is on strike. President inquires about state of negotiations and expresses hope that strike can be settled quickly as it is having a bad effect on the economy.
—(3) to Jones, the Director of the Office of Management and Budget, who is asked a specific question about the budget that has been brought to the President's attention.

10:00—Two defeated congressmen, members of the President's political party, arrive to learn whether the President has any jobs for them.

10:20—Congressmen leave and President calls the Commissioner of Education to inquire about the status of a particular education bill that interests the President.

10:30—Newly appointed American ambassador to Sweden drops in to say good-bye to President and to ask whether he has any special instructions. The President has none, but they chat for a few minutes about political conditions in Sweden.

10:45—President leaves office for an adjoining room where the relatives of five men killed in military action are awaiting him. President gives a short speech and presents the Purple Heart award to the families of five men. Cameramen record the ceremony.

11:15—President returns to his office to find his Special Assistant for National Security Affairs waiting. Assistant briefs him quickly on the present status of four international crises that have been occupying the attention of the President. President listens carefully, asks a few questions, but finds no new situation that would require a policy decision by him at that moment.

11:50—President leaves office and returns to his room on the second floor. He has a quick lunch, talks briefly by telephone with his daughter in New York, and lies down for a short nap.

2:00—President returns to his office to find that a group has assembled to observe his signing a new gun-control law. While cameramen record the event, he uses many pens to sign his name, giving the pens away to those who aided in passing the bill. President makes a brief speech.

2:40—President steps to the Cabinet Room, where the Council of Economic Advisers is awaiting him. They discuss plans to slow down the inflation that is affecting the country. President agrees to move quickly on one of their recommendations.

3:15—President returns to office and greets a young Iowa girl who presents him with a valentine. It is recorded by the cameramen; the picture will appear in most daily newspapers on Valentine's Day.

3:25—President invites White House reporters into his office and agrees to answer their questions for fifteen minutes. But first he uses five minutes to announce his plans for overseas travel in the near future. Some correspondents are unable to crowd in, and fifteen minutes is much too short a time to answer all the questions they have. Nevertheless, this brief meeting makes certain that the President will receive frontpage newspaper coverage the following morning.

3:45—Presidential aide rushes in with a top-secret CIA report containing information on guerrilla activities in a sensitive Latin-American nation, one of the four foreign policy crisis areas that the President has been concentrating on. President scans the report quickly and places a call to the CIA Director with instructions concerning the kind of additional information that he needs.

4:15—President receives the Foreign Minister from an Asian country. The Foreign Minister has spent several days meeting with the Secretary of State. His meeting with the President is more formal and official than for the purpose of conducting business, but the two men visit for a time.

4:45—A congressman enters the President's office. He has been trying to have an Army base reopened in his district. The President agrees to think carefully about the matter and let him know his decision soon.

5:00—Secretary brings in more mail and documents requiring the President's signature.

5:15—President's personal physician enters. The doctor concludes, after a brief examination, that the President has fully recovered from a cold.

5:30—President leaves for his room to change for a Lincoln Day dinner that evening. As he changes, he pores over his notes for the speech he is to deliver at the dinner.

6:30—He arrives at the hotel, eats dinner, and presents his speech.

10:00—President returns to White House and, feeling the need for some exercise, bowls for forty-five minutes.

10:45—Returns to his bedroom with a folder of "night-time" reading of memoranda and brief reports. He reads for one hour, marking questions and writing marginal notes that will suggest actions to be taken in the near future.

11:45—Turns out his light and falls asleep.

F. The President as Decision-Maker

The significance of presidential decision-making was understood well by John F. Kennedy, who once observed:

> A President must choose among men, among measures, among methods. His choice helps determine the issues of his Presidency, their priority in the national life, and the mode and success of their execution. The heart of the Presidency is therefore informed, prudent, and resolute choice—and the secret of the presidential enterprise is to be found in an examination of the way presidential choices are made.

Theodore C. Sorensen, a top-level assistant to President Kennedy, noted that decision-making is central to the presidential role:

> The President's entire existence is a continuous process of decision—including decisions not to decide and not to take action—decisions on what to say, whom to see, what to sign, whom to name, and what to do, as Commander-in-Chief

Both quotations from T. C. Sorensen, *Decision-Making in the White House* (New York: Columbia University Press, 1963).

289

and diplomatic chief, as legislative leader and political leader, as a moral leader and a Free World leader, and in taking care that the laws be faithfully executed. Every policy announced is the sum of many decisions, each made in a different mold and manner.

Types of Presidential Decisions

The scope of presidential decision-making is enormous. A President makes decisions about laws, about the appointment of men to office, about the relationship of our nation with other nations, about how to finance government programs, about national defense, about the space program, about the solution of farm problems and city problems, and so on. These decisions may range from the seemingly trivial to the obviously momentous, from deciding whom to invite to a White House luncheon to deciding whether to send troops to Vietnam. While most small decisions can be handled by assistants, decisions in which the stakes are high usually reach the President. As President Eisenhower told John F. Kennedy, upon introducing him to the White House, "There are no easy matters that will come to you as President. If they are easy, they will be settled at a lower level."

The great importance of many presidential decisions is a burden to any officeholder. As we shall see in the next section, during the Cuban missile crisis of 1962, President Kennedy had to make decisions about "life or death" affecting whole nations, or even mankind. President Truman's decision to provide massive economic assistance to Western Europe through the Marshall Plan was the first step in a rapid rise out of the rubble of World War II. Some observers believe that in the absence of this Marshall Plan both France and Italy would have fallen under Communist control.

President Lyndon Johnson meets in the Cabinet Room with his economic advisers.

Factors That Influence Presidential Decision-Making

Decision-making means choosing among possible courses of action. It also refers to the search for alternatives, to decisions about what problems will be treated, and to how policy decisions will be put into effect. Each President goes about the process of decision-making in a different way. However, there are several factors which influence the decisions of all Presidents and are common to decision-making in general. The factors that influence presidential decision-making can be considered under three major categories: the circumstances of the decision, the individual characteristics of the decision-makers, and other limitations.

Circumstances of the Decision

Some decisions the President faces can be anticipated. The President knows for several days or weeks that a decision will have to be made, and he can therefore prepare for it. For example, the President learns that Congress wants to increase the education budget by $200 million. He may decide to warn Congress that he will veto a bill authorizing such an increase in funds for education. Expecting that the bill will pass Congress despite his warning, the President may have several weeks to explore what the political consequences of a veto might be. He can even have his veto message written in advance of the time he needs it. This decision can be carefully planned.

Some decisions are made after years of study. Special presidential commissions, task forces, and congressional committees may have studied and shaped a proposal before it requires a final decision by the President. The bill to change the Post Office from a department in the executive branch into a public corporation came after years of study.

Before leaving for an assignment in Vietnam, Gen. Creighton Abrams (left) meets with President Johnson and Gen. Earle Wheeler, Chairman of the Joint Chiefs of Staff.

Unfortunately the President and his advisers do not always have the luxury of much time to select the problems they wish to deal with and to search for solutions. Many decisions are made in a crisis situation. In September, 1970, the Palestine Liberation Front "skyjacked" three jet airplanes and held the passengers hostage. President Nixon was presented with an unexpected and delicate problem. Plans to rescue the hostages and to prevent further such incidents had to be developed rapidly.

Decisions are undoubtedly affected by the amount of time available in which to make decisions. When a crisis is unexpected, when the stakes are high, and when time is short, it is not possible to study all the possibilities in detail nor to consult with many people. The President must make his decision under unsatisfactory conditions, frequently depending upon sketchy information and being less than certain of the probable outcomes of his policy choice.

The kind of decision that is made depends also upon the importance the decision-maker assigns to the situation. Much of the controversy over the war in Vietnam stems from a disagreement over the importance of the North Vietnamese invasion of South Vietnam. President Johnson and Secretary of State Dean Rusk believed that the defense of South Vietnam was vital to American interests. They saw the war in Vietnam as part of a general effort to extend Communist control throughout Southeast Asia and to drive American influence out of the area. Moreover, they believed their policy to be in keeping with the policies of Presidents Eisenhower and Kennedy. Critics of their policy argued that no major American interest was at stake, that the fight was primarily a civil war, and that we should stay out of it. However, the fact that President Johnson and his principal advisers considered the Vietnamese struggle crucial to American interests greatly influenced American military and diplomatic policies.

Individual Characteristics of Decision-Makers

Very little is known for certain about the influence of personality upon the behavior of decision-makers. Nevertheless, it seems likely that certain traits are important. Is the President willing to take risks? Does he show a need for power? Is he intelligent? creative? Does he have a feeling of self-esteem?

President X is creative and intelligent and employs intelligent and creative assistants. President Y tends to carry forward policies from the past. Which of these Presidents would seem to have the greater number of solutions to choose from when problems arise? A President who wants to be surrounded by "yes-men" will likely produce different decisions than a President who encourages debate among his assistants.

Decisions are likely influenced by the social background and experience of the decision-maker. President Eisenhower organized his White House staff along lines he had used successfully as a military general. It is not surprising that he found problems that involved partisan political affairs most annoying and uninteresting. He had no experience in politics prior to becoming President and preferred to delegate partisan matters to others while he dealt with issues he viewed as more important.

Other Presidents, arriving in office after a lifetime of political activity, may take a quite different view of the office. Upon assuming office following President Kennedy's death, President Johnson concentrated upon domestic problems: civil rights, education, poverty. At first, he showed relatively little interest in foreign affairs. Only after his election in 1964 did he begin to shift his attention to foreign affairs.

Presidential decisions may also be influenced by the personal beliefs of the President. If he believes that communism is the greatest threat facing the United States, he may interpret many problems as part of a Communist conspiracy and treat them accordingly. Some Presidents may have genuine concern for the plight of minority groups in the United States, while others merely demonstrate concern officially because it is expected of the role. Because of their attitudes it is likely that these two types of Presidents would have quite different policies toward minority groups. President Hoover believed firmly in American values of individualism and private initiative. He believed that government should stay out of economic affairs as much as possible. His personal beliefs may have prevented him from making decisions that could have reduced the impact of the economic depression in 1930. Other Presidents have believed that the Federal government should try to help solve economic and social problems. Their beliefs have helped to expand the scope of governmental activity.

Other Limitations on Decision-Makers

No individual, least of all the President of the United States, is totally free to decide what he will do. Like any other individual in a society, he is influenced by forces in his environment. These forces include rules, status relationships, public opinion, available resources, and external decision-makers.

Rules. A major limitation upon presidential decision-making power are the rules—laws and customs—that define the rights and duties of the Chief Executive. Both the Constitution and laws passed by Congress set limits upon presidential actions. Customs developed over almost two hundred years influence presidential behavior.

American political leaders are expected to play politics according to the "rules of the game." Thus, no President may appoint someone to a major office, such as a Federal judge, without the consent of the Senate. This limitation is stated in the Constitution. President Lyndon Johnson wanted to appoint Francis X. Morrissey to the position of Federal judge. Morrissey was a personal friend of Senators Edward Kennedy and Robert Kennedy. They had recommended this appointment to Johnson. However, after investigating the background and qualifications of Morrissey, a Senate majority believed that he would make a poor judge. Consequently, President Johnson withdrew Morrissey's name and chose another man for the job. In this case the President's decision-making power was limited by the Senate's constitutional right to confirm or reject his appointments.

Customs, as well as laws, influence presidential decision-making. For example, the custom of "senatorial courtesy" has been followed faithfully over the years. "Senatorial courtesy" refers to an unspoken pledge among the Senators not to consent to a nomination of a man disapproved by the Senator of the President's party from the state affected. For example, if Iowa has a Republican Senator and the President is a Republican, he must consult with that Senator about whom to nominate, say, as a Federal judge or marshal in Iowa. This is a custom, not a law. But Presidents tend to abide by this rule.

Status relationships. Every status, or position, in a society involves relationships with people occupying other statuses, or positions. The status of father involves relationships with wife and mother and with children. The President is head of the executive branch. His status gives him authority over other executive officials. His assistants in the White House Office—his personal staff—have especially close relationships with the President. How the President gets along with his staff—and how members of his staff get along with each other—is bound to affect the President's decision-making. He is also limited by the attitudes and skills of his subordinates. Are they skillful in analyzing crucial issues? Do they give him all the facts he needs, or do they hide some unpleasant things from him?

Since the President's time is limited, he can concentrate on only the most pressing problems which arise. He depends upon assistants to identify those issues that he must decide. And he will expect his subordinates to settle less important problems. Moreover, the President has assistants who assemble the facts he needs to make a decision and present this information to him in a form that can be easily and rapidly understood. No President has the time to read long reports. Thus, his staff must boil information down to brief memos. In selecting problems, in helping decide who will see the President, in determining the facts the President will hear, the presidential staff undoubtedly influences presidential decisions.

Moreover, the various bureaus and departments of the executive branch frequently have their own policies, their own view regarding what the President's decision should be. Often these are policies inherited from a previous administration. While the President theoretically can command an agency

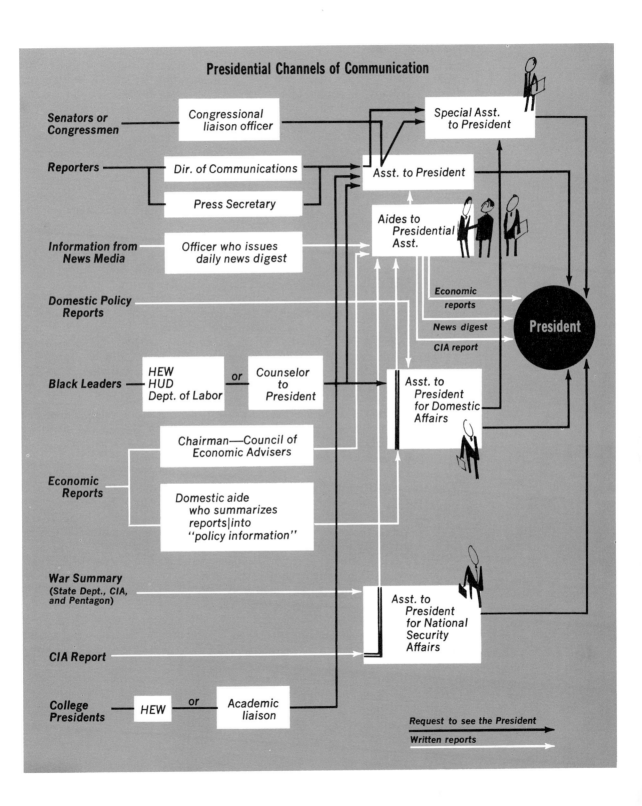

Presidential Channels of Communication

Senators or Congressmen — Congressional liaison officer — Special Asst. to President

Reporters — Dir. of Communications

Press Secretary

Asst. to President

Information from News Media — Officer who issues daily news digest

Aides to Presidential Asst.

Economic reports

News digest

CIA report

Domestic Policy Reports

President

Black Leaders — HEW HUD Dept. of Labor — or — Counselor to President

Asst. to President for Domestic Affairs

Chairman—Council of Economic Advisers

Economic Reports

Domestic aide who summarizes reports|into "policy information"

War Summary (State Dept., CIA, and Pentagon)

Asst. to President for National Security Affairs

CIA Report

College Presidents — HEW — or — Academic liaison

Request to see the President

Written reports

or department to carry out his own policies, in practice he must listen to their advice. Many of the bureaus and departments have staunch supporters in Congress. This sometimes makes it politically unwise for the President to meddle with them, for he might anger congressional leaders by doing so. And the President can remove only the top bureaucrats. Others are protected by civil service regulations. Therefore, the President finds that he not only has power, but power sometimes has him. He depends upon the departments to provide information and to implement his policies. In the process he must sometimes negotiate with his subordinates.

Status relationships in the Bay of Pigs incident. An example of the way advisers can affect decisions occurred in April, 1961, in the Bay of Pigs incident. Upon taking office President Kennedy found he had inherited a plan to use Cuban refugees to invade their homeland to oust Fidel Castro. The plan called for a two-stage attack. First, airplanes would destroy Castro's air force. This attack would be conducted from air fields in Guatemala by Cuban refugee pilots using planes donated by the United States CIA (Central Intelligence Agency). The planes were to be painted with the symbols of the Cuban air force. The public was to be informed that the pilots were defectors from Castro's air force rather than Cuban refugees trained by the CIA. Second, after Castro's air force had been destroyed, a force of about 1500 Cuban refugees was to mount an invasion of Cuba to liberate their homeland from Communist rule. The planners assumed that the invasion would spark uprisings throughout Cuba of citizens dissatisfied with Castro's rule.

The invasion took place on April 17. Within two days it was smashed completely by Castro's forces. What had gone wrong with President Kennedy's decision? Many factors contributed to this failure, but chief among them were faulty information, lack of clear communication among top-level presidential assistants, and incompetence in carrying out the decision.

There was no spontaneous uprising of Cuban citizens against the Castro government. Prior to the invasion, and unknown to the President, Castro had arrested potential leaders of such an uprising. Also, Castro had more support among the Cuban people than President Kennedy had been led to believe.

President Kennedy had been given inaccurate estimates of Castro's military strength. CIA and military advisers had told him that at the moment Castro's military force was slight. They stressed that soon Castro would receive massive arms shipments from the Soviet Union. They urged that the Cuban-refugee invasion take place immediately, before Castro's forces acquired large supplies of modern weapons. Unknown to these presidential advisers, and thus unknown to President Kennedy, Castro's military forces were already well armed, sufficient to defend their territory against the Cuban-refugee force. The small invading army became bogged down in the marshes of the Bay of Pigs.

Obviously, President Kennedy had been misinformed by those who reported to him. His decision was based upon faulty information provided by his subordinates. But perhaps more importantly, President Kennedy had in-

herited a policy to which the CIA was committed. President Kennedy's own assistants were too new to their jobs to be confident in their judgments. They permitted the project to go through without serious challenge.

Often a President has difficulty getting subordinates to carry out his decisions with enthusiasm or competency. President Franklin D. Roosevelt expressed the frustration he felt from time to time when trying to influence those who served under him.

> The Treasury is so large and far-flung and ingrained in its practices that I find it is almost impossible to get the action and results I want—even with Henry [Morgenthau] there. But the Treasury is not to be compared with the State Department. You should go through the experience of trying to get any changes in the thinking, policy and action of the career diplomats and then you'd know what a real problem was. But the Treasury and State Department put together are nothing compared with the Navy. The admirals are really something to cope with—and I should know. To change anything in the Navy is like punching a feather bed. You punch it with your right and you punch it with your left until you are finally exhausted, and you find [it] just as it was before you started punching.*

Many observers believe that the most important skill demanded of a President is the ability to persuade others to act. Presidential power is the power to persuade others to help him make and carry out decisions. These "others" include members of the President's executive staff and the enormous Federal bureaucracy commanded by the President and his chief aides.

Public opinion. Public opinion is an ever-present social force influencing presidential decisions about crucial issues. Abraham Lincoln is reported to have said that with public opinion on his side he could do anything. But in the face of public opposition he could do nothing.

Public opinion is a complex phenomena. On some issues it can almost be said that the public has *no* opinion. The public seems uninformed about the issue, is apathetic, or is simply willing to follow the President's leadership. An example of such an issue might be whether to renew the cultural exchange agreement with the Soviet Union. Probably most Americans would support the President in whatever choice he made. In other cases a decision seems to be forced upon the President by the power of public opinion. For example, from 1917 to 1933 the United States refused to grant diplomatic recognition to the government of the Soviet Union, primarily because of the American public's opposition to communism.

In addition to general public opinion, there are special groups whose opinions are especially influential. These groups have very strong views about certain issues. They also have enough influence in Congress to cause political problems for a President who ignores them. One example of such a group is the "China lobby." The China lobby consists of people who strongly favor Nationalist China and who despise Communist China. The China lobby includes missionaries, teachers, and businessmen who once lived in China or

*Clinton Rossiter, *The American Presidency.* (New York: Harcourt Brace Jovanovich, 1960), pp. 60–61.

President Nixon appeared on television in 1970 to rally public support of an Administration decision to send American and South Vietnam troops into Cambodia.

who have close ties to China. Any effort by the President to extend diplomatic recognition to Communist China is certain to provoke their hostile opposition.

Thus, public opinion is a major force on presidential decision-making. Because of this, Presidents take steps to be informed of it and to create it. President Lyndon Johnson was a "poll watcher." He gauged the public view of his decisions by reading the results of national political attitude surveys. Most Presidents have been avid newspaper and magazine readers in order to assess public opinion. Moreover, they look to editorial columns for views that support the decisions they want to make.

Through televised press conferences, televised speeches to the nation, press releases, and participation in public ceremonies, Presidents attempt to shape public opinion. Recent Presidents have appeared on television to inform the public about any new or bold decision. For example, in November, 1969, President Nixon addressed Americans via television regarding his plans to end the war in Vietnam. President Kennedy spoke to the nation to enlist public support for the passage of a civil rights law in 1963. And President Roosevelt, in pre-television days, used the "fireside chat" over radio to influence public opinion behind the bold new economic programs of his "New Deal."

Available resources. Presidential decisions are also limited by available resources. Presidents cannot undertake projects without the necessary materials, money, or skills. The availability of money, materials, technicians, and highly skilled scientists were all necessary for the decision to "send a man to the moon." Congress has much to say about the availability of resources for such decisions.

The President obtains funds to finance his programs through vote of Congress. He must convince Congress of the need for certain programs if he is to obtain resources to put them into operation. For example, President Truman's skill in influencing a previously hostile Congress to vote funds for the Marshall Plan was the crucial first step in carrying out his decision to aid war-torn Europe financially. Of course, the President's command of resources depends upon the abilities and productivity of the nation's people. Without productive people, the most vigorous President would be doomed to a lack of resources to carry out decisions.

External decision-makers. Especially in matters of foreign policy, the President does not always initiate the action. He is often responding to an action by another nation. When he chooses a course of action, he must always estimate how foreign decision-makers will react to his decision. Their response will most likely prompt him to undertake a new round of decisions.

The presidential decisions made during the unsuccessful invasion of Cuba in April, 1961, provide a good example of the influence of external decision-makers. Kennedy's decisions were formed in part by his judgments about the reactions of other decision-makers. The leaders of the Soviet Union had pledged to prevent the overthrow of Castro by invasion. Kennedy had to consider that a Cuban invasion by American forces might lead to war with the Soviet Union. Kennedy also had to consider the reactions of other Latin-American countries. Would their friendship with the United States be damaged as a result of a Cuban invasion by our nation? How would other nations with close ties to the United States react?

It should be clear that presidential decision-making is a complex problem and involves much more than the President sitting behind his desk, answering "yes" or "no" to questions. Presidential decision-making involves many people in selecting issues to be resolved, defining and classifying the problems, getting accurate information about the issues, posing alternative solutions, choosing the best alternatives, implementing the policies, and evaluating their consequences. In this activity the President is a major but by no means the sole performer.

G. The Cuban Missile Crisis

When, if ever, should nuclear weapons be used? This question has haunted every American President since Harry S. Truman ordered the atomic bombing of two Japanese cities in 1945. For twelve days in 1962 from October 16 until October 28, President John F. Kennedy faced daily the decision of whether to use nuclear weapons in defense of the national interest. During this time President Kennedy had to decide between war and peace, between life or death for millions of people. The following case illustrates many aspects of presidential decision-making.

Background of the Crisis

Why was the President forced to consider the awful possibility of nuclear warfare? The answer to this question must begin with a brief discussion of relations between the United States, Cuba, and the Soviet Union. Since 1959 Cuba had been ruled by Fidel Castro, a Communist dictator. Castro had won power during a revolution in which he had overthrown the autocratic government of Fulgencio Batista, a military dictator.

Soon after Castro took power, relations between Cuba and the United States became strained. Finally, formal communication between the two nations was ended; diplomatic relations were broken. The conflict between Cuba and the United States encouraged Castro to cooperate with the Soviet Union. The Soviet Union began to send weapons and military advisers to build up the armed power of Cuba.

American political leaders watched the Cuban arms build-up with grave concern. Rumors circulated that the Soviet Union was sending nuclear missiles to Cuba. However, Soviet leaders assured President Kennedy that Cuba would not receive offensive nuclear weapons.

On Tuesday morning, October 16, President Kennedy discovered that Soviet promises not to install nuclear missiles in Cuba were false. The Soviet leaders, including Premier Nikita Khrushchev, had deceived him.

Aerial Photographs Reveal Missile Sites

McGeorge Bundy, a special presidential adviser, gave the bad news to Kennedy. The President called a meeting of his chief advisers at 11:45 A.M. in the Cabinet Room. CIA Deputy Director Marshall Carter showed the President photographs of the Cuban missile sites. These photos proved beyond doubt that the Soviet Union had supplied Cuba with powerful offensive weapons to point at the United States. The President asked this group of

President Kennedy confers with his brother, Attorney General Robert F. Kennedy, on the missile crisis.

advisers to meet together regularly until a final decision had been made about this Cuban missile crisis. During most of this time they would meet without the President, although he would be kept informed of their progress.

The advisory group was the Executive Committee of the National Security Council, or EXCOM. EXCOM consisted of the Secretary of State, the Secretary of Defense, the director of the Central Intelligence Agency, the Secretary of the Treasury, President Kennedy's adviser on national security affairs, and his chief legal adviser on the White House staff. Other members were the Under Secretary of State, the Deputy Under Secretary of State, the chairman of the Joint Chiefs of Staff, the Assistant Secretary of State for Latin America, the President's adviser on Russian Affairs, the Deputy Secretary of Defense, and the Assistant Secretary of Defense. Also meeting with EXCOM from time to time were Vice President Lyndon Johnson; Adlai Stevenson, Ambassador to the United Nations; Kenneth O'Donnell, Special Assistant to the President; Donald Wilson, Deputy Director of the United States Information Agency; and Attorney General Robert F. Kennedy.

The first meeting of the EXCOM was spent discussing the problem. During the meeting President Kennedy issued the following orders to the group:

(1) Take more photographs of the missile sites in order that progress on construction and expansion of the sites could be charted. Daily flights over Cuba were to be scheduled to obtain a continuing supply of pictures.

(2) Put aside all other tasks in order that complete attention can be devoted to solving the problem of the Cuban missile sites.

(3) Maintain complete secrecy about this crisis until a final decision is made.

Between Tuesday, October 16, and Friday, October 19, the members of EXCOM devoted most of their time to the Cuban missile crisis. They met daily to discuss the problem, and they worked individually and in small groups to clarify their thinking. While EXCOM met, new aerial photographs showed some disturbing facts. As of Wednesday, October 17, the Cubans had constructed 16 missile sites with 32 missiles that could hit targets over 1000 miles away. These missiles were aimed at several important American cities and were capable of reaching these targets within a very few minutes after being fired. Military experts estimated that they could kill as many as 80 million Americans.

EXCOM Suggests Six Possible Solutions

At first the EXCOM considered six alternative solutions to the problem:

(1) Do nothing.

(2) Use negotiations with the Soviet leaders to work out a deal. For example, agree to remove United States missile bases in Turkey in exchange for Soviet removal of the missiles in Cuba.

(3) Try to work out a deal with Castro. Warn him that military force could be used against him.

(4) Use ships and aircraft to blockade Cuba, to prevent new shipments of military supplies from being sent there, and to put pressure on the Cubans to remove the missile sites.

(5) Launch an air strike to destroy the missile sites.

(6) Launch a full-scale invasion to destroy the missile sites and overthrow the Castro government.

EXCOM considered the strong and weak points of each of these solutions. From their discussion, four of the six suggested solutions were eliminated: the first, second, third, and sixth (in the above list). Several people in the group favored the fourth solution—a blockade. Others favored solution number five—an air strike. At first the majority of EXCOM favored an air strike. However, by Thursday night, October 18, the majority of the group favored a naval blockade.

At 9:15 o'clock that night, representatives from EXCOM presented the two solutions to the President. He heard arguments for the two positions and then instructed the EXCOM to study the two proposals again and report back to him on Friday.

Two Proposals Are Studied Intensively

On Friday morning EXCOM members decided to split into two groups—each favoring one of the two proposals. Each group wrote a paper that presented in detail the strong points of its solution. Then the two groups exchanged papers and criticized each other's arguments. Finally the papers were returned to the original groups for rewriting. This work continued all day Friday.

During the Cuban missile crisis in October, 1962, President Kennedy met with Army Chief of Staff Earle Wheeler (center) and other officers to discuss the Army's general readiness.

The main arguments of the group favoring an air strike were as follows:

An air attack against the missile sites would destroy them quickly and completely. The threat to our cities would be removed entirely. The Communists would have warning, from this bold step, not to challenge the United States like this again.

The air strike would be accompanied by a presidential address to the nation in which the action would be explained. At the same time Premier Nikita Khrushchev of the Soviet Union would be notified. Advance notice of the bombing would be given to Cuba through the United Nations. The United States government would call for a high level meeting of leaders from the United States and the Soviet Union to settle the problem and to prevent the air strike from leading to worldwide nuclear warfare.

The naval blockade idea should be rejected. Setting up a ring of warships around Cuba to prevent new arms shipments is like "locking the barn door after the horse has run away." A naval blockade cannot guarantee that the missiles will be removed; an air attack can guarantee this.

Here are the main arguments of those favoring a naval blockade:

The most important arguments for the naval blockade are the arguments against an air attack. An air strike would destroy the nation's moral leadership around the world. It would make the United States appear to be an aggressive, war-like nation picking on a weak neighbor. Furthermore, thousands of people, including defenseless women and children, would suffer casualties as a result of the attack.

The air strike would kill not only Cuban soldiers but also Soviet military advisers and technicians working at the missile sites. This could provoke a Soviet military response that could lead to an exchange of nuclear weapons between the United States and the Soviet Union.

The air strike cannot guarantee destruction of the nuclear weapons and missile sites in Cuba. An air strike would have to be followed with an infantry invasion of Cuba in order to be sure that the missile sites would be removed. This would lead to the death of thousands of American soldiers and the loss of millions of dollars in materials. And it could lead to worldwide warfare between the United States and the Soviet Union.

Most of President Kennedy's military advisers favored an air attack. General Curtis LeMay, Air Force Chief of Staff, argued strongly for the air strike. Robert McNamara, Secretary of Defense, was the main spokesman for those favoring a naval blockade.

President Kennedy was faced with the decision of choosing between the two alternatives presented to him by the EXCOM. He called a meeting of the National Security Council, including all members of the EXCOM, for 2:30 on Friday, October 19. The meeting continued until 5:10 P.M. The President heard arguments for an air strike and a naval blockade. He was informed that preparations had been made to carry out either decision quickly.

President Kennedy Makes a Decision

The majority of those present at the National Security Council meeting favored a naval blockade. The President decided in favor of the naval blockade. He reasoned that the blockade would show the Soviets that he meant business, that this Soviet challenge to the United States would be met. The blockade would give the United States a point of strength from which to bargain with the Soviets for the removal of the missiles. However, the blockade was a limited response. It gave the Soviets much opportunity to bargain their way out of the situation without a military response. And it gave the United States a chance to escalate the conflict if the blockade failed. By contrast, the air strike was an unlimited response. The chance that it could lead to total war was too great.

Now the decision had to be carried out. Various assistants to the President supervised different actions related to carrying out the decision. A team of writers prepared a presidential address to the nation to be given on Monday. Military chiefs prepared the armed forces for action. State Department leaders prepared messages to American allies, to American ambassadors in foreign nations, to the United Nations, and to the Soviet Union.

The President met with the National Security Council on Sunday, October 21, at 2:30. He checked the diplomatic messages and the military preparations that had been made during the past day and a half. The Navy Chief of Staff was asked to describe plans for the blockade. The President reviewed the draft of his speech and made several changes in it.

On Monday, October 22, the President met with several key groups to inform them of developments and to gain their support. He met with his Cabinet and with twenty top leaders of Congress. At 6:00 P.M. the Soviet Ambassador, Anatoly Dobrynin, was informed of the proposed naval blockade.

Influencing Public Opinion on the Decision

At 7:00 P.M. the President spoke to the nation. He informed the American people that the Soviet Union had built missile sites in Cuba and that missiles were pointed at American cities. He told of his decision to meet the Soviet

challenge. He called the proposed blockade a quarantine in order that the decision would sound less warlike. He stressed that all ships carrying offensive weapons to Cuba would be stopped on the high seas and turned away. He declared that the missile sites must be taken from Cuba. President Kennedy hoped to arouse the support and the courage of the American people with words such as these:

> The nineteen thirties taught us a clear lesson. Aggressive conduct, if allowed to go unchecked and unchallenged, ultimately leads to war.
>
> This nation is opposed to war. We are also true to our word.
>
> Our unswerving objective, therefore, must be to prevent the use of these missiles against this or any other country; and to secure their withdrawal or elimination from the Western Hemisphere.
>
> Our policy has been one of patience and restraint, as befits a peaceful and powerful nation which leads a worldwide alliance. . . .
>
> We will not prematurely or unnecessarily risk the course of worldwide nuclear war in which even the fruits of victory would be ashes in our mouths, but neither will we shrink from that risk at any time it must be faced.*

On Tuesday, signs of support for the President's decision were shown both in the nation and around the world. Newspaper editorials and telegrams to the White House were overwhelmingly favorable. The main allies of the United States wired support. And, most important, the nations of the Organization of American States voted to support the action of the United States in this crisis.

The Naval Blockade Begins

The "quarantine" went into effect at 10:00 A.M. on Wednesday, October 24. The world waited tensely as several Soviet cargo ships, accompanied by submarines, moved toward the American naval blockade. Would the Soviet ships turn back? If they refused to turn back, what would the Americans do? Would naval warfare break out? Would nuclear war start? Questions such as these played on the minds of informed people all over the world as leaders of the two super powers, the United States and the Soviet Union, braced for the world's first nuclear confrontation.

Throughout this crisis President Kennedy had to consider how the Soviet leaders would react to his moves. He believed strongly that he must not put them in a position where they would have to fight in order to "save face." Yet he realized that he must not back down from his reasonable demands. Somehow he had to chart a course that would win his objective of removing the Soviet missile sites from Cuba without plunging the world into war.

At dawn on Thursday, October 25, a Soviet tanker came into contact with American ships. After identifying itself, it was allowed to pass. The President, believing that weapons were not aboard the tanker, was anxious not to provoke the Soviets unnecessarily. At dawn on Friday, October 26, a Soviet ship was stopped, and Americans boarded and searched it. It was carrying only trucks and truck parts, so it was passed on to Cuba. However,

* The New York Times, October 23, 1962, p. 18. Copyright 1962 by The New York Times Company. Reprinted by permission.

The Organization of American States (OAS) is a mutual defense treaty organization of the Latin-American republics and the United States.

the boarding and searching showed the Soviet leaders that the President was prepared to back up the blockade with forceful action. Later on Friday, sixteen Soviet ships turned back from the voyage to Cuba. Since Wednesday, they had stopped dead in the water, just short of a confrontation with the American ships. The Soviet decision to send them away appeared to be a victory for the naval blockade.

The Soviet Union Makes a Response

However, disturbing news was reported from Cuba. The missile sites were still there and more were being constructed. Perhaps an air attack or an invasion would be necessary to get rid of the missiles. On Friday evening, October 26, a letter from Premier Khrushchev arrived. It said that the Soviet Union would consider removing the missiles from Cuba in return for a promise by the United

A Soviet ship with fifteen bombers pulled out of Cuba is on its way home a few weeks after the end of the missile crisis. The Soviet crew voluntarily opened the fuselage crates for U. S. aerial inspection.

States that Cuba would not be invaded then or in the future. The EXCOM met on Saturday morning to write an encouraging reply to Khrushchev. Before this job was completed, another letter from Khrushchev arrived. It suggested that the United States remove its missiles from Turkey in exchange for Soviet removal of missiles from Cuba. No mention was made of the previous letter.

While the EXCOM discussed the latest letter from the Soviet Union, a United States reconnaissance plane (U-2) was shot down while taking photographs over Cuba. Military leaders pressured the President to respond with an air strike against a missile site. President Kennedy resisted this pressure. He decided to try, one last time, to reach a peaceful settlement.

The President decided to reply to the first letter from Khrushchev, received on Friday, and to ignore the second letter. In his letter to Premier Khrushchev, President Kennedy agreed to end the naval blockade and to promise not to invade Cuba in return for removal of the missiles from Cuba.

On Sunday morning, October 28, Khrushchev's reply to the President's proposal was received. He agreed to accept President Kennedy's terms. The Cuban missile crisis had ended, thirteen days after it had begun. President Kennedy refused to boast publicly of a victory over Khrushchev. An important part of his strategy had been not to put the Soviet leaders into a corner so that they would have to fight to get out. Rather, he attempted to use just enough force to achieve a limited objective—removal of the Soviet missiles from Cuba. He tried to stop short of provoking a war.

Consequences of the Decision

President Kennedy's policy achieved its immediate goals—removing the threatening missiles from Cuba while avoiding war. But its long-range effects are harder to evaluate. For example, this policy decision did not change the relationships between the United States and Cuba. Indeed in 1970 there were reports that the Soviet Union was helping Cuba build bases for submarines armed with nuclear weapons. Perhaps from the apparent success of Kennedy's policy other American leaders concluded that the Soviet Union could be influenced successfully in the future by the use of threats. In short, it is very difficult to be absolutely certain about what is a "good" decision or a "bad" decision because the long-range consequences of decisions are unknown. A decision-maker can never be certain what might have been accomplished if a different policy had been chosen instead.

Circumstances for the decision:

1. Was this a decision that could be made in advance or was it a crisis decision?

2. How did the amount of time available for making the decision influence the consideration of alternative policies?

Individual characteristics of the decision-makers:

3. What clues can you find that reveal how President Kennedy interpreted the build-up of Soviet missiles in Cuba? How might this interpretation have influenced his decision? What other interpretations were possible?

4. What personal values seemed to be held by President Kennedy that may have influenced his decision?

5. To what degree might the approach President Kennedy adopted toward solving the problem have affected the final decision?

Other limitations on decision-makers:

6. In what ways did "rules" influence the decision process?

7. What examples can you find that status relationships may have influenced the decision?

8. What evidence can you find that President Kennedy was sensitive to public opinion?

9. In what sense did available resources make this decision possible?

10. How was the decision influenced by anticipated reactions of external decision-makers?

H. What Are the Characteristics of a "Great" President?

In this chapter we have studied the presidential role. We have examined factors that influence the recruitment of Presidents; we have looked at the role demands of the office; and we have learned that one of the principal activities of the President is making decisions—decisions that cannot be made by any other person. As President Truman once said about the Presidency: "The buck stops here." The "buck" cannot be handed on to another.

But we have not yet decided what qualities a President must have in order to be a great President. In the opening lesson of this chapter you were asked to list ten qualities that you believed to be most desirable for a President to have. Now that you have studied about the President's job, make a new list of ten qualities you believe a person would need to be a great President. Prepare this list without referring to your original list. When you have finished, compare the two lists—the one you have just completed with the one you composed when you began the chapter. In what ways is your second list different from your first? How can you account for these differences?

Historians Rank the Presidents

One way to think about the traits necessary for a great President is to think about past Presidents, how they have been evaluated, and why people thought that they were excellent, average, or mediocre. Perhaps, a consideration of past Presidents will provide clues to the qualities needed in Presidents today.

In 1962 Professor Arthur M. Schlesinger reported a survey of seventy-five scholars of American history, including two who work in British universities.* These scholars were asked to rank the American Presidents up to that time according to how good they thought the Presidents had been and which ones they thought would leave an enduring mark in history. The historians were asked to evaluate the men as Presidents and not base their judgments on any other aspects of the man's life, including other professional activities, that he might have been involved in either before or after he was President.

Since the poll was conducted in 1962, Presidents Kennedy, Johnson, and Nixon were not included in the study. Moreover, William Henry Harrison, who died within a month of his inauguration, and James Garfield, who served little more than six months before he died, were excluded because they had served so little time that it made judgments about their performance difficult.

Each of the scholars used his own judgment according to several criteria. The criteria were as follows: What was the nature of the times in which the President was in office; did the President demonstrate a creative approach to

*Arthur M. Schlesinger. "Our Presidents: A Rating by 75 Historians," *New York Times Magazine*, July 29, 1962.

his management of the office; did he seem to be in control of events or was he the victim of events; did he use his opportunity as President to advance the general welfare; how successful was he in staffing important government positions; was he properly attentive to the nation's interest in relationship to the rest of the world; and, finally, how significantly did he affect the future destiny of the nation?

There is no necessary reason why you should accept the judgments of these historians any more than you might accept the judgments of your classmates. Nevertheless, these seventy-five scholars were all careful students of American history. They knew the administrations of each of the Presidents very well. Therefore, while we might disagree with them about their judgments of the Presidents, you may be interested in learning how they ranked the Presidents on the basis of their knowledge and their judgments about presidential role performance.

Five Presidents were listed as *great*. Listed in order, they were Abraham Lincoln, George Washington, Franklin Delano Roosevelt, Woodrow Wilson, and Thomas Jefferson.

Six Presidents were considered *near great*: Andrew Jackson, Theodore Roosevelt, James Polk, Harry Truman, John Adams, and Grover Cleveland.

Twelve Presidents were considered *average or mediocre*: James Madison, John Quincy Adams, Rutherford B. Hayes, William McKinley, William Howard Taft, Martin Van Buren, James Monroe, Herbert Hoover, Benjamin Harrison, Chester A. Arthur, Dwight David Eisenhower, and Andrew Johnson.

Six Presidents were judged to be *less than average* quality: Zachary Taylor, John Tyler, Millard Fillmore, Calvin Coolidge, Franklin Pierce, and James Buchanan. Finally, two Presidents were judged to be *totally unfit* for the office: Ulysses S. Grant and Warren G. Harding.

Characteristics of the "Great" Presidents

It might be interesting to look more closely at the five Presidents who were ranked as great by these historians and see what, if anything, they had in common. Such an analysis might contribute to our ability to judge a President's potential for historical prominence while he is still in office.

With the exception of George Washington, all of the five "great" Presidents were vigorous, active politicians. Each of them sought the Presidency and worked hard to attain it. They bestowed and withheld political favors. They knew when to browbeat the opposition, when to bargain, and when to stand firm. They knew when it was appropriate to concede something that was relatively unimportant in order to achieve more significant goals. Each of the five men worked hard to make the office of the President an important political position. George Washington put the Presidency on a strong course. The others left the Presidency a stronger, more powerful position than before.

In exercising strong presidential leadership, each encountered opposition from Congress and the Supreme Court. Each offended important economic interests or aroused long-standing prejudices of the American public. Each was accused, during his time, of seeking to undermine the Constitution and to impose a dictatorship on the country. Nevertheless, while each of these men aroused strong opposition from certain quarters, they were all popular Presidents. Each was reelected to a second term, and Franklin D. Roosevelt was elected to a third and fourth term.

With the exception of Abraham Lincoln, all came from the upper-level of society. With the exception of Washington and Wilson, the Presidents were not outstanding administrators. They were primarily interested in the political aspects of the office and most would have agreed with President Roosevelt that the office "is preeminently a place of moral leadership."

In short, the President who will be remembered in history as a "great" President is not one who views the office primarily in negative terms, that is, in terms of what he cannot do. If he sees his role as primarily that of a caretaker or as a reed to be blown here and there in response to popular causes of the moment, he is likely to be judged badly by history—at least by those historians who participated in this study. According to the historians, the "great" Presidents were strong Presidents, ones who battled with various groups in the society, with the Congress, and with the courts to achieve goals they believed important for all Americans. They were men who were able to see beyond the immediate present and were able to build for the future.

1. Do you agree with the criteria used by the historians?

2. How else might Presidents be rated? How would the use of different criteria change the ranking of Presidents made by the historians?

chapter 14

The Congressional Role

More than 200 million people live in the United States. In any given year 535 of these Americans will occupy leadership roles in American politics as congressmen.* One hundred of these will be United States Senators, and 435 will be members of the United States House of Representatives.

A. The Recruitment of Congressmen

Do all Americans have the same chance of becoming a congressman? Or are people who have certain characteristics more likely to be elected to Congress than people without these characteristics?

Below are two cases of people hoping to become members of Congress. Decide in each case which of the two is more likely to be elected.

Case 1. Who Will Succeed Congressman Nelson?

Representative Robert Nelson is a Republican from Clearwater, Oregon. He is retiring at age 88 from the House of Representatives, where he served as chairman of the House Committee on the Interior for over forty years. He represents a rather conservative Oregon district in which a majority of people live in small towns and on farms. His major concerns in Congress have been conservation of water and forests and internal security against the menace of communism.

Who will replace Representative Nelson? The Republican party has not lost an election in Congressman Nelson's district in this century. Receiving the GOP nomination in this district almost insures election. Below are descriptions of two men who are seeking the GOP nomination.

David Glasgow is 48 years old. His ancestors were among the first settlers in Clearwater. He went to college in Oregon, where he also received his law degree. He has a law firm in Clearwater, but finds time to be active in the American Legion and the Little League. His father is a business executive in Clearwater. David Glasgow has been on the Clearwater town council for six years.

*In one sense all 535 members of Congress—both Senators and Representatives—are congressmen. However, it has become customary to use the term Congressmen to refer to members of the House of Representatives only. Therefore, in this section when the term Congressman is capitalized, it is meant to refer to members of the House of Representatives; when congressman (with c in lower case) is used, we are referring to members of Congress generally.

Mathias Beaman is 68 years old. He has been a small farmer for his entire life near Clearwater. His father was also a farmer until his death. Mathias Beaman was the eldest of eight children, and barely managed to complete high school. Mathias Beaman believes he would be a real representative of the people. He hasn't had time to belong to any community organizations, but that is only because he works so hard, he says.

Question: Which of these men do you believe will most likely receive the Republican nomination for Congressman? Why?

Case 2. Who Will Replace Senator Miles?

Senator Irwin Miles is an 89-year-old Democrat from New York State, a state with a liberal political tradition. Serving for over forty-five years in the Senate, he has always been identified with the liberal wing of the Democratic party. New York State contains many small towns and several large cities including, of course, New York City. The people who elected Miles are most often first-, second-, or third-generation Americans who still identify strongly with their Italian, Jewish, or Irish background. Senator Miles has been a strong advocate of civil rights and liberties as well as an active member of the labor movement before coming to public life.

Who will be selected to replace Senator Miles? The Democratic party is confident that it will win the Senate seat after Senator Miles's retirement. Two men who wish to run for the Senate on the Democratic ticket are described below.

Timothy O'Hara is 43 years old, the great-grandson of an Irish immigrant, and the son of a business executive in New York City. O'Hara's family has made much progress in three generations. Timothy O'Hara went to Columbia University in New York for his college education and law degree. He now works in the District Attorney's office in Manhattan. His interest in law led him to organize free legal clinics throughout the ghettos in New York. O'Hara finds time for the Boy Scouts and being a marshall at the St. Patrick's Day Parade. He is a close political and personal friend of Senator Miles and promises to continue Senator Miles's crusades in the Senate.

Matthew Jacobs is 59 years old. He owns a small food processing company in Binghamton, a small city in upstate New York. He is the son of a Russian immigrant. His father worked as a clerk in Binghamton. Matthew Jacobs finished high school and received two years of college credit through correspondence courses. He has been active in Binghamton's school board for three years. He believes he can best represent the little man in politics.

Question: Which one of these two men do you believe will most likely receive the Democratic nomination for Senator from New York State? Why?

Rules Affect the Recruitment of Congressmen

Every organization has a set of formal and informal rules that affect which people are likely to become its members. For example, football is traditionally considered in American culture to be a game for males, not females. Moreover, other things being equal, physically large boys are more likely to become football players than are small boys. Also, the chances of different boys becoming members of a school team may be affected by scholastic rules. The school may require that only boys whose grades are above a certain level can be members of an athletic team.

Rules also govern who becomes a member of Congress. Because of these rules every citizen does not have the same chance of being elected to Congress, just as every student does not have the same chance of becoming a member of the football team. Some of these are formal rules in the Constitution. Other rules are informal and are found in tradition and custom. There are still other rules that stem from the requirements of the congressman's job.

Rules on Age, Citizenship, and Residency

The Constitution requires that a person must be at least 25 years of age to be a member of the House of Representatives and 30 years of age to be a Senator. In fact, congressmen tend to be considerably older than the constitutionally prescribed minimum age. The typical Senator is in his late fifties and the typical Representative in his early fifties. In contrast, the average age of the American voter is about 43.

Another constitutional requirement is that a person must be a citizen for at least nine years before he is eligible to serve in the Senate and at least seven years to be eligible for the House of Representatives. Moreover, informal rules appear to support the formal rule to put a further handicap upon naturalized citizens becoming members of Congress. While about 7 percent of Americans are naturalized citizens, only about 2 percent of the Senators elected in a ten-year period after World War II were naturalized citizens.

The Constitution requires only that a member of Congress be a resident of the state from which he is elected. Yet custom decrees that a candidate for the House must actually have a residence in the congressional district that he wants to represent. In the same state, District A may have many qualified people eager to serve in Congress while District B has many fewer potential candidates. Competition for a seat in Congress is less in District B because

custom decrees that outstanding men and women in District A can compete in District B only by moving their residence to that district.

Informal Rules Affecting the Recruitment of Congressmen

A majority of adult Americans can meet the age, citizenship, and residency requirements set forth in the Constitution for members of Congress. Yet if we look at the kinds of people who actually become congressmen, it is clear that the American voters set other standards for these national lawmakers.

Sex status. Men are more likely to become members of Congress than are women. Historically, women have been discriminated against in American politics. Throughout most of American history women were not permitted to vote in elections. Today women enjoy the same formal legal status in politics as men. Because of tradition, however, women continue to be "second-class citizens" in many ways. More than 50 percent of Americans are women, but the membership of both the House and the Senate is overwhelmingly male. If women were represented in the House of Representatives equal to their number in the society, there would be over 215 congresswomen. In fact, in recent years the number of women in the House has averaged around 15, or about 3 percent of the House membership.

Race. Whites are more likely to become congressmen than nonwhites. Until recently, when Senator Edward Brooke was elected to the Senate from Massachusetts, there had been no black Senators since the period of Reconstruction following the Civil War. In the House the number has been about five Negroes in each Congress (or 1 percent of the House membership), although blacks count for more than 10 percent of the national population.

An exception to the general proposition that whites are more likely to become congressmen than nonwhites is found in the case of the Hawaiian congressional delegation. Since Hawaii became a state, the majority of its congressmen have been, and probably will continue to be, Oriental or of mixed white-Asian heritage.

Religious affiliation. Protestants are more likely to become congressmen than Catholics and Jews. In a study conducted in the 1950's, 59 percent of the American public defined themselves as Protestants, 34 percent as Roman Catholics, 6 percent as Jewish, and 1 percent as "other." A study of 100 Senators living in the post-World War II period found that 88 percent were Protestants, 11 percent Catholic, and 1 percent Jewish.

Education. Highly educated people are more likely to become congressmen than the less educated. In recent years about 90 percent of all Senators and about eight out of ten Representatives have had some college training. Over half of all recent congressmen have either been to law school or have done some other form of post-college work.

Socioeconomic status. People from high socioeconomic status background are more likely to become congressmen than people from lower socioeconomic background. About 95 percent of the recent Senators and 90 percent of the Representatives have come from middle and upper-middle-class backgrounds. Congressmen tend to have professional and business backgrounds (high-status

At left, a glimpse of the Documents Room. Above is the Mace, the symbol of authority in the House of Representatives.

occupations). Most congressmen have had incomes in the middle and upper-middle range before coming to Congress. Every Congress, in addition, has some very wealthy men. A study in 1968 found that at least one-fifth of the Senators were millionaires. But very few congressmen are members of the working class.

Occupation. Congressmen are more likely to be recruited from certain occupations than from others. Lawyers predominate. The legal profession is closely related to the political career of a congressman. A lawyer has an expert knowledge of the law, and the main job of a congressman is lawmaking. A lawyer who leaves his job for a few years to become a congressman probably improves his abilities as a lawyer. When he returns to his job, after a time in Congress, he finds that he has lost nothing and has probably gained in skills and in contacts with important people.

By contrast, many other occupations are not closely related to the job of a congressman. And a man who spends several years in Congress loses time and opportunity in developing his own career.

In 1964, lawyers made up 66 percent of the Senate and 57 percent of the House of Representatives. But lawyers made up less than one-tenth of 1 percent of the national labor force. The second largest occupational group in Congress are businessmen, about 10 percent of the membership. The occupations of farming, education, and journalism each account for about 5 percent of the membership of Congress.

Political experience. People with much experience in politics and government are more likely to become congressmen than people with little or no experience. Congressmen are not likely to be political amateurs. A study of post-World War II Senators revealed that on the average a Senator had held about three public offices and devoted about ten years of his life to governmental service before being elected to the Senate. Many of them had been law-enforcement officers or state legislators before becoming Senators.

"Joiners." People who are active in many voluntary associations are more likely to become congressmen than people who are not. Members of Congress, like other political leaders, tend to be "joiners." They are more likely than the average citizen to be members of such voluntary associations as the Masons, Knights of Columbus, Rotary Clubs, veterans' organizations, and the like.

> **1.** Can you explain why these formal and informal rules regarding recruitment exist? For example, what is there about American society that explains why women are underrepresented in Congress? Why are young people and people from lower socioeconomic classes underrepresented?
>
> **2.** Do you think these recruitment rules are fair or just? It is estimated that because of these rules only about 5 percent of Americans have a significant chance of becoming a member of Congress. Is this good, or do you feel the rules should be changed so as to broaden the range of people who have a good chance of becoming a member of Congress?
>
> **3.** What effect do you think these recruitment rules have upon American politics and government? Do you think American politics would be different if congressmen were recruited from a broader range of people? For example, would it make any difference if there were more women in Congress? more blacks? more poor people?

B. Congressmen Play Many Roles

How many times have you heard someone say, "There ought to be a law. . . ."? Deciding what Federal laws are needed is primarily the responsibility of congressmen. Article I of the United States Constitution granted "all legislative powers" of the central government to a Congress consisting of a House of Representatives and a Senate. These "legislative powers" include establishing post offices, levying taxes, regulating interstate commerce, declaring war, and establishing Federal courts below the Supreme Court. These, and several other activities, are part of the legislative powers invested in Congress by the Constitution.

Congressmen are often called lawmakers. We are most aware of those duties performed by congressmen that relate directly to passing laws: writing and introducing bills, hearing testimony from witnesses, working in committees, debating and voting in the House or Senate. In fact, nearly every official action taken by a congressman relates in one way or another to his primary responsibility as a lawmaker.

Nevertheless, much of a congressman's day is spent on activities that are not directly related to legislation currently under consideration by Congress. He may respond to letters from constituents who are complaining about certain government regulations. He may call upon an official in a Federal agency to secure needed information. Or he may give a speech at a Veteran's Day dinner in his home state.

Therefore, the "congressional role" actually consists of several roles. Before looking at the primary role, that of lawmaker, let us examine three other congressional roles.

The Congressman as Ombudsman

For many years the Scandinavian countries have had an official called an *ombudsman*. His job is to help citizens who are having some kind of trouble with the government. In our country where would the following people turn for help?

Mrs. Mary Jones, a 72-year-old widow living on Social Security, normally gets her check from the Social Security Administration on the fifth of each month. It is now April 15, and her check has not arrived. She has called the local Social Security office in her city, and they have informed her that a check of the records indicates that her check was prepared at the usual time. The young man in the office tells her he cannot understand what might have happened to her check.

James Black operates a small radio station. At lunch on Tuesday a business acquaintance told him that the Internal Revenue Service had just issued a new tax ruling that may apply to Mr. Black. When Mr. Black returned to his office, he called the local Internal Revenue office to inquire about the matter. The people he spoke to were friendly, but they told him that they have no specialist in their office that could advise him on just how the new ruling would affect his business.

The Zabachi family came from Eastern Europe twenty years ago, and Mr. Zabachi has worked as a janitor in a school since then. One afternoon Mrs. Zabachi suffered a stroke and died shortly afterward. Their son John is in the army and stationed in Europe. Mr. Zabachi, of course, wants to tell his son of the mother's death and have him come home for the funeral. He knows that his son is in Mannheim, Germany, but the family has only a stateside military postal address.

Our Federal government has no officials called ombudsmen to handle such problems. In each of these cases and many thousands like them, it is likely that the people will turn to their Congressman or Senator for advice. Mrs. Jones could ask her Congressman to find out what happened to her Social Security check and help her get another one if the first one was lost. Mr. Black can write or call to learn where he can obtain the information he needs. Mr. Zabachi (or perhaps a friend or the family clergyman) might send a telegram to their Congressman to learn how John can be contacted and whether an emergency leave can be granted.

Approximately 10 percent of a Congressman's time is spent dealing with constituent problems (*Table 1*, page 321). In addition, each member of Congress has one or more staff members in Washington who spend nearly all their time dealing with constituent requests. Most congressmen also have offices in their home districts. The staff member assigned to that office must spend much of his time with constituent problems.

Members of Congress are the nearest equivalent to an *ombudsman* in the American political system. It is a role which congressmen play with mixed feelings. Requests for help from constituents often seem excessive, and often the information and advice is easily available elsewhere. (For example, high school students who correspond with congressmen seeking help in writing term papers.) Nevertheless, work of this type wins friends and will be remembered at election time.

Political Educator and Campaigner

Members of Congress are elected political leaders. To remain leaders, they must maintain a following. At regular intervals (every two years for Congressmen and every six years for Senators) they must submit to a new election. No matter how long or how faithful their service, they must stand and be judged by the electorate. Few, if any, members of Congress can afford to move to Washington and forget the voters back home.

A study of the average Representative revealed that he spent 5.6 days per month in his home district while Congress was in session and made an average of 7.3 radio and 3.5 television appearances per month.* Many Representatives and Senators publish a regular newsletter describing their activities and points of view on current issues to send to constituents. Finally, each member of Congress visits personally with some constituents, either in Washington or in his home district, each month.

Members of Congress look for every possible way to keep their name and image in the voter's mind. They welcome invitations to speak to civic clubs and banquets. They are present at the unveiling of statues and the dedication of new buildings. They pose for pictures and prepare press releases for local newspapers. They appear at county fairs, football games, and Fourth of July picnics. Some congressmen send congratulations to high school and college graduates and condolences to surviving members of a family at the time of a death. In every way possible a member of Congress tries to remind voters that he is alive, well, and working in Washington with only the voters' best interests at heart.

During an election year the political educator and campaigner role increases in importance. It may even affect the way other roles are played. For example, it may become increasingly difficult to keep enough members of the House or Senate to make a quorum (the number required to be present when a vote is taken) because so many members are in their home districts conducting their political campaigns.

A congressman's political campaigner role may lead him to vote differently on bills in Congress in the months preceding an election than he would at other times. For example, some people believe that the Omnibus Crime Control bill passed by the Congress in 1970 might not have passed at all, at least in its present form, had not many Senators and Representatives been fearful of how their vote against it might have been viewed by their constituents.

*Donald G. Tacheron and Morris K. Udall, *The Job of the Congressman.* (New York: Bobbs-Merrill, 1966), p. 281.

NEWS

1232 Longworth House Office Bldg., Washington, D. C.
Area 202 225 3065   Zip Code 20515
207 Federal Bldg Greensboro, N.C.   Zip Code 27401
Area 919 272 1161

CONGRESSMAN RICHARDSON PREYER

Sixth District, North Carolina

June 12, 1970

An anti-air pollution bill co-authored by 6th District Congressman Richardson Preyer was approved overwhelmingly this week by the U. S. House and sent to the Senate. The measure would expand the fight on air pollution by $775 million over the next three years.

The bill will set national air quality standards on cars, industrial plants, fuels, and planes. The authorized spending ceiling for federal programs under the clean air legislation act of 1967 will increase from approximately $96 million to $200 million for the fiscal year beginning July 1.

"It is time to stop talking and to take concrete action," Preyer said during debate on the House floor Tuesday. "The situation is not hopeless despite some doomsday prophets, and I think the human race can solve it with the proper efforts and proper programs. I think this bill is a fine step in that direction."

The amount of spending would be boosted to $250 million for next year and to $325 million the following year. Preyer indicated that the passage of the bill would not be a total solution to the problem.

"The 1970 amendments to the Clean Air Act do what we know how to do, no more no less," he said. "They offer no final solution, but it does represent the most significant legislation ever passed...to meet the problem of air pollution in this nation."

During discussion of the bill proponents estimated that automobiles alone dump 90 million tons of pollutants into the air.

The Tar Heel legislator noted that setting national standards was one of the key points of the bill. "The national standards will be the minimum standards and states are free to insist on higher standards," he added. "Further, the bill attacks government pollution, and says all government installations must conform to state and national standards."

The pollution measure will cut through some of the red tape plaguing the enforcement of the 1967 act. "The maximum time in which each state must come forward with a plan under this act is 360 days," Preyer noted, "not four years as under the old act."

"We are embarking now on a new experiment in government, an experiment to determine whether we are wise enough to direct our affairs in a way which recognizes the essential interdependence of man and his environment."

A congressman keeps in touch with the voters "back home" primarily as a way of winning reelection. But some of his self-serving activities also help educate the public. A representative's newsletters to his constituents, the speeches and tours he makes in his district or state, the publications and documents he supplies to constituents also serve important educational functions in American democracy.

Members of Congress are political educators, and many consider their educational services to be an important part of their job. Virtually all congressmen feel that they have some responsibility to inform and politically educate the people they represent.

Investigator of, Consultant to, and Lobbyist for the Executive Branch

When a law is passed, Congress does not lose interest in it. Members of Congress are interested in how the law is administered. When the law is administered poorly, congressmen are likely to hear complaints from constituents. Therefore, many members of Congress believe that one of their most important roles is to check on the activities of the executive branch of government.

Members of Congress have a number of ways of exercising control over the executive branch. Congress can create, alter, and abolish agencies. It can grant or withhold funds from agencies. It can prohibit certain agency actions. Even the appointment of Cabinet officials and some other top bureaucrats must receive approval by the Senate before becoming effective.

On the left, House Minority Leader Gerald Ford and Senate Minority Leader Hugh Scott, along with other Republican congressional leaders, confer with President Nixon on the progress of the Administration's legislative program.

Congressmen not only supervise or check on the administrative branch but also frequently act as consultants for the administration. A congressman who serves on the same congressional committee for many years becomes an expert in the legislation handled by that committee. A long-time member of the House Armed Services Committee may know more about certain aspects of the military establishment than does an Assistant Secretary of Defense testifying before the committee. Moreover, a few congressmen have even exchanged roles: resigning from Congress to become a Cabinet member or winning election to Congress after having served in the executive branch. Congressman Melvin Laird was recognized as an expert on national defense. He resigned his House seat to become Secretary of the Department of Defense when President Nixon took office in 1969. Senator Symington was once Secretary of the Air Force before being elected to the Senate. Thus, upon his election, the Senate acquired an expert on defense matters.

A congressman may also serve as kind of a lobbyist for a particular executive department or bureau. (A lobbyist is a person who is hired by some group—labor union, farm organization, teachers' association, etc.—to get favorable legislation passed and unfavorable bills defeated through contact with legislators.) A member of the House Veterans Affairs Committee, for example, may work extra hard to get other congressmen to support legislation desired by the Veterans Administration. A member of the House Committee on Agriculture may lobby for measures supported by the United States Department of Agriculture.

The Department of Defense is an example of a Federal agency that cultivates the friendship of important Senators and Representatives and depends upon them to rally congressional support for defense appropriations. Once an agency has convinced a key member of the appropriate committee that its requests are justified, it may count upon the congressman to rally support within the Congress. Moreover, a friendly committee chairman can help influence the public as well. When people are invited by a congressional committee to testify for and against a particular bill, the chairman may arrange witnesses friendly to the department's position to have ample time to develop their arguments while critics of the department are given scant attention. Thus the committee chairman can influence the flow of news that Americans will receive about the topic under investigation.

C. The Legislative Role

While the roles described in the preceding lesson are important and occupy much of a congressman's time, he is first and foremost a lawmaker. As a lawmaker, he is also a political decision-maker.

Time Devoted to the Legislative Role

Most of a congressman's time is devoted to his legislative role. One study found that the average representative spent 59.3 hours per week at his job while Congress was in session. The amount of time he devoted to various

Table 1. Typical Work Week of a United States Congressman

Hours	Activity	Percent of Work Week
15.3	Attending sessions of the House of Representatives	25.8%
7.2	Legislative research and reading	12.1
7.1	Committee work on legislation	12.0
7.2	Answering mail	12.1
5.1	Handling constituent problems	8.6
4.4	Visiting with constituents in Washington	7.4
3.5	Committee work outside of committee meetings	5.9
2.4	Leadership and party functions	4.0
2.7	Writing chores, speeches, magazine articles, etc.	4.6
2.3	Meeting with lobbyists and lobby groups	3.9
2.1	Press work, radio and TV	3.5
59.3		99.9%

activities is shown in *Table 1*. Which five or six of the activities listed in *Table 1* seem to be most directly related to the legislative role? Using these five or six categories, compute the total percentage of time an average Congressman devotes directly to his legislative role.

It is not surprising that members of Congress devote such a large percentage of their time to strictly legislative matters. The legislative demands made upon Congress are enormous. Members of the First Congress (1787–1789) introduced only 144 bills. Since that time the volume of bills introduced in each Congress has grown sharply, reaching a peak with the 66th Congress (1909–1911), during which 44,000 separate bills were introduced. Today each Congress is likely to receive more than 25,000 bills—both public and private—during its two-year term. The First Congress passed 108 public bills. Today between 600 and 1000 public bills are likely to be passed by the two sessions of a Congress. It is apparent that simply introducing a bill is no guarantee that it will become a law. In fact, most bills do not become laws. The vast majority expire somewhere along the legislative path.

The legislative role of a congressman may be analyzed according to the following tasks:

1. Deciding upon a bill to introduce, drafting the bill, and introducing it.
2. Lining up political support for one's bill.
3. Studying bills that have been introduced by others, including reading arguments for and against the measure; listening to lobbyists, colleagues, constituents, party leaders, and representatives of the executive branch.
4. Working in committee on legislation, including listening to witnesses, discussing bills with committee colleagues, testifying before other committees, and drafting amendments to bills.

A "public bill" is of concern to the entire nation. A "private bill" is for the benefit of a specific individual, e.g., a bill to permit the immigration of a person beyond the usual quota.

321

CONGRESSIONAL DISTRICT REAPPORTIONMENT IN INDIANA

BEFORE 1966

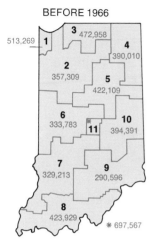

AFTER 1966

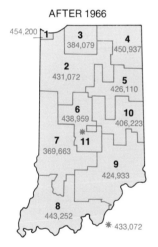

Population figures based on the 1960 Census.

One Congressman elected from each District.

Indiana's congressional districts were redrawn in 1966 to make each district more equal in population. Can you guess why Districts 1 and 11 are so small in area?

5. Participating in and listening to floor debate on bills.
6. Voting on the measure.

The way these tasks will be performed is influenced by a number of formal and informal rules.

The Influence of Formal Rules on the Legislative Role

The most apparent influences on legislative behavior are the rules which specify the legislative role. Most of the major rules can be found in the Constitution (Article I, p. 534). Other rules have been established by the Congress itself.

A bicameral legislature. The Constitution established a two-house (bicameral) legislature consisting of a Senate and a House of Representatives. The states were to be represented equally in the Senate (two Senators per state), but in proportion to population in the House of Representatives. Today a few of the smaller states have only one Representative each, while California—the most populous state—was entitled to 43 members of the House of Representatives beginning in 1972.

A necessary result of having a bicameral national legislature rather than a unicameral (one-house) body is that both houses must pass the identical bill—down to the commas and periods—before it can be sent to the President for his signature and thereby become law. Therefore, either the House of Representatives or the Senate can halt legislation desired by the other body. (In 1970, for example, the two houses failed to agree on a constitutional amendment providing for the direct election of the President, and the measure therefore failed.) Because the two houses must pass the identical bill or resolution, either the House of Representatives or the Senate can halt legislation desired by the other body. This means that much negotiation and compromise must occur between the two houses on many bills before they are ready for final passage.

Special duties of each house. The Constitution also gave special responsibilities to one house that it did not give to the other. For example, all tax bills must start in the House of Representatives. This has led to a very powerful House Ways and Means Committee that deals with all tax measures. The Constitution provides that all treaties must be approved by the Senate. (Approval by the House of Representatives is not required for treaties.) This provision has led to the establishment of a strong Senate Foreign Relations Committee that is much more influential than the House Committee on Foreign Affairs.

Terms of office and areas represented. Both Senators and Representatives are chosen by direct election. Representatives are elected for two-year terms from congressional districts created by the legislature of the state in which the district is found. Senators are elected for six-year terms by the residents of the state as a whole.

The total number of Representatives allotted to each state is based upon the total population of the state. Today, theoretically, there should be one Representative for approximately each 485,000 people. Nevertheless, some congressional districts represent much more than this figure and others less. Two Senators are chosen from each state in state-wide elections. As senatorial terms are staggered, voters of a given state are seldom asked to vote for both Senators in any one year.

The fact that Representatives are elected for a two-year term by voters in a specific district is an important influence on their role behavior. A Congressman must begin to think about the next election almost immediately after winning the last one. This requires that he devote special attention to legislative affairs that are important to his constituents. The fact that a Congressman is elected from a single district (for example, a section of a large city or several rural counties) means that he is more likely to feel responsive to a particular kind of constituency than a Senator who is elected by the entire state.

Size of the two houses. The First Congress consisted of a Senate of 26 members (two for each of the original thirteen states) and a House of Representatives of 65 members. With the addition of states the Senate has grown to nearly four times its original size. But the House of Representatives has increased more than six times. Finally in 1929 the Congress determined that the House should remain at 435 members. Chiefly because of the difference in size of membership, a Senator ordinarily serves on two major committees while a Representative serves on only one. Also debate on the floor of the House is strictly limited, while the Senate has been reluctant to pass rules that would interfere with unlimited debate.

Both houses of Congress have elaborate rules governing lawmaking procedures. In general, because of its greater number of members, the House tends to have more restrictive rules than does the Senate.

The Influence of Informal Rules

The legislative role is also influenced by a number of informal rules. These represent a series of expectations that new members must learn quickly if they are to be accepted by their colleagues in the Congress.

Courtesy. Over the years a special system of courtesy has evolved that is distinctive to the Congress and is followed by all its members. Neither Senators nor Representatives may direct personal criticism at each other, regardless of how much they may disagree with one another. While they may disagree vigorously in debate, they must always speak politely when referring to their opponent. Moreover, all remarks made on the floor are, technically, addressed to the presiding officer. Therefore, a member of Congress is always addressed in the third person on the floor of the Senate or House. This custom enables congressmen who differ on an issue to attack the arguments put forward by the other side without appearing to be making a personal attack on the individual who disagrees with him.

These are scenes from the Senate wing of the Capitol. At left is a Senate reception hall. Below are books in the Senate Document Room.

Following is an extract from a discussion that occurred on the floor of the Senate on January 22, 1969. The discussion was about Senate Concurrent Resolution 3, which urged the President to make relief supplies available to the people of Biafra. Some of the long speeches have been edited in order to focus your attention upon the forms of courtesy used by the Senators:

Mr. SCOTT. Mr. President, will the distinguished Senator yield?

Mr. PEARSON. I am happy to yield to the Senator from Pennsylvania.

Mr. SCOTT. I congratulate the Senator from Kansas and those who have joined with him in a proposal . . . which recognizes that the great heart of America is enlisted wherever famine, hunger, disease, and tragedy of this sort become pervasive and so burdensome that the local authorities and local governments involved are either unable or in some cases unwilling to meet it.

Therefore, I most heartily commend the distinguished Senator for having brought this matter to the attention of the Senate. . . .

Mr. PEARSON. I thank the Senator from Pennsylvania.

Mr. BYRD of West Virginia. Mr. President, will the Senator yield?

The VICE PRESIDENT. The time of the Senator from Kansas has expired.

Mr. BYRD of West Virginia. Mr. President, I ask unanimous consent that the distinguished Senator from Kansas may be permitted to proceed for three additional minutes.

The VICE PRESIDENT. Without objection, it is so ordered.

Mr. BYRD of West Virginia. Mr. President, I wish to join in applauding the distinguished Senator from Kansas and the able Senator from Massachusetts [Mr. Brooke] for having provided the leadership in preparing this concurrent resolution, and I congratulate them on acquiring the great number of sponsors—among whom I am one—who have joined in cosponsoring the resolution. . . .

Mr. KENNEDY. Mr. President, I should like to identify myself with the remarks of the distinguished Senator from Kansas. I am a cosponsor of the concurrent resolution. . . .

Mr. PEARSON. Mr. President, I ask unanimous consent to respond to the Senator from Massachusetts for 1 minute.

The VICE PRESIDENT. Without objection, it is so ordered.

Mr. PEARSON. I thank the Senator from Massachusetts for his cosponsorship of the proposal. I think he recognized, in joining us, that we were seeking to attack the problem of mass starvation. The Senator from Massachusetts, as I recall, was perhaps the first Senator to speak in the Chamber on this subject. . . .*

*Congressional Record, Vol. 115, No. 14 (January 22, 1969), S729–S732.

Senator Alben Barkley once advised a freshman Senator that if he thought a colleague was stupid, he should refer to him as "the able, learned and distinguished senator." If he *knows* he is stupid, he should call him "the *very* able, learned and distinguished senator."

We should recognize that such forms of courtesy serve an important function for members of the Congress. The issues debated in Congress are sensitive issues about which Americans have strong feelings. In order for laws to be passed that will enable the government to cope with these issues, the members of Congress must cooperate. Even if you know a man is a fool, you cannot call him one because that would wound him and likely make him a lasting enemy. While you may disagree with another member on the current issue, you may need his support at another time. Therefore, great care is given to keep debates and arguments focused upon the issues and carefully steered away from the personalities of the individuals involved.

Apprenticeship. Both the House and Senate expect new members to "take a back seat" and let others do most of the talking. Taking a "back seat" is literally true in the Senate, where seating is assigned according to seniority and the most recently elected Senators are assigned desks at the back of the chamber.

New members are expected not to participate in debate within the chamber. Occasionally, if the debate is about an issue on which a freshman member has a special knowledge, he may speak briefly. Usually, however, the debate is conducted and managed by veterans of the House and Senate.

Specialization. Closely related to the issue of apprenticeship is the custom of specialization. While in one sense all members of Congress are specialists in making laws, no member of Congress can be fully informed about all the issues that will be covered by bills in any single year. For example, on a single day, July 30, 1969, the following bills and resolutions were introduced in the Senate:

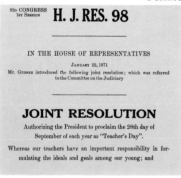

(1) Senator Gaylord Nelson (Wisconsin) introduced a bill (S. 2729) to amend the Federal Food, Drug, and Cosmetic Act to provide for the establishment of a national drug testing and evaluation center. The bill was referred to the Committee on Labor and Public Welfare.

(2) Senator Quentin Burdick (North Dakota) introduced a private bill (S. 2730) to provide assistance for one of his constituents. It was referred to the Committee on the Judiciary.

(3) Senator Warren Magnuson (Washington) introduced a bill (S. 2731) to provide for the protection, alteration, reconstruction, relocation, or replacement of highway bridges, trestles, and other structures over the Columbia and the Snake rivers. It was referred to the Committee on Commerce.

(4) Senator Abraham Ribicoff (Connecticut) introduced two private bills (S. 2732 and S. 2733) to provide relief for two of his constituents. The bills were referred to the Committee on the Judiciary. He also introduced a bill (S. 2734) together with three other Senators that would grant the consent of Congress to the establishment of the Connecticut-New York railroad passenger transportation compact. This bill was referred to the Committee on the Judiciary.

(5) Senator Gale McGee (Wyoming) introduced a bill (S. 2735) that would provide for the transfer of certain public lands in Wyoming to the

people who live on it. The bill was referred to the Committee on Interior and Insular Affairs.

(6) Senator Theodore Stevens (Alaska) submitted three bills:

S. 2736 would amend the Internal Revenue Code of 1954 to permit certain employees to establish qualified pension plans for themselves in the same manner as if they were self-employed. This bill was referred to the Committee on Finance.

S. 2737 would authorize an increase in the average cost of dwelling units in certain Federally assisted housing in Alaska. This bill was referred to the Committee on Banking and Currency.

S. 2738 would amend the Interstate Commerce Act in order to extend regulations of the act to carriers previously not covered by its provisions. This bill was referred to the Committee on Commerce.

(7) Senator Vance Hartke (Indiana) along with twenty-three other Senators introduced Senate Resolution 228, which called upon President Nixon to resubmit the Geneva Protocol to the Senate for advice and consent. The Geneva Protocol was written in 1925 and signed by the United States representative but never ratified by the Senate. The Geneva Protocol was a ban on the use of all gases and bacteriological weapons during wartime. Concern over American stockpiling of weapons of this type led some Senators to call upon the President to send the Geneva Protocol to the Senate for action, thereby putting the United States on record against the use of such weapons.

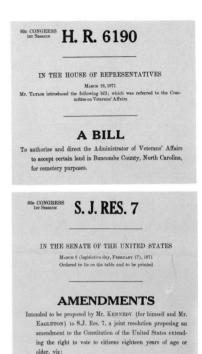

On the same day that these bills and resolution were introduced in the Senate, other bills were being presented to the House of Representatives. Throughout the morning various committees met to hear testimony on bills previously submitted or worked to rewrite bills. On the Senate floor that afternoon debate centered on a bill that would give the Department of Defense permission to spend $20 billion.

No single Senator or Representative can hope to be fully informed about all of these issues. The best he can do is become expert on (a) topics that come before the committees on which he serves and (b) issues that are of major concern to his own constituents.

In 1970 there were sixteen standing committees in the Senate and twenty-one in the House. The committee system was devised as a technique for handling the mass of legislative proposals coming before Congress each year. Most Congressmen belong to only one standing committee; Senators belong to more than one. Therefore, a relatively new member of the House representing an agricultural district in Kansas might be a member of the Post Office and Civil Service Committee. As a member of that Committee he would become a specialist in Post Office and civil service matters. As a representative from an agricultural district, he would feel also an obligation to be fully informed about agricultural legislation.

A standing committee is a committee that is permanently provided for by House or Senate rules. A standing committee may be compared to special committees created for unusual circumstances.

The custom, therefore, is for members of Congress to become expert on only certain topics that come before Congress. Often congressmen must vote

Copyright 1971 by Herblock in the *Washington Post*

"Enter and kneel!"

Copyright 1960 *St. Louis Post-Dispatch*, reproduced by courtesy of Bill Mauldin

"Play ball!"

While the House Rules Committee generally aids the flow of important measures, it does at times—as Mauldin points out—obstruct the legislative game. What point is Herblock making in the cartoon on the left?

on measures about which they have little knowledge or understanding. On such occasions they turn to others for advice on how to vote.

Seniority. *Apprenticeship* and *specialization* are related to the practice of seniority in Congress. Seniority is the custom of giving privileges on the basis of length of time served in a legislative body. It takes a number of forms. For one, members who have served longest have first choice for committee assignments when vacancies occur on committees. Some committees are more important, hence more desirable, than others. In the House, "Rules," "Ways and Means," and "Appropriations" are considered to be especially important committees. Since 1946 no first-term member has been assigned to the Rules Committee.

The Rules Committee is very important because it decides the order in which bills will be considered, the amount of time allowed for debate, and whether or not a bill may be amended from the floor. More important, it decides which bills will be brought up for a vote at all. Bills introduced in the House are first screened by the other standing committees. But even after this process there are more bills than the House can properly consider and vote upon. The Rules Committee will ordinarily advance the bills desired by the leadership of the majority party in the House.

Seniority also determines the committee chairmanships. The committee member of the majority party in the House or Senate who has served longest on the committee receives the chairmanship. Seniority determines where members sit at the committee table and affects their opportunities to participate, with freshmen members having the least opportunity to take part in debate.

328

Standing Committees of Congress in 1970

HOUSE COMMITTEES

Agriculture	House Administration	Post Office and Civil Service
Appropriations	Interior and Insular Affairs	Public Works
Armed Services	Internal Security	Rules
Banking and Currency	Interstate and Foreign Commerce	Science and Astronautics
District of Columbia	Judiciary	Standards of Official Conduct
Education and Labor	Merchant Marine and Fisheries	Veterans Affairs
Foreign Affairs		Ways and Means
Government Operations		

SENATE COMMITTEES

Aeronautical and Space Sciences	Commerce	Judiciary
Agriculture and Forestry	District of Columbia	Labor and Public Welfare
Appropriations	Finance	Post Office and Civil Service
Armed Services	Foreign Relations	Public Works
Banking and Currency	Government Operations	Rules and Administration
	Interior and Insular Affairs	

The customs relating to *seniority, specialization,* and *apprenticeship* tend to center power in the hands of those congressmen who have served the longest. Those who defend these customs assert that they assure that Congress will have the advantage of wisdom resulting from experience. Those who oppose these customs claim that they tend to give congressmen with conservative political ideas too much power and that they prevent fresh ideas from being considered.

Reciprocity. Often bills are introduced that are of little concern to some members of Congress. They do not really care very much whether the bill passes or not. In such a situation a member may be willing to vote the way a colleague wants him to vote in hope that the colleague will return the favor at some time in the future. Therefore, I might vote to build a new post office in your district if you will vote for a dam in my district. Such a practice is sometimes referred to as "logrolling." In short, it is a practice of doing favors for others in anticipation of receiving favors in return.

> Reciprocity: a giving of something of equal value in return for a favor.

Personality Affects Legislative Role Behavior

Formal rules and customs have considerable influence on the way a congressman will play his role. Nevertheless, the rules and customs affect 535 different personalities in almost as many different ways. It is not surprising, therefore, that no congressman plays his role in exactly the same way as do

The Legislative Reorganization Act of 1946 reduced the number of standing committees, provided committees with staff members, required the registration of lobbyists, forbade certain kinds of private bills and raised congressional salaries.

other congressmen. Each congressman brings his own personality to Washington, D.C., and this will influence how he interprets the legislative role.

For example, in 1946 the Legislative Reorganization Act created a Senate Committee on Government Operations, which in turn established a Permanent Subcommittee on Investigations. Little was heard of this subcommittee until 1952, when Wisconsin's Senator Joseph R. McCarthy became its chairman. Under McCarthy's leadership the subcommittee undertook a series of investigations of alleged Communists in the Federal executive branch. Senator McCarthy had attracted public attention in February, 1950, as a result of a speech he delivered in Wheeling, West Virginia. In it he claimed that the Department of State was full of Communists and that he and the Secretary of State knew their names. For the next four years he was the object of fear by some, adoration by others, and much publicity.

In 1954 the Senate censured him—largely because he violated certain informal rules of the Senate, not because of his anti-Communist activities—and his power waned. The subcommittee he had headed reverted to its former quiet role. It is clear that the activity of the subcommittee had been influenced strongly by Chairman McCarthy. Other chairmen before and after, with different personalities, behaved quite differently.

Members of Congress are relatively free to decide how they will spend their time—which aspects of their role they will emphasize. One congressman may spend most of his time dealing with committee affairs while another devotes more time to meetings with constituents. One congressman may come to be identified primarily as a spokesman for a particular point of view or cause (for example, civil rights), for a particular pressure group or lobby (for example, the American Legion), or for the executive branch. Some may become party leaders in the House and Senate. Some may become recognized as skilled legislative strategists and compromisers who know how to get bills passed. (President Lyndon Johnson had such a reputation when he was majority leader of the Senate.) One may seek a reputation as a statesman who stands above partisan conflict; while others are remembered as great orators or as intellectuals who wrote books and articles about their work. These and other variations on the congressional role are possible. Rules, custom, and personality all play their part in determining how the legislative role will be played.

Senator Joseph McCarthy is here giving testimony at a televised hearing held by his Senate subcommittee in the spring of 1954. The hearing dealt with a dispute between McCarthy and the Army. At McCarthy's right is Attorney Joseph N. Welch, counsel for the Army.

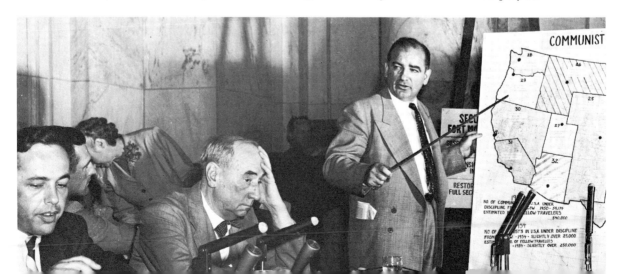

Summary. What, then, is a Senator or a Congressman? He is a legislator, an ombudsman, a political campaigner and educator, and an investigator. But he is also a father and husband—when he can find time. Whatever else one can say about members of Congress, the vast majority are very busy, *public* men and women. They work in a city where politics is the principal business. Dinners, luncheons, even casual conversations are used for political purposes. When a member of Congress travels, he is often recognized as a public personality; people seek him out, requesting advice and favors. He receives more mail than he can answer personally; he has more to read than he will ever have time for. With insufficient information, often depending upon the advice of trusted friends and colleagues, he often must make decisions that will affect the lives of millions of Americans. He must appear to be both the servant of his constituents while remaining their leader. He must often compromise while appearing to stick by his principles. He must not lose his patience but remain at all times courteous with his colleagues and constituents, reserving his frustrations for the only group of people absolutely loyal to him—his staff and family. A successful member of Congress is a political man—an appropriate product of a democratic political system.

D. A Typical Day in the Life of a Member of Congress

In the previous two lessons you learned about four roles played by members of Congress. Below is printed a typical day's schedule in the life of a hypothetical United States Senator. While we have selected a Senator for the exercise, a Representative's schedule would be similar in many ways, although the institutional setting would be different.

Your task is to analyze the typical schedule according to the four roles treated in the two previous lessons. An additional role—father and husband—has been added, since some of a Senator's activities each day would relate to that role. Some of the items on the schedule may require more than one role designation. The roles are:

Legislator (L)
Ombudsman (O)
Political Educator and Campaigner (PEC)
Investigator of, Consultant to, and Lobbyist for the Executive Branch of the
    Government (IC)
Father and Husband (FH)

Senator Brown's Calendar—March 10, 19—

6:30—Awakened, read the *Congressional Record* and two local newspapers.

7:45—Had breakfast with my wife; she drove me to Senate Office Building.

8:45—Arrived at office. Staff already there; dictated replies to the 25 most important letters selected from a stack of telegrams and letters 15 inches high; met with administrative assistant and other members of staff regarding day's agenda.

Congressional Record

United States of America

PROCEEDINGS AND DEBATES OF THE 92ᵈ CONGRESS, FIRST SESSION

Vol. 117   WASHINGTON, THURSDAY, FEBRUARY 11, 1971   No. 16

House of Representatives

The House was not in session today. Its next meeting will be held on Wednesday, February 17, 1971, at 12 o'clock noon.

Senate

THURSDAY, FEBRUARY 11, 1971

(Legislative day of Tuesday, January 26, 1971)

The Senate met at 11:45 a.m., on the expiration of the recess, and was called to order by the President pro tempore (Mr. Ellender).

The Chaplain, the Reverend Edward L. R. Elson, D.D., offered the following prayer.

Almighty God, by whose providence this Nation was brought forth and in whose will it has been preserved, keep us ever mindful of Thy goodness and mercy which has been over us from the beginning until now. As with grateful hearts we honor the heroes of old, spare us from merely admiring the past when we would be doers of great deeds in the present. Help us to lift high the banner of freedom in our time not only in eloquent phrase but in practical programs. Let the mantle of Washington and of Lincoln fall upon their sons in this age. In faith and hope that sends a shining ray far down the future's broadening way, send us to our tasks here, our travels and our talks beyond, with hearts aglow with the inspiration of Thy spirit.

In the Master's name. Amen.

THE JOURNAL

Mr. MANSFIELD. Mr. President, I ask unanimous consent that the Journal of the proceedings of Wednesday, February 10, 1971, be approved.

The PRESIDENT pro tempore. Without objection, it is so ordered.

COMMITTEE MEETINGS DURING SENATE SESSION

Mr. MANSFIELD. Mr. President, I ask unanimous consent that all committees be authorized to meet during the session of the Senate today.

The PRESIDENT pro tempore. Without objection, it is so ordered.

POSTAL SERVICE PASSPORT APPLICATION FEES

Mr. MANSFIELD. Mr. President, I ask unanimous consent that the Senate proceed to the consideration of Calendar No. 6, S. 531.

The PRESIDENT pro tempore. Is there objection?

There being no objection, the bill (S.

ment and shall continue in effect until June 30, 1975.

EXECUTIVE SESSION

Mr. MANSFIELD. Mr. President, I ask unanimous consent that the Senate go into executive session, to consider certain nominations on the Executive Calendar.

The PRESIDENT pro tempore. Is there objection?

There being no objection, the Senate proceeded to consider executive business.

NATIONAL CREDIT UNION BOARD

The legislative clerk proceeded to read sundry nominations to the National Credit Union Board.

Mr. MANSFIELD. Mr. President, I ask unanimous consent that the nominations be considered en bloc.

The PRESIDENT pro tempore. Without objection, the nominations will be considered en bloc; and, without objection, they are confirmed.

ED EDMONDSON

90TH CONGRESS H-97

9:45—Called the Veterans Administration about a problem concerning a constituent who had been denied treatment at a Veterans Hospital.

9:55—Talked for five minutes by long-distance telephone to a newspaper editor from one of the major city newspapers in my state. As a result of call, newspaper has agreed to support a bill I am sponsoring.

10:00—Attended meeting of Senate Aeronautical and Space Sciences Committee; listened to and questioned witnesses who appeared there to support the space bill being considered by the Committee.

10:45—Was called from Committee room to talk to a constituent who is looking for a job in Washington and who wondered whether I could help him.

11:00—Returned to Committee room in time for testimony by Director of the National Aeronautics and Space Agency; questioned him very closely about published reports that much money is being wasted by rushing the program to land a man on the moon.

12:00—Went to Senate floor for opening of the day's Senate business; gave a five-minute speech urging the President to find a way to stop the hijacking of American commercial airplanes to Cuba; this speech, suggested by my administrative assistant, is certain to be given a play in the newspapers and on TV news and attract favorable publicity.

12:30—Left Senate floor to have lunch with a group of businessmen from a community in my state who want help in securing a "model cities" grant from the government.

1:45—Returned to Senate and listened to debate on farm bill.

2:00—Spotted a Senate colleague who is sponsoring a bill that is opposed by important groups in my state. We left the floor, and I tried to talk him into dropping some of its most objectionable features; had little success, but we agreed to meet again tomorrow.

2:30—Returned to Senate floor to vote on compromise amendments to farm bill under consideration by the entire Senate.

3:00—Left Senate floor to talk to a constituent who would like an appointment to West Point for his son; told him to go to my office where application forms would be given to him.

3:20—Returned to Senate floor to vote on two additional amendments to farm bill; voted "nay" to one and would have voted "nay" to the other but for party leadership who asked for a "yes" vote on it.

3:45—Dictated letters to my secretary in room off the Senate floor.

4:15—Returned to Senate floor for last vote of the day.

4:30—Returned to office; placed five long-distance telephone calls that had come in during the day; signed letters.

5:30—Placed telephone calls to six Federal agency officials regarding problems facing several of my constituents.

6:45—Returned to Senate to have three editorials from newspapers in my state placed in the appendix of the *Congressional Record.* I try to make certain that at least one editorial from each newspaper in my state is printed in the *Congressional Record* sometime during the year.

7:30—Arrived at downtown Washington hotel for dinner with the chancellor of the state university; he is interested in obtaining support for an expensive new science laboratory on the campus.

10:30—Took a briefcase full of committee work home; read and worked on committee business for more than an hour.

11:45—Had a glass of milk, visited with my wife and went to bed.

E. The 1964 Civil Rights Act: A Case Study in Legislative Role Behavior

On July 2, 1964, President Lyndon B. Johnson signed the Civil Rights Act. Exactly one year before, President John F. Kennedy had urged Congress to pass a strong civil rights law. From July 2, 1963, to July 2, 1964, much had occurred to influence the passage of civil rights legislation. These events leading to the passage of the strongest civil rights law in a century provide an opportunity to observe how the legislative role is played.

Civil rights was not a new issue for lawmakers in 1963. Each year from 1945 to 1957, a bill dealing with civil rights was introduced in Congress; and each time it failed. Through executive action and as a result of Supreme Court decisions, the civil rights of ethnic minorities, especially black people, had become increasingly recognized. Nevertheless, efforts to pass laws against racial discrimination had failed. Although civil rights bills were finally passed in 1957 and 1961, they were so weakened by compromise that they failed to achieve their purpose.

Apparently President Kennedy had not intended to make civil rights a major part of his legislative program in 1963. The issue was not mentioned in his State of the Union message. Probably he was more concerned about getting other bills passed, including an important tax-reduction plan. But he had not foreseen how important the issues surrounding civil rights would become to Americans that year.

Public Opinion Becomes Aroused

In 1963 a storm of "black protest" was sweeping the Southern part of the United States. "Freedom rides," "sit-ins," boycotts, "freedom marches," and picketing were focusing the attention of the nation upon the complaints of black people and their demands for legal changes. It was the centennial year of Lincoln's Emancipation Proclamation. One hundred years had passed since Lincoln proclaimed his famous "Freedom Now" edict. But most Negroes in the United States, especially in the South, did not feel free in 1963. They pointed to the segregation system that kept them from using public facilities on equal terms with whites. They pointed to the caste system of the South

Civil rights demonstrators at Selma, Alabama, dramatized the need for Negro voting registration in the South.

that kept Negroes at the lowest levels of the American society. In 1963, as in 1863, black protesters were shouting "freedom now."

Several organizations were providing effective leadership for the black protesters of 1963. The dominant leader was Baptist minister Dr. Martin Luther King, Jr. At the head of his Southern Christian Leadership Conference (SCLC),

Dr. King marched into Birmingham, Alabama in April, 1963. He called Birmingham the most "segregated city in America."

For the next two months Americans watched while Birmingham suffered racial turmoil. When city officials refused Dr. King permission to lead his followers on peaceful marches through the city to demonstrate the opposition of blacks to the segregation practices in Birmingham, he and his followers marched anyway, breaking the law. They were met with fire hoses and police dogs. Many black protesters were arrested, including Dr. King, but the protest marches continued. Violence erupted on May 11 when the home of Dr. King's brother was bombed. In September, the 16th Street Baptist Church in Montgomery was bombed and four Negro girls killed. A short time later, two Negro boys were shot and killed by whites in Birmingham. Further, Medgar Evers, a black protest leader in Mississippi, was fatally shot outside his home.

The nation was shocked by this violence. Many whites around the country were angered by the sight of peaceful black demonstrators being clubbed by

white policemen, water-hosed by white firemen, and bitten by police dogs. Sympathy for Dr. King's cause began to grow. This sympathy was often expressed in letters to congressmen urging support for a civil rights law that would end segregation. *A climate of public opinion favorable to passage of a civil rights law was beginning to develop.*

A Bill Is Introduced

On June 11, 1963, President Kennedy appeared on network television to help build public opinion in support of his proposed legislation. He told the American people:

> It ought to be possible for every American to enjoy the privileges of being American without regard to his race or his color. In short, every American ought to have the right to be treated as one would wish his children to be treated. But this is not the case.
>
> The Negro baby born in America today, regardless of the section of the nation in which he is born, has about one-half as much chance of completing high school as a white baby born in the same place on the same day, one-third as much chance of completing college, one-third as much chance of becoming a professional man, twice as much chance of becoming unemployed, about one-seventh as much chance of earning $10,000 a year, a life expectancy which is seven years shorter, and the prospects of earning only half as much.
>
> This is not a sectional issue. Difficulties over segregation and discrimination exist in every city, in every State of the Union, producing in many cities a rising tide of discontent that threatens the public safety. . . . This is not even a legal or legislative issue alone. It is better to settle these matters in the courts than on the streets, and new laws are needed at every level, but law alone cannot make men see right.
>
> We are confronted primarily with a moral issue. It is as old as the scriptures and is as clear as the American Constitution.
>
> The heart of the question is whether all Americans are to be afforded equal rights and opportunities, whether we are going to treat our fellow Americans as we want to be treated. If an American, because his skin is dark, cannot eat lunch in a restaurant open to the public, if he cannot send his children to the best public school available, if he cannot vote for the public officials who represent him, if, in short, he cannot enjoy the full and free life which all of us want, then who among us would be content to have the color of his skin changed and stand in his place? Who among us would then be content with the counsels of patience and delay?
>
> One hundred years of delay have passed since President Lincoln freed the slaves, yet their heirs, their grandsons, are not fully free. They are not yet freed from the bonds of injustice. They are not yet freed from social and economic oppression, and this Nation for all its hopes and all its boasts, will not be fully free until all its citizens are free. . . .

Within a few days following President Kennedy's address, two identical bills, S. 1731 and H.R. 7152, drafted by the Attorney General's office and carrying the endorsement of President Kennedy, were submitted to the Senate and House of Representatives. Over 150 other civil rights bills were introduced in 1963. But because S. 1731 and H.R. 7152 had the backing of the President, this was the bill Congress would consider, oppose, defend, strengthen, weaken, rewrite, and finally pass.

The House of Representatives Acts on the Bill

House bill 7152 was referred to the Judiciary Committee, which in turn assigned it to a subcommittee for study. Congressman Emanuel Celler, the subcommittee chairman, was also chairman of the House Judiciary Committee. Celler, a Democrat from Brooklyn, and William M. McCulloch of Ohio, the senior Republican on the Judiciary Committee, provided important leadership in the subcommittee hearings.

Congressman Celler, an outspoken supporter of civil rights, represented a district populated by ethnic, racial, and religious minority groups. Representative Celler also had a long and close relationship with the Democratic party leadership and could be depended upon to support party positions.

Congressman McCulloch, a Republican, represented an Ohio district with very few Negro voters and a constituency which appeared to have little interest in civil rights legislation. For Representative McCulloch, civil rights in 1964 had become a matter of personal belief. He was eager to see a strong civil rights law passed because he thought it was the right thing to do.

To the surprise of everyone concerned, including the committee's leaders, Celler and McCulloch, the subcommittee strengthened rather than weakened the administration bill. In fact it added a section on fair employment which had not been included in the original bill.

Paul Conrad in the *Denver Post* © 1963

"Stand back, everybody! He's got a bomb."

Brooks in *The Birmingham News*

Awaiting Orders

On the left, Conrad comments on the use of force against Birmingham blacks. The Brooks cartoon points to a big increase in government interference with business—property rights—under a strong civil rights law. This cartoon appeared in March, 1964, during Senate debate on the bill.

Conrad cartoon by permission of the Register and Tribune Syndicate

While the bill would undergo further changes, deletions, and additions before it was finally signed into law, the main provisions of the bill approved by the subcommittee remained essentially unchanged. The five main features of the bill were as follows:

337

Voting: The bill provided far more effective enforcement of the right to vote in Federal elections. The misuse of literacy tests and registration forms to disqualify voters on racial grounds was forbidden.

Public Accommodations: Hotels, motels, and other lodging places with more than five rooms were required to serve all customers regardless of race. Racial discrimination was also outlawed in restaurants, lunchrooms, theaters, sports arenas, and other places of entertainment which affect interstate commerce. Private clubs were not covered by the law.

Public Places: Discrimination and segregation were outlawed in public places such as parks, playgrounds, pools, and libraries.

Schools: The United States Attorney General was given power to bring to court all complaints of school segregation.

Employment: All individuals, regardless of race, were to have an equal opportunity to get a job. Employers, labor unions, and employment agencies were prohibited from discriminating on the basis of racial identity.

The bill was approved in the subcommittee by an interesting coalition of Congressmen. Liberal Democrats who had spoken for years, unsuccessfully, for a strong bill were joined by Northern Republicans, who did not wish the Democrats to take complete credit for it. In addition, a few anti-civil rights Southern Democrats voted for the strengthened bill in the belief that because it *was* strong it could be more easily defeated later.

Since the Judiciary Committee contained a larger number of Southern Congressmen, it was more conservative on civil rights issues than either the subcommittee or the House of Representatives as a whole. Chairman Celler anticipated that the Committee would try to weaken the bill or defeat it altogether, as they had done with previous civil rights bills. Attorney General Robert Kennedy, testifying before the Committee, urged the members to consider a milder form of the bill than the one approved by the subcommittee. He reasoned that a weaker bill would have a chance of passing, while a strong bill would surely be defeated.

Not all civil rights supporters agreed with the Attorney General. The National Association for the Advancement of Colored People (NAACP) continued to press for strong legislation. When, to the surprise of everyone including Chairman Celler, a strong bill was approved by the Judiciary Committee, Attorney General Kennedy gave much of the credit to two Republican Congressmen, McCulloch and House Minority Leader Charles A. Halleck of Indiana. It was important that the Attorney General acknowledge the efforts of the Republicans in particular, since bipartisan support would continue to be needed if the bill were to succeed.

Death of a President

Two days after the House Judiciary Committee had approved the bill, a tragic event occurred which would have a great impact on the passage of this bill. On November 23, 1963, President Kennedy was assassinated. Only five days after his death, President Johnson clearly spelled out his strong

338

support for a civil rights law. In a funeral address to Congress the new President said:

> No memorial oration or eulogy could more eloquently honor President Kennedy's memory than the earliest possible passage of the civil rights bill for which he fought so long. We have talked long enough in this country about equal rights. . . . It is time now to write the next chapter—and to write it in the books of law.

During the first half of 1964, President Johnson used all of his persuasive talents to gain congressional approval of the civil rights bill. In his first State of the Union message the President put passage of a civil rights law at the top of his list of priorities. He said: "Let this session of Congress be known as the session which did more for civil rights than the last hundred sessions combined."

Challenging the Rules Committee

In the meantime H.R. 7152 had encountered opposition in the House Rules Committee. The Rules Committee determines the order in which bills approved by House committees will be brought to a vote on the floor of the House. It also decides on the "rules" for the debate on each bill: for example, how much time those favoring passage of the bill and those opposing the bill will be allotted for floor debate. The chairman of the House Rules Committee was Howard W. Smith of Virginia, a strong opponent of civil rights legislation. In the past he had successfully stopped most strong civil rights bills from reaching the House floor for consideration.

In an attempt to bypass the Rules Committee, Representative Cellar filed a *discharge petition.* A discharge petition releases a committee from considering a certain measure. The petition is placed on the Speaker's desk, where the members of the House can sign it. If more than half of the total membership signs the petition, a bill can be taken away from a committee and brought directly to the floor. President Johnson made it clear that he favored the discharge petition. He even made personal telephone calls to some of the House members who had failed to sign it. Rather than have the bill taken out of the Rules Committee by the discharge petition, Chairman Smith of Virginia finally agreed to hold hearings on the bill. Following other attempts at delay by the chairman, the Rules Committee voted to send the bill to the House floor.

Ordinarily the task of managing a bill backed by a Democratic President on the House floor would have fallen to Democratic "party whip" Hale Boggs of Louisiana. However, as most of his constituents strongly opposed the bill, responsibility for floor leadership passed to an organization called the Democratic Study Group, comprised of Northern liberals in the Democratic Party. They created an elaborate network of monitors to make certain that the bill's supporters would be present when they were needed. During the course of the floor debate almost a hundred amendments designed to weaken the bill were presented without success. Finally, on February 10, 1964, the bill passed the House by a vote of 290–130.

The cartoon depicts Rules Committee Chairman Howard Smith placing obstacles in the way of passage of the bill by the House.

"In charge of arrangements."

Reprinted by permission of the *Philadelphia Evening and Sunday Bulletin* and F. O. Alexander

"Whip" is the name given to the assistant floor leader of each party. His special duty is to see that members support their party on important issues.

H.R. 7152 Goes to the Senate

Senate leaders had decided to try to delay debate on a civil rights bill until one had cleared the House. They were fearful that the anger and bitterness certain to arise over the civil rights issue might lead to the defeat of other important legislation. Moreover, the leaders had mapped a strategy that would

In the early stages of work on the Civil Rights Bill in Congress, a massive public demonstration was arranged by civil rights leaders. The March on Washington took place in August, 1963. In the center of the front line is Martin Luther King, Jr.

allow the House bill to bypass the Senate Judiciary Committee, where it would surely be delayed. Usually, when a bill is introduced in either chamber, it is assigned to a committee. However, when a bill has passed the House, it can be intercepted at the door of the Senate chamber and placed directly on the Senate calendar. This is a very rare step, since it bypasses entirely the Senate's committee system. Senate Majority Leader Mike Mansfield of Montana decided that the importance of this bill justified his taking this unusual action. He elected to "meet the bill at the door." Mansfield's decision was challenged by Senator Richard Russell of Georgia, the leader of the Southern bloc. But Mansfield's move was supported by the Senate, and the bill was brought directly to the floor of the Senate for debate. But getting the bill to the Senate floor for debate was only the first skirmish in the battle that lay ahead. Now the civil rights supporters had to overcome a filibuster.

Filibuster and cloture. A filibuster is an effort by one or more Senators "to talk a bill to death." The Senate has a tradition of permitting debate to continue on proposed legislation until every Senator who wishes to speak has had an opportunity to do so. As compared to the House, which sharply limits the time set aside for debate, arguments on legislation can continue indefinitely in the Senate. In practice few Senators take advantage of the chance to extend debate because they do not want to inconvenience their colleagues. But, occasionally, when an issue is very important to a group of Senators who fear the bill will pass if brought to a vote, they will literally hold the floor, dividing the speaking chores, and prevent a vote from being taken.

The only way a filibuster can be broken is by a vote of *cloture,* or *closure.* This requires that two-thirds of the Senate vote in favor of ending debate. A vote of this size is rare.

Since no other legislation can be considered during a filibuster and since a vote of cloture rarely succeeds, a filibuster, or the threat of a filibuster, can be a powerful bargaining tactic of the opposition. Supporters of a bill may be willing to compromise rather than face a long delay by filibuster. In the past a filibuster had been used successfully to defeat or to greatly weaken each civil rights bill that had reached the Senate floor.

As debate began, most Senators seemed to favor the bill; and most of these planned to vote for cloture when it became necessary to do so. A smaller group of Senators opposed the bill and would vote against cloture because the filibuster was their best chance to defeat the measure. Most of these Senators were from the South. They were joined by a few Northern and Western conservatives. The leader of this latter group was Senator Barry Goldwater, a candidate for the Republican nomination for President. He argued that the public accommodations and the fair employment sections of the bill were unconstitutional.

Bipartisan support in the Senate. Senator Hubert Humphrey (Democrat) and Senator Thomas Kuchel (Republican) were the co-leaders of the pro-civil rights forces. Humphrey had wisely asked Senator Thomas H. Kuchel of California, the Republican Whip, to be co-chairman. By this move the bill appeared to be sponsored equally by Republicans and Democrats.

Humphrey and Kuchel assigned each section of the bill to a pair of Senators, a Democrat and a Republican. It was their job to see their section through floor debate as well as to defend it against weakening amendments. Each Senator was given favorable publicity in his hometown newspapers, thereby committing him more completely to the bill.

Cooperation of many kinds was needed to insure the bill's passage. Humphrey later wrote in his book, *Beyond Civil Rights: A New Day of Equality:*

> We had to cooperate as Republicans and Democrats. We had to work together as liberals, moderates, and conservatives. We had to maintain close and favorable relations with "the other house" [the House of Representatives] lest their rejection of our changes in the bill force a conference, and thus another vote, and thus another filibuster.*

The record for a single speech was held for many years by Robert La Follette (18 hours in 1908). The record was approached by Huey P. Long (15 hours) in 1935, and finally exceeded by Wayne Morse (22 hours) in 1953.

*Hubert H. Humphrey, *Beyond Civil Rights: A New Day of Equality,* (New York, Random House, 1968), p. 87.

Humphrey was especially careful to maintain courteous relations with the opposition. No personal attacks were permitted. If the debate were not kept on a high and serious level, uncommitted Senators might be offended. Humphrey gave an example of the extent to which he tried to keep on friendly terms with the Southern Senators:

> Nearing the point of recess on a day in March, for example, after he had just made a speech ridiculing every title of the bill and I had answered him, he [Sen. Willis Robertson of Virginia] walked over to me . . . and offered me a Confederate flag for my lapel. I accepted the flag as graciously as I could, and I praised Senator Robertson not only for his eloquence and his great knowledge of history and law, but also for his wonderful . . . gentlemanly qualities and his consideration to us at all times.

The Southerners would not give in easily. For six weeks they refused to allow a vote—even on an amendment to the bill.

The role of Senator Dirksen. A key individual in the ultimate success of the bill was Senate Minority Leader Everett Dirksen of Illinois. Dirksen, one of the most important leaders of the Senate, was especially influential with conservative Republicans who would provide the swing vote on cloture. Representing a midwestern state with a conservative area in the southern part of the state and a big city in the north, Dirksen had no previous record of staunch support for civil rights. The black voters of the second and third wards of Chicago regularly opposed his reelection.

The late Senator Everett Dirksen (right) and House Minority Leader Charles Halleck each had a major role in this case. They are seen here in their weekly news conference, dubbed "The Ev and Charlie Show," which was designed to balance the heavy publicity given to the Democratic President.

During the spring of 1964 the mail from his constituents, around 10,000 letters and cards, ran two to one against the bill. On March 26 he attacked the bill on the Senate floor. Dirksen said he could not vote for the fair employment or public accommodations sections. He suggested that as many as seventy amendments might be necessary before he could support the bill.

Having established himself as a severe critic of the House bill, Senator Dirksen began to play another kind of role. In the weeks following his March 26 speech, he met regularly with Senate leaders, including Humphrey and Kuchel, and Justice Department officials in an effort to reword the bill so that it would win the support of as many Senators as possible. Each section of the bill was subjected to careful analysis. As the debate continued, it became clear that the essential features of the House bill would be preserved, but new language was found for some of the sections. Finally, two months after his March 26 speech, Senator Dirksen offered a substitute bill in the form of an amendment. The "Dirksen-Mansfield substitute," as it came to be called, was backed by the coalition of civil rights organizations lobbying for the bill, the Justice Department, and conservative Republicans.

The five main provisions of the bill, including the public accommodations and the fair employment sections, had been preserved. The principal changes were to allow local and state governments that had their own antidiscrimination agencies time to act before the Federal government could intervene. Also in cases where Federal funds were withheld from a program because of a discriminatory practice, the withholding of funds would apply only to those governmental units directly guilty of the discriminatory practice and not to the larger units, such as a state, of which they were a part.

The Senate Passes the Civil Rights Bill

While the new bill now satisfied most of the uncommitted Senators, Humphrey needed a few more "ayes" before he would risk a vote on cloture. He agreed to postpone the cloture vote until a group of conservative Senators could present their amendments to the Dirksen substitute. Only one of the amendments (to allow trial by jury in certain contempt cases) passed, but the conservatives were satisfied that their views had been recognized.

On June 10, with all Senators present, the cloture vote was taken. Seventy-one Senators (four more than necessary) voted for cloture. Senator Clair Engle, Democrat of California, who had just undergone a brain operation was wheeled into the Senate chamber to cast his vote. Although he was unable to speak, he indicated by pointing to his eye, his "aye" vote for the bill.

After the cloture vote passed, the Senators could speak for only one hour on the bill and its amendments. As a delay tactic, the Southerners demanded roll call votes on nearly every amendment. On one day roll was called thirty-four times, setting a new record. On June 16 the opponents introduced 33 amendments: 14 by Strom Thurmond of South Carolina, 8 by Sam Ervin of North Carolina, and 7 by Russell Long of Louisiana. All were defeated.

On June 20 the civil rights bill passed the Senate. Seventy-three of the one hundred Senators voted for the bill. Those who opposed it included

Crook in *Newsday*, Long Island. Reprinted by permission.

"The ultimate weapon."

eighteen Southern Democrats, three border state Senators and Senator Goldwater plus the five Senators who were supporting his candidacy for the presidential nomination. The debates in the Senate filled 2890 pages of the *Congressional Record* and absorbed 736 hours and 10 minutes—a total of 83 days.

As the Senate had passed a version of the bill that was different from the one passed by the House, it had to be returned to the House for reconsideration. To avoid a conference committee and another possible filibuster in the Senate, the House elected to accept the Senate version by a vote of 289–126.

The President Signs the Civil Rights Act

On July 2, 1964, President Johnson spoke to the nation before signing the Civil Rights Act.

This is a proud triumph. Yet those who founded our country knew that freedom would be secure only if each generation sought to renew and enlarge its meaning. . . .

We believe that all men are created equal—yet many are denied equal treatment. We believe that all men have certain inalienable rights—yet many Americans do not enjoy these rights. We believe that all men are entitled to the blessings of liberty—yet millions are being deprived of those blessings, not because of their own failures, but because of the color of their skins.

The reasons are deeply embedded in history and tradition and the nature of man. We can understand without rancor or hatred how this all happened. But it cannot continue. Our Constitution, the foundation of our Republic, forbids it. The principles of our freedom forbid it. Morality forbids it. And the law I will sign tonight forbids it. . . .

With the President's signature, the Civil Rights Bill became the Civil Rights Act of 1964. From that moment, any state or city law that conflicted with the Civil Rights Act could not be enforced. Thus, many state and city laws that provided for segregated restaurants, hotels, parks, theaters, and public washrooms were now swept off the lawbooks.

In a prior lesson you learned about some of the rules and personality factors that influence legislative role behavior. Apply what you have learned to this case study.

1. What *formal rules* were important to the outcome of the Civil Rights Act of 1964.

President Johnson uses several pens to sign the civil rights bill as congressional leaders look on.

2. What *informal rules* were observed in considering this legislation?

3. Give examples in which personality and personal belief were important to the passage of the law.

F. Factors That Influence Congressional Decision-Making

A congressman must make many decisions each day: who to see, what reports to read, what meetings to attend, what requests to honor, and many others. Each of these decisions is part of playing the congressional role. There are many opportunities for a congressman to contribute to policy making. By his speeches he may help influence public opinion that will lend support or opposition to public policies; in his committee work he may help shape future legislation. But he most clearly acts as an official decision-maker when he votes "aye" or "nay" to a bill brought to a vote on the floor of the Senate or House of Representatives. Therefore, in this lesson we shall focus primarily upon those factors that cause a Senator or a Representative to vote for or against a bill.

How does a congressman make up his mind to vote for or against a bill? What factors limit his choices? What factors work upon him to produce a decision?

No political scientist could ever analyze thoroughly and exactly the factors that cause a congressman to make a particular decision. Probably even the congressman himself is not fully aware of the forces that influence him. Nevertheless, we can identify categories of social factors that seem to influence decision-makers, the degree of influence they have varying by people and situation. These social factors are (1) rules, (2) status relationships, (3) public opinion, and (4) the social situation. These social factors interact with the personal beliefs of a congressman to produce a decision.

Rules

In section C (pp. 320–321) we examined many of the rules that influence how the legislative role will be played. These same formal and informal rules undoubtedly have some influence on the final decisions a congressman will make. These rules will not be reviewed here.

However, there are additional rules that are influential. For example, congressmen are not given an opportunity to decide whether they favor civil rights, aid to education, better health for citizens, as abstract ideas. They must always decide how they stand on the issues in a specific bill that has reached the floor of the House or the Senate and that requires a decision.

For example, a Senator who favors good schools over poor schools must decide whether he wishes to have financial support for better schools to come from the Federal government, whether he is prepared to spend as much money as the bill calls for, whether he wishes to spend money for the particular types of programs specified in the bill, and so on. He can try to amend the bill, to add sections he favors and eliminate or change sections he dislikes. However, it is very difficult for a single congressman to gain enough support to amend a bill during debate on the floor. The bill probably represents many compromises that have been worked out in the committee sessions and that have broad support. Supporters of the bill do not like to have others tinker with a bill they believe has sufficient support to pass in its present form.

Nevertheless, amendments can be added to a bill during debate. The addition of a particular kind of amendment, called a "rider," may cause additional problems for the congressional decision-maker. Imagine that you are a Senator who favors a bill to establish programs providing for free hospital care for the elderly. You intend to vote for the bill. But the House version of the bill contains a rider that has no relationship to medical care. The rider calls for a general salary increase of 6 percent for all Federal employees. You oppose the rider but are warned that unless the Senate accepts the House version of the bill, the medical care bill will not pass the House. You must either vote against the medical care bill because you dislike the rider, try to get the rider removed, or vote yes, accepting the pay increase in order to get the medical care bill you want. You cannot vote for only a part of the bill. In short, the decision that a congressman makes is influenced in part by the rules that govern the legislative process.

In the illustration on page 347 you can observe the progress of the Smith-Jones Education bill from its introduction to its approval by the President. Only the most important legislative steps are shown in the illustration, but note how the bill has changed in form as it winds its way through the two houses of Congress.

Status Relationships

A congressman's status relationships (p. 294) may influence his decision-making. A member of Congress has three main types of status relationships that influence his decisions: (1) with other members of the Congress, (2) with the executive branch of the government, and (3) with political party leaders.

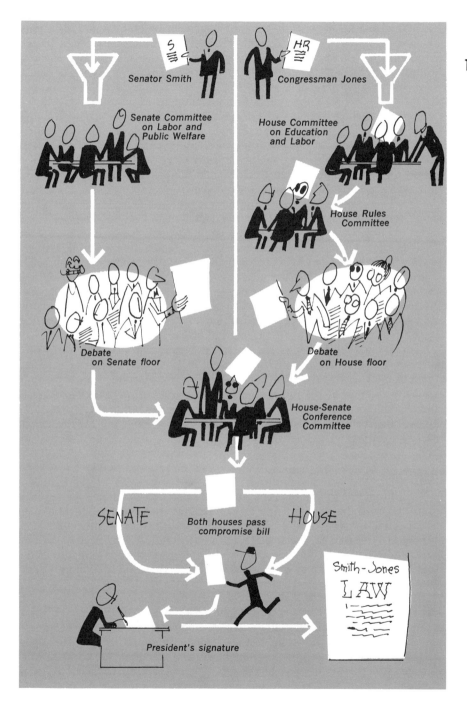

The Story of the
Smith-Jones
Education Bill

Senator Smith

Congressman Jones

Senate Committee
on Labor and
Public Welfare

House Committee
on Education
and Labor

House Rules
Committee

Debate
on Senate floor

Debate
on House floor

House-Senate
Conference
Committee

SENATE

HOUSE

Both houses pass
compromise bill

Smith-Jones
LAW

President's signature

Status relationships with congressional colleagues influence decision-making in a number of ways. First of all, there is a strong tendency to accept the report of the committee that was responsible for the bill. No congressman can study all of the legislation that comes before Congress. Therefore, he tends to depend upon the committee's view, especially when the committee was able to write a bill that had unanimous support among the committee members.

Secondly, congressmen are subjected to and participate in "logrolling" practices. "Logrolling" refers to the practice of exchanging support for legislation a colleague wants in return for getting support for a bill you want passed. Thus, Congressman Smith might vote for a new airbase in Congressman Jones's state on the understanding that Congressman Jones will vote for a shipyard facility Congressman Smith wants for his state.

Finally, a number of Senators and Congressmen have acquired reputations of high integrity and great ability on certain issues. Congressmen who are uncertain which way to vote may ask such individuals for advice.

Executive status relationships refer to the interaction that a congressman has with the President and his representatives from the Federal bureaucracy. Congressmen seek the advice of the heads of Federal bureaus when considering a decision. Also, the President or the chiefs of bureaus in the executive department may try to push a particular point of view on congressmen concerning pending bills. For example, President Lyndon Johnson worked hard to influence congressmen to support the civil rights bill of 1964.

Party status relationships refer to the interaction of a congressman with leaders of his political party both in and out of Congress. If state or national leaders of the congressman's party have taken a strong public stand on some issue before Congress, the member of Congress will face pressure from these leaders to support this stand with a vote for or against a bill. These pressures may take the form of refusing to support a congressman's bid for reelection unless the congressman goes along with the official position of his political party.

Public Opinion

Public opinion influences a congressman's decision-making. Both national public opinion and the public opinion of a congressman's district or state may influence him; but constituency influence, the influence of the home district, is strongest. The Senator's state or the Representative's district contains the votes that can reelect or reject a member of Congress in his bid to retain office. Thus, a congressman must be responsive to the views of the voters "back home" if he wants to be reelected.

This does not mean that a congressman bends like a reed in the wind before every pressure from his constituents. A state or a congressional district usually contains several different and conflicting social groups. The congressman usually identifies with some of these groups rather than others. He hopes that those he favors can muster enough votes at election time to keep him in office. Moreover, special-interest groups representing national or local opinion may exert pressure on a congressman from time to time. Nevertheless,

"Maybe in the next mail we'll find one in favor of your position, Senator."

the impact of the lobbyist, the representative of the interest group, has often been exaggerated. Unless the lobbyist is supported by a large segment of public opinion or by important individuals in Congress or the Federal bureaucracy, by himself he usually will not have a great impact upon a congressman's decisions.

Social Situation

The social situation at a particular moment can have a major impact on a congressman's decision. The "mood" of the nation, issues receiving attention by newspapers and television, and the actions of national leaders are all important. For example, fear of war has an impact on the amount of funds Congress appropriates for the military. In 1970 concern for "law and order" led to the passage of a strong legislative program aimed at fighting crime. In the same year growing concern over air and water pollution led to the consideration of bills aimed at meeting these problems.

Personality of Congressmen

The rules and social factors described above do not affect all congressmen the same way. Congressmen react differently to the same social forces because of differences in their personalities.

Some congressmen are pessimistic about the future while others are optimists. Some congressmen believe that progress is made by strong governmental leadership, while others think the "government which governs least, governs best." Some congressmen may think of themselves as "mavericks," isolated individuals defending the good of the nation against the passions of the mob. They may consider bargaining over issues to be compromising their principles. Yet others may see themselves as "great compromisers" who can be counted upon to arrive at a solution to which all can agree. Naturally a congressional leader who thinks of himself as a "maverick" may be expected to reach different decisions on specific issues than a "great compromiser."

Four models of congressmen. Some political scientists believe that members of Congress can be divided into four types, or models: (1) *trustee*, (2) *delegate*, (3) *partisan*, and (4) *politico*.

A Senator or Representative who is a *trustee* may be thought of as one who follows his own conscience. Such a person may believe that he understands the issues better than the voters who sent him to Washington. He may feel that his constituents would vote as he does, if they knew what he knows.

A *delegate* on the other hand is a member of Congress who believes he was sent to represent the views of the people in his district or state. He will vote the way the "people back home" want him to vote, even when he disagrees with their judgment.

A *partisan* is a representative who is loyal to the party platforms on which he was elected and loyal to the party's line on legislation.

A *politico* is one who combines the three types cited earlier. On some occasions a politico votes his conscience (acting as a trustee); on other occasions he votes as directed by his constituents (acting as a delegate); and on still other occasions he votes as the party directs (acting as a partisan). How he votes in any given situation will depend upon the circumstances.

Classify each of the four speakers below according to one of the four types described above. In what ways would a congressman's conception of his role influence his decisions?

> *Congressman Rogers:* I think we have an obligation to represent the people who sent us to Congress. I won't support any legislation that is not supported by at least a majority of the citizens of my district.

> *Senator Smith:* The voters in my state elected me to the Senate because of the kind of man I am. They trust me to make wise decisions in their behalf. They expect me to spend six years tending to public business and vote the way I think is best.

> *Senator Chavez:* There are some issues about which my constituents know nothing and care even less. I vote in whatever way I please in such cases— hopefully the way I think is best for the whole country. In other matters, mostly domestic issues such as civil rights, my people know exactly how they think I should vote and watch that I vote their way. I would be a fool to go against their wishes.

350

Senator Green: I think one has an obligation to support the party. The President has been trying to stuff a program through Congress to show the American public how great his party is. I think those of us in the other party must stand firm and resist the President. His program would be far too costly, anyway.

Political scientists are not sure which of these types (*trustee, delegate, partisan,* or *politico*) would most accurately describe most members of Congress. Probably, no congressman always behaves according to only one model. Probably a congressman sometimes acts as a *trustee,* other times as a *delegate,* and still other times as a *partisan.* Hence, the *politico* model may be the most accurate. In any event, how a congressman interprets his role surely is one influence on the decision he makes.

Now that you understand some of the factors that influence congressional decision-making, you will most likely have an even better understanding of the case study, "The 1964 Civil Rights Act." Reread the case study and complete the following exercises.

1. What rules were significant in influencing the passage of the Civil Rights Act of 1964?

2. List examples in which status relationships influenced the passage of the bill.

3. Which congressmen seemed to be most influenced by public opinion? Did public opinion influence congressmen differently?

4. What factors in the social situation influenced the passage of the bill?

5. Provide examples in which the personalities of key congressmen were significant.

G. What Decision Is Best?

Former Senator Paul Douglas once described congressional decision-making as follows:

> When the committee hearings and the important books and articles on a proposal are read; when the mail has been appraised; when the briefs and arguments have been weighed; when the wise men, living and dead, have been consulted, the Senator still faces that task of moving his own lips to say yes or no. On the clerk's list, his name stands out in all its solitude. And that is the way he must vote.
>
> It is also, I believe, the primary way in which he decides beforehand how he is going to vote. His hour of decision is not seen by the outer world. It can come in the dead of night, in periods of reverie in one's office after the day's work is done, over the breakfast or dinner table with one's family, or in a taxicab ride to or from the Capitol. It is at these times, I believe, that the final decisions which affect the life of the nation are generally made. The tension of the roll-call merely expresses the decision which . . . widely differing men, with different background, have already made in the quiet of their individual consciences.*

New York Times Magazine, April 30, 1950. Copyright 1950 by the New York Times Company. Reprinted by permission.

Congressmen make many decisions each day. Sometimes they must make decisions when they have had little opportunity to study the issue themselves and must rely upon the advice of others. Sometimes they have little interest in the topic and care little whether the bill is passed or defeated. But congressmen also face issues that are extremely important to the future of the United States, issues in which millions of American lives can be affected by the outcome. Often the "right" decision in such a case is unclear. They cannot predict exactly what will happen if they make one choice rather than another. Often different values are at stake. Passing a law to draft men into the army may strengthen national security, but it may also weaken individual freedom and choice. These are the kinds of issues Senator Douglas believes Senators resolve "in the quiet of their individual consciences."

The story that follows is about a mythical Senator who faced such a decision. Your task is to imagine yourself in his place, having to decide the issue he must resolve. How would you vote if you were in his place? Throughout the story you will have opportunities to make up your mind on the basis of what you learned about the issue to that point. You may find that your opinion shifts as you continue through the story. You may change your mind as often as you wish until the end of the story. Then, you must finally choose, and there can be no turning back.

"Let Your Conscience Be Your Guide"

"What? I'm sorry, dear. I didn't hear what you said," Senator Richard Williams apologized as he became aware that his wife was speaking to him. "Excuse me; what were you saying?"

"I said: How do you intend to vote on the Diego Resolution? I assume that's what is on your mind, that's why you rolled and tossed about in bed all night, mumbling in your sleep."

"I really don't know," he replied. "The situation in Ersatz seems certain to get worse before it improves. The Ersatz government acts as though it's paralyzed; it has lost control of the capital city. In the meantime the revolutionaries continue to kidnap Americans and other foreigners and to hold them as hostages. I am afraid that many of the hostages will be killed unless the Ersatz government gives in to the rebels. But would the hostages be any safer then? I don't trust the rebels or the government. We have helped that corrupt government so long that it expects us to come to the rescue in every one of its crises—but at least we can work with it. If the revolutionaries win, they'll probably seek friendly ties with the Soviet Union or China; Americans will be driven out, and American-owned properties in Ersatz will be taken by the revolutionaries with no compensation to the American companies."

A newscaster describes the situation. Senator Williams got up from his chair and turned on the morning television news in time to hear the news announcer say: ". . . But the President believes that if the Senate passes the Diego Resolution, it will give him the freedom he needs to deal with the current uprising in Ersatz.

"Very simply the Diego Resolution asks the Senate to endorse the President's plan to move a navy task force to a position ten miles off the shore of Ersatz in order that it will be available if needed. The resolution does not say specifically what the navy will do after it is there, only that it would be 'ready to take whatever actions are necessary to protect American lives.' Some sources believe that the navy is already on its way to Ersatz. It is unclear this morning how the vote scheduled for 12 noon will be decided.

"Many in the Senate fear that if they approve the resolution, the President will take that as a green light to invade Ersatz, and the United States may find itself involved in a local war that might continue for months or even years. They remember a number of years ago when President Lyndon Johnson interpreted the Tonkin Resolution as a vote in support of policies to widen the war in Vietnam. These Senators are cautious about giving such a blanket endorsement again, because they feel the President abused the power and made many decisions that should have been decided by Congress. These Senators also argue that there are many measures the American government can take to insure the safety of Americans in Ersatz without giving the President the power called for in the Diego Resolution. On the other hand, Senators favoring the resolution argue that the President needs a vote of support to strengthen his hand in dealing with a very delicate problem: how to protect the lives and property of Americans and prevent a Communist takeover of Ersatz without invading the country.

"At this moment the vote looks very close. We may not know the outcome until the very end when Senator Richard Williams makes his decision. At last word Senator Williams was still undecided, despite the fact that he is a member of the President's political party and backed him for the Presidency. It may be that the final vote will be 51–49, with Senator Williams casting the deciding ballot."

"Sounds like a real thriller, doesn't it?" said Senator Williams sarcastically as he pulled on his coat and opened the door. "Stay tuned to that station and learn Senator Williams's choice! Well, it's likely to be a hard day. I'll be home for dinner."

Williams hears further news. As he drove to his office, Senator Williams listened to the latest news from Ersatz on his car radio. . . . Five more Americans had been kidnapped, making a total of fifty-three Americans who had been taken from their cars, from their homes, and in a few cases right out of their offices. Thus far, only men had been captured, leaving behind terror-stricken wives and children. . . . Air Force General George Patrick had been quoted as having recommended dropping paratroopers into Ersatz to rescue the Americans, followed by helicopters to airlift all the Americans out. The Department of Defense denied any such plan . . . Meanwhile the Soviet Union said that it was studying the situation very carefully. Russian diplomats warned that the problem would become very serious if the United States intervened in Ersatz in any way.

"It's not getting any better," Senator Williams thought. "The revolutionaries seem to be moving about the city at random with little opposition from the Ersatz police or government troops. Within a few hours the government may fall. Some—maybe many—Americans will be killed. But what will the President do if we pass the Diego Resolution and give him a blank check to use the navy as he thinks best? If he invades, the rebels will probably kill those Americans being held hostage. We might even have to keep forces there to support the present government. What would the Soviet Union and China do if we took such action? What would other Latin-American nations do if we were to invade one of their neighbors? Has the President tried all possible channels of communication between American diplomats and the rebel leaders? Don't we have any allies who might try to negotiate in our behalf so that force wouldn't be necessary?

On the basis of what you know now, how would you vote—
for or against the Diego Resolution?

As he slipped through the side door of his office, Senator Williams was met by his secretary. "Hi boss. Glad you're here. The office is a madhouse. People are stacked up in the outer office waiting to see you, and the telephone is ringing constantly. I think everyone in the nation wants to tell you how to vote or be the first to learn what you are going to do."

"How do people want me to vote?" Senator Williams asked.

"I would estimate that opinion is about 2-1 in favor of your voting for the Diego Resolution and supporting the President. But it is sometimes hard to tell. For example, you received a long telegram from the faculty of Sinclair College urging you to vote in such a way that (1) no American lives will be

lost, (2) there will be no risk of war, (3) American honor will be preserved, and (4) the President is supported. I'll let you figure out how they want you to vote."

"I wish I had a choice like that. What I fear is that if we don't act, someone will be killed; but I'm also afraid that if we do intervene even more people might die. And would American honor be enhanced or tarnished if we sent an invasion force into such a small, defenseless nation? Who is waiting to see me?"

"About twenty reporters and one television crew!"

"Tell them I will have no statement to make until after I vote. Who else is waiting?"

"Probably fifteen other people, including Mrs. Fletcher, whose husband is one of the hostages in Ersatz, and Joe Flynn, a representative from Allied Electrical Corporation. As you know, Mr. Flynn's company not only contributed heavily to your last campaign but also owns considerable property in Ersatz. Incidentally, Mark Jones, the editor of the *Globe* in your hometown, wants you to call."

Williams grants some interviews. For the next two hours Senator Williams met with fourteen people and placed or received eight telephone calls. The most difficult interview was with Mrs. Fletcher, who began to weep as soon as she entered the office, pleading with the Senator not to support the Diego Resolution for fear that her husband would be murdered. She urged a policy that would give the revolutionaries what they wanted if they would free the hostages. Joe Flynn, on the other hand, argued that the Senator should back the President and vote for the Diego Resolution. He pointed out that the fifty-three captured Americans were in serious danger regardless of what action was taken. No one could predict what the rebels might do. What was certain was that property in Ersatz owned by Americans would be taken over by the new government if the revolutionaries won.

Between interviews Senator Williams called Mark Jones. The *Globe* editor wanted to know how the Senator intended to vote so that the paper could carry the story on the front page that evening. Editor Jones also expressed his own opinion that the most important factor to consider was that the United States should take a firm stand and make it clear that it would not stand by quietly when its citizens were threatened.

> On the basis of what you have learned thus far, how would you vote—
> for or against the Diego Resolution?

As his last visitor was leaving, Senator Williams's secretary rushed into the office and said: "The President is calling. He's holding on line 9."

Senator Williams picked up the phone, punched line 9, and said: "Good morning, Mr. President."

"Hi, Dick. Sorry to bother you. I know you're very busy. But I thought I'd call before you went over to the Senate. Can I count on your vote today?

"I really don't know, Mr. President. I think it is a very messy situation. I'd like to support you, but I am not sure that the Diego Resolution is good for you or the country. The present government of Ersatz lacks strong popular

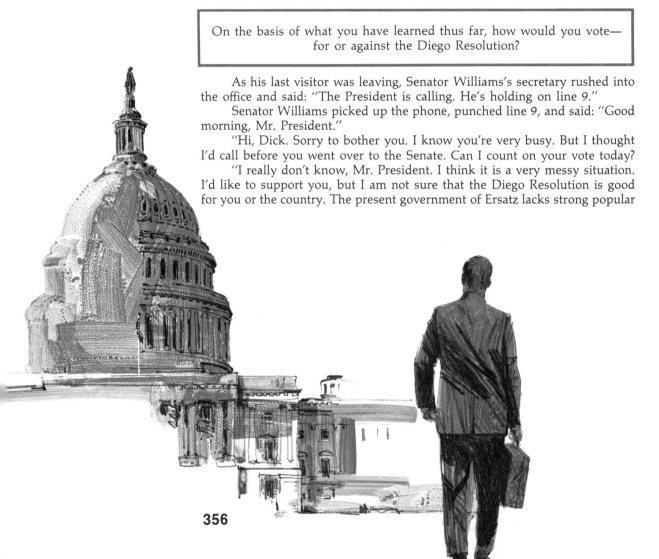

support. I despise the rebels' terrorist tactics, but I'm not sure the United States should intervene in just this way.

"Look, Dick, I need your vote. It's going to be close. Let me give you some information that hasn't been made public. We think we have found where the revolutionaries are holding the American hostages. It's in the countryside, a few miles outside the capital city. Ersatz government troops cannot free them because the revolutionaries would surely have advance warning of the attack hours before it came off. However, I think we have a good chance of dropping our own paratroopers in at night, freeing the hostages, and capturing the revolutionary leaders before they know what hit them.

"It's risky, but doing nothing is risky too. We have a message from the rebels that starting today they will execute one American every six hours until the government agrees to free all of the political prisoners it is holding and enters into negotiations with them.

"Dick, I need your vote. You'll have to trust me in this matter. A lot of people are depending upon us to do the right thing. Incidentally, drop by the White House at 5:00 P.M., and I'll fill you in on the plans to free those Americans. I'll see you later."

"Good-bye." Senator Williams returned the telephone to its stand.

> On the basis of what you have learned thus far, how would you vote—for or against the Diego Resolution?

Roll call had already begun when Senator Williams left his office to walk to the Senate. Just before leaving, he had a call from the Senate majority leader (his own party leader) urging him to support the President. In the view of the majority leader, the Diego Resolution would become an important political issue. In his view most Americans favored taking some action to save the hostages. A political party that seemed to lack the courage to act would risk losing a lot of votes in the next election. Moreover, if Williams wanted any help from the President on any of his own projects, he should plan to support the President today.

As Senator Williams strode toward the Senate chamber, he was met in the hallway by one of his assistants.

"It looks close, Senator. I think your vote will tip the balance. Incidentally, I just heard on the radio that one of the hostages—a guy named Fletcher—was found. He had been murdered."

Senator Williams entered the Senate just in time to hear the clerk call his name.

"Senator Williams: Do you vote aye or nay on the resolution before the Senate?"

> How would you vote?

chapter 15

The Role of Supreme Court Justices

Each year the United States Supreme Court receives about 4000 requests to review court decisions made by judges in other courts. Most of these requests are refused. During any single year the Supreme Court agrees to consider and offer opinions on less than 200 cases. Why are some cases accepted while others are refused? What happens when the Supreme Court agrees to hear a case? How do Supreme Court justices arrive at their decisions? Who are the justices; what kind of people are they; how do they become members of the Supreme Court? These are among the many questions that will be considered in this chapter. But first we must learn what function is served by the Supreme Court. The following case study provides some clues about the place of the Supreme Court in the American political system and the impact its decisions can have on American life.

A. Case Study: Banning Prayer in the Schools

Prior to 1960, prayer and Bible reading were a normal part of opening exercises in many public schools. Probably most Americans did not give much thought to the practice. Most of those who did seemed to approve of it.

Madalyn Murray, a 41-year-old divorcee with two sons, lived in Baltimore, Maryland. Her oldest son, 14-year-old William, was a student at Woodbourne Junior High School. One day in September, 1960, he returned home from school with a complaint that led eventually to an important and controversial United States Supreme Court decision on June 17, 1963.

William Murray complained that he was required to say prayers with his ninth-grade classmates at school. This daily compulsory religious exercise offended him. William had been brought up to be a nonbeliever, an atheist. He protested that as a nonbeliever in religion he should not have to participate in the daily recitation of prayer. He asked his mother to complain to school authorities. William said to his mother, "They are praying in school. If you don't insist that I protest, you are a hypocrite. Do I have to pray in school or not?"*

*Bynum Shaw, "Nevertheless, God Probably Loves Mrs. Murray," *Esquire,* October, 1963.

The Case Begins

Mrs. Murray first tried to change the school rule by contacting the school authorities. She petitioned the Baltimore Board of Education to ask that William be excused from the classroom during religious exercises. Dr. George B. Brain, superintendent of schools in Baltimore, answered Madalyn Murray's petition. He said that Bible reading and prayer in the schools were required by a 1905 school-board rule that stated:

Each school, either collectively or in classes, shall be opened by the reading, without comment, of a chapter in the Holy Bible and/or the use of the Lord's Prayer.

No one had ever challenged the rule before. The superintendent said that if William Murray did not want to participate, "he could remain in his seat in respectful silence."

Neither Madalyn Murray nor her son were pleased with the superintendent's decision. To protest his decision, Mrs. Murray took her son out of school on October 2, 1960. On October 28 William returned to school after the school board agreed to refer the case to the Maryland Attorney General.

The Attorney General ruled that Bible reading and praying in school was legal and that any student leaving a class to avoid it could be accused of truancy.

Mrs. Murray and son William are photographed in Hawaii a year after the Supreme Court decided the Murray case. She said she and her family were "fleeing for our lives."

He also ruled that any student who objected to Bible reading and praying could be excused from participating.

Madalyn Murray was satisfied with the Attorney General's ruling. Her son asked to be excused from the religious exercises in school and in accordance with the ruling was not required to participate. At this point Mrs. Murray and her son considered the matter ended. But some people in the community felt otherwise, and the conflict was renewed.

Public Reaction Keeps the Case Alive

The Murray protest against prayer in the schools had become front-page news. The Attorney General's favorable ruling angered some Baltimore residents. William's schoolmates beat him up for daring to protest against prayer in the school. He was jeered and made a social outcast. Vandals threw bricks through the windows of their home. Some people sent obscene letters and made threatening telephone calls.

If these angry people had been willing to "live and let live," the Murray protest against prayer in the schools might have ended. But the abuse directed against her family led Mrs. Murray to fight back. She said, "I decided that the whole country was sick, and one relatively sane person had to make a stand." She decided to fight for a court decision that would eliminate compulsory Bible reading and praying from the public schools.

Mrs. Murray had very few political resources. She had become a social outcast. She had no powerful organization behind her. No administrative or legislative groups seemed interested in supporting her cause. She decided to turn to the courts.

The Case Enters the Courts

Mrs. Murray began by hiring an attorney, Leonard Kerpelman. Because he believed in her cause, he charged very little for his services. Mrs. Murray filed a petition in the Superior Court of Baltimore asking for the ending of "sectarian opening exercises from the Baltimore public schools." She claimed that for a student opposed to prayer to be merely excused from class (as then permitted by the school board) caused the student "to lose caste with his fellows and to be subjected to reproach and insult." She argued that prayer exercises in the school violated religious freedom "by placing a premium on belief as against non-belief."

Attorney Kerpelman argued before the Superior Court of Baltimore that the 1905 rule was contrary to the First and Fourteenth Amendments to the United States Constitution. Therefore, the "rule" should be declared illegal.

Following are the portions of the First and Fourteenth Amendments that the lawyer said were violated.

> *First Amendment:* Congress shall make no law respecting an establishment of religion or prohibiting the free exercise thereof. . . .
>
> *Fourteenth Amendment:* No state shall make or enforce any law which shall abridge the privileges or immunities of citizens of the United States; nor shall

any state deprive any person of life, liberty, or property, without due process of law; nor deny to any person within its jurisdiction the equal protection of the laws.

The Superior Court of Baltimore ruled against the Murrays on April 28, 1961. The judge decided, after reviewing the evidence, that Bible reading and prayer in the Baltimore public schools was legal and could continue. William Murray could refuse to participate in the religious exercise, but he would have to respect the right of other students to participate.

Mrs. Murray and her lawyer were unwilling to accept this decision. They believed that they could argue successfully that the school-board rule was unconstitutional. They appealed their case to the Maryland Appellate Court, the highest court in the state of Maryland. After long argument and study, the Court voted 4-3 to uphold the school-board rule. The majority of the judges argued that since William Murray was not forced to participate, the religious activities in school did not violate his basic rights under the Constitution of the United States.

The Supreme Court Accepts the Case

Mrs. Murray and her lawyer refused to quit. They believed that they were right and that they could obtain a fair hearing from the highest court in the land. They appealed the verdict, and the United States Supreme Court agreed to hear their case.

Through their attorney, the Murrays argued before the Supreme Court that their rights to freedom of religious choice had been violated by the 1905 rule of the Baltimore school commissioners that required "reading without comment a chapter in the Holy Bible and/or the use of the Lord's Prayer." The Murrays argued that this rule was "in violation of their rights to freedom of religion under the First and Fourteenth Amendments and in violation of the principle of separation between church and state contained therein."

The Supreme Court announced its decision on June 17, 1963. By a vote of 8 to 1, the Supreme Court declared unconstitutional the Maryland rule that the Lord's Prayer or the Bible be required for religious exercises in public schools. The Supreme Court decided that the "Maryland rule" contradicted both the First and Fourteenth Amendments to the Constitution and was therefore illegal.

Justice Clark wrote the majority opinion of the Court. It contained the following statements:

> Once again we are called upon to consider the scope of the provision of the First Amendment to the Constitution which declares that "Congress shall make no law respecting the establishment of religion or prohibiting the free exercise thereof. . . ." In light of the history of the First Amendment and of our cases interpreting and applying its requirements, we hold that the practices at issue and the laws requiring them are unconstitutional under the Establishment Clause, as applied to the states through the Fourteenth Amendment. . . .

The place of religion in our society is an exalted one achieved through a long tradition of reliance on the home, the church, and the inviolable citadel of the individual heart and mind. We have come to recognize through bitter experience that it is not within the power of the government to invade that citadel, whether its purpose or effect be to aid or oppose, to advance or retard. In the relationship between man and religion, the state is firmly committed to a position of neutrality. The breach of neutrality that is today a trickling stream may all too soon become a raging torrent. . . .

Concurring with Justice Clark, Justice Douglas said:

The vice of . . . such arrangements under the Establishment Clause [see the First Amendment] is that the state is lending its assistance to a church's efforts to gain and keep adherents. . . .

Such contributions may not be made by the State even in a minor degree without violating the Establishment Clause. . . .

Justice Potter Stewart was the only Supreme Court member who voted to uphold the practice of religious activities in the Baltimore schools. In his dissenting opinion he wrote:

. . . permission of such [religious] exercises for those who want them is necessary if the schools are truly to be neutral in the matter of religion. And a refusal to permit religious exercises thus is seen, not as the realization of state neutrality, but rather as the establishment of a religion of secularism, or at the least, as government support of the beliefs of those who think that religious exercises should be conducted only in private.

". . . and if it isn't unconstitutional."

Shanks in *Buffalo Evening News*

Steps in the Development of a Legal Case:
Murray v. The Board of School Commissioners of Baltimore City

The Problem: William Murray was required to participate in Bible reading and prayer in school against his wishes.

Steps Taken to Resolve the Problem

1. Madalyn Murray appealed to school authorities.
   Result: She lost the decision. (October, 1960)

2. Madalyn Murray appealed to the Maryland Attorney General.
   Result: Partial but not totally satisfactory decision. (November 2, 1960)

3. Madalyn Murray appealed to the Superior Court of Baltimore.
   Result: She lost the decision. (April 28, 1961)

4. Madalyn Murray appealed to the Maryland Appellate Court.
   Result: She lost the decision. (April 6, 1962)

5. Madalyn Murray appealed to the United States Supreme Court.
   Result: She won the decision. (June 17, 1963)

The net effect was to reverse all previous decisions against Mrs. Murray which required her son to be in classrooms where prayer and Bible reading took place.

The Impact of the Murray Case

The Supreme Court had decided in favor of Madalyn Murray. This decision meant that not only was the Baltimore school rule unconstitutional, but by implication all similar rules in other cities and states were also in violation of the Constitution. Following this decision, many schools voluntarily ended Bible reading and prayer in the classroom. In other cases new court suits were begun to test state and local statutes. In still other cases community and school leaders searched for ways to continue religious exercises without violating Supreme Court rulings. For example, some schools used the prayer delivered in Congress each day and printed in the *Congressional Record.* Some political leaders started a movement to overturn the Supreme Court decision by advocating a constitutional amendment which would permit prayer in the public schools.

1. Why did Madalyn Murray appeal to the Supreme Court?
2. What impact did the decision in her case have on other people?

3. Why in the American political system are issues such as this resolved in the courts rather than in other ways?

4. List some ways in which decision-making in the Supreme Court differs from decision-making in Congress or by the President.

B. The Primary Function of the Supreme Court:
To Interpret the Law

Heading the judicial branch of the Federal government is the Supreme Court of the United States. It is composed of a Chief Justice and eight Associate Justices.

The Constitution established only the Supreme Court and gave Congress power to set up "inferior," or lower, courts.

The Supreme Court is chiefly an *appellate* court. This means that it seldom begins a case (conducts a trial), but rather it reviews cases already tried in some lower court—either a lower Federal court or a state court. But before focusing upon the Supreme Court, it is important to gain some understanding

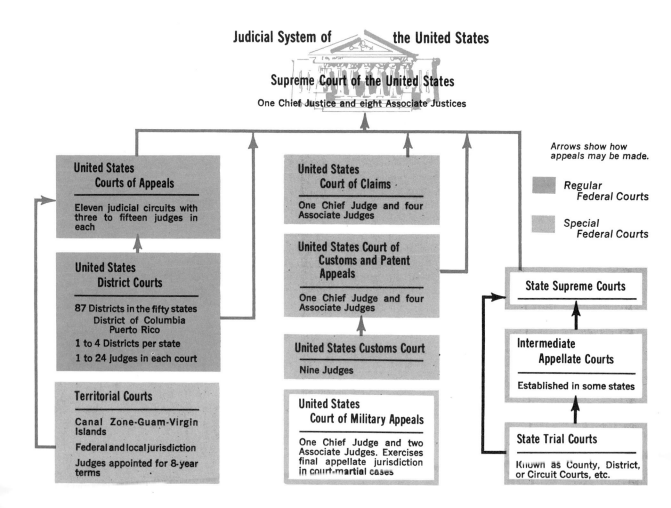

Judicial System of the United States

Supreme Court of the United States

One Chief Justice and eight Associate Justices

Arrows show how appeals may be made.

Regular Federal Courts

Special Federal Courts

United States Courts of Appeals

Eleven judicial circuits with three to fifteen judges in each

United States District Courts

87 Districts in the fifty states
District of Columbia
Puerto Rico
1 to 4 Districts per state
1 to 24 judges in each court

Territorial Courts

Canal Zone-Guam-Virgin Islands
Federal and local jurisdiction
Judges appointed for 8-year terms

United States Court of Claims

One Chief Judge and four Associate Judges

United States Court of Customs and Patent Appeals

One Chief Judge and four Associate Judges

United States Customs Court

Nine Judges

United States Court of Military Appeals

One Chief Judge and two Associate Judges. Exercises final appellate jurisdiction in court-martial cases

State Supreme Courts

Intermediate Appellate Courts

Established in some states

State Trial Courts

Known as County, District, or Circuit Courts, etc.

about the entire system of courts in the United States. In this way one can better understand the role of Supreme Court justices.

The Work of Trial Courts

Courts in the United States may be divided into two general categories: (1) trial courts and (2) appellate courts. State trial courts generally serve one or more counties and are known by various names, such as county, district, circuit, and superior courts. Also part of the state trial court system are municipal courts, which handle violations of city ordinances.

Every state also has at least one Federal trial court, known as the Federal district court. It handles cases involving Federal law. The Federal district court may also be used to settle disputes between citizens of different states but only when the amount involved is over $10,000. (Mr. A of St. Louis brings a suit in the Federal District Court of Eastern Missouri asking $15,000 in damages for injury in an auto accident against Mr. B of Cairo, Illinois.)

Criminal and civil cases. Trial courts, as the name implies, conduct trials. Cases tried in court are either *criminal* or *civil* cases. In a criminal case government officials acting for society accuse someone of committing a harmful act (crime) against society. In court the judge, or judge and jury, hear the accusation, listen to and examine the evidence, and decide if the prosecution has proved the commission of a crime beyond reasonable doubt. If the jury's verdict is "guilty as charged," the judge passes sentence—says what penalty, within the statutory limits, the defendant must suffer.

Civil cases are disputes between two or more parties, usually over money or property, as in the auto-accident case cited above. In a civil case one party (the plaintiff) charges the other (the defendant) with causing some harm. Each party has his own attorney to argue the case in court. The government has no interest except to insure fair play in the settlement of the case.

Determining the facts and applying the law. In the typical court case the plaintiff (the government in criminal cases) charges the defendant with wrongdoing. Much of the trial time is spent in *determining the facts:* Did the accused actually commit some wrongful act? Was the wrong committed intentionally or through negligence? Was the defendant sober or intoxicated? sane or mentally disturbed? How much harm or pain did the plaintiff actually suffer? And so on.

To establish the facts, American courts use the *adversary system.* This is a contest in which lawyers for each side try to present a strong case to support their client's interests. An attorney will emphasize certain evidence and ignore other evidence. He will voice objections whenever he thinks he sees possible mistakes in the conduct of the trial which may hurt his client. He will argue how the law should be interpreted to benefit his client most. Supporters of the adversary system believe that this contest between lawyers in the courtroom brings the facts out into the open.

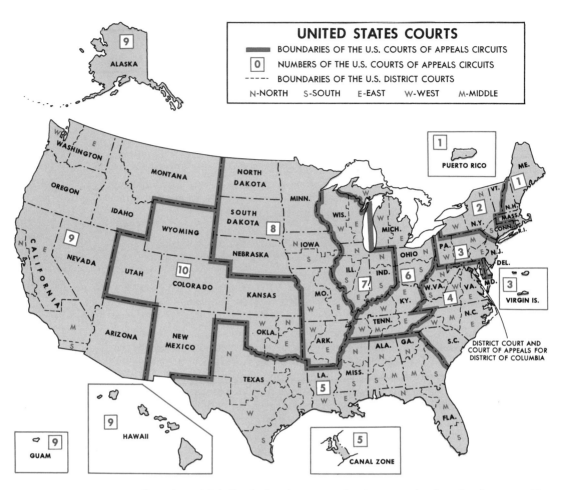

In a jury trial the judge instructs the jury on the law in the case. He points out, for example, that if the jury believes the facts to be thus and so, it must return a verdict (judgment in a civil case) against the defendant. In a trial without a jury the judge, of course, determines both the facts and the law in the case.

The Work of Appellate Courts

The defendant in a criminal case and either party in a civil case may appeal to a higher court if dissatisfied with the decision in the trial. Appellate courts—ones that handle appeals from trial courts—exist at both the state and Federal levels. The highest appellate court in a state is generally known as the state supreme court. Many states have an *intermediate appellate court* to share the work.

Most cases appealed from the Federal district courts go to one of the eleven United States Courts of Appeals. The United States Supreme Court, the highest appellate court in the land, accepts appeals from the United States Courts of Appeals, certain other Federal courts, and state supreme courts. But it chooses very carefully the cases it wants to hear and decide.

In an appellate case the court does not hold a new trial. Instead, it looks over the record of the trial and hears arguments of the lawyers on why the decision should stand or be changed. If an error in proceedings is discovered, the case may be returned to the lower court for a new trial.

To illustrate how a case moves from a lower court to the Supreme Court, let us assume that a city has passed an ordinance banning the showing of "X"-rated movies. A theater owner schedules such a movie and shows it to his customers. The police raid the theater, arrest the owner, take the film, and bring the manager before the city judge who fines him $100 for breaking the law. The theater owner appeals this decision to a higher court. In appealing the case, he is not likely to dispute the "facts." He appeals because he believes the judgment violates his constitutional rights. He may think that a higher court will agree with him and using prior rulings of the Supreme Court as a guideline will decide in his favor.

If the state appellate court ruled against the defendant, his lawyer might then appeal to the United States Supreme Court. If the case were accepted by the Supreme Court, the issue before the Court would not be the specific facts of the case. Rather, the issues would relate to the meaning of obscenity, the rights of a community to pass laws dealing with pornography, the rights of an individual to run his own business, freedom of speech; in short, the nature of the law that applies to the case. When the Supreme Court decides, it will rule only on the specific case. But afterwards the "opinions" of the justices will join the body of law to be used by other judges to decide similar cases.

In this way the Supreme Court acts as a kind of umpire for other units of government and many contending groups. Opinions on what is an obscene, or pornographic, movie vary widely from city to city, from state to state, and among public officials. This leads to different laws and regulations that may conflict with each other. By attempting to define obscenity, by establishing some criteria for determining what can be shown and what can be denied permission for showing, the Supreme Court helps to set a standard throughout the United States regarding what is legal and what is illegal.

Interpreting the Law

The primary function of the Supreme Court is to interpret the law. All laws in the United States must conform to the basic principles of the United States Constitution. Therefore, neither Congress nor state and local governments may make laws that violate the Constitution. And the President must not administer laws in such a way as to violate the Constitution.

What does it mean to "interpret" the law? To answer this question, we need first to understand that many words and phrases in the Constitution are somewhat vague and general. For example, the Constitution gives Congress power "to regulate commerce . . . among the several States." For many years the Supreme Court interpreted this phrase to mean that interstate commerce began when goods were loaded for shipment across state boundaries and ended when the goods arrived at their destination. Then in 1937 the Court decided that interstate commerce also included the manufacturing process if the goods were produced for sale across state lines. The Court made this broader interpretation of "commerce . . . among the several States" in upholding a Federal law regulating labor relations in industry. Through Court interpretation the "commerce power" of Congress is much broader today than it was in the nineteenth century.

Many other phrases in the Constitution can also have various interpretations. Does "freedom of speech and press" mean absolute freedom, or are some limitations permissible? If the latter, what are the limits and how can they be justified? States may not deny citizens "equal protection of the law." But what is equal protection? The Constitution says, "No person shall be . . . deprived of life, liberty, or property, without due process of law." The Supreme Court has often had to wrestle with the meaning of "due process of law." Chief Justice Charles Evans Hughes once said, "We are under a Constitution, but the Constitution is what the judges say it is." It is clear that interpreting the law is more than reading the Constitution and applying it as a yardstick to a particular case.

"Has anybody seen my copy of the Constitution?"

Not only is the Constitution subject to differing interpretations, but laws passed by Congress and state legislatures also often have vague language. A law may be clearly constitutional and yet contain a vague clause which needs clarification. If a court case hinges on the meaning of this particular clause in the law, the judge conducting the trial and the court reviewing the decision on appeal must say what they believe the words mean. To do this kind of interpreting, judges will sometimes go to the legislative records to try to find out what the legislators actually had in mind. Supreme Court decisions are sprinkled with such expressions as these:

> The history of congressional consideration of this problem leaves little if any room to doubt. . . .
>
> The history of this legislation emphatically underlines this fact. . . .
>
> Congress did not intend to . . . .

These are the kinds of complex issues that regularly face Supreme Court justices. The decisions they make are more than interpretations of law. And their "opinions" have far more influence than the opinions of others. Supreme Court justices are important *political decision-makers* in our society. They often make policy decisions that are as important as laws passed by Congress and the President. Many of their decisions affect American life profoundly.

C. Some Rules and Procedures Affecting Judicial Decision-Making

How do Supreme Court justices make their decisions? What factors lead them to make one choice rather than another? Why do Supreme Court justices often disagree among themselves about the best decision to make?

In previous lessons on *official decision-makers* you learned that a number of factors influence decisions. These factors include formal and informal rules and procedures, customs and norms, social forces, and personal beliefs. We shall examine each of these factors in studying decision-making in the United States Supreme Court. We begin with some important formal rules set forth in the Constitution and Federal laws.

Size of the Court and Tenure of Justices

One rule is that Congress has the authority to determine the number of justices to serve on the Supreme Court. Today the Court is composed of eight Associate Justices and one Chief Justice. The size of the Supreme Court has some influence on its decisions. A one-man Court or a fifty-man Court would require different procedures and might lead to different policy choices. The Court is sufficiently small that it can hold discussions as a group. Unlike the Congress, major decisions are not delegated to committees. Except when deciding whether to accept a case or not, judicial decisions are made by majority vote. The fact that judicial decisions can be reached by a simple majority vote rather than by a unanimous vote or even a two-thirds majority vote influences

In the 1930's the Supreme Court declared unconstitutional several major laws passed by Congress as a part of President Franklin Roosevelt's New Deal program. Anticipating further difficulties unless he could get new members on the Court, President Roosevelt asked Congress to enlarge the Court. He wanted one new justice for every present one over age 70. Roosevelt's "court-packing" plan failed to pass, but Congress did provide an attractive retirement plan for Federal judges. And President Roosevelt soon had a Court more to his liking.

Cartoon by "Ding" Darling. Courtesy of Mr. John M. Henry, secretary of the Ding Foundation, Des Moines, Iowa

That's the kind of sailor he is.

the decisions that are made. It certainly makes the task of reaching decisions on cases much easier than if all or two-thirds of the justices had to agree.

The Constitution states that Federal judges "shall hold their offices during good behavior." This means that a judge can only be removed from office if there is evidence of his misbehavior. Once appointed to the Court, a justice has the most secure job in the world. He alone decides when he will retire, if ever. While he is subject to impeachment for "bad behavior," throughout the history of the Supreme Court no justice has ever been removed by impeachment proceedings.

Permitting justices to hold their jobs without competing in elections was intended to make them free and impartial judges. Once selected, they are obligated to no one for their jobs.

Undoubtedly, lifetime appointment does influence decision-making by the justices, not only because they are relatively free from the political pressures that affect other officeholders, but also because lifetime tenure encourages justices to remain active until they are very old men. In some instances justices have refused to retire even when it has become apparent to others that their declining health and mental capacity has begun to interfere with their capacity to make judgments. In recent years, generous retirement policies have helped ease some men "off the bench."

The Rule on Real Cases

Another important formal rule is that the Supreme Court will hear only *real* cases. This means that to test a law in court a person or group must actually violate it or show that they are *directly affected* by it. Merely because one does not like a law is insufficient grounds for testing it in court.

The *spending power* of Congress is particularly difficult to challenge in the courts. Suppose you believe that the Constitution gives Congress no authority to spend money on urban renewal. The only way that this spending affects you directly is that a small part of the taxes you pay goes for this program. The Federal courts would not accept a case brought by you or by any group of taxpayers challenging the urban renewal program, since your interest is not unique and personal but is shared by all citizens generally.

The rule on *real cases* also means that a Supreme Court justice cannot make decisions until presented with a case calling for a decision. It is reported that Justice Felix Frankfurter once wrote a decision and then waited for the "right" case to appear to which he could apply it. The right case did not appear, so he published it after his retirement as an article in a law review.

The rule on real cases bars the Supreme Court from offering "advisory opinions" about pending legislation. While the President and Congress might like to have the Court's advice on the constitutionality of bills, the Court's only answer can be: Pass the law if you wish. If it is later brought before the Court, then we will offer our opinion about its validity.

Rules on the Supreme Court's Jurisdiction

A court is said to have *jurisdiction* over a case when it has the right to hear and decide it. As we have seen, the Supreme Court has broad *appellate jurisdiction* (the right to review a case tried in a lower court). It may review the following kinds of cases:

1. *Disputes involving the Constitution, Federal laws, and treaties.* Examples: (a) A citizen claims that a state law (or city ordinance, or school-board ruling) violates the Constitution. (b) A citizen believes that he was deprived of some constitutional right in his trial in state or Federal court. (c) A lawyer claims that a state law violated by his client should be voided because it conflicts with a Federal statute or a treaty on the same subject.
2. *Admiralty and maritime cases.* Crimes committed on the high seas and disputes between shipowners or between merchant seamen and officers are examples. Maritime cases are handled in Federal courts and can be reviewed by the Supreme Court.
3. *Cases in which the United States is a party.* Examples: (a) Mr. X sues the Postal Service for injuries suffered in an accident with a postal truck. (b) The government sues a contractor in a dispute over a building contract.

4. *Cases between citizens of different states.* As we saw on page 365, Federal district courts handle some cases in this category. The Supreme Court is unlikely to review such a case, however, unless it involves some constitutional issue.

Cases in the above categories would all have been handled in some lower state or Federal court. They would be reviewed by the Supreme Court only if the justices believed that an important issue was involved. Besides its appellate jurisdiction, the Supreme Court has *original jurisdiction* over three kinds of cases. That is, the case actually begins in (is tried by) the Supreme Court. (1) Cases affecting diplomatic representatives of other nations may be tried by the Supreme Court. Such cases are very rare. Diplomats enjoy immunity from state and Federal criminal prosecution, and a diplomat who breaks the law will be asked to return home. Occasionally a diplomat may be involved

Over the entrance of the beautiful Supreme Court Building is the motto "Equal Justice under Law."

in a civil suit, but effort would be made to settle such a case out of court. The Supreme Court handles (2) *suits between states* and (3) cases involving *a state and the Federal government.* In 1963 the Supreme Court settled a dispute between Arizona and California over use of waters from the Colorado River basin. A recent state-Federal case involved the ownership of public lands in Hawaii.

"Legal" Questions versus "Political" Questions

The Supreme Court decides only "legal" questions; it will not decide "political" questions. The difference between a legal question and a political question is not always easy to determine. For example, in 1946 in the case *Colegrove* v. *Green,* the plaintiffs charged that they were being discriminated against by the State of Illinois because some Illinois congressional districts had much larger populations than did others. Therefore, in one district a Congressman might represent twice the number of people as the Congressman from another district.

The Constitution leaves the task of determining the size and shape of the electoral districts to the states. Over time the districts that included large cities increased greatly in size when compared to the rural districts. State legislatures, often dominated by rural legislators, proved reluctant to alter the congressional districts. Those who were able to control the size and shape of the electoral districts could greatly influence the outcome of elections. In *Colegrove* v. *Green,* the Supreme Court decided it could not interfere in this matter as it was essentially a *political question.*

In the case *Baker* v. *Carr* (1962) the Supreme Court reversed the decision of a three-man district court in Tennessee that had based its ruling on the Supreme Court's own prior decision in *Colegrove* v. *Green.* In *Baker* v. *Carr* the plaintiffs protested that a 1901 Tennessee statute which apportioned the members of the General Assembly among the state's 95 counties had the effect of depriving them of their rights, since their vote counted less than the votes of citizens in other districts. The majority on the Supreme Court ruled in their favor, claiming that the issue was not a political question. The plaintiffs were being denied "equal protection" guaranteed by the Constitution. Justice Frankfurter and Justice Harlan dissented vigorously, accusing the Court of entering into matters that were beyond its proper responsibility.

In brief, a "political question" is any question the Court chooses not to decide for that reason. A question becomes "legal" when the Court decides it does have jurisdiction. A political question at one point in time may become a legal question at a later time. In general the Court will avoid deciding such political issues as whether a current war is "legal," questions of foreign policy, and so on.

Informal Rules

In addition to the formal rules described above, informal rules or customs also influence judicial decision-making. One such rule requires that individuals who wish to influence the court's policy choices must use lawyers. The judicial process is largely a private domain for lawyers. Only lawyers are recruited for the Supreme Court. The candidates are suggested to the President by the United States Attorney General (a lawyer), sometimes after consultation with a committee of the American Bar Association (the major professional association of lawyers). The President's nominee must be approved by the Senate Judiciary Committee (the one committee in Congress restricted to lawyers). Except for the litigants (plaintiffs and defendants) themselves, who may not even be present when their case is being argued, only lawyers may address the Court. The Court's decisions are written in a technical manner intended primarily for other lawyers. No other part of American society has been carved out as the special domain of a professional elite as is true of the courts.

If an ordinary citizen attempts to influence the Court's decision by writing a letter or by petitioning the Court, he may be found to be in "contempt of court." At least, the Court does not consider such efforts to be proper. Nevertheless, the Court may accept *amicus curiae* ("friend of the court") briefs that are intended to influence its decisions. Such briefs, written by lawyers on behalf of organizations that favor one side or the other in the contest before the Court, are an accepted part of the judicial process. Moreover, writing articles for law reviews is an acceptable way to influence the thinking of a justice. In the past, a few organizations with cases pending before the Court have paid for law review articles that supported their side. It is clear that ordinary people do not have the same access to the justices as do lawyers.

Another informal rule is that Supreme Court justices should not engage in partisan politics. This does not mean that individual justices never take part in political discussions. The justices have many friends in Congress and in the Federal agencies. Moreover, it is common for justices to dine at the White House. It would be impossible to avoid all political discussion in Washington, D.C., if they made an effort to do so. Nevertheless, Supreme Court justices are expected not to give active support to one political party against another, to campaign on behalf of a presidential or congressional candidate, or to take sides in a political issue before the Congress.

Some Important Procedures

Formal and informal rules play a major part in determining how judicial decision-making takes place. Within this framework the Court itself has established certain procedures which influence the decisions of the justices. These procedures specify how a case will be handled by the Court. We look at these procedures under the following headings: (1) initiation, (2) oral argument, (3) conference, (4) opinion writing, and (5) post-decision alternatives.

Initiation. Few cases begin in the Supreme Court, as we have seen. When the court exercises appellate jurisdiction, the cases must somehow get the Court's attention. The usual method is called *certiorari.* To illustrate, an attorney thinks that his client's constitutional rights were violated by the police and therefore the man did not get a fair trial. The attorney applies for a *writ of certiorari.* This is an order from a higher court to a lower one requesting that

An attendant prepares the conference room where the justices meet to decide what cases to review and what decisions to hand down in cases already heard.

the record of a case be sent up from the lower court. When the Court receives the application (or petition), the justices will review it. If at least four justices agree to review the case, a *writ of certiorari* is granted. Then the case is scheduled for a hearing.

Some cases reach the Supreme Court by means of a "certificate." Certification is used when the judges of a lower court are equally split on a decision, or when the case is of such importance that they feel the Supreme Court should make the initial judgment. In all cases in today's Court, "certificates" are accepted, placed on the docket, and acted upon.

The Supreme Court reviews only a very small proportion of the cases that appear in court each year. It has been estimated that more than 250,000 cases are filed in Federal courts each year, and more than a million cases are filed in state and local courts. From this total of more than approximately 1,250,000 cases annually, the Supreme Court will receive approximately 4000 applications for review. The majority are denied. The Court hears arguments on 150–160 cases each year.

Time and money are factors in court cases. It may take from two to five years before a case is finally decided in the Supreme Court. And the cost of a single trial in the Federal district court with appeal to the United States Court of Appeals and application for *certiorari* has been estimated to be no less than $15,000. The case *Brown* v. *Board of Education* (p. 393) reportedly cost the NAACP $200,000.

Therefore, the first step in judicial decision-making is deciding whether to accept the case for a hearing. A decision not to hear a case is itself a decision, since the decision reached by a lower court is thereby permitted to stand.

Oral argument. Once a case is accepted by the Court, parties to the case are notified of the time for the hearing. The Supreme Court justices have all the evidence that was presented earlier in the lower court, sometimes running to several volumes. But the Supreme Court also sets aside some time for the contestants in the case to present their arguments. Lawyers for each side prepare carefully documented "briefs" that explain their positions, referring to other cases like theirs that have been decided favorably. Usually the counsel for each party gets one hour for oral argument before the Court.

Conference-decision. During the period that the Supreme Court is in session, its schedule calls for sessions devoted to oral arguments for two weeks followed by two weeks of recess. The period of recess is devoted to writing opinions and studying appeals and petitions. Argument sessions are held from Monday through Thursday. Friday is the day the Supreme Court justices meet in conference.

The following description of the judicial conference is adapted from an address delivered by former Justice Tom Clark to the American Bar Association in 1956.

Conferences are held in an oak-paneled conference chamber around a rectangular conference table at which are placed nine chairs, each bearing the name-plate of a member of the Court.

The Court meets in this room in conference at 11 o'clock each Friday morning during or preceding an argument week and usually does not adjourn until after 5:30. The only persons present at the conference are the justices. It is feared that if secretaries, clerks, or pages were to be present, the decisions might become known too early, thus harming the decision-making process.

The Chief Justice begins the conference by calling the first case and discussing it, thus presenting his views first. After the Chief Justice, each associate justice is given the opportunity to speak in turn, moving from the justice who has served the longest to the justice most recently appointed.

After discussion, a vote is taken. Each justice has a large docket book that is kept locked when not in use. Each justice records his vote in his docket book. Since the time of Chief Justice Marshall, the formal vote begins with the most junior associate justice and continues to the most senior associate justice. The Chief Justice votes last, a procedure just the reverse of the discussion procedure. Five votes are required to decide a case and four votes to grant a *writ of certiorari.*

One of the notable features is that the justices as a group participate in each decision of the Court. This means that the time allowed for the discussion of some matters is necessarily very short. If some cases require an hour's discussion, other matters are likely to be disposed of quickly. However, each of the items on the day's agenda has been considered privately by the justices before the conference.

Opinion-writing. Decisions of the Court are announced to the public as "opinions." Once a decision has been voted upon, someone must write the "opinion" of the Court. If the Chief Justice voted with the majority, he will decide which of the associate justices is to be assigned to write the majority opinion. Occasionally, he will assign the task to himself. If the Chief Justice did not vote with the majority, the most senior associate justice who voted with the majority will decide who shall write the majority opinion.

More is involved in deciding who will write the majority opinion than simply dividing up the work load. The way the opinion is written may determine the final outcome of the case. The writer of the opinion realizes that he is writing a statement that will be used as a precedent for other cases. Moreover, he must try to make the decision as acceptable to the public as possible. Finally, he will use the opinion to try to hold the majority of the justices together and to win the support of one or more dissenting justices, if possible. A well-written opinion may pick up support from justices who had originally been opposed to the decision.

	A Typical Two-Week Schedule for Supreme Court Justices				
	Monday	Tuesday	Wednesday	Thursday	Friday
Week One	Hear oral arguments on cases	Hear oral arguments on cases	Hear oral arguments on cases	Hear oral arguments on cases	Conference
Week Two	Announcements of decisions and publication of opinions	Research and writing of opinions	Research and writing of opinions	Research and writing of opinions	Conference

The task of writing opinions may be the most difficult one a justice has. In some cases months are consumed in researching cases, writing opinions, and circulating drafts to colleagues. A justice who agrees with the decision but disagrees with the statement written for the majority may write his own opinion (called a concurring opinion). Those who oppose the majority frequently write *dissenting opinions*. Only after much discussion and argument is the final decision of the Supreme Court on a case known and the various opinions published.

Few things are more secret than the process by which opinions are formulated. Apparently some justices write the first draft themselves and circulate it among others for advice. Some ask their law clerks to write drafts of opinions; the justice may include some of their views in his final version.

Post-decision alternatives. What happens after the Supreme Court has announced its opinion on a case? At least five alternatives are available to the disappointed party to a case:

(1) He can apply for a rehearing. If the decision was close (5–4), a change in personnel on the Court or a change in the social situation might alter the view of the Court in the future.

(2) Congress may get around the Court by passing new legislation that has the same purposes as the original legislation but is constitutional.

(3) Since the Court does not *decide* cases (it sends *opinions* back to lower courts), the individual can return to the lower court and ask for a new hearing.

(4) The decision of the Court might be ignored. If the decision is unpopular (for example, rulings on school desegregation), some people may choose to ignore it.

(5) The Constitution can be amended. In the late 1960's some members of Congress sponsored a proposed constitutional amendment to permit prayer and Bible reading in public schools in order to upset the Court's ban on such activity (pp. 358–363).

There are occasions in which the Supreme Court may order a lower court to take a certain action. More commonly, the Supreme Court asks the lower court to review its decision, taking the Supreme Court's *opinion* into consideration.

D. Application of the Law to Specific Cases: a Judicial Norm

Carved on the front of the Supreme Court building in Washington are the words "Equal Justice under Law." This phrase summarizes a very important standard, or norm, of judicial behavior. American judges are not expected simply to decide a case by asking, "What would be best for everyone concerned?" Rather, they are expected to ask, "What does the law say about a case like this?" Then if the meaning of the law is not entirely clear, the judges have the duty to say what they think the words of the law mean.

Let us see how this norm, or informal rule, applies to the Baltimore school-prayer case. When the Supreme Court agreed to review this case, their concern was not with such questions as these: Are certain children emotionally upset by religious exercises in the schools? Do more children benefit from religious exercises than are hurt by such practices? Would striking down this law have any good or bad results? These would be useful questions for lawmakers to ask when deciding whether to require or forbid religious exercises in the public schools. But the question facing the Supreme Court was simply whether the Baltimore school-board rule on religious exercises was consistent with the highest law of the land, the Constitution of the United States.

What Is "the Law"?

Justices of the Supreme Court are expected to base their decisions on the law. The highest law in the United States is the Constitution. All other laws—Federal, state, and local—must be in substantial agreement with the Constitution. Very many of the cases reaching the Supreme Court involve

disputes over whether a law passed by Congress, a state legislature, or a local governing body is in agreement with the Constitution. Other cases reaching the Court have to do with the
behavior of officials. For example, did the police make a legal
arrest, or did the judge conduct the trial according to the rules.
In the school-prayer case the question was whether the school
officials were acting legally in requiring religious exercises.

In following the judicial norm of basing decisions on the
law, justices of the Supreme Court look at the Constitution and
any other *written laws* (statutes and ordinances) which apply to
the case. But "the law" consists of more than constitutions and
laws passed by legislative bodies. *The law also includes prior court
decisions.* When the justices studied the Baltimore school-prayer
case, they looked at various earlier rulings by the Supreme Court
on the religion clause of the First Amendment. These earlier
decisions on related cases are called *precedents.* When the Court
made its decision in the Murray case, its ruling became a new
precedent for settling other similar cases.

Following is a case which illustrates how judges look at the
written law (in this case certain sections of the Constitution) and
at precedents in arriving at a decision. You are to play the role
of judge in the situation. Following a brief summary of the facts
of the case, appropriate sections of the Constitution are provided.
You will also read some precedents which the lawyers arguing
the case want you as judge to consider. You should write a
statement telling how you think the case should be resolved.
Your decision must be based on how you think the law (the
portions of the Constitution and the precedents) applies to the
specific case.

By Schochet. Copyright 1970
by Saturday Review, Inc.

"The book I banned twenty
years ago is now required
high school reading."

Case: Applying the Due Process Clause of the Constitution

Henry is arrested and charged with breaking into a poolroom. Henry
states that he is innocent. He also claims that he is too poor to pay for a lawyer
to defend him in court. He asks the state government to provide a lawyer for
him. The government refuses. Henry is tried in court, without a lawyer to help
him, and is found guilty.

Henry complains that his trial was unfair because he did not have the
help of a lawyer. He declares that poor men cannot get equal treatment before
the law because they cannot afford to hire lawyers. He says that American
law courts favor the rich and that American law is a rich man's law. He demands
that his conviction be overturned. The state government refuses to listen to
him, but the United States Supreme Court decides to hear his case.

As one of the Supreme Court justices you must consult a number of
laws. Pay particular attention to the following sections of the Constitution.

In all criminal prosecutions, the accused shall enjoy the right to a speedy and public trial, by an impartial jury of the State and district wherein the crime shall have been committed, which district shall have been previously ascertained by law, and to be informed of the nature and cause of the accusation; to be confronted with the witnesses against him; to have compulsory process for obtaining witnesses in his favor, and to have the assistance of counsel for his defense.—*Sixth Amendment*

All persons born or naturalized in the United States and subject thereof are citizens of the United States and of the State wherein they reside. No State shall make or enforce any law which shall abridge the privileges or immunities of citizens of the United States; nor shall any State deprive any person of life, liberty, or property, without due process of law; nor deny to any person within its jurisdiction the equal protection of the laws.—*Fourteenth Amendment*

When Henry's case reached the Supreme Court, he was represented by a lawyer. The state government was also represented by lawyers. In arguing the case, the lawyers on each side cited the following precedents.

Powell v. *Alabama* (1932): Seven Negro boys were accused of assaulting two white girls aboard a freight train in Alabama. They were found guilty and sentenced to death. They were not advised of their right of counsel, nor were they offered court-appointed counsel, or the opportunity to communicate with their relatives. It was only after they had been convicted that they were offered adequate legal counsel. The Supreme Court reversed the conviction, indicating that the due process clause of the Fourteenth Amendment had been violated.

Johnson v. *Zerbst* (1938): In this Federal court case the government had failed to provide a lawyer for a defendant accused of counterfeiting. Up until 1938 it was generally understood that where a person desired assistance of counsel, but for lack of funds or any other reason was not able to obtain a lawyer, the court was not obligated to furnish him with an attorney unless it was a *capital* case (one punishable by death). In this case the Supreme Court said that the defendant had the right to have a lawyer in *any criminal case in Federal court.*

Betts v. *Brady* (1942): Betts was accused of robbery in Maryland, and he asked the state court to provide him with a lawyer, since he was unable to pay for an attorney. The judge refused, on the ground that it was not the practice to appoint counsel for poor defendants except in murder and rape prosecutions. The Supreme Court upheld the conviction, concluding that "appointment of counsel is not a fundamental right, essential to a fair trial."

Do you agree with Henry that his trial was unfair? Should his conviction be overturned? Explain your reasons.

Checking Your Decision

In the preceding case Henry was tried in court for a criminal offense, without a lawyer, and was found guilty. He complains that his rights under the Constitution have been violated because he did not have the help of a lawyer at his trial.

According to a recent Supreme Court interpretation of the Sixth and Fourteenth amendments to the Constitution, Henry was deprived of his constitutional rights. The Sixth Amendment declares that persons accused of crimes have the right to obtain the help of a lawyer to defend them in court. The Fourteenth Amendment says that no state can deprive a person of his liberty "without due process of law." One aspect of "due process" is the right to have an attorney.

The Sixth Amendment names several requirements for criminal trials *in Federal courts.* They must be (a) speedy, (b) public, and (c) by an impartial jury. The person on trial must (d) be told what he is accused of, (e) have the right to see the witnesses against him, (f) have the right to obtain witnesses in his favor, and (g) have the right to have a lawyer. Without certain of these features it would be difficult to have a fair trial—to have "due process of law." The question in the preceding case is whether all of these requirements are essential to a fair trial. If any of the Sixth Amendment's requirements are basic rights essential to a fair trial, they are covered by the Fourteenth Amendment's due process clause. And the Fourteenth Amendment requires state and local governments to give citizens protection of basic rights.

Since Henry was too poor to hire a lawyer, and the state government would not provide him with a lawyer's services at its expense, Henry was convicted "without due process of law," without "the equal protection of the laws," and in violation of the Sixth Amendment provision that "the accused shall enjoy the right to assistance of counsel for his defense."

The case *Gideon* v. *Wainwright* was very much like the situation described above. Clarence Earl Gideon was arrested and charged with breaking into a poolroom in Panama City, Florida, on August 4, 1961. He declared that he was innocent. During his trial the following dialogue took place:*

*Lucius J. Barker and Twiley W. Barker, Jr., *Freedoms, Courts, Politics: Studies in Civil Liberties,* © 1965. By permission of Prentice-Hall, Inc. Englewood Cliffs, N.J.

The Court: What says the Defendant? Are you ready to go to trial?

The Defendant: I am not ready, your Honor.

The Court: Did you plead not guilty to this charge by reason of insanity?

The Defendant: No, sir.

The Court: Why aren't you ready?

The Defendant: I have no Counsel.

The Court: Why do you not have Counsel? Did you not know that your case was set for trial today?

The Defendant: Yes, sir, I knew that it was set for trial today.

The Court: Why, then did you not secure Counsel and be prepared to go to trial?

The Defendant: Your Honor, . . . I request this Court to appoint Counsel to represent me in this trial.

The Court: Mr. Gideon, I am sorry, but I cannot appoint . . . Counsel to represent you in this case. Under the laws of the State of Florida, the only time the Court can appoint Counsel to represent a Defendant is when that person is charged with a capital offense. I am sorry, but I will have to deny your request to appoint Counsel to defend you in this case.

The Defendant: The United States Supreme Court says I am entitled to be represented by Counsel.

The Court: (Addressing the Reporter) Let the records show that the Defendant has asked the Court to appoint Counsel to represent him in this trial and the Court denied the request, and informed the Defendant that the only time the Court could appoint Counsel to represent a Defendant was in cases where the Defendant was charged with a capital offense. The Defendant stated to the Court that the United States Supreme Court said he was entitled to it. (Addressing the Defendant) Are you now ready to go to trial?

The Defendant: Yes, sir.

In this manner, at the start of his trial, Clarence Gideon raised the question of whether his trial was legal. He claimed that his constitutional rights were being violated. He was too poor to hire a lawyer and the state refused to appoint one for him. The trial judge ruled that his constitutional rights were being respected. The state was not obligated to provide Gideon with a lawyer.

The jury eventually found Gideon guilty, and he was sentenced to five years in the Florida State Prison. However, Gideon continued his efforts to win his freedom. On October 11, 1961, he appealed to the Florida Supreme Court, but was refused a hearing.

Gideon next appealed to the United States Supreme Court. The Supreme Court granted Gideon a hearing and appointed Abe Fortas, a famous attorney appointed to the Supreme Court in 1966, to argue Gideon's case. Fortas argued:

> An accused person cannot effectively defend himself. The assistance of counsel is necessary to "due process" and to a fair trial. . . .
>
> To convict the poor without counsel while we guarantee the right to counsel to those who can afford it is also a denial of equal protection of the laws.

The Supreme Court agreed with Fortas. Justice Hugo Black delivered the opinion of the Court. He said that the "due process" clause of the Fourteenth Amendment protects a person from being sent to jail in disregard of his basic rights. Justice Black devoted most of his remarks in the majority opinion to the *Powell* and *Betts* cases (p. 380). He said, "We think the Court in *Betts* was wrong . . . in concluding that the Sixth Amendment's guarantee of counsel is not [one of the] fundamental rights" covered by the Fourteenth Amendment's due process clause.

After the Supreme Court decision, the state of Florida gave Clarence Gideon another trial. This time, W. Fred Turner, a local attorney, was named by the court to defend him. This time the jury returned a verdict of "not guilty."

. It is important to note that in the case described above, the Supreme Court sought to *apply* and to *interpret* the law. The justices are not free to make any kind of decision they want. Their decisions must be logically related to the Constitution, to statutes, or to precedents. Thus, one of the features of judicial decision-making is making decisions on the basis of law.

Capital offense: a crime punishable by death.

In The Supreme Court of The United States
Washington D.C.
Clarence Earl Gideon
        Petitioner,
        vs.
H.G. Cochran, Jr., as
Director, Divisions
of corrections State
of Florida

Petition for a writ
of Certiorari Directed
To The Supreme Court
State of Florida.

No. 890 Misc.

OCT. TERM 1961

U.S. Supreme Court

To. The Honorable Earl Warren, Chief
Justice of the United States
        Comes now The petitioner, Clarence
Earl Gideon, a citizen of The United States
of America, in proper person, and appearing
as his own counsel. Who petitions this
Honorable Court for a Writ of Certiorari
directed to The Supreme Court of The State
of Florida. To review the order and Judgement of the court below denying The
petitioner a Writ of Habeus Corpus.
        Petitioner submits That The Supreme
Court of The United States has The authority
and Jurisdiction to review The final Judgement of The Supreme Court of The State
of Florida the highest court of The State
Under sec. 344(B) Title 28 U.S.C.A. and
Because The "Due process clause" of the

Gideon spent hours in the state prison library consulting law books. Then he penciled this petition asking the Supreme Court to hear his case.

E. *Stare Decisis:* Another Judicial Norm

As you have learned, judges are expected to look both at statutory law and at precedent (earlier decisions on similar or related cases) in reaching a decision. We now focus on the use of precedent in reaching court decisions. A second major judicial norm (informal rule) is *stare decisis,* which means "let the decision stand." In effect, this rule tells the judge to be consistent, to pay close attention to earlier decisions on related cases.

The Florida judge who told Clarence Gideon that the state was not obliged to provide him with a lawyer was following the *stare decisis* norm. In 1961 the precedent which most nearly fit Gideon's case was *Betts* v. *Brady* (p. 380). In that case the Supreme Court said that a state judge was not obliged to offer a defendant in a noncapital criminal case a court-appointed lawyer.

The *stare decisis* norm is more binding on lower courts than on the Supreme Court. The practice of following precedents gives stability to the legal system. Imagine the confusion if judges could decide cases any which way. Lawyers would be unable to prepare cases for their clients. Parties in a court case could not be sure of their rights. A legal *system* could really not exist without the following of precedents. But new social conditions sometimes require new interpretations of the law. Thus most of the really important decisions of the Supreme Court are those which set new precedents or which modify in some way an old precedent.

When the Supreme Court modifies existing precedent, as it did in the *Gideon* case, it does not ignore previous decisions. Justice Black, speaking for the majority in the *Gideon* case, said that the precedent of *Betts* v. *Brady* was mistaken. He said that the Court in 1942 should have ruled in favor of Betts by following the precedent established in 1932 in *Powell* v. *Alabama* (p. 380), in which the Court ruled that the seven boys had failed to receive a fair trial for lack of legal counsel. In fact, Justice Black in 1942 had written a dissenting opinion in the *Betts* case in which he emphasized the *Powell* v. *Alabama* precedent.

In short, while the Supreme Court does give new interpretations to the law—makes new precedents—it tries very hard to find earlier precedents in support of its new decisions.

The norm *stare decisis* is a powerful influence on judicial decision-making. The lawyers appearing before the Court build their cases by finding prior decisions which hopefully the justices will accept. Each Supreme Court justice listens to the arguments presented by the opposing lawyers. One justice may be impressed by a particular set of precedents, and another justice by another set of prior decisions. And when a justice gets the assignment to write the Court's decision in a case, he will be careful to show how the present decision is based on precedent.

You Be the Judge: Escobedo v. Illinois

When the Supreme Court in 1963 in *Gideon* v. *Wainwright* decided that a criminal defendant in a state court had to be furnished a lawyer, the Court still did not answer all the questions about assistance of counsel. One unanswered question was this: Just when in the criminal proceedings must the accused have access to a lawyer? This question came before the court in 1964 in the case of *Escobedo* v. *Illinois.*

You are to imagine yourself a member of the Supreme Court in 1964. A brief description of the case follows. The pertinent sections of the Constitution and a number of precedent decisions are cited. You are to write an "opinion" explaining how the case should be resolved.

The crime and the arrest. On the night of January 19, 1960, Danny Escobedo's brother-in-law was fatally shot. At 2:30 the next morning Escobedo, his sister Grace (wife of the deceased), and two friends of Danny's—a Mr. Chan and a Mr. Di Gerlando—were arrested. They were taken to a Chicago police station and questioned by detectives for over fourteen hours. None of those arrested made a statement, and a lawyer they had called managed to secure their release at 5 o'clock in the afternoon of the same day they were arrested.

The police believed that Escobedo and his friends had killed Grace's husband because she hated him. But the police had no proof, only guesses. On January 30 Benedict Di Gerlando, who was again in police custody and who was later indicted (formally accused) for the murder along with Escobedo, told police that Danny had fired the fatal shots. Between 8 and 9 o'clock on the night of January 30, Escobedo and his sister were again arrested and taken to police headquarters. On the way to the police station one of the arresting officers said to Danny that Di Gerlando had told the police that Escobedo had fired the fatal shots. The officer told Danny that he might as well admit to the crime. To this Escobedo replied: "I am sorry but I would like to have advice from my lawyer."

The lawyer's testimony. Upon arrival at the police headquarters Escobedo was hurried into a questioning room with his hands tied behind his back. Shortly thereafter, Escobedo's lawyer arrived. At the trial, Escobedo's lawyer described the events in these terms:

> On that day I received a phone call from the mother of another defendant and pursuant to that phone call I went to the Detective Bureau at 11th and State. The first person I talked to was the sergeant on duty at the Bureau Desk, Sergeant Pidgeon. I asked Sergeant Pidgeon for permission to speak to my client, Danny Escobedo. . . . Sergeant Pidgeon made a call to the Bureau lockup and informed me that the boy had been taken from the lockup to the Homicide Bureau. This was between 9:30 and 10:00 in the evening. Before I went anywhere, he [Pidgeon] called the Homicide Bureau and told them there was an attorney waiting to see Escobedo. He told me I could not see him. Then I went upstairs to the Homicide Bureau. There were several Homicide Detectives around and I talked to them. I identified myself as Escobedo's attorney and asked permission to see him. They said I could not. . . . The police officer told me to see Chief Flynn, who was

on duty. I identified myself to Chief Flynn and asked permission to see my client. He said I couldn't see him because they hadn't completed questioning. . . . I filed an official complaint with Commissioner Phelan of the Chicago Police Department. I had a conversation with every police officer I could find. I was told at Homicide that I couldn't see him and I would have to get a writ of habeas corpus. I left the Homicide Bureau. . . . at approximately 11:00 [Sunday morning]. I had no opportunity to talk to my client that night. I quoted to Captain Flynn the Section of the Criminal Code which allows an attorney the right to see his client.

The Illinois statute then in effect provided in part that:

All public officers . . . having the custody of any person . . . restrained of his liberty for any alleged cause whatever, shall except in cases of imminent danger of escape, admit any practicing attorney . . . whom such person . . . may desire to see or consult. . . .

Other testimony. Escobedo testified that throughout the questioning he repeatedly asked to see his lawyer and that the police replied that his lawyer "didn't want to see" him. The police testified that throughout the questioning Escobedo was handcuffed in a standing position. Moreover, evidence was introduced to show that Escobedo was upset because he had not slept well for more than a week. Other testimony revealed that during the questioning Officer Montejano, who grew up in Escobedo's neighborhood and knew his family and who spoke to Escobedo in Spanish, told him that he and his sister could go home (and they would be held only as witnesses) if Danny pinned the crime on Di Gerlando.

Escobedo testified that he finally accused Di Gerlando of the murder because of the promises made by Montejano. In turn, Montejano denied making any such promises.

Another police officer testified that during the questioning the following occurred:

> I informed him of what Di Gerlando told me and when I did, he told me that Di Gerlando was lying and I said, "Would you care to tell Di Gerlando that?" And he said, "Yes, I will." So I brought . . . Escobedo in and he confronted Di Gerlando and he told him that he was lying and said, "I didn't shoot Manuel, you did it."

At this time Escobedo, for the first time, admitted to having *some* knowledge of the crime. Later he made other statements that further indicated his connection with the murder plot. An Assistant State's Attorney was summoned to take a statement. This person, an experienced lawyer, took the statement by asking carefully framed questions designed to assure that Escobedo's answers would be accepted as evidence. Escobedo said that he and his friends had planned to kill his brother-in-law because Grace wanted to get rid of him. Escobedo also said that he had offered Di Gerlando $500 to kill Grace's husband. According to his statement, Chan was a lookout for the job.

Escobedo was convicted of murder and sentenced to twenty years in prison. He appealed his conviction to the Supreme Court, saying that any statements made during the time he was not allowed to see his lawyer should not have been used against him.

Constitutional Provisions and Precedents

This case involved the "assistance of counsel" clause in the Sixth Amendment and the due process clause of the Fourteenth Amendment (p. 380) just as the *Gideon* case did. Also involved was a part of the Fifth Amendment which declares that "No person . . . shall be compelled in any criminal case to be a witness against himself. . . ."

This latter provision means that a person may not be *forced* to sign a confession or take the witness stand in his own trial. If he supplies testimony, he must do so voluntarily. This clause in the Fifth Amendment originally applied only to the Federal government. But over the years the Supreme Court decided that the right not to testify against oneself (called *self-incrimination*) was a fundamental right protected by the due process clause of the Fourteenth Amendment. It therefore applied to state governments as well as the national government.

Why might the police sometimes prefer that a call to the arrested person's attorney be postponed? How do you think the cartoonist feels about the issue?

In the *Escobedo* case the Supreme Court justices cited a number of precedent cases—either in the majority opinion or in the dissenting opinions.

Bram v. *United States:* On December 13, 1867, while on board ship to Halifax, a sailor named Brown was accused of murder. He implicated a fellow sailor, Bram, in the crime. Bram was put in irons and held prisoner on board ship until arrival at port. At Boston, Bram was charged with the crime. During the testimony presented at the trial, it was discovered Bram had been taken into a room, stripped of his clothing, and ordered to answer questions. Bram was convicted, but appealed to the Supreme Court, and the Court held that the confession made by Bram was involuntary and therefore inadmissible as evidence. He was released.

Powell v. *Alabama* (1932): See page 380.

Hamilton v. *Alabama:* The petitioner was refused the right to counsel in an assault case. He was convicted and sentenced to death. The Supreme Court reversed the Alabama decision saying "only the presence of counsel could have enabled this accused to know all the defenses available to him."

Ward v. *Texas:* In June, 1942, Ward was harassed by the police for a confession. He was taken to several jails in different counties and held for an extended period of time until he finally confessed. The Supreme Court held that the use of the confession at the trial voided the conviction.

Haley v. *Ohio:* Haley, a 15-year-old boy, confessed to committing a murder after five hours of questioning, starting at midnight, by police officers working in relays. The officers did not inform him of his rights. In 1948 the Supreme Court

388

ruled that the confession should be disregarded because it was involuntary and violated the boy's rights under the Fourteenth Amendment.

Spano v. *New York* (1957): Vincent Spano was convicted of murdering a former professional boxer after the man had walked out of a bar with some of Spano's money that had been lying on the counter after Spano had paid for a drink. Spano followed the boxer outside; the boxer beat Spano, kicking him in the head. Spano got a gun, killed the boxer, and then turned himself over to the police, bringing his lawyer with him. After the lawyer left, the police questioned Spano for several hours, finally getting a confession that was used in his trial. He was convicted but the Supreme Court overruled the decision, saying the confession was not voluntary.

Cicenia v. *Lagay* (1958): The Supreme Court upheld a lower court's decision convicting Cicenia of murder. Cicenia said he was denied his right to consult his lawyer until he had confessed. He also said he had not been permitted to inspect his confession before pleading.

White v. *Maryland:* In April, 1963, White was arrested on a charge of murder and pleaded guilty without having the advice or assistance of counsel. Counsel was later appointed, and he pleaded not guilty at his formal "arraignment." However, the guilty plea made at the preliminary hearing was introduced in evidence at his trial, and he was sentenced to death. The Supreme Court held that the absence of counsel when the guilty plea was entered violated White's rights under the due process clause of the Fourteenth Amendment.

Haynes v. *Washington:* In May, 1963, Haynes was convicted on a robbery charge and sentenced to prison. He objected, in his appeal, to the use as evidence of a written confession obtained after sixteen hours of being held "incommunicado" and after being told he could not call his wife until he signed the confession. The Supreme Court held the evidence was obtained involuntarily and reversed the lower court's decision.

Gideon v. *Wainwright* (1963): See pages 381–383.

How would you decide the case? Was Escobedo deprived of his rights? What precedent opinions did you draw upon to reach your decision?

F. The Influence of Social Forces and Personal Belief on Judicial Decision-Making

The norms, rules, and procedures described earlier apply to all justices alike. Nevertheless, justices do not always agree about what is a good decision. And sometimes a decision believed to be "good" at one time is reversed years later by another group of justices. Probably these differences can be accounted for by changes in the social situation and by new justices who have different personal beliefs than their predecessors. Supreme Court justices, like other men, are influenced by values, attitudes, and beliefs widely held during the time in which they live. They are likely to take advantage of knowledge

acquired by recent social science research and will be influenced by current social theories.

The following case study illustrates the influence of social forces on judicial decision-making. After you have read the case, answer the following questions:

1. How may the concept "political culture" be used to explain the reversal in decision?

2. How would you use the opinions expressed by Justice Brown and Chief Justice Warren to demonstrate that social forces influence the decisions of Supreme Court justices?

3. If social forces influence judicial opinions, what advice would you offer regarding the recruitment of judges?

The Segregation Decisions of 1896 and 1954

In the latter part of the nineteenth century, segregation was established firmly in the South. A civil rights law had been passed in 1875. This law said that segregation was illegal. It said that Negroes could not be stopped from using public services on equal terms with whites. But this law was declared "null and void" by the United States Supreme Court in 1881. In the South a social and political system based on unequal treatment of the races was a fact of life. Public opinion throughout the nation was either hostile to or indifferent about the problems of the Negro.

A very important case about segregation came to the United States Supreme Court in 1896. It was called *Plessy* v. *Ferguson*. Homer Plessy was a very light-skinned man with a one-eighth Negro heritage. He lived in Louisiana, where segregation laws existed. One day he bought a train ticket and entered a passenger car having a sign that read, "For Whites Only." He took a seat in the car. This simple action, a man with dark skin sitting in a passenger car reserved for whites, broke one of Louisiana's segregation laws. The train conductor ordered Plessy to leave the seat and to move to a passenger car reserved for Negroes. Plessy refused to move and was arrested. He was taken to jail to await trial. At his trial, Plessy was found guilty of breaking a Louisiana law.

Plessy appealed this decision to the United States Supreme Court. He claimed that the segregation laws of Louisiana violated the Fourteenth Amendment of the Constitution. Plessy said that the segregation laws should be declared unconstitutional and that his conviction for breaking these laws should be overturned.

Following is Section 1 of the Fourteenth Amendment:

> All persons born or naturalized in the United States, and subject to the jurisdiction thereof are citizens of the United States and of the State wherein they reside. No State shall make or enforce any law which shall abridge the privileges or immunities of citizens of the United States; nor shall any State deprive any person of life, liberty, or property, without due process of law; nor deny to any person within its jurisdiction the equal protection of the laws.

390

This amendment says that *all* persons shall have "the equal protection of the laws." Plessy said that Negroes were not given the same protection of the laws as were white people. He claimed that the Louisiana segregation laws contradicted the Constitution, that they prevented Negroes from enjoying "the equal protection of the laws."

The Supreme Court did not agree with Homer Plessy. It decided that segregation laws did not contradict the Fourteenth Amendment if the separate facilities provided for Negroes were equal to the facilities provided for whites. This decision was called the "separate but equal" doctrine. The vote of the Supreme Court was 7 to 1 against the appeal of Homer Plessy. Justice John M. Harlan voted for Plessy's appeal and against the majority opinion of the Court. Justice David J. Brewer did not vote.

Justice Henry Brown wrote the majority opinion of the Court. He said:

> The object of the Fourteenth Amendment was undoubtedly to enforce the absolute equality of two races before the law, but in the nature of things it could not have been intended to abolish distinctions based on color, or to enforce social, as distinguished from political, equality. . . . Laws permitting, and even requiring, [the separation of the two races] in places where they are liable to be brought into contact do not necessarily imply the inferiority of either race to the other. . . . The most common instance of this is connected with the establishment of separate schools for white and colored children. . . .
>
> Gauged by this standard, we cannot say that a law . . . [requiring] the separation of the two races in public conveyances is unreasonable.

Justice Brown's opinion argued that separation of the races did not stamp "the colored race with a badge of inferiority." The majority felt that while the courts must ensure the civil and political rights of both races, the Plessy case was an issue of social equality. The Court concluded that "If one race be inferior to the other socially, the Constitution of the United States cannot put them upon the same plane."

Citizens' Council, Jackson, Miss.

"Judicial tyranny."

© 1970, Don Wright, *The Miami News*

"Really, now—you can't hold it there forever."

Cartoonist Wright pictures the desegregation rulings of the Court as bitter medicine that must be swallowed. The cartoon on the left represents the view of groups organized in the South in the 1950's to delay desegregation. They argued that the Court was trimming away states' rights.

Justice Brown noted that segregation of Negroes was a way of life in the South. He noted that Negroes were considered inferior by whites. He concluded that the Constitution could not be used to change the beliefs of whites about Negroes. He interpreted the Fourteenth Amendment to mean that segregation could be practiced. The Supreme Court decision in the *Plessy* v. *Ferguson* case buttressed the segregation system.

In practice the "separate but equal" doctrine meant separate and *unequal*. Separate black schools were not as good as separate white schools. For example, in 1940 the Southern state governments spent about twice as much money for the education of white children as they did for the education of black children. As late as 1960–1961, the state of Mississippi was spending $81.86 per white child in average daily attendance compared to $21.77 for Negro children. Similar examples could be provided about other supposedly "separate but equal" facilities to show that the *Plessy* v. *Ferguson* case merely legitimized the unequal treatment of Negroes.

In 1954 the *Plessy* v. *Ferguson* decision, as it applied to segregated schools, was overturned in the case known as *Brown* v. *Board of Education of Topeka, Kansas.* In a vote of 9 to 0, the Supreme Court decided that "separate but equal" public schools violated the Fourteenth Amendment. The Court decided that segregated public schools denied Negroes "the equal protection of the laws."

Chief Justice Earl Warren wrote the unanimous opinion for the Court. Justice Warren said:

> . . . minors of the Negro race, through their legal representatives, seek the aid of the courts in obtaining admission to the public schools of their community on a nonsegregated basis. In each instance, they had been denied admission to schools attended by white children under laws requiring or permitting segregation according to race. This segregation was alleged to deprive the plaintiffs of the equal protection of the laws under the Fourteenth Amendment. . . .
>
> The plaintiffs contend that segregated public schools are not "equal" and cannot be made "equal," and that hence they are deprived of the equal protection of the laws. . . .
>
> In approaching this problem, we cannot turn the clock back to 1868 when the Amendment was adopted, or even to 1896 when *Plessy* v. *Ferguson* was written. We must consider public education in the light of its full development and its present place in American life throughout the Nation. Only in this way can it be determined if segregation in public schools deprives these plaintiffs of the equal protection of the laws.
>
> Today, education is perhaps the most important function of state and local governments. . . . It is required in the performance of our most basic public responsibilities, even service in the armed forces. It is the very foundation of good citizenship. . . . In these days, it is doubtful that any child may reasonably be expected to succeed in life if he is denied the opportunity of an education. Such an opportunity, where the state has undertaken to provide it, is a right which must be made available to all on equal terms.
>
> We come then to the question presented: Does segregation of children in public schools solely on the basis of race, even though the physical facilities and other "tangible" factors may be equal, deprive the children of the minority group of equal educational opportunities? We believe that it does. . . .
>
> To separate them from others of similar age and qualifications solely because of their race generates a feeling of inferiority as to their status in the community that may affect their hearts and minds in a way unlikely ever to be undone. . . .
>
> We conclude that in the field of public education the doctrine of "separate but equal" has no place. Separate educational facilities are inherently unequal. Therefore, we hold that the plaintiffs . . . are . . . deprived of the equal protection of the laws guaranteed by the Fourteenth Amendment.

Chief Justice Warren said that segregated schools for Negroes were not and could not be equal to white schools. Warren pointed to the inequality of educational opportunities in our society today. He asserted that segregation by race, "generates a feeling of inferiority as to their status in the community that may affect their hearts and minds in a way unlikely ever to be undone." This conclusion was based on current theories of psychology and sociology. Warren based his decisions on the Fourteenth Amendment and current ideas about the relationship of a social environment to equality of opportunity.

The Influence of Personal Beliefs on Judicial Decision-Making

A changing social situation may help explain why a Court will reverse the opinion of a Court fifty years before, but it does not explain why nine justices serving on the same Court have trouble reaching agreement upon the case before them. This can best be accounted for by examining the personal beliefs of the justices.

Each Supreme Court justice is a unique individual, whose personality was shaped by a set of unique personal experiences. While the role of Supreme Court justice is the same for the eight associate justices and nearly the same for the Chief Justice, each member gives his own interpretation to the role. And each member tends to view the current social situation through his own perspectives.

Some justices have tended to take the side of individuals in cases involving possible violations of civil rights and liberties, believing that individuals need to be supported against attacks by government on their freedom. Other justices tend to give greater weight to protecting the majority. For example, in a case involving the use of evidence gained by wiretapping, some justices may believe that such evidence cannot be used in court because it was gained illegally. They would consider wiretapping a clear violation of the personal freedoms of the individual. Therefore, although the evidence suggests the accused is guilty, these justices might decide that he must go free because he was convicted with illegal evidence. Other justices, concerned about the increase of crime, may feel that intrusion on one's freedom through the use of electronic "bugging" is justified if it helps curb crime. These judges are more willing to accept evidence acquired through wiretapping and therefore to uphold the verdict of the lower courts.

Some justices believe that the Court should actively support policies aimed at ending racial discrimination. Other justices believe that such questions are usually political questions and should be settled by political processes.

Justices may also differ in how the "facts" are to be interpreted. In recent years the Supreme Court has heard a number of cases dealing with pornography. After looking at alleged indecent pictures and films and reading books that are considered pornographic, the Court continues to have difficulty establishing a standard definition of "hard-core pornography." The Court's difficulty stems from the fact that justices have trouble both defining pornography for themselves and getting other justices to accept their definition.

394

In *Jacobellis* v. *Ohio* (1964) the Court found that a certain movie was not pornographic as had been found by the lower court. In his concurring opinion, Justice Potter Stewart said, "I shall not attempt to further define the kinds of material I understand to be embraced within that shorthand description [of pornography]; and perhaps I could never succeed in intelligibly doing so. But I know it when I see it." Many decisions are influenced by how the justice "sees it," that is by his own personal beliefs.

G. What Kinds of People Become Supreme Court Justices?

In the previous lesson you learned that it makes a difference *who* the judge is. Rules, procedures, and norms all serve to shape the judicial role, but the personal beliefs of the justice interact with each of these influences, leading him to make decisions that are often different from those of his colleagues on the bench. Therefore, decisions made by the Court are in large part products of the kind of men they are. Who are the justices? What kind of training have they had? What are their social class origins? What prior political experiences have they had? Answers to these and to other questions are suggested by the tables that follow. The data are from an article by John R. Schmidhauser, "The Justices of the Supreme Court: A Collective Portrait." After reading each table, write your answers to the questions that are provided.

One important influence on any person—including judges—is the socioeconomic status of his family in his early years. A major factor which social scientists use to measure the socioeconomic status of families is the *occupation* of the father or chief breadwinner. Schmidhauser found the following occupational backgrounds of the fathers of Supreme Court justices from 1789 to 1957.

Schmidhauser in *Midwest Journal of Political Science*, Vol. 3.1 (February, 1959), pp. 2–37, 40–49. Adapted by permission of the Wayne State University Press.

Occupations of Fathers	1789–1919		1920–1957	
High status occupations	**63**	*93%*	**19**	*83%*
Merchants or manufacturers	9		5	
Bankers or financeers	1		0	
Wealthy farmers, plantation owners, land speculators	20		3	
Lawyers	14		6	
Clergymen	8		2	
Physicians	7		1	
Miscellaneous	4		2	
Low status occupations	**5**	*7%*	**4**	*17%*
Small farmers	4		3	
Mechanics and laborers	1		1	
Number of justices	68		23	

1. What generalizations can you make about the social-class origins of Supreme Court justices as measured by father's occupation?

2. Are there significant differences between the social-class origins of justices appointed prior to 1920 and after 1920?

Where the Supreme Court justices were born and their ethnic background also interested Schmidhauser. Up to 1957 all but six justices were born in the United States. Five were born in Europe and one in Asia, but the latter was not of Asian ethnic background. Thurgood Marshall in 1967 became the first Negro justice. All justices up to 1967 had European ethnic backgrounds.

Place of Birth	1789–1919		1920–1957	
United States	62	91%	21	91%
Europe	3		2	
Asia	1		0	
Type of Community of Birth				
Urban	22	33%	11	48%
Small town	24	36%	10	43%
Rural	21	31%	2	9%
Ethnic Origin of Family				
English or Welsh	41	60%	11	48%
Scotch-Irish	16	23%	6	26%
Irish	2		3	
French	4		0	
German	3		1	
Dutch	2		0	
Scandinavian	0		1	
Iberian	0		1	

1. What conclusions can you make about where justices were born?

2. Since 1920 a much smaller proportion of justices have come from a rural background. How do you account for this fact? What differences might this fact make on the decisions of the justices?

3. How do the ethnic backgrounds of Supreme Court justices compare with those of Presidents and members of Congress?

4. What differences might it make to judicial decisions if the ethnic origins of justices were different?

5. All justices from 1789 to today have been male. Why have women been excluded? Would decisions likely have been different if women were Supreme Court justices?

It is hardly surprising that all the Supreme Court justices were lawyers at some time or other before their appointment to the Court. Schmidhauser investigated the legal education of the justices and the primary kinds of legal activity which each justice engaged in before his appointment to the Court.

Types of Legal Education	1789–1919		1920–1957	
Law school of high standing	17	25%	15	65%
Law school of average standing	7	10%	6	26%
Private apprenticeship and study under a prominent lawyer or judge	43	63%	1	4%
Self-taught	1		1	
Types of Legal Practice	**1789–1919**		**1920–1957**	
Primarily politicians (officeholders)	37	54%	12	52%
Primarily state or Federal judges	21	31%	3	13%
Primarily corporation lawyers	7	10%	4	17%
Primarily non-corporate practice	3	4%	0	
Teaching or research in the law	0		4	17%

1. Is it likely that a person with no legal training would become a justice?

2. How would you account for the differences in legal education of justices since 1920 with those appointed earlier in our history?

3. What kinds of lawyers are most likely to be selected as Supreme Court justices? What influence might this have on judicial decision-making?

All but one of the 91 justices studied by Schmidhauser had held some kind of political post prior to his appointment to the Court. The following table shows the *highest* political post held by the ninety justices with such experience. Many justices have held numerous political positions.

	1789–1919		1920–1957	
Federal political careers	35	52%	20	87%
Executive branch	19		12	
Congress	7		5	
Judicial branch	9		3	
State political careers	28	42%	3	13%
Executive branch	7		1	
Legislature	6		0	
Judicial branch	15		2	
Political party management or presidential elector	4	6%	0	

1. Try to account for the fact that the Federal judiciary has been a less promising road to the Supreme Court than the executive branch.

2. Why is the Federal government a more promising route than state or local government?

3. Why has the state judiciary been a more promising route than state executive or legislative branches?

In summary, write a paragraph containing a profile of a "typical" Supreme Court justice. Then speculate about the possible effect on judicial decision-making of having people of the "typical" characteristics on the bench. If other kinds of people were to be selected as justices, would different decisions be a likely result?

H. The Appointment of a Chief Justice: Two Case Studies

Imagine that you are the President of the United States. A Supreme Court justice has written to you announcing that he will retire at the close of the present term of the Court. You have asked your Attorney General to prepare a list of possible candidates from which you may choose one to nominate to the Senate.

Following are three names that he has given you. Each has been checked with the Committee on the Federal Judiciary of the American Bar Association and has been awarded a high rating. Moreover, each name has been presented informally to members of the Senate Judiciary Committee, and you have been assured that any of the three can win confirmation. Therefore, you can appoint successfully any of the three. Whom would you appoint and why?

Candidate A: Mr. Brown is a well-known law school professor and a specialist on the Supreme Court. He has written many distinguished articles and books on the Court. More of his students have been chosen to serve as clerks to Supreme Court justices than those of any other law professor. He is a close personal friend to three of the present justices. Mr. Brown has not campaigned for or held any political office. Moreover, he is not identified closely with any political party, as he feared partisan political activity would interfere with his scholarship. He is fifty-five years old.

Candidate B: Mr. Smith is your Attorney General. He is a long-time political ally and friend. He has spent most of his life in political office—first as a state legislator, then as a Congressman, and later as governor. When you were elected President, he left a profitable private practice to become Attorney General. He has always been active in state and national politics, and you think alike on most political matters. He has never been a judge; he is fifty-seven years old.

Candidate C: Mr. Jameson is a Federal district court judge. You appointed him only two years ago at the urging of his friend, Senator Strongarm. The Senator had reminded you that without his state's electoral votes, you would not be President. Senator Strongarm's support was important in his state; it was easy to pay your debt by appointing Jameson. Now, Strongarm would like to see Jameson appointed to the Supreme Court. While Jameson is a hard-working, competent judge, you have not always liked his decisions, especially those relating to civil rights and the treatment of criminals. He is fifty-six years old.

Whom will you nominate and why?

President Johnson Nominates a Chief Justice

In June, 1968, Chief Justice Earl Warren sent a letter to President Lyndon B. Johnson, indicating he would like to retire from the Supreme Court at a time "effective at your [the President's] pleasure." President Johnson replied that he would accept Warren's resignation at a time that a suitable successor could be found.

This exchange of letters touched off an intense political battle. Some observers believe that Warren, knowing that President Johnson was not planning to run for the Presidency and believing a Republican candidate might win, decided to retire prior to the close of Johnson's term of office in order that he might appoint Warren's successor. Some commentators believe that Warren wished to maintain the liberal strength on the Court and thought his opportunity to do so would be greater if President Johnson chose his successor. If Warren were to wait until February, 1969, to retire, someone with more conservative political attitudes might be chosen to succeed him. A judge with more conservative views would be less likely to make decisions favored by Warren.

Warren's letter was sent at a time that the Supreme Court's popularity was very low. The table below contains evidence of the popularity of the Court in the summer of 1968. Many Americans were unhappy with recent decisions of the Court and expressed their displeasure to their congressmen.

"In general, what kind of rating would you give the Supreme Court—excellent, good, fair or poor?"

	Latest %	July, 1967 %
Excellent	8	15
Good	28	30
Total Favorable	36	45
Fair	32	29
Poor	21	17
Total Unfavorable	53	46
No Opinion	11	9

Source: George Gallup. "High Court Gets a Low Rating," *The Washington Post*, July 10, 1968. Reprinted by permission of the American Institute of Public Opinion (The Gallup Poll), Princeton, New Jersey.

Acting on Chief Justice Warren's letter, President Johnson decided to nominate Justice Abe Fortas, who had been appointed to the bench by Johnson in 1965, to the post of Chief Justice and to nominate Homer Thornberry, a long-time Texas friend of the President, to fill the "vacancy" left by Fortas, if and when he was ratified by the Senate as Chief Justice. As both Fortas and Thornberry had been close associates of the President, it was clear to the Senators that confirmation of these two appointments would support Johnson's policies and would likely continue the present decisions of the Court.

A number of Senators expressed opposition to the nomination of Fortas and Thornberry, but the strongest opposition came from Senator Strom Thurmond of South Carolina. Thurmond had been a major critic of the Supreme Court, especially its decisions on civil rights. Moreover, Senator Thurmond, formerly a Democrat, had become a Republican because he disagreed with most of the policies of the national Democratic party. Finally, Thurmond was a supporter of Richard Nixon, the Republican candidate for President. Not only did Thurmond dislike Johnson's nominees, he hoped to postpone a nomination to the Supreme Court until Richard Nixon became President.

Throughout the debate on the Fortas nomination, little was said about Fortas's technical qualifications for the job. He was generally admired as a competent attorney. The principal criticism directed at Fortas related to his political views and his close association with President Johnson.

On July 18, Fortas appeared before the Senate Judiciary Committee for an inquiry into his "qualifications" for the job of Chief Justice. For nearly two hours Senator Thurmond attacked the Court and Fortas personally for past Court decisions. A description of a portion of that hearing follows:

> Thurmond pressed Fortas for his opinion on a 1957 ruling that freed confessed rapist Andrew Mallory of Washington. Fortas was appointed to the Court in 1965.
>
> "Why did he go free? Do you believe in that kind of justice?" the Senator [Thurmond] demanded.
>
> "Mallory! Mallory! I want that name to ring in your ears. Mallory!" he shouted. "A man who confessed a crime and the Court turned him loose on a technicality. Do you as a Justice of the Supreme Court condone such a decision as that?"*

* *Washington Post*, July 19, 1968. Reprinted by permission of The Washington Post. Copyright 1968.

The hearings revealed that Fortas had been asked to advise President Johnson from time to time on "fantastically difficult" decisions concerning Vietnam and the urban crisis. Some Senators worried whether this was a good practice for an associate justice to have such a close relationship to the President. Fortas replied:

> Since I have been a Justice, the President of the United States has never, directly or indirectly, proximately or remotely, talked to me about a matter before the Court or that might come before the Court. The President has done me the honor on some occasions to ask my help on a few critical matters having nothing whatever to do with a legal situation.

A third criticism aimed at Fortas was his interpretation of the judicial role as related to the Constitution. Senator Sam Ervin (Democrat of North Carolina) expressed his opposition to the Fortas view in a letter to the *Washington Post*, August 9, 1968:

> Let me assure you that I was courteous to Justice Fortas throughout the hearing and treated him just exactly like I would have liked to have been treated had our positions been reversed.
>
> In my deliberate judgment, the cases make it plain that in the performance of his work as an Associate Justice, Mr. Fortas has undertaken to carry into effect the words he spoke at American University on March 20, 1968. At that place and time he declared:
>
> > "But the words of the Constitution were not written with a meaning that persists for all time. Words are static symbols.
> >
> > Words may be carved in impervious granite, but the words themselves are as impermanent as the hand that carved them. They reflect light and shadow, they are modified by rain and sun, they are subject to the changes that a restless life brings upon them. So the specific meaning of the words of the Constitution has not been fixed and unchanging. They never will be fixed and unchanging.
> >
> > The Constitution is not static. But the changes in those words— changes in the meaning of those words—have not, as one might think, been arbitrary or haphazard."
>
> After reading these words of Justice Fortas, I wondered why George Washington, Benjamin Franklin, James Madison, Alexander Hamilton, and the other good and wise men who framed the Constitution put provisions in that document requiring Supreme Court Judges to take oaths to support a Constitution whose words Justice Fortas says have no fixed meaning, and specifying that the Constitution can be amended, i.e., changed only by the joint action of Congress and the States.

The review of the Fortas nomination continued into September. The Senate Judiciary Committee requested that Justice Fortas appear a second time for another round of questions. In the following letter to the Judiciary Committee, Fortas gave his reasons for refusing a second appearance before the Committee.

> My dear Mr. Chairman:
>
> I acknowledge receipt of your telegram advising me that a number of members of the Senate Judiciary Committee have expressed the desire that I return for further interrogation, as described in the telegram, relating to the President's nomination of me for the post of Chief Justice of the United States.
>
> I appeared before your committee initially, despite the lack of precedent for such appearance, because of my profound respect for the Senate and my view that such appearance might aid the Senate in the performance of its constitutional duty to advise and consent concerning judicial nominations. I hope

that during the interrogation of me by members of the committee, my respect for the Senate as well as my profound and unshakable devotion to the Court and the Constitution was evident. I believe that, now, my proper course of action is respectfully to decline to appear again at the request of some members of the committee for the further interrogation described in your telegram.

Sincerely yours,

Abe Fortas

There was concern among the pro-Fortas members of the Senate that sufficient strength might be mustered by the anti-Fortas Senators to stage a filibuster when the nomination was brought to the floor of the Senate. The Republican presidential candidate, Richard Nixon, said he opposed the filibuster on the Fortas nomination, but he did not say whether he was for or against the nomination. The Democratic presidential candidate, Hubert Humphrey, attacked Nixon for "making a deal" with Strom Thurmond to block the nomination of Fortas for Chief Justice. Senator Thurmond denied such a deal.

On September 17, 1968, by a vote of 11–6, the Senate Judiciary Committee recommended to the Senate that Justice Fortas be confirmed as Chief Justice of the United States. Although the Committee had recommended his confirmation, Fortas's nomination had to be approved by the entire Senate. Senate Majority Leader Mike Mansfield (D-Mont.), expecting a filibuster, said he would let the debate continue for about a week before attempting to force an end to the filibuster by invoking cloture, a device used to stop unlimited debate in the Senate and requiring a two-thirds vote of the Senate members. Some wondered whether two-thirds of the Senate would vote for cloture, ending the filibuster.

On September 27 a Republican-led filibuster was launched in the Senate against a motion to call up the nomination of Abe Fortas for Chief Justice of the United States. The Republicans were joined by some southern Democratic Senators.

The pro-Fortas Senators were dealt a blow the next day on September 28, when Senator Dirksen, the Senate Republican leader, said he would not only not vote for debate-limiting cloture, but also said he might oppose confirmation of Fortas if cloture were invoked. To those pro-Fortas Senators who were counting on Senator Dirksen to carry essential Republican votes, this action came as a complete surprise. Earlier, Dirksen had said he would definitely vote for confirmation of Fortas.

Some people believe that Dirksen had political reasons for changing his views. They noted that Dirksen had not liked the Supreme Court decision in the case *Witherspoon* v. *Illinois*, in which the Court held that a man cannot be sentenced to death by a jury from which members *opposed* to capital punishment have been excluded. Fortas voted with the majority in deciding this case. Under the precedent of this case, Richard Speck, who was sentenced to death for killing eight student nurses in Chicago in 1966, was appealing his death verdict. Some believed Dirksen would be hurt in his campaign to gain reelection as

402

Senator from Illinois if he supported a man who made it possible for a convicted murderer to appeal his case and perhaps go free.

On Tuesday, October 1, the cloture vote was taken and fell fourteen votes short of being successful. In the opinion of many liberals supporting the Fortas nomination, his chances were finished. On Wednesday, October 3, Fortas requested that President Johnson withdraw his name from nomination. His letter follows below:

Justice Abe Fortas (left) at the witness table awaiting questioning by members of the Senate Judiciary Committee. At the right, Senator Thurmond is shown while making criticisms of Fortas toward the end of the Committee's hearings.

My dear Mr. President:

I note the failure of the motion to end the filibuster in the Senate with respect to my nomination as Chief Justice of the United States. The 1968 term of this Court begins, according to law, on Monday, October 7. I will, of course, be participating in its work as Associate Justice.

In view of these circumstances, I ask you to withdraw my nomination as Chief Justice. Continued efforts to secure confirmation of that nomination, even if ultimately successful, would result in a continuation of the attacks upon the Court which have characterized the filibuster—attacks which have been sometimes extreme and entirely unrelated to responsible criticism.

Attacks of this sort would be especially inappropriate and harmful to the Court and the Nation if they should continue while the Court is in session,

403

engaged in the adjudication of issues of great importance to the Nation as well as the litigants.

I do not want to provide the occasion for a situation of this sort. My action in submitting this request for withdrawal should avert the danger that it will occur; and I hope that my withdrawal will help to put in motion a process by which there will be an end to destructive and extreme assaults upon the Court.

I appreciate the confidence in my qualifications which led you to nominate me as Chief Justice. I wish particularly to thank my colleagues at the bar and in the law schools for their support, and to express my appreciation to those members of the United States Senate who have supported me.

I pray that we shall see, in all of our Nation, renewed dedication to the principles of fairness and justice and moderation, without which our democracy cannot continue.

It is in this spirit that I respectfully ask that you honor my request for withdrawal of my nomination as Chief Justice of the United States.*

* *The Washington Post*, October 2, 1968. Reprinted by permission of The Washington ton Post. Copyright 1968.

> Sincerely,
>
> Abe Fortas

The attempt to nominate Abe Fortas as Chief Justice had failed. President Johnson decided not to send another nomination to the Senate. He decided it would be best to have Earl Warren continue as Chief Justice, at least until a new President was in office.

Less than a year after withdrawing his name from nomination to the position of Chief Justice, Abe Fortas resigned as Associate Justice.

President Nixon Appoints a Chief Justice

On May 26, 1969, President Nixon announced his choice to succeed retiring Chief Justice Earl Warren. President Nixon nominated Warren Earl Burger to be the fifteenth Chief Justice of the United States. Who was Judge Burger? Why had President Nixon selected him?

Prior to the Burger nomination, speculation had centered on men much more closely allied to President Nixon, such as his Attorney General John Mitchell and former Attorney General under President Eisenhower, Herbert Brownell. Both of these men were highly qualified, and their political views seemed to be close to those of Mr. Nixon.

In contrast President Nixon chose one whom he knew only slightly. Some reporters suggested that criticism of the Johnson-Fortas relationship led President Nixon to choose someone whose views were like his own but who was not tied closely to him.

Chief Justice Burger was born on a Minnesota farm of immigrant parents. He worked his way through school, earning highest honors in the process. He graduated from the St. Paul Minnesota Law School in 1927, began to practice law in Minnesota, and became active in the Republican party.

Chief Justice Burger first met Richard Nixon at the 1948 Republican National Convention. At that time Burger was a strong supporter of Minnesota Governor Harold Stassen for the presidential nomination. At the 1952 convention Burger urged the Minnesota delegation to support Eisenhower. As Richard Nixon was the nominee for Vice-President with Eisenhower in 1952, Burger's support indirectly helped Nixon gain national prominence.

When Eisenhower was elected in 1952, he rewarded Burger with a post as Assistant Attorney General. Four years later Burger accepted an Eisenhower appointment as Federal judge of the Washington, D.C., Court of Appeals. He continued to serve on the Court of Appeals until President Nixon selected him for the position of Chief Justice.

Nixon and Burger have held similar critical views of recent Supreme Court decisions. They both have said that the Court has been too protective of the rights of accused individuals at the expense of law-abiding citizens. For example, during his campaign for the Presidency, Richard Nixon frequently criticized the Supreme Court for its decisions on criminal cases. Nixon charged that Supreme Court decisions, such as in the Escobedo case (pp. 384–389), were "seriously hamstringing the peace forces in our society and strengthening the criminal forces." He called for the protection of the "first civil right of every American, the right to protection in his home, business and person from domestic violence. . ."

Meanwhile, Judge Burger delivered a commencement address at Ripon College that caught Nixon's attention. In that address Judge Burger said, "Government exists chiefly to foster the rights and interests of its citizens—to protect their homes and property, their persons and their lives."

President Nixon also favored a dissenting opinion Burger wrote in 1957. In that decision the majority reversed a conviction because police delayed taking the defendant before the judge. Burger dissented, arguing that "under

Members of the Supreme Court in 1971 were, left to right, John M. Harlan, Thurgood Marshall, Hugo Black, Potter Stewart, Chief Justice Warren E. Burger, Byron R. White, William O. Douglas, Harry A. Blackmun, and William J. Brennan, Jr.

the guise of protecting legitimate individual rights, the majority [of the Court] abandons the balance we are charged with maintaining between individual rights and the protection of the public."

Apparently President Nixon had found a nominee whose views were very similar to his own. The American Bar Association approved of Judge Burger and said so in a letter to Senator James Eastland, chairman of the Senate Judiciary Committee. The hearing to secure confirmation before the Senate Judiciary Committee went smoothly. Some of the testimony follows:

> *Senator Eastland:* Do you think the Supreme Court has the power to amend the Constitution of the United States by judicial interpretation?
> *Judge Burger:* No; clearly no. It has no power to amend the Constitution.
> *Chairman Eastland:* Does the Supreme Court have the power to legislate judicial interpretation?
> *Judge Burger:* I think as you put the question, clearly it has no such power. No court has that power.
>
> • • •
>
> *Senator Eastland:* Is it your philosophy that the Constitution of the United States has a fixed, definite meaning, that does not change but stays there until it is amended as the Constitution provides that it be amended?
> *Judge Burger:* Well, within the confines of a limited hearing, Senator, Mr. Chairman, it might call for a lecture . . . to meet all points of that, but surely it is the duty of the judges, all judges, to read the Constitution and try to discern its meaning and apply it.

Approval of the Senate Judiciary Committee and the full Senate were secured easily. And on June 23, 1969, retiring Chief Justice Earl Warren swore in his own successor.

> Answer the following questions on the basis of information presented in the two preceding case studies.
>
> **1.** Why did President Johnson nominate Abe Fortas to be Chief Justice? Why was his nomination opposed so strongly?
>
> **2.** Why did President Nixon nominate Warren Burger to be Chief Justice? Why was his nomination approved easily?
>
> **3.** It is sometimes said that a great judge is one who makes great decisions. How do Presidents and Senators decide whether a particular candidate is likely to produce great decisions?

chapter 16

The Role of Federal Bureaucrats

Suppose there is a large building which you have never been able to enter. Every half hour the doors of the building open, and a new car is pushed out. This happens day after day, month after month. Without ever going into the building you can be reasonably certain that the building is an automobile factory.

Government is a bit like that building. Most of us never get inside. We see only what comes out the doors. But what does come through the doors? What is the "product" of government? Among other things, money and orders to spend money. Government spends money for many things including aircraft carriers, school books, public parks, and cancer research.

Government also issues other kinds of orders. It decides what rates may be charged for certain utilities such as gas, electricity, and telephone. Government also may decide whether two companies can combine to make a larger company or whether a railroad can stop its passenger service. Government orders are frequently directed not to individuals but to institutions and corporations. Most of what comes from government seems to be (a) directives to act or not to act and (b) money to support these directives.

What Is the Federal Bureaucracy?

Many of the directives of modern government emerge from doors marked "administrative agencies." The administrative agencies are what is sometimes called the Federal bureaucracy, the largest component of government (in terms of number of people). The various executive departments like the Departments of Commerce, Defense, Justice, Interior, and Transportation are examples of administrative agencies. The administrative agencies are not simply messenger boys for the President—or for the Congress. They play a part in governmental decision-making, a very important part. These agencies touch all our lives, in ways partly visible and in other ways not so visible.

It seems useful to know as much as possible about the agencies of the Federal government, and this includes knowing something about the behavior of people who work in them—in other words, knowing something about "bureaucratic role." However, defining bureaucratic role is much more difficult than defining presidential role, congressional role, and judicial role. It is fairly easy to study the President and what he does, since he is only one man. Although the Congress has 535 members and the Supreme Court nine, it is relatively easy to describe the congressional role and the judicial role. An examination of bureaucrats is more difficult because there are so many more of them and the range of their activities is more varied.

Today the Federal government employs nearly three million civilian employees. Many of these are bureaucrats. These people differ from each other in many ways. Some are specialists in agriculture, some are lawyers specializing in patent and copyright law, others are medical doctors who are specialists in drugs. The list of occupations seems endless. Hundreds of jobs that exist outside government can find their match within the government.

Who Is a Federal Bureaucrat?

We shall define a Federal bureaucrat as a professional civilian employee of the government who has a responsibility for carrying out programs authorized by the President and the Congress or for supervising those who carry out such programs. A bureaucrat can be someone who is a member of the President's Cabinet, such as the Secretary of Defense. He can be head of a bureau or be a *program officer,* a person who has the direct day-by-day responsibility for managing a Federal program. In short, all of those people who have responsibility for making bureaucratic policy or who influence or carry out bureaucratic policy are included. We shall not include in our definition everyone who works for the government. Among the people who are Federal employees but not bureaucrats are secretaries, clerks, janitors, cooks, and chauffeurs.

A. The United States Office of Education as a Bureaucracy

Perhaps the best way to begin a study of bureaucracy is to look at one. Since we cannot take you on a trip to Washington to study a Federal agency first hand, we shall do the next best thing: give you a kind of map, an organization chart, of one bureaucratic agency—the United States Office of Education.

The United States Office of Education (USOE) is one of the divisions of the Department of Health, Education, and Welfare (HEW). The chart on pages 410–411 shows USOE as it was in February, 1970. Since that time it has been partially reorganized several times. This chart gives us a glimpse of what a bureaucracy is like. As you study the organization chart for this Federal agency, answer the following questions:

1. What does USOE do? Make a list.

2. Make a list of adjectives which you think describe USOE.

3. One of the activities administered by USOE is the "Trainers of Teacher Trainers" (TTT) program. This program provides grants of money to universities seeking to improve their teacher-training courses. Suppose that you accepted a job in the USOE and were assigned to work as a program officer in the TTT program. Your duties might include negotiating with university officials seeking funds from USOE to improve their teacher-training courses, evaluating programs you were supporting to learn if they

were performing satisfactorily, meeting with your colleagues to help make policy for the program, and defending the program both within the agency and to outsiders. Put yourself in the role of a program officer for the TTT program, and answer the following questions:

    a. Who are your supervisors? Which individuals do you see regularly? Which ones do you think you would seldom meet?

    b. In what branch, division, and bureau do you work?

    c. If you had an opportunity to accept a promotion to become head of the "Basic Studies Branch," would you take it? What factors would influence your decision? If you took the job, do you think your feelings about the TTT program would change? If so, in what ways?

    d. You have just learned that the Bureau's budget has been reduced by 10 percent from the amount of money available last year. What would be your response? What might you do to make certain that your program did not suffer?

    e. The President of the United States is a Republican. You also are a Republican and voted for the President. In fact, you resigned your position as a teacher in a university to accept the job with the Office of Education in part because you wanted to join the "President's team," to help the President carry out his programs. You have just learned that in order to save money, the President has decided to reduce sharply or abolish entirely all programs designed to improve the training of teachers. What is your reaction to this information?

4. Suppose a congressman wrote a letter to the Commissioner asking what USOE was doing to promote international studies, especially exchanges of students and scholars. Whom would the Commissioner consult for advice in drafting a reply?

5. What do you think are the functions of the Office of Public Affairs and the Office of Legislation?

B. Characteristics of Bureaucracy and Bureaucratic Role

What do you think of when you hear the term bureaucrat? It is not ordinarily something you call a friend. Americans frequently use the term to describe a government official whom they believe to be lazy, inefficient, insensitive, and ignorant. People have referred to bureaucrats as the "pin-headed guideline writers" in Washington, or talked of bureaucratic "red tape" and bureaucrats from Washington who "can't park their bicycles straight but who tell us how to run our schools and businesses."

While the term "bureaucrat" is often used in an insulting way, social scientists use the term bureaucracy simply to refer to a particular kind of work organization system that has emerged in modern, industrialized societies. Bureaucracy developed in response to the need in complex, modern societies for skillful, efficient, honest, and fair management. All large organizations,

My Cabrera

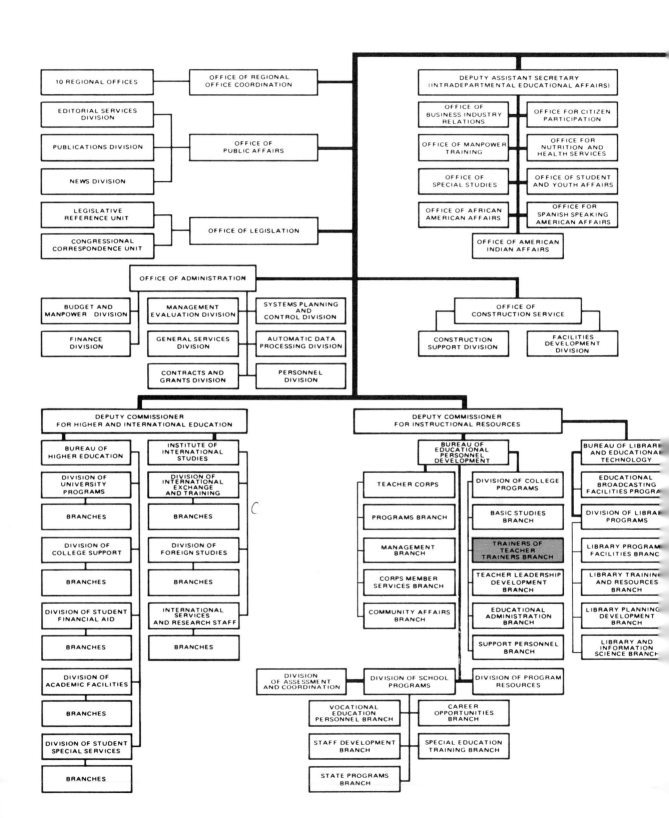

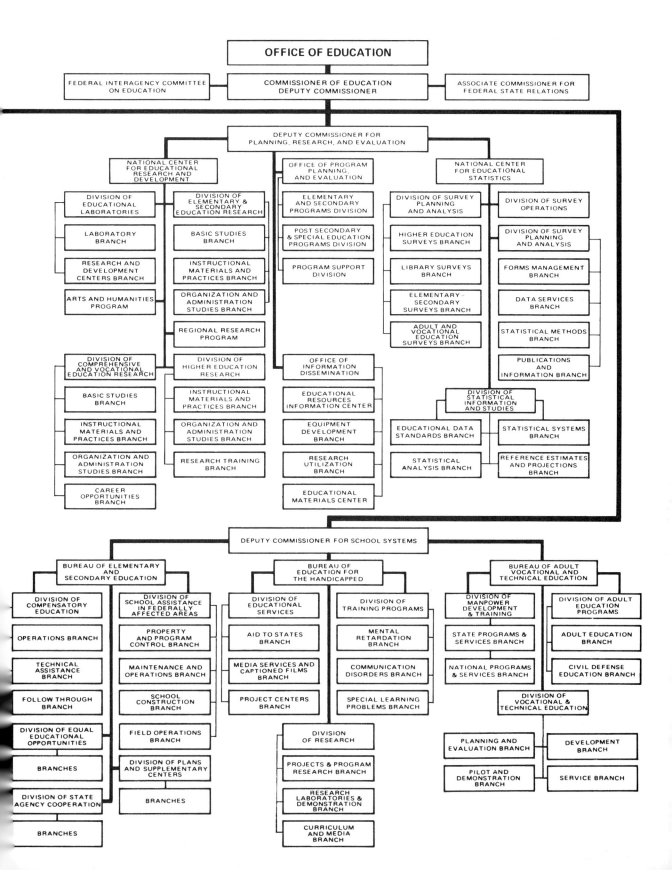

OFFICE OF EDUCATION

FEDERAL INTERAGENCY COMMITTEE ON EDUCATION

COMMISSIONER OF EDUCATION
DEPUTY COMMISSIONER

ASSOCIATE COMMISSIONER FOR FEDERAL STATE RELATIONS

DEPUTY COMMISSIONER FOR PLANNING, RESEARCH, AND EVALUATION

NATIONAL CENTER FOR EDUCATIONAL RESEARCH AND DEVELOPMENT

OFFICE OF PROGRAM PLANNING, AND EVALUATION

NATIONAL CENTER FOR EDUCATIONAL STATISTICS

DIVISION OF EDUCATIONAL LABORATORIES

DIVISION OF ELEMENTARY & SECONDARY EDUCATION RESEARCH

ELEMENTARY AND SECONDARY PROGRAMS DIVISION

DIVISION OF SURVEY PLANNING AND ANALYSIS

DIVISION OF SURVEY OPERATIONS

LABORATORY BRANCH

BASIC STUDIES BRANCH

POST SECONDARY & SPECIAL EDUCATION PROGRAMS DIVISION

HIGHER EDUCATION SURVEYS BRANCH

DIVISION OF SURVEY PLANNING AND ANALYSIS

RESEARCH AND DEVELOPMENT CENTERS BRANCH

INSTRUCTIONAL MATERIALS AND PRACTICES BRANCH

PROGRAM SUPPORT DIVISION

LIBRARY SURVEYS BRANCH

FORMS MANAGEMENT BRANCH

ARTS AND HUMANITIES PROGRAM

ORGANIZATION AND ADMINISTRATION STUDIES BRANCH

ELEMENTARY – SECONDARY SURVEYS BRANCH

DATA SERVICES BRANCH

REGIONAL RESEARCH PROGRAM

ADULT AND VOCATIONAL EDUCATION SURVEYS BRANCH

STATISTICAL METHODS BRANCH

DIVISION OF COMPREHENSIVE AND VOCATIONAL EDUCATION RESEARCH

DIVISION OF HIGHER EDUCATION RESEARCH

OFFICE OF INFORMATION DISSEMINATION

PUBLICATIONS AND INFORMATION BRANCH

BASIC STUDIES BRANCH

INSTRUCTIONAL MATERIALS AND PRACTICES BRANCH

EDUCATIONAL RESOURCES INFORMATION CENTER

DIVISION OF STATISTICAL INFORMATION AND STUDIES

INSTRUCTIONAL MATERIALS AND PRACTICES BRANCH

ORGANIZATION AND ADMINISTRATION STUDIES BRANCH

EQUIPMENT DEVELOPMENT BRANCH

EDUCATIONAL DATA STANDARDS BRANCH

STATISTICAL SYSTEMS BRANCH

ORGANIZATION AND ADMINISTRATION STUDIES BRANCH

RESEARCH TRAINING BRANCH

RESEARCH UTILIZATION BRANCH

STATISTICAL ANALYSIS BRANCH

REFERENCE ESTIMATES AND PROJECTIONS BRANCH

CAREER OPPORTUNITIES BRANCH

EDUCATIONAL MATERIALS CENTER

DEPUTY COMMISSIONER FOR SCHOOL SYSTEMS

BUREAU OF ELEMENTARY AND SECONDARY EDUCATION

BUREAU OF EDUCATION FOR THE HANDICAPPED

BUREAU OF ADULT VOCATIONAL AND TECHNICAL EDUCATION

DIVISION OF COMPENSATORY EDUCATION

DIVISION OF SCHOOL ASSISTANCE IN FEDERALLY AFFECTED AREAS

DIVISION OF EDUCATIONAL SERVICES

DIVISION OF TRAINING PROGRAMS

DIVISION OF MANPOWER DEVELOPMENT & TRAINING

DIVISION OF ADULT EDUCATION PROGRAMS

OPERATIONS BRANCH

PROPERTY AND PROGRAM CONTROL BRANCH

AID TO STATES BRANCH

MENTAL RETARDATION BRANCH

STATE PROGRAMS & SERVICES BRANCH

ADULT EDUCATION BRANCH

TECHNICAL ASSISTANCE BRANCH

MAINTENANCE AND OPERATIONS BRANCH

MEDIA SERVICES AND CAPTIONED FILMS BRANCH

COMMUNICATION DISORDERS BRANCH

NATIONAL PROGRAMS & SERVICES BRANCH

CIVIL DEFENSE EDUCATION BRANCH

FOLLOW THROUGH BRANCH

SCHOOL CONSTRUCTION BRANCH

PROJECT CENTERS BRANCH

SPECIAL LEARNING PROBLEMS BRANCH

DIVISION OF VOCATIONAL & TECHNICAL EDUCATION

DIVISION OF EQUAL EDUCATIONAL OPPORTUNITIES

FIELD OPERATIONS BRANCH

PLANNING AND EVALUATION BRANCH

DEVELOPMENT BRANCH

BRANCHES

DIVISION OF PLANS AND SUPPLEMENTARY CENTERS

DIVISION OF RESEARCH

PILOT AND DEMONSTRATION BRANCH

SERVICE BRANCH

DIVISION OF STATE AGENCY COOPERATION

BRANCHES

PROJECTS & PROGRAM RESEARCH BRANCH

BRANCHES

RESEARCH LABORATORIES & DEMONSTRATION BRANCH

CURRICULUM AND MEDIA BRANCH

including churches, businesses, labor unions, and professional associations, have bureaucracies. Simply stated, bureaucracy is a way of organizing employees so that they can carry out the programs of the organization in an orderly fashion.

While all large organizations have bureaucrats, in this chapter we are concerned only with the bureaucracy of the Federal government and the people who work in it. First we examine some features of the bureaucracy itself; then we look specifically at the bureaucratic role.

The Federal Bureaucracy Is Large and Complex

In 1792 the Federal government had only about 800 civilian employees; over 600 of these worked in the Treasury Department. Today the Federal government employs nearly three million civilian employees. If we add military personnel, more than five million men and women are on the Federal payroll.

In addition to the Federal government, there are 50 state governments, around 3000 county governments, 18,000 municipal units, 18,000 townships, 19,000 public school districts, and 18,000 special districts of various kinds. Most of these units of government employ bureaucrats. It has been estimated that one of every six American workers (including members of the armed forces) is on a government payroll.

Why has the governmental bureaucracy grown so large? In the United States today, government is expected to do hundreds—even thousands—of different jobs. Most of them are carried out by administrative agencies. As our nation has grown in size, so too has the demand for governmental services. The government delivers our mail, inspects the food we eat and the homes we live in, regulates our transportation, and licenses our entertainment. It certifies our birth and supervises our burial. There is scarcely a human activity that is not in some way touched by a governmental regulation.

Not only has the size of the bureaucracy grown, but bureaucratic tasks have become increasingly specialized and complex, as society has become more industrialized. Federal bureaucrats tend to be highly trained specialists. Among

the small society   by Brickman

What does this political cartoon suggest about the growth of governmental bureaucracy?

© Washington Star Syndicate, Inc.

Federal bureaucrats one can find specialists in African languages who work in the State Department, marine biologists employed by the Department of Interior, and space scientists who work for the National Aeronautics and Space Administration.

The Bureaucracy Operates Almost Like a Fourth Branch of Government

A typical chart of the executive branch of the government, such as the one on page 414, shows the Cabinet departments and most other Federal agencies as directly responsible to the President. Yet a few years ago, President Johnson is reported to have said that while there are 2,867,356 Federal employees, "on a good day maybe 100 are working for the President." How does one account for such a statement? Why is it that the President lacks firm control over the actions and policies of the Federal agencies?

In most areas of governmental activity the President has no specific policies—for example, public health, railroad regulation, airports, meat inspection. He does expect the Federal officials who are responsible for tasks in these areas to meet their responsibilities and not to embarrass his administration. In such areas, bureaucrats largely develop their own policies, policies that are carried forward from one presidential administration to the next.

This does not mean that most bureaucrats are free to do whatever they choose. Quite the contrary. The people with whom the agency works most directly must be satisfied. The Office of Education will try to satisfy educators; the Department of Agriculture will try to keep farmers content. And each agency must keep congressmen happy, since Congress can provide generous funds for an agency or abolish it. Some agencies, such as the Federal Bureau of Investigation, are very popular with Congress and are treated generously. Other agencies, such as the Agency for International Development, which handles foreign aid, seem always on the defensive and must constantly prove their worth to Congress.

Sometimes the Army Corps of Engineers, which has responsibility for certain flood-control and conservation projects, can get congressional support for programs the President may oppose. When President Eisenhower tried to hold the line on the budget for the Army Corps of Engineers, the Engineers had their funds restored by congressmen eager to have dams and recreational facilities constructed in their districts. And Congress at times appropriates money for military equipment desired by generals and admirals but opposed by the President.

The result is a very complex set of relationships. Most agencies seek the favor of Congress, from whom they get their funds; and many agencies operate with little interference from the President's office. In some areas in which the President has a definite policy, such as foreign relations, he must struggle with department officials—plead, threaten, and persuade—before his policies are carried out faithfully.

Nearly every President has expressed exasperation at one time or another with the difficulties in getting a policy carried out. This has led to the presidential practice of appointing White House aides whose duties often compete with

"Now let me be quite precise in this respect. The Federal Reserve is independent, and the new chairman, who will be sworn in here tomorrow, is one of the most independent men I know."—Pres. Nixon, Jan. 30, 1970.

"However, I hope that independently he will conclude that my views are the ones that should be followed."—Nixon at swearing-in ceremonies the next day.

Quoted in TIME, March 1, 1970

The Executive Branch of Our Government

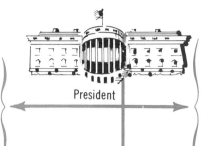

President

Cabinet Departments

State	Labor
Treasury	Health, Education, and Welfare
Defense	
Justice	Transportation
Interior	Housing and Urban Development
Agriculture	
Commerce	

Executive Office

The White House Office
Office of Management and Budget
Council of Economic Advisers
National Security Council
Domestic Council
National Aeronautics and Space Council
Office of Economic Opportunity
Office of Emergency Planning
Office of Science and Technology
Council of Environmental Quality
    and others

Regulatory Agencies

Federal Communications Commission

Interstate Commerce Commission

Federal Power Commission

Securities and Exchange Commission

Federal Trade Commission

Atomic Trade Commission

Federal Reserve Board

National Labor Relations Board

Corporations

Federal Deposit Insurance Corporation

Export-Import Bank

Tennessee Valley Authority

Postal Service

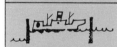
St. Lawrence Seaway

Panama Canal Company

Other Independent Agencies

Agencies in the tinted boxes tend to have greater independence from presidential control than do the others. Members of regulatory agencies serve for fixed terms (usually seven years). Government corporations have some financial independence.

and overlap the responsibilities of officials who head the regular agencies and departments. For example, each recent President has employed special foreign-policy advisers who supply him with information he may have trouble obtaining from the State Department, who suggest alternatives to policies presented to him by State Department officials, and who frequently serve to encourage the State Department to greater activity. In short, the President must often appoint individuals to posts in which their only loyalty is to him because bureaucrats may have loyalties to their agency, the Congress, or many special-interest groups as well.

The Federal Bureaucracy Makes and Interprets Rules

Federal agencies do more than "administer" laws. Frequently, they "legislate." For example, the Department of Health, Education, and Welfare has created a set of guidelines for school desegregation that are used to decide whether school districts are eligible to receive Federal funds. These guidelines have the force of law. In order for schools to receive funds, they must abide by these agency-created rules.

Agency officials also become involved in lawmaking when they help draft legislation to be introduced into Congress, testify before Congress, and provide technical information needed by congressmen who are preparing legislation. Congressmen acknowledge that it is nearly impossible to pass legislation without first seeking the advice—and often the support—of the appropriate agency.

In some agencies bureaucrats also have a judicial function. A few agencies function almost like courts, settling tax-claim disputes, trade disagreements, and many other matters. Nearly all agencies are engaged in "interpreting the law." While agency decisions frequently may be appealed in the courts, on a day-to-day basis parties affected by bureau decisions tend to consider them forceful enough to abide by them.

Some Features of the Bureaucratic Role

While the special talents required to fill particular positions within the bureaucracy differ greatly, some features of the bureaucratic role are essentially the same whatever the position.

Chain of command. All bureaucracies are organized according to a *hierarchy,* a kind of pyramid of levels of authority in which higher status people with greater authority supervise the work of people with lesser status. In the organization chart for the Office of Education you had a chance to observe the chain of command in such a hierarchy.

In a bureaucracy, status, prestige, authority, and responsibility are identified with the office rather than with the individual who occupies the position. In other words, the Commissioner of Education has the right to demand responses from division and bureau heads not because of who he is but because of the position he holds.

Channels of communication. The pattern of formal communication among bureaucrats is also hierarchical. For example, suppose you were a program officer in the Office of Education and you wanted to tell the Commissioner your feelings about a particular agency policy. It would be most unusual for you to have an interview with the Commissioner or to write him a note. Ordinarily you would communicate your opinion to your immediate supervisor, who in turn would pass it along to his superior.

In the preceding lesson you were asked to decide whom the Commissioner might consult if he had to write a letter to a congressman about USOE's international studies program. The typical way this would be handled would be for the Commissioner to give a copy of the letter and a memo regarding the information he wanted to one of his assistants. The assistant would then send the memo on to the Deputy Commissioner for Higher and International Education. He in turn would pass the word to the Associate Commissioner for International Studies, who in turn would give direction to his chief of the Division of International Exchange and Training. The Division chief would give it to the man in charge of the Educational Exchange Branch, who might assign the task to one of his program officers. The program officer would write the first draft of the letter and would give it to the branch chief. The branch chief might add to or modify the letter and then forward it to the head of the Division. Thus, the letter would finally find its way back to the Commissioner's desk after it had been passed on by everyone in the Office of Education's "chain of command."

This system of distributing information is important in a bureaucracy. First of all, it keeps everyone who needs to know informed about how a particular issue is being handled. Secondly, each level of the bureaucracy has a different outlook on the problem. For example, the Commissioner of Education cannot be as familiar with the details of the exchange program as the officer who administers it. On the other hand, each program officer may be too close to his own program to see the big picture. Only the top administrators who have overall responsibility for many programs may be able to see how they all fit together to form a unified Federal program.

Within every bureaucracy there are also *informal* levels of authority and *informal* communications systems. Some individuals have a reputation for making wise decisions and are consulted regularly whether they are exactly in the chain of command or not. Moreover, in the cafeteria, driving to work in a car pool, or playing golf on Saturday, agency officials share ideas, communicate plans informally, and influence the decisions made within their particular agency.

The influence of rules. Another typical feature of a bureaucracy is its elaborate system of rules. There are rules for hiring people, for firing people, for promoting people, for vacations, for sick leave, and for travel. The bureaucracy has rules for using consultants, for avoiding conflicts of interests, for managing contracts, and for nearly every other aspect of bureaucratic life. As compared to the presidential, congressional, and judicial roles in which formal rules may be less important than informal rules, the Federal bureaucratic role is influenced strongly by many formal rules which determine what bureaucrats can and cannot do.

Bureaucrats subject to cross-pressures. If there is a "military point of view," it is most likely to be found in the Department of Defense. The Department of Agriculture vigorously defends programs for farmers and opposes efforts by the administration to spend more money on the cities if it means reducing aid to farmers.

Within any agency an individual may be expected to show complete loyalty to the agency's causes if he wishes to advance his career. Especially when the agency's and the President's views are in disagreement, the bureaucrat may find himself in a cross-pressure situation. If he is a very high policy-maker, such a conflict may become public knowledge, leading to his resignation or dismissal if he is unable to settle the conflict in any other way.

For example, in 1970, a high-ranking official in the Justice Department disagreed with the desegregation policy of the President and the Attorney General. This official had been appointed by the previous President and his primary loyalty was to his division of the Justice Department rather than to the new President. After unsuccessfully attempting to convince the Attorney General to return to policies similar to those of his predecessor, he called a news conference at which he stated his disagreements with the Administration. He was then asked to resign.

Bureaucrats find themselves in other kinds of cross-pressure situations. Some agencies were established "to promote and to regulate" certain activities. Naturally, this means that the agency will have an unusually close relationship with the people who are most frequently involved in this activity. For instance, many of the officials in the Office of Education are former teachers, university professors, and school administrators. Many are or were members of professional educational associations and have formed close friendships or have been co-workers with people presently in the educational field. When they make policies for education, it may be difficult for them to set themselves apart from their own prior experiences and the interests of friends and professional associates. They may find it difficult to evaluate a problem objectively because of this.

An agency tends to work out "alliances" with its constituents. The term "military-industrial complex" is used to describe the relationship that has developed over the years between the various armed services and the major industries that supply them with materials. For example, military officers who have worked within the Federal government for many years often retire from the armed forces to accept appointments with companies which manufacture military equipment. They return to Washington seeking contracts for their companies from their former colleagues in the government. While bureaucrats are expected to be impartial in their assignment of defense contracts, their friendships with people in the defense industry make it difficult for them to remain unbiased.

This problem takes another form as well. Bureaucracies are supposed to be governed by formal, hierarchical relationships and by formal rules. This presumably avoids favoritism and makes certain that everyone is treated equally. This also makes bureaucracies seem cold and impersonal. However, bureaucrats are also expected to take a personal interest in their various constituencies in order to satisfy as many people as possible. But "taking a personal interest" in someone opens the bureaucrat to charges of playing favorites. These cross-pressures often make the job of the bureaucrat difficult.

C. Recruitment of Federal Bureaucrats

Who are the people who become bureaucrats in the Federal government? What are their backgrounds? How are they similar to, or different from, people who do not work for the government?

We can separate them into two general categories. One category consists of career officials who have entered government service through one of the career systems: (a) the Federal civil service, (b) the foreign service, or (c) the military service. The foreign service consists of a relatively small number of people who belong to a special career system in the Department of State. Customarily young people are recruited into the lowest levels of this service

Federal civil service jobs are open to those who can demonstrate their fitness by competitive examination. The exam may be a written test, including skill demonstration as shown here for clerk-typists; or it may be an evaluation of education and work experience.

and gradually through experience work their way up to more important positions—even the rank of ambassador.

The military service is probably the best known Federal career system in the United States. A very large number of men and some women spend some time in the military service during their lifetime. They may be drafted into one of the branches of the military, or they may enlist. Except for those who have had special training or have unusual special skills (for example, doctors), most people enter the military service at the lowest ranks and through experience and further training win promotions to higher ranks.

The Federal civil service is by far the largest system for civilian employees in the government. Today nearly 3 million civilians are employed by the Federal government. Around 93 percent are members of the Federal civil service system. Of course, many of the people covered by civil service do not fit our definition of bureaucrat. The civil service includes nearly everyone who works for the Federal government, including guards, cooks, clerks, and postmen. In this chapter we concentrate primarily upon those people who are in the Federal civil service, not with the foreign service and the military service.

Political Appointees

The second category of Federal employment consists of *political appointees.* Of the total number of people employed by the Federal government, they represent only a very small proportion. An estimate in 1968 put the number of posts filled by presidential appointment at 2150. A majority of these require the approval of the Senate. They include Cabinet officers, assistant secretaries in the various executive departments, ambassadors, and special advisers to the President.

Civil service employees differ in one major way from political appointees. Civil service employees tend to have made a lifetime career of their jobs. Those holding high positions have earned them through years of experience in their departments, and they continue to hold their jobs from one presidential administration to another regardless of who wins an election.

Political appointees, on the other hand, are often selected because their political views are like those of the President. They tend to be appointed to the top policy-making positions in government in order to ensure that the policies within each department conform as much as possible to what the President wants. Political appointees rarely are experts in the technical aspects of the departments they head. They depend upon their career civil service advisers for technical information. Rather, their job is to worry primarily about the political effects of decisions made in their departments.

For example, the Secretary of Defense and his principal subordinates are political appointees. They are not expected to be experts in military strategy. They can rely upon career military officers, including the Chiefs of Staff, for this kind of advice. However, to make certain that decisions by military career officers conform to the policies of the President, it is considered important to have civilians directing the Defense Department. The President would thus appoint civilians who are able to put the military advice they receive into a

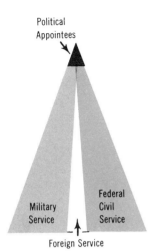

Political
Appointees

Military
Service

Federal
Civil
Service

Foreign Service

**A Diagram of
Federal Employment**

general policy-making strategy that will be acceptable to both civilian and military leaders.

Political appointees rarely spend many years in any one post. When a new President takes office, especially when he is from a different political party than his predecessor, political appointees resign and are replaced. Occasionally, a political appointee may serve in several different posts during his lifetime. Robert Finch began as Secretary of Health, Education, and Welfare in the Nixon Administration but was later shifted to special presidential assistant in the White House. Elliott Richardson was moved from a political appointee post in the State Department to the position vacated by Finch at the Department of Health, Education, and Welfare.

The diagram at the left shows us roughly how the Federal bureaucracy is divided.

As you can see, political appointees make up a very small proportion of the people who work for the Federal government. However, their placement at the top of the pyramid emphasizes their influence on policy-making in the Federal government. There are more people in the lower ranks of the government than at the higher ranks. Although there are fewer political appointees, they tend to wield far greater power in proportion to their total number than do the career service employees.

Nevertheless, we shall see later that top career service administrators are important decision-makers and often have as much influence on policy within a particular department as does the politically appointed department head.

Some Characteristics of Bureaucratic Decision-Makers

The range of activities represented by the Federal bureaucracy and the number of people employed by the government limit the generalizations we can make about Federal bureaucrats. Moreover, the government does not seek data on the ethnic identity, religious affiliation, and political party preference of its employees. Therefore, this information is not available to us. Despite these handicaps, some useful generalizations can be made.

Both men and women are employed as Federal bureaucrats. However, men occupy the highest ranks in the Federal civilian bureaucracy far out of proportion to their number in the total adult population. A 1959 study found that 10,851 men and 145 women held appointments in the highest ranks of the civilian bureaucracy. Recent efforts to recruit more women into executive positions in government has probably altered this ratio to some degree, but it remains true that a high-ranking Federal bureaucrat is much more likely to be a man than a woman.

Federal bureaucrats come from all regions of the nation. A 1959 study found that the region of birth of Federal executives was nearly identical to that of the population as a whole. Contrary to some popular belief, most Federal bureaucrats are not born in Washington, D.C.

Federal bureaucrats tend to be well educated. A study that compared the education of Federal bureaucrats to adult males and to business leaders revealed the following data:

Educational level	Adult Males (1957 data)	Bureaucrats (1959 data)	Businessmen (1952 data)
Less than high school	46%	*	4%
Some high school	17	1%	9
High school graduation	21	4	11
Some college	7	14	19
College graduation	9	81	57

*Less than 0.5 percent.

Source: W. L. Warner, P. P. Van Riper, N. H. Martin, and O. F. Collins, *The American Federal Executive* (New Haven: Yale University Press, 1964), p. 354.

Bureaucratic decision-makers tend to be well-educated persons who through training and experience have become experts in particular fields of knowledge.

D. Bureaucrats as Decision-Makers

Most Americans are aware that the President, members of Congress, and Supreme Court justices make important decisions. Americans are less aware that thousands of bureaucrats daily make decisions whose effects are often as great as decisions of the President, the Congress, and the Supreme Court. If we consider just the total number of decisions made annually, the Federal bureaucracy is a more important source of political decisions than the other branches of government combined.

Kinds of Bureaucratic Decisions

Bureaucrats make many kinds of decisions. Some decisions relate to the gathering and processing of information. Many decisions reached by Congress and the President are based on, or influenced by, technical information which bureaucrats make available. For example, President Kennedy's decisions in the Cuban missile crisis in 1962 depended in part upon information provided by the Central Intelligence Agency (CIA). A few years ago the Office of Education supported a study on the relationship of racial segregation in schools and the ability of children to learn. The findings of this study, known as the "Coleman Report," provided evidence in support of legislation, judicial decisions, and bureaucratic policies aimed at integrating public schools. Studies by the Public Health Service on the effects of smoking have led to a number of regulations aimed at discouraging the use of cigarettes.

Bureaucrats also decide which programs they wish to support and which people they will provide with money to carry them out. In the late 1950's and early 1960's, the policy of the national government was to stress the teaching of science, mathematics, and foreign languages in the public schools. In the

In 1969 the United States Surgeon General, William Stewart, appeared before the House Commerce Committee to urge for strong health warnings on cigarette packages and advertising.

late 1960's emphasis shifted to vocational training, minority-group education, and the training of the handicapped.

Each change in emphasis meant new bureaucratic decisions about which people and which agencies would receive Federal money. These decisions also influenced instruction in schools. Such decisions must often be approved by the President, and Congress must pass legislation enabling the bureau to carry through its policies. But the decisions to enter into such programs are usually made first by bureaucrats.

Very important decisions are made by bureaucrats when they issue agency regulations. In 1964 the Federal Trade Commission (FTC) issued a regulation which directed the tobacco industry to include the following warning in all cigarette advertisements: "Cigarette smoking is dangerous to health and may cause death from cancer and other diseases." While this regulation, particularly as it related to cigarette advertising, was overturned later by Congress, one result of the FTC action was a requirement that a health warning appear on all cigarette packages. The FTC took this action in response to medical research data linking cigarette smoking to certain kinds of cancer and heart disease.

An important characteristic of bureaucratic decisions is that they are often accommodational decisions. The decision-maker seeks a solution that will make the greatest number of people happy. Let's assume that a particular agency is in charge of regulating the discharge of pollutants into the air. On the one hand, one might expect that the agency would pass regulations that would eliminate all air pollution by industries. But many groups would consider such a decision unreasonable, since it might force certain industries to close down entirely. On the other hand, to do nothing would anger the health groups that are worried about air pollution. Therefore, agency officials will try to make an accommodational decision. They will establish regulations that tend to reduce the amount of pollution, making the health groups partly happy.

422

However, they will not make the regulations so strict that the industries cannot afford to comply with them. Neither side will be totally satisfied nor completely unhappy with the resulting regulations. Since reaching such accommodational decisions is primarily a political process, bureaucrats are indeed political decision-makers.

Who Are the Decision-Makers?

Not everyone who works in a government agency makes policy decisions. On the other hand, policy-making is not limited to the people at the very top. In some cases many people may participate in the decision process. The idea for a new program may begin with a program officer who seeks the branch chief's approval and so on upward through the agency until it is approved as agency policy.

On some questions the top leaders of an agency merely approve what has already been worked out by subordinates. In other cases the decision may be viewed as having serious political implications and may require much thought by top management before it is approved, modified, or rejected. For example, decisions made within the Department of Health, Education, and Welfare concerning welfare programs, Medicare, or school desegregation are often closely watched by politicians, newspaper and television reporters, and interested citizens. A controversial HEW decision often gets widespread public attention and reaction. In some cases the decision on a policy may be made at the top and handed down for subordinates to administer.

There seems to be a simple rule we can follow in understanding some aspects of bureaucratic decision-making. A decision which is noncontroversial, in keeping with agency policy, and primarily concerned with carrying out current programs is most likely to be made by people in the middle ranks of the bureau without much review by supervisors. A policy which has great political implications, is likely to be controversial, is a departure from the agency's ordinary practices, and may be criticized by the President or the Congress is more likely to be made by the top men in the agency after listening to the advice of subordinates.

Factors That Influence Bureaucratic Decision-Making

The factors that influence decision-making in a bureaucracy may be grouped into three general categories: the circumstances leading to a decision, the characteristics of the decision-maker, and other factors.

Circumstances leading to a decision. Among the circumstances that influence a decision are (1) the time available to make the decision, (2) the seriousness of the problem, and (3) the competing values that are part of the problem.

A sudden crisis may call for a quick decision. Perhaps there has been an airplane accident. Help must be sent immediately to the survivors, and investigators must begin determining the cause of the accident. In other cases an agency may have months or even years to work on a solution to a problem.

Programs intended to curb the use of harmful drugs are one such example. Many agencies have spent years studying the research on the effects of drugs on the body, working to restrict the sale of drugs, and finding effective treatments for drug addiction.

The seriousness of the problem is also a factor in the decisions that are made. For example, as long as drugs were used by a minority of the population, many decision-makers gave other problems more attention. As the use of drugs increased and began to spread into the middle class and among teen-agers, decision-makers began reexamining their policies. Recently there has been a tendency among health officials to recommend that law-enforcement officials take a new look at the penalties for use of marijuana and heroin to decide if they ought to be equally harsh. Public officials are looking into programs which treat heroin addicts with less powerful drugs such as methadone and evaluating other new treatment programs.

Competing social values also influence decisions. For example, competing values appear on the question of reducing or eliminating the penalties for possession and use of marijuana. Some people contend that marijuana is no more harmful than alcoholic beverages. But even if there is a risk to health, they say, such a risk is a personal matter. Perhaps they believe that government should interfere as little as possible with an individual's right to do what he wants with his life. This belief in personal freedom—noninterference by government—is one value on the issue of penalties for possession of marijuana. A competing value is expressed by those who believe that government has an obligation to establish and enforce regulations against harmful products.

Individual characteristics of decision-makers. The decisions are also influenced greatly by the individual decision-maker's personal beliefs, by his own social background and prior experience, and by his personality. A decision-maker with strong opinions about what is right and wrong is likely to behave differently from one who is less confident that he knows what is the "right" thing to do in each circumstance. The decision-maker who is aggressive, ambitious, and likes to act decisively will likely influence decisions in ways that are different from one who is content with existing policies and takes new actions only when they cannot be avoided. Some bureaucratic leaders like to lead dramatically and are happiest when caught up in fights over new programs. Others prefer to avoid publicity and to apply pressure behind the scenes.

A decision-maker's understanding of the problems he faces is also influenced by his social background and prior experience. Imagine three bureaucrats faced with the same general question: How can we best spend public money to improve the schools? One bureaucrat is a Mexican-American male raised in the barrio of Los Angeles. The second is a woman and a former teacher who taught primarily in suburban high schools. The third is a male college professor who formerly taught Latin and Greek at an Eastern college. Each of these people may answer the question differently and propose somewhat different policies for carrying out their decision.

Other factors. These include rules, status relationships, public opinion, available resources, and external decision-makers.

Bureaucratic decision-making is influenced by rules. Federal programs cannot be undertaken unless Congress passes legislation authorizing them. A bureaucrat cannot simply make decisions on matters he believes are important unless he is given the authority to do so.

Nevertheless, the authority granted to an agency by Congress is sometimes vaguely stated. This is done deliberately because Congress cannot foresee every circumstance that will arise. Therefore, it passes legislation which is flexible enough to leave many of the specific decisions to the bureaucrats. For example, the Federal Aviation Administration is charged by law with the "promotion, regulation, and safety of civil aviation . . . ." This makes it clear that it is not responsible for automobiles and trains, but how it "promotes" and "regulates" aviation can be interpreted in different ways.

Bureaucratic decision-makers are also bound by rules and procedures for reaching decisions. For example, there are rules requiring that hearings be held on decisions reached by regulatory agencies, rules regarding how and in what form policy decisions must be announced, rules regarding the selection and payment of advisory panels of outside experts, and rules for many other items. For decisions to stand up they must be arrived at according to acceptable procedures and must be within the authority of the agency.

Status relationships. Bureaucrats have important status relationships with five groups: the President, members of Congress, members of the agency itself, bureaucrats in other government agencies, and important constituencies outside of government.

On many issues the President has no announced policy, and the bureaucratic decision-maker has considerable freedom of action. In other cases a general presidential directive—for example, a freeze on hiring new people or an order to reduce spending by 10 percent—will certainly affect decisions. In some cases the President will announce a policy decision, and all bureaus must somehow try to bring their programs into line. An announcement by the President that he will take steps to prevent further pollution of the air by automobiles could lead to a number of different actions by Federal agencies. Some agency might begin to prepare legislation on this matter. The agency which purchases government vehicles may decide to require that all new cars bought by the government must have effective anti-pollution devices by a certain date.

Each bureau has to worry about its relationships with Congress, especially those congressional committees that hold hearings on the legislation desired by the agencies. Certain congressmen may be very important in determining the fate of certain kinds of legislation. If these congressmen disapprove of the legislation, it is not likely to pass.

In 1971 Representative Edith Green of Oregon, head of the House special subcommittee on education, was a key member whose support was needed for education legislation. Senator John Stennis and Representative Edward

Bureaucrats from the
Department of Defense
(foreground) testify at
a hearing held by a
subcommittee of the House
Armed Services Committee.

Hébert were key congressmen serving as chairmen of Armed Services Committees in the Senate and House respectively. Their support was required for the authorization of funds for the Department of Defense.

Top bureaucratic decision-makers spend much of their time in Congress testifying before committees and in private meetings with members of Congress. Without support in the Congress an agency is severely handicapped.

Bureaus also try to maintain good relations with other bureaus. For example, efforts by the Federal Trade Commission to force cigarette companies to indicate in their advertising the harmful effects of cigarette smoking encountered opposition from the Department of Agriculture and initial opposition from the Federal Communications Commission. The Department of Agriculture was annoyed because one of its programs was to support the production and sale of tobacco. Warnings on cigarette packages as required by the FTC would likely damage the sale of tobacco.

The Federal Communications Commission regulates the radio and television industry. These companies get much of their income from cigarette commercials. FTC interest in extending health warnings to radio and television advertisements about cigarettes could result in a loss of income for the radio and TV industry. Thus any bureaucratic decision-maker must consider how his decision will affect other bureaus. This means that important policy decisions often require negotiations among leaders from several bureaus.

Bureaucratic decision-makers also have status relationships with subordinates and supervisors within their own bureaus. It is frequently necessary to alter a decision somewhat in order for it to gain acceptance and support within the agency. A subordinate may be reluctant to carry out a decision unless he feels that he has been consulted and his views taken seriously. A decision-maker must also plan ways to influence his superiors.

Nevertheless, there are many times in an agency when a decision that one or more people vigorously opposed becomes policy despite their opposition. The bureaucrat then has only two choices: either accept the policy and try to carry it through; or, if it has become a matter of deep moral principle, resign and seek employment elsewhere. Accommodation to the policy is the most typical response.

Finally each bureaucrat has status relationships with certain "constituents." In a sense all Americans are constituents of each bureaucrat as all must live under the policies and regulations produced in the agencies. But some people and some organizations are more directly affected by bureaucratic decisions than others. These most "concerned" people make up the bureaucrat's constituency.

The Department of Labor is especially sensitive to the views of organized labor. The Office of Education consults with educational organizations such as the National Education Association and the American Association of Colleges of Teacher Education. The Department of Commerce is alert to the interests of businessmen; the Federal Aviation Administration to airplane manufacturers, airport managers, and airline companies; the Department of Agriculture to farmers. Many more illustrations could be provided to support the major point: When making a decision the bureaucrat must take into account the reactions of his "constituents."

Public opinion. Opportunities for decision-making are influenced by public opinion. Problems of pollution have existed for many years, but public opinion was not aroused on this issue until the late 1960's. Bureaucrats now make decisions on problems of air and water pollution that were not even considered a decade ago.

Available resources. Every decision is influenced by available resources, including time, money, and people. A bureaucrat may have a great idea for solving a problem, but if he lacks the resources to carry it through, it will die. Many people regret the passing of good passenger train service in the United States. Perhaps there are bureaucrats in the Department of Transportation who have excellent plans for providing fast, low-fare, efficient, and comfortable train service for passengers. But without large sums of money from Congress the plans will not be carried out.

External decision-makers. Each bureaucratic decision-maker must remain alert to other decision-makers over whom he has no control. Some of these were referred to in the topic on status relationships above. But there are other external decision-makers. They include state and local officials, business executives, even foreign leaders.

Before a recommendation is made to raise the tariff on foreign automobiles entering the United States, bureaucrats consider the probable response of government officials in the countries affected by this change in tariff policy. For example, will these countries strike back by raising their tariffs?

These are many of the factors which decision-makers must consider in reaching their decisions. The following case provides an opportunity to apply some of these factors.

When Is a Ham a Ham?

The national government makes many decisions each day on many kinds of issues. A few years ago the government had to make a policy decision on such a commonplace commodity as ham, the kind you might buy at the supermarket. This case is about the making—and remaking—of a policy decision about ham. The key decision-maker was the head of the Agricultural Research Service of the United States Department of Agriculture (USDA).

Years ago Congress passed a Federal meat inspection law to protect consumers against the sale of unfit and improperly labeled meat. The law applied only to *interstate* commerce (goods moving across state lines), but when the law was passed the major packers and processors of meat were engaged in interstate business.

If meat is to be inspected and judged, it is essential to have standards. Some of these are easy to state. Spoiled meat, for example, should not be approved, or meat from diseased animals, or meat prepared in filthy places. Congress could have written such standards into the Meat Inspection Act. But there are other possible standards. Congress can say that "adulterated meat shall not be approved for sale in interstate commerce." But what, specifically, is adulterated meat?

Because it could not anticipate all the questions of this kind, Congress authorized the Department of Agriculture to *issue regulations* defining such things as adulterated meat. These regulations are actually laws, and violators of the regulations are punished. Within the Department of Agriculture, the adminis-

At work in a packing plant is a meat inspector for the United States Department of Agriculture.

trator of Agricultural Research Service was given power to make these regulations. In other words, he is a decision-maker. In reaching decisions on regulations, he is legally obliged to follow certain procedures set forth in another law, the Administrative Procedures Act of 1946.

A bureaucratic ruling on ham. On December 30, 1960, the administrator issued a new regulation, changing the definition of ham. Before that date, a ham was defined as a cured-pork product that could not have any added water (that is, the ham could not weigh any more than it did before it was cured). After December 30, 1960, under the new policy, a ham could be "watered," by adding enough water to make it weigh as much as 14 percent more than before curing.

Why was this new policy adopted? And what were the effects of this decision?

At least three factors led to the new policy: First, technological developments and scientific discoveries made it possible to pump extra water into a ham.* Second, partly because of these developments, a lot of watered hams were being sold in intrastate commerce (not moving across state lines) by the end of the 1950's. Some of these hams, not subject to Federal regulation, were less than 80 percent meat and more than 20 percent water. Water is cheaper than ham, and these intrastate hams could be sold for less than hams prepared under the Federal meat inspection regulations. This led to the third reason for the new Federal policy: pressure by meatpackers for the Department of Agriculture to change the rule. Their business was being hurt by intrastate ham producers. Some of the big packers even went into the watered-ham business, using local branch plants to cure hams so they would not enter interstate commerce. This was an effort to avoid Federal inspection and control.

In response to a request from the meatpackers, the head of the Agricultural Research Service set up a task force to review the existing meat inspection requirements. Starting in September, 1960, the group was instructed to consider the rule, or standard, regulating the water-content of a ham "from the viewpoint of consumer protection and current production and marketing practices."

This group apparently examined a "consumer survey" made by the American Meat Institute, the trade association of the meatpacking industry. The survey claimed that there was a consumer demand "for jucier smoked meats." So USDA—or specifically M. R. Clarkson, the acting administrator of the Agricultural Research Service—changed the standard defining a ham.

It is impossible to know the precise reason behind the change. Clarkson and his advisers may have felt that they should listen to the American Meat Institute because it was a powerful spokesman for the meatpackers. Or they may have decided that a failure to change the rule would only drive more ham

---

*Until the 1930's hams were cured by soaking them in brine for up to two months. Later, someone invented a pump that would inject the curing liquid into the blood vessels of a fresh ham, making possible a quick cure. Then, in the 1950's, it was discovered that by adding certain phosphates to the curing liquid, hams could be made to absorb a lot of water without dripping or looking wet. Now a ham could be pumped, or watered, to bring its weight up to as much as 125 percent of its uncured weight.

production into the intrastate market, where there would be no Federal inspection. They may have actually been convinced that the consumer wanted a juicier product. In any event, a policy was made, by a bureaucratic decision-maker, in response to a problem that he had to face.

But the policy did not stick. The December 30 decision created a controversy, and on October 18, 1961, it was reversed. A new rule was issued, and a ham moving in interstate commerce was once again defined as a pork product whose weight "shall not exceed the weight of the fresh uncured article."

Why did Clarkson change his policy? The essential answer is "countervailing political pressure," pressure that was stronger than the force exerted by the meatpackers.

Opposition forms. Even before the December 30 ruling, an interest group representing hog farmers was attacking the watering of ham. The October, 1960, issue of the *National Hog Farmer* urged, "Let's Not Sell Water at the Ham Counter," and pointed out that "every dollar that the housewife spends for water at the ham counter is a dollar that she won't buy pork with." And pork consumption in the United States was gradually dropping, as consumers spent more and more of their money for beef instead. By the 1960's the average amount of pork consumed per person in the United States was five pounds per year less than in 1930.

Soon after the December 30 rule was issued, it was criticized in the publication of a farm cooperative in the corn-hog country of the Midwest.

A packing-plant worker is pumping curing liquid into fresh hams.

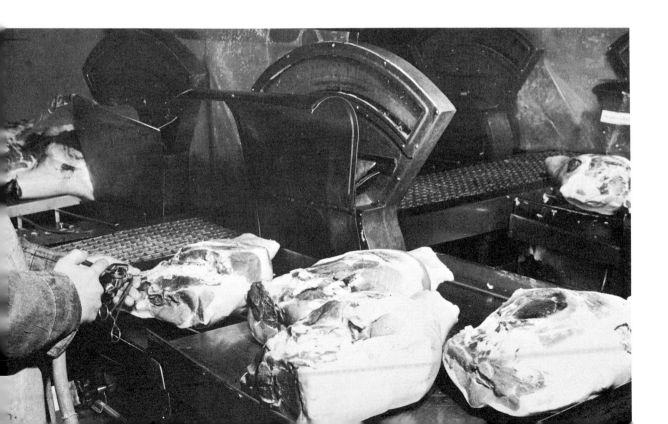

Within a couple of months the matter had also come to the attention of Consumers Union, a product-rating organization that distributes information about the quality of consumer goods. A feature article in the Union's magazine, *Consumer Reports*, described "The Great Ham Robbery."

Meanwhile, complaints were coming to the Department of Agriculture from other sources, including quantity purchasers of meats, such as chain stores, and the associations representing restaurants and hotels. And citizens were writing their congressmen to complain. City dwellers had read the *Consumer Reports* article, and hog producers had read about the ruling through various farm journals.

Thus, the matter came to the attention of the new Secretary of Agriculture, Orville Freeman. Mr. Freeman came to office in January, 1961, following the election of President John F. Kennedy. Freeman, a Democrat, replaced a Republican Secretary of Agriculture. Sometime during the winter of 1961 he told the press he was looking into the matter.

On March 28, 1961, Clarkson issued a notice that hearings would be held on the revised meat regulation. "Any interested person" was invited to "present any views, facts, or arguments—orally at one or more of the hearings, or . . . [by sending] . . . a written statement of comments to the Administrator, Agricultural Research Service," not later than May 22, 1961.

During April and May, hearings were held in Philadelphia, Atlanta, Chicago, Denver, Portland, Minneapolis, Los Angeles, and Washington. The December 30 rule was sharply criticized. It became quite clear that many more people—and a lot more interest groups—were opposed to watered ham than were in favor of "juicier" pork products.

The result was almost inevitable. On August 31, Clarkson issued a notice that the December 30 rule was being cancelled. As of November 17, 1961, a ham moving in interstate commerce could not weigh more than it had weighed before being cured. The Great Ham Issue had run its course. And a bureaucratic decision-maker, having made a policy in the form of a rule, had also reversed that policy.

1. Who was the key decision-maker? Do you think others participated in the decision? If so, who might have been involved?

2. Which groups profited most by each decision? In what way does knowing that there was a change in the political party in the White House between the two rulings help explain the change in the decision?

3. Is this an example of a decision made during a crisis or was there time to consider alternative policies?

4. How did different opinions on what was good for consumers affect the two different rulings?

5. How did rules and procedures influence the decision?

6. What status relationships appear to be especially important in this case?

7. What effect did public opinion have on the outcome of the case?

8. In your view which of the two rulings was the better example of an "accommodational decision"?

E. Aircraft Noise: A Problem for Bureaucratic Decision-Makers

Most policy decisions begin with the need to solve a problem. This case study concerns the problem of aircraft noise and the efforts of the Federal Aviation Administration (FAA) to establish new regulations on the amount of aircraft noise that would be allowed. We shall first consider the problem. Then we shall examine how the FAA dealt with the problem.

The Problem Is Noise

Here are the words of a man living half a mile from Kennedy Airport, one of the major airports in the New York City area. Like millions of others who live near commercial airports, this man is bothered by a very modern problem—aircraft noise.

> They are using the runway tonight! Wish you were here! Ho, man, I wish you could feel the walls. When they take off, it is like they were shooting at us. It's like they were firing guns at us. I really mean it. Everything vibrates. It's vibrating right now. There are cracks in the walls. The beams are giving way in the basement. The floor slants. I am constantly repairing and plastering the place. If you were here, you could smell the fuel. They have been using the northeast runway for two weeks, and that means we are catching it.*

*Quotation from Robert Sherrill, ''The Jet Noise is Getting Awful,'' *New York Times Magazine* (January 14, 1968), pp. 24–25.

Propeller aircraft are noisy enough. But beginning in 1958 the airline companies began changing over to jets, and passengers liked them. By 1970 there were around 2000 commercial jet liners flying the skies over the United States. On short runs of a few hundred miles, the jets fly at altitudes ranging from 20,000 to 30,000 feet. On longer routes they cruise at 30,000 to 40,000 feet. At these altitudes the jets cannot be heard on the ground, although you may see a white streak across the sky. It is when they are close to the ground or on the ground that they pollute the local environment with their characteristic wild roar.

At busy airports the noise for ground crews is continuous. It is so destructive that "ear defenders" must be worn by anyone outside of buildings. For people who live near busy airports, the sound is almost as continuous. For example, at O'Hare field near Chicago, aircraft take off and land on the average of once every 40 seconds. The noise pollution caused by O'Hare aircraft is shown in the map on the next page.

In 1965 the area within which the noise at O'Hare was objectionable included a population of 236,000 with 86 schools and 4 hospitals. By 1975 increases in traffic and in population will result in an affected population of 432,000 with 142 schools and 6 hospitals.

By 1970 there were 259 airports handling jet aircraft, and the amount of air traffic continues to expand. Millions of people are already affected, and many more millions will be affected by the end of the 1970's.

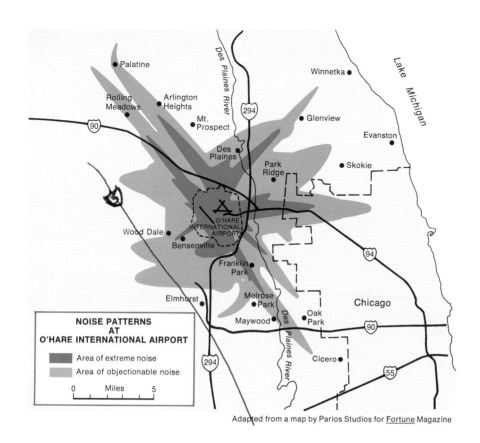

NOISE PATTERNS
AT
O'HARE INTERNATIONAL AIRPORT

Area of extreme noise
Area of objectionable noise

0   Miles   5

The map shows noise
patterns at Chicago's
O'Hare Airport in 1969.

Adapted from a map by Parios Studios for <u>Fortune</u> Magazine

How Much Noise Is Too Much?

There is no single scale for measuring noise. Instruments that measure noise actually measure the intensity of the sound in a unit called the *decibel.* But since the human ear and brain do not hear noise in exact proportion to its intensity, various other kinds of scales have been invented that try to approximate the actual annoyance level of noise. Among the scales is one called the *PNdb,* which means perceived noise. Another scale is the "A" scale written *dbA.* This scale emphasizes the sound intensities associated with higher frequency tones, as these are the tones that tend to be most annoying. Following are some sample levels of various kinds of noises as shown on a *dbA* scale: (These are the levels measured at distances from which people would most commonly hear these noises.)

Rustling leaves . . . . 20 dbA
Conversation . . . . 60 dbA
Vacuum cleaner . . . . 69 dbA
Heavy diesel truck . . . . 92 dbA
Power lawnmower . . . . 98 dbA
Thunder clap . . . . 135 dbA
Take-off blast of Saturn Five moon rocket . . . . 180 dbA

433

There is a strange thing about these scales for measuring noise. According to these scales it appears that a diesel truck (92 dbA) makes only half again as much noise as ordinary conversation (60 dbA). Common sense tells us that this is certainly not the case. In fact, *every increase of 10 decibels means a doubling of the intensity of the sound.* Ninety-two dbA (the truck) is over eight times louder than ordinary conversation.

How much noise is too much? Eighty decibels is considered to be the maximum level for comfort. At 85 decibels, hearing damage may occur if there is prolonged exposure. At 95 decibels, serious or even complete hearing loss can occur with continuous exposure. Remember that 95 decibels is twice as loud as 85 decibels. Remember, also, that 105 decibels is twice as loud as 95 decibels. A large, four-engine Boeing 707, one of the most commonly used jet airliners, produces from 107 to 120 decibels on takeoff. The same aircraft produces approximately 120 decibels during its landing approach, or eight times the recommended maximum level for comfort (80 dbA).

Jet engines can be quieted. Research has shown that a Boeing 707 fitted with sound absorbing material inside the engines will have a landing approach noise level of 105 decibels instead of the usual 120 decibels. To do the necessary work on present airplanes, however, would cost about $1 million per plane, and airline officials are not enthusiastic about investing such sums. They argue that this would increase airplane operating costs by about 5 percent because of the modifications.

Even 105 decibels, of course, is more noise than anyone wants. For that matter, 85 decibels is too much noise, and that's how much you will hear if you are a half a mile to the side of a jet runway as the 707 climbs away from the airport.

Some Costs of Excessive Noise

What are the costs of all of this noise? If a number of the law suits now pending in courts are settled in favor of those complaining, airport operators (usually the city governments) will have to pay millions of dollars to private citizens. For example, in 1968 ten families living hear the Los Angeles International Airport sued the city for $400,000 on the grounds that they had suffered permanent hearing damage and emotional disturbance from the noise of jet planes at landing and takeoff.

But the costs are hard to measure in dollars. Open-air concerts along the Potomac near Washington National Airport and concerts in the Hollywood Bowl and in a number of other cities have become almost inaudible. The loss cannot be measured in money. A concert is a priceless thing to some, a worthless thing to others.

Some people argue that modern urban man is already adapted to the increasing noisiness of his world. After all, such arguments go, electronically amplified music often reaches a level of 120 decibels, and young people pay for the privilege!

Meanwhile, back on the drawing board are plans for an airplane that will not just disturb people near airports. It will have the capacity to disturb everyone along its entire flight path. The noisy world is going to get noisier.

Supersonic Planes Promise More Noise

Today's jet aircraft cause disturbance when they are near the ground. When they are at their cruising altitude traveling at a speed of 550 miles an hour (a *sub*sonic speed), they cannot be heard on the ground. Tomorrow's supersonic jet transport (the SST) is another story. It will cruise at speeds

Housing Boom

The American SST project came to an abrupt halt in 1971 when Congress refused to extend the Federal subsidy for development of a supersonic transport plane.

Paul Conrad cartoon reprinted by permission of the Register and Tribune Syndicate

435

ranging from 1400 to 1800 mph. Whether the SST will be allowed to fly that fast over populated areas is a serious question.

Even though such aircraft will cruise at an altitude of 65,000 feet (twice the altitude used by present jets), they will produce noise on the ground. It will not be jet-engine noise. Instead, it will be total airplane noise, caused by the shock of the big airplane forcing its way through the air at supersonic speeds.

The shock wave produced by an aircraft flying at supersonic speeds is continuous and is heard as a sharp explosion as it reaches the ground. Think of it this way. Suppose the airplane is trailing a very large blanket long enough to reach the ground and 30 to 50 miles wide. It is along the trailing edge of the "blanket" that the sound effect of the airplane is felt. The trailing edge of the "blanket" doesn't touch the ground immediately under the aircraft but some distance to the rear so that it is only after the plane has passed that the shock wave touches the ground. And the shock is felt not just in a single point directly under the flight path but for the entire width of the "blanket," a distance as much as 25 miles on each side of the flight path. If the plane flies across the continent, the explosive bang will be heard by millions of people, since the bang zone is 50 miles wide and several thousand miles long in such an instance.

By the 1960's such bangs, or sonic booms, were caused only by military supersonic aircraft. But a Russian SST, the Tupelev 144, had its first flight on January 31, 1968. Britain and France have cooperated in the development of an SST, the Concorde. Its first flight was in March, 1969; and it was scheduled to be in regular use by 1973.

Work on an American SST also began in the 1960's. The airplane builder, the Boeing Company, expected to have the airplane available for regular use by 1980. The Federal government provided most of the money for the development of the SST. By 1970 it had already invested more than $700 million in the airplane. Then in 1971 Congress voted to cancel the subsidy.

People who supported the development of an American SST argued that the "superiority" of the American aviation industry can only be maintained by developing such an aircraft. They also argued that the SST would create thousands of new jobs in the aircraft industry.

Opponents of the SST argued that, in spite of promises that the plane would not be allowed to fly at supersonic speeds over populated areas, the airlines know that it is only through such use that they will be able to make a profit. This situation will bring pressure on the government to relax the rules restricting supersonic flight over populated areas if the SST is ever revived.

The American SST was designed to be larger than the Tupelev and the Concorde—280 feet long in contrast to the Concorde (193 feet) and the Tupelev (180 feet). The American SST would have been faster than the European versions, 1800 miles an hour rather than 1400 to 1500; and it would have carried more passengers—280 instead of 130. Because of its greater size, it would create a somewhat louder boom than the Tupelev and the Concorde. Noise during takeoff of the American SST was estimated at 117 decibels.

The aircraft industry suffered a tremendous blow when work was halted on an American SST, shown under development in the Boeing plant in Seattle.

The Federal Aviation Administration

Stand on the west steps of the Capitol in Washington and look toward the Washington Monument. Somewhat to the left of your gaze will be a row of bright, modern-looking Federal office buildings along Independence Avenue. One of them, a ten-story building, houses the Department of Transportation. On the upper floors of the building are the offices of the Federal Aviation Administration (FAA).

The FAA is the Federal government's administrative arm in matters of aviation. The agency licenses pilots, mechanics, and aircraft; issues rules about the operation of aircraft; trains and employs more than 20,000 air-traffic controllers; assigns air space for various types of aircraft; operates navigation aids; and concerns itself with airport safety.

The Federal Aviation Administration is charged by law with "the promotion, regulation and safety of civil aviation. . . ." The law under which the FAA operates is the Federal Aviation Act of 1958. Sometimes new problems arise, and the law fails to provide the regulatory authority required for the agency

437

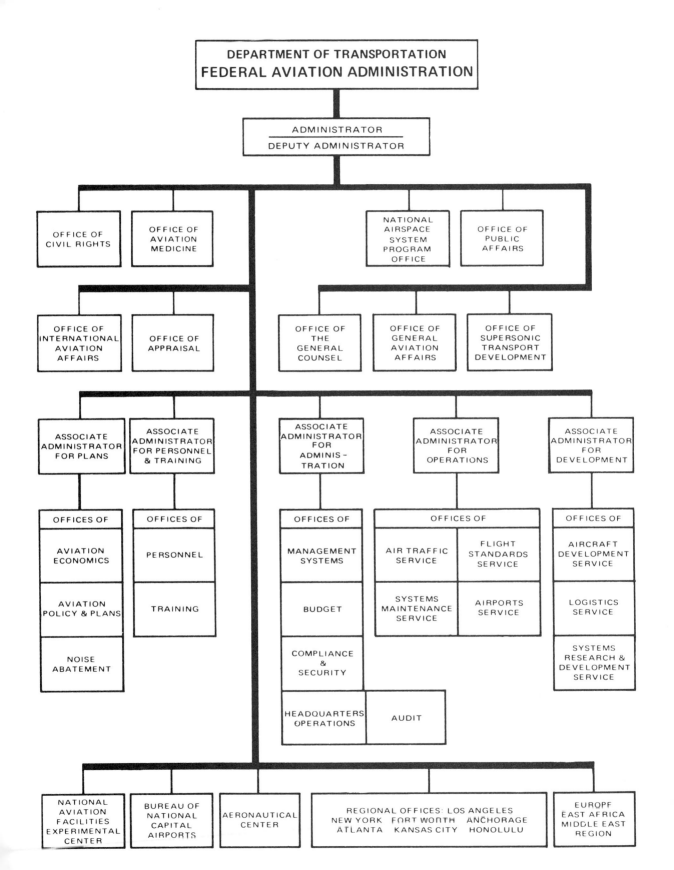

to act. This has been the case with the aircraft noise problem. Congress was asked to provide an amendment to the Federal Aviation Act of 1958 in order to authorize the FAA to issue regulations concerning aircraft noise. Congressional hearings were held, and a new law was passed giving the FAA the necessary authority. The new law (p. 441) was Public Law 90-411, approved July 1, 1968.

Congress also provides the means to *promote* aviation. It votes money to support particular developments. The SST was one such development. Presidents Kennedy, Johnson, and Nixon supported the development of an American supersonic transport. The FAA reflected this policy of support by maintaining an office of supersonic transport development. The FAA was a strong supporter of the SST and felt that such support was a part of the agency's responsibility to promote civil aviation.

Thus, the FAA must operate under conflicting goals. On the one hand it is seeking ways to reduce aircraft noise. On the other hand it is promoting the development of advanced aircraft which may increase noise.

In 1970 the office of SST development, at the end of the main hall on one of the top floors of the building, was a plushly furnished office, with carpets and modern furniture clearly designed with visitors in mind. On the same floor, down a branching hall, was the more work-a-day office of Noise Abatement (noise reduction). The acoustic engineers, the physicists, and the other specialists who have helped develop the FAA's regulations on aircraft noise work here.

Almost 50,000 people work for the FAA. Of these about 2700 work in the Washington, D.C., offices. The jobs range from that of clerk-typist to top policy-makers. Most of the people who work for the FAA are civil service employees.

The Federal Aviation Administration is a very technical operation. That is, many of the employees have (and require) a high level of technical training. It is difficult to think of technicians as "bureaucrats." And most of them probably do not think of themselves that way. The decisions made within the FAA are based largely on sophisticated technical studies performed by FAA technical experts or by outside consultants. Yet, in spite of the sophisticated technical research, many FAA decisions are ultimately *political* in nature. A decision like the aircraft noise rule affects all of us, and it was made by those "bureaucrats in Washington."

The FAA Makes a Decision on Aircraft Noise

The data for studying this example of decision-making in the Federal bureaucracy consists of an excerpt from an interview with an official who works in the Noise Abatement office in the FAA plus some documents that trace development of the decision that led to a new regulation on aircraft noise. The interview provides an opportunity to see how the problem was viewed by someone inside the agency. The documents tell us something about the constituencies to which the agency responds and about the relationship between the agency and Congress.

Public Law 90-411 Amending the Federal Aviation Act of 1958

The law on page 441 relating to aircraft-noise abatement was passed on July 21, 1968. As you read the law, answer the following questions:

1. If you were an aircraft manufacturer, could you tell from reading public law 90-411 the exact amount of noise that will be permitted by the Federal government in approving a new aircraft you are designing?

2. What is the purpose of this law?

FAA Announces Plans for New Noise Regulations

Public announcements of new decisions and policies of Federal agencies are published in the *Federal Register.* The following announcement appeared in the *Federal Register* on January 11, 1969.

1. What is the relationship between P.L. 90-411 and this announcement?

2. Which of the factors influencing bureaucratic decision-making is being demonstrated by this announcement?

3. Who would you predict would be most eager to have the information contained in this announcement?

Department of Transportation Federal Aviation Administration

Noise Standards: Aircraft Type Certification
Notice of Proposed Rule Making

The Federal Aviation Administration is considering the adoption of a new Part 36 of the Federal Aviation Regulations prescribing aircraft noise standards for subsonic transport category airplanes, and for subsonic turbojet powered airplanes regardless of category. . . .

Interested persons are invited to participate in the making of the proposed rule by submitting such written data, views or arguments as they may desire. . . . All communications received on or before March 12, 1969, will be considered by the Administrator before taking action upon the proposed rule. The proposals contained in this notice may be changed in the light of comments and will be available . . . for examination by interested persons.

Public Law 90-411 adds new section 611 to the Federal Aviation Act of 1958. This section provides that "the Administrator of the Federal Aviation Administration, after consultation with the Secretary of Transportation, shall prescribe . . . standards for the measurement of aircraft noise and sonic boom and shall prescribe . . . such rules and regulations as he may find necessary to provide for the control and abatement of aircraft noise and sonic boom, including the application of such standards, rules, and regulations in the issuance, amendment, modification, suspension, or revocation of any certificate authorized by this title" (Title VI).

FAA Issues New Aircraft Noise Standards

On November 12, 1969, the FAA announced new regulations on the control of aircraft noise. The document on page 443 represents the first page

Public Law 90-411
90th Congress, H. R. 3400
July 21, 1968

An Act

82 STAT. 395

To amend the Federal Aviation Act of 1958 to require aircraft noise abatement regulation, and for other purposes.

Be it enacted by the Senate and House of Representatives of the United States of America in Congress assembled, That title VI of the Federal Aviation Act of 1958 (49 U.S.C. 1421–1430) is amended by adding at the end thereof the following new section:

Aircraft noise control.
72 Stat. 775.

"CONTROL AND ABATEMENT OF AIRCRAFT NOISE AND SONIC BOOM

"SEC. 611. (a) In order to afford present and future relief and protection to the public from unnecessary aircraft noise and sonic boom, the Administrator of the Federal Aviation Administration, after consultation with the Secretary of Transportation, shall prescribe and amend standards for the measurement of aircraft noise and sonic boom and shall prescribe and amend such rules and regulations as he may find necessary to provide for the control and abatement of aircraft noise and sonic boom, including the application of such standards, rules, and regulations in the issuance, amendment, modification, suspension, or revocation of any certificate authorized by this title.

"(b) In prescribing and amending standards, rules, and regulations under this section, the Administrator shall—

Administrative provisions.

"(1) consider relevant available data relating to aircraft noise and sonic boom, including the results of research, development, testing, and evaluation activities conducted pursuant to this Act and the Department of Transportation Act;

80 Stat. 931.
49 USC 1651 note.

"(2) consult with such Federal, State, and interstate agencies as he deems appropriate;

"(3) consider whether any proposed standard, rule, or regulation is consistent with the highest degree of safety in air commerce or air transportation in the public interest;

"(4) consider whether any proposed standard, rule, or regulation is economically reasonable, technologically practicable, and appropriate for the particular type of aircraft, aircraft engine, appliance, or certificate to which it will apply; and

"(5) consider the extent to which such standard, rule, or regulation will contribute to carrying out the purposes of this section.

"(c) In any action to amend, modify, suspend, or revoke a certificate in which violation of aircraft noise or sonic boom standards, rules, or regulations is at issue, the certificate holder shall have the same notice and appeal rights as are contained in section 609, and in any appeal to the National Transportation Safety Board, the Board may amend, modify, or reverse the order of the Administrator if it finds that control or abatement of aircraft noise or sonic boom and the public interest do not require the affirmation of such order, or that such order is not consistent with safety in air commerce or air transportation."

72 Stat. 779.
49 USC 1429.

SEC. 2. That portion of the table of contents contained in the first section of the Federal Aviation Act of 1958 which appears under the center heading "TITLE VI—SAFETY REGULATION OF CIVIL AERONAUTICS" is amended by adding at the end thereof the following:

"Sec. 611. Control and abatement of aircraft noise and sonic boom."

Approved July 21, 1968.

of a news release announcing the new regulations. The diagram below indicates the top noise levels permitted by the new regulation.

1. Which group interested in regulations relating to aircraft noise gained the most by this decision?

2. Explain the new regulation in terms of the concept "accommodational decision."

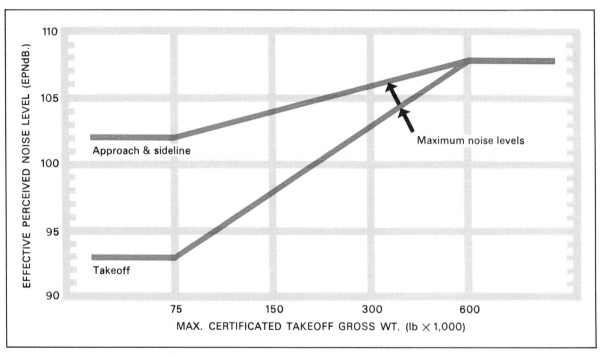

Allowable noise limits, shown above on chart, are based on aircraft's certificated gross takeoff weight. Maximum for 600,000-lb. aircraft is 108 EPNdB. The above chart is based on a drawing from *Aviation Week & Space Technology*, November 17, 1969, page 35.

FAA Comments on the Noise Abatement Rule

In a document called "Introduction to the Noise Rule," issued November 13, 1969, the FAA explained further the new aircraft noise abatement regulation and published a summary of the comments it had considered in reaching its decision.

Summary of public comments. The FAA received a total of 1428 public comments in response to the notice published in the *Federal Register* (p. 440). One major group contained approximately 1000 comments from individuals,

DEPARTMENT OF TRANSPORTATION

NEWS

FEDERAL AVIATION ADMINISTRATION
WASHINGTON, D.C. 20590

69-124

FOR IMMEDIATE RELEASE   Area Code 202--962-6461

12 November 1969

NOISE CERTIFICATION STANDARDS FOR NEW AIRCRAFT
ADOPTED BY FAA

"We have taken the important first step in reversing the escalation of
aircraft noise around airports," Secretary of Transportation John A. Volpe
said today, as he announced a new Federal Aviation Administration regulation
that establishes noise standards and maximum noise levels for all new subsonic transport airplane type designs, including some airplanes already
under development.

"The new regulation will result in an approximate halving of the noise
around airports," the Secretary added.

The noise limits prescribed in the new rule are as much as 10 EPNdB
(effective perceived noise decibels) less than those for the noisiest aircraft
presently in service. This represents an approximate halving of perceived
noise when measured on a logarithmic scale.

The new rule establishes the top maximum EPNdB to 93 and 108 EPNdB
depending on the type and size of the aircraft. Today's largest aircraft are
operating at 110 to 120 EPNdB at comparable measuring positions.

(over)

In this news release the
FAA announced its new
regulations on aircraft
noise.

citizen associations or committees, and local airport authorities. However, approximately 960 of these comments were identical form letters from the Los Angeles area. The other major group included comments from aviation trade associations, aircraft manufacturers, and aircraft operators.

Both groups agreed that the standards in the notice should be changed, but for directly opposite reasons. The first group argued that Congress intended greater reductions in noise levels than those proposed by the FAA. The second group felt that the statutory requirement to prescribe "technologically practicable and economically reasonable" noise standards could only be met at noise levels higher than those proposed.

Comments from private citizens and FAA replies. The document "Introduction to the Noise Rule" summarized the various comments received and replied to issues raised. Excerpts from the document follow.

from *The Wall Street Journal*

(1) The 960 form letters from the Los Angeles area stated that the noise standards should be "based on the technology *available* instead of that which would be most advantageous to the airlines."

The FAA replied that it agreed "that available technology must be applied in the reduction of aircraft noise. The noise standards in this amendment are intended to accomplish this result [in keeping] with the requirement in Section 611 (b) (4) that the Administrator must consider whether the standards are economically reasonable and technologically practicable."

(2) Several comments requested that protection against sonic boom be assured.

The FAA replied that "while not a part of this rulemaking action, study of the sonic boom problem is continuing so that appropriate action can be taken specifically in that area."

(3) "One comment stated that the FAA should limit the noise levels to those that do not exceed industrial health standards, . . . and the FAA should permit local standards to prevail if they are [stricter] than FAA standards."

The FAA replied that the goal of achieving noise levels not exceeding industrial health standards can be largely achieved by its ruling. But it recognized "that certain locally desired noise levels might not be achievable within the [limitations of the requirement] that economic reasonableness and technological practicability be considered. . . . This being the case, the FAA . . . recognizes the right of state or local public agencies, as the proprietors of airports, to issue . . . restrictions with respect to the permissable level of noise that can be created by aircraft using their airports."

(4) One citizens' association sent the FAA the results of a noise study indicating that the introduction of commercial passenger traffic at their local airport would have large costs for their community and that the published noise limits would not be acceptable. They requested limits of 90 to 95 EPNdb.

The FAA replied that it was convinced after thorough study that the current knowledge in the field of aircraft noise reduction simply does not permit the attainment of 90 to 95 EPNdb noise levels for the larger aircraft within the limits of the requirement that "economic reasonableness and technological practicability be considered by the Administrator in issuing noise abatement regulations."

Comments from state and local authorities. The document "Introduction to the Noise Rule" then took up some comments received from state and local public officials. To each of the issues raised in these comments the FAA gave a reply.

(1) One airport commission pointed out that the FAA notice represents "no more than the first step toward an ambitious goal." The commission concluded that, in issuing noise standards, the FAA should recognize the views of the airport's neighbors as well as the views of the aviation industry.

The FAA replied that it agreed and had "fully reviewed each of the many comments received from [persons] directly affected by aircraft noise. . . . These public comments have greatly assisted the FAA in determining . . . that the many and substantial costs to be imposed on the air transportation industry by this amendment are reasonable and appropriate."

(2) One commentator stated that the proposed levels are not adequate because they are not socially acceptable.

The FAA replied that under the legal regulations "socially acceptable noise levels can only be required insofar as they [put] economically reasonable burdens on the aircraft industry and are technologically practicable."

(3) One comment from a city manager stated that the FAA should "take a more militant stand in favor of the general public and opposed to the private monetary interests of airlines and aircraft manufacturers."

The FAA's answer was that it "does not intend to 'favor' or 'oppose' any segment of the public in its noise abatement activities. Rather, the FAA intends to impartially administer the language of [the 1968 noise-abatement amendment to the Federal Aviation Act] in the light of the pertinent statements of congressional intent concerning the public law. . . ."

The FAA concluded the summary with the following remarks: "The FAA intends to ensure that its noise abatement regulatory program requires aircraft manufacturers to achieve the greatest noise reductions that are consistent with the economically reasonable limits of noise reduction technology. . . ."

1. What individuals or groups seemed to be most interested in the new FAA regulations? May these be considered FAA "constituencies"?

2. What specific concerns and criticisms did each of these groups have?

3. What kinds of arguments does the FAA use to justify its position? What clause in Public Law 90-411 (p. 441) did the FAA cite most frequently?

An Interview with an FAA Official

After the publication of the new regulation on aircraft noise, some FAA officials were interviewed. As you read the brief excerpt from one of these interviews, keep the following questions in mind.

Circumstances for the decision

1. Was the noise-regulation decision an example of a crisis decision?

2. Identify the competing values that had to be resolved successfully by the decision.

Individual characteristics of the decision-makers

3. What kinds of people work in the Office of Noise Abatement and how did this affect the kind of decision that was reached?

Other factors in decision-making

4. What *rules* or *procedures* are referred to in the interview?

5. What *status relationships* are discussed in the interview and what effect did these relationships seem to have on the FAA decision?

6. What influence did *public opinion* have on the outcome?

7. In what sense were *available resources* a factor in the decision?

8. What *external decision-makers* were taken into consideration.

Interviewer: Give me some idea of how this office fits into the Federal Aviation Administration.

FAA Official: O.K. Well, the FAA's Office of Noise Abatement is an element of the Office of Plans under the Administrator for Plans, who in turn reports directly to the administrator of the FAA, Mr. Schaffer. Our office has to do primarily with the establishment of aircraft noise regulations, including both the problems of aircraft noise and sonic boom. In addition to the regulatory activities that we have, we conduct research and development programs which we hope will assist in implementing our regulations; and our only goal, of course, is to make aircraft and air commerce as compatible as possible with the airport environment and the environment of the population as a whole. We hope to do the best job we can on lowering aircraft noise levels.

Interviewer: Tell us how the noise-abatement rule came about.

FAA Official: . . . Around the latter part of 1966, the FAA was aware of the considerable concern that the public had and the industry was also beginning to share this concern about ever increasing aircraft noise. To get legal authority to make any improvements or to pass any rules and regulations in this area, we had to go to the Congress and request this legal authority. The Congress, of course, had pressures brought on them by various citizen groups, by airport owners, by interested parties in creating aircraft noise legislation.

In July, 1968, after [a lengthy period] of committee hearings, the Congress enacted Public Law 90-411, which is the law which gives the administrator of the FAA the legal authority to prescribe rules and standards for aircraft with respect to both noise and sonic boom. O.K.,

446

so then in its response to this public law we have just . . . issued our first rule on the certification of new transport-category aircraft with respect to noise.

What this means is that we have, working with the NASA (National Aeronautics and Space Administration), using the information from our research programs, working with the local government groups, the airport operators, citizen groups, with the aircraft industry, the transport association, . . . we have in this office developed what we believe to be the "technologically reasonable" and "economically viable" upper levels for future aircraft. These levels are prescribed in the rule. This rule, which consists of about 150 pages, describes methods for measuring aircraft noise, methods for evaluating aircraft noise, and then finally the permissible upper bounds and maximum levels for new aircraft.

Implementation of the rule is the responsibility of Federal Aviation Administration regional offices. The call that I was on just before you came in was to our western region which is now in the process of reviewing the certification procedures for the Boeing 747 aircraft. Now this rule has an effective date of 1 December 1969. The Boeing 747 aircraft is attempting to get a type certificate by 15 December.

Interviewer: They will not be bound by this rule?

FAA Official: They *will* be bound by this. In other words, our rule becomes effective before their type certificate becomes effective. The Boeing Company has actually been put on notice that they will be bound, but the manner in which they are bound will be somewhat different than aircraft which were put on notice after 1 January 1967. You see, the Boeing 747 was well into its design cycle before January, 1967. That was roughly the date when the industry was put on notice that the FAA was seeking this rule-making authority. So, what this means is that they started their design, and they didn't have available to them the latest acoustic techniques. So they didn't have the opportunity to include these latest advances into their early design phase. As a result, the Boeing Company may initially not meet our levels. O.K., so the 747 may not come under those limits right now, but they will be required to work with the administrator of the FAA and to establish a date or a time at which they will meet those levels in the near future.

Interviewer: Are most of the people who work in this office basically aeronautical engineers?

FAA Official: Well, we have a kind of interesting mixture. We have aeronautical, electrical, physicists, and acousticians. And then we have . . . well old flying pilots, . . . and all of these different disciplines are sort of necessary to be responsive to the many factors. . . .

Interviewer: How many professional level people are there now?

FAA Official: Let's see, the total staff is thirteen and that's ten professional.

Interviewer: Are these the people who handled the development of the rule?

FAA Official: Basically, these are the people. Now the rule is not just the product of this staff, but it is truly the product of this staff working together with the public. And the way we have done this in the noise office is we have actually set up task forces. These are members of civic groups, of airport communities, Airline Pilot Association, Aircraft Industry Association of the American Transport Association. And we have worked with these groups in task force meetings over the past, oh, year and a half, two years. I would say those meetings occurred only every other month roughly on an average. These groups have prepared their independent recommendations which we have digested . . .

Interviewer: . . . I know there was a lot of community citizen complaint in the Los Angeles airport area. Would someone representing that complaint be on a task force?

FAA Official: . . . the airport operators are there, so they are the ones that, of course, receive the complaints. Right now we have had in the present task force the lawyers of the city of Chicago, for example, the ones that are meeting with the public and putting the pressure on the airport operators.

Interviewer: That's the only representative of the public?

FAA Official: . . . The New York, Hempstead area has been a very active group . . . these groups run in the order of 35 people. We have people from all over the country . . . but the groups that are most involved are from New York, Chicago, and Los Angeles. The public obviously gets its word in very strongly through the congressional mails. The congressmen that have the most active citizen groups are the ones that are, well, obviously most responsive to it, and they are the ones that are insuring that the FAA is in fact responsive to the needs of the citizen groups.

Interviewer: Well, what's happening right now? I heard you say that you are hearing from people?

FAA Official: Well, most of the response so far has been through the press. I have had about three or four congressional inquiries. I think there was one press release that said the Aircraft Industries Association was going to sue the Federal Aviation Administration . . . and then on the other side I think there has been, I'm not sure it's the Hempstead group . . . that suggested that the FAA has sold out to the Boeing Company. So, from our point of view, if we can get about equal complaints from all sides, we feel we might have done a good job on rule making. Because in the noise business . . . we are not going to make anybody happy. . . . So, if you do make one group happy . . . say you make the aircraft manufacturers completely happy . . . then that means that you haven't put enough burden on them. And so if the responses are just about equally squeezing on us, then we have a feeling we might have done a good job.

Interviewer: Is that a consideration while the rules are being devised?

FAA Official: Well, from a realistic standpoint the considerations are first technological . . .; then this public law . . . this 90-411 was a little bit unique in that they cautioned us to be absolutely sure that everything that we were doing was "economically reasonable." Now that is very vague. . . .

Interviewer: That's support of the industry.

FAA Official: Yes, but it is more than that, because it supported the gross national product of the United States, because the industry is part of that gross national product. So, if we do something that wrecks the industry, we are also wrecking the United States. So, we've got to be realistic from that standpoint. I mean, obviously, you could evade noise by keeping the aircraft on the ground; that would be about the most extreme thing that one could do.

Interviewer: How does the rule handle the sonic boom situation?

FAA Official: The present rule is a subsonic rule, so it does not handle the sonic boom situation. The sonic boom, I believe, will be addressed in the supersonic transport rule. And right now the administrator of the FAA, Mr. Schaffer, and Mr. Volpe, Secretary of the Department of Transportation, have both stated that there will be no supersonic over-land flights by commercial SST's until it can be proven that the sonic boom levels or character can be demonstrated to be acceptable to the public. Now, exactly what is "acceptability" is very difficult to say, but I think . . . this statement does sort of notice that the first generation of SST's will probably not fly supersonically over land.

Interviewer: In the case of citizen groups opposed to the SST . . . has there been any direct contact between this office and such groups?

FAA Official: Well, obviously there is considerable correspondence, and I think at times these people have been invited to come and make their views known to us. Occasionally, well, I guess it gets to a point that after you have heard their story there is [nothing further to be gained from listening to them].

Interviewer: Do you ever get a situation in an office like this where individuals would find themselves personally in some disagreement with the policy? Does this ever happen?

FAA Official: Boy, that sounds like a "have-you-quit-beating-your-wife" type of question.

Interviewer: Well, no—what I am asking is that this is a very technically oriented operation, and yet the decisions at the very top have to be very political while taking the technical into consideration. So, there must be occasions when the technical people find themselves not quite totally in agreement with the policy decision.

FAA Official: Well, we could imagine a situation where the technicians say, "Boy, I could squeeze an extra five decibels out of that aircraft, if you

At a news conference held late in 1970 by a Senate opponent of the SST, the author of a booklet on sonic booms, Charles Shurcliff, urged defeat of a measure to continue funding of the project. Early in 1971 Congress voted that the SST subsidy be ended.

let me increase the direct operating cost by 50 percent." And this would be an economically unrealistic burden. Now, this kind of a situation could occur, but I can't think of any specific examples right off hand. Obviously rule-making must necessarily be a compromise. . . .

1. Was the decision leading to new noise regulations primarily a "technical decision" or a "political decision"?

2. As an agency in the executive branch of the government, the FAA administers laws passed by Congress. Can you find any evidence in this case that the FAA "legislates" and "interprets laws" as well as administers laws?

3. Do you approve of the decision reached by the Federal Aviation Administration? Explain your answer in terms of the factors that influence bureaucratic decision-making.

F. Bureaucracy and Democracy: Can They Get Along?

Bureaucracy seems to be a fact of life in a modern nation. Bureaucratic structures exist not only in government but in all large organizations. They exist to help organizations operate as efficiently as possible.

Nevertheless, there are features of a bureaucratic system which seem inconsistent with the values of democratic societies. The purpose of a bureaucratic system is to accomplish the goals of an organization in the most efficient manner possible. But in a democracy efficiency is not always the primary goal of the society. Opportunity to dissent, the rights of individuals, and the need to find decisions that will accommodate the interests of as many people as possible are very important considerations. Sometimes the desire for efficiency can lead to limitations on these democratic values.

The tension between democracy and bureaucracy has led some people to fear the growth of bureaucracy, because they believe it threatens democracy. Others see bureaucracy as an effective means for accomplishing democratic purposes. In the imaginary roundtable discussion which follows, you will have an opportunity to consider various arguments on this issue. Do you think that democracy and bureaucracy are compatible?

Roundtable Discussion

Helen: It seems to me that bureaucracy and democracy are by nature incompatible. In a democracy a citizen chooses the policy-makers through open elections. But bureaucratic officials are not elected. A few are appointed, and most get their positions through the civil service examinations. Bureaucrats make many decisions that affect us, but we have no way to control these decisions or the people who make them.

Sydney: I agree with some of your ideas, Helen, but disagree totally with your conclusions. In my opinion bureaucracy is essential to the smooth functioning of democratic government. The purpose of government is to produce programs that we want. Such programs cannot be carried out without trained, qualified people to manage them.

Helen: Agreed! But what controls do we have over these policies?

Sydney: There are many controls. First of all, bureaucrats must remain sensitive to public opinion, and there are always plenty of reporters around eager to find stories it can print about the bureaucracy. Secondly, bureaucrats can only go as far as the Congress and the President want them to go—and we elect both the President and members of Congress.

Eldridge: I don't know. It seems to me to be a bad idea to have a Washington elite make policy for all of us when it isn't representative of Americans.

Miriam: I think you raised two questions: one, what is an elite? and two, is the bureaucracy representative of Americans? If you mean by *elite* a group of people who are technically qualified to make decisions in a field, then I think the bureaucracy is a kind of an elite—and we should be grateful for it. It is true that bureaucratic decision-makers as a group

The accommodational decisions of bureaucrats often seem to be patchwork. Are such decisions in keeping with democracy?

"The Patchwork Quilt"

are better educated than the population as a whole and better educated than leaders in business as a group. And I prefer to have qualified leaders to unqualified ones. Regarding your second question, I think the bureaucracy *is* generally representative of typical Americans—more so than Congress at least. Bureaucrats come from many regions of the country and a variety of social classes. As compared to some European countries where government leaders usually come from the upper classes, American bureaucratic leaders tend to come from the same social groups as all other Americans.

Eldridge: What irritates me most is the whole impersonal nature of the bureaucracy. They make you feel like you are just a number to them. But I am *me!*

Sydney: I know. I have had the same feeling at times. But, in fact, part of making certain that everyone is treated equally—that no one receives special favors—is to handle each case by the same procedures. A fundamental American value is that everyone is entitled to equal justice under law. This means that everyone must be treated alike—even though you are certain that yours is an exceptional case.

452

Eldridge: I can understand that, but it's also true that while it's very hard for an individual to influence bureaucratic policy, a group of powerful people acting together can win exceptions to, or changes in, the rules.

Helen: That's true. Each agency does have its own constituencies to which it pays special attention. It seems to me that all of us are subject to policies that are a result of deals between special-interest groups and their contacts within the bureaucracy.

Sydney: In a sense that's true, but these groups often counteract and balance off each other. Anyway, Helen, most of democratic politics is making compromises. It seems to me that you are really saying that democracy and bureaucracy fit together.

Eldridge: But doesn't that make it difficult to get good policies? For example, suppose that some industry is dumping waste containing mercury into a river. Downstream others are getting their drinking water from the river. The industry wants to dump mercury; the people who are drinking the water expect the water to be pure. More than likely the bureaucracy will make an accommodational decision: limit the amount of mercury that can be released into the river but not force the industry to stop the practice altogether. In the meantime, people are slowly dying from their drinking water.

Sydney: I suppose it might happen, but it's a strange argument for you to make, Eldridge. Earlier, you feared a Washington elite would force policies on Americans. In this case you want it to force a policy on the industry. Accommodational decisions are at the heart of the democratic process. If the public doesn't like a particular decision, it is the citizen's responsibility to make his views known. That's what democracy is all about; that's how we can make the bureaucracy responsive to our needs.

"Everybody's organized but the people."

John Gardner asks you to join him in forming a mighty "Citizen's Lobby" concerned not with the advancement of special interests but with the well-being of the nation.

I know that many of you share my concern over what is happening to our country.

That is why I am coming to you; to ask you to join me in forming a new, independent, non-partisan organization that could be an effective force in rebuilding America.

It will be known as Common Cause.

It will not be a third party, but a third force in American life, deriving its strength from a common desire to solve the nation's problems and revitalize its institutions of government.

Wherever you touch the public process in this country today, almost without exception, you will find a failure of performance.

The air we breathe is foul. The water we drink is impure. Our public schools are in crisis. Our courts cry out for reform. Race conflict is deepening. Unemployment is rising. The housing shortage has driven rents through the roof.

The things that government is supposed to do, it is not doing. The things it is not supposed to do—interfering with the lives and liberties of its citizens—it is doing.

How we can work together in Common Cause.

The first thing Common Cause will do is to assist you to speak and act in behalf of legislation designed to solve the nation's problems. We will keep you up to date on crucial issues before Congress. We will suggest when and where to bring pressure to bear.

Common Cause is an outgrowth of the Urban Coalition Action Council. Operating under a governing board of extraordinary diversity (mayors, leaders from business, labor, minority and religious groups), the Action Council proved to be astonishingly effective in influencing major legislation.

So we know from first hand experience that citizen action can get results.

I shall not attempt to list here all the issues with which Common Cause will be concerned.

We believe there is great urgency in ending the Vietnam war now. We believe there must be a major reordering of national priorities, and that the Government cannot go on spending $200,000,000 a day for "national defense". We believe the problems of poverty and race must be among our first concerns. We will call for new solutions in housing, employment, education, health, consumer protection, environment, family planning, law enforcement and the administration of justice.

We intend to take the phrase "Common Cause" seriously. The things that unite us as a people are more important than the things that divide us. No particular interest group can prosper for long if the nation is disintegrating. Every group must have an overriding interest in the well-being of the whole society.

One of our aims will be to revitalize politics and

After spending the last 5 years in Washington as Secretary of Health, Education & Welfare and as Chairman of the Urban Coalition, John Gardner is convinced that only an aroused and organized citizenry can revitalize "The System" and change the nation's disastrous course.

government. The need is great. State governments are mostly feeble. City government is archaic. The Congress of the United States is in grave need of overhaul. The parties are virtually instruments of the popular will. We can [...] obsolescence.

Most parts of the system [...] they cannot respond [...] so ill-designed [...] waste taxpayer [...] frustrate [...]

The so [...] councils [...] ber of C [...] that mig [...] more rest [...] ful, hard [...] We can p [...]

Skeptics [...] things." [...]

States has changed in dramatic ways since its founding. Why should we assume it has lost the capacity to change further?

The political parties have changed even more dramatically since the birth of the Republic. They can change again.

Many of you share my anger at institutions and individuals that have behaved irresponsibly. But, if we're going to focus our anger, a good place to begin is with ourselves.

We have not behaved like a great people.

We are not being the people we set out to be. We have not lived by the values we profess to honor. And we will never get back on course until we take some tough, realistic steps to revitalize our institutions. We had better get on with it.

In recent years we have seen too much complacency, narrow self-interest, meanness of mind and spirit, irrational hatred and fear. But as I travel around the country, I see something else. I see great remaining strength in this nation. I see deeper reserves of devotion and community concern than are being tapped by present leadership. I see many, many Americans who would like to help rebuild this nation but don't know where to begin.

I invite you to be among the first to join us in Common Cause.

We cannot and should not depend on big contributors. The money to support our work must come from the members themselves.

We therefore ask you to enclose a check for $15 with your membership application.

If you can afford more, send an additional contribution. [...] and active membership, we can begin [...] America. —*John [...] Gardner*

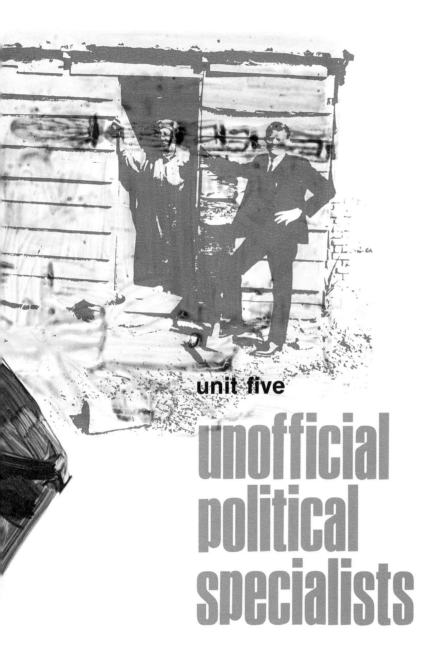

unit five

unofficial
political
specialists

chapter 17

The Role of Unofficial Political Specialist

An unofficial political specialist is a person who does not hold a position in government but who devotes much time and effort to attempts to influence public policy decisions. Who are unofficial political specialists? What are their rights and duties? What social forces influence their political behavior?

A. Who Are Unofficial Political Specialists?

The following case presents some clues about the roles of several unofficial political specialists. As you read, try to decide who the unofficial specialists in this case are and what they do.

Does Shoreline Need New Airport Facilities?

Walter Simko, president of the Shoreline Chamber of Commerce, picked up his copy of the *Shoreline Evening Herald* and turned to the editorial page. He began to read "Culp's Column," a daily feature written by Lester Culp. As he read, Walter Simko became more and more annoyed.

"Martha," he shouted to his wife, "listen to what this fool Culp says about the airport issue."

> For nearly one year, the City Council has been discussing whether or not to build new city airport facilities. Conflicting opinions about this issue have been presented to the City Council.
>
> The Council meets tomorrow to discuss the airport issue. Responsible citizens of Shoreline must contact their councilmen and urge them to oppose airport expansion.
>
> Our present airport is large enough to serve a city like Shoreline. Money for airport expansion can be put to better use building new schools and parks. While only a few higher-income people would benefit from enlarging the city airport, all of Shoreline citizens would benefit from new educational and recreational facilities. The people of South Side need a new elementary school. Our city needs a larger library and civic center.
>
> In addition, expanding the city airport would greatly increase air traffic to our city. This would cause discomfort to the people of Shoreline, since more and bigger jets landing here mean more noise and air pollution. Therefore, we must urge the City Council to reject the proposals to build new airport facilities here.

After reading "Culp's Column" to his wife, Simko phoned Roger Rand, the city councilman who represents his district.

456

"Hello, Roger, this is Walter. Did you read 'Culp's Column' in the *Evening Herald?*"

"Yes, Walter, I did," said Roger Rand. "Culp's arguments are certain to cause trouble for us at the city council meeting tomorrow night."

"Why don't you contact Max Douglas and arrange for him to testify before the Council," said Simko. "Douglas can present a convincing argument in support of airport expansion."

"I agree, Walter, and I'll see that Douglas is there," replied Rand.

"Fine," said Simko. "I'll see you tomorrow."

The "Expansionists" State Their Case

The next evening George Geddes, president of the Shoreline City Council, called the meeting to order. After disposing of other business, Geddes called upon Max Douglas to testify about the need for new airport facilities. Following are excerpts from a transcript of this portion of the Council meeting:

Geddes: Mr. Max Douglas is here tonight as a representative of the Branis Corporation, the engineering-consultant firm hired by the airport authority to do a study of Shoreline's future airport needs. Mr. Douglas, we are pleased that you are able to be here to help us this evening.

Douglas: I am pleased to be of service to you.

Geddes: What are your opinions about the airport issue, Mr. Douglas?

Douglas: First of all, Mr. Geddes, we of Branis do not propose an entirely new airport. The present site has too much invested in it with the new terminal just finished last year and the two million dollars you are now spending for runway expansion. Nevertheless, my company believes that Shoreline, with its rapid growth rate, must plan now for 1990, before it's too late to take advantage of its current airport investment. By 1990 Shoreline will need a major airport facility capable of handling international carriers.

We base our position on facts. The number of air passengers from Shoreline is growing rapidly. In 1952 only 9 percent of this area's air passengers came from Shoreline. By last year over 40 percent did. This, in round numbers, meant that 750,000 Shoreliners flew somewhere last year. Many had to drive forty-five miles to Freetown to get a flight because they could not get reservations at the Shoreline Municipal Airport. The simple fact is that the present airport facilities are not adequate to handle the needs of Shoreline's own population. And this is not counting the needs of the rest of the surrounding metropolitan area.

Geddes: Mr. Douglas, some critics of your proposal have said that the increased noise and air pollution caused by increased jet aircraft traffic would outweigh any advantages connected with expansion of our airport. What do you think?

Douglas: As an aeronautical engineer, naturally I keep up on the latest scientific information on noise and pollutant control. I predict that given the time and effort being expended, we will have jet noise licked in another year. As for air pollution, this is a more difficult problem. But I predict that science will solve this problem too in the near future. And concerning jet noise, our readings in the airport neighborhood, one mile from the runways show that the noise has never exceeded 50 decibels, which is not harmful.

Geddes: I agree, Mr. Douglas, that you may in time control some of the irritating accompaniments of jet flights. But what about the decline in the value of properties located near airports? How do you assure people who live in houses near the airport that they are safe?

Douglas: Statistics on deaths caused by planes reveal that most deaths result during landings. But these deaths, statistics also tell us, occur in areas within a quarter of a mile of the landing strip. The expansion plans we suggest take this factor into account. Land within the danger zone would be purchased and cleared.

Geddes: Thank you for your help, Mr. Douglas.

After the city council meeting, Walter Simko went to a nearby restaurant where he met Councilman Rand. The two men ordered sandwiches and coffee and discussed the meeting.

"Douglas did a fine job tonight," said Simko. "I'm sure his testimony will convince many doubtful citizens of the need to expand airport facilities."

"His testimony also seemed to make a good impression on the three councilmen who are still undecided on this issue," said Rand.

"By the way, I've decided to answer Culp in the *Evening Herald*," said Simko. "I've written a letter to the editor, and it should appear in the paper tomorrow. Look for it, Roger."

Walter Simko's letter appeared in the next edition of the *Evening Herald*. It pointed out that a larger airport would mean more money and more jobs for Shoreline residents. The letter also argued that problems of air pollution

458

and noise would probably be solved by scientists in the near future and concluded with the following statement:

> We should not lose sight of our great opportunities because of a few possible problems. The opportunity for Shoreline must be seized now, or it may soon be lost to another, more aggressive community in our area.

It was signed "Walter Simko, President of the Shoreline Chamber of Commerce."

Simko meets with resistance. Marshall Levy, director of the Safe and Sane Airport Committee, read Simko's letter in the *Herald*. He smashed his fist down hard on his kitchen table. "Simko thinks he's won his battle for an expanded airport, but we'll create some new problems for him and his cronies when we hold our anti-airport demonstration."

"Right! We'll shake up old man Simko tomorrow," replied Kent Elliot. "When Simko and his friends on the city council realize that the people are against their airport plans, they'll have to change their minds and see things our way."

On the following day Marshall Levy led a march of more than 5000 demonstrators. They chanted slogans and carried signs protesting the airport expansion and denouncing the Branis Corporation, Walter Simko, and the Chamber of Commerce. The marchers halted in front of City Hall.

The Opposition Presents Its Petition

Marshall Levy walked up the steps of City Hall and spoke through a bull horn:

Attention, Mayor Curtis and members of the City Council. You had better listen to us if you want to keep your jobs. We represent people power, and we are against spending valuable city funds to expand the airport for the benefit of Walter Simko and a few other local big shots.

For six months we have been meeting in local schools, clubrooms, and churches to study the problem of air transportation and its effect on our environment. Over 10,000 citizens have signed our petition against further expansion of airport facilities in any part of the Shoreline metropolitan area. We are here today to deliver this petition to you, Mayor Curtis.

Here are just a few of our reasons for opposing increased air traffic in Shoreline:

1. Jet planes pollute the air with carbon monoxide and nitrogen oxides which produce smog, lung diseases, and hurt our local truck-garden industry.
2. Jet landings and takeoffs produce noise levels of up to 110 decibels. Medical experts have told us that an 85 decibel level, if continuous, is enough to create serious emotional disturbances in people.
3. Two invaluable public facilities—the Sands Wildlife Refuge and the Placer State Hospital for the mentally ill—will be made useless by an expansion of the present airport.

I could go on, but let me close by urging all of you to make your opinions known to your councilmen. United we can preserve our environment. Otherwise our city council may approve this monstrous plan that threatens the pleasant environment we all share in Shoreline. Mr. Simko and others of his kind must stop thinking only in terms of dollar bills. We must not ruin our environment in order to increase the profits of a few businessmen.

Levy's speech ended with a tremendous roar of approval from the crowd.

The following day the *Shoreline Evening Herald* reported the demonstration at City Hall. The newspaper also announced that the councilmen planned to vote on the airport issue at the next Council meeting. Would the editorial by Lester Culp and the demonstration of the Safe and Sane Airport Committee influence their thinking? Or would the testimony of Max Douglas and the arguments of Walter Simko sway their votes? How will the airport issue be resolved?

1. Which of the individuals in the Shoreline case are playing the role of unofficial political specialist?
2. What is the role of unofficial political specialist?
3. Why do individuals play the role of unofficial political specialist?
4. What factors are likely to influence the behavior of an unofficial political specialist?

460

Many Kinds of Unofficial Specialists

Thus far in our study of political behavior, we have looked mainly (a) at the voters who elect officials and (b) the officials they elect. However, if we stopped here, we would have difficulty understanding much that happens in political life, for there are many "middlemen" in the political system.

The middlemen, or *unofficial political specialists,* are people who do not hold official positions in government, but who nonetheless play an important part in influencing public policy decisions. While most public policy must receive final approval from people who hold public office, congressmen, city council members, and so on, these decisions may be strongly influenced by informal or unofficial political specialists.

In this unit we will look at some of the roles of unofficial specialists. We will speculate on who they are, how they become influential, and how they use their political resources to influence others. Our study is complicated by the fact that unofficial specialists differ from each other almost as much as they differ from people with little influence. This makes it difficult to make generalizations about them. However, to simplify our investigation, we have divided unofficial specialists into four main categories: (1) lobbyists, or those who represent interest groups; (2) commentators, or people who present political news and viewpoints to the public through the mass media; (3) experts, or people who serve as authorities on specialized fields of knowledge; and (4) leaders of political parties.

B. Who Becomes an Unofficial Political Specialist?

There are few generalizations which can be made about unofficial political specialists. An analysis of the socioeconomic status of lobbyists, reporters, editors, publishers, party leaders, and scientific experts would no doubt show a wide variety of social backgrounds, educational preparation, wealth, and occupational status. However, while on the whole, unofficial specialists are less likely to come from the upper-middle and upper social classes than public officials are, their income tends to be somewhat higher and their education somewhat better than average.

People with many political resources tend to become unofficial specialists more often than people with few resources. One reason some people are more influential than others is that they have a larger number of political resources. While not all rich, high status people use their resources to influence policy, many do. The poor, the uneducated, and lower status people can also become influential, but lack of money and connection requires the development of other resources to do so. To compensate for limited political resources, a person with few resources usually joins with others who share his goals. Through good organization and leadership such a group may develop effective political resources.

Unofficial specialists tend to have many of the social characteristics of the groups they represent. This fact helps to explain why there are so many different kinds of unofficial specialists. Negroes occupy the positions of leadership in most civil rights groups. Labor leaders are usually recruited from the lower middle class or working class. The National Association of Manufacturers attracts businessmen to its positions of leadership. Political party leaders also tend to reflect the composition of their own party in their locale. For example, the Democratic party in Chicago depends upon Catholics, Polish-Americans, Negroes, and blue-collar workers for its election victories. It is, therefore, not suprising to find Catholics, Polish-Americans, Negroes, and labor leaders occupying positions of leadership within the party.

The general manager of WBZ-TV in Boston is shown taping one of the station's editorials, which are usually aired twice a day.

While unofficial political specialists seem to have little in common, they do share a belief that government policy, at least in their own area of interest, is important. They care about issues, election outcomes, and policy decisions. Unofficial political specialists are also likely to be better informed than the casual spectator about political issues, about the way government works, and about politics in general.

Before continuing, check your understanding of the term "unofficial political specialist" by identifying the individuals below that you think would fall within our definition of *unofficial* political specialists.

Legislative Director for Connecticut State Rifle and Revolver Association.

Governor of Illinois.

Republican grocer who votes in every public election but does nothing else "political."

Editor of local newspaper who writes editorials about various political issues.

Doctor who testifies before a committee of the state legislature on the effects of marijuana.

State legislator who hears that testimony.

Democratic party leader who influences the position the Democratic candidate takes on Vietnam.

Wealthy businessman who never dabbles in politics.

Taping a rebuttal to a WBZ-TV editorial is Mrs. Katherine Kane, who disagreed with what the station had to say about a summer program which she was directing for the city of Boston.

463

C. How Do Unofficial Political Specialists Behave?

A social role, you will recall, is a set of expectations about the behavior of a person occupying a particular position, or status. The role of an unofficial political specialist may be thought of as what people expect such a specialist to do and what they expect him not to do.

The roles played by various kinds of unofficial political specialists differ widely because there are so many different kinds of such specialists. But they do have several important characteristics in common. A party leader, a lobbyist, and a newspaper editor are all expected to try to influence policy. Most government officials and most citizens view a lobbyist's attempts to influence policy as part of his job. And, while some may disagree with what an editorial says, they would not challenge the right of the editor to try to influence people in this way.

> **1.** How might the county chairman of a political party exercise his influence in ways that would be acceptable to most people?
>
> **2.** What are some ways he might exercise influence that would clearly *not* be acceptable?

An unofficial political specialist is expected to be influential, but to exercise his influence according to the "rules of the game." Sometimes the rules are not even very clear, but the best guide is the experience that comes from watching politics and observing the reactions to the attempts of other unofficial political specialists to influence policy. Effective unofficial political specialists sense what the rules are and learn to be influential without violating them.

Unofficial Specialists Use Many Skills

Some men have a knack for bargaining and making compromises. Others are persuasive speakers. Still others have a talent for mobilizing and organizing people to work on a certain job. The ability to write in a clear and interesting way, to communicate effectively over television, to research and analyze a certain issue, or to draft a bill in precise legal language—these are other important political skills.

These same skills are valuable in many roles besides political ones. A businessman may need to know how to bargain well, and a salesman needs to be persuasive. A football coach must be able to organize his team and get a maximum effort from each player. Scholars may use their analytical skills for research unrelated to politics. And movie stars, as well as television commentators, must be attractive and communicate well. Unofficial political specialists use these same skills to influence public policy. That is the difference.

Few political specialists possess all the skills needed in political activities. Usually unofficial political specialists concentrate on using their particular talents to best advantage, whether it be writing, bargaining, persuading, organizing, or something else. But no unofficial specialist can hope to be very effective unless he has one or more of these skills.

464

The activity of unofficial political specialists takes many forms, but most of what they do can be classified as (1) *bargaining* with decision-makers—usually official political specialists, (2) working for the *selection* (by appointment or election) of men they want as decision-makers, and (3) *developing resources* for use in future bargaining or in future attempts at influencing the selection of decision-makers. To bargain successfully with decision-makers, or to influence the selection of new decision-makers, an unofficial political specialist needs political resources.

The right-hand column of the exercise below lists five valuable skills. Any unofficial political specialist might like to excel in each of these skills. Yet certain skills are needed more than others by any particular unofficial political specialist. Which *one or two* skills would be of particular importance for each of the unofficial political specialists listed in the left-hand column?

POSITION	SKILL
1. Legislative lobbyist for Pennsylvania Motor Truck Assn.	A. Organizing and mobilizing people
2. County chairman of Republican party	B. Personal persuasion
3. Newspaper reporter	C. Research and analysis of problem
4. Highway engineer testifying before state legislature	D. Bargaining
5. Representative of American Farm Bureau discussing policy with Secretary of Agriculture	E. Writing ability

How Do Unofficial Political Specialists Influence Policy?

Following are three examples of how unofficial political specialists try to influence policy. After reading these examples, answer the questions which follow each one.

Example A. Roy is running for president of his senior class. Abe is president of the Lettermen's Club, composed of all boys who have earned athletic letters. Abe would like for the senior class to set aside a portion of the class dues to sponsor a senior-class float in the annual Homecoming parade. He tells Roy that if Roy will advocate using some of the class treasury for this purpose, the Lettermen's Club will support him for class president.

What is the issue? What policy is Abe seeking? What resources has Abe used in his bargaining? How has Abe tried to influence policy?

Example B. The policemen's union in New York City is asking for higher wages for its members, but the city government will not meet their demands. Union leaders call for a work slowdown. The next day 25 percent of the city's policemen call in to say they are "sick." City government leaders enter into emergency negotiations with leaders of the police union.

> What is the issue? What policy is the police union seeking? What resources can the union leaders use in their bargaining? How have the union leaders tried to influence policy?

Example C. A large southern newspaper has always supported the Democratic candidate for President, but this year it has not endorsed either party's candidate. The paper's editorials state that it is withholding endorsement because neither candidate has come out strongly against busing to achieve integration of the schools. The editorials also hint that the candidate who promises to oppose the use of Federal funds to "force" integration will receive the newspaper's endorsement.

> What is the issue? What policy is the newspaper seeking? What resources does the newspaper have at its disposal? How have the newspaper editors tried to influence policy?

chapter 18

Interest-Group Representatives

Interest-group representatives usually have a strong personal interest in the policy that their group is working for. A Negro civil rights leader has probably been developing attitudes about social injustice since early childhood. A leader of the National Rifle Association may not have such early commitment; but once he is a leader of the organization, its policy objectives become his own.

Leaders of interest groups often act as *lobbyists. A lobbyist* is a person who tries to influence the passing or rejecting of laws. (This term stems from the fact that individuals who try to influence lawmaking often are seen in the halls, or lobbies, of legislatures.)

A. A Tightly Knit Organization

The following case study is about the activities of an interest group, the Connecticut State Rifle and Revolver Association, and its lobbyists. As you read try to identify the unofficial political specialists, their policy objectives, and their methods of influencing policy-makers.

A New Firearms Bill Arouses an Interest Group

Dan Juliani was the first to hear about the bill. Through his former activities as president of the Connecticut State Rifle and Revolver Association, and then as legislative director of the organization, he had come to know many Connecticut legislators and their staff members. He had a reputation as a discrete, trustworthy man. Legislators drawing up bills affecting firearms would frequently come to him to ask for information and advice and to sound out his organization's position on their proposals. This time the sponsor of the bill did not check with him, but Juliani heard about it quickly enough anyway. And he did not like what he heard.

The leaders of the Connecticut State Rifle and Revolver Association were prepared for such a bill. Their organization had watched carefully as similar proposals, requiring registration of all firearms and licensing of all gunowners, had been introduced in other state legislatures in the wake of President John Kennedy's assassination. As representatives of the gunowners and firearms dealers in Connecticut, the Association's leaders strongly opposed such restrictions.

Control of firearms would, they reasoned, inconvenience the members of their organization in several ways: (1) Sportsmen might find it harder to buy guns and could be required to obtain licenses or to register their weapons.

(2) Transportation of guns across state lines or even within the state might be restricted. (3) Gun control legislation would weaken the organization's efforts to interest new members in gun sports. (4) Sales of weapons might decline, hurting gun dealers and the state's large firearms manufacturing industry.

The leaders were committed to fight any bill which threatened to restrict the sale, ownership, or transportation of guns; and the bill Juliani had spotted looked like their first big fight.

Senator Harrison A. Williams, Jr. (Dem., N.J.) in his office in 1968 looks over a mountain of mail received after the assassination of Senator Robert F. Kennedy. Most of the letters urged stronger Federal gun-control measures.

Juliani reported his findings to James E. Murray, III, the current legislative director of the Connecticut State Rifle and Revolver Association. They agreed at once that the bill was totally unacceptable to the Association. Its leaders were anxious to keep Connecticut as free of gun-control laws as possible. Their organization's effectiveness would surely be tested now. As Murray wrote later in *The American Rifleman,* "Time was against us. If certain news media had learned of the pending bill, and had made it a major issue, the battle might have been lost before it had even begun." But this was the kind of challenge their tightly knit organization had been preparing for.

The Gun Lobbyists Provide A New Bill

Juliani and Murray first went to Dr. John Blake, the legislator who was sponsoring the proposed bill. Blake listened to their views on his bill. He admitted that he had little knowledge of firearms legislation. The chief of police in his home district had merely described a local problem concerning firearms and suggested that the legislature do something about it.

BOOKMARKS

Many opponents of strong gun-control laws contend that private ownership of firearms is a worthy part of the American culture. But Bill Mauldin sees American history as marked by too much violence: murder, assassination, dueling, and lynching. What do you think?

Murray carefully selected a committee representing all segments of the shooting sports to cooperate with Dr. Blake in obtaining new firearms legislation. Dr. Blake further agreed to give the Association time to draft its own bill. In just three days the Association had prepared its own "model" bill. The revised bill was quite different from the original and in every way more favorable to the "gun" interests in Connecticut.

Dr. Blake quickly agreed to substitute the Association's draft for his own much stronger bill, which had called for the registration of all guns and the licensing of owners. The new bill had more lenient registration conditions and called for the creation of a Board of Permit Examiners to review complaints of individuals who had been denied handgun permits.

Through skillful intervention the leaders of the Association had been able to turn an unacceptable proposal into a bill which was, in fact, more favorable to their interests than existing laws.

Cartoon by Lou Grant. Copyright 1968, Los-Angeles Times Syndicate

To make the bill more attractive to legislators who were concerned about the increase in street crimes, penalties for use of weapons in violent crimes were increased. But instead of having to renew pistol permits every year, sportsmen under the revised bill would be granted permits for a five-year period. And, best of all for the Association, no registration of firearms or additional licensing would be required of their members.

Gun Lobby Uses Other Resources

Round One had gone to the Association before most legislators or the press were even aware of the issues. Nevertheless, much work still lay ahead for the Association before its own substitute bill could become law. The legislation was introduced to the Joint Committee on the Judiciary. The Rifle and Revolver Association quickly rounded up speakers to testify in its behalf. Years of experience had enabled the gun lobbyists to select speakers who sounded reasonable and intelligent and to screen out witnesses who might appear as crackpots or extremists.

The first real objection to the bill came from the state police, who wanted a broader definition of weapons considered "deadly and dangerous" than the present bill contained. They also objected to the Association's draft on several other grounds. Once again the Association swung into action. Immediately following the hearing, Murray contacted representatives of the Connecticut State Police and other opposition groups. Through informal discussions with these people, Murray was able to pinpoint objections to the Association's bill and to make some technical changes in its language. The end of the legislative session was drawing near, however, and basic differences of opinion still had not been resolved. Until some agreement could be reached, the bill stood little chance of passage.

With only days to spare, a subcommittee of the Judiciary Committee was established to meet with interested parties to work out a compromise. The negotiations resulted in the agreement of the Association (a) to return to the old definition of dangerous and deadly weapons and (b) to allow the local authorities (rather than the state police) to issue handgun permits. In return, it was agreed to establish a Board of Permit Examiners (which was to include representatives from the Rifle and Revolver Association and Ye Connecticut Gun Guild) with the power to take evidence; to issue, revoke, or reinstate permits; and to force local issuing authorities to follow the orders of the Board.

All interested parties seemed satisfied with the result. The amended bill passed the legislature without major opposition. And the new law actually benefited the members of the Rifle and Revolver Association. How did they do it? Murray attributed the Association's success to tight organization and able leadership which enabled them to influence the legislators successfully.

B. The Squeaky Wheel

The political techniques of interest-group leaders vary. Some interest groups, such as the Connecticut State Rifle and Revolver Association, have vast political resources. They have ample money, good organizational skills, and many contacts with important public officials. They can use and support one or more full-time lobbyists.

Other interest groups have few political resources. They are unable to maintain a professional lobbyist. The Navajo Indians of the southwestern United States can be viewed as an interest group with few political resources.

The Reservation of the nation's largest Indian tribe covers over 15 million acres in the area shown below.

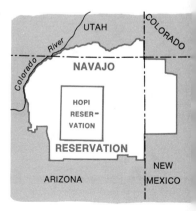

Commissioner of Indian Affairs in the Nixon Administration was Louis R. Bruce, seen here meeting with Indian people at Rough Rock Demonstration School.

Following is a case study about a representative of the Navajo Indians who plays the role of unofficial political specialist.

Problems of the Navajo Tribe

The Navajo were once a proud tribe who called themselves *Dineh,* which means "the people." Even today the pride remains in the face of widespread poverty. Seven out of every ten adults are unable to read or write the English language. It has been estimated that over half of those able and willing to work are unemployed. Most families live in hogans made of logs and adobe. Few have running water or electricity.

For many years Congress promised to appropriate more money to correct these conditions, but the promises meant little to most Navajo, who heard similar promises all their lives. Only in recent years has the Federal government made a determined effort to raise the tribe's living standard. Health care is a prime concern. Governmental health services have been spread too thin to control trachoma, an eye disease which leads to blindness. Tuberculosis, infant mortality, and malnutrition are other critical health problems on the Navajo reservation.

Over $50 million is now spent each year, primarily on health and education. Approximately 90 percent of Navajo children are now in school, compared with about 50 percent in 1952. Recent programs have been launched to help the Navajo live in modern American society without loss of the rich Navajo cultural heritage. Furthermore, mineral deposits—coal, gas, oil, uranium, helium—have provided an income of several million dollars a year to the tribe, and a few large industries have constructed plants near the reservation to take advantage of the labor supply. Still, the job is far from done.

Faced with economic difficulties and uncertainty in government policy, the Navajo have taken steps to help themselves. At Window Rock the tribal council meets four times a year to wrestle with the affairs of the tribe. Representatives elected in hard-fought campaigns assemble at the new hogan-shaped building in their boots, plaid shirts, and Western hats. The women council members wear the colorful long skirts and handwoven shawls of Navajo tradition.

Aside from managing the internal affairs of the tribe, the council must give attention to the tribe's relationship to the Federal government. The government has, at times, been cruel or negligent, and at other times tried to do for the Navajo what they could do for themselves. One of its members, whom we shall call Maria Begay, has devoted many years to improving health conditions for the Navajo. Her work brings her into contact with a variety of government agencies.

Maria Confers with a Bureaucrat

Maria Begay sat impatiently in the easy chair in the corridor outside an office in the Health, Education, and Welfare building in Washington, D.C. It had been a long trip from Window Rock, Arizona, but she had made it many times before. Her appointment was for 10 o'clock this morning; and, as usual,

472

the Public Health official was running behind schedule. Slowly, she smoothed the folds in her colorful Navajo dress. She knew what to expect when the door finally opened. There would be no surprises this morning—no instant victories, no quick defeats. She would return to Window Rock with little new to report, but with the hope that her presence in Washington would have some effect in the long run.

"Come in, Maria, it's good to see you again," said the balding middle-aged man approaching her with hand outstretched. "Hello, Mr. Drew," responded Maria, "why are you so jovial—you must know why I'm here?" Drew ushered her into his inner office and poured them both a cup of coffee. "I can guess," he smiled.

"What happened?" Maria was reserved, polite, but direct. She had never really understood why government officials smiled when they had trouble, but put on long faces when things went well.

"We got caught, Maria. It's as simple as that. When we gave you assurances last spring that funds for the new hospital in Tuba City would be included in this year's budget, there wasn't a doubt in my mind about it. But take a look at this." He handed her a memo from the Bureau of the Budget stating that all governmental agencies were expected to trim their proposed budgets for the next fiscal year by 20 percent, by order of the President. "You know

On a Navaho Reservation in northern Arizona a father plows a furrow and his daughter follows behind dropping seeds of corn and pressing them into the ground with her foot.

the reasons as well as I. The war. Trying to save something of the poverty program. The election this fall."

"Mr. Drew," Maria began slowly, "you talk of poverty. You have seen the Navajo Reservation. Where is Federal money needed more than in our area? You have published the statistics yourself. In our land two babies die at birth for every one of yours. In our land five times as many people have tuberculosis. I have worked for the last six years for this hospital. The Tribal Council has given it top priority on our list of public health improvements. Now you tell me it will have to wait because it is in the 20 percent that is expendable. Do you expect me to tell my people that?"

Maria was restrained but firm. She had not come to Washington to hear why the grant was not included this year. She had come to try to get it put back in the budget, if possible, or at least make certain it would be in next year.

Maria Becomes a Squeaky Wheel

There is an old saying that "it is the squeaky wheel that gets the grease." Bureaucrats and other government officials have a pretty good idea of which wheels are going to squeak and cause them trouble. This is just another way of saying that they usually know which leaders will complain loudly about their decisions and which will accept them without too much protest. If Drew had cut another portion of his budget, Maria Begay would be happy; but someone else would probably be in his office tomorrow. However, he expected to get less pressure from Maria and the Navajo than from the others.

Maria was there today to show him that such an expectation was wrong. And whether or not she could change his mind about this year's appropriation, she certainly could make it clear that the needs of the Navajo could not be disregarded without provoking a reaction from her.

Maria operates without large financial resources. She does not have the legal skill to draft legislation. She could probably not launch a campaign to bring in 500 letters to congressmen, let alone 500,000. She cannot rely upon having members of her tribe scattered through the committees of Congress, although she has found some congressmen who are more sympathetic to her demands than others. But she has developed tactics which stretch her thin resources as far as they will go in influencing government policy.

How Maria Uses Her Resources

First, she appeals to the consciences of public officials. Most Americans have a deep sense of guilt about the treatment of the American Indian. Maria points to government promises made but not kept through the years. She compares the living standards on her reservation with those in the nation at large and appeals to an official's sense of fair play. And Maria is well suited for this job because she is a full-blood Navajo, the granddaughter of a tribal chieftain, and a life-long resident of the reservation.

Maria is persistent, year after year, in pushing for her cause. Bureaucrats cannot ignore her demands, although they may try to put her off. As she works,

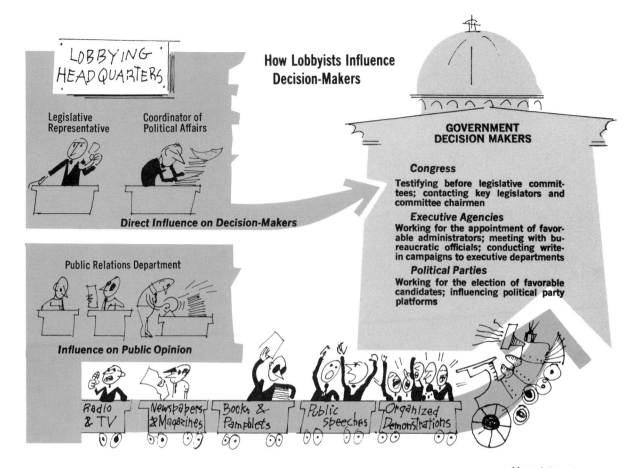

How Lobbyists Influence Decision-Makers

LOBBYING HEADQUARTERS

Legislative Representative

Coordinator of Political Affairs

Direct Influence on Decision-Makers

Public Relations Department

Influence on Public Opinion

Radio & TV

Newspapers & Magazines

Books & Pamphlets

Public Speeches

Organized Demonstrations

GOVERNMENT DECISION MAKERS

Congress
Testifying before legislative committees; contacting key legislators and committee chairmen

Executive Agencies
Working for the appointment of favorable administrators; meeting with bureaucratic officials; conducting write-in campaigns to executive departments

Political Parties
Working for the election of favorable candidates; influencing political party platforms

Many interest groups maintain lobby headquarters in Washington. Some lobbyists will make direct contacts with congressmen and bureaucrats, while others will engage more directly in public-opinion activities aimed at putting public pressure on government officials.

she develops experience and understanding of the ways of government. It may be easy for a public official to tell her "no" the first time, but it is not so easy the second time, for she then has answers for his arguments.

Finally, although Maria does not have vast resources, she does have one resource the Federal government needs. Federal agencies desire information about the needs of the Navajo and what the priorities should be. They need to know what Navajo leaders are thinking and doing. As a representative of her tribe, Maria provides such information. She also stirs up her members or calms them down. If none of her demands are granted, she manages to get enough publicity and get the ear of enough congressmen to make life miserable for the Public Health Service and the Bureau of Indian Affairs. If, on the other hand, she gets support from these agencies, she tells her people of the progress being made through cooperation with the Federal government. Which way would you rather have it if you were an official in the Public Health Service? Maria Begay has few resources, but she uses them skillfully.

1. What is the main issue in this case?
2. What policy is Maria Begay seeking?

3. What political techniques does Maria Begay use?

4. What is the relationship of political techniques to political resources? (Consider both "A Tightly Knit Organization" and "The Squeaky Wheel" as sources of information for answering this question.)

C. The Activists

Some interest-group leaders do not have direct access to public policy makers as the gun lobbyists or Maria Begay did. They try to influence public policy by influencing public opinion. Following is a case study about interest-group leaders who are trying to influence public opinion.

Background of the Case

In the fall of 1967, Gail Lewis was a 20-year-old sociology major at a midwestern state university. Gail believed quite strongly that the United States should not have troops fighting in Southeast Asia. She was convinced that all American forces should be withdrawn at once. Many of her fellow students at the university shared her objections to the Vietnam conflict. However, none of them seemed to feel there was anything they could do to influence the Federal government's policy. They reasoned that since they were not old enough to vote, could not afford to pay for a professional lobbyist to plead their cause, and had no experience in political organizing that there was little they could do.

One of Gail's closest friends was Ron Abernathy, a 23-year-old graduate student at the university. Ron also opposed American involvement in Vietnam. He was well-informed about the history of Southeast Asia and often talked to Gail and other students about the previous occupation of the area by the French and their defeat at Dien Bien Phu. He deplored the large-scale bombing of North Vietnam by American planes and believed that President Johnson was making a tragic mistake by allowing the war to become larger by sending more and more troops overseas. Abernathy would be losing his student deferment at the end of the following year, and he had not yet decided whether he would resist induction or not.

One day Ron and Gail were drinking coffee in the Student Union. Ron had just finished a newspaper article which reported that President Johnson had ordered more troops into Vietnam. After explaining to Gail what he thought the new troop movements meant, he told her of a project he had been mulling over.

"You know, Gail," said Ron, "I think the public has begun to have serious doubts about this war. If those of us who feel strongly about it can organize to dramatize what is happening it could really shake things up. No administration can continue to carry out a military policy that has strong public opinion against it. If we could just convince people to speak out against the war, it might just make the government change its policy. There's no organization on campus for the specific purpose of protesting our involvement in Vietnam. I think it's up to us to organize one."

"Well," replied Gail, "I'm not sure it will do much good. I can't see how a few students with no money, no votes, and no connections are going to be listened to on this campus, much less in Washington. All the people in government care about is their popularity ratings with the voters."

"But don't you see," Ron argued, "if we can show the President that the war is unpopular with the American people, then we may have some effect on foreign policy. We've got to publicize our opposition in every way we can so that we can get people reading and hearing about the war and talking about it among themselves."

"It's worth a try," Gail agreed, "but I have my doubts."

Formation of the "People's Lobby"

For the next two months Ron and Gail talked with friends about organizing an antiwar protest organization. They contacted the National Mobilization Committee to End the War in Vietnam, the coordinating organization for many antiwar groups throughout the country. They found that the "Mobe" welcomed a campus chapter. They formed a small group called the "People's Lobby" with Abernathy as chairman. But time had been short and not much was accomplished before final exams and summer vacation. The coming year would determine the success "People's Lobby" and the hundreds of other organizations like it springing up across the country would have in changing national policy.

Throughout the summer Ron and Gail were busy devising plans for attracting members to the organization and dramatizing their protests to students, faculty, and community residents. Both Ron and Gail agreed that although they could not afford to buy time for television commercials or put advertisements in the local newspapers, they could find other ways of publicizing their position on the war. They felt that there were many students at the university who shared their frustrations about the war, but who doubted that students would ever be able to influence political decisions. If they could convince these students to join the People's Lobby, they might be able to build an effective protest organization.

When school began again in the fall, Ron called a strategy planning session. About sixty students showed up for the meeting. A few were members of radical campus organizations. The rest were of all types—from bearded hippies to clean-shaven fraternity members.

Ron opened the meeting by saying, "If you are opposed to the war, and want its immediate end, then join us in finding ways of accomplishing this goal. The People's Lobby wants peace now, if that's what you who are here this evening also want, then you've come to the right place. Our job tonight is to make plans for the coming year. I'd like to hear some ideas from you people about how you see this organization."

A heated debate followed. Some people at the meeting wanted the organization to pick peace candidates and become involved in political campaigns for these candidates. Others felt the Peace Lobby ought to be devoted to canvassing local neighborhoods and talking to townspeople about the group's

opposition to the war. The majority, however, wanted protest activities to focus on the university campus. This group wanted to sponsor educational forums on the war, hold peace rallies, and try to interest faculty members in joining them in their protest. When this group finally persuaded most of the others to accept these goals, the leader of the radical students shouted that the violence of the war should be met with more violence and that simple protest would get them nowhere. The most radical students then walked out. However, most of the group remained, and the Peace Lobby was off to a shaky, but promising start.

The People's Lobby Goes into Action

Throughout the year the People's Lobby became more and more active. They sponsored speakers and folksingers who came to campus to participate in a teach-in on Vietnam. They picketed army recruiters when they came to the school to try to enlist students. When a leading chemical company sent representatives to the college to interview students for jobs, People's Lobby staged a sit-down strike in the building to publicize the fact that the company was a manufacturer of napalm (the jelly-like substance used in United States firebombs in Vietnam). And they threatened to lead a student strike and disrupt classes if the college officials did not agree to cancel the school's research contracts with the United States Department of Defense for development of military weapons.

In moments of depression, Ron wondered how effective they really were. It seemed far-fetched that their activity in one college could have any effect at all upon the nation's foreign policy. They certainly were not well-organized. There was not even an up-to-date list of who belonged to the organization. The group had very little money. Meetings and rallies were announced by word of mouth or on mimeographed sheets because newspaper advertising was too expensive. But the results of their sit-ins were always reported in next morning's paper, and the group quickly became known throughout the campus and the community. On one occasion, when two of their members had been arrested for blocking a doorway during a sit-in, the local television station had run a half-hour special on People's Lobby, including interviews with Ron and the college president.

The American Public Reconsiders Vietnam

Public opinion was changing. Opinion surveys that showed the American people strongly supporting President Johnson's handling of the war only a few years back indicated, by late 1967, that only 28 percent of the people still approved. Mass demonstrations, such as those waged by the People's Lobby, were surely not the only reason for declining support of an unpopular war. During 1967 alone, 9353 American servicemen had been killed—more than in the six previous years of the war combined. The nation had been spending over $2 billion a month on the conflict and had lost more than 3000 planes and helicopters. The price of attempting to bring democracy to a shaky regime on the other side of the world was beginning to be felt by all.

The Peace Lobby and other protest groups around the country did everything they could to stir up reaction against the war. In October, 1967, the National Mobilization Committee organized a demonstration in Washington which drew between 55,000 and 150,000 protesters to the Lincoln Memorial from all over the country. David Dellinger, chairman, declared that the demonstration was "a beginning of a new stage in the American peace movement in which the cutting edge becomes active resistance." And Dr. Benjamin Spock, well-known author of books about child-rearing, said: "We are convinced that this war which Lyndon Johnson is waging is disastrous to our country in every way and that we, the protesters, are the ones who may help save our country if we can persuade enough of our fellow citizens to think and vote as we do."

As new protest groups formed through the nation, it became clear that a small but very committed minority was so strongly opposed to the war that they were willing to face arrest, if necessary, to make their point. Lacking the resources and connections to change government policy from the inside, they chose instead to try to influence the opinion of people everywhere. And, at least in part, they succeeded. In November, 1967, President Johnson complained that the "bullying" tactics of some of his Vietnam critics amounted to "irresponsible dissent" and called them "extremely dangerous to our national interest." But early in the next year he made the first major move to reduce the level of fighting by ordering a halt to the bombing by American planes of most of the territory in North Vietnam. At the same time he declined to run for another term as President and stepped up the search for a negotiated settlement of the war. The protest movements and demonstrations around the country had contributed to changing public opinion. Public opinion, in turn, certainly played a major part in President Johnson's decisions.

1. What policy were Ron and his friends seeking?

2. Compare and contrast the political behavior of Dan Juliani, Maria Begay, and Ron Abernathy. How can you account for differences and similarities in the way they play the role of unofficial political specialist?

3. Evaluate the methods used by the activists to influence public opinion? Are there rules of the game for protest leaders as there are for other interest-group representatives? Explain.

Illustrations on the next page tell something about the diversity of interest groups and of their activities. Many lobbyists work for a particular segment of the economic community, such as bankers, car dealers, and farmers. On the other hand, "Common Cause" seeks to promote what its leaders consider to be the *general* welfare. The salaried representatives of interest groups carry on activities like those shown here: arranging an annual banquet for state legislators; preparing copy for advertising and news releases; publishing trade journals like *Cars & Trucks* magazine; and operating the interest group's headquarters office.

chapter 19

Representatives of the Mass Media

From their earliest years most Americans are aware of the mass media. Newspapers, television, and radio are among our most important links with the outside world. The daily newspaper contains a tremendous variety of information. So do nightly local television news programs. What movies are in town this weekend? What is the United Nations doing about the latest Middle East crisis? What is on sale at which department stores? Who is favored in the Super Bowl? What was the city council's decision about repaving Main Street? How will the weather be tomorrow? Have they caught the man who robbed the corner grocery last week?

Few of us stop to consider how important the men who publish a newspaper or produce television programs may be in the political life of the community and the nation. Who are these men and how do they influence politics?

A. Newspapermen as Unofficial Political Specialists

Most journalists begin their careers as relatively low-salaried reporters. Today many reporters, even on the smaller papers, have a college degree, perhaps in journalism, history, or political science. As a good reporter becomes more successful, he may take a reporting job with a larger, better-paying newspaper, or he may move into an editorship on his own paper.

Editors as Unofficial Political Specialists

Newspaper editors may have several kinds of responsibilities. They decide which of the many stories coming from the wire services will be run and where they should go in the paper. Even *The New York Times,* which is one of the largest American newspapers, can publish only a small proportion of all the information available to it each day. The decision whether or not to print a story about a public official charged with income-tax evasion can have important consequences for politics. And if it is printed, it will make a difference whether it appears on page one or page five. When stories are too long for the space allotted, an editor will delete the paragraphs he believes are least essential. Or if a reporter files a story that the editor believes is unbalanced, or not clearly written, the editor may rewrite a portion of it. Letters to the editor may flood the newspaper office, making some selection necessary to decide which of these to print.

Another important job of the editor is writing editorials. A news story is supposed to give a factual, unbiased account of an event. An editorial, on the other hand, expresses the position or opinion of the newspaper on the issues of the day. By reading the editorial column the reader can determine just where the newspaper stands and what the arguments for the position are.

The endorsement of *The New York Times* in its editorial columns is eagerly sought by presidential candidates and may be an important factor in the election. But the endorsement of the *Danville News* may be just as important to a man running for district attorney in his county. While most newspaper readers do not pay a great deal of attention to editorials and the arguments they present, some do—and these few may be particularly influential.

Editors are not entirely free to express their own opinions in an editorial. There are several competing pressures on an editor. He is an employee of the publisher or owner of the paper. As editor he will also feel a responsibility for the economic well-being of the newspaper—both in terms of its circulation and its advertising income. Any position he takes may offend his publisher, his readers, or potential advertisers.

The editorial position which newspapermen often adopt in editorials is that of "watchdog" of the rights of the public. For example, when politicians are found to be involved in illegal business transactions or to have associations with prominent underworld figures, an editor may write an unfavorable editorial about the politician without offending his readers or his employer. Editorial writers strongly endorse prosperity, good government, and projects which promise to help the business community and most of their readers.

However, when there is sharp division in a community on an issue such as school desegregation, editorial stands are likely to be more cautious. The editorial writer who launches an anti-smoking campaign may run the risk of offending cigarette advertisers. These kinds of considerations often encourage the editorialist to write primarily about issues of "morality," that is, issues with which most of the public can easily identify and agree on who is right and who is wrong.

Reporters as Unofficial Political Specialists

Reporters can also be unofficial specialists without ever expressing their opinions on the editorial page of a newspaper. In some cases, reporters can influence public opinion through their skillful investigation of how well government officials serve the public. In recognition of the part the newspaperman can play in influencing public decisions, each year the highly respected Pulitzer Prize is awarded to a newspaper for "disinterested and meritorious public service." The case which follows describes such work by reporters on the *Chicago Daily News*. The *Daily News* won the Pulitzer Prize in 1956 for the publication of the case described below. This case gives us an inside look at the way in which a reporter performs his role as unofficial political specialist and the impact this role can have on the political life of a community.

A Careful Accounting

Basil Walters, executive editor of the *Chicago Daily News*, was sitting in his office one morning in May, 1956, when he received a visit from Michael J. Hewlett. Hewlett was running for state auditor on the Democratic ticket in the upcoming November election. He opposed the Republican incumbent. Hewlett had come to tell Walters some facts and some gossip he had uncovered while doing research for his campaign.

His information was the following: (1) The incumbent's department, the state auditor's office, was receiving more money from the state budget than under any of its previous directors. (2) Yet the appropriations to the state auditor's office seemed to be disappearing more rapidly than usual. (3) The incumbent was reported to be living extravagantly. (4) Hewlett had a list of fifteen people whom he claimed were on the state auditor's payroll. However, these people were not actually working for him.

While Hewlett's information could have the makings of an important story, Walters was also well aware that Hewlett hoped to defeat the incumbent state auditor in the November election, perhaps by uncovering a scandal which would turn the voters of Illinois against him. Although Executive Editor Walters realized that Hewlett was a prejudiced informer, he felt this tip was worth looking at more closely. He relayed the information he had received to a *Daily News* reporter at the state capital in Springfield.

Checking the facts. Reporter George Thiem began his investigation by checking the charges of payroll padding. He went to the state auditor's office and examined the list of employees. None of the fifteen employees Hewlett had mentioned was listed. Thiem then went to the state auditor and asked him specifically about one of the people Hewlett believed to be illegally on the state auditor's payroll. The auditor denied the charge. Thiem then examined the records in the state treasurer's office. The paycheck records indicated that, despite the state auditor's denial, several of the fifteen had been drawing checks from his office.

About the same time, Thiem received a telephone call from a friend at the statehouse. His informant said that the state auditor had told his employees not to talk with the reporter from the *Daily News.* This aroused Thiem's suspicions further. He turned to an investigation of the reports of lavish living and reckless spending. He found that the state auditor had paid a $5200 hotel bill with a warrant, or guarantee of payment, issued by his own office. Thiem knew that each state warrant issued should have a voucher in the government's files authorizing the payment of the warrant and stating its purpose.

Thiem returned to the state auditor's office and asked permission to go through the auditor's vouchers. The state auditor replied that there were too many files for any reporter to go through. However, the state auditor did agree to allow Thiem to examine any specific voucher if he could provide a serial number for the one he wanted to see. For a short while, Thiem's investigative efforts seemed to be blocked. It seemed unlikely at this initial stage of investigation that he could find enough specific information to ask for a voucher by number. But Thiem had a lucky break. Someone in the auditor's office had seen the check for $5200 as it was being processed. Thinking it rather odd, he had copied down the check number. When he heard about Thiem's inquiry, he passed along the exact information Thiem needed.

The reporter returned to the state auditor's office and asked to see the file of vouchers. The office manager replied that there was no such file, that they kept only the originals, which were stored in a warehouse. Thiem then visited the warehouse. There a clerk quickly found the voucher Thiem was looking for. It did not reveal any evidence which could be of use to Thiem in uncovering a story.

A lucky conversation. However, while at the warehouse, Thiem began talking with a career official who proudly offered to show him how the entire filing system operated. As the official explained the filing system, Thiem came across an account from the state auditor's department which was especially interesting to him. This account had received a two-year appropriation of $197,000. With less than a year gone, only $8.33 remained in the account. Thiem copied down the serial numbers of all the larger checks. But he had no way of knowing who the checks had been sent to, and without this information he could go no further. He had no way of proving that the state auditor was involved in illegal activities. Nonetheless, at this point Thiem reported his findings to the county attorney of Sangamon County, the county in which Springfield is located. The attorney said he would take an official look.

Thiem had by this time learned that the state treasurer's office maintained a file listing the recipients of all checks. Armed with a list of suspect check numbers, Thiem went through this file and found the names of firms or individuals to whom a dozen checks had been written. Thiem's research indicated that all the recipients were people with whom the state might normally be doing business. There was still no proof that the state auditor had been involved in illegal activities.

The editors make a decision. At this point the editors of the *Daily News* had a difficult decision to make. Although Thiem had uncovered some rather suspicious information, he had no solid facts with which to write a story accusing a public official of graft. To do so would have opened the *Daily News* to charges of libel. The publishers decided to publish a story listing the checks, the recipients, and the amounts as a feature on how the state auditor performs his job. The story did not accuse the state auditor of any wrongdoing.

The story received little attention from the average reader. However, a Chicago attorney who read the story contacted the *Daily News* to say that a check for $9000 listed as having been sent to him never reached him. Furthermore, he said that the state did not owe him any such amount. This gave Thiem another lead.

He had learned that the state treasurer's office kept a microfilm list of all cancelled checks. Thiem went through the files until he found the check for $9000 issued to the Chicago attorney. The check along with the next fourteen checks on the film had all been endorsed by typewriter. The total amount of the checks was $178,000. The existence of fifteen consecutive checks endorsed by typewriter was too unlikely to be a coincidence. The explanation was clear: the state auditor and his associates were writing checks to pay nonexistent bills and cashing the checks themselves.

Investigation climaxes. The *Daily News* assigned every available reporter to contacting the people to whom the fifteen checks in question had supposedly been sent. Six of those contacted made statements to *Daily News* reporters that they had never received the checks and had no payments coming. Staff reporters also obtained pictures of the checks from the microfilm. Before the editors printed the story, the political editor of the paper went to Springfield to give the state auditor a copy of the story that was about to be published. The state auditor expressed surprise that anything was wrong.

The *Daily News* story appeared on the front page of the paper. It contained statements from those the reporters had contacted and pictures of the checks. The same day that the *Daily News* story appeared, the governor put armed guards around the state records. The state auditor was later arrested, tried, and sent to prison.

Syndicated Columnists as Unofficial Political Specialists

The syndicated columnist is a special kind of editorial writer. The writers of syndicated columns comment on political issues. The term "syndicated" means that local papers across the country can purchase the rights to reprint the columns. The "Evans-Novak Report," "The William Buckley Column," and "The Washington Merry-Go-Round" by Jack Anderson are three examples of well-known syndicated columns.

Following is a description of two political columnists, Jack Anderson and Drew Pearson. Prior to Mr. Pearson's death in September, 1969, they worked together on their news column, "Washington Merry-Go-Round," for over twenty years. This column, which is continued by Jack Anderson, appears daily

486

in over 600 newspapers. Each day over 50 million people read papers containing the column. Many Washington politicians read the column, even though they may disagree with the viewpoints they find there. They read the column in order to be aware of the public image of political affairs that is projected in "The Washington Merry-Go-Round."

In 1971 these were some of the prominent syndicated political columns in American newspapers.

Drew Pearson and Jack Anderson specialized in exposing unethical or immoral behavior among politicians in Washington, D.C. Bureaucrats, congressmen, lobbyists, even the President, were potential targets of the Pearson-Anderson investigations. As a result of their investigations, Pearson and Anderson were hated by many public figures. Over the years many doors were slammed in their faces. They lost count of the number of times they were sued for libel. However, they never lost any of these law suits.

Pearson and Anderson received from 200 to 300 letters daily with evidence of some shady deal or unethical act involving public officials. The letter writers asked the columnists to publicize these wrongdoings.

A staff of eight, including secretaries and investigators, aided Pearson and Anderson in verifying these reports. The staff did most of the tedious leg-work of interviewing and researching to obtain and check information. Facts were checked and double-checked before they were used in a column. Pearson and Anderson did the actual writing of the column as well as personally conducting some of the more delicate sleuthing operations.

In Herbert Klurfeld's book *Behind the Lines: The World of Drew Pearson,* Pearson's view of his role as a syndicated columnist is summarized:

> It is the job of the news columnist to uncover and report to the public news that politicians try to keep hidden from public view. The public has the right to be informed as fully as possible about political affairs.

The news columnists must expose the wrongdoings of public officials so that public opinion can influence the government to correct these wrongdoings.

The news columnist must praise outstanding public officials so that the public can maintain faith in those who serve the government well.

The news columnist must try to influence public officials to make decisions that serve the public interest.

Drew Pearson also expressed his views about his role as an unofficial political specialist in a memo dictated to his staff in 1958. Excerpts from that memo, which also appears in *Behind the Lines,* follow:

Remember that ever since politicians became politicians, the thing the public was not supposed to know has taken place in the private lobbies and the smoke-filled rooms. Yet, what is hidden from the public is usually what the public is most entitled to know about, and the job of a good newspaperman to report. . . .

• • •

However, it is also important to remember that the government is neither all good, nor all bad. There are bureaucrats who are a credit to mankind. It is your job to discriminate.

• • •

Government is only as good as the men in it. And since men are human, they are subject to all the frailties that make up mankind—laziness, inefficiency, greed, graft, temptation.

• • •

But they are also subject to great effort, sacrifice, inspiration. It is your job as a newspaperman to spur the lazy, watch the weak, expose the corrupt. You must be the eyes, ears, and nose of the American people.

1. Why can newspapermen be called unofficial political specialists?

2. What are the rights and duties of newspapermen as unofficial political specialists?

3. What are the main political resources and techniques of a newspaperman?

B. The Political Cartoonist as Unofficial Political Specialist

Political cartoons can also be editorials. As you know, an editorial is an article that expresses an opinion about something. Newspapers have editorial pages where political opinions are discussed. Political cartoons are also found on the editorial pages of most newspapers. Often the cartoon of the day will be related to an issue discussed in one of the editorials.

Political cartoonists try to influence public opinion. They use political symbols to represent political opinions, values, and attitudes, and to represent different nations, groups, and roles. For example, Uncle Sam or an eagle is used to represent the United States. An elephant is the symbol of the Republican party and the donkey symbolizes the Democratic party. An olive branch or dove is a symbol for peace. An arrow or hawk is used to symbolize war.

Following is an example of the use of symbols in a political cartoon. The eagle is a symbol of the United States of America. The bear is a symbol of Russia. The hammer and sickle on the bear's back is a Communist symbol. The "gulch" that separates the eagle and the bear is a symbol for the differences

Why would most Americans react differently from most Russians to the symbols shown in this cartoon?

Bruce Russell. Copyright, 1946, Los Angeles Times. Reprinted by permission.

"Time to Bridge That Gulch."

in political values and attitudes that have made the governments of the Soviet Union and the United States oppose one another. The caption "Time to Bridge That Gulch" means that the man who drew the picture believed that Russians and Americans should be more friendly toward one another.

The relationship of a written editorial to a political cartoon is shown on the following page. Both the political cartoon by Burck and the editorial, "Clean Air and Water Is a Right," appeared on the editorial page of *The Chicago Sun-Times* on July 13, 1970. Both the editorial and the cartoon present value judgments about the topic of environmental pollution.

489

Often the cartoonist and editorial writer make a joint attack on a particular problem as shown on this page.

"BYAAACH!"

Clean Air and Water Is a Right

The new Pollution Control Board has its work cut out for it. As *The Sun-Times* has pointed out in its news columns and on this page, Illinois does not have one stream or lake where the water is clean enough to drink, to swim in or to fish in. The air we breathe is filthy and getting worse.

As we noted on this page on Friday, more and more communities are faced with the problem of what is the more important, a clean environment or jobs in industries that foul the air and water?

Illinois is faced with that problem today. We expect the new Pollution Control Board to come down on the side of a clean environment as the right of every citizen.

Study the following political cartoons and answer these questions.

1. What opinions are presented in each of the cartoons?

2. How does the cartoonist portray his opinions?

3. Which of the cartoons present controversial opinions?

4. Do you agree or disagree with the opinions presented in each cartoon? Explain.

5. How is question 4 different from questions 1–3?

490

Two Parties and a Plank

Ficklen in *The Dallas News,* by permission

A political cartoon usually consists of three main parts: (1) One or more *main characters* appear in a cartoon. The character may represent a real person or stand for a group of people, an organization, a nation, etc. (2) Other symbols are added to convey the cartoonist's mood or opinion. (3) *Captions* or *labels* are added to enable the reader to choose, among the variety of meanings a symbol can convey, the one the cartoonist intended. The caption, usually brief, often summarizes the cartoonist's point of view.

Bill Crawford, reprinted by permission of Newspaper Enterprise Association

"Well, That Just About Does It!"

As Nearly as We Can Translate, It Says: "We Are Agreed in Principle on Preventing the Spread of Nuclear Weapons; however . . . ."

492

C. Television Commentators as Unofficial Political Specialists

Commercial television has come to play a major part in the leisure-time activities of most Americans. For many adults as well as children, television has brought the movie theater, the sports arena, and even the schoolroom into the home. Television news broadcasts have taken over many functions of the newspaper in providing information about political issues and policy decisions.

Many adults who do not regularly read a newspaper will have the television on during newscasts; and even though they may not watch closely, they are certain to get glimpses of major news events from time to time. What the viewer sees, because it is so vividly portrayed, may impress him.

Because television news broadcasts can and often do influence our opinions about political issues, the people who produce and present them are important unofficial political specialists. Unlike newspaper editorialists, however, they seldom actively seek to persuade us to change our opinions or even take a definite position on an issue. The influence of television news shows is more subtle. The kinds of pictures we see of an event and the way in which the newscaster describes and explains it will probably influence our opinions about it. If the event is related to a significant political issue, such as pollution, our opinions about the issue may be influenced.

Critics of television programming charge that most newscasters do not realize how influential they are or do not take their responsibility seriously. Some critics say that television news programs increase people's awareness of, and feelings about, events without increasing their understanding of these events.

Producing the News for Television

People within the television industry often explain why this happens with the following arguments:

(1) Television is primarily an entertainment medium. Most people watch television to relax, to be amused, not to be educated. Network executives who make the major decisions about news programs are well aware of the public's attitude toward television. Consequently network executives may evaluate news programs in much the same way as they would a comedy show such as "Laugh In" or a western series such as "Bonanza." That is, they will ask, "Will it get sponsors and attract audiences?" If it does not, then it must either be changed or be replaced.

In reality, it is unlikely that any network would do away with its news departments altogether, because they bring considerable prestige to the network. However, no matter how informative and worthwhile a program is, if it receives low weekly ratings and fails to obtain sufficient sponsors, it will quickly be replaced by some other format. This is the only way a network can survive in the intensely competitive television industry.

Nixon and Kennedy held a TV debate in the 1960 election campaign.

(2) News programs are expensive to produce and must attract high-paying sponsors. Well-known news announcers are paid salaries between $50,000 and $80,000 a year. Television personalities such as David Brinkley or Walter Cronkite receive even higher salaries. Another large expense is the cost of maintaining communication networks of reporters and commentators spanning most of the world and transporting crews and cameras to wherever the news is breaking. To pay for these expenses, news programs sell air time for commercials. The larger the audience for a program, the more expensive its advertising. On CBS a one-minute spot commercial during a National Football League game may sell for as much as $75,000. While news departments are not expected to compete with popular sports events, network executives do expect a news show to have an audience large enough to attract high prices for its commercial time.

(3) Consequently network news shows are usually produced by men with one eye on the ratings and the other on the budget. They know that the most important ingredients of success will be getting film footage that attracts the attention of many viewers and hiring an "anchor man" or newscaster who appeals to a large audience, much as a movie star might. They also know that research has shown that the audience prefers a commentator who will be reassuring by taking the edge off disturbing news. In short, while television newscasters may devote much time to research and reporting the news, they must also concern themselves with presenting it to the viewers in ways that may be entertaining or at least not too alarming.

Getting the Picture

Television adds a visual dimension to more traditional forms of journalism. Because of this the picture tends to dominate the thinking of producers. Producers constantly keep in mind that to be interesting the shots must have action. It also helps if they are unusual or sensational in some way. Battles, riots, and protest marches make good pictures, but the background behind the issues usually does not. The viewer of the news show will see what is happening, but may still be left wondering why it happened.

In 1967–1968, NBC and CBS each spent more than $2 million a year covering the Vietnam war. Correspondents found out early in the war that when they tried to cover a political story, or a report on economic aid to Vietnamese villagers, these filmclips were pushed aside to make way for battle action shots, pictures of badly wounded American soldiers, or piles of dead Vietnamese. If they want their material to go on those thirty minutes of air time each day, they have to "shoot bloody"—but not too bloody. As one man put it, "We go on the air at suppertime."

No one knows exactly how this kind of coverage affects the attitudes of the American people toward war in general. Some argue that by bringing the horror of war into the living room of millions of Americans, television has stripped away the glamor of combat and diminished the taste of many viewers for United States involvement in foreign military adventures. Others think that the vivid pictures may have an "immunizing" effect—that viewers grow accustomed to seeing death and suffering each evening and become conditioned to it, confident that they have seen the worst. These commentators believe that by withholding the most sickening scenes the networks are really painting a deceptively mild picture of the agony of warfare.

The effect of television coverage of Vietnam upon public support for the war is somewhat clearer. Since most Americans in the late 1960's had already formed opinions about American policy in Vietnam, network programs probably only reinforced their existing attitudes. The person who favored American involvement and a forceful military policy would focus his attention on pictures of Americans being killed or wounded and call for an even stronger military response. Another man who opposed American involvement would be more likely to recall pictures of soldiers setting fire to huts in a village and burning native women and children out of their homes. He would likely cite these scenes as examples of the injustices of an "unnecessary war."

Many Considerations Affect a News Show's Format

Very little of the material used on television news programs comes from first-hand accounts of television correspondents. Much of it is rewritten from information received from the major wire services—Associated Press, United Press International, and Reuters. Network reporters can write original material for only the most important stories. Television writers are often paid a $25 to $150 fee for each item used on an evening news program. As a result of these factors, news commentators are often tempted to move hastily from one topic to the next without much digging for facts behind a story. In an effort to be entertaining, they may neglect important facts and analyses of the news which might give the viewer an entirely different perspective on an issue.

Network news programs seldom present anything comparable to newspaper editorials. The Federal Communications Commission requires television stations to present both sides of controversial matters, and an interest group that feels it has been slighted can demand "equal time" to present its side of the matter. As a result, producers will try to be fair in their coverage of the news; but this fairness often means that commentators cannot offer their own opinions or interpretations. This noncommittal attitude may be interpreted by some viewers as approval of what is happening, or at least as evidence that their favorite television news personalities do not care very much one way or the other.

"We Have Partially Stated the Problem"

There are many situational factors which influence the role of the television commentator as unofficial political specialist. The way in which a commentator sees his role as unofficial specialist can also influence his performance. The example which follows describes the way in which one commentator saw his role as unofficial political specialist.

In May, 1968, a national television network aired a documentary entitled "The Forgotten American," concerning the plight of the Navajo. It was sharply critical of the role of the Federal government in general, and the Bureau of

Experts believe that the debate had a big influence on Kennedy's victory.

495

Indian Affairs (BIA) in particular. Two major points emerged from the documentary. First, it argued that many Indians have been unable to assume a socially and economically equal position in the mainstream of American life. Second, it placed the blame upon the Federal government for adopting a paternalistic program, for emphasizing the white man's culture in its educational program, and for depriving the Indian of his rich cultural heritage.

The response was strong and quick. Most viewers applauded the presentation as a blow struck for the Navajo against the injustices of history and the clumsiness of the Federal bureaucracy. Leaders of the Navajo tribe were not so certain. They were proud of the progress their tribe had made over the last quarter-century, and protested in their official newspaper, *The Navajo Times,* that the CBS report had not reflected this progress. They were also uneasy about the suggestion that the functions of the Bureau of Indian Affairs be transferred to the Department of Health, Education, and Welfare. Tribal leaders had, after all, learned to live with the BIA. They criticized it often, but they also understood it, believed in its dedication to their own best interests, and valued its experience with Indian affairs. They were by no means as sure of HEW.

Reaction came pouring in to the television network from around the nation. One of the millions of viewers, a young white man who had grown up on the campus of a Federal Indian boarding school, expressed his disagreement with the treatment of the problem in a letter to the commentator who narrated the show. He objected to the network's failure to portray the progress that had been made, their use of questionable sources, and their portrait of the BIA. Most of all, however, he criticized the network's failure to offer any constructive alternatives to present government policies. Agreeing that paternalism was not an entirely satisfactory solution, he asked how the news commentator proposed to bring the Navajo into the mainstream of American white culture and still preserve their Indian cultural identity. The commentator's reply provides some insight into the way television newsmen view their role.

May 20, 1968

Dear Mr. _____:

Thank you for your thoughtful letter and criticism of our broadcast "The Forgotten American."

Basically, I think we have an obvious difference in point of view. We never intended to "prescribe any treatment" or "offer any constructive alternatives." In the flood of information buffeting the average American, we simply had one function, as we saw it. As subsequent articles in the *National Observer,* week of May 6, *Time Magazine,* May 14 issue, and *The Christian Science Monitor* of Tuesday, May 14, have reemphasized our basic points, we simply aimed to show that the American Indian has a plight that should be of concern to all of us. I think we did that by concentrating on the Navajo, the largest Indian nation.

As for your comments on the conflict between paternalism and indifference and your further remarks regarding the costs and problems facing solutions,

Paternalism: acting as a father might, protecting and guiding his immature children.

496

you totally overlook the moral obligation we have, thanks to solemn treaties which span the history of our nation—treaties which consistently have been violated and often used as excuses to exploit both the Indian and his land. Against that backdrop, I believe the Indian has a valid claim on our resources.

As you noted early in your letter, your personal experience may, indeed, give you a bias regarding the Bureau of Indian Affairs because, just as it does consist of some "deeply concerned and dedicated public servants," it may also contain some bureaucratic hacks in the positions of power and responsibility, usually reserved for white employees of the Bureau.

I refer to a report still not released by the President's Task Force on American Indians—"too many BIA employees were simply time servers of mediocre or poor competence who remained indefinitely because they were willing to serve in unattractive posts at low rates of pay for long periods of time; that too many had unconsciously anti-Indian attitudes and are convinced that Indians are really hopelessly incompetent and their behavior reflects this assumption."

That report recommends the BIA's functions be transferred to the Department of Health, Education and Welfare.

In conclusion, I do not think we have done these people and our subject "a grave injustice." We have partially stated the problem; we have aroused public reaction, and we trust that that will lead to the evolvement of alternative courses of action. In my opinion, that would be in the best tradition of good journalism for, in the last analysis, it is the public which must feel the concern and provide the alternative.

Sincerely,

1. Which of the following statements do you believe accurately reflect the television news commentator's view of his role as an unofficial political specialist?

    a. Television commentators should search for and present constructive alternatives to present policy.

    b. Television commentators should strive to arouse public feeling on issues and trust that the public will provide alternative courses of action.

    c. Television commentators should probe difficult issues, such as the dilemma of how to bring Indians into white culture, while preserving their own native culture.

    d. Television commentators should provide an unbiased account of issues in documentaries, examining all sides of the question.

    e. Television commentators should remind Americans of their moral obligations.

    f. Television commentators should not concern themselves with what effect they have upon public opinion.

2. In what ways is the television commentator's role as unofficial political specialist similar to and different from the role of newspaper editorialist, syndicated columnist, and newspaper reporter?

chapter 20

The Expert as Unofficial
Political Specialist

By now it should be clear that public officials are not the only shapers of public policy. Important as they are, their decisions are influenced by pressures from interest groups, by the mass media investigating political activities, and by many other forces. The expert, behaving as an unofficial political specialist, is among the most important influencers of public policy decisions. Who are the experts? How do they affect public policy?

A. Who Are the Experts?

A familar example of the use of experts is in criminal trials. A ballistics expert may be called to the witness stand to testify whether a bullet found at the scene of the crime was fired from a gun in the possession of the defendant. Psychiatrists may be called to examine a defendant and testify whether he is sane or insane. These are men who have special knowledge which is helpful to a judge or jury in deciding the guilt or innocence of the accused.

In a similar way experts playing the role of unofficial political specialist are people who have special knowledge useful in making decisions about political affairs. The specialities of experts vary as widely as the subject matter of politics itself. It is, indeed, difficult to think of any kind of expert whose services might not at some time be useful to public officials in deciding questions of public policy. One scholar specializing in the history of the English novel was surprised not long ago when he was asked to testify before a congressional committee debating censorship and obscenity bills. A scientist specializing in guided missiles may provide information that will help a congressional committee decide whether a proposed missile defense system will work well enough to justify an appropriation for it. Agricultural economists may be asked to predict what a certain change in farm legislation will do to wheat prices next year.

Experts Perform Their Roles in Different Ways

Many experts are employed by the government on a full-time basis to help make and administer policy. Most of these become well-paid bureaucrats in the various bureaus and offices of local, state, and national government. But even outside the official positions in government one finds many men who contribute their specific and often technical knowledge to the policy-making process. A sociologist may be called upon to testify before Congress about

498

the relationship between unemployment and urban riots. A physicist writes an article in a popular magazine questioning the foolproof nature of the safety devices on H-bombs and asking that the government not build bases for these nuclear warheads near large cities. A noted astronomer appears on television with a list of scientific mysteries that a manned landing on the moon might resolve and then calls for larger appropriations for the space program. The private, non-profit RAND organization carries out a detailed study of the feasibility of building a new swing-wing fighter plane for the military. Employees of the Brookings Institution in Washington, D.C., prepare assessments of various trouble-spots around the world for policy makers to ponder. All of these men are using the special knowledge they possess as experts to influence official policy.

Many experts acting as unofficial political specialists are either scientists or engineers. Approximately 60 to 70 percent of all scientists and engineers with advanced degrees are directly or indirectly employed by the Federal government. A few years ago the National Science Foundation counted a total of 128,000 scientists and engineers actually on government payrolls—about 8 percent of all white-collar government employees. But of this number, only a few hundred are continually asked to give advice on policy matters. Studies have placed the size of this expert elite at between 200 and 900.

Who Are the Influential Experts?

Science magazine once complained in an editorial, "Only those who circulate . . . in the right circles, who have the right connection, are likely to be called on to give advice. . . ."

What, then, are the "right circles"? During and just after World War II the United States experienced fantastic development in science and technology. Nuclear weapons and power systems, radar, guided missiles, transistors, computers, commercial television, and space satellites were all developed in this period. Scientists frequently worked in large teams at a few laboratories and large universities throughout the country on such projects. The experts came to know each other well, and leaders emerged who were willing to spend part of their time advising government on policy questions. Many of these men have held a long succession of leadership posts, and some are still influential today.

So important has scientific knowledge become to government that approximately $16 billion is spent each year on science-related projects alone. Much of this amount goes to agencies like the National Science Foundation or the National Aeronautics and Space Administration. These government bodies, in turn, channel the money into hundreds of corporations, universities, and other non-profit organizations in exchange for information. Just as the army may contract with a munitions company for a certain kind of ammunition, the Food and Drug Administration may provide money to faculty members at a medical school to conduct research on the physiological effects of marijuana. Many of the experts classified as unofficial specialists are paid by the United States government to do research.

Frequently experts are asked by government officials to testify or perform certain kinds of jobs for the government. They may work regularly as professors, doctors, or in other private professional positions, and only occasionally work for the government as a sideline. But some rely more heavily upon government, moving from one contract to the next in an endless succession of jobs.

1. Which of the following persons would you think of as playing the unofficial political specialist role of "expert"?

a. A journalist who writes feature stories about various government agencies for a newspaper.

b. A chemist who testifies before a committee of the state legislature about ways of reducing water pollution.

c. An architect designing a new public-housing project.

d. A safety engineer who prepares a report on the effectiveness of seat belts in reducing automobile injuries for General Motors executives to use in congressional testimony.

e. A political scientist specializing in the Soviet political system who is paid $150 a day for one week to consult with State Department officials about American foreign policy.

f. An employee of the Department of Agriculture inspecting and stamping meat in a packing plant.

g. An aeronautical engineer estimating for the Department of Defense what the cost of developing a new experimental supersonic fighter plane will be.

h. A lobbyist for the American Tobacco Company trying to convince a congressman that the health warning on all cigarette advertising is not necessary.

i. A cancer researcher doing an experiment for the Public Health Service on the relationship between lung cancer and cigarette smoking.

2. Can you identify any experts in your own community who have used their knowledge to influence public policy decisions?

B. How Do Experts Affect Policy?

An expert influences the policy-making process by providing certain facts or making predictions that official decision-makers want to consider before making policy decisions.

Sometimes experts are called upon to be *consultants.* That is, they are asked by government leaders to help them make policy decisions. Occasionally experts become *political activists.* They decide to take part in public activities aimed at influencing the government. Following are two case studies of experts as unofficial political specialists. As you read these cases try to decide what the unofficial political specialist role of "expert" is.

500

Case 1. Ralph Nader Crusades for Auto Safety

Since 1968 Federal law has required new cars to have shoulder harnesses, head rests, emergency blinkers, recessed door knobs, and all-round interior padding. But Ralph Nader had been pushing the issue of automobile safety into the halls of Congress since 1959. Almost singlehandedly this young lawyer, who did not own a car, provoked national auto-safety legislation.

Ralph Nader became interested in auto safety in 1959 when he was studying auto-injury cases as a senior at Harvard Law School. His studies led him to the engineering departments of Harvard and Massachusetts Institute of Technology to gather data on automotive technology. As Nader compiled more and more facts, he became convinced that the law treated the driver unjustly. In most accident cases the law found the driver guilty. Nader's facts suggested that many times an accident happened because of defects in the car, not because of the driver's errors.

After graduation from Harvard Law School, Nader began practicing law in Hartford, Connecticut. He continued his research on automobile safety. He read everything he could find on auto accidents, auto engineering, and automobile manufacturing corporations. Soon he was writing articles and making speeches to civic groups on the subject. He earned recognition when he testified before the auto-safety committees of both the Massachusetts and Connecticut legislatures. But Nader was frustrated. Neither the public nor the lawmakers were responding to the issue of automotive safety. He felt he was not reaching the appropriate audience. Nader became convinced of the futility of local crusading.

Ralph Nader (left) and a group of his "Raiders," a name coined by newsmen for the young men and women who have helped Nader in his efforts to get stronger consumer legislation.

In 1964 Nader had a chance to carry his crusade to the national government. Daniel Moynihan, Assistant Secretary of Labor, invited Nader to Washington as a consultant. He wanted Nader to write a report on what the government could do about auto safety.

Nader's book launches safety crusade. Nader's research led him to write more than the usual government report. After completing it, he left the Labor Department to write a book of his own on auto safety. The book, *Unsafe at Any Speed*, was published in late 1965.

Farris. Copyright 1970, Saturday Review, Inc.

"I had a nightmare last night. I dreamed
I went over to Nader's Raiders."

In his book Nader concluded that manufacturers try chiefly to please the public through styling design. He charged that they are only secondarily concerned with the safety design of their products.

Nader used the Chevrolet Corvair as a glaring example. General Motors had designed this car to compete with European economy cars which were taking an increasing share of the American market. Nader argued that the Corvair's rear suspension system was not strong enough to withstand stress slightly more than normal. He gathered various kinds of evidence to support his claims, emphasizing the more than 100 lawsuits filed by Corvair owners around the country.

In one Chicago case General Motors had made an out-of-court settlement with an injured person. Nader argued that the corporation had made such a settlement to avoid a court order requesting the company to make public all test and engineering information on the Corvair.

In another case a California highway patrol officer testified that he had seen a Corvair rear suspension snap, causing the driver to lose control.

Nader accused the manufacturer of failure to include a device invented by one of its own researchers to correct the weakness of the car's rear suspension system.

He called attention to an accessory produced by a small California firm to correct and stabilize this automobile's rear suspension. Why, asked Nader, should an owner have to purchase such an accessory?

Nader's charges attract nationwide attention. *Unsafe at Any Speed* became a best-seller. President Johnson decided to include this growing public issue of auto safety in his State of the Union message of 1966. He mentioned auto safety in only one sentence, but it was enough to open the doors to new legislation which Nader had been suggesting.

In March, 1966, President Johnson urged Congress to establish a six-year highway safety program, including Federal safety standards for new cars and trucks. Earlier in the session several congressmen had proposed bills on the same subject. Editorials in newspapers across the country quickly gave added support for such legislation.

Nader received an invitation from the Senate Commerce Committee to testify at a hearing on proposed auto-safety legislation. In his testimony he urged stronger legislation than that proposed by the President. Among other things he pointed out that automakers had known for twenty years that windshield "safety" glass could be penetrated upon an impact at a speed as low as 12 miles per hour. He read the results of a study of 177 fatal accidents in which medical authorities determined that 40 percent of the victims would have survived if they had been wearing lap seat belts. He urged that seat belts should be required as regular equipment on all cars.

Nader's political activities brought disturbances to his private life. He received strange phone calls. Friends told him of investigators who had been asking questions about his private life. He discovered that detective agencies in at least three cities had been investigating him, and they refused to say who had hired them. Upset by Nader's harrassment, Senator Ribicoff (Dem., Conn.), a member of the Senate Commerce Committee, warned the major auto manufacturers about a Federal law which provided heavy penalties for intimidation of a congressional witness.

Almost immediately two companies denied any connection with the investigation of Nader. With public attention growing, General Motors officials announced that they had ordered a routine investigation of Nader. Their purpose, they said, was to find out if Nader had any connections with attorneys representing persons suing General Motors over defects in the Corvair. But the GM officials admitted finding no evidence of such connections.

Tom Darcy in *Newsday* (Long Island)
Reprinted with permission

"On the brighter side, one of our 296,000 cars with defective brakes and headlights may be purchased by Ralph Nader."

The private investigation of Nader did reveal a man totally involved in a cause. Nader, the investigators found, lived in a $80-a-month boarding house in Washington. He had no private telephone, but shared a common hallway phone with other boarders. He ate in modest restaurants, usually alone; and worked a 20-hour day. His room was crowded with periodicals, scientific reports, file cabinets, and notes. He supported himself entirely on fees received from his writing and speaking on the topic of auto safety.

Reports of the undercover investigation of Nader brought him more public attention. Invitations to appear on TV talk shows began to come his way, and he used these opportunities to explain his safety crusade.

The campaign received further impetus during the Commerce Committee hearings when General Motors announced that it was calling in 1.5 million 1964 and 1965 models to correct sticky throttles. The company had learned that under snowy conditions the throttles of these cars might freeze. A few days later the Ford Motor Company recalled 30,000 cars to correct a defect that could cause brake failure.

By these actions the auto manufacturers intended to demonstrate their concern with safety. Such voluntary action would presumably show that government regulation was unnecessary. But public reaction simply increased. Congressmen began to receive record amounts of mail supporting auto-safety legislation.

Safety Campaign Results in New Legislation

As a result the Senate Commerce Committee reported in nearly record time a bill that was stronger than the President had requested. Nader's influence could be seen in many parts of this bill. At the Committee's request he had written sections of the bill. The auto industry also won some concessions. An amendment permitted the companies to exchange information about safety devices in cars. (The Federal antitrust laws generally forbid dealings between companies that would reduce competition.) The Senate unanimously supported the bill.

In August, 1966, the House also passed the bill by a 371-to-0 vote. By September the bill was ready to be signed by the President. It established mandatory Federal safety standards for all new motor vehicles and tires. Nader had won his long fight to influence a public policy about auto safety. With 200 other guests representing Congress, auto manufacturers, and safety organizations, Nader witnessed President Johnson's signing the bill into law. Nader and other guests each received a pen used by the President as part of the bill signing.

The New York Times of September 10, 1966, carried Nader's statement to the press: "With the signing . . . President Johnson launches the Federal government on a great lifesaving program. . . ."

Case 2. Dr. Gatch Helps the Hungry

In 1957 a new doctor, Donald E. Gatch, moved to Beaufort County, South Carolina. Dr. Gatch had not been in the county long before he began telling leading citizens about the hungry, disease-ridden black people he discovered and treated in the county. He asked repeatedly why something was not being done to aid these undernourished people. However, the leading citizens were convinced that any man who worked could survive in Beaufort County. "No one has to go hungry," they were fond of saying.

Some white people in the county felt Dr. Gatch exaggerated the real situation. Other people were sure he was a radical or a Communist planted in their midst to stir up trouble. The other doctors of the county also believed that Gatch exaggerated the seriousness of disease and hunger among Negroes. Despite Dr. Gatch's persistent arguments in support of actions to help poor people, the leading citizens of Beaufort County ignored him.

In November, 1967, Dr. Gatch was invited to testify, as an expert consultant, before the Citizens' Board of Inquiry into Hunger and Malnutrition in the United States. The "Citizens' Board" was a private organization established to study the hunger problem and to make policy recommendations on the issue. Dr. Gatch's testimony at the hearing in Columbia, South Carolina, made newspaper headlines. The leading citizens of Beaufort County could no longer ignore his pleas to aid the poor.

Dr. Gatch provides expert testimony. At the hearing Dr. Gatch said that he had seen children dying of starvation, that most of the black children of

During his investigation of hunger, Dr. Gatch talks with a Beaufort County resident about conditions in the area.

his area suffered from worms, and that families were living in hovels worse than the pigsties of his native Nebraska.

Gatch filled his testimony with facts and figures from his own investigations and from Public Health Surveys of Beaufort County. He said that over 70 percent of the adults and 80 percent of the children under five years of age whom he had examined in Beaufort County had intestinal parasites. Further, he claimed that every day he saw cases of such diseases as rickets, scurvy, beri-beri, and pellegra among his poorer Negro patients.

Dr. Gatch declared that local and state authorities had ignored his pleas for help. Further, they refused even to believe his facts about disease and hunger in the county. He asked the "Citizens' Board of Inquiry" to take Beaufort County's case to the Federal government. He described his own fruitless attempts to get money for the county. Private and public agencies had turned him down. He felt that Beaufort County needed a crash program to provide food, basic health education, decent housing, and jobs.

Members of the "Citizens' Board" decided to see Beaufort County for themselves. They relayed their shocked reactions to the national news media. More outsiders came to see. Overnight Dr. Gatch became Beaufort County's

Dr. Gatch found that inadequate housing was also a problem of many of the poor people he visited.

unofficial tour director. A nationally televised documentary titled "Hunger in America" featured Dr. Gatch leading the cameras through his daily rounds. Dr. Gatch also met with reporters from South Carolina newspapers and *The New York Times* and writers from *New Republic* and *Esquire* magazines.

Life in Beaufort became difficult for Dr. Gatch after his testimony and the national attention that followed it. Most white people in his community shunned him. Other doctors in Beaufort County publicly condemned his testimony. He was forced to stop using the Beaufort County Memorial Hospital. The staff refused to serve him or his patients. He received threatening calls.

The "Citizens' Board" before which Dr. Gatch had testified wrote a report about their investigations. This report, *Hunger: U. S. A.*, received nationwide attention. A copy of the report was sent to every member of Congress.

To study the problem, the Senate created a special committee, chaired by Senator McGovern (Dem., S. Dakota). The Senate Select Committee on Nutrition and Human Needs set hearings for February, 1969.

A South Carolina senator speaks out. Just before the Senate subcommittee's hearings were to be held, Senator Ernest Hollings of South Carolina spent ten days touring his state's poverty areas. He spent some of his time in Beaufort County with Dr. Gatch. On February 18, 1969, two years after Dr. Gatch had testified before the Citizens' Board of Inquiry in Columbia, South Carolina, Senator Hollings told the Senate committee of his recent trip through his home state. A portion of his testimony follows.

> Mr. Chairman, . . . I have been asked today to report on my recent visit to South Carolina hunger and poverty areas. . . .
>
> There is hunger in South Carolina. In Beaufort County I visited a shack in which sixteen persons lived and there was no light, no heat, no running water—hot or cold, no bath, no toilet. The entire store of food consisted of a slab of fatback, a half-filled jar of locally harvested oysters, and a stick of margarine. Dr. Kenneth Aycock, our state health official who was accompanying me, [made an initial diagnosis of] a man in the house as suffering from pellagra, a disease supposedly nonexistent in this country. In the same house one small child had rickets and another was recovering from scurvy.
>
> At our next stop I talked with an 83-year-old man who supports a wife and three children on a $40-a-month welfare check. Two of the children receive hot lunches at school by paying 35 cents a day. The cost of these children eating lunch is $14, out of a total family income of $40. When I pointed out that Congress had provided a free lunch program, Thomas C. Barnwell, from whom you will hear later, said, "Well, Senator, that hasn't trickled down this far yet. Maybe we are just too far down the coast. Anyway, we haven't got it."
>
> In the five areas I visited, there are literally hundreds of hungry families who never heard of food stamps. But perhaps this is a blessing, for if they did, they wouldn't qualify anyway. They can't afford the initial cost. . . .
>
> Nor is the problem simply one of race. . . . I saw white hunger, white poverty, and white slums in Riverside and Greenville, Black Bottom in Columbia, and in Beaufort and Chesterfield counties. . . .

Hunger: U. S. A. was published as a book by Beacon Press, Boston, in 1968.

507

The testimony of Senator Hollings had a great impact. Within the month the Secretary of Agriculture ordered free food stamps given to the poor. The press praised Hollings for his courage in making ugly facts public. Governor Robert E. McNair pledged new state programs for the poor and hungry of South Carolina. More money and professional help arrived in Beaufort County from the Office of Economic Opportunity. A child-care clinic was opened. Nutrition teachers traveled from home to home explaining how to prepare healthy meals. A pre-school program began.

After going to the state capital to testify before the Citizens' Board of Inquiry, Dr. Gatch returned to his medical practice. In contrast to Ralph Nader, who has made a career of playing the roles of expert and political activist, Dr. Gatch became involved in temporary political activity to solve a particular social problem.

1. What is the unofficial political specialist role of "expert"?

2. Dr. Donald Gatch and Ralph Nader were both "consultants" and "political activists" in these cases. Provide one example from each case of Gatch and Nader acting as consultants and as political activists. What are the similarities and differences in the political behavior of the expert as consultant and the expert as political activist?

3. Why did Gatch and Nader decide to play the role of "expert"?

4. What were the results of Gatch's and Nader's political behavior? Why?

C. Other Aspects of the Role of Expert

In the two previous cases, both Nader and Gatch were experts acting on their own to get the government to make policy changes. Experts are also often asked by special-interest groups to give opinions on policy issues which concern these special interests. The role of the expert in this situation is to make the claims of the interest group appear more valid by associating his knowledge and prestige with it. Naturally interest-group members will try to find an expert who not only has a strong technical or scientific knowledge of his field, but also shares the political attitudes of those he represents.

One example of the way in which an expert's political attitudes can influence his interpretation of the facts can be seen by comparing the attitudes of two top nuclear scientists on American defense policy.

In the 1950's the United States faced a real dilemma in its defense policy. Should it spend millions of dollars to develop and install the best and biggest missile system possible, or should it rely instead upon trying to negotiate a nuclear-test-ban treaty with other countries in the hope that the superiority it already had in missiles would not be matched by others. Without further testing it was assumed that no other country could match the nuclear power of the United States.

The debate raged, and those on each side of the issue produced a set of experts to support their position. Two eminent nuclear physicists—Dr. Edward Teller and Dr. Hans Bethe—were typical of the experts who entered the debate. These two men, each of whom had helped develop the hydrogen bomb, held opposite opinions on the issue. The argument centered around the question of establishing inspection systems for nuclear testing.

Bethe believed that a reliable system could be developed. He proposed a detailed plan that included 200 inspection stations equipped with sensitive technical instruments for detecting violations. Teller believed that a nation could find ways to cheat on such a system. Could the proposed equipment for measuring seismic movement (earth vibrations) detect the differences between an earthquake and a nuclear explosion? Teller doubted it. Bethe, on the other hand, was convinced the inspection system would work and thought, in any event, that the Soviet Union would not dare risk being caught cheating.

In the following quotations each states his position:

> *Bethe:* "I believe, therefore, that it is technically *feasible* to devise a system of detection stations and inspections which give reasonable assurance against clandestine testing, with the possible exception of very small, decoupled tests."

> *Teller:* "This is the impasse at which we find ourselves today. We can say simply, surely, and clearly that if we agree on test cessation today, we have no way of knowing whether the Russians are testing or not. *There are no technical methods* to police a test ban."

Political Beliefs Influence Opinions

Each scientist's assessment reflected his political views. Bethe strongly favored nuclear disarmament and had fought hard against the strategy of "limited" nuclear war then being discussed in Washington. Teller supported a strategy of "limited" use of nuclear weapons when necessary to protect the interests of the United States. He had long opposed nuclear disarmament of any kind. Their conflicting views about the workability of an inspection system were surely, in part, a result of their larger beliefs about the kind of foreign policy America should follow. And this is a political question, not a scientific one. It is often difficult for scientists to separate their scientific knowledge from their opinions about what policies their nation should, or should not, pursue.

When one expert contradicts another, as happened in this case, the first question asked is: "Which one has his facts straight and which one doesn't?" Since the political leaders who must make defense decisions seldom know enough physics to determine that directly, they must take an indirect approach: "Which one has the best reputation as an expert?" But in this case both Bethe and Teller appeared to be equally qualified. Both had many other scientists supporting them.

The usual effect on policy-making, when highly respected experts contradict each other, is that *the decision is then made on other grounds.* In this case the debate shifted (a) to moral arguments about nuclear warfare and (b) to political considerations of the prospects of cooperation with the Soviet Union. When two experts cannot agree on the technical questions they are trying to answer, the effectiveness of both in political policy-making is weakened. When most experts agree (as, for instance, when virtually all German scientists agreed that no nation could develop a working atomic bomb before the end of World

War II), they may play a very important role in the policy-formation process, even though they may, upon occasion, all be wrong.

Experts Not Particularly Qualified to Make Value Judgments

Policy-makers, as we have seen, must very often turn to experts for facts upon which to base decisions. But if experts are so important to the process, why not put them in charge of policy-making?

To a certain extent the American political system does allow experts to make policy. But when this happens, the expert is not an *unofficial* political specialist but is rather an official political leader. Many experts are bureaucrats with some decision-making power. The United States Commissioner of Education will almost certainly be an expert in education, and he will make numerous policy decisions. Sometimes he will rely on his own expertise; other times he will solicit help from other experts. But the Commissioner of Education does not have a free hand in making national educational policy. He does not decide how much the government will spend on education next year, nor what programs the money will support. These are *value judgments* made in Congress.

Experts are not uniquely qualified to decide basic questions of value. Scientists and other experts can provide useful information on the costs and possible benefits of additional manned space flights to the moon. But these experts have no special competence in deciding whether additional large expenditures in space exploration are more important than building more low-cost housing or spending tax money in other ways.

Unofficial political specialists acting as experts may, of course, have strong feelings about value questions. An expert on taxation may believe strongly that certain changes should be made in the Federal income tax. Suppose he is called to testify before a congressional committee as a tax expert. He will be expected to provide accurate facts and predictions. If he omits certain facts, or distorts the facts, so that the committee will propose tax changes which the expert values, he is not doing his assigned job. If there is suspicion that he is giving biased answers, his reputation as an expert will suffer.

Most experts will not consciously distort the facts. But two experts will not necessarily interpret the same body of facts in exactly the same way. We saw how Dr. Teller and Dr. Bethe each arrived at recommendations which fit his view of the way things *should* be. In the political world the line between facts and value judgments is not always clear. And experts do sometimes— perhaps frequently—let their own values influence the advice they give.

What happens if strongly opinionated experts do most of the advising on matters of public policy? We can expect that their recommendations will reflect their value preferences.

1. What are the limitations of expert advice in the making of public policy?

2. Why may two experts disagree about an issue?

3. How do official political leaders decide which decision to make when experts disagree about solving the problem?

chapter 21

Political Party Leaders

Political party leaders perform various duties which influence, either directly or indirectly, the recruitment of public officials and the shaping of public policy. Following are three cases about the role of political party leaders as unofficial political specialists.

A. Political Party Leaders in Action

As you read the following cases, consider these questions: (1) Who becomes a political party leader? (2) What do party leaders do? (3) Why do people become party leaders?

Case 1. Leo Trask Calls the Shots

Leo Trask paced the kitchen of his large farmhouse, deep in thought. His political future might well be at stake. He had to move with the sure instinct developed over forty-five years of dabbling in Democratic party politics. This was not a normal year. Some Democrats on the slate might have a chance for election in this solidly Republican county. But with this ray of hope came problems. The county Democratic party, which Trask had guided for the last nineteen years, was split; and his leadership was being challenged.

How different it seemed from former times. Trask smiled as he thought back to his first years as county chairman of the Democratic party. He got the job because no one else wanted it. There were, after all, only a handful of Democrats in the county; and most of them saw little point in voting, much less running for office. But through the years the county seat had grown, bringing hundreds of outsiders in from neighboring states to work in its small factories. And, one by one, Trask's Republican farm neighbors had sold their land and moved to the more comfortable life of the city.

It all had to make a difference in the politics of the county, and the last election showed just how much. Democratic candidates had won the office of county coroner and tax assessor and even came close to winning a seat in the city council of the largest town. Things looked just as good this year. Or at least they did until the reform movement started up.

It all began with a young school teacher who decided Trask had not been doing as much as he should to promote the Democratic party in Scottston. "What does he know about it?" mused Leo. "Why, he only moved to Douglas County three years ago. Did he see the days when the Democrats were lucky to win even one vote in some precincts? You bet your sweet life he didn't—but now that things are looking up, here he is, saying that he can run things better.

511

Complaining because ol' man Trask doesn't hold regular meetings of the party leaders and wasn't able to find candidates for a couple of offices this year. I've half a mind to let him try it. Would do him good to call a hundred people trying to find one who's willing to run for dog catcher and probably get clobbered at that."

But it was the other end of the ticket that troubled Trask tonight. The reform Democrats had selected their own candidate for the state legislature in a bold attempt to take control of the party away from Leo. Trask's own choice had been an attractive young pharmacist, well known throughout town, but a newcomer to politics. In the county Democratic convention last month, precinct workers had seen quite a fight between the two camps, with Leo's candidate, Wes Miller, emerging with just enough votes to win the nomination.

The reformers said a newcomer to politics could not win the general election. Now Leo had to prove that he could. A defeat for Miller would make it even more difficult for Trask to hold onto his county chairmanship next time around. But Miller seemed intent on beating himself. Leo interrupted his day dreaming and reached for the telephone.

"Hello, Wes," growled Trask, "I'd like for you to stop by my place first thing in the morning."

"Well," Miller hesitated, "I'm supposed to be out at the shopping center shaking hands."

"Wes, my boy," said Leo, "you can shake hands 'till the cows come home, and it ain't going to do you no good unless you and I have a little talk. Try to be here around seven, and I'll have the coffeepot on."

The next morning Wes Miller sipped his coffee uneasily as the old pro spread out the precinct maps on the kitchen table. They chatted about which areas looked good and where there might be trouble in the county. They went over their schedule for newspaper advertisements and their plans to stretch the thin party finances to buy a few spots on local television. But this was old stuff, and Wes knew this was not why Trask had asked him over. Finally Trask got to the point.

Wes Miller gets a political education. "Wes," he said, "you've got a great political future ahead of you. You have a respectable business, good looks, sensible head, you're young, and you don't rub people the wrong way. I'm getting old, even uglier than I used to be, and probably couldn't pull a hundred votes in this county for state legislator. But I've got one thing you haven't got. I know the politics of this county like the back of my hand. I know the people—who they are, where they live, how they think, what they want. And, Wes, when you got up in front of that dinner club the other day and told them you favored tighter gun-control legislation in this state, I could just hear the votes switching away from you. We've still got more Republicans than Democrats in this county. And we've still got more farmers than big-city types. Most of them got their first rifle on their eighth birthday, and their pappy showed them how to shoot it by plunkin' hedge apples out in the pasture. They been hunting ever since. Now you're coming along and telling them they're going to have to get a license for that rifle or have the state register it with a lot of fancy paperwork. It ain't going to sit well at all."

"But, Leo, it just so happens that I believe we *do* have to have tighter gun control in this country. Look at the crime figures, the accidental deaths by guns, the assassinations of national figures over the past few years. Surely you can see that our society is at a point now where it just can't go on selling guns to any Tom, Dick, or Harry that wants one."

"What I see," countered Trask, "is that you're going to lose this election if you make an issue out of this. And I'm not given to spending the party's money and my time backing losers. You'd better decide right now whether you want to win this election so you can do something up there in the state capital, or whether you want to spend the rest of your life counting out pills for old ladies with back aches. If you want to win, you don't go around saying every fool thing that comes into your head."

Wes thought for some time, then spread his hands pleadingly. "What can I do? I'm already on record on the gun-control issue."

"My boy," Trask said with the air of a father who had just scolded his son and was now preparing to guide him back on the path of truth and wisdom, "you don't have to lead the charge *against* gun control. Just play the issue down.

Better yet, muddy the water a little. Next time the question comes up, tell them you are only concerned about crime in the big cities and only meant that *pistols* should be registered. Tell them you believe in the right of every law-abiding man to own a gun. Leave yourself a little room to maneuver if you do get elected. You can do what you darn please, once you walk through the door that says 'State Assembly'; but my job is to get you that far."

The election. Late into election night a few weeks later, Trask sat in a wooden chair in the county courthouse where the votes were being counted. The room was full of familiar faces he had seen on election days over the years. But there were new faces too, including some of the reformers in his own party. It had been a hard week. Decisions had to be made about how to spend remaining party funds. Last-minute literature had to be distributed in the right places, precinct captains had to be urged to get their workers out ringing doorbells, and jittery candidates who felt they weren't getting enough support from the party had to be soothed.

Today he had to organize a car pool to get Democratic voters to the polls and provide babysitters for others. There had been the usual last-minute check at the polls and the drive to get voters who had not yet voted out while there was still time. But this was the one day of the year that Leo Trask enjoyed most.

As the returns came in, Trask noted that things were going pretty much according to plan. It was still a Republican county, although the Democrats picked up a local office here and there and finally won a seat on the Scottston city council. But Miller's race for the state legislature was close. According to the figures Trask had scrawled on the pad in front of him, he had a chance. As the vote from the outlying areas came in, it looked more and more like he might make it.

A party worker handed him the returns from the small town of Ogden. Trask knew before anyone else in the room what they meant. Ogden had delivered 40 percent of its vote to Miller, better than the Democrats had ever done there before. Miller was in, and Trask flashed the victory sign to Wes across the room. He leaned back in his chair and chuckled to himself. That would take the steam out of those young rebels. It looked like they were going to have to put up with Leo Trask as Democratic county chairman for a while longer.

Case 2. Joseph Scarpito Uses His Resources

What does the chairman of a state political party organization do? Why does he do it? We can find answers to these questions in the following description of the role of Joseph Scarpito, state Democratic party chairman of a northeastern state.

Joseph Scarpito has been chairman of the Democratic party in this state since 1965. He built a position of power and prestige through clever use of patronage. For example, many important people in this state owe political debts to Scarpito. And he has always known how to make collections on these debts.

Candidates for office are approved or disapproved by him. He has the final word about who is or is not appointed a judge. Jobs at all levels of the state government are granted only with his approval.

Joseph Scarpito maintains his position of political power through hard work. He works at his job seven days a week and twelve to fifteen hours a day. He likes his job and enjoys the competition and the excitement of political activity. He enjoys the exercise of power and the prominence that it brings to him.

Though Scarpito is a very powerful political figure, he is no dictator. He must bargain and compromise to maintain his position and to settle conflicts. But he brings vast political resources to the bargaining table. And he seldom fails to get something from his political deals.

Scarpito's job varies, depending on whether the Democratic party is in or out of power. When his party is out of power, then Scarpito has the final say on all party disputes. He is the highest authority in the party organization. However, when a Democrat is governor, then Scarpito plays the role of adviser and servant. He assists the governor in carrying out his policies. Sometimes this role is difficult because it may force Scarpito to do things that he disagrees with.

Scarpito is in politics because he loves to exercise power and he loves competition. He has no burning desire to crusade in behalf of his fellow man or to promote any high ideals. His main political goal is to remain state chairman. This means he must manage the party organization efficiently, so that the party can win elections and control patronage.

Case 3. Theodore Williamson—Loyal Republican

"Theodore Williamson, Attorney at Law," read the small gold plaque on the door. The name was well-known throughout Dalton. For twenty years Ted Williamson had practiced law in his third-floor suite in the First National Bank building. When a businessman faced bankruptcy, when a real-estate developer wanted a change in the local zoning ordinances, when a wife considered divorce, the word went out: "Better see Ted Williamson. He'll know what to do."

Williamson usually did know what to do. There were not many problems that he had not faced before with one of his clients. He knew the leaders of Dalton well. The businessmen, lawyers, and doctors of Dalton were all among his friends. He had been urged several times to run for mayor but chose not to, though he would almost certainly have been elected. He preferred to move behind the scenes. If not everyone knew how many strings he could pull, so much the better.

Dalton is a city with more Republicans than Democrats, and Williamson has been a life-long, loyal member of the Republican party. As a lawyer he could set his own schedule and devote some of his working day to party matters. His wide range of acquaintances and the respect city officials had for him were valuable to the party. He could always be counted upon to come up with a list of well-known individuals who might back an unknown candidate or contribute to his campaign.

Assuming party leadership. So valuable was he to the Republican party in Dalton that strong pressure arose last year for him to run for city chairman of the party. "It is his duty to the party," said friend after friend. "There is no one else who can do as well." Williamson publicly expressed reluctance, but privately he found the idea of heading the city party organization exciting. Finally he agreed to serve, and won the position easily.

This last year had been a busy one. With general elections coming up, Williamson searched for able and appealing candidates. He quietly sought pledges of campaign contributions from businessmen and other donors. Party contacts throughout the state had to be renewed. And he carefully went through the local party organization checking on the past and present performance of precinct captains and other subordinates—gauging their strengths and weaknesses in an effort to make the best possible use of each man's talents in the hectic campaign days ahead.

Issues also received his attention. His sense of what would concern the voters in the weeks before the election would be crucial in deciding how to fill the ticket. He saw this as a "law and order" year in which the public would like candidates who talked tough on matters of law enforcement and had public records of opposition to militant protest groups. There would be other local issues, such as urban renewal. He wanted to find a way of presenting the urban renewal issue that would put local blacks, the churches, and the Chamber of Commerce all on his side.

Tonight, however, Ted Williamson's thoughts were on the Republican National Convention in Miami, Florida. He had almost declined the appointment as an uncommitted delegate to the convention because of the responsibility of party business in Dalton and his own law practice. But something—perhaps the promise of excitement—prompted him to accept. Some delegates in his state were elected, but most were named by the party caucus as he had been.

Williamson looked at the clock, neatly stacked the papers on his desk, and locked the office door behind him. He had worked later than usual tonight, clearing his desk for the trip. Tomorrow his junior law partners could take over the routine office work. He would be helping to select his party's next nominee for President.

The nominating convention. On the plane to Miami, Williamson noticed a fellow delegate from a neighboring town. They had met once several years ago on business, and Williamson had filed his name in the corner of his mind for a day like today. Names were important in this game. Williamson reintroduced himself and sat down beside the man. They chatted about the prospects of the various candidates. Richard Nixon appeared to have the inside track, but many people in their state favored Nelson Rockefeller or Ronald Reagan, who had just announced that his "hat was in the ring."

Williamson had still not definitely decided which candidate he favored. He would listen tomorrow to each candidate's appeal before his state delegation. He also wanted to size up the political leanings of the other delegates

from his state before committing himself. If the delegation were evenly split, his vote might become important to the governor, who was supporting Rocke-feller. He liked the idea of being important to the governor. A man never could tell when he could cash in on such political credit.

During the next two days in Miami, Williamson sized up the situation as best he could amidst the confusion. First came the usual decisions on the rules of the convention, followed by a discussion of the party platform that had been drafted by a committee of party leaders. But what the platform called for was so vague that Ted couldn't see much to fight about. Still, some groups insisted that it be strengthened here or a line be taken out there. It would be forgotten quickly enough anyway.

No one really seemed to know what was going on. He talked with other delegates, but they knew no more than he did. He was buttonholed by some workers for Rockefeller, Nixon, and Reagan and learned that each of the three expected to win the nomination. Except for one, brief conversation with the governor of his state and handshakes with a few others, he met none of the well-known leaders of his party. When he could, he thumbed through newspaper accounts of the convention or flipped on the television in his hotel room.

The more he saw and read of Ronald Reagan, the more he liked him. "Here is a man who stands for the right things and makes a good appearance to boot," thought Ted. He joined with several other Reagan supporters in his delegation in an effort to get most of their state's votes in the Reagan column. Just as their campaign was gaining momentum, Reagan withdrew from the race. Nelson Rockefeller's strength was also slipping, and it began to seem that Richard Nixon would be the nominee.

The governor called a caucus of the state delegation and announced that he was switching to Nixon and said he hoped the entire state delegation would vote unanimously for Nixon. He pointed out that it would be to the advantage of the state to get on the bandwagon early. Ted Williamson was not enthusiastic about Nixon as a candidate, but there was little else to do. Nixon would not hurt the local ticket in Dalton. He might even help it.

Back from Miami. Williamson boarded a return flight for Dalton the morning after Nixon's acceptance speech. Already he was planning ways to sell Nixon to voters at home. Perhaps he could even arrange for a brief appearance by the presidential candidate on his campaign swing through the state.

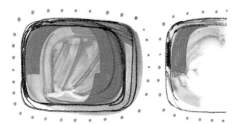

As he stepped off the plane in Dalton, Williamson spotted a photographer for the local paper who had been sent out to record the return of the delegates. Flashbulbs popped as Ted proudly displayed the large "Nixon for President" button on his lapel and raised two fingers of one hand in a confident "V" for victory.

On the basis of information presented in the previous cases, speculate about answers to the following questions. Match your speculative answers against information provided in the remainder of this chapter.

1. What is the role of a political party leader?

2. What are the typical characteristics of individuals who become political party leaders?

3. Why do certain individuals want to play the role of political party leader?

4. How can political party leaders influence public policy decisions?

B. Political Parties and the Role of Party Leader

The Founding Fathers have been justly praised for their exercise of keen insight in framing the Constitution of the United States. But they did not foresee what has come to be one of the most fundamental elements of American politics. Nowhere in the Constitution is there a provision for the political party. Citizens were to have direct control of their government without need of intermediate organizations. In fact, the framers of the Constitution feared that political parties would create divisions within the country which might tear the Union apart. Yet parties emerged, almost inevitably; and political scientists today suspect that almost every political system has some kind of organization that does the job that American political parties have come to do.

The Function of Political Parties

Political parties are different from all other political or social organizations in that their primary effort is to elect men to public office. The goal of party leaders is to win and maintain control of the government, thereby permitting party members to exercise political power. An interest group like the National Rifle Association tries hard to influence public policy, but it does not systematically attempt to control government decision-making by electing its own people to public office. We have seen how the mass media may affect policy on certain issues, but television commentators seldom actually run for office. It is left to the political parties to recruit, select, and support candidates for public office.

The political party system differs somewhat from country to country. In some nations a single party, run by a small group of men, controls the government. Crucial policy decisions are as often made within the party organization as through regular governmental channels in such countries. In such one-party countries elections are a formality where the nominees of the party are automatically assured election.

At the other extreme are countries with several different political parties, no one of which has enough support among the people to win a majority by itself. In these multi-party systems the parties tend to support very different policies. Each advances its own program and has its own distinct set of ideas. Competition may be intense, but two or more parties will have to agree to cooperate in order to win control of the government.

Somewhere in between these two examples falls the American party system. Two major political parties—first the Democratic and then the Repub-

Thomas Nast in *Harper's Weekly*

America's first great political cartoonist, Thomas Nast, originated the elephant symbol of the Republican party. He also helped to popularize the Democratic donkey, which had appeared in cartoons as early as the 1830's.

lican—have emerged in the United States; and one or the other usually wins control of the government. Membership is voluntary, but any eligible voter can join merely by registering to vote. No dues are required. A member does not have to agree strongly with the ideas of the party he joins. And members may even switch now and then to vote for candidates of the other party. American parties, just like all political parties, concentrate upon selecting and electing their candidates to public office. Unlike a one-party system, however, once the candidates get elected, the party has little control over their performance. At the national level, and in many states and cities (although not all), the Republican and Democratic parties compete in elections. The party that wins at each of these levels is called the "majority" party. The party that loses is referred to as the "minority" party.

Political Parties Provide the Nation with Leaders

American parties are important because they help select the men and women who will become government officials and work to get them elected. In the presidential election of 1968 the Republican party searched its ranks for hopeful candidates, including governors, mayors, and senators, and selected Richard Nixon, a former Vice-President, as its standard bearer. The Democratic party after consideration of Hubert Humphrey, Eugene McCarthy, and George McGovern, finally selected Humphrey. Following the nominations of these two men—Nixon and Humphrey—the machinery of each party moved into high gear to get them elected. And much the same process was being carried out in countless state and local elections across the country.

But parties are important in the political process for another reason. We have seen how issues arise in politics and how groups form on all sides of any issue. How can all of these various interests be expressed in public policy? Parties provide an important key. To win an election, a political party must appeal to as many interests as possible without alienating others that already support it. So it must find candidates that will be attractive to a wide range of interests. It must also draw up a platform and encourage its candidates and office holders to take stands on issues which will gain support for the party. As a result, both parties in America have to find ways to smooth over the differences between conflicting interest groups where possible and combine these various interest groups into a majority. By narrowing the choice of the individual voter down to one of two candidates—Republican or Democrat, the American two-party system has taken a big step toward reducing the conflict that might arise in a society which embraces many strong and diverse interests.

There are vast differences between the kind of parties that compete for public office through electoral campaigns and those which do not compete for public favor. A revolutionary organization dedicated to overthrowing a government by force and abolishing competitive elections is sometimes called a "party," but it is different from the political parties we are considering.

Similarly, one frequently sees small minor parties which nominate and run candidates for public office but with no real expectation of victory. Most American parties in history, such as the Federalists and the Whigs, failed to survive for long once they stopped winning elections. Some, such as the Socialist party, persist but use elections as a means of advertising their programs or ideology rather than as a serious attempt to gain control of the government.

For the party in a competitive system (such as the American political system) the crucial goal is attaining public offices. In the process the party must make concessions on policy and candidates to voters or interest groups that might be tempted to support the other party. Thus deciding on the tactics necessary to win an election represents crucial decisions for party leaders. In the 1964 presidential election the Republican party, with Senator Barry Goldwater as its presidential nominee, directed its appeal toward the southern, midwestern, and western states, largely ignoring the East and alienating the Negro voters. The failure of that strategy became fully apparent only after Democrat Lyndon Johnson rolled to a landslide victory. Disagreement among Republican party leaders over the way in which the Goldwater campaign had been conducted threatened for a time to weaken seriously the effectiveness of the party. Party leaders are constantly called upon to make value judgments on such tactical matters, and this fact creates constant tension within the party.

Political Party Organization

Millions of Americans consider themselves Republicans or Democrats, but their party activity seldom goes beyond casting an occasional vote. Only a very small percentage of American citizens are very active political participants. Many of these will be in positions of party leadership.

"Party leader" can mean anything from National Chairman to a precinct captain responsible for a few city blocks of voters. The formal organization of our two major parties differs in many details, and varies from one state to the next, or even from city to city. However, some generalization can be made. Let us look briefly at several of these party leadership positions, or statuses.

National chairman. Officially he is chosen by the National Committee, but in practice he is selected by the party's presidential nominee. His major job is to help manage the presidential campaign. He raises funds for candidates and oversees a staff which prepares campaign literature and maintains a speaker's bureau. He may also settle arguments among his party's candidates or other leaders. As official spokesman for the party, he is a frequent target for criticism from within and without his own party. He has little influence in selecting his party's candidates or setting policy and little control over party leaders at other levels.

National, state, and county committeemen. One man and one woman from each state is appointed to serve on the national committee of each major party. The national committee members as well as state and local members usually have earned their positions in return for past services rendered to the party. Their influence varies, but those who have most influence are likely to hold other positions in the party as well.

Congressional campaign committees. These are relatively independent bodies which assist Senators and Congressmen as they battle for reelection.

State chairmen. They are responsible for building a year-round organization at the state level. They must find able candidates, get them elected, and keep up the image of the party.

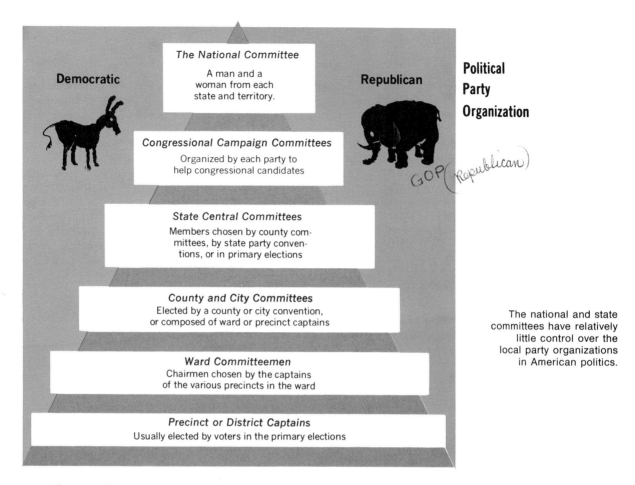

Political Party Organization

Democratic — Republican

GOP (Republican)

The National Committee
A man and a woman from each state and territory.

Congressional Campaign Committees
Organized by each party to help congressional candidates

State Central Committees
Members chosen by county committees, by state party conventions, or in primary elections

County and City Committees
Elected by a county or city convention, or composed of ward or precinct captains

Ward Committeemen
Chairmen chosen by the captains of the various precincts in the ward

Precinct or District Captains
Usually elected by voters in the primary elections

The national and state committees have relatively little control over the local party organizations in American politics.

County chairmen. They often are the real power in local politics. They maintain control of the local party organization and head the county committee. Chairmen of larger counties or cities may wield great influence in state and national politics as well.

Precinct captains. These are party leaders in local neighborhoods. They work with city or county chairmen in recruiting candidates and getting out the vote. At the precinct level much of the real work of politics is carried on. The precinct is the smallest electoral unit, usually including a few hundred voters in the same neighborhood. Yet, in highly competitive areas, the precinct captain is an important cog in the party machine. He organizes a small band of volunteer party workers to register potential voters for his party, distributes campaign literature, canvasses the neighborhood to make personal contact with the voters, or holds social gatherings in which his neighbors can meet the current crop of candidates.

From the diagram of party organization above, you may get the impression that a party is like an army with commands flowing down from generals at the top, and with foot soldiers waiting at the bottom to carry them out.

In some states the election ballots carry a party symbol. Above are some of the symbols which have appeared in recent years on New York ballots.

Nothing could be further from the truth. In actual fact, there is surprisingly little coordination among the various levels of the party, and leaders at each level jealously guard their own freedom of action. A county chairman has local issues and a set of local candidates to worry about, and he may be more concerned with them than about who the state's next senator will be. Friction among leaders at the various levels is frequent in both parties. Likewise the national committee has virtually no authority over state, county, or city leaders.

How can one call this kind of party an organization at all? Europeans accustomed to much more tightly knit, well-disciplined parties ask this question often. The answer lies in a general commonness of purpose felt by members of a party at all levels, some interaction among leaders in an otherwise decentralized system, and a sense of identification with one party or the other that most Americans begin to develop at an early age.

What Do Party Leaders Do?

Many crucial decisions are made within political parties. The voter will have a choice between the Republican and Democratic candidate, but these two nominees will have been selected from a larger group of possible candidates by their political parties. Strategy adopted during a campaign by party leaders may have an effect upon later policy positions of their candidate, should he be elected to office.

Party leaders will also be influential in determining who gets "patronage" positions. Patronage is the practice of permitting a public official to appoint men of his choice to work in certain government jobs as payment for their support. While civil service (which hires on the basis of qualifications for the position without regard to party membership) has greatly reduced the number of patronage jobs in recent years, there is still enough patronage possibilities at most levels to permit the party to reward its most faithful helpers.

Most of what party leaders do has one aim—winning elections. For a National Chairman this may mean month after month of travel around the country, greasing the party machinery, meeting new candidates and leaders, spotting trouble in the organization, and trying to patch up the worst problems. There will be high-level conferences in which campaign strategy is discussed, schedules are worked out, and offended politicians are soothed.

For the precinct captain, winning elections may mean knowing the voters in his precinct personally and keeping a set of cards—one for each household in his precinct—on which he will record the name of the family living there, whether they are registered and with which party, how they have voted in the past, whether they can be counted upon for party work or campaign contributions, and any other information that may be useful. It will mean conducting registration drives to make certain that new families in his precinct (especially those who indicate a preference for his party) are eligible to vote. Later he may follow up by going from house to house throughout the precinct to distribute information on the candidates and to make a personal appeal for support of his party. He may also be called upon to arrange social gatherings, to conduct telephone campaigns, or to make mailings to voters in his precinct.

Local party leaders also provide certain services for the people of their community. For example, a recent survey of precinct leaders in one New Jersey county found them carrying out all of the following tasks:

R. T. Frost, "Stability and Change in Local Party Politics," *Public Opinion Quarterly*, Vol. 25 (Summer, 1961), pp. 231–232.

1. Help unemployed get work.

2. Help people get public jobs on a highway crew, the fire department, or police force.

3. Show people how to get their Social Security benefits, welfare payments, and unemployment compensation.

4. Help citizens with problems like rent gouging, unfair labor practices, zoning, or unfair assessments.

5. Help a neighborhood to get a needed traffic light, more parking space, or more policemen.

6. Run clambakes and other get-togethers for interested people, even though no political campaign is involved.

7. Help citizens who are having difficulties with the law.

8. Help newcomers to the community get adjusted and find places to live and work.

9. Work with some of the other party's leaders to reduce friction and keep the campaign from getting too rough.

10. Help young men with military service problems.

In return for services such as these, the party leader would expect support for his candidates in local elections.

Wide variations in role behavior. Not all precinct captains perform their jobs faithfully. In many areas of the country one party is so dominant that there is little incentive for either party to wage a big election campaign. Even in areas where the two parties are rather evenly matched, leaders may have little enthusiasm for the hard work their job calls for. After studying the actual work of precinct workers in cities today, one political scientist came to this conclusion:

James Q. Wilson, "The Economy of Patronage," *Journal of Political Economy*, Vol. 69 (August, 1961), p. 337.

> Relatively few precinct workers canvass their areas vigorously or frequently. Once they acquire a patronage job and become a member in good standing of the local political club or ward headquarters, they often concern themselves more with the social and fraternal advantages of membership (getting away from the wife a few nights a week, playing cards with "the boys," and swapping political yarns). . . . Precinct workers canvass principally their friends and a small group of voters who are well known and who can be relied upon.

This view is supported by a careful study in which 142 precinct leaders in Detroit, Michigan, were interviewed. When asked about specific tasks they had performed, these precinct leaders answered as shown in the table on the next page.

Party Leadership Tasks	Percent Responding "Yes"
Has done something to get voters registered	71%
Kept some kind of records of voters in precinct	47
Has fairly complete records of own supporters and independents	20
Knows whether voters in precinct are registered or not	37
Uses records to check voters at polls on election day	12
Has helpers for precinct work	67
Had meetings of these precinct workers during campaign	32
Participated in fund raising in precinct	9
Contacted people in precinct by telephone	16
Conducted door-to-door canvassing	29
Distributed literature in precinct	46
Has had contact with county leaders	40
Has had contact with congressional district leaders	67

D. Katz and S. J. Eldersveld, "The Impact of Local Party Activity on the Electorate," *Public Opinion Quarterly*, Spring, 1961.

Precinct leaders and workers are the link between the relatively small group of higher party leaders and the people. State and county chairmen know that for their party to be most effective, it must be well organized at the grass roots. Precincts must be manned by able and energetic leaders if a party hopes to mobilize its potential vote on election day.

At higher party levels, leadership is a full-time job. Of course, elected public officials have a great stake in maintaining a strong party organization and will devote part of their time to party matters. A governor may be the formal head of the party in his state and will be influential in determining party policy and selecting nominees. But he will depend heavily upon city, county, and state party leaders who are not burdened by responsibilities of public office and can devote all of their time to party matters.

The activities of party leaders at all levels, then, are directed toward ensuring the election of their candidates in upcoming elections. But this may mean different things for leaders in different positions. The precinct leader will be expected to establish contact with the voters in his neighborhood, performing small services for them where possible with an eye to getting supporters of his party to the polls. County, state, and national party leaders will be concerned with questions of campaign strategy, party finances, and recruiting likely candidates to run for office.

As with any organization, friction will arise as to who should be nominated, where the money should go, where candidates should make personal appearances, and what campaign tactics will be most effective. There is very little effort made to maintain the loyalty of party workers. However, those who are loyal to the party and who work hard are often rewarded by the party for their efforts.

Judging by our account of party leaders thus far, they do not seem as concerned about how public issues should be decided as do interest group representatives, mass media representatives, and even experts acting as unofficial political specialists. This does not mean that party leaders do not have strong opinions about public policy. However, at times these opinions must take a back seat to the job of getting the party's nominee elected. Still, we have seen that who party leaders select as candidates and what strategy is followed during a campaign may influence the policy-making process indirectly in the years ahead.

At this point you should refer to the speculative answers you made about the role of political party leader in response to question 1 on page 519. Which of your speculations can be supported with evidence presented on pages 524–526. In light of this evidence, what changes do you need to make in these speculative answers?

C. The Characteristics of Political Party Leaders

Thousands of Americans are actively engaged in party politics. In most of the nation's 3000-odd counties both major parties have leaders at work. And supporting each county chairman will be from a dozen to a hundred or more precinct captains. Are these leaders representative of the general population? Or are certain kinds of people attracted to party leadership positions?

Socioeconomic Status and Personality Traits

Party leaders are drawn from a variety of racial and ethnic backgrounds, income and educational levels, and occupations. Yet certain characteristics tend to stand out.

In terms of occupation, party leaders tend to come from the ranks of lawyers, realtors, salesmen, and businessmen. In rural areas, of course, farmers are well represented.

Thomas M. Watts studied party leaders in fifteen Indiana counties and found a variety of occupations represented as shown in the table.

In this Indiana sample both parties drew heavily from the legal profession, but farmers were represented more heavily in the leadership of the Democratic party, while manufacturing executives made up the largest single group in the Republican leadership.

A quite different pattern was found by political scientist Samuel C. Patterson in Oklahoma. There, attorneys and businessmen formed the backbone of the Democratic leadership, while farmers and ranchers were more heavily represented in the Republican party. Patterson also found that most leaders of both parties had at least some college education, and a sizable majority earned an annual income of over $10,000.

Table from T. M. Watts, "Application of the Attribution Model to the Study of Political Recruitment: County Elective Offices," in W. J. Crotty, ed., *Approaches to the Study of Party Organization.* (Allyn and Bacon, 1968).

Occupations	Republican	Democratic
Lawyers	16	14
Farmers	8	18
Bankers	7	6
Insurance representatives	4	3
Manufacturing executives	18	5
County or city officeholders	8	8
Contractors	4	1
Union officers and stewards	0	5
Miscellaneous (all others)	18	21
	83	81

In short, party leaders tend to have many of the same characteristics as other unofficial political specialists—relatively high status, education, and income. They also reflect the characteristics of their own party members in their region of the nation. They are likely moreover to come from families which have been politically active in past generations.

It is not coincidence that lawyers, realtors, insurance agents, and businessmen frequently find their way into a party leadership role. These occupations call for skill at negotiating and at balancing conflicting interests. These skills are needed by political parties, since a party must also find ways of getting differing groups to cooperate. Professional and business people are also likely to have more than usual contact with political conversation and a better understanding of the political rules of the game. Notice too that the occupations most represented among party leaders are those which permit the person to take a few hours out of the middle of the day to devote to party matters. Employees who have a fixed work-day find it less easy to become party leaders.

For some people, politics represents a path for professional or business advancement. A young lawyer who wants to become a district attorney, or perhaps a judge, will eventually have to enter the political arena. Others may be able to use their political reputation or connections to their own business advantage. For example, a realtor active in party politics will meet a great many people and be known to many others. He may even sell property to a few of them. He may get a chance to transact business for the city or county. But most of all, party leadership requires that same instinct for human relationships that is important for public officials and other unofficial political specialists.

Party Leaders and Political Issues

Party leaders tend to have somewhat more intense opinions about political and social issues—and are more likely to act upon their beliefs politically—than the average citizen. And, as you might assume, their opinions are less likely to change. Their knowledge about issues and their interest in the political world is far higher than is the case for non-leaders.

In the late 1950's Herbert McClosky and his colleagues conducted a study comparing the attitudes of party leaders to those of their followers. Each of the respondents to their survey was asked whether he favored an increase or decrease in various government activities: Federal aid to education, farm price supports, taxes on business, foreign aid, and so on.

The findings contained some surprises. Democratic and Republican leaders were far apart on most of the issues, but the rank-and-file Democrats and Republicans were much closer together. In general, Democratic leaders and followers both tended to favor more public ownership, more government regulation of business, more welfare, more taxes on business, and a more active foreign policy. But more Democratic *leaders* than *followers* favored these policies. And more Republican leaders than followers opposed these same policies. Democratic followers favored the stated policies only slightly more than did the Republican followers. Most striking of all, Republican followers were generally closer to the Democratic leaders than to their own Republican leaders!

It is this pattern of political opinion that provides a key to understanding much about party politics in the United States. Party leaders and candidates must go where the votes are. And most citizens have more moderate views on policy issues than do the party leaders. People who become impatient with political parties and candidates for not taking strong stands on every issue do not appreciate the fact that a party must win if it is to survive. And the way to win is usually by doing a better job than the other party of attracting voters who are moderate in their political views.

At this point you should refer to the speculative answers you made about the characteristics of party leaders in response to question 2 on page 519. Which of your answers can be supported with evidence presented on pages 527–528? In light of this evidence, what changes do you need to make in these speculations?

D. Why Do Men Work for Political Parties?

To win elections (with all that entails in the way of recruiting and selecting candidates, seeking campaign funds, organizing the campaign, getting voters registered and out to vote, and a host of other activities) a political party must have a group of devoted workers who come to the aid of their party year after year. How do they attract these people? There are several inducements a party can offer its more active members.

Major Incentives for Party Activists

Patronage is a major incentive for some party leaders to devote their time to party matters. The hope of being appointed to a position in government if their candidates win, or the desire to keep the job they already have, spurs some men and women to work loyally for their party in elections. Although patronage is not so important as it once was, American parties still reward their most faithful leaders with jobs more frequently than does any other party system in the world.

Closely related to patronage is the notion of *preferments*. Preferments are concrete rewards that can be handed out by officials in administrative or executive positions to members of their own party. The owner of a small printing establishment who is also a party leader may find juicy government or party printing contracts coming to his company. An officer of a construction firm frequently takes great interest in party politics in hope that his firm will receive preference when the time comes to decide what company will pave the city streets or build the new courthouse. An active member of the party in power may also get preferential treatment when government agencies are deciding where to build new sidewalks or sewers. It is not unusual for the party in power to take special care of neighborhoods where party leaders live.

Many people become active in party life because they are hoping for a *political career*. Knowing that the party controls the nominating process, they must first establish themselves as loyal party workers before they can claim the nomination. Even after election to public office, the ambitious person may

Local party leadership, especially as city chairman or county chairman, offered relatively greater opportunities for economic rewards in the past than today. Civil service exams have reduced job patronage in many localities, and laws now generally require competitive bidding on public contracts. Perhaps the most notorious political boss in American history was Boss Tweed of New York City. Nast's attacks on the Tweed Ring helped bring several indictments—and Tweed's eventual imprisonment.

Some political bosses have been both party leader and public official. Boss Hague served as mayor of Jersey City for thirty years, retiring in 1947. For many years he was a member of the Democratic National Committee. Boss Crump of Tennessee held political power in Memphis and eastern Tennessee for forty years but served as mayor only about ten years. Both of these twentieth-century bosses are pictured on the opposite page.

Harper's Weekly, January 6, 1872

CAN THE LAW REACH HIM?—THE DWARF AND THE GIANT THIEF.   by Th. Nast

still keep a hand in party operations in order not to be forgotten when opportunities to run for higher office arise.

Party leaders may find that their political activity results in certain *economic rewards* in their own business or occupation. Contacts made through the political party may be especially helpful to lawyers, insurance salesmen, real-estate brokers, or small businessmen or storekeepers in attracting more clients or customers.

Those who are cynical about politics assume that most party leaders are active because they want the kinds of rewards we have mentioned. While incentives of this kind may be important for some, they are by no means the only reasons people become party leaders. Let us look now at some other things the political party has to offer its leaders.

Other Rewards of Party Participation

Some people may be attracted to positions of party leadership because of the psychological rewards the party can supply. The party may represent an opportunity for an individual to mix with people slightly higher on the social ladder than he or she customarily meets, thereby providing increased social status for an individual. For the lonely or the bored the party supplies friends and a way of keeping busy. Some may find the opportunity to meet or associate with powerful officials attractive in itself, and others will enjoy the excitement of the political battle and relish getting the "inside dope" about what is happening in the political world. Still others may see party service as a way of fulfilling their civic duty. They derive satisfaction from the knowledge that they are doing something constructive for community or country.

Some party leaders are initially attracted to these positions by a hope of influencing *policy-making.* We have seen that most unofficial political specialists are interested in policy questions. And if American parties are not the most effective way for people to get specific policies passed, they do at least provide a means by which men can work indirectly for the kinds of decisions they consider important.

Personal beliefs and values may also be important in attracting men to work for a political party. We have seen that the two American parties differ to some degree on the things their members (and especially their leaders) think are important and valuable. The liberal may see the Democratic party as a place where he can work toward distributing social services more equally. Similarly the strong conservative may find the Republican party an organization through which he can combat what he considers governmental encroachment upon individual freedom.

Finally, once a party leader has identified strongly with his party and worked hard for it, just serving it loyally and seeing it prosper may give him satisfaction. The *welfare of the party* becomes an important end in itself, and its victories may seem personal victories for the party leader.

Of course, no political party can provide all of these rewards to each leader, even if it wanted to. At certain times a party will have to rely heavily upon the psychological incentives. In other situations it may offer the promise of jobs or other economic benefits. People are attracted to the role of party leader for many reasons, and no two leaders will be interested for exactly the same reason. The variety of incentives that parties may offer assures them a leadership of men and women of various skills, personal goals, and viewpoints working together on behalf of their party.

So far we have looked at the kinds of things parties have to offer their leaders as incentives, but we might approach the question of why people work for parties in another way. Several investigators have asked party leaders why they devote much time to party affairs. In one such study of precinct leaders in Wayne County, Michigan, leaders were asked what kinds of satisfaction they received from party work. Their responses are described in the table on the next page.

Frank Hague (above) and Edward Hull Crump (below) built up very successful political machines in their areas.

531

Type of Satisfaction	Democrats	Republicans
Social contacts	63%	47%
Political fun and inside information	12	8
Business, economic, and political gain	1	1
Moral and philosophical satisfactions	4	3
Ideological or issue satisfactions	3	17
No satisfactions received	15	22
Unclassified	2	2
Total	100%	100%

Adapted from S. J. Elders-veld, *Political Parties* (Chicago: Rand McNally, 1964), p. 278.

As you can see, a variety of incentives are important to precinct leaders in Wayne County. Social contacts were mentioned by far more of the leaders than any other kind of satisfaction, although smaller percentages in both parties viewed political fun and ideological or issue satisfactions as their major motivation. A sizeable proportion of the leaders in both parties indicated that they received *no* satisfaction from party work.

Some party leaders, of course, prove to be more effective than others. A precinct captain who does not turn out the expected vote for his party in his own precinct year after year will not be in a strong position when it comes time for the party to dispense rewards. Likewise, leaders who show good judgment in spotting able candidates, who have a gift for picking the right campaign strategy, or who energetically solicit contributions for the party will almost certainly advance in the party organization and may eventually run for office themselves. Parties have a job to do, and one way their leaders can make sure it is done well is by distributing most of the rewards to the workers who have contributed most to winning elections.

At this point you should refer to the speculative answers you made about why individuals want to play the role of political party leader in response to question 3 on page 519. Which of your speculations can be supported with evidence presented on pages 529–532? In light of this evidence what changes do you need to make in your speculative answers?

E. How Do Party Leaders Affect Public Policy?

Naturally the organizations which nominate candidates for public office and play such an important part in whether they win or lose the election will have an impact upon public policy. But interested as party leaders may be in political issues, their influence on major policy questions is probably not strong.

Perhaps the chief reason party leaders do not exercise strong direct influence upon public policy is that they put other considerations first. Few issues are important enough to them to risk losing an election. Party leaders develop an intense loyalty to their party, and one of the surest ways to lose the respect of other leaders in the party is to fail to support a candidate because of his stand on a certain issue. Governor Rockefeller's failure to strongly endorse Barry Goldwater in 1964 may well have cost Nelson Rockefeller the presidential nomination four years later. Party leaders do not quickly forget those who place their own preferences or beliefs above the welfare of the party.

There may be important differences among party leaders in the same party on current issues. A party is not like an interest group, such as the National Rifle Association, in which all representatives agree quite closely on the policy they are working for. The Democratic party in 1968 found itself badly split between those leaders who supported the Johnson administration's war effort in Vietnam and those leaders who did not.

Even when party leaders agree on a certain issue, they are not often in a good position to put pressure on elected officials. Party organization is strong just before elections, but in the periods between elections only a skeleton of the organization remains. Yet, government officials have to deal with issues all twelve months of the year. It is extremely difficult, therefore, for party leaders to maintain any kind of steady influence.

From the party's point of view, it is not always wise to emphasize the issues anyway, at least in very specific terms. There may well be more chance of offending a voter who would have supported your party than of converting a voter who leans toward the other party by coming out with a precise program or a clear-cut stand on a certain issue. As a result, parties and their candidates tend to say just enough about the issues so that voters will think them informed and responsible in meeting the problems of the day.

Platforms and candidates may be intentionally vague. It is safer to favor "an honorable solution to the war in Vietnam" (which is, after all, what everyone wants) than to try to spell out exactly *how* one would try to gain an "honorable solution," since each solution invites criticism from someone. But a candidate cannot overdo this, or he may be branded by the mass media as indecisive, insincere, or unwilling to take a stand. Much of his task is trying to *appear* to take wise and strong positions on the issues without really committing himself too far. The party leaders behind him realize his dilemma and will try to leave him freedom to maneuver. It is not surprising, then, that party leaders have little systematic effect upon public policy.

The main way that party leaders affect policy is through their effect on elections. Party leaders help to nominate and select candidates and to manage and carry out election campaigns. Through these activities they indirectly influence public decisions. By helping to put Candidate A rather than Candidate B into public office, they contribute support to certain policy decisions that Candidate A will make in office.

At this point you should refer to the speculative answers you made about the influence of party leaders in public policy decisions in response to question 4 on page 519. Which of your speculations can be supported with evidence presented on pages 532–533? In light of this evidence, what changes do you need to make in these speculative answers?

of the United States, in order to form a more perfect union, establish justice, insure domestic tranquillity, provide for the common defense, promote the general welfare, and secure the blessings of liberty to ourselves and our posterity, do ordain and establish this CONSTITUTION for the United States of America.

ARTICLE I · LEGISLATIVE DEPARTMENT

Section 1 · Congress

All legislative powers herein granted shall be vested in a Congress of the United States, which shall consist of a Senate and House of Representatives.

Section 2 · House of Representatives

Election and Term of Members • The House of Representatives shall be composed of members chosen every second year by the people of the several States, and the electors in each State shall have the qualifications requisite for electors of the most numerous branch of the State Legislature.

Qualifications • No person shall be a representative who shall not have attained to the age of twenty-five years, and been seven years a citizen of the United States, and who shall not, when elected, be an inhabitant of that State in which he shall be chosen.

Apportionment • Representatives and direct taxes shall be apportioned among the several States which may be included within this Union, according to their respective numbers, which shall be determined by adding to the whole number of free persons, including those bound to service for a term of years, and excluding Indians not taxed, three-fifths of all other persons. The actual enumeration shall be made within three years after the first meeting of the Congress of the United States, and within every subsequent term of ten years, in such manner as they shall by law direct. The number of representatives shall not exceed one for every thirty thousand, but each State shall have at least one representative; and until such enumeration shall be made, the State of New Hampshire shall be entitled to choose three; Massachusetts, eight; Rhode Island and Providence Plantations, one; Connecticut, five; New York, six; New Jersey, four; Pennsylvania, eight; Delaware, one; Maryland, six; Virginia, ten; North Carolina, five; South Carolina, five; and Georgia, three.

Vacancies • When vacancies happen in the representation from any State, the executive authority thereof shall issue writs of election to fill such vacancies.

The words printed in the margins in this kind of type explain some of the more difficult passages. The parts printed in color are no longer in force.

Margin notes:

Six reasons are given here for the establishment of our Constitution.

A bicameral legislature.

Representatives are to be chosen for two-year terms by the electors (voters) who are permitted to vote for members of the lower house of their own state legislature.

The number of representatives per state is determined by its population.

"All other persons" refers to slaves. Amendment XIV changed this "three-fifths compromise" provision.

A census of the population shall be taken every ten years to determine how many representatives each state shall have. The 1970 ratio was one representative for about each 465,000 persons.

House vacancies shall be filled by a special election called by the governor of a state.

534

Officers; Impeachment • The House of Representatives shall choose their Speaker[1] and other officers; and shall have the sole power of impeachment.

Section 3 · Senate

Number of Senators: Election • The Senate of the United States shall be composed of two senators from each State, chosen by the legislature thereof, for six years; and each senator shall have one vote.

Divided into Three Groups • Immediately after they shall be assembled in consequence of the first election, they shall be divided as equally as may be into three classes. The seats of the senators of the first class shall be vacated at the expiration of the second year; of the second class, at the expiration of the fourth year; of the third class, at the expiration of the sixth year, so that one-third may be chosen every second year; and if vacancies happen by resignation, or otherwise, during the recess of the legislature of any State, the executive thereof may make temporary appointments until the next meeting of the legislature, which shall then fill such vacancies.

Qualifications • No person shall be a senator who shall not have attained to the age of thirty years, and been nine years a citizen of the United States, and who shall not, when elected, be an inhabitant of that State for which he shall be chosen.

President of Senate • The Vice-President of the United States shall be president of the Senate, but shall have no vote, unless they be equally divided.

Officers • The Senate shall choose their other officers, and also a president *pro tempore,* in the absence of the Vice-President, or when he shall exercise the office of President of the United States.

Trials of Impeachment • The Senate shall have the sole power to try all impeachments. When sitting for that purpose, they shall be on oath or affirmation. When the President of the United States is tried, the Chief Justice shall preside; and no person shall be convicted without the concurrence of two-thirds of the members present.

Judgment in Case of Conviction • Judgment in cases of impeachment shall not extend further than to removal from office, and disqualification to hold and enjoy any office of honor, trust, or profit under the United States: but the party convicted shall nevertheless be liable and subject to indictment, trial, judgment, and punishment, according to law.

Section 4 · Both Houses

Manner of Electing Members • The times, places, and manner of holding elections for senators and representatives shall be prescribed in each State by the legislature thereof; but the Congress may at any time by law make or alter such regulations, except as to the places of choosing senators.

[1]The Speaker, who presides, is one of the representatives; the other officers—clerk, sergeant-at-arms, postmaster, chaplain, doorkeeper, etc.—are not.

Amendment XVII in 1913 provided for *direct* election of senators.

One-third of the senators are elected each two years.

Senate vacancies are filled by the governor. Such appointees serve until a new election is held (see Amendment XVII).

The Vice-President serves as presiding officer in the Senate but may vote only in case of a tie.

The Senate elects a temporary president to serve in the Vice-President's absence or when there is no Vice-President.

If an impeached person is found guilty, he is removed from office and not permitted to hold any Federal office. If he has broken any laws, he may be tried for these violations in a court, just as any other person.

Today all our states hold elections for Congress on the first Tuesday after the first Monday in November, in the even-numbered years.

Meetings of Congress • The Congress shall assemble at least once in every year, and such meeting shall be on the first Monday in December, unless they shall by law appoint a different day.

Section 5 • The Houses Separately

Organization • Each house shall be the judge of the elections, returns, and qualifications of its own members, and a majority of each shall constitute a quorum to do business; but a smaller number may adjourn from day to day, and may be authorized to compel the attendance of absent members, in such manner, and under such penalties, as each house may provide.

Rules • Each house may determine the rules of its proceedings, punish its members for disorderly behavior, and, with the concurrence of two-thirds, expel a member.

Journal • Each house shall keep a journal of its proceedings, and from time to time publish the same, excepting such parts as may in their judgment require secrecy; and the yeas and nays of the members of either house on any question shall, at the desire of one-fifth of those present, be entered on the journal.

Adjournment • Neither house, during the session of Congress, shall, without the consent of the other, adjourn for more than three days, nor to any other place than that in which the two houses shall be sitting.

Section 6 • Privileges and Disabilities of Members

Members are paid by the Federal government, and they have the power to set their own pay.

They may be arrested for law violations but not for civil suits while Congress is in session. They may not be sued for anything they say in Congress.

During his term of office a member may not be appointed to any Federal job which was created or for which the pay was increased during that term. And no member may hold another Federal office while in Congress.

Pay and Privileges of Members • The senators and representatives shall receive a compensation for their services, to be ascertained by law, and paid out of the treasury of the United States. They shall in all cases, except treason, felony, and breach of the peace, be privileged from arrest during their attendance at the session of their respective houses, and in going to and returning from the same; and for any speech or debate in either house they shall not be questioned in any other place.

Prohibitions on Members • No senator or representative shall, during the time for which he was elected, be appointed to any civil office under the authority of the United States, which shall have been created, or the emoluments whereof shall have been increased, during such time; and no person holding any office under the United States shall be a member of either house during his continuance in office.

Section 7 • Method of Passing Laws

Tax bills must begin in the House but the Senate may propose changes.

A bill passed by Congress must be sent to the Presi-

Revenue Bills • All bills for raising revenue shall originate in the House of Representatives; but the Senate may propose or concur with amendments as on other bills.

How Bills Become Laws • Every bill which shall have passed the House of Representatives and the Senate shall, before it become a law, be presented to the President of the United States; if he approve, he shall sign it, but if not, he shall return it, with his objections, to that house in which it shall have originated, who shall enter the objections at large on their journal, and proceed to reconsider it. If after such reconsideration two-thirds of that house shall agree to pass the bill, it shall be sent, together with the objections, to the other house, by which it shall likewise be reconsidered, and if approved by two-thirds of that house, it shall become a law. But in all such cases the votes of both houses shall be determined by yeas and nays, and the names of the persons voting for and against the bill shall be entered on the journal of each house respectively. If any bill shall not be returned by the President within ten days (Sundays excepted) after it shall have been presented to him, the same shall be a law, in like manner as if he had signed it, unless the Congress by their adjournment prevent its return, in which case it shall not be a law.

Resolutions, etc. • Every order, resolution, or vote to which the concurrence of the Senate and House of Representatives may be necessary (except on a question of adjournment) shall be presented to the President of the United States; and before the same shall take effect, shall be approved by him, or being disapproved by him, shall be repassed by two-thirds of the Senate and House of Representatives, according to the rules and limitations prescribed in the case of a bill.

dent for his approval and signature. If he disapproves, he returns it with his objections to the house where it started (veto). Congress may pass a bill over his veto by a two-thirds vote of each house.

The President can let a bill become a law without his signature. But a bill sent to the President in the last ten days of a session of Congress is dead (by "pocket veto") if the President does not sign it.

The President's approval is likewise required on resolutions and other matters (except adjournment) passed by both houses.

Section 8 • Powers Granted to Congress

Powers of Congress • The Congress shall have power:

To lay and collect taxes, duties, imposts, and excises, to pay the debts and provide for the common defense and general welfare of the United States; but all duties, imposts, and excises shall be uniform throughout the United States;

To borrow money on the credit of the United States;

To regulate commerce with foreign nations, and among the several States, and with the Indian tribes;

To establish a uniform rule of naturalization, and uniform laws on the subject of bankruptcies throughout the United States;

To coin money, regulate the value thereof, and of foreign coin, and fix the standard of weights and measures;

To provide for the punishment of counterfeiting the securities and current coin of the United States;

To establish post offices and post roads;

To promote the progress of science and useful arts, by securing, for limited times, to authors and inventors the exclusive right to their respective writings and discoveries;

To constitute tribunals inferior to the Supreme Court;

To define and punish piracies and felonies committed on the high seas, and offenses against the law of nations;

These are the "enumerated powers" of Congress.

Federal tax rates must be the same in all states.

This is the "interstate commerce clause."

Naturalization and bankruptcy laws.

Congress determines our system of measurements.

Securities are government bonds and notes.

Patent and copyright laws.

Congress may set up other Federal courts

Congress, rather than the states, has power over crimes committed at sea.

To declare war, grant letters of marque and reprisal, and make rules concerning captures on land and water;

To raise and support armies, but no appropriation of money to that use
shall be for a longer term than two years;

To provide and maintain a navy;

To make rules for the government and regulation of the land and naval
forces;

To provide for calling forth the militia to execute the laws of the Union,
suppress insurrections, and repel invasions;

To provide for organizing, arming, and disciplining the militia, and for
governing such part of them as may be employed in the service of the United
States, reserving to the States respectively the appointment of the officers, and
the authority of training the militia according to the discipline prescribed by
Congress;

To exercise exclusive legislation in all cases whatsoever over such district
(not exceeding ten miles square) as may, by cession of particular States, and
the acceptance of Congress, become the seat of the government of the United
States, and to exercise like authority over all places, purchased by the consent
of the legislature of the State in which the same shall be, for the erection of
forts, magazines, arsenals, dockyards, and other needful buildings;—and

Implied Powers • To make all laws which shall be necessary and proper
for carrying into execution the foregoing powers, and all other powers vested
by this Constitution in the government of the United States, or in any department or officer thereof.

Section 9 • Powers Forbidden to the United States

Absolute Prohibitions on Congress • The migration or importation of
such persons as any of the States now existing shall think proper to admit,
shall not be prohibited by the Congress prior to the year one thousand eight
hundred and eight, but a tax or duty may be imposed on such importation, not
exceeding ten dollars for each person.

The privilege of the writ of habeas corpus shall not be suspended, unless when in cases of rebellion or invasion the public safety may require it.

No bill of attainder or ex-post-facto law shall be passed.

No capitation, or other direct, tax shall be laid, unless in proportion to
the census or enumeration hereinbefore directed to be taken.

No tax or duty shall be laid on articles exported from any State.

No preference shall be given by any regulation of commerce or revenue
to the ports of one State over those of another; nor shall vessels bound to, or
from, one State, be obliged to enter, clear, or pay duties in another.

No money shall be drawn from the treasury, but in consequence of
appropriations made by law; and a regular statement and account of the re-
ceipts and expenditures of all public money shall be published from time to
time.

No title of nobility shall be granted by the United States: And no person holding any office of profit or trust under them, shall, without the consent of the Congress, accept of any present, emolument, office, or title, of any kind whatever, from any king, prince, or foreign state.

Section 10 · Powers Forbidden to the States

Absolute Prohibitions on the States · No State shall enter into any treaty, alliance, or confederation; grant letters of marque and reprisal; coin money; emit bills of credit; make anything but gold and silver coin a tender in payment of debts; pass any bill of attainder, ex-post-facto law, or law impairing the obligation of contracts, or grant any title of nobility.

Conditional Prohibitions on the States · No State shall, without the consent of the Congress, lay any imposts or duties on imports or exports, except what may be absolutely necessary for executing its inspection laws; and the net produce of all duties and imposts, laid by any State on imports or exports, shall be for the use of the treasury of the United States; and all such laws shall be subject to the revision and control of the Congress.

No State shall, without the consent of Congress, lay any duty of tonnage, keep troops, or ships of war, in time of peace, enter into any agreement or compact with another State, or with a foreign power, or engage in war, unless actually invaded, or in such imminent danger as will not admit of delay.

ARTICLE II · EXECUTIVE DEPARTMENT

Section 1 · President and Vice-President

Term · The executive power shall be vested in a President of the United States of America. He shall hold his office during the term of four years, and together with the Vice-President, chosen for the same term, be elected, as follows:

Electors · Each State shall appoint, in such manner as the legislature thereof may direct, a number of electors, equal to the whole number of senators and representatives to which the State may be entitled in the Congress: but no senator or representative, or person holding an office of trust or profit under the United States, shall be appointed an elector.

Proceedings of Electors and of Congress · The electors shall meet in their respective States, and vote by ballot for two persons, of whom one at least shall not be an inhabitant of the same State with themselves. And they shall make a list of all the persons voted for, and of the number of votes for each; which list they shall sign and certify and transmit sealed to the seat of the government of the United States, directed to the president of the Senate. The president of the Senate shall, in the presence of the Senate and House of Representatives, open all the certificates, and the votes shall then be counted. The person having the greatest number of votes shall be the President, if such

Congress may not grant titles of nobility. Nor may any public official accept a title, office, or pay from a foreign country without the consent of Congress.

Certain powers are forbidden to the states, either because these powers belong to the Federal government or because they are things no democratic government should do.

The states may not, without the consent of Congress, tax goods entering or leaving the state except for small fees to cover the expense of inspection. Any profits from an interstate commerce tax would have to go to the Federal treasury.

The states may not tax the cargo of ships, keep troops or warships, make compacts with other states or with foreign countries, or engage in war, unless invaded, without the consent of Congress.

Federal officials may not serve as presidential electors.

The manner of electing the President and Vice-President was changed by Amendment XII. The change was made because in 1800 Thomas Jefferson and Aaron Burr both received the same number of electoral votes, even though the electors number be a majority of the whole number of electors appointed; and if there be more than one who have such majority, and have an equal number of votes, then the House of Representatives shall immediately choose by ballot one of them for President; and if no person have a majority, then from the five highest on the list the said house shall, in like manner, choose the President. But in choosing the President, the votes shall be taken by States, the representation from each State having one vote; a quorum for this purpose shall consist of a member or members from two-thirds of the States, and a majority of all the States shall be necessary to a choice. In every case, after the choice of the President, the person having the greatest number of votes of the electors shall be the Vice-President. But if there should remain two or more who have equal votes, the Senate shall choose from them by ballot the Vice-President.

Time of Choosing Electors • The Congress may determine the time of choosing the electors, and the day on which they shall give their votes; which day shall be the same throughout the United States.

Qualifications of President • No person except a natural born citizen, or a citizen of the United States at the time of the adoption of this Constitution, shall be eligible to the office of President; neither shall any person be eligible to that office who shall not have attained to the age of thirty-five years, and been fourteen years a resident within the United States.

Vacancy • In case of the removal of the President from office, or of his death, resignation, or inability to discharge the powers and duties of the said office, the same shall devolve on the Vice-President, and the Congress may by law provide for the case of removal, death, resignation, or inability, both of the President and Vice-President, declaring what officer shall then act as President; and such officer shall act accordingly until the disability be removed, or a President shall be elected.

Salary • The President shall, at stated times, receive for his services a compensation which shall neither be increased nor diminished during the period for which he shall have been elected, and he shall not receive within that period any other emolument from the United States, or any of them.

Oath • Before he enter on the execution of his office, he shall take the following oath or affirmation:—"I do solemnly swear (or affirm) that I will faithfully execute the office of President of the United States, and will, to the best of my ability, preserve, protect, and defend the Constitution of the United States."

Section 2 • Powers of the President

Military Powers; Reprieves and Pardons • The President shall be commander in chief of the army and navy of the United States, and of the militia of the several States, when called into the actual service of the United States; he may require the opinion, in writing, of the principal officer in each of the executive departments, upon any subject relating to the duties of their respective offices; and he shall have power to grant reprieves and pardons for offenses against the United States, except in cases of impeachment.

Treaties; Appointments • He shall have power, by and with the advice and consent of the Senate, to make treaties, provided two-thirds of the senators present concur; and he shall nominate, and by and with the advice and consent of the Senate shall appoint ambassadors, other public ministers and consuls, judges of the Supreme Court, and all other officers of the United States, whose appointments are not herein otherwise provided for, and which shall be established by law; but the Congress may by law vest the appointment of such inferior officers, as they think proper, in the President alone, in the courts of law, or in the heads of departments.

Vacancies • The President shall have power to fill up all vacancies that may happen during the recess of the Senate, by granting commissions which shall expire at the end of their next session.

The Senate is given the special powers of approving treaties and presidential appointments.

Pag-aralan

This is intended to prevent the President from appointing officials, except temporarily, without the Senate's consent.

Section 3 • Duties of the President

Message; Convening of Congress • He shall from time to time give to the Congress information of the state of the Union, and recommend to their consideration such measures as he shall judge necessary and expedient; he may, on extraordinary occasions, convene both houses, or either of them, and in case of disagreement between them with respect to the time of adjournment, he may adjourn them to such time as he shall think proper; he shall receive ambassadors and other public ministers; he shall take care that the laws be faithfully executed, and shall commission all the officers of the United States.

At the opening of each session of Congress the President sends or delivers his "State of the Union" message. He also sends special messages from time to time.

Section 4 • Impeachment

Removal of Officers • The President, Vice-President, and all civil officers of the United States, shall be removed from office on impeachment for, and conviction of, treason, bribery, or other high crimes and misdemeanors.

ARTICLE III • JUDICIAL DEPARTMENT

Section 1 • United States Courts

Courts Established; Judges • The judicial power of the United States shall be vested in one Supreme Court, and in such inferior courts as the Congress may from time to time ordain and establish. The judges, both of the Supreme and inferior courts, shall hold their offices during good behavior, and shall, at stated times, receive for their services a compensation which shall not be diminished during their continuance in office.

Federal judges hold indefinite terms, but they may be removed by impeachment.

Section 2 • Jurisdiction of United States Courts

Federal Courts in General • The judicial power shall extend to all cases, in law and equity, arising under this Constitution, the laws of the United States, and treaties made, or which shall be made, under their authority;—to all cases

This describes the kind of cases which are to be handled in the Federal courts.

affecting ambassadors, other public ministers, and consuls;—to all cases of admiralty and maritime jurisdiction;—to controversies to which the United States shall be a party;—to controversies between two or more States;—between a State and citizens of another State;—between citizens of different States;—between citizens of the same State claiming lands under grants of different States, and between a State, or the citizens thereof, and foreign states, citizens or subjects.

Supreme Court • In all cases affecting ambassadors, other public ministers and consuls, and those in which a State shall be party, the Supreme Court shall have original jurisdiction. In all other cases before mentioned, the Supreme Court shall have appellate jurisdiction, both as to law and fact, with such exceptions and under such regulations as the Congress shall make.

Trials • The trial of all crimes, except in cases of impeachment, shall be by jury; and such trial shall be held in the State where the said crimes shall have been committed; but when not committed within any State, the trial shall be at such place or places as the Congress may by law have directed.

Section 3 • Treason

Treason Defined • Treason against the United States shall consist only in levying war against them, or in adhering to their enemies, giving them aid and comfort.

No person shall be convicted of treason unless on the testimony of two witnesses to the same overt act, or on confession in open court.

Punishment • The Congress shall have power to declare the punishment of treason, but no attainder of treason shall work corruption of blood, or forfeiture, except during the life of the person attainted.

ARTICLE IV • RELATIONS OF THE STATES TO EACH OTHER

Section 1 • Official Acts

Full faith and credit shall be given in each State to the public acts, records, and judicial proceedings of every other State. And the Congress may by general laws prescribe the manner in which such acts, records, and proceedings shall be proved, and the effect thereof.

Section 2 • Privileges of Citizens

The citizens of each State shall be entitled to all privileges and immunities of citizens in the several States.

Fugitives from Justice • A person charged in any State with treason, felony, or other crime, who shall flee from justice, and be found in another State, shall, on demand of the executive authority of the State from which he fled, be delivered up, to be removed to the State having jurisdiction of the crime.

Amendment XI took away the right of private citizens to bring a law suit against a state in a Federal court.

Certain kinds of cases must be handled by the Supreme Court directly. Cases handled by the lower courts may be reviewed by the Supreme Court, but Congress may change the appellate (review) power.

This section on how trials shall be held is strengthened by the Bill of Rights, especially Amendment VI.

Treason is very strictly defined. Conviction requires the testimony of two persons to the same specific act, or confession in court by the accused.

Punishment for treason may not extend to one's descendants.

The states are required to honor each other's laws, records, and legal decisions.

Each state must offer fair treatment to citizens of other states.

The process of returning an accused person to a state from which he has fled is called "extradition."

542

Fugitive Slaves • No person held to service or labor in one State, under the laws thereof, escaping into another, shall, in consequence of any law or regulation therein, be discharged from such service or labor, but shall be delivered up on claim of the party to whom such service or labor may be due.

This was the basis for the fugitive slave laws. This provision became ineffective with the adoption of Amendment XIII.

Section 3 • New States and Territories

Admission of States • New States may be admitted by the Congress into this Union; but no new State shall be formed or erected within the jurisdiction of any other State; nor any State be formed by the junction of two or more States, or parts of States, without the consent of the legislatures of the States concerned as well as of the Congress.

New states may not be formed by dividing or joining existing states without the consent of the state legislatures and Congress.

Territory and Property of United States • The Congress shall have power to dispose of and make all needful rules and regulations respecting the territory or other property belonging to the United States; and nothing in this Constitution shall be so construed as to prejudice any claims of the United States, or of any particular State.

Congress has authority over Federal territory and property.

Section 4 • Protection of the States

The United States shall guarantee to every State in this Union a republican form of government, and shall protect each of them against invasion, and on application of the legislature, or of the executive (when the legislature cannot be convened) against domestic violence.

A republican form of government is interpreted to mean a representative government governing by will of the people.

The Federal government is required to protect the states against invasion and, when the states so request, against domestic violence.

ARTICLE V • AMENDMENTS

How Proposed; How Ratified • The Congress, whenever two-thirds of both houses shall deem it necessary, shall propose amendments to this Constitution, or, on the application of the legislatures of two-thirds of the several States, shall call a convention for proposing amendments, which, in either case, shall be valid to all intents and purposes, as part of this Constitution, when ratified by the legislatures of three-fourths of the several States, or by conventions in three-fourths thereof, as the one or the other mode of ratification may be proposed by the Congress; provided that no amendment which may be made prior to the year one thousand eight hundred and eight shall in any manner affect the first and fourth clauses in the ninth section of the first article; and that no State, without its consent, shall be deprived of its equal suffrage in the Senate.

Amendments may be proposed by a two-thirds vote of each house of Congress or by a national convention called by Congress at the request of two-thirds of the states. Amendments may be ratified by legislatures of three-fourths of the states or by conventions in three-fourths of the states.

No amendment may deprive a state of its equal vote in the Senate.

ARTICLE VI • GENERAL PROVISIONS

Public Debt • All debts contracted, and engagements entered into, before the adoption of this Constitution, shall be as valid against the United States under this Constitution, as under the Confederation.

Debts and obligations made by the United States before the adoption of the Constitution were to be honored.

543

Supremacy of Constitution • This Constitution, and the laws of the United States which shall be made in pursuance thereof; and all treaties made, or which shall be made, under the authority of the United States, shall be the supreme law of the land; and the judges in every State shall be bound thereby, anything in the Constitution or laws of any State to the contrary notwithstanding.

> The Constitution, laws, and treaties of the United States are supreme. Judges in every state are bound by them.

Official Oath; Religious Test • The senators and representatives before mentioned, and the members of the several State legislatures, and all executive and judicial officers, both of the United States and of the several States, shall be bound by oath or affirmation to support this Constitution; but no religious test shall ever be required as a qualification to any office or public trust under the United States.

> All public officials, state as well as national, shall promise to support the U.S. Constitution.

> Religion may not be used as a qualification for holding a Federal office.

ARTICLE VII • RATIFICATION OF THE CONSTITUTION

Ratification • The ratification of the Conventions of nine States shall be sufficient for the establishment of this Constitution between the States so ratifying the same.

> The Constitution was to go into effect when approved by nine states.

Done in convention, by the unanimous consent of the States present, the seventeenth day of September, in the year of our Lord one thousand seven hundred and eighty-seven, and of the independence of the United States of America the twelfth.

In witness whereof, we have hereunto subscribed our names.

George Washington, President, and Deputy from Virginia

New Hampshire	New Jersey	Delaware	North Carolina
John Langdon	*William Livingston*	*George Read*	*William Blount*
Nicholas Gilman	*David Brearley*	*Gunning Bedford, Jr.*	*Richard Dobbs*
	William Paterson	*John Dickinson*	*Spaight*
Massachusetts	*Jonathan Dayton*	*Richard Bassett*	*Hugh Williamson*
Nathaniel Gorham		*Jacob Broom*	
Rufus King	Pennsylvania		South Carolina
	Benjamin Franklin	Maryland	
Connecticut	*Thomas Mifflin*	*James M'Henry*	*John Rutledge*
	Robert Morris	*Daniel of St. Thomas*	*Charles C. Pinckney*
William Samuel	*George Clymer*	*Jenifer*	*Charles Pinckney*
Johnson	*Thomas Fitzsimons*	*Daniel Carroll*	*Pierce Butler*
Roger Sherman	*Jared Ingersoll*		
	James Wilson	Virginia	Georgia
New York	*Gouverneur Morris*	*John Blair*	*William Few*
Alexander Hamilton		*James Madison, Jr.*	*Abraham Baldwin*

Attest: *William Jackson*, Secretary

544

AMENDMENTS

ARTICLE I

Religion, Speech, Press, Assembly, Petition • Congress shall make no law respecting an establishment of religion, or prohibiting the free exercise thereof; or abridging the freedom of speech, or of the press; or the right of the people peaceably to assemble, and to petition the government for redress of grievances.

Congress may not set up an official church or pass laws limiting worship, speech, the press, assembly, and the right to petition.

ARTICLE II

Militia • A well-regulated militia being necessary to the security of a free State, the right of the people to keep and bear arms shall not be infringed.

The right of the states to maintain a citizens' militia is guaranteed.

ARTICLE III

Soldiers • No soldier shall, in time of peace, be quartered in any house, without the consent of the owner; nor in time of war but in a manner to be prescribed by law.

Limits the army's right to take over private housing.

ARTICLE IV

Unreasonable Searches • The right of the people to be secure in their persons, houses, papers, and effects, against unreasonable searches and seizures, shall not be violated, and no warrants shall issue, but upon probable cause, supported by oath or affirmation, and particularly describing the place to be searched, and the persons or things to be seized.

This clause limits the right of the government to search and take custody of persons and property. Specific warrants for search and arrest are required.

ARTICLE V

Legal Protection of Accused Persons • No person shall be held to answer for a capital, or otherwise infamous crime, unless on a presentment or indictment of a grand jury, except in cases arising in the land or naval forces, or in the militia, when in actual service in time of war or public danger; nor shall any person be subject for the same offense to be twice put in jeopardy of life or limb; nor shall be compelled in any criminal case to be a witness against himself, nor to be deprived of life, liberty, or property, without due process of law; nor shall private property be taken for public use, without just compensation.

Guarantees grand-jury indictment in Federal trials (except military trials). Prohibits double jeopardy and self-incrimination. Requires due process of law (fair legal procedures) and fair payment for private property taken for public use.

ARTICLE VI

Right to Trial • In all criminal prosecutions, the accused shall enjoy the right to a speedy and public trial, by an impartial jury of the State and district wherein the crime shall have been committed, which district shall have been previously ascertained by law, and to be informed of the nature and cause of the

Trials shall be speedy and public, by impartial juries, in the district and state where the crime occurred. The accused shall be told of the

charges against him, be allowed to face the witnesses
against him and call defense
witnesses, and have a
lawyer.

accusation; to be confronted with the witnesses against him; to have compulsory process for obtaining witnesses in his favor, and to have the assistance of counsel for his defense.

ARTICLE VII

Jury trial is guaranteed in
civil suits when the matter
amounts to more than $20.

Suits at Common Law • In suits at common law, where the value in controversy shall exceed twenty dollars, the right of trial by jury shall be preserved, and no fact tried by a jury shall be otherwise re-examined in any court of the United States than according to the rules of common law.

ARTICLE VIII

Bail, Punishments • Excessive bail shall not be required, nor excessive fines imposed, nor cruel and unusual punishments inflicted.

ARTICLE IX

The listing of these rights
does not mean that other
rights may be disregarded.

Reserved Rights • The enumeration in the Constitution of certain rights shall not be construed to deny or disparage others retained by the people.

ARTICLE X

Powers not given to Con-
gress are reserved to the
states and the people.

The first ten amendments
were proposed in 1789 and
adopted in 1791.

Reserved Powers • The powers not delegated to the United States by the Constitution, nor prohibited by it to the States, are reserved to the States respectively, or to the people. DIVORCE LAW EXAMPLE

ARTICLE XI

This preserves the right of
a state not to be sued without its own consent. Pro-
posed in 1794 and adopted
in 1798.

Suits against States • The judicial power of the United States shall not be construed to extend to any suit in law or equity, commenced or prosecuted against any of the United States by citizens of another State, or by citizens or subjects of any foreign state.

ARTICLE XII

The Twelfth Amendment
made some changes in the
method of electing the
President and Vice-Presi-
dent (see Article II, Sec. 1).
The major change was that
the members of the Elec-
toral College (called "electors") should vote separately
for President and Vice-
President.

Method of Electing President and Vice-President • The electors shall meet in their respective States, and vote by ballot for President and Vice-President, one of whom, at least, shall not be an inhabitant of the same State with themselves; they shall name in their ballots the person voted for as President, and in distinct ballots the person voted for as Vice-President; and they shall make distinct lists of all persons voted for as President, and of all persons voted for as Vice-President, and of the number of votes for each, which list they shall sign and certify, and transmit sealed to the seat of the government of the United States, directed to the president of the Senate;—the president of the Senate shall, in the presence of the Senate and House of Representatives, open all the certificates, and the votes shall then be counted;—the person having the greatest number of votes for President, shall be the President, if such number be a majority of the whole number of electors appointed; and if no person have such majority, then from the persons having the highest numbers not exceeding three on the list of those voted for as President, the House of Representatives shall choose immediately, by ballot, the President. But in choosing the President, the votes shall be taken by States, the representation from each State having one vote; a quorum for this purpose shall consist of a member or members from two-thirds of the States, and a majority of all the States shall be necessary to a choice. And if the House of Representatives shall not choose a President whenever the right of choice shall devolve upon them, before the fourth day of March next following, then the Vice-President shall act as President, as in the case of the death or other constitutional disability of the President. The person having the greatest number of votes as Vice-President, shall be the Vice-President, if such number be a majority of the whole number of electors appointed; and if no person have a majority, then from the two highest numbers on the list, the Senate shall choose the Vice-President; a quorum for the purpose shall consist of two-thirds of the whole number of senators, and a majority of the whole number shall be necessary to a choice. But no person constitutionally ineligible to the office of President shall be eligible to that of Vice-President of the United States.

ARTICLE XIII

Slavery Abolished • *Section 1.* Neither slavery nor involuntary servitude, except as a punishment for crime whereof the party shall have been duly convicted, shall exist within the United States, or any place subject to their jurisdiction.

Section 2. Congress shall have power to enforce this article by appropriate legislation.

ARTICLE XIV

Negroes Made Citizens; Protection of Citizens • *Section 1.* All persons born or naturalized in the United States, and subject to the jurisdiction thereof, are citizens of the United States and of the State wherein they reside. No State shall make or enforce any law which shall abridge the privileges or immunities of citizens of the United States; nor shall any State deprive any person of life, liberty, or property, without due process of law, nor deny to any person within its jurisdiction the equal protection of the laws.

Section 2. Representatives shall be apportioned among the several States according to their respective numbers, counting the whole number of persons in each State, excluding Indians not taxed. But when the right to vote at any election for the choice of electors for President and Vice-President of the United States, representatives in Congress, the executive or judicial officers of a State, or the members of the legislature thereof, is denied to any of the male inhabitants of such State, being twenty-one years of age, and citizens of the United

If no candidate for President wins a majority, the House of Representatives chooses a President from the three highest—with each state having one vote. If no candidate for Vice-President wins a majority, the Senate chooses from the two highest.

The phrase in color was changed by Amendment XX.

Article XII was adopted in 1804.

Adopted in 1865.

Citizenship was conferred on Negroes. States were forbidden to deny equal privileges to any citizen. The effect of Section 1 was to apply the basic protections in the Bill of Rights to the states as well as to the Federal government.

Section 2 provides that a state's representation in Congress may be cut if it denies the right to vote to any group of adult male citizens. This Section has never been applied.

States, or in any way abridged, except for participation in rebellion or other crime, the basis of representation therein shall be reduced in the proportion which the number of such male citizens shall bear to the whole number of male citizens twenty-one years of age in such State.

Section 3. No person shall be a senator or representative in Congress, or elector of President or Vice-President, or hold any office, civil or military, under the United States, or under any State, who, having previously taken an oath, as a member of Congress, or as an officer of the United States, or as a member of any State legislature, or as an executive or judicial officer of any State, to support the Constitution of the United States, shall have engaged in insurrection or rebellion against the same, or given aid or comfort to the enemies thereof. But Congress may, by a vote of two-thirds of each house, remove such disability.

Section 4. The validity of the public debt of the United States, authorized by law, including debts incurred for payment of pensions and bounties for services in suppressing insurrection or rebellion, shall not be questioned. But neither the United States nor any State shall assume or pay any debt or obligation incurred in aid of insurrection or rebellion against the United States, or any claim for the loss or emancipation of any slave; but all such debts, obligations, and claims shall be held illegal and void.

Section 5. The Congress shall have power to enforce, by appropriate legislation, the provisions of this article.

ARTICLE XV

Negroes Made Voters • *Section 1.* The rights of citizens of the United States to vote shall not be denied or abridged by the United States, or by any State, on account of race, color, or previous condition of servitude.

Section 2. The Congress shall have power to enforce this article by appropriate legislation.

ARTICLE XVI

Income Tax • The Congress shall have power to lay and collect taxes on incomes from whatever source derived, without apportionment among the several States, and without regard to any census or enumeration.

ARTICLE XVII

Direct Election of Senators • The Senate of the United States shall be composed of two senators from each State, elected by the people thereof for six years; and each senator shall have one vote. The electors in each State shall have the qualifications requisite for electors of the most numerous branch of the State legislature.

When vacancies happen in the representation of any State in the Senate, the executive authority of such State shall issue writs of election to fill such

Section 3 barred from Federal office any former Federal or state official who served the Confederacy in the Civil War.

Legalized the Federal Civil War debt. But voided all debts incurred by the Southern states and the Confederacy in fighting the war.

Adopted in 1868.

Adopted in 1870.

or Race Related

Permits Congress to levy income taxes. Adopted in 1913.

United States senators formerly were chosen by the state legislatures (see Article 1, Section 3).

Adopted in 1913.

vacancies: Provided, that the legislature of any State may empower the Executive thereof to make temporary appointments until the people fill the vacancies by election as the legislature may direct.

This amendment shall not be so construed as to affect the election or term of any senator chosen before it becomes valid as part of the Constitution.

ARTICLE XVIII

National Prohibition • *Section 1.* After one year from the ratification of this article the manufacture, sale, or transportation of intoxicating liquors within, the importation thereof into, or the exportation thereof from the United States and all territory subject to the jurisdiction thereof for beverage purposes is hereby prohibited.

Section 2. The Congress and the several States shall have concurrent power to enforce this article by appropriate legislation.

Section 3. This article shall be inoperative unless it shall have been ratified as an amendment to the Constitution by the legislatures of the several States, as provided in the Constitution, within seven years from the date of the submission hereof to the States by the Congress.

Forbade the making, selling, and transporting of intoxicating liquors. Ratified in 1919, it was repealed by the Twenty-first Amendment in 1933.

ARTICLE XIX

Woman Suffrage • *Section 1.* The right of citizens of the United States to vote shall not be denied or abridged by the United States or by any State on account of sex.

1920

Section 2. Congress shall have power to enforce this article by appropriate legislation.

Ratified in 1920.

ARTICLE XX

"Lame Duck" Amendment • *Section 1.* The terms of the President and Vice-President shall end at noon on the twentieth day of January, and the terms of senators and representatives at noon on the third day of January, of the years in which such terms would have ended if this article had not been ratified; and the terms of their successors shall then begin.

Section 2. The Congress shall assemble at least once in every year, and such meeting shall begin at noon on the third day of January, unless they shall by law appoint a different day.

Section 3. If, at the time fixed for the beginning of the term of the President, the President-elect shall have died, the Vice-President-elect shall become President. If a President shall not have been chosen before the time fixed for the beginning of his term, or if the President-elect shall have failed to qualify, then the Vice-President-elect shall act as President until a President shall have qualified; and the Congress may by law provide for the case wherein neither a President-elect nor a Vice-President-elect shall have qualified, declaring who shall then act as President, or the manner in which one who is to act shall be

Provided for the President to take office on January 20 and members of Congress on January 3 to reduce the time between an election and taking office. A "lame duck" is an official who continues to serve though not reelected.

Before on march

Congress is to meet once a year.

Provides for succession to the Presidency if the President-elect should die or fail to qualify before January 20.

Roosevelt is the last President elect to take office in march

549

selected, and such person shall act accordingly until a President or Vice-President shall have qualified.

Section 4. The Congress may by law provide for the case of the death of any of the persons from whom the House of Representatives may choose a President whenever the right of choice shall have devolved upon them, and for the case of the death of any of the persons from whom the Senate may choose a Vice-President whenever the right of choice shall have devolved upon them.

Section 5. Sections 1 and 2 shall take effect upon the fifteenth day of October following the ratification of this article.

Section 6. This article shall be inoperative unless it shall have been ratified as an amendment to the Constitution by the legislatures of three-fourths of the several States within seven years from the date of its submission.

ARTICLE XXI

The Repeal of Prohibition • *Section 1.* The Eighteenth article of amendment to the Constitution of the United States is hereby repealed.

Section 2. The transportation or importation into any State, Territory, or possession of the United States for delivery or use therein of intoxicating liquors, in violation of the laws thereof, is hereby prohibited.

Section 3. This article shall be inoperative unless it shall have been ratified as an amendment to the Constitution by conventions in the several States, as provided in the Constitution, within seven years from the date of the submission hereof to the States by the Congress.

ARTICLE XXII

Presidential Term • *Section 1.* No person shall be elected to the office of the President more than twice, and no person who has held the office of President, or acted as President, for more than two years of a term to which some other person was elected President shall be elected to the office of the President more than once. But this article shall not apply to any person holding the office of President when this article was proposed by the Congress, and shall not prevent any person who may be holding the office of President, or acting as President, during the term within which this article becomes operative, from holding the office of President or acting as President during the remainder of such term.

Section 2. This article shall be inoperative unless it shall have been ratified as an amendment to the Constitution by the legislatures of three-fourths of the several States within seven years from the date of its submission to the States by the Congress.

ARTICLE XXIII

Electors for the District of Columbia • *Section 1.* The District constituting the seat of Government of the United States shall appoint in such manner as the Congress may direct:

A number of electors of President and Vice-President equal to the whole number of senators and representatives in Congress to which the District would be entitled if it were a State, but in no event more than the least populous State; they shall be in addition to those appointed by the States, but they shall be considered, for the purposes of the election of President and Vice-President, to be electors appointed by a State; and they shall meet in the District and perform such duties as provided by the twelfth article of amendment.

Section 2. The Congress shall have power to enforce this article by appropriate legislation.

electors are to be chosen. In proposing this amendment, Congress made it clear that qualified residents of the District would get the right to vote for President and Vice-President.

Ratified in 1961.

ARTICLE XXIV

Poll Tax • *Section 1.* The right of citizens of the United States to vote in any primary or other election for President or Vice-President, for electors for President or Vice-President, or for Senator or Representative in Congress, shall not be denied or abridged by the United States or any State by reason of failure to pay any poll tax or other tax.

Section 2. The Congress shall have power to enforce this article by appropriate legislation.

Forbids use of poll tax as a requirement for voting in election of Federal officers.

Ratified in 1964.

ARTICLE XXV

Presidential Disability and Vice-Presidential Vacancy • *Section 1.* In case of the removal of the President from office or his death or resignation, the Vice-President shall become President.

Section 2. Whenever there is a vacancy in the office of the Vice-President, the President shall nominate a Vice-President who shall take the office upon confirmation by a majority vote of both houses of Congress.

Ratification completed in Feb., 1967.

Section 3. Whenever the President transmits to the President pro tempore of the Senate and the Speaker of the House of Representatives his written declaration that he is unable to discharge the powers and duties of his office, and until he transmits to them a written declaration to the contrary, such powers and duties shall be discharged by the Vice-President as Acting President.

Clarifies role of Vice-President when the President is disabled.

Section 4. Whenever the Vice-President and a majority of either the principal officers of the executive department or of such other body as Congress may by law provide, transmit to the President pro tempore of the Senate and the Speaker of the House of Representatives their written declaration that the President is unable to discharge the powers and duties of his office, the Vice-President shall immediately assume the powers and duties of the office of Acting President.

Thereafter, when the President transmits to the President pro tempore of the Senate and the Speaker of the House of Representatives his written declaration that no inability exists, he shall resume the powers and duties of his office unless the Vice-President and a majority of either the principal officers of the executive department or of such other body as Congress may by law provide, transmit within four days to the President pro tempore of the Senate and the Speaker of the House of Representatives their written declaration that the President is unable to discharge the powers and duties of his office. Thereupon Congress shall decide the issue, assembling within 48 hours for that purpose if not in session. If the Congress, within 21 days after receipt of the latter written declaration, or, if Congress is not in session, within 21 days after Congress is required to assemble, determines by two-thirds vote of both houses that the President is unable to discharge the powers and duties of his office, the Vice-President shall continue to discharge the same as Acting President; otherwise, the President shall resume the powers and duties of his office.

ARTICLE XXVI

Proposed in March, 1971. Ratification completed in record time on June 30, 1971.

Voting Age • *Section 1.* The right of citizens of the United States who are eighteen years of age or older, to vote shall not be denied or abridged by the United States or by any state on account of age.

Section 2. The Congress shall have power to enforce this article by appropriate legislation.

index

553

Scoble, Harry M., study by, 120–121

Scott, Hugh, *photo,* 319; quoted, 325

Secondary groups, voting and, 222–224

Segregation, racial: bus boycott case, 132–138; court decisions on, 390–394; in Gary, 173; state laws on, 158–160; in Tuskegee, 236, 237

Self-incrimination, 387

"Self-interested partisan" voter, 217–218

Senate, United States: in check-and-balance system, 250–251; Chief Justice and, 398, 400–404, 406; and Civil Rights Act of 1964, 336, 340–341; committees of, 327, 329, 330; decision-making case, 351–357; member's typical day, 331–333; recruitment for, 312–316; special powers of, 185, 187, 274, 278, 294, 319, 322; special rules for, 322–323. *See also* Congress

Senatorial courtesy, 294

Seniority, in Congress, 328–329

Senses, deciding facts with, 35

"Separate but equal" doctrine, 391–393

Separation of powers, 249, 251, 273; *diagram,* 79

Sex identity: of bureaucrats, 420; congressional recruitment and, 314; party preference and, 214–216, 225–226; political efficacy and, 33–34, *table,* 34; of presidential candidates, 269; roles and, 107; voting turnout and, 196, 197

Sherrill, Robert, quoted, 432

Shoreline airport case, 456–460

Situation: influence of, on voting, 231–232; tendency to vote and, 207–208

Sixth Amendment, 380, 387, 545–546

Skills, of unofficial political specialists, 464–465

Slander, cases on, 64–66, 77

Slogan, "black power" as, 112–116

Slum clearance, party views on, 227

Slums, case on, 124–129

Smith, Howard W., 339

Smith, Margaret Chase, 269

Smith v. *Allbright,* 203

Social detachment, tendency to vote and, 206, 207

Social environment, *see* Culture

Social forces, judicial decision-making and, 389–394

Social-group membership, *see* Group identification

Social science approach, 24–58

Social science inquiry, limitations of, 52–54

Social Security, 226, 227

Socialization, 100–116; defined, 100–101; loyalty and, 140, 146; personality and, 110–111; relationship to political behavior, 101–103; roles and, 105–110; socioeconomic status and, cases, 122–129. *See also* Political socialization

Socioeconomic status, 117–118; background of Supreme Court justices, 395; characteristics of, 117–118; of congressmen, 314–315; defined, 117; measuring, 119–120; of Montgomery blacks, 133; in open and closed societies, 118–119; of party leaders, 527–529; party preference and, 215–216, 225–226; of presidential candidates, 269–270; relationship to political behavior, 120–128; tendency to vote and, 206, 207; of unofficial political specialists, 461; voter turnout and, 196–197, 206, 207–208, 211

Somerville, Massachusetts, 128

Sonic booms, 436, 449

Sorensen, Theodore C., quoted, 289–290

South Carolina, case on hunger in, 504–508

Southern Christian Leadership Conference, 113, 159, 334

Southern states: political beliefs in, 87; voting rights in, 201–203

Soviet Union: as autocracy, 86; Cuba and, 296, 299–307; elections in, 168; recognition of, 297; scientific inquiry in, 54, 57; test-ban treaty and, 509; voting in, *photo,* 85

Spano v. *New York,* 389

Specialists, *see* Unofficial political specialists

Specialization, in Congress, 326

Speck, Richard, 402

Speech, freedom of, 153, 154

Spencer, Claude, 104

Spending power of Congress, courts and, 371

Spock, Benjamin, 480

SST Project, 435–437, 439, 450

Stare decisis, 384

State Department, 279, 301, 304, 415, 418–419

State government: in Amish school case, 94, 95, 97; in bus boycott case, 132, 133, 137; corruption case, 483–486; court system in, 364, 365–366, 367; election laws, 198–203; in federal system, 248–249; gun control case, 467–471; legislative reports, *illus.,* 219; in school prayer case, 359–363; West Virginia welfare case, 129–131

State of the Union message, 274, 281, 334, 339, 503

Status, socioeconomic, *see* Socioeconomic status

Status relationships: of Federal bureaucrats, 425–427; in Congress, 346, 348; in presidential decision-making, 294–297, *chart,* 295

Statuses, roles related to, 106, 108

Stennis, John, 425

Stevens, Theodore, 327

Stevenson, Adlai, 222, 223, 301

Stewart, Justice Potter, *photo,* 405; quoted, 362, 395

Stewart, William, *photo,* 422

"Street people," 70

Student government, cases on, 109–110, 257

Student protest, voting and, 231

Subculture, 91; Amish as, 91–99

Subsidies, governmental, 244–245, 246, 426, 436, 439

Supersonic transport planes, 435–437, 439, 450

Supreme court, state, 366

Supreme Court, United States: appointment of a Chief Justice, 398–406; in bus boycott case, 137; characteristics of members, 395–398; in check-and-balance system, 250, 251; Gallup Poll on, 399; law interpretation by, 367–369; *photo,* 405; place in Federal court system, 364–367; rules and procedures, 369–389; school prayer case, 358–363; social and personal influences on, 389–395; voting rights and, 199, 202–203

Survey Research Center of University of Michigan, 38

Sweden, voting in, 212

illustration credits

Drawings by Ken Jones/Graphics, Inc.
Charts and graphs by Visual Graphics

C D E F H I J 0 7 9 8 6 5 4 3 2
Printed in the United States of America